W9-AAW-121

NITSCHKE

NITSCHKE

EDWARD GRUVER

TAYLOR TRADE PUBLISHING
Lanham • New York • Oxford

First Taylor Trade Publishing edition 2002

This Taylor Trade Publishing hardcover edition of *Nitschke* is an original publication. It is published by arrangement with the author.

Copyright © 2002 by Edward Gruver

All photographs are used with permission of Vernon J. Biever.

All rights reserved.
No part of this book may be reproduced in any form or by any electronic or mechanical means, including information storage and retrieval systems, without written permission.

Published by Taylor Trade Publishing
A Member of the Rowman & Littlefield Publishing Group
4720 Boston Way
Lanham, Maryland 20706

Distributed by National Book Network

Book design and composition: Barbara Werden Design

Library of Congress Cataloging-in-Publication Data available.

ISBN 0-87833-271-5 (alk. paper)

∞ The paper used in this publication meets the minimum requirements of American National Standard for Information Sciences—Permanence of Paper for Printed Library Materials, ANSI/NISO Z39.48–1992.

Manufactured in the United States of America.

For Kathie and Patrice,
two of the best sisters a brother could have

CONTENTS

INTRODUCTION

THE VOICE, with its distinctive tires-crunching-over-gravel tone, was instantly recognizable on the other end of the phone.

"Hey, how's it goin', man?" Ray Nitschke asked. "How ya doin'?"

October 1995, and a long-distance phone call had been placed to the Oneida, Wisconsin, home of the Green Bay Packers' Hall of Fame middle linebacker to talk about his career. Nearly a quarter century had passed since the aging warrior had last worn the green-and-gold, a quarter century since he had last patrolled the field for the Packers during the Green Bay glory years, a time so special and romantic in the memory of those who were there that Packer guard Jerry Kramer likens it to Camelot.

Nitschke, Vince Lombardi, Bart Starr, Jim Taylor, Willie Davis, Willie Wood—they were the faces of victory in America's fastest growing sport during the sixties, and they created a national following by dominating their decade like no NFL team before or since. Lombardi led the Packers on a heady run of excellence—five league championships in seven years, an unprecedented and still unmatched three straight NFL titles from 1965 to 1967, victories in the first two Super Bowls over the rival American Football League.

Amid the sit-ins and drop-outs of the psychedelic sixties, the Packers were throwbacks to an earlier era. They embodied the Spartan qualities of teamwork and self-sacrifice, and their success inspired a generation of fans. Future actor Tommy Lee Jones idolized Kramer; the singer Meat Loaf wanted to be Fuzzy Thurston, Kramer's partner at pulling guard.

Nitschke understood the adulation. In an era of social and political turbulence, when riots were engulfing cities like Newark and Detroit, the town team from Green Bay stood as a symbol of excellence. At a time when U.S. troops were bogged down in the jungles of Vietnam, the Lombardi Packers were sweeping to victory with the power and precision of Patton's Third Army.

"The Lombardi teams wanted to get into the big games," said Nitschke, his gruff voice still carrying the growl that marked this lion in winter. "We had a great record in post-season games. We lost the first, but never lost another."

Not counting the meaningless "Playoff Bowl" held in Miami every year following the NFL championship game, the Packers won nine straight post-season games from 1961 to 1967. They became pro football's "Team of the Decade," the measuring stick for the dynasties that followed—Pittsburgh in the '70s, San Francisco in the '80s, Dallas in the '90s.

What set the Packers apart? To Nitschke, the answer was clear. Green Bay had an advantage no other team could claim at that time: a hard-driving force in a camel-hair coat who pushed them through practice and prowled the sidelines on game days.

"Lombardi represented preparation and hard work," Nitschke said. "Every game was important to him. So when we got to the real important games, we were ready to go, man. Every game was a championship, and that made it easier when we got to the big games because we weren't awed by it, we weren't nervous about it. We were more relaxed than the opponents, and in those years, we always played to our experience. That's how we handled it. That's what you work all season for, to get into the playoff games, and you don't want to blow it."

The Packers lost their first championship under Lombardi in 1960, then never lost another stakes game the next seven years. Their post-season games, played on ice-glazed fields under steel-gray skies, burn in the memory. They carried the NFL banner in the first two Super Bowls against the rival American League following the '66 and '67 seasons, and reinforced the notion of NFL supremacy by outscoring Kansas City and Oakland by a combined 68–24.

Green Bay's no-nonsense, no-frills style perfectly suited an era when pro football was still more of a game than a business, when players covered themselves with equal parts mud and glory.

"It was another day to go to work, man," Nitschke said. "One of the great things about football is that you don't cancel the games because of weather. It shows a little about yourself and about the character of yourself.

"Everybody can play in 50-degree weather, but can you play in 100-degree weather? Can you play in a windchill of 50 below? It's a test, a test of your character and your team's character, and you have to make adjustments. It's like life, you know. Things don't always go your way, and you have to make the right adjustments."

Nitschke's life was all about making the right adjustments. His father died when he was three; his mother when he was thirteen. Adopted and raised by his older brothers, Nitschke's teenage years in the urban cauldron of Chicago were undisciplined to say the least. He knocked downed slugs of whiskey and neighborhood toughs with equal vigor. His overriding redeeming quality was his ability on the playing field. He excelled in baseball, and in a high school state tournament hit what was estimated to be a 560-foot home run. He was offered a $3,000 signing bonus by the St. Louis Browns, but his first love was football. An all-star quarterback at Proviso East High in Maywood, Illinois, Nitschke was persuaded by both his older brother, Robert, and his high school football coach, Andy Puplis, a former Notre Dame back, to accept a football scholarship to the University of Illinois. Converted to fullback, Nitschke averaged 6.5 yards per carry and closed out his varsity career by rushing for 170 yards against Northwestern.

Though he had hoped to play for his hometown Chicago Bears, he was taken by the Packers in the third round of the 1958 NFL draft; a pick made possible because of a trade Green Bay had engineered with the New York Giants. Nitschke had to literally take out a map to find out where Green Bay was, and once he arrived in camp was converted to linebacker. It was an idea that suited him fine, since he always reasoned that on the football field, it was better to give than receive.

"I like contact," he said at the time. "It brings out the meanness in me."

Nitschke rode the bench his rookie year, and the Packers won just one game under head coach Ray "Scooter" McLean. In 1959, Green Bay hired Lombardi as its head coach and general manager.

Lombardi was the ultimate disciplinarian, and Nitschke, frustrated by his lack of playing time, remained the ultimate undisciplined player.

"Just call me the judge," he would shout when Lombardi was nearby, "'cause I'm always on the bench."

Lombardi's response was less than understanding.

"Hey, Nitschke."

"Yeah?"

"Shaddup."

"It was hard to miss Ray," Lombardi's son, Vince Jr., recalled. "He had that raspy voice, and he was always yelling and screaming."

Privately, the Packer coaching staff worried that Nitschke's wild ways might end in tragedy. Lombardi confided to friends that he thought Nitschke "might kill somebody" and threatened to trade his troubled middle linebacker in 1960.

"Raymond was headed for bad trouble," halfback Paul Hornung remembered. "His drinking was out of control."

Under the guidance of Lombardi and defensive coordinator Phil Bengston, Nitschke was molded from a player who tried too hard and was overly aggressive into one who combined punishing hits with perceptive reads. As the Packers drove to their first Western Conference title under Lombardi in 1960, Nitschke began splitting time in the starting lineup with Tom Bettis. In 1961, Nitschke played a pivotal role in Green Bay's 37–0 win over the New York Giants in the NFL title game. One year later, in a game that was more grudge match than rematch, Nitschke recovered two fumbles and forced an interception as the Packers beat the Giants 16–7 amid cyclonic winds and sub-zero temperatures at Yankee Stadium. Nitschke was named the game's Most Valuable Player, a fitting tribute to a man whose fierce play perfectly suited one of the most brutal defensive struggles in league championship history.

Nitschke's rising stature on the field was due in large part to his stability at home. His 1961 marriage to Jackie Forchette proved to be a major turning point in his life. To Jackie, he was always "Raymond," and friends recalled how just the sound of her voice lit a spark in her husband's hard-as-flint face. The couple eventually adopted three children—John, Richard, and Amy—and Nitschke's transformation from barroom brawler to doting dad was underway.

"It was the greatest thing I've ever seen," Hornung said. "He adopted three kids, became a model citizen, and just did a fantastic job turning his life around. I loved Raymond for that."

Stability in his personal life led to tremendous strides in his professional life. Aimed by Bengston and triggered by Lombardi, Nitschke combined the best elements of his forerunners—the strategy of Joe Schmidt, the strength of Bill George, the sideline-to-sideline pursuit of Sam Huff—and by the mid-sixties had become the best ever at his position. From 1964 through '66, Nitschke was named the league's top middle linebacker by two of the leading wire services at the time, the Associated Press and United Press International. He covered the field with a crablike scurry; a powerful, pitiless presence with an appetite for the ball or the man with it. Over the course of his 15-year career, he buried ballcarriers and blanketed receivers with equal fervor, and established himself as a premier ballhawk with 25 interceptions and 20 fumble recoveries.

With his huge shoulders and padded arms, his skinny calves and the big number 66 on his jersey, Nitschke became one of the ornaments of the modern NFL.

"I always thought his number was 99," wide receiver Tommy McDonald said. "When I was looking up after he had knocked me upside down, his 66 always looked like 99."

Nitschke's big-game battles with future Hall of Famers were legendary. He hand-fought Philadelphia center Chuck Bednarik in the 1960 NFL title game, engaged in mental gymnastics with New York quarterback Y.A. Tittle in '61 and '62, and shadowed Cleveland fullback Jim Brown over a field slick with icy mud in '65.

"To me, Ray Nitschke was the perfect definition of the word 'presence,'" said Steve Sabol, the president of NFL Films and an astute historian of the game. "When he was on the field, it was almost like there was an odor about him. You could smell it, you could feel it."

The sixties were a decade dominated by defense, by great gangs of four in Minnesota, Los Angeles, and Dallas, and by the middle men who lurked behind them. From the Purple Gang, Fearsome Foursome, and Doomsday Defense to Nitschke, Dick Butkus, and Willie Lanier, the NFL had never seen such a collection of defensive dominators. At the top of that impressive list in the eyes of the fans stood Nitschke and Butkus. They were warriors both, physical enforcers bonded by their past as Illinois natives and former Illini, by the Packers–Bears rivalry, by their ferocious play at middle linebacker.

"There was a mutual respect between us," Butkus remembered . "I liked his desire. Green Bay had some great players on defense, but at that time, the middle linebacker position was *the* impact position on the field. I think we played the game with the same intensity, the same desire."

Nitschke brought that intensity and desire to bear in the biggest games. When Green Bay met the Kansas City Chiefs of the rival American Football League in January 1967 in the first Super Bowl, the Age of Aquarius was in full swing. Anguish clashed with achievement, tradition with upheaval. Some saw that first AFL–NFL showdown as a reflection of the times, the Establishment versus the Rebels. Whatever, Nitschke became the first of the Super Bowl tough guys, and set a trend for future enforcers when he unnerved the Chiefs before what was officially billed as the AFL–NFL World Championship Game. The AFL to that time had never produced a middle man as violent and perceptive as Nitschke, and the Chiefs were wary of what to expect. "We had heard the stories about Ray's past," Kansas City guard Ed Budde recalled. "He was a wild man."

Nitschke lived up to his billing, helping Green Bay to a 35–10 victory that gave the cocky upstarts their comeuppance, at least for the time being. One year later, Nitschke provided the fire amid the ice as Green Bay made its historic run for a record third straight NFL championship. The Packers were nearing the end of their magnificent run; injuries and exhaustion were everyday companions. Power backs Taylor and Hornung were gone from the team, and many of their aging stars, including Nitschke and Starr, played virtually every game of their 23-game season hurt and heavily taped.

The marathon that was the '67 season provided the Packers with pro football's ultimate challenge, and through it all, there was Nitschke.

Nitschke, shouting at officials in the pewter-gray twilight of the Western Conference playoff against the favored Los Angeles Rams, imploring them, begging them, to let L.A.'s offense have a first down. "Give it to 'em," he snarled at the refs. "We're not ready to leave the field yet."

Nitschke, ignoring his frost-bitten feet one week later in the final, frozen moments of the epic Ice Bowl and exhorting Green Bay's offense from the sideline. "Don't let me down," he screamed, pumping his padded right fist in the brittle air. "Don't let me down!"

Nitschke, flipping Oakland fullback Hewritt Dixon heels-over-helmet to short-circuit a Raiders sweep two weeks later in Super Bowl II in the sun-drenched Miami Orange Bowl. A hit so explosive that Packers' public relations director Lee Remmel said it left the 220-pound Dixon trembling like a tuning fork. "Dixon wasn't a factor the rest of the day," Remmel said. Super Bowl II became one of the great games of Nitschke's career. Fighting off the blocks of Oakland center Jim Otto and guards Gene Upshaw and Wayne Hawkins, he made nine tackles that day. Five of those stops were solo, and of those, four came within three yards of the line of scrimmage, a defining stat for a middle linebacker.

The Packers' 33–14 win over Oakland marked the end of the Green Bay glory years. Lombardi stepped down as head coach the following February and died of cancer in 1970. One by one, Packer veterans retired or were traded. By 1972, the 36-year-old Nitschke remained one of the last links to the legendary Packer teams of the sixties. Few knew, as Packer trainer Domenic Gentile later revealed, that Nitschke had played his entire career on one good leg. His left leg had been injured so often in high school and college that the muscles had atrophied and never fully regenerated, leaving it 50 percent smaller than the right.

Nitschke retired after the '72 season, then built a life after football that saw him do many things but make a career of none. From 1975 to 1987, he appeared in 138 national television commercials, including the first Miller Lite Beer spot. He was a pitchman for Oldsmobile; did public relations work for Clairmont, a trucking firm; and worked as a good-will front man for a major Wisconsin dairy. Though he appeared an unlikely thespian, Nitschke was cast in two feature movies. In 1968, he played a character known only as "One" in *Head*, a movie featuring the TV rock group, the Monkees. In 1974, he was cast in the movie *The Longest Yard*, portraying a prison guard named Bogdanski.

That was the public Nitschke. Privately, he supported his wife's involvement with The Bridge, Inc., an organization dedicated to helping recovering alcoholics and their families, and he and Jackie were long-time co-chairpersons of the Cerebral Palsy Telethon. He became a born-again Christian in 1995, ending a long-time grudge he had held against God for the perceived injustice of losing his parents at such an early age. When he first joined the Packers, he alternated between jersey numbers 33 and 72. He was eventually given 66, and in later years Jackie would tell him that the change had occurred for a reason.

"You wore number 66, and there are 66 books in the Bible," she would tell him. "For some reason Raymond, you got that number."

In time, Nitschke traded Sunday morning tee times for time in prayer at the Bayside Christian Fellowship Church, and Amy remembered him having very strong views on abortion, and how much he was opposed to it.

"Dad was such a family man," she said. "Anything that dealt with children, he felt very strongly about. All three of us children were adopted, and he always felt there were better options out there than abortion."

Through time spent in church or with the children, in charitable causes or on the cruise trips they took every year, Ray and Jackie maintained a close partnership. When she died of cancer in July 1996, he was devastated.

"He was kind of lost after Mom died," his son Richard said. "He just kind of let himself go. Not physically, but mentally and emotionally."

Over the next two years Nitschke spent increasing time with Amy and his newborn granddaughter, Jacqueline Rae. He was traveling with them to visit friends in Venice, Florida, on Sunday, March 8, 1998, when he began suffering chest pains at around 12:30 P.M. He was rushed to nearby Venice Hospital, but at 1:30 P.M., the man who had been a heartbeat for so many causes was pronounced dead.

In death, Raymond Ernest Nitschke left a legacy that was both lasting and puzzling.

If, as Charles Dickens wrote in 1859, every human creature is constituted to be that profound secret to every other, then Nitschke presented the ultimate in profound contradiction. Off the field, he was the modern, urbane man—bespectacled and given to conservative business suits. Quiet and intelligent, he reposed in thoughtful, articulate conversation. He embraced friends and family in bearhugs that have become legend and were warmly remembered by his oldest son, John, at his father's service.

"Who here has ever been hugged by my dad?" John asked the assemblage that packed Bayside Christian Fellowship Church in Green Bay to pay their final respects. Seeing the high number of raised hands, John smiled. "Pretty neat, huh?"

Reverend Arni Jacobson, the pastor at Nitschke's church, remembered the most famous member of his flock as a pied piper of sorts, a Santa Claus with an ever-present cigar. Nitschke took seriously his obligations as an ambassador for pro football and role model for those looking to turn their lives around, and he took so much time in carefully signing autographs— "Ray Nitschke #66"—that during his playing days teammates kidded him, but always from a distance. "Hey Ray, what are you doing?" they would yell from the team bus. "Running for office?"

Nitschke always had a warm and ready smile for the children who approached him, but he loved to startle adults by suddenly taking on his grim football persona.

"Whaddya want?" he would say roughly, fixing the approaching person with a game-day stare that Sabol said was more than frightening. "He made Freddie from *Nightmare on Elm Street* look like a Muppet," Sabol said. Nitschke would quickly calm the trembling fan by throwing an arm around his shoulder and sharing small talk.

"He had some sort of unspoken relationship with the fans," former teammate Boyd Dowler said. "In the sixties we would play 30, 35 exhibition basketball games in and around Green Bay during the winter months. We would go into the locker room after the game and get showered up and he would say, 'C'mon let's go out and there and sign autographs,' and we would get out there and sit at the scorer's table. For the most part, we wanted to get out of there, but he would hang around and talk to the fans until the last person was gone. While the rest of us were somewhat detached, you know, out doing our own thing, Ray communicated a little better with the dyed-in-the-wool, hard-core Packer people. And they related to him a little more than they did to the rest of us."

Nitschke maintained a home in Oneida just outside of Green Bay, and never tried to shield himself from the public. The address—410 Peppermint Court—was well-known to Packer fans. His two-story brick house sat just 2.6 miles from the western city limits of Green Bay, and those seeking autographs or a few moments reliving the glory days would follow Highway 54 to Riverside Drive and then look for the house that sat on a slope facing east amid a collection of young trees, sumac, and other assorted brush.

Driving to his home was one way to contact the Packer legend. Simply picking up the phone was another. When Al Pahl was hired as the editor of *Ray Nitschke's Packer Report* in February 1986, he looked to get in touch with the Packer legend and introduce himself.

"I come to Green Bay, get out the phone book, and Ray Nitschke is in the *gaddamn* white pages," said Pahl, his midwestern accent still tinged with astonishment at that fact some 15 years later. "That just amazed me."

Nitschke maintained his connection with the Packers through his *Packer Report*, a publication he helped start in 1970, and by being a regular at Green Bay games, where team photographer Vern Biever remembered him heading down to the sideline to spur the team on.

"He was very much into the game even when he retired," Biever said.

"He'd be on the sidelines telling a player, 'Hey, you're not doing this properly,' or 'You should be doing this.'"

Amy witnessed the transformation her father underwent every time he entered Lambeau Field. Four season tickets were held in his name for every home game, and for years his seats were always the same—Section 16 on the Packers' side of the field, in-between the 35- and 40-yard lines in the north end of the field. The last decade of life, his seats were switched to Section 21 behind the opposing team's bench, near the 40–yard line on the south side of the field.

Regardless, just walking into Lambeau Field on game day stirred his inner passion.

"I know that he missed it really terribly," Amy said. "You could see it. Walking into Lambeau Field, he would almost become a different person."

It was a transformation reminiscent of his playing days. Game days in Green Bay would see Nitschke remove his front teeth, place them on the top shelf of his locker, and replace them with a gummy mouthpiece that gave his mouth a cruel, downward curve. Smears of eye black were substituted for his dark-rimmed glasses, yards of pads and tape took the place of his business suits. The carefully constructed autographs he handed out to fans were replaced by scrawled messages inside the knee pads of his gold football pants: *Beat Chicago*, he would write, or whatever team the Packers were playing that day. He covered his balding head with a battle-scarred green-and-gold helmet, and it was said at the time that when he peered at opponents through the bars of his full-cage facemask, he wore the look of a lifer peering through the prison bars of a padded cell.

"He was ugly with his facemask and no teeth," former Atlanta middle linebacker Tommy Nobis remembered, and ex-Dallas center Dave Manders said seeing Nitschke up close was a surreal experience.

"Probably one of the most ugliest and frightening sights was Ray Nitschke lined up in front of you," Manders said. "No teeth, sweating hard, breathing hard, talking a lot of rough B.S. And he didn't have any teeth to keep the saliva in his mouth. Just a real weird picture."

Minnesota quarterback Fran Tarkenton said once that Nitschke played with a gleam in his eye that no other defensive player of his era had. Pittsburgh Steelers halfback Preston Pearson remembered the gleam, remembered a 1970 game in Three Rivers Stadium when he took the ball from Terry Bradshaw on a sweep and out of the corner of his eye caught a heart-sinking glimpse of Nitschke closing in.

"I saw this monster only a moment before he hit," Pearson said. Nitschke exploded into the right side of Pearson's helmet, and the Steeler back's first thought was that a bomb had gone off inside his head. It was the kind of hit, Pearson said, that could break a man's back. As he was going down with Nitschke on top of him, Pearson saw the "gleam" that Tarkenton had talked about. Nitschke had a wild look in his eyes, Pearson said, and even more incredibly, seemed to be foaming at the mouth.

The devastating hit left Pearson stretched out on the snow-covered Tartan Turf. The next thing he was aware of was a Steeler trainer waving smelling salts under his nose and shouting, "You okay?" In 14 years of playing professional football, 14 years of playing with and against Joe Greene, Jack Lambert, Lanier, and Butkus, Pearson said the hit by Nitschke was the hardest he had ever endured.

Others backed up Pearson's testimony. Hall of Fame running back Bobby Mitchell recalled getting leveled by Nitschke, recalled what he described as the "tremendous force" of a body blow.

"Ray had tremendous strength," Mitchell said, "and he tried to make sure you felt his force."

Bears running back Ronnie Bull felt Nitschke's force as a rookie playing in Lambeau Field for the first time. The date was September 30, 1962, but to Bull, it remains as vivid nearly 40 years later as if it had happened yesterday.

"I was running around right end, and just as I planted my foot to cut upfield it was like a two-ton truck hit me," Bull said. "I got up looking for the truck, and there was Nitschke, smiling at me. It was a blind-side hit, and he caught me flush. It was the hardest I've ever been hit."

Three years later, Bull had another encounter with Nitschke, but this time it was memorable because of a hit Nitschke *didn't* deliver. "We're playing up in Green Bay again," Bull said, "and Willie Wood intercepts a pass. He's going across the middle and I'm chasing him, and just before I get there, the whistle blows. Somebody grabs me on my shoulder and I turn around and it's Nitschke. With his helmet on and no teeth, he's uglier than sin. And he just kind of smiles at me and says, 'Saved by the whistle.' I was so flabbergasted all I could say was, 'Yessir.' "

At a time when the Temptations scored a Motown hit with *Get Ready 'Cause Here I Come*, Nitschke was scoring direct hits on NFL ballcarriers and announcing each one. He would hunch over center before the snap, call out the offensive formation, call out the defensive signal, and then call out a running back or offensive lineman.

"Hey you," he would shout, pointing a threatening finger. "Yeah, you. I'm gonna git you."

When Nitschke and Bobby Mitchell were teammates at the University of Illinois, Nitschke always called Mitchell by his middle name, Cornelius. When the two played against each other in the NFL, Nitschke punctuated his tackles against Mitchell by announcing his presence.

"Cornelius!" he would shout. "Here I am, Cornelius!"

Nitschke's distinctive voice emanated across NFL battlefields for parts of three decades. He chattered constantly, in the locker room, on the practice field, on game days.

"Ray was our holler guy," recalled Willie Davis, Green Bay's Hall of Fame defensive end during the Lombardi years. "He would do a lot of talking and make a lot of noise, but he would also be the first to create an impression on a running back or a receiver with one of those Ray Nitschke kind of hits, where you could pick up that sound any place in the stadium."

One such hit occurred late in the third quarter of the epic Ice Bowl, when Nitschke pursued a Dallas sweep down the line and met halfback Dan Reeves at the line of scrimmage. The violent collision of pads caused a crackling sound that is clearly audible on the videotape of the game.

Bald and toothless, and with all the sympathy of a bill collector, Nitschke sacked quarterbacks and smacked running backs. He exuded an aura few others could match. When the Vikings opened their 1962 regular season on September 16 in Lambeau Field, rookie Mick Tingelhoff was starting his first NFL game at center. Spinning out of the huddle to lead the Vikings offense to the line of scrimmage on their first play, Tingelhoff immediately became aware of the man opposite him.

"He looked pretty bad," Tingelhoff said. "He didn't have his teeth in, and he was out there yelling and hollering. I didn't know what the hell was going on."

Nitschke's teammates sometimes felt the same confusion. When defensive tackle Mike McCoy played his first preseason game with Green Bay in 1970, Nitschke stood behind him, shouting instructions.

"Hey rookie! Watch the pass! Watch the run! Watch the draw!"

The ball was snapped, the offense ran a draw play, and the runner hacked out a few yards. After the players unpiled, Nitschke walked up to McCoy.

"I told you what they were going to do," he told the startled rookie.

"He liked to talk a little bull," Kramer said. "He had that distinctive voice—'Hey, man, let's go, let's do it, man.' But when I think of Raymond, I think of him more as a person than a player. His journey through life showed so much improvement. He had a rough childhood and he took it out on everyone. But he went from being half an ass to being a tremendous person, a beautiful, loving, giving person."

Bart Starr, whose career in Green Bay paralleled Nitschke's, remembered Nitschke's loud and sometimes abrasive personality, but he remembered the softer side of the man as well.

"On the field, Ray was one tough hombre," Starr said. "But off the field, as we walked from the practice field, he might be the first one on the team to help an elderly lady across the street. Just a marvelous personality. Couldn't be any tougher on the field; off the field, a perfect gentleman."

Indeed. There were two Ray Nitschkes. The man who belonged to the Green Bay Packers, and the man who belonged to Green Bay and the rest of the country.

This is the story of both of them.

T **HE WORLD** Raymond Ernest Nitschke was born into on December 29, 1936, offered a dichotomy of peace at home in the United States, instability abroad.

President Franklin Roosevelt had carried the November election in record fashion, winning every state but Maine and Vermont in a landslide victory over Republican Party candidate Alf Landon. Overseas, Edward VIII became king of England but abdicated his throne after the British government opposed his marriage to Mrs. Wallis Warfield Simpson. While FDR opened the Inter-American Conference in Buenos Aires, where Latin American nations consulted with the U.S. for "mutual safety," Hitler and Mussolini signed the Rome-Berlin axis. Italy annexed Ethiopia, and Germany occupied the Rhineland. Rightist uprisings against Spain's government began in Morocco and spread to Spain, and successful coups toppled governments in Greece and Nicaragua.

News from the old country was of particular interest to Robert and Anna Nitschke. He was of German ancestry; she was Danish. Both were solidly built; Robert was half a foot taller, with a thick shock of curly, light brown hair parted neatly on the left and combed over. He was given to wearing white open-neck shirts, dark cuffed slacks, and patent leather shoes. He favored a white fedora, and his rolled-up sleeves revealed thick forearms. He had broad shoulders and large hands, and the same wide mouth and sharp features that marked the Nitschke family. Anna was thickly built, with a round face and short, dark hair parted on the right and reaching to the tops of her shoulders.

In 1936, Robert and Anna's home was the top floor of a duplex in Elmwood Park, Illinois, a working-class suburb on the fringe of Chicago. Visitors to Elmwood Park today are drawn to Conti Circle, which has become ground zero for providing improved public facilities. But where the renovated library and civic center and recently added family aquatic center now stand, Conti Circle once featured a grand French fountain as the centerpiece of a tree-lined walkway. The community park was dedicated to the community in 1927 by real estate developer John Mills, with the stipulation it remain a place for passive recreation. At the time, Conti Circle was an open, grass-covered area of five acres. Neighborhood boys played baseball there, and on occasion dropped soap bars swiped from home into the fountain waters. The soap would drain into the pipes and come up out of the fountain as foam. The sight of the fountain spouting bubbles became something of a tradition in Elmwood Park, as did the sight of perpetrators who had lingered long enough to watch being chased away by police. Elmwood Park remained a wide-open area until 1973, when the Mills' last surviving heirs responded to the overtures made by town officials to lift the restrictive ban on the use of the park area surrounding the fountain. Conti Circle's development since then has transformed Elmwood Park from its appearance during the thirties, when Robert and Anna Nitschke, like the rest of America, were trying to cope with raising a family amid the Great Depression.

By 1936, the couple had two children—Robert Jr., age eight, and Richard, four. Four days after Christmas that year, the Nitschkes welcomed a third son, Raymond.

Life in Elmwood Park was not easy for the Nitschkes. The nation was still enduring hard times, and bread lines and soup kitchens were not far removed from the memory. Robert Nitschke carved out a living for his family with the Chicago Surface Lines, and while their life was no-frills, the Nitschkes never complained. How could they, Ray asked years later, when he and his brothers always had clean clothes and full stomachs?

In 1940, fate dealt a body blow to the Nitschke family. Robert Sr. was returning home from a union meeting when a trolley collided with his car. He was killed in the accident, and Anna was left to raise three growing sons on her own. With her husband deceased, Anna went to work for a relative, Pete Rasmussen. To the Nitschke kids, he was Uncle Pete, the owner of Pete's Place. Located on the corner of Grand Avenue near the railroad tracks in River Grove, Pete's Place was a tavern typical of the neighborhoods of Elmwood Park. The food was home-cooked, there was always a card game in the back room, and the same people showed up every Friday and Saturday night. The clientele was mixed, factory workers mingling with white-collar types, but they were all on a first-name basis.

"It was kind of a hard place to live because it was right near the railroad tracks," remembered Jan Smid, who grew up in nearby River Grove and was a long-time friend of the Nitschke brothers. "It wasn't the slums, but it was mediocre housing. It was a small town, and everybody knew everybody from the three or four towns around us."

Chuck Heyward, a friend of Richard Nitschke's who also lived in Elmwood Park, remembered the Nitschke's home as a "fixer-upper," located in a very poor section of Elmwood Park. Anna worked two jobs to support the family, yet despite his mother's absence from home, Ray grew extremely close to her. She was his life, and he recognized how hard she worked for her children. On most days, her only relaxation came after she had finished her shift as a waitress at Pete's Place. Taking a seat at the bar, she would relax with a beer before heading home. Years later, Ray remembered that as the only fun she seemed to have.

Anna's work ethic undoubtedly made an impression on her children. When he was old enough, Ray worked alongside his mother in Pete's Place, peeling potatoes and doing odd jobs. Times being what they were, he literally was paid in pennies for his work. But it was spending money, and he picked up a few extra coins from his grandmother. Anna worked long hours at the tavern, but by the time Ray was six, the family was struggling so much financially his oldest brother Robert, who was getting ready to start high school, went to work for the railroad to earn extra money for the family. He was just 14, but at six feet tall was big for his age. With his mother away at work, Robert often took on the role of family disciplinarian. He knew how to administer justice, but he also knew when to back off. On one occasion, Robert was disciplining Ray with the belt, and the thought crossed Ray's mind that if Robert hit him one more time, he was going to have an injured kid brother. Robert must have known it too, because he quickly ended the punishment.

Of the three brothers, Richard was the quietest. Because they were the same age, Smid hung out most with Richard. To Smid, Richard was more easy going than Robert, but when he told Ray "no" on occasion, Ray would listen. While friends would call the brothers "Bob" or "Rich" or "Ray," the brothers always called themselves by their full names. It was always "Robert," "Richard," and "Raymond."

While Robert and Richard had quickly grown to an impressive physical size, Ray was smaller and thinner. He was enrolled in Elmwood Park grade school, then transferred to Elm School. He had his father's facial features—the wide mouth, the prominent nose—and his thick shock of sandy hair was close-cropped on the sides with bangs hanging just above his eyebrows. A school photo shows him wearing a dark button-down sweater, horizontal-striped shirt and jeans cuffed at the ankles. His large, scuffed shoes protrude from the bottom of the desk.

"Ray was a tag-a-long," Smid said. "A skinny, scrawny, snot-nosed kid."

Little Ray was skinny but aggressive. He hung around the nearest playgrounds, playing football, basketball, and baseball with Richard and some of the older, bigger kids in the neighborhood. Since Robert was working and didn't have time for sports, Ray spent much of his free time with Richard. The two competed with one another constantly, and because Richard was older and bigger, he usually beat Ray at whatever game they were playing. The losses bothered Ray but didn't discourage him; he still competed hard with Richard, still tried to outdo him in football, basketball, and baseball, still worked hard to be better than Richard was.

Heyward, who went through grammar school and high school with Richard, remembered joining with kids their age from the neighborhood to play sandlot tackle football games in an empty lot on Fullerton Avenue and 78th Street in Elmwood Park. "Ray would come over and ask to play," Heyward recalled, "and we told him to run off because he was too small. He was very slim, didn't weigh much."

Ray's determination eventually become a trademark of his Hall of Fame career. Just as he grew used to taking on kids who outweighed him by 50 pounds in playground scuffles, Ray grew used to taking on linemen who outweighed him by the same amount during his NFL career. Just as he competed hard with Richard and was never satisfied with second place, Ray competed hard to become the starting middle linebacker in Green Bay and was never satisfied with being second-string.

By the time he was 13, Ray followed Richard's path to Proviso High School in Maywood. Elmwood Park didn't have a high school, so students graduating eighth grade had a choice of choosing between several high schools in the area. Richard had gone to Maywood, located some five miles from Elmwood Park, and played football there, and Ray decided to do the same. He was 13, just starting high school, when his mother was admitted to the hospital. Ray was stunned. For 10 years she'd had two jobs and had taken on the dual role of mother and father to her boys. Yet she had never taken time off for illness, never gone to the doctor. She was still young, just 41 at the time, and because of her youth and vigor, Robert, Richard, and Ray believed their mother would spend a few days in the hospital and then return home.

Later, the boys would find out that their mother had been bleeding internally but hadn't gone to the doctor. Anna had always been self-sufficient, and any time she had been sick, she had taken care of herself rather than seek medical treatment. A week after her admission to the hospital, Anna died of a blood clot. Her death devastated her sons. Robert was 21, Richard 17, and Ray 13, and when their mother passed, Ray said later it was as if the world had come crashing down on their shoulders. They were orphans, and at Anna's funeral, Ray overheard his aunts and uncles discussing which of the boys they would take in. "I'll take one," Ray heard one person say, "if you'll take another of the boys."

Robert and Richard, however, decided there would be no dividing up of the Nitschke boys. Together they would raise Ray, who was just starting his freshman year.

"Bob was a father figure," recalled Smid. "Their mom raised them, and then Bob took over when their mother passed. He was of age, and he took it upon himself to raise them and keep the house and family together."

Ray entered high school confused and angry over his mother's passing. He wondered why he had been orphaned, what he had done to deserve such a fate. "Why did she have to die?" he asked himself. She was the one who had given him all his love, the one he loved so much in return. He seethed at the loss of his mother, and without the discipline of his parents to help him deal with his anger, channeled his rage into street fights. He weighed barely 100 pounds as a freshman but grew up, as he said later, "belting the other boys in the neighborhood and getting belted back." He signed up for a Boy Scout troop, got into a fight at the first meeting, and was told to never come back.

By his own admission, Ray became a loner; he was against everyone and everything. He didn't seem to have any friends and didn't seem to want any either. All he knew is that every other kid in the neighborhood had a mother, and his had passed away. He spent hours after school and on weekends away from everyone else. He would take his football out to the park and kick it, chase it down by himself, and kick it again. He played basketball alone too. When winter storms covered the Chicago courts with snow, Ray would carry his shovel to the playground, clear the courts, and shoot baskets alone.

Ray used his shovel in other ways as well, earning spare change in the winter by clearing snow-filled sidewalks. Because his neighbors shoveled their own walks, he would head over to River Forest, an upper-class neighborhood where residents would pay to have their driveways and walks cleared. During the Christmas holiday he would go door to door in River Forest, singing carols until residents paid him to stop. In the summer, he returned to River Forest to mow lawns and picked up pocket change as a caddie at a local golf course. He found the pastoral settings of River Forest pleasing. His world in Elmwood Park was strictly steel and mortar—neighborhoods, schoolyards, playgrounds, city streets. Neither Robert nor Richard owned a car, so Ray rarely did any traveling. To him, anything ten miles outside the city limits could be classified as "the country." Since he had been kicked out of the Scouts, Ray was never able to take part in camping trips. Golf offered scenery he could appreciate, a chance to explore nature. Caddie Day offered something else, an opportunity to actually play the course. Nitschke, who owned an awkward but strong swing, developed a love for the game that remained with him the rest of his life.

When he wasn't caddying, he was delivering papers for the *Chicago Tribune*. The job was solitary, and Ray liked it. He would rise at 5:30 every morning, roll the papers up tight, and then send them spiraling toward porches. He saw every paper as a football and every delivery as a long bomb. His errant heaves shattered porch lights and windows, and early risers could mark his route by the sound of breaking glass and an irate customer's screech. In time, Ray lost so much money paying for broken property he could no longer afford to be a paper boy.

Sports provided Ray an outlet for his aggression and role models for him to follow. He had no one to look up to in the business world, so he turned his attention to the athletes making the headlines on the sports pages. He collected baseball and football cards and studied them with such intent he could rattle off player's statistics from memory. He knew, for instance, that when Chicago Bears fullback Bronko Nagurski retired in 1943, he had gained 4,013 yards rushing in a nine-year NFL career. Ray followed Chicago Bears football and Chicago Cubs baseball and since Wrigley Field served as the home field for both teams and was just a short bus ride from his home, he made the trip on several occasions to see firsthand the heroes he followed on the radio and in newsprint.

Ray attended his first Bears game at Wrigley Field in 1949. The Bears that season were a team in transition, much different than the '43 championship team that had captured his attention as a seven-year-old. Head coach George Halas had sold a young quarterback named Bobby Layne to the New York Bulldogs, and when veteran Sid Luckman contracted a thyroid condition that sidelined him for much of the season, Halas turned control of the Bears offense over to Johnny Lujack, a second-year pro out of Notre Dame. Lujack led the NFL in touchdown passes, completions, and yards, and he set an NFL record when he beat the Bears' crosstown rivals, the Chicago Cardinals, by throwing for 468 yards in a 52–21 win. Halas's "Monsters of the Midway" were a colorful team, renowned for their rough physical play. Linebacker Ed Sprinkle, nicknamed "The Claw" for his clothesline hits, symbolized the Bears' style. Ray grew enamored of the team's fierce, no-frills play, and dreamed about playing in the NFL for Halas and the Bears.

Ray had little ambition outside of sports and went to school only because he knew he had to. Classmates thought he came from a tough but loving home, yet since there was usually no one to go home to after school, Ray would head to his aunt's house or go off by himself. He walked alone, thinking about where his life was heading and what he was going to do. He was still small, but as he entered Proviso High he was determined to prove he was as good as anyone else, even the boys with mothers. He would prove it the only way he knew how: by being a better athlete than they were.

Proviso was, and is, a sprawling school district with a large student body. It draws students from a dozen different communities, and while the school has since been divided into Proviso East and West, in Ray's time it was one school with student attendance numbering more than four thousand. Located just ten miles west of Chicago, Proviso serves students from Maywood, Melrose Park, Broadview, and Forest Park. The school, a brown-brick building constructed in 1910, is situated on First Avenue in Maywood and over the years has undergone renovations in the form of two additions. The Proviso East/West split occurred on July 1, 1958, and Proviso West was founded in Hillside. The school's motto of "Peace, Pride, and Power" has long encouraged Proviso students to promote peace in their school community and the world; pride in their school, staff, and in the success of the students; and the tenet that knowledge is power.

Because of the large number of students in 1951, Proviso fielded three freshman football teams. Ray played on the C team, the least talented of the three. He was an underdeveloped 13-year-old, competing against boys aged 14 and 15. He became a fullback, and while the sight of a 100-pounder carrying a ball that seemed almost as big as he was didn't scare too many defenders, Ray never backed down from an altercation, on or off the field.

The void in his life continued to grow. He pushed himself to go to school and thought privately about running away from home. Robert and Richard were working, and while Ray loved them both, he saw them as being not much more than boys themselves. He went to school mainly to get away from his home life, but his lack of interest caused his grades to suffer. He needed a C average to stay eligible for sports, but with his mind occupied by his mother's death, he failed two subjects. When he returned to Proviso High for his sophomore season, he was told he was academically ineligible to participate. Since sports was one of the primary reasons why he was still going to school, Ray was jolted into improving his grades. He raised them enough to become eligible again his junior year, but for the rest of his life he regretted letting his grades slide and losing his eligibility during his sophomore season.

The year away from sports saw Ray change not just academically but physically as well. He had large feet and hands, as well as a sizable desire to be at the center of action for every sport he played. He wanted to control every game he played in, so he tried out for quarterback in football, center in basketball, pitcher in baseball. His oversized hands helped him excel in all three sports. The summer before his junior season Ray was throwing a football around the field when Proviso's varsity football coach, Andy Puplis, caught a glimpse of him while driving by. Ray uncorked a pass that Puplis later said flew "a country mile." That fall, Ray became the starting quarterback on the Proviso varsity.

Ted Leber, a sophomore at Proviso when Nitschke was a junior, saw the dramatic change in Nitschke from his sophomore to junior seasons.

"He was a 5-foot-9 guy, and over the summer, he became a 6-foot giant," Leber said. "Was he a tough guy? Sure. I'm sure there were times when people were ticked off at him because he was mean. And he didn't care. If somebody wanted a poke in the nose, he'd poke them in the nose. If somebody challenged him, he stood up to them. Ray was one bad sucker."

Heyward saw the change in Ray too after returning to Elmwood Park from the University of Louisville, where he was a teammate of a young, crewcut quarterback named John Unitas. "I had played football at Proviso and at the beginning of Ray's junior year I had come back to work out with the team before going to Louisville," Heyward said. "We had a drill where one back would post and the guy behind carrying the football would stiff-arm him, spin, and pull away. I posted for Ray one time and he practically knocked me over. Ray had grown up and was a lot stronger."

Jack Meihlan shared a study hall with Ray at Proviso, and the two would head off to the school's training room to work out together. Meihlan was an Illinois state wrestling champion but, at 127 pounds, was much smaller than the hulking Nitschke.

"He was supposed to be giving me a massage to loosen me up, and he'd be bouncing me around the wrestling mats," Meihlan said. "He would literally lift me off the mats and pound on me. I'd ask him, 'What the hell, Ray?' He was known to be kind of a rough kid, and he did have a temper. He clobbered one of the P.E. teachers at the school once."

Of all the authority figures at Proviso, Ray most admired Puplis. A former All-America quarterback at Notre Dame, Puplis inspired his rough-hewn quarterback with his gentlemanly ways. To a 15-year-old who had been lacking a father figure in his life since the age of three, Puplis provided a role model that later influenced Ray in his own future dealings with children.

"Andy Puplis was very soft-spoken," Meihlan remembered. "But he was a great leader and a fine educator. He was also a helluva football technician. We had some hellish football teams in the fifties."

Tony Fiovani was a freshman quarterback the year Nitschke was a senior. To Fiovani, Puplis was a coach that the younger players in the program were eager to play for.

"A lot of the assistant coaches at Proviso were from Maywood, so they already had their teams picked beforehand," Fiovani said. "And a lot of the kids they picked were Maywood kids. So you had a lot of guys playing out of position on the lower levels. But once we got to the varsity, Puplis would tell us, 'I'm going to keep my eye on you.' He was very fair, just a phenomenal guy. I just couldn't wait to get to practice. All the kids in the neighborhood wanted to play for him.

"He was real quiet, real mild-mannered, but a real good technician. He spent a lot of time with his quarterbacks, and he made athletes out of them.

I had him for study hall, and he would teach me how to read defenses, what to look for.

"Puplis made successes out of people because of his work as a coach and an educator. He probably saved Ray's life. Ray didn't have a father figure and Puplis filled that role. A lot of the success Ray had in his formative years was due to Andy."

Puplis showed Ray not only how to handle himself on the field but off the field as well. Nitschke was still feeling sorry for himself, still feeling resentful of others. He disliked those peers who seemed to have it all—a great family life, a new car, new clothes, plenty of money. Ray had none of those luxuries, and just to level the playing field, would level the egos of the rich kids whenever he could. If one of them did 10 pushups, Ray would do 15. If one of them ran a mile, Ray pushed himself a mile-and-a-quarter. He had an inner hunger to prove himself equal, and he knew the only place he could do it was in sports. He learned at an early age that nothing comes easy, but he found out that if a person is willing to give that extra effort, they can succeed. Whenever he became discouraged, whenever he felt like quitting, Ray gave himself a pep talk. "Uh-uh," he would say, "I'm not going to give up." That hunger to prove himself, to push himself to be better than the next guy, was an advantage he carried through the rest of his career.

"When Ray was a young person growing up, he had a fair amount of rage," said Al Pahl, who as editor of *Ray Nitschke's Packer Report* from 1986–95 became close to Ray. "His father had been taken from him at an early age and he literally was mad at God for a great number of years. Football was a way for Ray to channel that rage, even though I'm sure it was an unconscious thing. A kid at 15 years old doesn't make a conscious decision, 'Well, I better play football so I don't get my ass in a sling.' But it was football that kept his ass out of the sling."

Ray funneled his aggressive nature into football, prompting Puplis to call him the meanest kid he had ever coached. Puplis loved Ray's aggression on the field, but he sat him down on several occasions to talk about the virtues of controlling his temper to avoid being thrown out of games. It was fine to be aggressive on the field, Puplis told him, but if a player didn't harness his aggression he hurt not only himself but the team as well. Always eager to be where the action was, Ray made a lot of tackles on defense from his safety position but made a lot of mistakes as well. He often left his assigned position early, and smart quarterbacks would take advantage by floating passes over Nitschke's head to the receiver he was supposed to be covering.

"Ray played safety like a linebacker," Fiovani remembered.

Nitschke took the talks with Puplis to heart and realized that playing aggressively, playing "mean" as he put it, was fine since to him "mean" meant playing hard and never giving up. But he remained an abrasive, belligerent type, even to teammates.

"I had been a manager of the freshman and sophomore football teams," Leber said, "and at some point in my sophomore year I said, 'I can play as good as these third-stringers.' So I went out for football, and I was going through a drill where the quarterback puts the ball in your stomach. And Ray put that ball in my stomach and I collapsed. He did it on purpose because I was the smallest guy on the field and he didn't think I belonged there. And that was just Ray. He was a gentleman in later years, but then he was a mean S.O.B."

Leber carries a constant reminder of Ray's hard play just below his right knee, a quarter-inch scar courtesy of Nitschke's cleats. "I played safety against the varsity and he just ran right over me," Leber said. "I have this permanent scar because I tried and just couldn't stop him. I remember his mean streak in various forms. He picked up one of our first-string guards and threw him into a locker. I looked into the locker after the guy got up and it was halfway bent. Ray was a strong, tough guy."

Nitschke carried his aggressive style to the basketball court, playing that winter under Proviso varsity coach Joe Hartley. Hartley also coached the freshman C football team and remembered Ray as a skinny fullback from two years earlier. When he saw him on the basketball court, he took one look at Nitschke's oversized feet and thought he must be wearing his older brother's sneakers. But when Hartley looked closer at Ray's hands, he called assistant coach Ray Rice over.

"This kid's feet are for real," Hartley told Rice. "Take a look at the size of those hands."

Smid, who later played the line for the University of Illinois and has large hands, said Nitschke's hands were so large they engulfed everyone else's. "We'd shake hands," Smid said, "and I would look down and say, 'Where the hell is my hand?' "

In later years, Green Bay Hall of Fame cornerback Herb Adderley would express the same amazement at the size of Nitschke's bearlike paws. "He had huge hands," remembered Adderley, who played alongside Nitschke from 1961 to 1969. "Great hands. He didn't drop many balls that came his way. He and (tight end) Ron Kramer had the best hands on the team. I never saw Ron Kramer drop a pass in practice or during a game and Nitschke, very seldom would he have a chance for an interception and not get it."

Ray's growth spurt continued, and when he returned to play football his senior season, he added another 20 pounds in weight and two inches in height. He was now 6-foot-1, 190 pounds, with tremendous hand and arm strength.

"He got awfully big awfully fast," Meihlan said. "It was kind of strange because he lost his hair too, and he had always had a big head of sandy hair."

Ray's increased size and strength allowed him to throw a football a great distance, and throw it with great force. He once knocked the helmet off his receiver with one of his passes, leaving his teammate temporarily stunned by the impact.

"He threw the ball hard, no question," Leber said. "And there were a lot of times when he threw it too hard to one of the ends and the coaches would say, 'What do you expect? They can't catch that stuff.' "

Proviso had posted a 3–4 record during Ray's junior season in 1952, but the Pirates improved dramatically the following year. With Nitschke starting at quarterback, Proviso cruised to victories in its first four games of the season. Week Five saw Proviso trailing New Trier High, 29–18, as the fourth quarter approached its midway point. Nitschke looked up at the stands, saw fans filing toward the exits, and shook his head. He couldn't understand. He looked at the clock, saw there were eight minutes still remaining, and thought, "We're going to win."

Resisting the notion to use his arm strength to throw for deep scores, Ray relied on a short passing game. He finished with 153 passing yards in the fourth quarter alone and led Proviso to two touchdowns and a 30–29 comeback win. One week later, the Pirates settled for a tie against Highland Park, but with a 6–0–1 record, Proviso entered its final game of the season needing a win over Oak Park to become champions of the Suburban League. At the time, the Suburban League was considered the toughest high school league in Illinois. The championship game against Oak Park reflected the league's balance. Proviso trailed 19–14 in the final quarter, and the visiting Huskies had driven down to the Pirates 7-yard line. With seven minutes remaining, an Oak Park score would have clinched the victory. But the drive stalled on the 1, leaving Nitschke the option of engineering a 99-yard drive to the title-winning score or losing the championship. It was the kind of scenario Ray had been dreaming about for years, ever since his childhood days when he and his mother would go to the games to watch Proviso play Oak Park. Sitting in the stands with his mother, Ray was amazed at the physical size and talent of the high school boys, and he would dream of one day being one of them, being a Pirate and playing the Huskies.

Now the opportunity was his, and he looked to make the most of it. With a sell-out crowd of more than 7,000 fans rocking Proviso's home field, Nitschke dropped back from his own 1-yard line and fired an 11-yard completion to Pete Fiorito. Nitschke drove the Pirates to the Oak Park 1, thanks in large part to Fred Keys, who made several spectacular catches to keep the drive alive. With 1:03 remaining, Nitschke turned and handed off to Fiorito, who plunged in over right tackle for the game-winning score. Ray closed out his senior season with 50 completions in 99 attempts. He threw for 750 yards and nine touchdowns, rushed for an additional 213 yards, and averaged nearly five yards per carry. He had been named "Prep Player of the Week" during the regular season, and when his name appeared in the *Chicago American* newspaper, Ray clipped the article and showed it around Pete's Place. *Scholastic Coach* magazine tabbed Nitschke and Fiorito as honorable mention selections to their 1953 All-America high school football team.

Following the football season, Ray played center for Proviso's varsity basketball team. Hartley called Nitschke his "tiger," but had to suspend him for one game when Nitschke lost his temper and told the coach to go screw himself. He was reinstated because he was a good athlete and the team needed him.

"He wasn't that tall, maybe 6-1 as a senior," Leber said, "but he was tough under the boards. He got into position and he got his shots and got his rebounds and he hustled up and down the court."

Nitschke admitted later that while he wasn't the smoothest center who ever played, he did have good elbows. He took every game as a challenge to prove himself, and he would get angry with Hartley if the coach chose someone other than him to guard the other team's best frontcourt player.

"Ray was a competitor," Leber said. "Every inch of the way."

As a team, Proviso was solid but unspectacular, and the highlight of the season came in a game against Oak Park. With both teams using stall tactics, Proviso led at halftime, 6–2. Both teams loosened up in the second half, and the Pirates walked off with a 41–30 victory. Albert Lee Stange, who started at the guard position and overshadowed Nitschke both athletically and socially, was the star of the team. Stange, who went by his middle name Lee, ranked sixth in the conference in scoring and was named all-conference. He later went on to pitch 10 years in the major leagues and compiled a 62–61 record with four American League teams.

Nitschke's personal highlight came in a game against St. Edwards, when he scored a school-record 36 points. That mark remained a school record for 17 years, until Dave Roberts surpassed it during the 1970–1971 season. At season's end Nitschke was passed over for all-conference honors but did gain an honorable mention selection.

"Ray could shoot a basketball," remembered Boyd Dowler, a teammate of Nitschke's in Green Bay from 1959 to 1969. "We used to play exhibition games during the off-season in Green Bay and he could really shoot. He had real good hands, and a lot of athletic ability."

In the spring, the Proviso baseball team advanced to the state championship game against Bloomington. Nitschke had earned a reputation as a strong-armed pitcher; Leber thought Nitschke's fastball was the most explosive he had ever caught at the high school level.

"He was a great pitcher," said Leber, a catcher on the Proviso team. "He had the fastest ball I ever caught. And every time he threw it, it hurt."

The state championship game was played at Tom Conners in Peoria, and while Nitschke didn't pitch, he batted third and started in leftfield. He contributed to the Pirates' win with a massive home run over the centerfield fence. The Proviso school newspaper, *The Pageant*, described the ball as having traveled "a stated distance of 700 feet." Actually, the distance was later estimated at 560 feet, but it was a tremendous blow nonetheless. Nitschke batted .500 in the state tournament and his baseball skills impressed major league scouts. The *Chicago Tribune* named him to the paper's Second Team All-State squad, and the St. Louis Browns offered him a professional contract and $3,000 signing bonus. The money was tempting to Ray, as was the idea of someday playing major league baseball. He'd always enjoyed the game and found it easier to play than football. But he saw baseball as a game for individualists. Football, he thought, required more teamwork and was more physical, two intangibles that appealed to him.

Until he reached his senior year in high school, Nitschke hadn't given much thought to what he wanted to do after graduation. He didn't think seriously about college, simply because no one he was close to had ever continued their education beyond high school. To people with blue-collar backgrounds like the Nitschkes, college was for the rich kids who lived in River Forest, the kids whose driveways he used to shovel and whose lawns he used to mow. Since college didn't appear to be an option, Ray never prepared himself academically while in high school. He didn't take prep courses, merely went through the motions in classes like math and composition. When he found a course he liked, as in history, he usually did well in it.

"When I was tutoring him in math he was not bright, but he didn't study either," Leber said. "He showed himself to be a competitor and an outstanding performer, and I think everybody thought he could be a great ballplayer of some sort. But we all thought that he would flunk out because he was that kind of guy."

Meihlan agreed, and he recalled that the talk among Nitschke's classmates at Proviso was about "how the hell he was going to get through it because he had so many problems with school work."

Ray considered the baseball offer from the Browns and also thought about joining the military or going to work in a factory or with a construction crew. They were jobs, he thought, that didn't require a lot of schooling.

When he first got to Proviso, Ray had been mistrustful of his teachers. If he had problems in their course and the teacher would try to help him, he would wonder to himself why were they trying to help him. "Why should they bother with me?" he thought. He had been trying to just get through high school, to keep his grades up just so he could remain eligible to play sports. His outlook on college changed, however, when he began receiving offers for football scholarships to major universities. With the baseball offer from the St. Louis Browns still on the table, and with scholarship offers from football coming from various universities and colleges, Ray had a decision to make. Once again, Puplis provided direction.

"Go to college, Ray," Puplis said. "Get an education. Make something of yourself. Take advantage of your God-given ability."

The $3,000 baseball offer from the Browns was hard for Nitschke to turn down; to him, it seemed like all the money in the world. If he didn't take the money now, Ray thought, he might never see that much money in a lump sum the rest of his life. His respect for Puplis was so strong, however, that if his coach told him to go to college, it must be the right thing to do.

Nitschke turned down the Browns' offer, then turned his focus on deciding which college he should attend. Since he had only maintained a C average at Proviso, some schools weren't interested in him. Ray visited several universities, including the University of Miami, but his desire to play for a Big Ten school and in the Rose Bowl influenced his decision to accept a scholarship to play football at the University of Illinois. In high school, he had written an English theme paper about the Rose Bowl. As he pondered his future, the Fighting Illini featured a great player in J. C. Caroline, and the fact that Puplis had sent other Proviso players to Illinois and that the Illini coach was Ray Eliot were a positive factor in Ray's mind. Nitschke had met Eliot at an all-state football dinner hosted in the Executive Mansion in Springfield by Governor William G. Stratton. Eliot quickly became one of Nitschke's mentors, much like Puplis had been.

When he committed to Illinois, Nitschke believed firmly he was about to fulfill a long-time dream. With him at quarterback, he thought, the Illini would win the Big Ten, qualify for the Rose Bowl, and then win that game as well.

The Rose Bowl was still the number one bowl game at the time, and Nitschke wanted to be the quarterback who won it. That would be his way of showing everyone at Proviso that Ray Nitschke was as good as anyone, as long as he was playing football.

TWO

FOOTBALL had earned Ray Nitschke a full scholarship to the University of Illinois. But it would take two full years before the blue-collar kid from Elmwood Park would believe he really belonged in college.

By the time he enrolled at Illinois in the fall of 1954, Nitschke was showing signs of social growth. His senior year at Proviso High had seen him excel as a three-sport athlete, and Nitschke started to shed his loner status. His athletic ability allowed him to feel more like an equal, and he began hanging around his peers at the local pizza parlors and drugstores. Once he reached college, however, Nitschke again began feeling out of place. He had grown up on the urban fringe of Chicago, and with the university situated in a rural setting, Nitschke saw himself as a big-city guy among hayseeds. Because he had lived in Elmwood Park, people assumed he was street-wise and tough, and Nitschke not only went along with that stereotype; he tried to live up to it. He started smoking, favoring Chesterfield cigarettes and pipe tobacco, and began drinking regularly. Nitschke and alcohol were a combustible mix, and he didn't handle liquor well. A few beers and Nitschke would begin mouthing off. On several occasions, he went from trading barbs to trading fists.

Nitschke's troubles his first two years in college weren't confined to off-the-field activities. He majored in physical education because it was the field of study that interested him the most, but it didn't take long for him to realize he wasn't prepared academically for his courses. He had never done much homework at Proviso and didn't really know how to study. Classes at the university were larger than they had been in high school, the pace was quicker, and for the most part didn't have the same one-on-one relationship with college professors that he had at Proviso. His status as a scholarship athlete was both help and hindrance. Some of his professors, particularly those in the physical education department, gave Nitschke extra help because they wanted to see him remain eligible to play football. Other teachers, however, denigrated him as a dumb jock, and Nitschke believed they were tougher on the student-athletes than on the regular students. One professor, upon finding out that Nitschke was a football player, made him sit in the back of the classroom by himself.

Nitschke struggled through his courses, and English and botany proved particularly difficult for him to grasp. He had never been good in English, couldn't write very well, and the only thing he knew about botany was that his aunt had cooked similar-looking plants and served them in his Uncle Pete's tavern. The customers at Pete's Place didn't care about the private lives of the greens they were eating, and Nitschke didn't know why he had to study them in botany.

When Chuck Heyward returned to Illinois from Louisville to take a summer job with Coca-Cola, he saw Nitschke hitch-hiking along the road and picked him up. During their ride home Heyward asked how things were going. Football's going okay, Nitschke said, but his grades weren't so good.

Feeling somewhat like a big brother, Heyward offered Nitschke some advice.

"Now, Ray," he said. "You've got to work on those grades because you can't make a living playing football."

Nitschke's academic difficulties were compounded by his lack of available study time. Along with becoming a member of the Illini's 60-man freshman football team, he took a job to earn a little spending money and made $50 each month working in the school's athletic association laundromat. Nitschke found help for his studies from two sources. The Illinois Alumni Association hired a tutor to assist with his studies, and Jan Smid, his roommate, did what he could to speed Nitschke's acclimation to the quicker pace of college life. The captain of the Illini's varsity football team and an All-America guard, Smid was three years older than Ray. They had known each other for years, Smid having grown up in River Grove not far from Nitschke's neighborhood in Elmwood Park, and he had been a friend of Ray's older brother Richard.

To Ray, Smid was like a big brother. And like an older brother, Smid was always trying to ditch Ray. "I always told him to stay the hell away from me," Smid said. "I didn't want him hanging around with me."

Smid saw Nitschke as an outgoing kid and knew he had a reputation for trouble as well. "He was a hell-raiser," Smid said. "When you have the kind of life he did, you're around a different element. But he was a good guy. I never had any problems with him. I'd tell him to shut his face and he'd shut up."

Nitschke credited Smid with helping him smooth his transition from being a well-known star in high school to being just another face in the crowd in college. The transition was less difficult on the football field, where Nitschke started at quarterback for the freshman team and quickly made a name for himself as a physical player who relished contact.

Nitschke wasn't graceful but he was effective, particularly when he broke from the pocket and ran with the ball. One writer observed that Nitschke "didn't run to daylight, he ran to flesh." Nitschke's physical play made him perfect for the special teams, and he was used as a punt returner. In the course of returning one particular punt, Nitschke collided with a large lineman on the opposing team, and the force of their contact reverberated throughout the stadium. Both men recoiled from the blow, but while Nitschke recovered to gain extra yardage, he saw his would-be tackler falling stiff and motionless.

As a quarterback, Nitschke loved to throw the long bomb, and in fellow freshman Bobby Mitchell he found a wide receiver with the speed to outrun defenders and the sure hands to haul in the deep ball. A star running back and wide receiver with the Cleveland Browns and Washington Redskins from 1958 to 1968, Mitchell and Nitschke formed a future Pro Football Hall of Fame combination on the Fighting Illini freshman team. The two practiced together constantly, Nitschke heaving long passes to the end zone and Mitchell hauling them in, and they looked forward to the time they'd become eligible to play varsity and be an All-America quarterback– receiver combination.

"At that time, freshman couldn't play on the varsity team," recalled Mitchell. "I had been seeing this big guy walking around and I thought he was a linebacker or a lineman, but as it turned out he was a freshman quarterback. We talked and all, and when the freshmen practiced against the varsity, Ray and I would tear them up. Ray would throw the ball about 60 yards in the air and I would run under it and catch it. The freshmen were killing the varsity and they didn't know what to do about it.

"So that's how we got started together, and we both made the varsity the next year and we had a good time together. We played together those three varsity years and I got to know him real well. We would ride each other all around the campus. My middle name is Cornelius, and he was the only one on the team who knew it. I'd be walking across the campus and hell, I'd be a quarter of a mile away and I could hear him screaming. '*Cornelius! Cornelius, where ya goin'?*' People would be looking around and I'd say to Ray, 'Shut up, man!' "

A sudden lack of depth in the Illini running game caused head coach Ray Eliot to reshuffle his offense the following season. Joe Gorman, the Illini's starting fullback, was declared ineligible before the first day of practice, and three days later, Gorman's replacement, Don Kraft, was hospitalized with an appendectomy. With his team down to just one fullback in Danny Wile, Eliot went looking for backfield depth. Remembering the running ability Nitschke had displayed as a freshman quarterback and how he enjoyed running the ball, Eliot called Nitschke into his office.

"Which would you rather be," Eliot asked Nitschke, "the second-string quarterback or my first-string fullback?"

Nitschke's heart sank. He knew that as a sophomore he was deep on the quarterback depth chart behind the more experienced Hiles Stout and Em Lindbeck. Yet while Eliot didn't believe Nitschke could beat out either Stout or Lindbeck for the starter's job, Nitschke did believe it.

"Coach," he said, "I'd rather be the first-team quarterback."

Eliot was unmoved. "Ray," the coach said, "as of now, you're not a quarterback on this team. You're a fullback."

Realizing his dream of quarterbacking the Illini in the Rose Bowl was over, Nitschke broke down and cried in Eliot's office. "Cried like a baby," Mitchell remembered. "But when he was moved to fullback and linebacker, that changed his whole career."

Later, Nitschke would see the justification in his coach's decision. It was a decision made in part because Nitschke lacked the touch on his passes to be an accomplished quarterback at the major college level. No one doubted his arm strength, and in later years the Packers would be amazed at how far he could throw the football. Boyd Dowler, who played quarterback at the University of Colorado before being converted to a wide receiver by Green Bay head coach Vince Lombardi, swore Nitschke could throw the ball 70 yards in practice. Green Bay defensive coordinator Phil Bengston knew of Nitschke's days as a high school quarterback and entertained the notion of making his middle linebacker available to Lombardi as an emergency quarterback if the Packers were ever faced with a sudden shortage.

Every Saturday morning during the regular season, some of the Packers would loosen up before their light workout with a long-throw contest. Even on a team loaded with former and current quarterbacks like Dowler, Bart Starr, Zeke Bratkowski, Paul Hornung, and Willie Wood, there was no doubt who would win.

"Ray won it every year," Starr said. "And it was really funny because what we were doing was seeing who would throw for second place. He literally could just hurl the ball into space. It was unbelievable how far he could throw it."

Asked if Nitschke had any "touch" on his short passes, Starr laughed. "Are you kidding? He'd kill you with the shorter passes," he said. "He'd throw the ball right through you, and I think that was his intent."

Eliot had seen Nitschke zipping his passes around the Illinois practice field, had seen Illini receivers struggling to catch the short throws. Tom Haller eventually became the Illini quarterback, and his strength and throwing accuracy are best reflected in the fact that he later became a major league catcher and played 12 years with the San Francisco Giants, Los

Angeles Dodgers, and Detroit Tigers. He was a member of the 1962 Giants team that lost a seven-game World Series to the New York Yankees, batting .286 in 14 at-bats with one home run, three RBI, and four hits.

Eliot knew Nitschke lacked the necessary skills to lead the Illini offense, and he knew that Ray's grades were so low his freshman year he had to go to summer school just to remain eligible for football. Carrying nine credits, the maximum number allowed at Illinois at the time, Nitschke studied harder than he ever had and earned passing grades in both English and botany. Because of his difficulties in the classroom, Illini coaches weren't sure Nitschke was going to be able to remain academically eligible to play as a sophomore.

The other factor in Eliot's mind was that in 1955, the college game was still one of single-platoon football. Free substitution, instituted in 1941, had been eliminated in 1953. Coaches responded to the rules change by reverting to the single-platoon, meaning players started on both offense and defense. On the change of possession, offensive linemen became defensive linemen, receivers played the secondary and running backs became linebackers. Often, the fullback became the middle guard when the offense switched to defense.

Eliot had watched Nitschke closely in practice, had seen how much the 18-year-old sophomore enjoyed the physical contact during scrimmages. To Eliot, Nitschke was a vicious player, and his aggressive attitude was something the coach was looking for in his fullbacks and linebackers.

"Ray was a tough, hard-nosed football player," Smid remembered. "And he got bigger and nastier."

Nitschke might have been more opposed to switching positions had he not respected Eliot as much as he did. Dark-haired, with clear glasses and a wide, bright smile, Eliot was known as "Mr. Ilini." He held the position of head coach at U of I longer than anyone other than the legendary Bob Zuppke and had graduated from Illinois in 1932 as a three-year letter-winner at the tackle position. After coaching at Illinois College in Jacksonville, Eliot returned to the university in 1937 as an assistant under Zuppke. When Zuppke retired in 1942, Eliot took over as head coach. His teams won Big Ten titles in 1946, '51, and '53, and Rose Bowl victories on New Year's Day in '47 and again in '52.

With his gray fedora, light gray blazers, V-neck sweaters, and patterned ties, Eliot was the picture of authority. He gained a reputation as a motivator and toured the country giving speeches at coaching clinics. To players like Nitschke, Eliot was both father figure and football coach, and he inspired his teams with a simple nine-word motto that in time became a mantra:

"Anything you *think* you can do," Eliot would say, "you *can* do."

In later years, Mitchell would see Nitschke socially, see him with his dark-rimmed glasses, receding hairline, and conservative business suits, and be struck by the influence Eliot had on Nitschke. "I couldn't believe how much they looked alike," Mitchell said with some astonishment. "Ray had become Coach Eliot."

Eliot's influence on his players was evident long after they had left the school, Smid said.

"Eliot made me, as far as I'm concerned," he said. "And he probably made Ray too. He was an inspirational person. He'd get you all worked up for a game, and you would be ready to go through a brick wall for the man. Could he get you up for a game? Oh, yeah. And that was something I missed after I got out of school. When I played a post-season game, I'd say 'Where the hell is Ray Eliot?' "

"Eliot was a Knute Rockne type," Tony Fiovani remembered. "He was a rah-rah, a real motivational speaker. He'd get you so fired up you'd want to run through the door for him."

Nitschke benefited from playing under Eliot at Illinois, and then playing under Lombardi in Green Bay. "Lombardi was hell on wheels," Smid said, "and Ray Eliot was like that too. He was the leader, and he kept you focused and got you to play above your head."

In later years, Nitschke would talk with some amazement to Fiovani about the great run of coaching he had received at Proviso and Illinois, and in Green Bay. "Puplis, Eliot, and Lombardi," Nitschke would say to Fiovani. "Can you find anything better?"

Nitschke took Eliot's inspirational words to heart, and they helped carry him through the difficult transition from quarterback to fullback. He hadn't played fullback since his freshman year at Proviso, and he struggled to reacquaint himself with the technical aspects of the position. As a quarterback the past four years, he had played the game in an upright position. Now, he was down in the three-point stance again, the fingers of his right hand digging into the grass and dirt as he positioned himself in the proper stance—weight balanced on the balls of his feet; right arm forming a tripod with his feet; shoulders squared and back parallel to the ground; head up and eyes looking straight ahead and not to the area to he's going to run.

Every running back has his own distinctive style of running, but all good runners have explosion out of their stance and quickness to the hole. Nitschke wasn't exceptionally quick off the snap and lacked the natural feel for running laterally along the line of scrimmage. He had difficulty absorbing the coaching points of his new position, and it would take two years before Nitschke finally felt comfortable again playing fullback.

"Ray was an offensive-minded guy," Mitchell said, "and once he couldn't quarterback he set out to become a great fullback. But he didn't have that kind of speed and elusiveness to be a great runner."

Even though he was no longer a quarterback, playing varsity football in the Big Ten was the realization of a dream Nitschke had held since he first became a fan of the conference as a boy in the mid-forties. Growing up in Illinois, he had watched the Illini on television several times—in 1948, when Illinois made its first appearance on regional TV and dropped a 6–0 decision to Minnesota on October 16; on New Year's Day in '52, when the Illini defeated Stanford 40–7 on NBC, a game made historic by the fact that it was the first national network telecast of any bowl game and the first national telecast of a college game; and again in 1953 and '54, when the Illini were carried regionally by NBC and nationally by ABC, respectively. So Nitschke knew the history of Big Ten football, knew how it had become arguably the most competitive conference in the country.

American football had been born on the eastern college campuses of Princeton and Rutgers, Harvard and Yale, and the game was nurtured by men like Walter Camp and Amos Alonzo Stagg, Pop Warner and Percy Haughton. Architects of the game—their formations, shifts, and special plays—proved key to the sport's strategic evolution. But it was the midwestern schools, Chicago and Illinois, Michigan and Minnesota, that brought college football to what many considered to be its highest level. After Illinois coach Bob Zuppke, in his thick German accent, declared the Big Ten the "anchor of amateur athletics in America" in the mid-twenties, many viewed his words not as an idle boast, but as a statement of fact.

Coached by Camp, Yale had become college football's first dynasty, dominating the game from 1872 to the turn of the century. But in 1901, Fielding Yost became the first midwestern coach to snatch supremacy away from eastern teams. A master of rapid motion on and off the field, he was called "Hurry Up" Yost and his famous "Point-a-Minute" Michigan teams proved a mirror image of the man. With Yost driving his players—"You're not movin' out there," he would shout, "ya think we got all day?"—the Wolverines overwhelmed opponents. At Ann Arbor in 1904, Michigan defeated West Virginia 130–0, prompting a West Virginia newspaper to headline its account of the game with the words, "Horrible Nightmare." In the 1901 Rose Bowl, the inaugural Tournament of Roses game, Michigan was on its way to an overwhelming win when Stanford coach C. M. Fickert requested the game be stopped. "No sirree," Yost replied. "Let's get on with it." With close to eight minutes left and Michigan leading 49–0, the Wolverines team captain finally agreed to end the game when Stanford pleaded exhaustion.

In 1903, Michigan tied with Minnesota 6–6 in a game that became historic for two reasons. In order to stop Yost's "Point-a-Minute" offense, legendary Golden Gophers coach Dr. Harry Williams employed what is recognized as the first four-man defensive backfield in history. Because the forward pass was rarely used at the time, most college teams stacked the line with nine men to stop the run. Once a runner broke the initial line of defense, however, he was usually on his way to a big gain. To combat Wolverine back Willie Heston, a game-breaker and consensus All-America choice, Williams put just seven men on the line and kept four back. The alignment frustrated Yost, whose team had been winning games that season by scores that staggered the imagination—88–0 over Ferris Institute, 79–0 over Beloit, 76–0 over Albion, 65–0 over Ohio Northern, 51–0 over Indiana. When the Minnesota game ended with the Michigan supermen having scored just six points, Yost was in such a rush to get his team out of town he left behind the brown plaster jug used to supply his team with fresh spring water. Spotting the jug on the departed Michigan sideline prompted one Minnesotan to chidingly remark, "Yost loft his 'yug.' " Minnesota's team trainer followed up by sending a note to his opposite at Michigan, telling him the Gophers had the jug and challenging Yost and the Wolverines to try to get it back the next season. The challenge led to the creation of the Little Brown Jug trophy, given annually to the winner of the Minnesota–Michigan game.

Yost and Michigan set the standard for midwestern football, and through the years men like Zuppke, Iowa coach Howard Jones, Northwestern's Pappy Waldorf, and Minnesota's Bernie Bierman built powerhouse teams that competed for national supremacy. Zuppke's 1923 Illinois squad featured a sophomore named Harold Grange, a redhead whose name in the Roaring Twenties would become as synonymous with college football as Babe Ruth's was with baseball, Jack Dempsey's with boxing. Zuppke once said that All-America players were often made "by a long run, a weak defense, and a poet in the press box." But when it came to Grange, who in Zuppke's thick Berlin accent, was pronounced "Grench," the hard-crusted Illini coach acknowledged that has was coaching the greatest player in college history.

"I will never have another 'Grench'," Zuppke said, "but neither will anyone else."

From Ann Arbor came word that Yost and his Michigan men were unimpressed with the Illini superstar. "All Grange can do is run," Yost snapped. At the time, the statement was akin to saying that all Dempsey could do was punch. Grange responded on game day, running for five touchdowns and 402 yards on 21 attempts. He also threw a touchdown pass, showing Yost he could do more than just run, and personally

accounted for six touchdowns as Illinois christened its new stadium with a
39–14 win before a jam-packed crowd of 66,609.

Stagg called Grange's performance the "most spectacular single-handed performance ever delivered in a major game," and the magnificent redhead rode it into legend. Everything about Grange captured the imagination of the sporting public. His uniform number, 77, was the most famous in football. He was lyricized by the most influential sportswriter of his time, Grantland Rice, who immortalized Grange as "The Galloping Ghost" and seemed mesmerized by Grange's sweeping end runs out of the single wing:

> *A streak of fire, a breath of flame,*
> *Eluding all who reach and clutch;*
> *A gray ghost thrown into the game,*
> *That rival hands may never touch;*
> *A rubber bounding, blasting soul*
> *Whose destination is the goal—*
> *Red Grange of Illinois!*

Led by Grange the Illini offense, with its single-wing and split time, wide sweeps, and novel trap blocks, became the talk of college football. Zuppke once told football historian H. A. Applequist in 1943 that his contributions to the game also included the spiral pass from center to the backs, the screen pass, forward and backward lateral passes, guards protecting the passer, and the formation of the huddle. His greatest contribution, however, could be found in the football itself. Cutting the design from leather in his own workshop, Zuppke remodeled the rounded, bloated footballs of the time into a more streamlined version to suit the modern passing game.

Ray Eliot had been a guard on Zuppke's Illini teams from 1929 to 1931, and in 1941 served as line coach for his aging mentor. When Zuppke stepped down prior to the '42 season, Eliot took over as Illinois head coach. In 1946, the Illini emerged as one of the nation's most improved teams and finished 8–2 to capture the Big Ten title. Illinois capped the season by defeating a previously unbeaten UCLA team, 45–14, in the Rose Bowl. The Illini captured the Big Ten title in 1951 with a 9–0–1 record, the program's first unbeaten season since 1927, then crushed Stanford 40–7 in the Rose Bowl. In 1953, the season before Nitschke's arrival on campus, Eliot guided the Illinois to a 7–1–1 record and a share of the Big Ten championship. The title was the Illini's eleventh conference crown, and the third for Eliot since 1942.

At the start of the 1955 season, Illinois was picked by various observers to supplant Ohio State as Big Ten champions. Captained by future NFL star J. C. Caroline, the Illini opened the season September 24 at the University of California. Playing behind Wile at fullback, Nitschke came off the bench and proved pivotal in the win. Over the summer, Eliot had added a series of "belly" plays to his T-formation offense. The inside belly play is a hard, quick-hitting play in which the quarterback fakes a handoff to the fullback, influencing the flow of the defense in one direction, then gives a reverse handoff to the halfback, who then runs counter to the flow of the defense. The fullback's fake is key, since he must convince the defense that he is the lead runner on the play. The play is most effective against defensive tackles who read and react to the initial flow of the offense.

Eliot had planed to save his belly series for Ohio State, but decided to open the season with it against California. Pulling on the Illini's bright orange helmet that was *sans* facemask and his number 32 jersey, Nitschke smashed fearlessly into the line time and again, selling the fake so well the belly play broke for several sizable gains. California defensive tackles grew increasingly frustrated chasing Nitschke along the line of scrimmage only to realize too late that he didn't have the ball.

Illinois won its opener 20–13 and Eliot was so impressed with Nitschke's play against California he started him the following week in the Illini's home opener against Iowa State. Dressing in the Illini's home colors—dark blue jersey with orange numerals, bright orange pants—and making his varsity start before a throng of 43,457 fans, Nitschke came out anxious and overeager. He fumbled twice in the early going but, rather than become overcautious as some sophomores might have, Nitschke instead became more determined, displaying the same tenacity that had caused him to compete extra hard against his brothers as a kid, the same tenacity that had caused him to outperform many of his peers at Proviso High. He scored three touchdowns and gained 88 yards on 12 carries to lead the Illini to a 40–0 win. Nitschke's hard play prompted one sportswriter to label him the "Proviso Pounder" in his account of the game. When he returned to classes Monday, Nitschke found he had been transformed almost overnight from a nameless, faceless sophomore into one of the Illini's more recognizable players.

Illinois followed the big win over Iowa State by traveling to Ohio State. The Buckeyes were the defending Big Ten and Rose Bowl champions and had gone through the previous season unbeaten and untied. Despite losing Nitschke to a charley horse suffered in practice the week before the game, Illinois was confident entering the game, believing that a victory over OSU would pave the way for the Illini to win the Big Ten. Ohio State, however, had other ideas. Coached by Woody Hayes and led by All-America halfback Howard "Hopalong" Cassady and guard-linebacker Jim Parker, the Buckeyes were a powerful unit that had won the conference in 1954 with a 9–0 record and beaten USC 20–7 in a rain-drenched Rose Bowl. Cassady was enjoying a Heisman Trophy and Maxwell Award season, and was on his way to final totals of 958 yards rushing and 15 touchdowns. With Cassady providing the breakaway threat in Hayes' "three-yards-and-a-cloud-of-dust" offense and a thunderous crowd of 82,407 providing a deafening roar, Ohio State rolled over Illinois, 27–12.

Still struggling with his charley horse injury, Nitschke sat out the next game as well, a 21–13 win at home over Minnesota, then returned to the lineup for the Illini's road trip to Michigan State. The Spartans were led by quarterback Earl Morrall, a player Nitschke would become more familiar with in the NFL. Morrall had gone to Michigan State on a football and baseball scholarship. But after committing five errors at third base against Wisconsin, he decided football would be his sport of choice. In 1955 Morrall accounted for 1,047 yards of total offense and was in the midst of leading Michigan State to a 9–1 record and a 17–14 win over UCLA in the Rose Bowl. From his linebacker position, Nitschke spent much of the afternoon chasing down Morrall, but the Spartans earned a 21–7 win.

Playing opposite Nitschke that day was Spartans center Dan Currie. Like most college players of that era, Currie played offense and defense, and while his job on offense often saw him taking on Nitschke with blocks, his job on defense was to stop Nitschke's bull-like rushes. Ironically, Currie and Nitschke would later be part of a 1958 Packers draft that included fullback Jimmy Taylor and guard Jerry Kramer and is still considered by many to be the best in franchise history.

"I played against Ray for three years when he was at Illinois," Currie recalled. "The NCAA wanted to give the smaller schools a chance, so they figured it would be a penalty for the big schools to have their players play both ways. So we knew each other quite well before we ever ran into each other at Green Bay."

The loss to Michigan State summed up a season that fell far below the Illini's own expectations. Illinois followed by falling to Purdue 13–0, a game marked by a steady Illinois rain and by Nitschke's own difficulties in dealing with the Boilermakers' huge offensive linemen. The Illini defense featured a six-two alignment—six down linemen and two linebackers. Since there isn't a middle linebacker in the six-two, Nitschke always positioned himself over the opposing team's guard or tackle. Against Purdue, Nitschke was startled when he saw the Boilermaker linemen get down in their three-point stance, pick their heads up, and although he was upright, look him straight in the eye because of their great size. Battered physically by Purdue's huge tackles, Nitschke spent a long day picking himself up off the muddy turf.

"He worked so hard at becoming a fullback that he was just another guy at linebacker," Mitchell said. "You couldn't look at him and say this guy was going to be great. There was no way you could get a read on him in college."

Upset by his performance, Nitschke took his revenge out on Michigan in Week Seven of the regular season. He knocked a Wolverine running back unconscious in the first quarter, and the Illini defense held a Michigan passing game that had produced 289 yards and three scores a week earlier to just three completions in 22 attempts in a 25–6 victory.

Nitschke's development as a linebacker was aided by his work with Chuck Studley, his position coach. A standout guard-linebacker with the Illini's 1951 Rose Bowl team, Studley was a strict disciplinarian with a forceful personality. He would grab players by their shoulder pads, and shout in their faces. To Fiovani, Studley was not unlike Lombardi—and Nitschke responded to his coaching.

"Ray got along real well with Studley," Fiovani said.

Following the home win over the Wolverines, Illinois earned a 17–14 win at Wisconsin in a game carried regionally by CBS, Nitschke's first televised collegiate game. The Illini closed their campaign with a 7–7 tie at Northwestern. The Illini finished with a 3–3–1 record in the Big Ten and a 5–3–1 overall mark, but Nitschke's first year on the varsity had left his coaches impressed with his on-field development.

"He improved steadily as a linebacker," Nitschke's 1956 bio reads in the Illini's press book, "and by the end of the season had convinced coaches of his defensive ability."

Impressed them so much that Eliot began telling NFL scouts about Nitschke.

"Ray Eliot was telling NFL scouts that he had a guy he thought could play pro football," Mitchell said. "They asked about me and he said, 'No, he can't play.' He told them to pass me up, that I wouldn't be any good to them. But he said Ray was the one guy that he had that could go pro. He told them, 'Obviously, Nitschke would have to play defense.' He hadn't seen enough of Ray to say he was going to be a great linebacker. No one could. But Ray took that determination that he had offensively and put it into his head defensively.

"One other thing about him. From day one, you could see he had that leadership in him, and he always wanted to express that. I think that came from being a quarterback in high school. He had that leadership thing in his head. Everybody would say, 'Ray, shut up. You don't know what you're talking about.' And that would bother him because he felt he knew what he was talking about. He'd say something and we'd say 'Ray, shut up,' and he'd go right on talking. When he knew for a fact that the only way he was going to play this game was to play defense, then he worked at it."

Nitschke was known around the campus for his hard play and hard drinking, though he was disciplined enough not to imbibe as much during the football season.

"During the week before the game, I seldom saw him drink," Mitchell said. "He was true to his sport. But on the weekends, when his brothers got together, they went farther than beer. If he did anything during the week it was probably just a beer. I'm proud to say that for him. He didn't have his nose red the week of a game."

The off-season was another story. Nitschke frequented assorted Champaign taverns, and his hangouts included Kamm's Annex and the Tumble Inn. The latter proved notable, since it was at the Tumble Inn that Nitschke met Al Herges, a man who, like Andy Puplis and Ray Eliot, would become a role model for Ray. Herges and his wife, Lorraine, had three children—Nancy, Butch, and Peter. Herges took to the rough-hewn Nitschke, and took him home on Sundays to have dinner with the family and relax and talk. Nitschke saw in Herges a father figure, and Herges saw in Nitschke a young man who really had no home life. Hanging out with the Herges family helped Nitschke get away from the pressures of college life. He appreciated Herges so much Ray gave him the baseball cards he had collected since grade school. Some day, Nitschke told Herges, NFL teams will have player cards like major league baseball teams did.

"You'll see my picture on one of them," Nitschke said.

Herges smiled. "Sure, Ray. Sure I will."

That Nitschke was already thinking ahead to playing pro football was indicative of his intense drive to succeed, to prove himself. Mitchell saw the inner drive that Nitschke had, saw the various sides of the boy who was becoming a man.

"I watched him change," Mitchell said. "At Illinois, he was a pretty violent guy. His brothers would come down and they'd turn out all the other bars. Ray became a very close guy with the chief of police, he was with him so much. Our sophomore year, he and another player on our team, Abe Woodson, got in a fight. The fight spilled outside and all around the building, and we all followed it. Abe was backing up and Ray was coming forward the whole time, and Ray couldn't hit him. Abe would hit him two or three times then duck and run back, and Ray just kept coming. It didn't matter what Abe did, Ray just kept coming. Finally, Abe picked up the top of a big trash can and hit Ray over the head with it. It didn't really hurt him, and even Ray had to laugh. It just showed how tough Ray was. You couldn't hurt him, and Abe just got tired of hitting him.

"Back in those days, with the racial situation the way it was, there were a number of places on campus that I couldn't go. But Ray didn't care where it was, we were together. And if we went into a place and somebody said, 'Get outta here,' Ray said, 'Shut up!' That was a helluva thing, and we knew when we were with Ray nobody was going to bother us. He never talked about race, never cared about it. It didn't bother him. Ray was just one of the guys.

"He kind of grew up without a mom and dad, and he and his brothers had to make it on their own. They fought for what they needed and protected their baby brother, although he grew to be bigger than them. Oh, they were rough guys. When they came to the university, Coach would send word to Ray. 'Now tell them damn brothers to cool it! We got a game this weekend and I want you on the field, not in jail.' He'd get excited when they'd show up. He got in fights, and usually they were pretty quick. He'd hit you once and that would be it."

In later years, Green Bay defensive captain Willie Davis remembered Nitschke as someone who saw past the color of a person's skin, an attribute that was of particular importance in a decade as emotionally charged with racial issues as the sixties were.

"Ray went out of his way to help make the minority players feel at home in Green Bay," Davis said. "Green Bay wasn't as diversified in the early sixties as it would be years later, but Ray was one of those guys that the rookies could go talk to."

The Illini opened the '56 season with a 32–20 win at home over California, then promptly dropped three straight. Included in that skein was a 26–6 defeat at home against Ohio State on October 13. The date was significant for Nitschke, who picked up what would become a future trademark on the opening kickoff. Hustling down the field in his facemask-less helmet, Nitschke caught a Buckeye helmet in the mouth. The collision caused two of his teeth to break off and go flying; the other two were dangling by their roots. A teammate shoved a wad of cotton in Nitschke's mouth to slow the flow of blood, and Ray played on—played the whole 60 minutes while spitting blood all over the field. At game's end, Nitschke headed back to the deserted field and began scouring the scarred field for his missing teeth. "How am I going to look with no teeth?" he thought.

His thoughts were interrupted when someone approached and asked Nitschke what he wanted the missing teeth for.

"I want them because they're mine," he said, growling through blood-caked gums.

Nitschke never did find them, and eventually he replaced the missing teeth with a false plate. In future years, his toothless face terrorized NFL opponents, and on occasion, he would startle unsuspecting Ohio State alums by suddenly yanking his bridgework out upon introduction.

"That's what your school did to me," he would say, then issue a gummy grin.

On October 27, Illinois welcomed top-ranked Michigan State to Champaign. The Spartans were the defending Rose Bowl champs, having beaten UCLA 17–14 on Dave Kaiser's 41-yard field goal with seven seconds remaining. Experts listed the Spartans as 21-point favorites over the Illini, and the first half did little to dispel that lopsided line. Illinois trailed 13–0 at halftime, but Eliot opened up the offense in the third quarter. Rather than be restricted to just blocking for halfback Abe Woodson, Nitschke was given a chance to run the ball, and he responded by ripping off a 38-yard gain. The big play set the stage for a Woodson touchdown, and the Illini rallied to score twice more while shutting the Spartans out.

The upset of the No. 1 team in the country proved to be the last highlight of the season for Illinois. The Illini tied Purdue 7–7 the following week, lost to Michigan 17–7, tied Wisconsin 13–13, and fell to Northwestern 14–13 to finish 1-4-2 in the conference and 2–5–2 overall. Nitschke's numbers were a little more rewarding. He had gained 255 yards on 48 carries and averaged an impressive 5.7 yards per carry. He had also been used as a punter, averaging 32.2 yards per kick.

Defense, however, remained his forte. Viewers who had seen the Illini's two televised games his junior season—against Ohio State and Purdue—didn't have the benefit of slow-motion replays that future generations did, so Nitschke's play at linebacker went largely unnoticed by the fans. Coaches around the conference, however, knew that Nitschke was emerging as one of the top linebackers in the Big Ten. By his senior season, he had grown to almost full maturity, standing 6-foot-3 and weighing 225 pounds. Nitschke was still outweighed by as much as 70 pounds by various Big Ten offensive tackles, but three seasons of varsity football had taught him how to deal with the size disadvantage.

Nitschke learned how to sidestep would-be blockers, how to shed linemen by taking a step or two to either side to avoid full contact. He learned, too, to make ballcarriers remember who it was that was leading the Illini in tackles.

"Each time I tackled somebody, I tried to make sure that when he got up and walked away he'd remember Ray Nitschke," he said later. "And I don't mean socially."

Purdue halfback Len Wilson remembered. After being stopped hard by Nitschke in a Week Six game in Champaign, Wilson told a sportswriter he had never been hit as hard during his career as the hit he had taken from Nitschke.

The 1957 season got off to a difficult start for both Nitschke and the Illini. They opened the season with a 16–6 loss at UCLA, and Nitschke was demoted to second-string fullback for the home opener the next week against Colgate. Jack Delveaux, who later went on to play pro football in the Canadian Football League, was promoted to first-string fullback but was injured in a practice scrimmage the week before the game. Eliot returned Nitschke to the first string, and Ray responded. On his first carry of the game, he burst through the middle of the line for a 32-yard pickup. He followed with an 11-yard touchdown run, the first of his three scores in a 40–0 win.

Illinois lost three of its next four games to quickly fall out of contention in the Big Ten and eventually finished with a 3–4 record in the conference and a 4–7 mark overall. The last game of the season provided Nitschke with a fitting finale to his college career. Before hosting Northwestern on November 23, Nitschke had been talking with Bert Bertine, a sportswriter from the *Champaign–Urbana Courier*. The conversation centered on Nitschke's career, and Ray told Bertine he would be satisfied if he could break off just one long run for a score. In practice that season, Nitschke once rambled 99 yards for a touchdown, and he came close to repeating that against Northwestern. Taking the handoff, Nitschke hit off right tackle, picked up blocks from Dick Nordmeyer and Percy Oliver at the line of scrimmage and a downfield block by Rich Kreitling, then shook a tackle by Nick Andreotti en route to an 84-yard TD. At the time, his run was the second-longest in Illini history behind Buddy Young's 93-yard jaunt against the Great Lakes Naval Station in 1944.

Nitschke capped his afternoon with a three-yard scoring run and finished with a career-high 170 yards gained. His final statistics from his senior season included 514 yards on 79 carries, a 6.5 yards per carry average, and five rushing touchdowns. He also caught a touchdown pass and led the team in punting, averaging 32.7 yards per kick. Nitschke hoped his numbers would earn him a nomination to the All-America team. Along with playing in a Rose Bowl game, being an All-America player was a goal Nitschke had since his childhood days in Elmwood Park, when he spent fall weekends reading Big Ten football stories in the sports pages.

Nitschke took his case to the Illini's public relations director, but was turned down. Because Illinois had a losing record, the university didn't think it had a chance to have two of its seniors named to the All-America team, so it was decided to push for just one: Rod Hansen, a two-way end. Hansen didn't make All-America either, but he did make first-team Big Ten. Nitschke had to settle for being named to the Big Ten's second team, but he did gain solace that Cleveland Browns head coach Paul Brown, considered at the time to be the leading football authority in the country, included Nitschke on his list of college seniors the NFL was most interested in drafting and called Nitschke the best linebacker in college football.

Otto Graham, who had quarterbacked Cleveland to seven league championships before retiring in 1955, agreed with his former coach. Serving as head coach of the College All-Star team that would face the NFL champion Detroit Lions in the annual preseason opener in Chicago's Soldier Field, Graham named Nitschke to his roster. The College All-Star lineup that season offered a who's who of future NFL starters: Nitschke, Currie, Jim Taylor, Jerry Kramer, Gene Hickerson, Bobby Mitchell, Lou Michaels, and Wayne Walker. With Mitchell scoring two touchdowns and the College All-Stars outrushing the NFL champions 179–3, the collegians earned a 35–19 win.

Nitschke also played in the Senior Bowl, an experience made memorable for him because it was the first time the game was broadcast nationally and the first time he was ever paid for playing football. He returned home to await the 1957 NFL draft , the first four rounds of which would be held December 2.

For someone who had grown up in Illinois and followed the on-field exploits of Bronko Nagurski and Sid Luckman, there was only one NFL team Nitschke could see himself playing for, only one team he wanted to run on the field with.

The Chicago Bears.

THREE

ON DECEMBER 2, 1957, representatives of the 12 National Football League teams held the first four rounds of their annual college draft. Players who weren't selected in the first four rounds would have to wait until January 28, 1958, when the NFL would hold rounds five through thirty.

The split draft was relatively new to pro football. Until 1956, the NFL held a one-day draft in mid-January; the actual date fluctuated on a year-to-year basis throughout the early 1950s, ranging from as early as January 17 to as late as January 28. In 1956, league officials decided to split the draft into two rounds and move the first three rounds two months earlier in order to give NFL teams an even start with the Canadian Football League, which was looking to upgrade its talent by signing name players from U.S. colleges and universities.

Like hundreds of other college football players in 1957, Ray Nitschke anxiously awaited news of the NFL draft. He knew he could play in the NFL if given the chance, and he wanted more than anything for that chance to come with his favorite team, the Chicago Bears. As a six-year-old in 1943, Nitschke had followed a Bears team featuring Sid Luckman at quarterback, Bronko Nagurski at fullback, and Bulldog Turner at center. On December 26 of that year, he had cause to celebrate three days prior to his seventh birthday, when Chicago claimed a 41–21 win over Washington in the NFL championship game.

Winning the Western Conference for the fourth straight year, these were the Bears of "Monsters of the Midway" fame. The team was coached by George Halas, whose career as an end, coach, and owner paralleled the rise of the NFL. He was the "Papa Bear," and to Chicago-area youths like Nitschke, Halas was football. Halas had attended the University of Illinois, played in the Rose Bowl in 1919, and been named the game's Most Valuable Player. On September 17, 1920, Halas was in Canton when the NFL held its first organizational meeting. For the next three decades he was instrumental in the league's growth but by 1955 had decided in favor of a younger coach. Long-time assistant Paddy Driscoll, who was just two years younger than the 59-year-old Halas, took over and led the Bears back to the NFL title game. Chicago was embarrassed by the New York Giants 47–7 on an icy field in Yankee Stadium, and when the Bears struggled to a 5–7 finish the following season, Halas returned as head coach.

Nitschke sat through the first two rounds of the '58 draft hoping Halas and the Bears would select him. It was a long shot, since Nitschke had starred at linebacker in college, and Chicago was already strong at that position. NFL teams at that time usually drafted players to shore up a weakness, and with veterans Bill George and Joe Fortunato, the Bears had two linebackers of all-pro caliber. Nitschke knew the Bears were loaded at linebacker and wasn't entirely surprised when Chicago used its first two picks to select West Virginia guard Chuck Howley, who would later become a linebacker for the Dallas Cowboys, and Southern Methodist end Willard Dewveall. Dewveall later created a stir when in 1961 he became the first player to voluntarily move from the NFL to the young American Football League, playing out his option with the Bears and joining the Houston Oilers.

Nitschke was startled, however, when he was selected by the Green Bay Packers in the third round. Green Bay's first two choices had been Michigan State center Dan Currie and Louisiana fullback Jim Taylor. The Packers' first pick in the third round was North Carolina State back Dick Christy, and Green Bay used its second pick of the third round, obtained in a trade with the Giants, to select Nitschke. The pick surprised Ray, since one of the few things he knew about the Packers from following their games against the Bears was that they had two solid linebackers in Bill Forester and Tom Bettis. In the Packers, Nitschke was joining a team that had gone 3–9 the previous season and finished last in the Western Conference.

Coached by former Marquette boss Lisle Blackbourn, Green Bay was quietly assembling the nucleus of a great team. Quarterback Bart Starr and offensive tackles Forrest Gregg and Bob Skoronski were products of the 1956 draft; Heisman Trophy winner Paul Hornung and tight end Ron Kramer were the team's top two picks in '57; Nitschke, Taylor, Currie, and guard Jerry Kramer were drafted in '58. Green Bay almost lost Nitschke to the Canadian Football League, however, when he balked at a contract Blackbourn offered following Ray's appearance in the North–South Shrine game. The deal Blackbourn brought to Nitschke was for a $7,000 contract. When Nitschke heard what other college players were signing for, he took Green Bay's offer as an insult. Unimpressed with both the contract and Blackbourn's handling of the negotiations, he resisted the Packer coach's attempts to get him to sign quickly. Nitschke turned his attention from the NFL to the CFL. The Toronto Argonauts had also drafted him, and Nitschke booked a flight to Canada to talk with Toronto team representatives.

Before he left, however, Nitschke made a phone call that would change his life. Contacting Packer talent scout Jack Vainisi, Nitschke told him he was flying to Toronto to talk with Argonaut officials. Vainisi's response was immediate. Urging Nitschke not to go, he arranged to meet with Ray over dinner in Chicago.

Nitschke and Vainisi liked and respected one another, and the Packer scout offered a contract that, while worth only a little more money than the original deal Blackbourn had offered, also promised Ray a $500 bonus upon signing.

The fact that Vainisi had flown to Chicago to meet with him proved to Nitschke that the Packers really were interested in him and eventually proved more persuasive than the $500 signing bonus. Nitschke put the money to good use; he used $300 of it to purchase a 1954 Pontiac, then drove by the home of Al Herges, whose family had adopted Nitschke as one of their own during his playing days at Illinois. Spotting Al's son, Butch, playing basketball in the yard, Nitschke approached him with the remaining $200 of his bonus money in his hand.

"Buy your mom, your brother, your sister, your dad, and your aunt some clothes," Nitschke told Butch, then returned to his car and drove off.

Nitschke's quiet act of gratitude belied the Packer scouting report that labeled the Illinois linebacker "a mean cuss." It was an attitude that the rookie carried into training camp in 1958. He cruised into camp in his Pontiac, a big-city guy taking in a small town. He was still a loner, still carrying a chip on his shoulder, and his abrasive attitude soon alienated members of the town and the community. Nitschke talked too loud, drank too much, and started too many barroom brawls. His childhood insecurities, all stemming from the fact that his mother had been taken away from him, still dogged him. If he was in a bar and had a couple of drinks, Nitschke's mood turned dark and ugly. He would see another patron sitting close to him as an infringement of his privacy. If someone gave him a wrong look, Nitschke took it as a challenge. If someone smiled at him, he would see it as though they were laughing at him.

"Ray was a real loud, kind of obnoxious guy," remembered defensive back Bobby Dillon, a four-time All-Pro who intercepted a Packer team record 52 passes from 1952 to 1959. "He and his brothers would come up to Green Bay and raise hell from time to time. The stories were all around town."

Nitschke carried the same chippy attitude into the clubhouse. When he first arrived in camp, Nitschke saw that the Packers were a team divided. There were various factions on the club, four or five players in each group, all going in their own direction and fraying the fabric of team togetherness. Nitschke stood alone, off to one side, a faction unto himself. Whatever his problems away from the game, he was a determined, aggressive player once he took the field. Blackbourn had promised Ray he would get a shot at either defensive end or outside linebacker, but when the Packers fired

Blackbourn in the off-season and replaced him with assistant Ray "Scooter" McLean, Nitschke was used primarily as a backup to Bettis in Green Bay's four-three defense.

By 1958, the four-three had become the standard defense in the NFL and the middle linebacker was its linchpin. Great middle men like Sam Huff in New York, Bill George in Chicago, and Joe Schmidt in Detroit popularized the position, which grew out of the fertile mind of defensive strategist Steve Owen. As head coach of the New York Giants, Owen had sat in the stands in Philadelphia's Municipal Stadium on the night of Saturday, September 16, 1950, taking notes as the Cleveland Browns of the defunct All-America Football Conference destroyed the two-time NFL champion Eagles. Owen studied how the Browns attacked coach Greasy Neale's five-four "Eagle" defense by spreading them wide with sideline passes and pounding the thinned-out middle with 238-pound fullback Marion Motley. The result, a 35–10 upset by the upstarts, brought a revolutionary response from Owen.

With his team scheduled to face the Browns in two weeks, Owen drew up a six-one-four defense that had his ends, Jim Duncan and Ray Poole, flexed and dropping into coverage, and his middle guard, John Cannady, off-set from the line of scrimmage. With Duncan and Poole dropping to the flat to take away Cleveland quarterback Otto Graham's flare passes, and with the off-set Cannady providing a more difficult target for the Browns' trap blockers, Owen's defense opened in umbrella fashion and dealt Cleveland coach Paul Brown his first pro shutout, 6–0.

Owen's "Umbrella Defense" proved to be more than a one-game gimmick. He had used a similar scheme back in 1934, when he huddled with Columbia University coach Lou Little prior to the Giants' 1934 title game against the unbeaten Bears. The Bears romped into the frozen Polo Grounds as defending league champions. The year before, fullback Bronko Nagurski surprised the Giants in the NFL championship game with flip passes at the line of scrimmage to end Bill Karr, and Chicago's strategic passing paved the way to a 23–21 win. One year later, Chicago entered the '34 title game as the first unbeaten and untied team in NFL history. Owen looked to put an end to the Bears' 13-game win streak, and came up with a five-three-two-one defense in which he positioned a third linebacker, Johnny Dell Isola, behind the noseguard. Isola's presence over the middle took away Nagurski's short passes and proved pivotal as New York upset Chicago, 30–13. Owen's five-three-two-one defense remained popular in the NFL for the next decade, until pass-oriented teams like the Los Angeles Rams of the 1940s showed its vulnerability in the secondary. His Umbrella Defense, however, was better balanced and endured longer. By the end of the 1950s, virtually every NFL team was running the four-three-four defense that stemmed from Owen's Umbrella concepts, and the middle linebacker became the dominant defensive figure in the game.

Nitschke liked being in a position that was the focal point of the defense, but he struggled to learn the nuances of his new position. Middle linebackers were similar to tight ends in that they had to be hybrids. Just as tight ends had to be big and strong enough to serve as a sixth lineman on blocking plays and quick and agile enough to serve as receivers on passing plays, linebackers had to be strong enough to stop the run and quick enough to defend against the pass.

Nitschke's primary responsibility as a linebacker at Illinois had been stuffing the running games of Big Ten opponents. His defense against the run served him well in his first Packers' training camp, when he butted helmets for the first time with another rookie, Louisiana fullback Jim Taylor. Taylor was 6-foot-2, 215 pounds, and seemingly cast out of iron. One of the NFL's early practitioners of weight training, he attacked defenders with his ferocious running style. Football, Taylor said, is a game of contact. As a running back, he had to make defenders respect him, and he did that by trying to punish them before they punished him. The idea, he said, was to give more than he got. "It's either them or you," Taylor said.

"Jimmy Taylor loved contact," said Dillon, who recalled a game against Chicago where Taylor broke through the line on his way to a touchdown. "He could have scored easily," Dillon said, "but he saw a Bear at the two-yard line headed for him and ran right over him. We said, 'What's going on with you?' and he said, 'Aw, you've got to sting 'em a little bit.'"

Taylor was all high knees and lowered shoulders, and Nitschke was impressed with the fullback's power and pistonlike leg drive. Nitschke said later that he hurt when he tried to tackle Taylor. To Nitschke, Taylor was a tiger, one of the toughest and most determined men he had ever encountered.

"Both of them went a hundred percent, all the time," Dillon said. "Taylor would just as soon run over somebody and Ray would just as soon hit you. That's what made them good ballplayers."

Nitschke's aggressiveness in camp turned off many of the Packers' veteran players, but it earned him the respect of the coaching staff. Prior to the last cut that summer, Nitschke approached McLean and said that if he was going to be released, could the coach let him know right away so he could try to catch on with another NFL team?

"Ray," McLean said, "we're going to keep you."

Nitschke was the fifth linebacker on a club that usually carried just four, but McLean liked what he had seen in camp. Nitschke was assigned to the special teams, the "suicide squads" of pro football. But when Bettis went down with an injury in the first exhibition game, Nitschke started the rest

of the preseason and the season opener against the Bears. Nitschke's first
official game in the NFL was played Sunday, September 28, before a sellout
crowd of 32,150 in Green Bay's City Stadium. He played with a sense of
wide-eyed wonder. In later years, he recalled the Bears' center Larry Strickland, "must have been six-foot-seven." Strickland, in reality, was 6-foot-4,
but Nitschke's recollection indicates the awe that most rookies feel when
playing their first league game in the NFL.

Chicago beat Green Bay, 34–20, and the loss proved to be a foreshadowing of the Packers' season. Green Bay tied with Detroit, 13–13, the following week, and lost to Baltimore and Washington before eking out a
38–35 win at home over Philadelphia. It was the Packers' first victory of the
season—and their last. The team was young and inexperienced; against the
Eagles, Green Bay frittered away most of its 38–7 lead before holding on for
the win. McLean was too nice to discipline the veterans he had grown close
to in his years as an assistant, and the players took advantage of their
coach. The Packers followed their win over the Eagles with a humiliating
56–0 loss at Baltimore, and even an aggressive rookie like Nitschke saw no
need for further optimism that season. Green Bay dropped its final seven
games of the season to finish 1–10–1, and McLean was fired as head coach.

Nitschke was embarrassed by the Packers' season, and assessed his own
performance with the same bottom-line approach. He had played aggressively, but his inexperience frequently left him out of position and he often
ended up hitting the wrong people.

"Ray was a real active guy," said Dillon. "He was kind of wild, but he
had a lot of ability. He liked to make tackles everywhere, and sometimes he
was out of position."

Nitschke started the first four games of the regular season, and felt he
made an immediate statement for his hard play in his debut game against
the Bears. When Nitschke left the field that day, he hoped the Chicago veterans knew the name of the rookie playing middle linebacker.

Nitschke's final game as a starter came in Week Four against Washington. Redskins fullback Johnny Olszewski blasted his way to 156 yards
rushing against the Packers, and Green Bay coaches blamed Nitschke for
the 37–21 defeat. Nitschke wasn't so sure; he often found himself wrapping
up Olszewski well beyond the line of scrimmage, indicating to him that the
Packer front wasn't doing its job. Nitschke took the benching grudgingly
and took out his frustrations the rest of the season as a kamikaze member of
the suicide squad.

By season's end, the Packers were in shambles. "We had a terrible year,"
Dillon said. Center Jim Ringo thought the team was "a hellhole," and halfback Paul Hornung heard stories that coaches around the league were for-

ever threatening their players with trades to Green Bay. "It was the Siberia of pro football," Hornung said.

Amid the team's turmoil, Nitschke felt he had played hard enough to look back with some pride on his rookie campaign. On December 28, he settled back along with millions of other nationwide viewers to watch NBC's telecast of the NFL championship game between the Baltimore Colts and New York Giants in historic Yankee Stadium. The game became an instant classic, and by the time it ended with Colt fullback Alan "The Horse" Ameche galloping into the gathering darkness of the end zone in overtime, Baltimore's 23–17 victory had stamped the NFL on the nation's collective consciousness.

Pro football was about to enter a new era, and so were the Packers. One month to the day after he had served as the Giants' offensive coordinator in the championship game, Vince Lombardi was named Green Bay's new general manager and head coach. Nitschke's response to the hiring mirrored that of many others.

"Who the hell," he thought, "is Vince Lombardi?"

When Lombardi accepted the Packers' job, one of the first things he did was contact long-time friend Ed Breslin. Knowing Lombardi had grown tired of being an assistant coach and longed to be in charge of his own team, Breslin told him, "It's what you've always wanted."

"Yeah," Lombardi remarked, "and the first thing I'm gonna do out there is build a defense."

For much of his football life, Lombardi had concerned himself with the offensive side of the game. As a senior on the 1932 St. Francis Academy team in Brooklyn, he played halfback on offense and was a two-way guard. Though small by today's standards at 168 pounds, Lombardi was squat and powerfully built, particularly in the upper body. His hard hits earned the respect of teammates who had sought to test him—"This guinea (hits) like the Fifth Avenue El," one stunned teammate remarked—and Lombardi's no-frills, no-nonsense play as a two-way guard helped St. Francis finish the season with one of the best records among New York's private schools. The lone loss in their six-game schedule came in the season opener, when Lombardi and Co. were outdueled by Erasmus High School and its sensational sophomore quarterback, Sid Luckman. Luckman later went on to star for Columbia University and became a Hall of Fame quarterback for the Chicago Bears.

With the help of Dan Kern, a 24-year-old Fordham University graduate who tutored Vince in Greek, Lombardi gained a football scholarship to Fordham, at the time the largest Catholic university in the country. He became a member of the famous "Seven Blocks of Granite" line and was coached by a staff that included head coach Jim Crowley and line coach

Frank Leahy. Both Crowley and Leahy were protégés of Notre Dame legend Knute Rockne. Crowley was one of Rockne's "Four Horsemen" and Leahy later became one of the most successful coaches in Fighting Irish history. After graduating in June 1937, Lombardi played guard for several semipro teams, including a Wilmington, Delaware, squad that met NFL teams like the New York Giants and Washington Redskins in exhibition games. He later became head coach at St. Cecilia High School in Englewood, New Jersey, winning 32 straight games with the brutal single-wing power plays made famous by Jock Sutherland at the University of Pittsburgh. Lombardi's education in offensive football continued when he became an assistant at West Point, learning the innovative passing game as taught by Army assistant Sid Gillman, whom Lombardi replaced in 1949, and overall team preparation from head coach Earl "Red" Blaik.

Lombardi left West Point in 1954 to become offensive coordinator of the New York Giants. In his five-year stay in New York, he helped coach the Giants to two Eastern Conference titles and one NFL championship. His first season as offensive coordinator saw New York improve its record from 3–9 to 7–5 and their point production from 179 points to 293. In 1956, the Giants won the Eastern Conference with an 8–3–1 record, and Lombardi's offensive game plan helped New York romp past Chicago in the NFL championship game. Two years later, in Lombardi's final season with the team, New York beat Cleveland in a playoff game to decide the Eastern Conference, then dropped a 23–17 decision to Baltimore in the overtime classic.

Because he had spent the majority of his career on the offensive side of the ball, Lombardi didn't understand the techniques, the steps and drops, of defensive football. In 1957, he had spent a long afternoon on the sidelines watching a San Francisco defense coached by coordinator John Phillip (Phil) Bengston frustrate his offense in a 27–17 defeat. The date—Sunday, December 1—is significant because it is generally regarded as the birthday of the blitz. The memory of 49er linebackers Karl Rubke, Matt Hazeltine, and Marv Matuszak swooping in on New York quarterback Charlie Conerly and forcing five fumbles remained prominent with Lombardi, and when he was named head coach and general manager of the Packers, the first assistant he hired was Bengston.

A tall, chain-smoking Swede, Bengston became the ice to Lombardi's fire. He had begun his coaching career in the 1930s at Missouri under Don Faurot, the father of the Split-T offense. In the forties, Bengston coached at Stanford under Clark Shaughnessy, who had introduced the Man-in-Motion-T. Bengston broke into the NFL in 1951, when 49ers coach Buck Shaw named him San Francisco's new line coach. Shaw was fired following the '54 season, and Bengston then worked under Red Strader for one season and Frankie Albert for two. When Albert quit coaching at the end of the '57 season, the 49ers named Howard "Red" Hickey his successor. Hickey and Bengston were cordial to one another, but there was little chemistry between the two men. The day after Hickey was named head coach, Bengston walked into Hickey's office, congratulated him, and following an awkward moment of forced smiles, said what both men were thinking.

"It isn't there," Bengston said. "It just won't work."

By the time the 49ers announced later that day that Bengston would not be back with the club, he had already cleared out his desk and was heading home to Minnesota, his coat pocket stuffed with a list of NFL teams who might be in the market for coaches.

Bengston contacted the Packers about their head coaching vacancy and was assured by club president Dominic Olejniczak that he would be seriously considered for the position. When the Packers named Lombardi their new head coach and general manager, Bengston phoned Vince. Lombardi wasn't in, so Bengston left a message. Shortly thereafter, Bengston's wife, Kathryn, took a call, and handed the phone to her husband. On the other end of the line was the former Giants' assistant coach, whose voice was tinged with an unmistakable New York accent.

"How *ah* you, Phil? This is Vince *Lombahdi.*"

Lombardi told Bengston he was putting together a new coaching staff in Green Bay and needed someone with experience to handle the defense.

"We're going to start from the bottom up and build a winning team here," Lombardi said. "If you're interested, why don't you come out to Green Bay for an interview?"

When Bengston joined the Packers, he was 45 years old, the same age as Lombardi, and had the reputation as a "career assistant." His long tenure in San Francisco and thinning black hair earned him the nickname "Old Dad." Bengston and Lombardi shared some similarities—both were Catholic, both had been successful assistants in the NFL, both were students of the game who demanded excellence from their players. But it was their differences that made them such a dynamic coaching duo. Lombardi's interest lay in coaching offense; Bengston's in defense. Lombardi was passionate, Bengston calculating. Lombardi was volcanic, Bengston placid as a mountain lake.

As a tactician and defensive strategist, Bengston has never received his full due from NFL historians. Mostly, he's remembered as the man who replaced Lombardi as head coach in Green Bay and presided over the fall of the Packer dynasty. It's an unfair legacy, since Bengston was inheriting an aging team wrung dry by years of Lombardi's emotional coaching style and pressure-packed games. In many ways, Bengston's situation in taking over the '68 Packers resembled that of Ray Handley in taking over the '91 Giants from Bill Parcells. Like U.N. troops at the Yalu River, they were tired veterans trying to hold off fresh attackers with depleted forces.

Bengston was not only Lombardi's chief lieutenant during the Green Bay glory years; he was chiefly responsible for fielding a unit that ranks among the greatest in history and has sent five of its members to the Pro Football Hall of Fame. In 1967, when the Packers won an unprecedented third straight title and second straight Super Bowl, nine of the eleven members of the unit Bengston put on the field had been named all-pro in their career.

During his stay in New York, Lombardi had worked side by side with Tom Landry, a quiet, intellectual Texan whose work with the Giants defense led many to consider him the leading defensive strategist in the game. A former defensive back and assistant coach with the Giants in the early fifties under Owen, Landry had fine-tuned his coach's Umbrella scheme and come up with the modern four-three. For five years in New York, Lombardi's offensive unit scrimmaged Landry's defense in Giant practices, and Lombardi watched the four-three in action on a daily basis.

When Lombardi left for Green Bay, he took his working knowledge of Landry's defense with him and implemented it as the base defense for the Packers. A symbolic seed had been taken from New York to Green Bay, and when Bengston was hired as defensive coordinator, he immediately refined Landry's version of the four-three to his own personality. Bengston taught his cornerbacks to play seven yards off the ball, backpedaling at the snap in a concept he called the "Fisherman Theory"—like patient fishermen, Green Bay corners had to wait until the precise moment to break on the ball and make their catch. The Packers also employed what Bengston called the "Victory" formation, a zone pass-coverage scheme employed in end-game situations.

When Bengston studied film of the Green Bay defense throughout the winter of '59, he found the Packers to be a collection of talented but tentative players. Because they had been burned by big plays for so many years, Green Bay defenders developed a safe, cautious approach. They were defensive in every sense of the word, Bengston said, the Switzerland of pro football defenses.

The challenge, as Bengston saw it, was to change the Packers' approach on defense from conservative to aggressive. Bengston had coached an attacking defense in San Francisco, and he planned to instill in his Packer players the belief that a modern defense must have an aggressive mindset. Defenses were equipped with their own formations, plays, and strategies. They could score points, win games, and ultimately win championships. Most importantly, Bengston thought, a successful defense must have a morale of its own, must have its own leader, its own goal, and its own reward.

Bengston's philosophy of an attacking defense fueled by an aggressive leader blended seamlessly with Lombardi's vision of the four-three. In New York, Landry's unit had been geared to Huff, and both Lombardi and Bengston believed that for the Packer defense to be as successful as the Giants' unit, Green Bay would need a dominant middle linebacker in the mold of Huff.

"When Lombardi left, he took the New York Giants' defensive playbook to Green Bay," Huff remembered. "In later years, Ray and I could talk the same language because we played the same position. In the four-three, your middle linebacker will be your leading tackler, and he should be because you're playing both sides of the field and in the middle. So you don't want to put a guy in there that doesn't like to tackle. And Ray was a hitter."

The Packers' new philosophy fit Nitschke perfectly. He had watched Green Bay's collapse the previous season. The team had a loser's complex, and Nitschke felt that some of the players lacked that extra spark. He believed the Packers lost late-game leads because they didn't believe they were good enough to win. Even though he was a rookie, Nitschke's assessment was an accurate one. Fellow linebacker Dan Currie later remarked that players hadn't expected to win in '58, and that it was understood that even when they tried their best they would most likely lose. The main objective, Currie said, was just to keep the game close.

Lombardi's staff, which studied more than 20,000 feet of film of the Packers and their opponents that first winter, recognized Green Bay's defeatist attitude and realized it was an outlook they needed to change when they met with their players for the first time in the training complex at St. Norbert College.

"Gentlemen," Lombardi began, "I have never been associated with a losing team and I don't intend to start now." Speaking in a deep, rough voice that halfback Paul Hornung thought sounded like authority itself and that sent chills up and down the spine of linebacker Bill Forester, Lombardi told his team they were going to start winning because they would out-work, outexecute, outblock, and outtackle every team on their schedule. Lombardi spoke at length about the need for professionalism, pride, and paying the price to win.

"I'm going to find thirty-six men who have the pride to make any sacrifice to win," he said. "If you are not one, if you don't want to play, then get the hell out."

The speech fired up his players. Forester felt ready to run outside and scrimmage without pads. Tackle Bob Skoronski said later he thought Lombardi's emphasis on professionalism had more to do with making Green Bay champions than anything Vince did from a coaching standpoint. Lombardi later confided to split end Max McGee that he had been "nervous as hell" about delivering that speech. He was worried, Lombardi said, that he would return the next day and find only a couple of players still in camp. Issuing his trademark alligator smile, Lombardi told McGee he was relieved to find that the entire team hadn't left him.

Nitschke was in the army during training camp, and didn't catch up with his new coach until the Packers' exhibition game against the Washington Redskins in Greensboro, North Carolina. Ray's reputation, however, did precede him, and when he arrived, Green Bay equipment manager Dad Braisher pulled him aside.

"Watch yourself, Ray," Braisher told him. "Don't do anything you're not supposed to be doing. This Lombardi is really tough."

After spending six months in the army, Nitschke wondered how much tougher Lombardi's camp could be than what he had just been through. He was quickly filled in by the other players. Players had been vomiting on the practice field the first couple of days, and the squad as a whole lost an average of 12 pounds per man. On the first day of practice, Lombardi took one look at Bettis and defensive tackle Dave Hanner and told them to lose 20 pounds in two weeks or "get the hell out of camp."

Bettis made weight, a fact that Ray realized later kept him from possibly becoming a starter earlier than he eventually did. Six weeks of army conditions had kept Nitschke in shape, but the second-year pro soon realized that while he may have been in shape by U.S. military standards, he was not in shape by Lombardi standards. To compensate, Nitschke drove himself physically and mentally. "You pushed yourself as hard as you could," he said, "and then you had Lombardi pushing you that much more."

Nitschke remained second-string behind Bettis and was confined largely to the special teams. Because he had missed the opening days of training camp due to army duty, Nitschke felt like he had not had a full opportunity to show Lombardi and Bengston what he could do on the field. All they had to go on, Nitschke thought, were films of Green Bay's games from the previous season, films showing Nitschke as an active, if overaggressive, rookie.

"The guy was so fast and so smart, but he was so eager he made a lot of mistakes," Dillon said. "He'd leave his position of where he was supposed to be and that would hurt the team sometimes."

The Packers opened their 1959 regular season on Sunday, September 27, against the Chicago Bears in Green Bay. A crowd of 32,150 filled City Stadium on a gray, wet afternoon. Lombardi had bolstered the Packers with a number of off-season signings and trades. He drafted Colorado quarterback Boyd Dowler and converted him into a flanker; the rookie went on to lead the team in receptions that season with 32. Lombardi dealt Billy Howton—an all-pro end and Green Bay's second-leading receiver the season before—to Cleveland in exchange for defensive end Bill Quinlan and defensive tackle Henry Jordan. In retrospect the deal was a steal for the Packers. Howton led the Browns in receptions that season but was out of football following the '63 season. Quinlan and Jordan went on to anchor the right side of the Packer defense through the early years of their dynasty, and Jordan has since become a Hall of Famer. Lombardi furthered shored up the defense by acquiring another future Hall of Famer, safety Emlen Tunnell from the Giants, and picked up offensive guard Fred "Fuzzy" Thurston in a trade with Baltimore coach Weeb Ewbank.

Trailing the Bears 6–0 midway through the fourth quarter, the Packers rallied to score nine points in the final seven minutes. Slogging through the mud, Taylor followed pulling guards Thurston and Jerry Kramer on a sweep left from five yards out to give Green Bay a 7–6 lead, and Jordan and Nate Borden combined to trap Bear quarterback Ed Brown deep in the end zone for a safety. Nitschke played a role in clinching the victory. On Chicago's free kick following the safety, the Bears kicked it short hoping to recover the ball, but Nitschke fell on it, securing the win as Green Bay ran out the clock.

For a team that had made a habit of losing close games and hadn't beaten the arch-rival Bears since 1957, the dramatic victory was cause for celebration. Lombardi was swept off the field on the shoulders of his players, and the *Green Bay Press-Gazette* lauded the first victory of the new regime with a headline that read "Gutty!" In his game-day story, Art Daley of the *Press-Gazette* wrote that the Packers' performance showed much promise for the future.

"This was more than just a triumph over Green Bay's archrival," Daley wrote. "It was the beginning of the new and fiery regime headed by thunderous Vince Lombardi, who was carried off the water-logged field by the joyous Bays after the game."

The Packers followed with wins over Western Conference foes Detroit and San Francisco. After three weeks of the regular season, Green Bay was giddy over a team that sat alone atop the conference standings. Reality resurfaced, however, in the form of a five-game winless streak. With a losing season staring him in the face, Lombardi switched quarterbacks, benching starter Lamar McHan and replacing him with backup Bart Starr. The move may have smacked of desperation at the time, but it was a master stroke. Green Bay swept to victory in its final four games, finishing with a 7–5 record to tie for third place in the conference.

Though the team celebrated its first winning season since 1947, Nitschke didn't see much room for joy. He had received little meaningful playing time and felt it was Lombardi, rather than Bengston, who wasn't giving him an opportunity to show what he could do. Game after game, Nitschke would sit on the bench, hoping the Packers would get so far ahead the coaches would be forced to put him in just to give Bettis a rest and prevent an unnecessary injury. Week ten, however, demonstrated to Nitschke just how little the coaching staff thought of him.

Leading Washington 21–0 in the fourth quarter, Nitschke waited for the call to get in the game. With time running out, he approached Bengston on the sideline and asked to be put in the game. Bengston shook his head.

"No," Bengston said. "We want the shutout."

As he sat on the sideline, Nitschke tried to see his benching as a learning experience. He watched how Bettis and opposing middle linebackers—Chicago's Bill George, Detroit's Joe Schmidt—played the position. Other times, however, Nitschke sulked. At the end of the '59 season, Lombardi and Nitschke were clearly at odds, and the 1960 season would see the second-year middle linebacker on the verge of being traded away from Green Bay.

FOUR

TO **VINCE LOMBARDI,** Ray Nitschke was the rowdy of the Green Bay Packers; big, rough and belligerent, with a love of contact.

"He has the proper temperament for a middle linebacker," Lombardi explained in his 1963 book *Run to Daylight*, "but maybe too much of it."

Lombardi acknowledged at the time that Nitschke had been "a problem to coach." The problems lay in Nitschke's behavior on and off the field. Still seething inside at the loss of his mother, Nitschke remained an undisciplined loner. His constant mistakes on the practice field infuriated Lombardi, who demanded perfection at all times. "Everyone makes mistakes," Lombardi would tell his players, "but not too many if you want to remain a Green Bay Packer."

"Great players have that instinct, you can call it a nose for the ball, and Ray had it," flanker Boyd Dowler recalled. "I used to laugh because he'd say 'I have a hunch, I have a hunch,' but then he'd run the wrong way, off on his own. He'd be extra aggressive because he wanted to show he should be out there playing. But it took him awhile to break into the starting lineup."

To defensive end Willie Davis, Nitschke's mistakes on the field were compounded by his problems away from the game.

"He was a guy who couldn't handle his alcohol and would get into trouble and barroom fights," Davis remembered. "He was frustrated those first couple of years until he really got his game underway. He was a guy with a pretty quick temper, and somebody would look at him and he'd be ready to punch him out. Some guys shouldn't drink because they can't handle the booze, and Ray was one of those guys.

"I think there was a point where Lombardi was ready to give up on Ray, because Ray had a tendency to make mistakes, and Lombardi detested mistakes. Some of Ray's more embarrassing moments came when he decided to play one of his hunches. He would go chasing out after a play he thought the offense was going to run only to have it be a different play. In the films, you would see him trying to sneak back to his position. "

Nitschke's wild, undisciplined ways led to his becoming one of the team's whipping boys. "He needs it," Lombardi said at the time, "and he can take it." The team's coaching staff struggled to find ways to reach their backup middle linebacker. Lombardi chewed him out and Nitschke took it. But he frustrated Lombardi by turning around and making the same mistake over again. Bengston offered a different approach, often throwing his arm around the shoulders of his defensive players as he issued quiet instructions. Of his four linebackers—Nitschke, Tom Bettis, Dan Currie, and Bill Forester—Bengston thought Nitschke promised to be the roughest and toughest of them all. He also told Lombardi that Nitschke might someday become the Packers' starting middle linebacker.

Lombardi had his doubts. He could see Nitschke was talented, but the Packer boss questioned his young linebacker's motivation. "Vince was incredibly intense and driven," guard Jerry Kramer said. "He'd chew your ass out for anything. And he and Raymond had some exchanges. But I think Coach saw in Raymond the same thing he saw in me, an ability we weren't using. We were comfortable in having made the team, and Vince could see that."

Nitschke's seeming comfort masked what he later described as an inner turbulence. He was still drinking, and it would take just a couple of shots of whiskey for him to become loud and obnoxious. He would sit by himself at a bar, toss back a few drinks, and then, as he once recalled, "say the wrong things to the wrong people." Before long, Nitschke would be breaking up the furniture and brawling with patrons. Lombardi feared for Nitschke's future, feared getting a phone call some day from the police.

"I remember in the beginning, Ray didn't have a whole lot of discipline," Vince Lombardi Jr. said. "He had all the tools but it took awhile for my father's message to sink in, to make sense to Ray. But you could see he had a lot of passion."

Nitschke entered the 1960 season as the Packers' fourth linebacker. For the first time since arriving in Green Bay, he had decided to stay in town during the off-season and not return to Chicago. While many of his teammates caught the first plane out of town following their return home from a season-ending win December 13 in San Francisco, Nitschke stayed in town. He still considered himself a big-city guy, but other than his older brothers he felt there was nothing for him to return home to. As long as he was making his living in Green Bay, he reasoned, he might as well remain there. With its close proximity to his home in Illinois, and with its family-oriented, small-town feel, Green Bay was beginning to grow on the former Chicago street tough. "It was a pleasant area," he said, "nice people, the whole bit."

He still wasn't happy about his lack of playing time under Lombardi, but he respected his coach as a man and as a leader of men. Upon his arrival in Green Bay, Lombardi had broken up the cliques that had developed under Scooter McLean and done away with the players who had caused internal problems. The result, Nitschke thought, was a healthy atmosphere where no one on the team was satisfied with playing close games, as they had been the year before, but were concerned only with winning.

Kramer said the team's attitude prior to Lombardi's arrival was that if they won, fine. If they didn't, well, there were more important things to do after the game.

"We were just a group of guys who had a horseshit season and didn't know how to win," Kramer said. "But when you look back, so many of the guys who would have greatness thrust on them were already on the team—Jimmy Taylor, Paul Hornung, Jim Ringo, Forrest Gregg. And then along came Vince."

Lombardi defeated the Packers' losing attitude by instilling in his players the belief that in his life they ranked only behind God and family. His players became his extended family, "my boys" as he called them, and they bought into his beliefs of self-sacrifice and teamwork. Split end Max McGee played many games where he may not have had even one catch, or even had a pass thrown his way, but if he had thrown a good block for Taylor or Hornung and the Packers had won the game, McGee was happy.

Nitschke, the loner, welcomed the feeling of family that Lombardi brought to the locker room. Defensive tackle Henry Jordan may have joked that Lombardi treated everyone on the team the same—"like dogs," Jordan said—but Nitschke saw it as the truth. Lombardi, he said, didn't care about his players' race, religion. or political beliefs. America was on the cusp of the socially conscious sixties, and still in the distance were the struggle for civil rights; freedom marches in Selma and Montgomery, Alabama; the Watts riots; and uprisings in Detroit and Newark, New Jersey.

When Lombardi was hired in Green Bay, the Packers had just one black player on the team, defensive end Nate Borden. Emlen Tunnell, an African-American athlete who had forged a Hall of Fame career with the New York Giants and was brought to Green Bay by Lombardi in 1959, said Borden was staying in a rental room so dirty and run-down that Tunnell said he wouldn't have kept his dog there.

"Vinnie changed all that," Tunnell said later. "He gave the people who were renting the room to Nate hell and then moved him into a decent place."

In his first meeting on the field with his team, Lombardi laid down the law about race relations within the team. "If I ever hear 'nigger' or 'dago' or 'kike' or anything like that around here," he said strongly, "regardless of who you are, you're through with me. You can't play for me if you have any prejudice."

Sportswriter Jimmy Cannon thought Lombardi in his own way was a great social scientist. "His dignity and grace in racial matters was almost totally neglected," Cannon wrote. "He made black and white people some neutral color."

At a time when NFL teams had quotas for the number of black players they would have on their rosters—the Redskins' quota, for instance, was two, the Giants' was six—Lombardi proved progressive in drafting and trading for African-American athletes. Before the start of the 1959 season, Lombardi acquired Tunnell from the Giants and defensive end Willie Davis from Cleveland. Davis, who later became defensive captain of the Packers and a Hall of Fame defensive end, joined defensive end Bill Quinlan and tackle Henry Jordan as three outstanding players Lombardi acquired from Cleveland Browns head coach Paul Brown. It was later suggested by some that Brown had helped Lombardi build the Packers into a contender because he felt an obligation to see Vince succeed after talking him up so much to Green Bay's search committee back in January 1959. When Jerry Atkinson, who was an executive committee member, contacted Brown for a reference on Lombardi, the Cleveland coach was effusive in his praise.

"Lombardi is a great football tactician and he is also a scrapper," Brown told Atkinson. "He'll get the most out of his men. He won't let anybody dog him."

Atkinson told the Cleveland coach the Packers were looking to hire "a Paul Brown of Green Bay." Would Brown, Atkinson asked, work closely with Lombardi and assist in setting up the new regime? Brown said he would, and in the next two seasons, delivered to Green Bay three members of the defensive line that would start for Green Bay in the 1960, '61, and '62 NFL championship games, as well as return specialist Lew Carpenter.

Said Atkinson, "I'll never forget what Paul Brown did for us, for Green Bay."

The presence of Davis at defensive end, free agent Willie Wood at free safety, and rookie Tom Moore, the team's top draft choice, as a backup halfback helped give Green Bay a new look at the start of the 1960 season. To Nitschke, however, there was little difference between the '59 and '60 campaigns. Through the Packers' six exhibition games, all of them victories, Nitschke was still confined largely to the special teams. He had come to camp prepared to take the starting job from Bettis, but the biggest impression he made early on occurred during a September practice. It was a humid day, and the skies over the two practice fields on Oneida Avenue grew dark with the threat of an approaching storm. Because it was so hot, Lombardi told his players they could take off their helmets and shoulder pads. The players put their equipment on the ground near a 25-foot steel structure that stood between the fields. It was regarded as a photographer's tower, but the Packers believed it had been built to allow Lombardi to occasionally watch practice from above and yell down at them.

As dark clouds rolled in from the west, a gusty wind carried in the first drops of rain. Nitschke hustled back to the base of the steel tower where he had put his equipment, and began putting his pads on to protect them from getting wet. He put his helmet on too, and the instant he pulled the hard plastic shell down over his head, a strong gust of wind caught the tower and tipped it over. A thousand pounds of steel scaffolding collapsed on top of Nitschke, sending him sprawling to the ground. A steel bolt drove through his yellow-gold helmet, four inches above his left temple. NFL helmets in 1960 were constructed of plastic with a web suspension that provided an inch of space between the top of the helmet and head. The bolt that punched through Nitschke's helmet stopped just short of his skull. "I put my helmet on to protect this," Nitschke said later, pointing to his bald head. "If I hadn't, I might have spent the rest of the season in the cemetery."

When the scaffolding collapsed, Lombardi and the players went running to the site, unsure of who was beneath it.

"Who's that guy on the ground?" Lombardi yelled.

As the players dug the mystery man out from beneath the pile of steel rubble, quarterback Bart Starr shouted, "It's Nitschke."

Lombardi looked relieved.

"Nitschke? He's all right. Everybody back to practice."

After seven weeks of the regular season, Nitschke was still playing second-string, still running down punts and kickoffs. Nitschke's playing time had increased during that time, and the Green Bay press, taking note of Bengston's four-linebacker rotation, dubbed them the "Fearsome Foursome," predating the popularized use of the term to describe the Los Angeles Rams front four of the late 1960s.

Nitschke continued to learn from Bettis, whom he considered his best friend on the team, and continued to study other linebackers from the sidelines to pick up playing tips. Nitschke's aggressiveness and toughness impressed Bengston and Lombardi, and when Green Bay dropped a 33-31 decision to the visiting Rams in Week Eight, Packer coaches decided a change was in order.

The next game on Green Bay's schedule was the annual Thanksgiving Day meeting in Detroit against the Lions. The Packers were locked in a four-game race for the Western Conference title with defending champion Baltimore, Detroit, and San Francisco, and the Green Bay defense was showing signs of weakening, having given up 33 or more points in two of its last three games. At practice during the short week before the Thursday game, Lombardi pulled Nitschke aside and told him the middle linebacking job was his.

"Go out there and do the best job you possibly can," Lombardi told him. "We're going to sink or swim with you."

Kramer said Lombardi's short conversation with Nitschke was a turning point for Ray professionally. "Now he had a goal," Kramer said, "and he went from a guy who was happy to be a part of the team to wanting to be a great linebacker."

Nitschke heard later that part of the reason for his being promoted was a locker room flare-up between Lombardi and Bettis. Davis, however, recalled another reason why Nitschke was given the starting job at middle linebacker. Opposing quarterbacks, Davis said, were taking advantage of the 6-foot-2 Bettis by completing passes over the middle just beyond the reach of his outstretched fingers. At 6-foot-3 and 235 pounds, Nitschke was an inch taller and 10 pounds heavier than Bettis, and with his long arms and huge hands, presented a larger obstacle in the middle for quarterbacks to contend with.

Nitschke's first start since being benched following the loss to Washington in 1958 didn't signal an immediate turnaround for the Packer defense. Detroit defeated Green Bay 23–10, but the Packers responded the following week by beating Chicago, 41–13. Heading to San Francisco for their third straight road game, Nitschke spent a frustrating Saturday afternoon trying to chase down 49ers halfback Hugh McElhenny in muddy Kezar Stadium. A future Hall of Famer, McElhenny was dubbed "The King" by 49ers quarterback Frankie Albert, who called McElhenny "the king of all runners." An open-field artist who slashed from sideline to sideline with sudden bursts of speed and an assortment of swivel-hip fakes and sidesteps, McElhenny often ran forty yards to gain five. NFL commissioner Pete Rozelle once called him the most exciting runner he had ever seen, and McElhenny left a lasting impression on the young Nitschke. "He was something to behold," Nitschke said later.

Despite McElhenny's success eluding Nitschke, the Packer defense still managed to shut out San Francisco, 13–0. Green Bay's win, coupled with Baltimore's 10–3 loss in Los Angeles—the third straight defeat for the Colts—dropped the two-time defending NFL champions out of first place in the West and allowed the Packers to take a one-game lead with one game left.

The following week, the Packers flew to Los Angeles for the season finale against the Rams. A victory would give Green Bay the Western Conference title. The team was quartered in Santa Monica. Looking to unwind, Nitschke went alone to a restaurant across the street from the hotel and ordered a drink from the bar, violating a team rule. Prior to his arrival, several Packer players had gained reputations for their love of the nightlife; Hornung was called "Picadilly Paul" for his frequenting of a nearby nightspot. Knowing the reputation some of his players had among the citizens, Lombardi put out a strict order that first season prohibiting them from standing at public bars.

"I don't care if you're drinking ginger ale and talking to a friend," Lombardi told his team. "It just doesn't look good if a fan sees you in the place."

"Vince had a serious problem with that," flanker Boyd Dowler remembered. "We weren't supposed to be at the bar if we were in a supper club or a restaurant."

The alternative was for players to drink at a table or booth. Nitschke knew about the directive, but decided, as he later put it, to "take a chance." He was standing at the bar, drinking and minding his own business, when Lombardi, Bengston, and defensive backfield coach Norb Hecker suddenly strode in. Startled, Nitschke realized there was nothing he could do. As the three men walked toward him, Nitschke rasped, "Hi, Coach."

Lombardi said nothing, but as they walked past him, Nitschke could see the back of Lombardi's neck beginning to redden. When the coaches sat down at a nearby table, Lombardi grabbed a handful of peanuts from a bowl on the table and squeezed them so hard he shattered the shells.

A round of drinks was sent to their table—scotch, bourbon, and beer—and when Lombardi informed the waiter they had yet to order, he was told the drinks had been sent by a patron at the bar. Looking over, Lombardi saw Nitschke grinning back at him. The Packer boss seethed for a minute, then told Bengston and Hecker, "Let's get out of here."

As the three men walked by Nitschke at the bar, Lombardi, still looking straight ahead, shouted, "You're all done! You're through! Get out of town!"

Nitschke could tell by the tone of Lombardi's voice the coach meant what he said. His only hope was that Lombardi would calm down enough to change his mind. Nitschke had seen it happen before; Lombardi had once embarrassed Kramer on the practice field by calling him "a cow." Later that same day, Lombardi saw a despondent Kramer sitting by his locker stall. Throwing his arm around Kramer's slumped shoulder, Lombardi told him, "Son, some day you're going to be the greatest guard in the National Football League." The short pep talk immediately lifted Kramer's confidence, and he became, along with Fuzzy Thurston, one of the keys to Lombardi's lead play, the power sweep. Kramer was also arguably the greatest drive-blocking guard of the sixties, and his omission from the Pro Football Hall of Fame remains an ongoing mystery.

Lombardi, however, never wavered from his plan to trade Nitschke. Realizing the Packers were on the verge of clinching the Western Conference title and how important Nitschke could be to their defense, Bengston and Hecker tried to persuade Lombardi to keep him. Lombardi was unmoved. "Get rid of him," he replied. Eventually, Bengston convinced Lombardi of Nitschke's value to the team. Lombardi, however, was now in a situation where he had to back down without losing face. Shrewdly, he decided to leave Nitschke's fate in the hands of his teammates. Lombardi announced that if the Packer players voted to keep Nitschke on the team, he would go along with their wishes.

"Vince said, 'Well, it's not going to be my decision, it's your decision' and walked out of the room," Hornung recalled. "How were we going to vote him off the team? We would have to be crazy. So when Vince left the room I stood up and said, "Well, I think we ought to just vote him off the team.' I think Ray was about ready to choke me. He didn't think that was too funny."

The decision was a smart one on Lombardi's part, since he knew which way the team would vote. "We knew we had him then," Hecker said later. The next day, the Packers voted 39–0 to keep Nitschke.

"I think my father wanted to get rid of him to make an example out of him," Vince Jr. said. "It was probably the culmination of a lot of things that had built up, but cooler heads prevailed. Still, I think my father would probably have thought the better of it a day or two later and not traded him."

On the final Sunday of the regular season, Green Bay defeated Los Angeles, 35–21, in the Coliseum. The victory was the Packers' third straight, and allowed them to win the Western Conference with an 8–4 record, one game better than Detroit and San Francisco.

That night, 11,000 fans crowded Austin Straubel Airport and withstood 12-degree cold to welcome their champions home from the West Coast. The title was the Packers' first since 1944, and the *Press-Gazette* celebrated by publishing the newspaper's first "extra" edition in 21 years. It sold out within hours. Green Bay mayor Roman Denissen proclaimed the Packers' conference title to be "the most wonderful thing that has happened to Green Bay in a long time."

The 1960 NFL championship game was scheduled for Monday, December 26, in order to avoid conflicting with Christmas Day. That the

Packers were playing the Philadelphia Eagles offered a bit of irony for Lombardi. In January 1958, he had been offered the Eagles' head coaching job. Vince McNally, the Eagles general manager, met him at a Philadelphia train depot and offered a short-term contract with an option for an extension if the club performed well. Lombardi was excited about the opportunity to finally become an NFL head coach, excited about the opportunity to coach Eagles' quarterback Norm Van Brocklin.

"Every time I see that guy coming on the field," Lombardi said, "I start shivering."

When Lombardi took the Eagles' offer back to Giants' owner Wellington Mara, Mara talked him out of accepting the position. The Eagles, Mara said, were run by meddling stockholders who weren't going to yield control of the club. Mara told Lombardi that the short-term contract wasn't sufficient to rebuild the Eagles and that he might be fired before the job was completed. To further induce Lombardi to stay with the Giants, Mara raised Vince's salary and improved his insurance policy. There was also the understanding that once Giants' head coach Jim Lee Howell stepped down, Lombardi would be named his successor.

When Lombardi informed McNally of his decision to stay in New York, the Eagles hired Buck Shaw, Bengston's former head coach in San Francisco, to take over as the new boss in Philadelphia. Lombardi remained one more year with the Giants, then went to Green Bay. One year later, the paths of Lombardi, Bengston, and Shaw converged once more, this time in Franklin Field to decide the NFL championship.

Like the Packers, the Eagles' turnaround was a remarkable one. In 1958, they had finished 2–9–1 and tied for last in the Eastern Conference with the Chicago Cardinals. It was the second-worst record in the NFL outside of Green Bay's 1–10–1 finish, but the following season saw both the Eagles and Packers improve to 7–5. In 1960, Philadelphia dropped a 41–24 decision to Cleveland in the league opener in Franklin Field, but led by Van Brocklin and two-way star Chuck Bednarik, the Eagles went on a white-hot winning streak.

"We won nine games in a row," Hall of Fame flanker Tommy McDonald noted, "but we were behind at halftime in six of them. Nobody really picked us to finish near the top or anything like that. I would have to say that Cleveland and New York had better overall teams than we did. We were just an average team, but we always pulled the game out in the third and fourth quarters. And then we started a little saying, 'Okay, the third and fourth quarter is ours. It's the Eagles' time.'"

The Eagles clinched their first Eastern Conference title in 11 years with consecutive wins over the rival Giants, 17–10 at Yankee Stadium on November 20, and 31–23 in Franklin Field the following Sunday. The rivalry between the Eagles and Giants has long been one of the most intense in the league, and perhaps never more so than in 1960. Philadelphia had dominated the Eastern Conference at the end of the 1940s; New York at the close of the 1950s. Their mutual dislike dated back some three decades, and prompted Giants' team physician Dr. Francis Sweeny to state on one occasion that every time New York played Philadelphia, "we have to bring at least one of our players home through the window."

The reference was to the practice at the time to load injured players onto the team train via a stretcher through an open window. When the Eagles traveled to Yankee Stadium for their first meeting with the Giants in 1960 Philadelphia was challenging New York's two-year reign as conference champions. Six straight victories had lifted the Eagles into first place, and the Giants trailed by one-half game. A crowd of 63,571 jammed into Yankee Stadium and rocked the historic structure as the Giants jumped to leads of 7–0 and 10–7 before the Birds battled back to tie the game at 10 and then take a 17–10 lead late in the fourth quarter. With two-and-a-half minutes remaining, New York rallied. A Frank Gifford reception carried the Giants to the Eagles' 49-yard line, and Gifford followed by gathering in a pass at the Philadelphia 30. The Giants' flanker was still on his feet and looking for more yardage when defensive back Don Burroughs drilled Gifford low and Bednarik belted him high. The force of the double-blow resounded throughout the huge stadium and lifted Gifford off his feet, parallel to the ground. When he landed, his helmeted head slammed the hardened turf with a sickening impact. The ball squirted free from his limp hands, and Chuck Weber covered it for Philadelphia. Bednarik's tackle not only knocked Gifford out of football for the next two seasons, it virtually knocked the Giants out of contention for the conference title. Photographers rushed to get pictures of Bednarik exulting over the fumble recovery, but to New York fans it appeared the Eagles' linebacker was celebrating his knockout blow over the prone Gifford.

Bednarik in 1960 was the last of the 60-minute men, a two-way starter at center and linebacker. As the Eagles' center, the 35-year-old Bednarik would be matched against the 23-year-old Nitschke in the NFL championship game. Nitschke's youth and inexperience in big games symbolized the Packers' plight as they got ready for their first post-season game. For Lombardi, the NFL championship game was his third since 1956, but his first as a head coach. He drove his players and coaches hard that week, telling them, "we haven't got a thing really won yet until we win in Philadelphia." When assistant Red Cochran asked at a team meeting if the coaches could leave a little earlier than their scheduled departure of 9 P.M.—"maybe 8:30?" Cochran asked—in order to get in an hour of Christmas shopping, Lombardi exploded.

Pounding his fist on the table, he shouted, "Red, you wanna be Santa Claus or you wanna be a football coach? There's no room for both."

Lombardi followed his own dictum; he and his wife Marie didn't even put up a Christmas tree that week. He eased up on Christmas Eve, which the team spent in a Philadelphia hotel. Concerned about his players being away from their families, he arranged for presents to be brought to his suite, and the team gathered there to open their gifts.

As game day dawned in Philadelphia, the Packers remained tense. NBC had paid $200,000 to broadcast the game nationally, and as Nitschke ran onto the field for pregame warm-ups, his mood reflected that of his teammates. This was a big game not only for the players and coaches, Nitschke thought, but for the Packer organization, which hadn't been in an NFL title game since 1944. Nitschke knew Green Bay had outstanding players, but he also realized they were still a young team, a team he believed was just on the verge of becoming great.

Some of the Eagles shared Nitschke's sentiment. Van Brocklin could see the potential the young Packers had and knew as he looked at his own team that the Eagles' leaders were aging pros making their last stand. "If we're ever going to win the championship," the Dutchman told his teammates, "it better be today."

Bednarik saw the promise in the Packers as well. From watching films, he knew they were a strong team with a lot of physical talent. "And they executed even then," he remembered. "You could tell they had some kind of spark."

Still, the Eagles weren't convinced the spark came from Lombardi. Unlike future Packer opponents, Philadelphia didn't enter their championship game in awe of the Green Bay boss.

"Vince?" Bednarik asked. "In 1960 he was just another coach."

McDonald agreed. "I didn't realize how great Lombardi was going to be," he said.

Franklin Field sparkled amid a warm sun and unseasonably comfortable weather conditions as the two teams prepared for the kickoff. The sudden change in temperature favored Philadelphia; the field, which had been frozen for nearly two weeks, thawed and turned the stadium floor slick and muddy. The slippery bog slowed the Green Bay ground game, and a questionable decision early by Lombardi cost the Packers three points when he went for the first down on fourth-and-two from the Eagles' six-yard line. Taylor, betrayed by the slick footing, was stopped at the five, and Philadelphia took over.

Green Bay regained the ball on another turnover, Nitschke eluding Bednarik's block on a draw play and submarining halfback Ted Dean.

Nitschke's hard hit forced a fumble, and outside linebacker Bill Forester recovered for the Packers. Five plays later, Paul Hornung kicked a 20-yard field for a 3–0 lead. The Packers upped their advantage to 6–0 in the second quarter on a 23-yard field goal by Hornung, but Van Brocklin brought the Eagles back. From his own 43, the Eagles' quarterback found McDonald free on a slant for a 22-yard gain to the Green Bay 35. On the next play, Van Brocklin connected with McDonald again, this time down the right side-line, and the Eagles end carried it in for the score and a 7–6 lead. Bobby Walston's 15-yard field goal and a 13-yard miss by Hornung as time expired allowed Philadelphia to take a 10–6 lead into halftime.

"They dominated us statistically," Bednarik said, looking back. "But we hung in there."

Game films show Nitschke battling Bednarik throughout much of the afternoon. Since the Packers played a straight four-three alignment for much of the game, only on occasion sliding their tackles head-up over Bednarik, the Eagles' center usually had a direct path to the Packers' middle linebacker on running plays.

"It was strictly a defensive battle," Bednarik said, "and I know Nitschke did a helluva job out there."

Eagles receivers kept a constant eye out for the Packers' middle line-backer whenever they ran crossing patterns over the middle, a patch of turf McDonald referred to as "Nitschke territory."

"When you went across the middle on him, you better bring your lunch with you," McDonald said. "If he could hit you, he was going to hit you. In those days, there was no five-yard limit beyond the line of scrimmage. And if the ball was in the air, you better watch your head."

Green Bay's scheme defensively was to shut off the Eagles' passing game by pressuring Van Brocklin with an array of stunts and blitzes. At San Francisco, Bengston had developed the blitz in 1957 while preparing for Giants' quarterback Charlie Conerly. "I decided that if we were going to stop Conerly," Bengston said, "we'd have to do it in the pocket rather than at the receiving end."

Bengston devised the blitz, code-named it "Red Dog," and sent his line-backers pouring in on Conerly. The scheme caught Lombardi, then the Giants' offensive coordinator, by surprise, and Bengston revised the strategy to use against Van Brocklin in the '60 title game. Green Bay's defensive coordinator decided that if the Packers were to defeat the Eagles' passing game, they would have to defeat it at its source. That meant getting to the Dutchman. Films show Nitschke stunting and looping on several occasions, clawing his way past Eagles guards Stan Campbell and Gary Huth. Van Brocklin, however, continually beat the blitz by holding the ball to the last second, allowing his receivers that precious extra moment to run their patterns. From the Green Bay sideline, Starr watched in fascination as Van Brocklin made big play after big play despite pressure from the Packer defense. "I was really in awe of him that day," Starr said.

Green Bay gained a 13–10 lead in the fourth quarter when Starr, showing the same poise he admired in Van Brocklin, connected with McGee for a seven-yard score. But the Eagles responded on their next series. Dean returned the kickoff 58 yards to the Packers' 39 before Wood made a touchdown-saving tackle. A defensive holding penalty took the Eagles to the 32, and Dean and fullback Billy Barnes each gouged out six yards against the Green Bay defense. With the ball at the 20, Nitschke slowed the Eagles' drive when he sacked Van Brocklin for a loss of seven yards. It was a momentary setback only. The gritty Dutchman dropped back again, seemingly daring yet another Packer blitz, and hit Barnes for a 13-yard gain. Barnes and Dean alternated smashing into the Green Bay defense, Dean finally put the ball in the end zone when he skirted left end from five yards out for a 17–13 lead.

There was just under 10 minutes remaining when Green Bay got the ball back, but the Packers' drive was short-circuited when Bednarik jarred the ball loose from McGee at midfield and then recovered the fumble. Determined to run out the clock, the Eagles put together another march. But Nitschke, who had stopped an earlier Eagles' drive by dropping Walston with a shoulder tackle on a third-down slant pass, helped stuff Barnes on third-and-four.

The tackle forced an Eagles' punt, and the Packers took over on their own 35 with 1:10 left. Starr passed for two first downs, but had to use two time-outs in the process. With 17 second remaining, the Packers were on the Eagles' 22 with no time outs left. Dropping back to pass, Starr saw his primary receivers covered, then swung a pass to Taylor. The Packer back broke several tackles as he bulled inside the 10, where Bednarik, who had slid over from his left linebacker position, was waiting.

"He was coming right at me, running like hell," Bednarik said. "I knew I had to make the perfect tackle. . . . If he gets by me, he scores."

Fullback and linebacker collided at the eight, a clash of future Hall of Famers, and Bednarik wrestled Taylor to the dirt. Spitting mud from his mouth, Taylor was fighting to get up and run one more play. Bednarik, however, wasn't moving.

"Get off me, you son of a bitch," Taylor growled, but Bendarik remained in place, watching the final seconds tick off the stadium clock. When the clock hands got to zero—"Those big, beautiful zeroes," a grinning Bednarik said later—he released Taylor from his grasp.

"Okay, you son of a bitch, you can get up now," Bednarik said. "This damn game is over."

As the Packers trudged off the field, Bednarik caught up with Taylor and Hornung. He told the muddied Packer backs they had a helluva team, and that they'd be back in the title game. The words were of small consolation; some of the Packers wept openly in the dressing room. They had dominated the game statistically, owning huge advantages in first downs (22–13), total yardage (401–206) and plays from scrimmage (77–48). Unsure at first of what to tell his team, Lombardi called them together in the middle of the room.

"Perhaps you didn't realize you could have won this game," he said. "We're men and we will never let this happen again. We will never be defeated in a championship game again. Now, we can start preparing for next year."

Nitschke was stung by the defeat, stung more when he heard the comments emanating from the Eagles' victorious locker room. According to Nitschke, Van Brocklin told reporters that the Packers' middle linebacker had been out of position at times, allowing the Eagles to create big plays. Nitschke, who felt he had prepared himself to play the game as well as he could at that stage of his career, believed he was getting blamed for the loss. Nitschke knew his aggressiveness had caused him to make mistakes during the game, but felt he had played as well as he could against a more experienced team.

In the days that followed, Lombardi, perhaps seeking to shield his players from too much blame, acknowledged he had made some coaching errors in the game. Of the decision to go for a first down rather a field goal early in the game, Lombardi told reporters, "I made the wrong guess."

Nitschke appreciated his coach's public stance and adopted the attitude that whenever the Packers again played a big game, he would play as if he had something to prove. He would prove, Nitschke said, that the loss to the Eagles was not his fault.

Pocketing the loser's share of the title game money, which in 1960 was $3,105.14, Nitschke returned home to Chicago for the off-season. Teaming up with Robert and Richard, the Nitschke brothers celebrated Ray's homecoming. The brothers never looked for trouble, Robert said later, "but a lot of guys in Chicago and the suburbs wished they'd never seen us."

The three drank and brawled together; if one got into a fight the other two quickly joined in. Unsuspecting street toughs soon realized that if they got into a fight with one brother, they soon had what Ray later called "eight hundred pounds of Nitschkes" on their hands.

The Nitschke brothers didn't always come out on top. Hornung remembered a time when the brothers were drinking and popping off around members of the Packers team. It was a mistake. Defensive end Bill Quinlan and linebacker Dan Currie, tough guys in their own right, carried the argument outside.

"Quinlan and Currie beat the shit out of them," Hornung recalled. "The Nitschke brothers didn't get the best of that one."

Ray's attitude at the time reflected his lifestyle. He didn't care what anybody thought of him; he had no real purpose in his life other than to have three square meals a day, a place to sleep, and a chance to tackle the guy running with the football on autumn Sundays.

Nitschke didn't know it, but his outlook on life was about to undergo a dramatic change.

FIVE

THROUGH the first 25 years of his life, Ray Nitschke's life had been influenced most heavily by the untimely deaths of first his father and then his mother. Everything that he was as the new year of 1961 dawned stemmed from his past. By his own admission, Nitschke was undisciplined, selfish, adolescent, and lacking confidence. He was plagued by serious personal problems, all of which had turned him into a loner who seethed with anger at what he believed was a "dirty trick" that life had played on him.

Nitschke's private frustrations led to public outbursts, and his reputation made him an unsavory character in Green Bay. He was considered by some a rowdy, a bully, someone people wanted to stay away from once he began drinking. People who knew Nitschke realized that even one drink could alter his personality and behavior; before long he would grow loud and obnoxious, and on occasion, vulgar. By 1961, Nitschke's reputation preceded him whenever he strolled into Green Bay bars and restaurants; some patrons would get up and leave at the sight of him coming through the front doors.

"I used to worry I might have bad breath," Nitschke said later, explaining the rush to the exit doors whenever he entered a Green Bay bar.

"He was crazy as hell," said Emlen Tunnell, who played safety for the Packers from 1959 to 1961. Chuck Lane, who served as the Packers' director of publicity in the 1960s, said over the course of an evening, when Nitschke was slightly over-served, he would start pitching folks through the windows of saloons and breaking bar stools over people's heads.

"He did a lot of things," Lane said, "that tended to discourage business."

Mike Manuche, a New York restaurant owner who was friends with Green Bay head coach Vince Lombardi, felt Nitschke's troubles were due in part because he had trouble expressing himself. "He would become violent and tear everything apart," Manuche said.

Green Bay halfback Paul Hornung thought Nitschke was headed for serious trouble. "He had a bad act early on," Hornung recalled. "We all stayed away from him because he was a pain in the ass."

Green Bay flanker Boyd Dowler knew about Nitschke's past, knew he had a rough upbringing in Chicago. "He was kind of a wild kid," Dowler said. "He was aggressive and outgoing, and he could get irritated and upset. And there were times early in his career when he'd be out roaming the streets. If he had kept drinking the way he was, it probably would have developed into a problem and it could have caused him serious trouble."

Because of his reputation, Nitschke found it difficult getting to know a waitress he had taken notice of in a Green Bay restaurant. The waitress was Jackie Forchette, a farm girl from Ewen, Michigan. One of seven children, Jackie was a middle child with two brothers and four sisters. Her father was a woodworker, and after moving briefly to California following her high school years, she returned home to be close to her ailing father. Ewen sits some 40 miles from the west end of the Upper Peninsula, and some 200 miles from Green Bay. Like most of Green Bay's citizenry, Jackie had heard about Nitschke, and she wasn't interested in meeting him.

She had grown up a practicing Catholic, and her first marriage had ended when her husband left her in New Mexico. After moving to Green Bay, she began dating again and was seeing someone when Ray first took an interest in her.

"At first, my mom didn't want to have anything to do with my dad when he started pursuing her," said Amy Klaas, the youngest of the couple's three children. "She had heard of him, she had heard of the way he had acted, and she didn't want to be associated with that kind of behavior and that kind of drinking. That's basically what it came down to."

Despite Jackie's lack of interest, Nitschke still pursued her. The first time he had seen Jackie, he had fallen for her. She was strikingly pretty, dark-haired with a pleasant smile and pleasing manner. One night, while Jackie was at a restaurant with her date, Ray walked in and sat down at the couple's table.

"So," Nitschke said to the man, "why don't you tell Jackie about your wife and kids?"

As the man sat there stunned, Nitschke told him, "Pay the bill on your way out."

"My dad had done some research on this guy and found out he was married and had some kids, and she didn't know anything about that," Amy said. "My dad stayed and had dinner with her, and the rest, as they say, is history. I guess she figured then that this guy isn't so bad."

By 1960, Jackie and her brother, Bruce, had taken an apartment in Green Bay. After Ray dropped Jackie off on the night of their first date, Bruce was in the apartment when he heard someone pounding on the front door.

"Who is it?" he called.

"It's Nitschke."

"Well, whaddya want?

"Your sister's got my car keys."

Bruce had yet to meet his sister's date face-to-face, and after he answered Nitschke in a way that was unsympathetic to his plight, he was shocked to see the size of the man outside his door. "He could have torn me up like nothing," Bruce recalled.

Other members of Jackie's family were not so easily impressed. When she took Ray home to Ewen to meet her father, Jackie introduced her new boyfriend as a pro football player.

"Well," her father answered, "he must not be any good. I've never heard of him."

Bruce could see the feelings developing between the couple. They both had been through rough times—Nitschke from his childhood days and Jackie from a failed first marriage.

"Ray had a hard upbringing," Bruce observed. "He didn't trust a lot of people. But he liked Jackie right off the bat. She was personable; if she was in a room and met 50 people, she could remember the name of every one of them."

Ray and Jackie were married on June 26, 1961, and later made their home on Neufeld Street in Green Bay, not far from Lambeau Field. The change in Nitschke was dramatic. He gave up drinking entirely, having realized that he was one of those people for whom even one drink is one too many. The turning point in his decision to stay away from alcohol had come prior to his marriage, when he was out with Jackie and the two survived a horrific traffic accident.

"It was a pretty good car wreck," Jerry Kramer remembered. "I think he rolled the car a couple of times. The story was, he almost killed Jackie. From that point on, he changed."

Nitschke quit alcohol cold, just as he had quit tobacco cold in college, and realized that just as he had disliked smoking, deep down he had disliked drinking just as much. It had been a crutch to cover up his loneliness and insecurities, a crutch he no longer needed now that he had Jackie. He had grown tired of getting into fights, tired of waking up the next morning feeling foolish and embarrassed by his previous night's behavior. Now that he was married, he realized he was no longer just representing Ray Nitschke; he was representing Jackie as well. It was time, he thought, to wise up, set a good example, and become a man.

Together, Ray and Jackie began planning for a family. Because Jackie could not have children of her own, they agreed early in their marriage that they would adopt. In 1963, they brought home a boy, John. Richard was adopted in 1966 and Amy in 1972. Nitschke became the father he had never really known. He doted on his children, and along with Jackie they gave him the love and support that had been missing from his life since his childhood.

"Having a family," Nitschke said later, "really solidified my life. Before I got married I was kind of runnin' them streets."

"He was a good dad," said Richard, named after his father's second-oldest brother. "He didn't get really involved with a lot of things we did because of the type of work he did. He was pretty tied up during the four or five months of the football season. But when he was around during the summer, we did things and it was good."

As children, John, Richard, and Amy heard the stories of their father's wild days, heard how he had reformed after marrying their mother. "My father was kind of rowdy, let's put it that way," Richard said. "He wasn't the kind of guy that you really wanted to go out drinking with. So after he got married and adopted my brother John, he quit drinking. He realized he had choices to make in life. He was going to be a father or he was going to be a bum. He made his choice and stuck by it."

And did so with the help of Jackie and Vince Lombardi.

"I think my mom really did have a big part in him simmering down," Amy said. "Her and Lombardi. Obviously, they were the two people my dad looked to at the time for any kind of guidance and strength."

Family life helped Nitschke focus on what was important to him, which was having someone to love and having someone love him. He was no longer concerned with himself only; now he was looking out for his wife and children. It was something he needed, he said. To care for somebody, to worry about somebody else.

"I know it had been hard for him growing up," Amy said. "And I think that's why he made it a point to make family such a big thing. We always had to eat dinner together. There wasn't any of that 'I'm going to eat now and sit up in my room later.' We *had* to eat dinner together. And there were times we had to do family things and couldn't get out of it."

As young children, John, Richard, and Amy learned to share their father with the people of Green Bay. It was disturbing at times, Richard said, but they eventually became accustomed to it.

"It was hard to go out to eat sometimes," he recalled. "You couldn't sit down to have a normal dinner like most people. I'm not saying it was real bad or anything; we got used to it, I guess. I know I became accustomed to it. My dad would just tell the people, 'Hey, my food's here now. When I get done eating you can come back.' "

Amy said the reason her father was so obliging was that when he was younger he couldn't imagine anyone ever wanting his autograph. "He told me once that when he was 16 or so he could never have believed that he would become what he did," she remembered.

Richard recalled times when his father would become angry at the sight of pro athletes refusing to sign autographs for kids. "Dad would sign anything for anybody," Richard said. "He would get aggravated by that, because without the fans, my father would say, you're nothing. You're out there doing your job, but they're writing your paycheck. Without their support, the club doesn't exist and you're out the door. In this day and age, I don't think that would happen, but when my dad played, that's the way it was."

The Nitschkes lived on Neufeld Street in Green Bay until the fall of 1970, when they moved to Oneida, where their home sat on the border of four different school districts. John went to a private school in Green Bay; Richard to a public school located in Pulaski some 25 miles away. Both played high school football, and while their father was supportive of their interests he never tried to push them in any particular direction.

"Just do what you want to do," he would tell them, "and do the best job you can."

He and Jackie regularly attended the boys' Little League baseball games and at home loved hanging out with the neighborhood kids. The boys would spend summer days playing wiffle ball in the street, and on those occasions when the ball would go down the sewer, the kids would call for Mr. Nitschke. Out Ray would come, and he would lift the sewer cap with one hand and hold it while one of the boys jumped down to get the ball. He and Jackie hosted barbecues, and Ray would cap the day by loading all the kids into the family station wagon and taking them out for ice cream. He loved to hold children—he would pick nine-year-old Bill Toogood up with one hand—but when he and Jackie brought Amy home in April 1972, Ray confided to friends he was afraid to hold his baby daughter because she was so small.

The change in Nitschke's off-field personality impressed those connected with the team. Lombardi said that marriage had settled Nitschke down, and teammates noticed the difference as well. The first couple of years when Nitschke wasn't married and wasn't playing much, Hornung said, had left Ray disgusted and hard to live with. Teammates didn't want to be around the brooding middle linebacker; at times, Nitschke seemed to want to fight his own teammates at the drop of a harmless crack.

"He was a nasty guy," Hornung said. "Shit, he didn't know what he was doing half the time. He thought he could drink, like all drinkers do. But we didn't want to be out with him when we he was drinking so we kept our distance.

"But once he stopped drinking, all that changed. When he got with Jackie, she straightened his act out. He stopped all that bullshit and became a great guy."

Al Pahl, a friend of the Nitschkes, thought Jackie had saved Ray from himself, and Kramer agreed.

"It all started with Jackie," Kramer said. "You have no idea how mean and nasty he was. When he had too much to drink, he would literally slap some lady in a bar and knock her on her ass. Anyone who was happy, he didn't like. But when Raymond met Jackie, he found love, and she brought a lot of good things into his life."

Kramer's relationship with Nitschke had been strained from the start. The two first met at the College All-Stars practice in the summer of 1958. Kramer was a guard from the University of Iowa and had been drafted by the Packers in the fourth round, one round behind Nitschke. Nitschke had been the 36th pick in the draft; Kramer was the 39th. At the All-Stars camp, Kramer made a half-joking reference to Nitschke's intelligence; a "smartass remark," Kramer said later, about Nitschke being a mental giant, a genius. Nitschke, who didn't need much prodding, didn't like Kramer's joke and jumped out of his chair. In a loud and menacing voice, he challenged Kramer to back up his remarks. Realizing he was wrong, Kramer backed down. When the two rookies reported later that summer to the Packers' training camp, their relationship remained strained. Nitschke hadn't forgotten the insult and always looked at Kramer as if he was a dog that had once bitten him.

The two had several verbal confrontations in their early years at Green Bay, and the situation finally reached a physical standoff at a team party. Both men had been drinking, and this time it was Nitschke who instigated the trouble. As he often did when he drank more than he should, Nitschke began spouting off. Sparks flew, and Nitschke asked Kramer if he wanted to take it outside.

"Hell, yes," Kramer said, then had second thoughts as he headed toward the door and saw Nitschke right behind him. Kramer had battled Nitschke in scrimmages and knew the power of Ray's forearms. "Oh, self," Kramer thought, "you are in trouble!"

Realizing that matters were about to get serious, Kramer figured he had better get his bluff in first. Turning around quickly, Kramer grabbed Nitschke by the throat, backed him up against a brick wall, and told him he was ready to tear his head off. "All right, you son of a bitch," Kramer told Nitschke, "I'm crazy enough to fight or drink. Whichever way you want it."

Nitschke looked at Kramer for a moment, then relaxed. "Naw, man, you're my teammate," Nitschke said. "I don't wanna fight you."

"We went back inside," Kramer remembered. "Fortunately for me."

The truce between Kramer and Nitschke remained an uneasy one, and through their years together in Green Bay, which ran from 1958 until Kramer's retirement in 1969, the two all-pros engaged in various scrimmage wars. By the mid-sixties, Kramer was arguably the best guard in the game; Nitschke the dominant middle linebacker. Every time they scrimmaged, Kramer knew Nitschke would be waiting for him, waiting with what Kramer called "that damned forearm of his."

Nitschke's forearms were ferocious weapons. Thick and meaty, he intensified their size and clubbing power by wrapping them in pads and fastening them in place with yards of tape. Films of Nitschke in the sixties show him using his forearms like scythes to cut through a cordon of enemy blockers and punish the ball carrier.

"You buckled it up when you went to see Raymond," Kramer said. "The first time he'd hit you, you'd be ticked off about it. But the next time you buckled it up because you knew he was going to deliver a hit."

"He and Jerry had some moments," defensive end Willie Davis remembered. "Ray made practice a little more aggressive than it should be, and Jerry would say, 'Why'd you do that, Ray?' And Ray's first reaction would be, 'Hey, man, just gettin' ready to play!' And the next thing you know Jerry would be saying, 'All right, you son of a bitch, let's get ready to play.' And it would get to be a real heated thing. But that was Ray. He had an attitude about the game and he played that way. He took no prisoners, and he fully expected that he was going to have some fights. And when someone would knock the crap out of him, he'd take it."

If Nitschke seemed ultra-violent on NFL Sundays, he was just as tough on teammates during the week. Center Bill Curry, who joined the Packers in 1965, said that Nitschke didn't care if it was Bart Starr or Paul Hornung, if they ran near him during a contact scrimmage, he was going to hit them. "He almost tore my head off a few times," Hornung remembered. "So I went after his knees. He had bad knees, and he got ticked off. I said, 'Bullshit, you're not going to tear my head off.' This was a Tuesday practice, and I said, 'Let's put the pads on and go full speed if we're going to do it this way. I'm not going to let him tear my head off.'"

"Lombardi said, 'You will *not* go after his knees.'

"I said, 'Bullshit, I won't. If he comes in after me I'm going for his knees. Let's all put the pads on and go full speed. That damn Nitschke runs around and tries to tear your head off.' But that's the way Ray was."

Red Cochran, who was the Packers backfield coach under Lombardi from 1959 to 1966, called Nitschke "gruff as hell" and thought he practiced the way he played. Cochran knew Nitschke didn't realize there was such a thing as half-speed, but he still took issue with Nitschke's rough treatment of Packer backs.

"Dammit, Nitschke," Cochran would shout during scrimmages. "Lay off my running backs!"

Green Bay tackle Forrest Gregg said if Packer linemen weren't careful when they scrimmaged Nitschke, they'd get one of his big forearms in their teeth. Kramer thought Nitschke used his forearms the same way Dillinger used a pistol—to intimidate people, to stop them.

At times, Kramer thought of Nitschke more as an opponent than a teammate. Nitschke, he said, seemed incapable of letting up, even against his own teammates. "He was always grabbing people, hitting people, throwing elbows," Kramer said.

Dowler used to look for Nitschke during practices, look for the elbows that were sure to come his way whenever his pass route carried him into Nitschke's territory.

"We're running our pass offense and I'd be going across the middle and Ray would throw a forearm at me," Dowler remembered. "I'd say, 'What the hell are you doing out here?'

"'Just making you better,' he'd say."

Like fullback Jimmy Taylor, Nitschke didn't know how to ease up when playing football, didn't know how to "brother-in-law it," the Packers' term for toning it down against teammates. And he never apologized for his aggressiveness. "I came to play," Nitschke said. "I came to practice."

Nitschke and Taylor were alike in their approach to football, and Nitschke looked up to Taylor. Just as Nitschke would explain his explosive charge into a running back by saying, "You want the ball carrier to be a little shy, and a little shyer the next time," Taylor adopted the same attitude toward defenders.

"You've got to sting 'em," Taylor would say. "If you give a guy a little blast, maybe the next time he won't be so eager."

In practice, the two men often collided in the Packers' nutcracker drill. On one occasion when Taylor was the ball carrier and it was Nitschke's job to stop him, Nitschke was screened by the blocker and Taylor galloped by, untouched. Lombardi stopped the drill and announced, "Mr. Nitschke, I have read that you are the best linebacker in the NFL. But after watching you just then I find it hard to believe. Now do it again!"

On the next play, an angry Nitschke grabbed the blocker by the shoulder pads, lifted him off the ground, and tossed him back into Taylor. Lombardi was sufficiently pleased. "Next group," he shouted. Cornerback Herb Adderley recalled the practice collisions between Nitschke and the running backs, recalled the short tempers that occasionally flared.

"Hornung, Tom Moore, Elijah Pitts, any of the running backs, Nitschke would jar them just to let them know, 'Hey, this isn't touch football,'" Adderley said. "At least once a week we'd have to pull Ray Nitschke and

Jimmy Taylor apart. Both of them were tough guys and they always wanted to prove that they were tough. So they would get into some kind of scuffle during the practice session."

Davis remembered days when Nitschke would be keying Taylor on a scrimmage play and after chasing him down, deliver a hit. "Ray was going to manage a little push or a whack that Jimmy thought was more aggressive than it should have been and the next thing you know they would be pushing and shoving," Davis said. "It was in their competitive juices. Those two could get into a pushing match over who wanted to stand in a particular spot."

Kramer recalled the scrimmage conflicts between Nitschke and Taylor, and thought that the occasional flare-ups stemmed from the fact that the two men were so much alike in their approach to the game.

"Raymond and Jimmy got pretty damn close to a fight a couple of times," he said. "Raymond was that kind of a practice guy, and Jimmy was too."

By 1961, Taylor had developed into one of the most punishing fullbacks in NFL history. "He'll kill you for a yard," one opposing player said. Once, when five Ram defenders piled on and drove him out of bounds, Taylor leapt from the pile, clapped his hands, and shouted, "Way to hustle, guys!"

"Taylor was a tough, mean S.O.B," remembered Eagles' linebacker Chuck Bednarik. "Tough and mouthy. When we beat them in 1960 and I made that tackle on him, I was excited and I looked at him and said, 'You can get up now, this damn game is over!' So they came back and played us two years later and just beat the shit out of us. And Taylor let me know it. He would come up to me and say, 'Hey, how do ya like that shit, heh?'"

To Giants' middle linebacker Huff, Taylor was like Nitschke in that they both played with a linebacker's mentality. "Jimmy Taylor loved to run over you," Huff said. "He'd kick you in the head with those knees."

Like Nitschke, Taylor had endured a tough childhood, one that involved the untimely death of a parent. Born in Baton Rouge, Louisiana, on September 20, 1935, Jimmy was still in grade school when his father passed away. His mother worked in a laundry to support her three sons, and Jimmy pitched in by taking on two paper routes. One required him to get up early every morning and deliver papers before school; the other saw him delivering papers immediately after school was over.

"I must have pedaled my bike a million miles," Taylor said later, and credited the hard work with developing his tremendous leg drive.

"Jimmy will let you grab a leg," Green Bay offensive line coach Bill Austin said at the time, "then ram it through your chest."

Taylor's upper body development began in high school, when he hired on as a roughneck on an offshore oil rig. Taylor's job involved handling heavy pipes, and he would sometimes be out on the boats for 10 to 12 hours before returning to shore.

"Toughest thing I ever did," he said.

Taylor played well enough at Baton Rouge High School to earn a football scholarship to Louisiana State University. Poor study habits caused him to flunk out following his freshman year, and he spent the next two years at Hinds Junior College in Raymond, Mississippi. Taylor reapplied to LSU, and played his final two seasons of college ball under head coach Paul Dietzel. Despite sharing the same backfield with Heisman Trophy winner Billy Cannon, who would go on to become the first superstar of the American Football League, Taylor impressed scouts as a fullback, linebacker, and place-kicker. As a senior he ranked among the nation's leaders in rushing and points scored. The Packers chose Taylor in the second round of the '58 draft, and he arrived in camp with the reputation of being absent-minded. Taylor had trouble remembering his new Packer teammates' names, and solved his problem by calling everyone "Roy" or "Rick" or "Reno." He took over as the Packers' top fullback on Sunday, December 7, 1958, in San Francisco, in the penultimate game of the regular season, and remained in the starting lineup until leaving the team following Super Bowl I.

Taylor often engaged in what Lombardi referred to as "jive talk," and his manner of speaking confused his head coach. When Lombardi would question him in film sessions about a missed block on a linebacker, offensive tackle Steve Wright said Taylor would reply, "Uh, well, Coach, I was standing around and I cut to the right and he was standing there right in front of me and I didn't know which way to go because I saw his fromish and then his kribish and when the tackle froused, you know, it happened so quick."

"What?" Lombardi would ask incredulously. "Does anybody know what he's saying?" Lombardi later complained to writer W. C. Heinz that Taylor "uses jive talk I can't understand."

Taylor angered Lombardi by smoking cigars in the back of the darkened room during film study. Wright thought Taylor smoked during the meetings because he knew it blew Lombardi's mind. Taylor would light his cigar, take a few puffs, and then hear Lombardi's voice cutting through the darkness. "Taylor, put that damn cigar out!" When Lombardi chastised Taylor for failing to carry out a fake properly, Taylor would infuriate his coach by taking a long drag from his cigar, flick the ash off the end of it, and remark, "Guess I'm washed up, Coach."

No one, however, found anything to complain about when Taylor carried the ball. He stood 6-foot and weighed 215 pounds and was one of the first players in the league to devote himself to a rigorous weightlifting and isometric training program. Taylor trained himself with the same monkish fanaticism that Marciano had used to rule the heavyweight division in the 1950s, and his body looked like it had been chiseled out of granite. Lombardi would bump into Taylor by accident and walk away feeling as if he had just bumped into a cast-iron statue. "Nothing gives," Lombardi said, and the Packers' head coach noticed that Taylor's neck and shoulder muscles were so heavily developed that when he wanted to turn his head he would have to turn his whole upper body as well.

Taylor's devotion to physical fitness impressed Nitschke. He was amazed that in camp during two-a-day practices Taylor would lift weights early in the morning before the first practice then lift again before the afternoon practice. Two-a-days under Lombardi were an annual period of agony for the Packers, but Taylor was the one player who seemed unfazed by the grass drills and contact scrimmages under the blazing sun. Despite being someone whom Nitschke thought didn't have too much natural ability, Taylor really pushed himself in an effort to become the best fullback in the game. To Nitschke, Taylor played the game as if he was convinced there was no one better than he was, and his determination and desire had a profound impact on Nitschke. If Taylor could play that hard on offense, Nitschke thought, then he could play that hard on defense.

Nitschke's decision to dedicate himself to getting the most out of his potential paid off in the summer of 1961. Before Lombardi welcomed his Western Conference champions back to camp, he issued a sobering warning to his players. "Football," he said, "is a hard-headed, cold business. If a player isn't as good as he was last year when he won the championship for you, he's got to go."

Since success could make players "fat-headed," they would have to come to camp with a singleness of purpose, a dedication to victory. "I can assure you," he told the media, "that our staff and players will have that again in 1961."

Green Bay added three key rookies in Adderley, defensive tackle Ron Kostelnik, and halfback Elijah Pitts. The Packers went 6–0 in the preseason for the second straight year and outscored opponents by a combined score of 146–69. They stumbled in the regular season opener, losing to Detroit 17–13 before a crowd of 44,307 in Milwaukee, but then won their next six games and nine of their next ten. The Packers won despite having Nitschke, Hornung, and Dowler called into the service due to the Berlin crisis. The fall of 1961 had seen tension between the United States and Soviet Union escalate over access to Berlin, and President John F. Kennedy responded by calling up U.S. Armed Forces Reserves and National Guard units. The buildup resulted in more than two dozen players from the NFL and AFL joining their respective units on active duty.

Nitschke and Dowler reported to Fort Lewis, Washington; Hornung to

Fort Riley, Kansas. Nitschke, along with a lot of other men from Wisconsin, was assigned to the 32nd Division. He was paid $85.80 a month to carry sacks of potatoes. Nitschke joked later that the army must have thought he had the muscles for such an important job. His biggest problem at first was finding a uniform shirt that would fit; the army had to special order one with a size 18½-inch neck.

Lombardi fretted over the loss of three front-line players to military service, and he pulled favors from the Kennedy White House to get them weekend passes so they wouldn't miss any games. Lombardi was on good terms with the Kennedys; in the 1960 Wisconsin primary, Vince and his wife Marie had gone to see JFK speak in Green Bay. The two men met, and Lombardi told the Democratic candidate, "I'm with you all the way." Ethel Kennedy said later that Lombardi's endorsement helped the Kennedy's cause in what was a key primary state. "A grateful President," she said later, "never forgot."

Nitschke ended up missing two games that season, and because he was often absent from practice, split time at middle linebacker on game days with Tom Bettis. Yet the everyday absence of three regulars was just one problem the Packers faced in 1961. Defensive tackle Dave Hanner underwent an appendectomy, but 10 days later was back in the lineup. Hanner, Nitschke said, had Lombardi's reluctant permission to miss one game. Kramer broke his leg during the season and Lombardi was forced to alter his offensive line. Gregg slid over from right tackle to Kramer's spot at right guard, and backup Norm Masters took over at the tackle position.

Despite having to juggle their lineup, the Packers won the games they had to win. In Week Two, they faced conference rival San Francisco and the famous "Shotgun" offense installed by 49ers' head coach Red Hickey. A top pass receiver during his playing days, Hickey had watched the solid defensive units in Green Bay, New York, Detroit, and Baltimore stunt the scoring of the standard T-formation offenses prevalent in the NFL in the early 1960s. Hickey's Shotgun formation involved a spread offense, with two wingbacks and a tailback playing quarterback. With its tailback plunges and wingback reverses, the Shotgun was fully loaded for the '61 season. The 49ers defeated Washington 35–3 in their season opener, and when Hickey brought the 49ers to Green Bay in Week Two, 38,669 jammed City Stadium to see if the Packers could jam the Shotgun. Green Bay did, winning 30–10, then followed with a 24–0 shutout of Chicago, and a devastating 45–7 victory over Baltimore in a game in which Hornung personally accounted for 33 points by scoring four touchdowns and kicking a field goal and six extra points. Prior to the annual Thanksgiving Day game in Detroit, Lombardi switched Adderley, who had been playing halfback, to cornerback. Because of the short week, Adderley received a three-day crash course in playing his new position from defensive coordinator Phil Bengston. Proving himself a quick study, Adderley turned the game against the Lions around with an interception that started the Packers on their winning drive in an eventual 17–9 victory.

The win over the Lions moved the Packers to within one game of their second straight Western Conference championship, and Green Bay hosted the Giants on December 3 with a chance to clinch the title outright. Both teams entered the game 9–2, and sportswriters called the showdown of the two conference leaders a preview of the NFL title game. Before a crowd of 47,012 in Milwaukee, the Packers staged a come-from-behind, 20–17 win to repeat as conference champions. Green Bay split their final two games to finish with a league-best 11–3 record, then prepared to rematch with the Giants, who behind star quarterback Y. A. Tittle had won the Eastern Conference with a 10–3–1 record, one-half game ahead of second-place Philadelphia.

The Packers had played in five NFL championship games prior to 1961, yet none had ever been held in Green Bay. Packer fans responded to the event, adorning store windows with signs that read "Titletown, U.S.A." When Huff saw the gold-and-green signs and car stickers, he laughed. "How about that," Huff said. "The hicks don't even know how to spell 'Tittle.'" Giants' fans came bearing signs of their own—"Tittletown, U.S.A." Sportswriters pointed out that the Packers and Giants had finished atop the league in both offense and defense. Green Bay's offense led the league in points scored with 391, and New York was second with 368. The Giants' defense led the NFL in fewest points allowed with 220, while the Packers were second with 223. Green Bay fans looking for good omens remembered that the Packers' previous NFL championship had come against the Giants, a 14–7 win in 1944.

The return of Nitschke and Hornung to the locker room for the title game lifted the spirits of the team. Hornung's personality, his rare combination of nonchalance and determination, inspired his teammates. He was the rogue son who could tweak Lombardi, the team's disciplinarian father figure. Hornung's free-and-easy lifestyle kept the Packers loose. Prior to a big game in San Francisco against the rival 49ers, Hornung followed a stream of emotional team speeches by standing up and saying, "Look, I came out here for two reasons. I took care of the first last night, now let's go out and beat the 49ers."

When Lombardi finished a chastising of Hornung by shouting, "What do you wanna be? A football player or a playboy?" Hornung wasted no time answering.

"A playboy!" he shouted back.

Hornung was handsome, and his blond, curly hair and blue eyes added luster to his nickname, "Golden Boy." He was also glib, and once, during his college days at Notre Dame, was caught by head coach Frank Leahy snuffing out a cigarette with his shoe.

"Do you see what I see near your shoe, Paul?" Leahy asked.

"Yeah, Coach, I see. But you take it. You saw it first."

Hornung loved the single life, and his advice to those getting engaged was to never get married in the morning. The reason? "You never know who you'll meet that night," Hornung said. When Hornung eventually married, he broke his own rule and was married before noon. But he had his reasons. "If it didn't work out," he said, "I didn't want to blow the whole day."

On bus trips to the stadium, Lombardi always demanded that his players be in their seats 15 minutes before the scheduled departing time. Lombardi's seat was in the front of the bus, at the right elbow of the driver, and latecomers invoked his wrath. When Hornung and teammate Max McGee, who also liked the nightlife, arrived late, Lombardi fumed.

"Where have you two been?" he asked.

Without breaking stride, Hornung replied, "Church." The remark broke Lombardi up.

Nitschke looked past Hornung's playboy ways and saw a player who was a tremendous field leader and clutch competitor. The bigger the game, Nitschke thought, the bigger Hornung played.

Game day in Green Bay brought sunny but sub-freezing temperatures, and a New Year's Eve day crowd of 39,029 filled City Stadium. On the field below, 50 stadium workers had spent the early morning hours clearing the field of 14 inches of snow and then covering it with 20 tons of hay to preserve footing before the warm-ups. To combat the 21-degree cold, infrared heating units were placed along the bench areas of both teams. Across the country, a national television audience settled in to watch the game on NBC, which had paid a record $615,000 for the exclusive rights to the game.

Unlike the previous year, when Nitschke had taken to the Franklin Field sod uneasy about the Packers' inexperience, he ran onto the frozen turf of City Stadium confident Green Bay could beat the Giants. Packer practices during the week had been crisp and precise, and the team was peaking, physically and emotionally. Nitschke knew he wasn't as sharp as he could be because of his missed practices, but splitting time with Bettis and playing on special teams had helped keep him reasonably well-prepared.

Running onto the field, Nitschke barely acknowledged the cold. He was concentrating on Tittle, whom the Giants had acquired from San Francisco in a trade. Tittle replaced Charlie Conerly as the starting quarterback in Week Two and had thrown for 17 touchdowns and 2,272 yards. Having coached in San Francisco when Tittle was there, Bengston knew all of his former quarterback's tendencies. He knew what pass patterns were Tittle's favorites, what play Y. A. was likely to call in a certain situation. As the Packers' middle linebacker, Nitschke would be engaging in a game of mental cat-and-mouse with Tittle. Knowing Tittle's habits beforehand gave Nitschke an advantage, and he took the field believing this title game was going to mark one of the great afternoons of his life.

Nitschke made his presence felt on the game's first play. A tape of the '61 championship shows him hustling downfield on the opening kickoff and slamming Giant return man Joel Wells to the frozen field. On NBC radio, play-by-play announcer Ray Scott provided the call on a play that helped set the game's tempo:

This crowd is really coming alive as Ben Agajanian comes toward the ball and this championship game is under way. . . . It is off to the left, it is going to land at the 15-yard line, picked up by Wells, gets away from one man, he's to the 20, 25 and he is collared from behind and flipped down around the 30-yard line. . . . Ray Nitschke makes the tackle. . . .

Nitschke and Bettis spent the afternoon alternating at middle line-backer, where they stared across center at Tittle. The key to stopping New York, Nitschke knew, was to prevent Tittle from completing his deep passes to streaking ends Kyle Rote and Del Shofner, and holding fullback Alex Webster in check. The Packer defense was successful on both counts through a scoreless first quarter, but they gained a break when Rote slipped past the secondary only to drop Tittle's pass.

Green Bay broke the game open in the second quarter, scoring 24 straight points. Hornung had been cleared from army duty on special orders from JFK—"Paul Hornung isn't going to win the war on Sunday," the president said, "but the football fans of this country deserve the two best teams on the field that day"—and Green Bay's glamour back scored the first points of the game when he veered off right tackle from six yards out on the opening play of the second quarter. Nitschke followed with an intercep-tion of a Tittle pass that had been tipped at the line by defensive tackle Henry Jordan. Backpedaling into the secondary, Nitschke clutched the flut-tering ball and returned it eight yards before Rote dragged him down from behind.

Scott made the call on NBC radio:

A spread formation now for New York. . . . Fading to pass is Tittle, he is looking, he's throwing, the ball is batted. . . . Intercepted by Nitschke! He's at the 34-yard line. Ray Nitschke intercepts a ball that was batted near the line of scrimmage. . . . Ray Nitschke, who had moved in at middle line-backer, carried it back to the Giant 34-yard line and the Packers are in great position. . . .

Nitschke's interception set up Green Bay's second touchdown, a 13-yard pass from Starr to Dowler. Taking advantage of a New York secondary that was forced because of injuries to play offensive halfback Joe Morrison at safety, Starr followed with a 14-yard touchdown pass to tight end Ron Kramer. Desperate to put points on the board before halftime, the Giants replaced Tittle with Conerly, a championship quarterback from years past. Conerly drove New York deep into Green Bay territory, but Nitschke and the Packer defense responded to the challenge. Fighting off the block of center Ray Wietecha, Nitschke combined with defensive end Bill Quinlan to shut down halfback Phil King's alley to the end zone at the Packers' 8-yard line. Nitschke then teamed with left linebacker Dan Currie to stop Webster's drive through the middle at the 6. Two plays later, halfback Bob Gaiters ran right on an option and overthrew Rote in the back of the end zone.

Nitschke and the Packer defense had held, and Hornung closed the half a short time later with a 17-yard field goal to give Green Bay a 24–0 lead. Nitschke opened the second half by taking Pat Summerall's short kickoff at the Packers' 18-yard line, and displaying the running style he had showed years before as a fullback at Illinois, tucked the ball under his right arm and barreled 18 yards upfield before slipping on the icy turf and being downed at the 36.

Nitschke's run brought a chuckle from Ray Scott, who opened the second half with the following call:

The sun is shining, but don't get me wrong, there's no heat wave in Green Bay. All things considered it's just about as much as we could hope for. We're ready to go. . . . Summerall comes to the ball, his kick is high and fairly short. It will land at the 20, be picked up and taken to the 25, 30, 35 and down falls . . . Ray Nitschke, I do believe. That's right, Ray Nitschke, who played some fullback in his football career but (is) known in professional football as a linebacker, takes a short kickoff, moves it to the 36-yard line where, trying to cut, he falls down. . . .

The Packers added 10 more points in the third quarter on a 22-yard field goal by Hornung and Starr's second TD pass to Ron Kramer, a 13-yarder that made it 34–0. Hornung's 19-yard field goal in the fourth closed the scoring at 37–0 and he finished the game with an NFL championship record 19 points. The Packer defense had done its job as well. Webster, who had rushed for 928 yards that season and averaged 4.7 yards per carry, was held to 19 yards rushing, and Tittle was limited to six completions in 20 attempts. Nitschke hounded Tittle all afternoon, and the result was that the Giants quarterback threw for just 65 yards while splitting time with Conerly. By game's end, New York's vaunted air attack had been limited to six first downs and 130 yards of total offense.

Giants' rookie Greg Larson played right tackle that day, and was shaken by the ferocity of Nitschke and the Green Bay defense.

"When we fell behind they knew we had to pass," Larson said after the game. "When they knew that, they came in swinging fists and elbows and yelling and looking crazy in the eyes. They came in screaming and screeching. It was the most frightening thing I ever saw in a football game, absolutely terrifying. We had no way to stop them. It was unending. They were like wild men. Play after play, pounding and slapping and punching. It was enough to make a man cry from the physical brutality of it all."

At the final gun, Lombardi was hoisted on the shoulders of his players. "Today," he told them, "you are the greatest team in the history of the National Football League." Later, as a cold dusk descended on Green Bay's New Year's Eve celebrations, Lombardi received a telegram from President Kennedy. "Congratulations on a great game today. It was a fine victory for a great coach, a great team, and a great town."

In the crowded Green Bay dressing room, defensive backs coach Norb Hecker paid special tribute to Nitschke. A review of the radio broadcast of the game reveals that Nitschke was credited with four solo tackles and one QB pressure. Hecker said later that it was Nitschke's hard hits that inspired the Packer defense.

"It sort of rubs off on the rest of the men and makes them want to hit harder," Hecker said. "You know how it is when you're in a fight and someone on your side gets in a big punch? It swings things your way. That's the way it is when Nitschke flattens someone."

Bengston thought Nitschke's hitting had given the Packers' middle linebacker a presence on the field, a presence opponents were becoming increasingly aware of. "It gets so they want to know where Nitschke is lined up on every play," Bengston said. "They become quite conscious of his presence."

Nitschke was overjoyed with the victory. He found it hard to describe the depth of feeling he was developing for his teammates. Strangers to one another not so long ago, they had been molded by Lombardi and the coaching staff into a group of men with a singleness of purpose and confidence in one another. A team that Nitschke knew had been on the verge of greatness since 1960 had realized their goal in one afternoon of near-perfect football—an afternoon, Nitschke felt, that couldn't be improved upon.

The Packers returned for the 1962 season seeking a second straight NFL championship and a third consecutive Western Conference title. For the third straight season they won every preseason game, then won their first 10 games of the regular season. The defense excelled, claiming consecutive shutouts in Weeks Two and Three and allowing just 14 points combined over the first four games. Even with Hornung below par physically because of a sore knee, the Packer offense scored a total of 100 points in its first three games, including finals of 34–7 over Minnesota and 49–0 over Chicago.

The Packers were strong, Jerry Kramer thought. And Lombardi went through that season with a gleam in his eye, a gleam that Kramer thought meant the Packers had better not do anything wrong. It was the gleam of a successful man seeking additional success.

Driven by Lombardi, the Packers reached their peak as a team. They were tough and experienced, and like the DiMaggio Yankees of the forties and early fifties, featured a clubhouse filled with H.A.s, the Yankees' term for "Hard Asses." They were hard men playing a hard game, a family of rough, rowdy brothers who battled opponents, and at times, each other. If Nitschke missed a tackle, for instance, Wood would let him know it in the huddle.

"Don't you ever let those running backs get to me again!," he would scream at Nitschke. From his free safety position, Wood had the best view of the play as it unfolded in front of him, and he didn't see why he had to make the tackles Nitschke should have been making. "He was getting paid twice as much as me," Wood said.

Wood stood 5-foot-10 and weighed 170, but he withered teammates with hard stares. Even Nitschke was frightened by Wood's cold looks. "I hate to miss a tackle," Nitschke said at the time, "because if I do, I know I'm gonna get a dirty look from Willie. He'll kill you with that look."

Some of the Packers, like Starr, were angelic assassins. Off the field, Starr was soft-spoken and courteous. But Zeke Bratkowski, who became Starr's backup in 1963, said once that Starr's personality changed once he lined up under center. "On the field, he'll cut your heart out and show it to you," Bratkowski said.

Starr ran an offense geared to power sweeps and off-tackle blasts; Lombardi called it "grinding meat." *Time* magazine described it as "rugged, old-fashioned blocking to open holes for rugged, old-fashioned ball carriers." Starr would slap the ball into Taylor's rock-hard stomach some 20 times a game, Hornung would take it 12 or 13 times, and Starr would throw the ball 25 times. "That was our offense," Hornung said.

"Those Packer teams of '61 and '62 were just fantastic football teams, if not the greatest of all time," Huff remembered. "There was no way you could go into Green Bay and beat 'em. They had Hornung and Taylor in the backfield, two Hall of Famers, and their line could *block*. They had to, because they had Lombardi coaching them and he made them a tough team."

Opposing coaches knew what the Packer offense was going to do; it was always Hornung into the strong side, Taylor into the weak side, and Starr carving up the defense with a ball-control passing attack. Otto Graham, who coached the College All-Stars from 1958 to 1963 and the Washington Redskins from 1966 to 1968, said it was never difficult to prepare a game plan for the Packers because they rarely tried to surprise opponents with anything new. "They just dared you to stop them," Graham said.

"The offense made it very easy for us," said Currie, an all-pro at left linebacker. "They'd get the ball and go eight-and-half minutes for a touchdown, and when the opposition can't get their hands on the ball, it kills them. It makes it very frustrating for them. "

At the heart of the Packers' precision offense was the power sweep. In the playbook, the call was "49-Sweep" when Hornung ran it to the right side; "28-Sweep" when Taylor ran it to the left. In time, it became known simply as the "Lombardi Sweep." It was Green Bay's bread-and-butter play, their top-priority play, the play they had to make go and the one opponents had to stop. Every team in the NFL had their own signature play. Chicago ran the pitchout for speedy halfback Willie Galimore and Cleveland the toss sweep for fullback Jimmy Brown. In Detroit, the Lions favored the fullback slant for Nick Pietrosante; in San Francisco, the 49ers ran the screen pass better than anyone else.

In Green Bay, the Packers ran the sweep, a play that had become a part of Lombardi during his days as a guard at Fordham, when he played against the single-wing sweep as run by the great Pittsburgh teams of Jock Sutherland. Lombardi's sweep incorporated the same qualities as Sutherland's, the same guard-pulling techniques, the same cutbacks by the ball carrier. Lombardi had run the sweep in New York when he had Frank Gifford, and when he took over in Green Bay, he saw in Hornung a halfback who was a bigger, stronger version of Gifford. The sweep was the first play Lombardi put into the Packer playbook, and he taught it with such force he sometimes punctuated his remarks by snapping the chalk in two.

"What we want," Lombardi would tell his team, "is to get a seal *heah*, and a seal *heah*, and run this play IN THE ALLEY!"

The Lombardi Sweep became the dominant play of the decade and served to influence a generation of future head coaches. Don Shula's Miami Dolphins featured the sweep in the 1970s, with Mercury Morris running strongside in Hornung's footsteps and Larry Csonka pounding the weakside just as Taylor had before him. The trend continued in the 1980s with Bill Parcells, Mike Ditka, and Bill Walsh running their versions of the Lombardi Sweep.

"That damn sweep worked because everybody on the team did his job," former Baltimore Colts coach Don McCafferty said once. It was a matter of Packer execution, McCafferty said, and it was the defenses who were getting executed. When a reporter asked if there was anything mysterious about the Packers' success with such a simple play, McCafferty shook his head.

"Just too damned good," he said.

In practice, Nitschke would watch as Green Bay's guards pulled from the line and began their calvary charge around the end with Hornung and Taylor hot on their heels. "Dapper! Dapper!" Nitschke would call out to Currie amid the thunder of cleats. "Look out, Dapper! Here they come!"

The Packers ran the sweep relentlessly in practice, and while other NFL teams finished each practice day by running wind sprints, the Packers closed their practices by running the sweep. Nitschke and the Green Bay defense saw the sweep so much in practice they grew to know the intricacies of it as well as the offense. That hard-earned knowledge paid off on game days. When opposing teams would try to sweep the flanks against Green Bay, the Packers' instant recognition of the play allowed them to shut it down. Nitschke consistently shot the gaps left by the pulling guards, and films show him running down Baltimore's Lenny Moore on a sweep right in Green Bay, wrapping up New York's Phil King on a sweep left in Yankee Stadium.

As a team, the Packers peaked in 1962. When they rematched with the Eagles in Philadelphia in Week 11, they rolled up 628 yards in a 49–0 win. Green Bay linemen whip-sawed Bednarik, their old antagonist, with powerful, precision blocks. It was payback for the '60 title game, Bednarik thought, and Packers' defensive coordinator Phil Bengston didn't disagree. "We had learned the lessons of 1960," he said.

Walking off the field at halftime, a weary Bednarik called out to Green Bay assistant coach Tom Fears.

"Hey, Tom, when are you going to put in the scrubs?"

Looking right through Bednarik, Fears replied coldly, "Chuck, we don't have any scrubs."

Watching Nitschke on that November 11 afternoon, Bednarik realized that the linebacker the Eagles had seen two years earlier in the NFL championship game had returned to Franklin Field as the veteran leader of the Green Bay defense.

"A linebacker is like a general," Bednarik recalled. "He's a guy that calls the defenses, he can see what the hell's going on from behind the line. He could actually grade those guys while the game's going on. You know, 'What the hell are you doing?' You're like a teacher behind there too, you know, 'Why don't you do this? or 'You've gotta do this.'

"I could see Nitschke was a helluva football player, and he did a helluva job at middle linebacker. He really stood out."

Lombardi called Nitschke "the spearhead of our defense," and recognized the importance of the position. Modern middle linebackers, Lombardi said, had to be mobile because they had gone from 300-pound giants rooted to the trenches to 230–240-pound freelancers who comprised the second line of defense. They also had greater opportunities for fame since they were now out in the open, where fans could see them taking shots at the ballcarriers. "It has made Sunday heroes," Lombardi said, "of the Schmidts, Nitschkes, Huffs, and the rest."

Lest Nitschke or any player get too comfortable with his new-found fame, Lombardi kept them in line. He reminded his team throughout the '62 season that since they were on top, everyone was looking to knock them off. "This is the real test," he would say. "This year you find out whether or not you're really champions."

On the practice field, in the film grading sessions, Lombardi pounced on every mistake. Jerry Kramer said Lombardi rode them unmercifully that season. As an assistant at West Point under Red Blaik, Lombardi had picked up the habit of addressing the young cadets as "mister." By the time he reached the NFL, he had developed a way of saying the word in the most cutting fashion. When one of the Packers made a careless mistake, Lombardi would look at him with disgust. "You really are something, you are *mister*," he would say with derision.

Lombardi's tough coaching methods insulated Nitschke and the Packers against outside pressure. Even a 26–14 loss in Detroit on Thanksgiving Day, the Packers' lone defeat of the season, failed to rattle them. For one of the few times during the Lombardi years, the Packers failed to match the intensity of their opponent. Several Packers had been left bloodied and dazed by the beating the Lions handed out that afternoon, and Detroit had run out to a 26–0 lead in a performance that ranks as one of the greatest in franchise history. "They came out of the chutes like they'd gone crazy," said Starr, who was sacked 11 times on the day. "It looked like there were 50 of them playing us instead of 11."

The Packers stopped the onslaught with two late touchdowns, but by game's end, they were physically beaten. When Starr asked his receivers late in the game which one could get open, McGee asked, "Why don't you throw an incomplete pass and *nobody* will get hurt." The remark left the battered Packers laughing in their huddle, and Bengston thought the moment proved Green Bay had turned the corner as a team. Even a loss as humiliating as this one had been, he said, had been just a momentary lapse, another step in the team's character building. Starr agreed. "We showed something in the second half," he said.

Lombardi later accepted the blame for the loss, calling it "coaching stupidity" for not adjusting to what the Lions were doing. Nitschke thought there was another reason. The Lions had all the momentum that day, he said. Detroit had been pointing to the rematch since October 7, when a late turnover led to a 9–7 Packers' victory in a game the Lions believed should have been theirs. Green Bay guard Fuzzy Thurston's mother had died before the Thanksgiving Day rematch, and his somber mood reflected that of the team. Green Bay was due for a letdown; they had won 18 straight games, including post-seasons and exhibitions, dating back to 1961, and they finally came up flat.

Still, Nitschke thought the Thanksgiving Day loss to the Lions helped the Packers. They were determined, he thought, not to let it happen again that season.

Confident that no defeat could destroy them, the Packers rebounded to win the conference title with a 13–1 record and became the first NFL team since the 1934 Bears to win 13 games in a season. Taylor led the NFL in rushing by pounding out 1,474 yards and an NFL-record 19 touchdowns. Starr led the league in passing and Wood led in interceptions. Eleven Packers were named all-pro, including four of their five starters on the offensive line.

In the East, the Giants repeated as conference champions, finishing first with a 12–2 record. For the second straight year, New York and Green Bay would meet to decide the NFL championship. For the second straight year, Nitschke would be matching wits with Tittle, who after 14 years of pro football, had suddenly become an overnight sensation by throwing for a league-record 33 touchdowns. It was a game that had been building for a full season, and when the Giants wrapped up their regular season with a 41–31 win over Dallas on December 16, a crowd of 62,694 fans rocked cavernous Yankee Stadium with a singular, tribal chant.

"Beat Green Bay . . . Beat Green Bay . . . "

SIX

OOD AFTERNOON, everyone. We are waiting for the Packers and the Giants to come out of the dugouts now, as 62,000-plus fans are on hand at Yankee Stadium. Repeating the weather situation, the temperature here is 20 degrees. There is a northwest wind, about 25 to 30 miles an hour, with occasional gusts. And down on the surface it becomes a problem, because it does swirl around.

"The Green Bay Packers are now being introduced individually as they take the field. . . ."

Listeners to NBC Radio announcer Ken Coleman's 1 P.M. broadcast of the 1962 NFL championship game on Sunday, December 30, 1962 could hear the thunderous boos that accompanied Yankee Stadium announcer Bob Sheppard's baritone introductions of the Packers' offense:

"At *quahteback*, Number 15, *Baht Stah* . . . "

In the visitors' dugout, Ray Nitschke stood with members of the Green Bay Packers defense awaiting their turn to take the field. To Nitschke, it was a miserably cold day, and as he ran gingerly across the field in his white Packer uniform with the yellow-gold helmet and pants, the howling wind rippled his warmup cape and churned up cyclones of dust from the dirt infield. The Packers' appearance on the Yankee Stadium turf also churned up memories of last year's 37–0 title game victory over the Giants, and the standing room-only crowd of 64,892 shook the stadium with chants of "Beat Green Bay . . . " as members of New York's famous defense were introduced.

For more than a week, New York City had become engulfed in the intense buildup given the Packers–Giants rematch. Newspaper stands were filled with issues of that week's *Time* magazine, whose cover carried a picture of a grinning Vince Lombardi. Across the cover were the words, "The Sport of the '60s," and if the NFL was in the process of gripping the imagination of the American sporting public, it was the bitter rivalry between dynastic teams like Green Bay and New York that was helping shape pro football's transformation. For the Packers, the '62 title game marked their third consecutive appearance in the NFL championship game. For the Giants, it was their second straight title game appearance, their fourth in five years and fifth in seven years.

From the moment Don Chandler's 16-yard field goal cleared the uprights at 4:10 P.M. Central Standard Time on Sunday, December 2, 1962, giving the Giants a 26–24 win over the Chicago Bears at Wrigley Field and the Eastern Conference title, the attention of New York's players and coaches turned automatically to one thought.

"Another showdown," New York quarterback Y. A. Tittle said, "with the Green Bay Packers."

For almost a full year, the Giants had lived with the memory of their shutout loss to Green Bay in the 1961 NFL championship game played the previous New Year's Eve, lived with the memory of Packer backs Jimmy Taylor and Paul Hornung combining for 183 yards rushing, with quarterback Bart Starr's precise passing game, with a Green Bay defense, led by Nitschke, that had both beaten up and shut down the most prolific offense in the Eastern Conference. When it was over, when the Packers had carried head coach Vince Lombardi off the field on their shoulders and Green Bay fans chanted "Titletown . . . Titletown" and tore down the goalposts, the Giants' mood was symbolized by a solitary New York player. Covered in ice and dirt, the player slumped wearily in front of his locker stall as reporters raced into the locker room. Amid the muttering and swearing, the despondent Giant offered what *Newark* (New Jersey) *Star-Ledger* sportswriter Jerry Izenberg later recalled as the only printable quote from the loser's side. Looking up at the horde of reporters crowding into the visitors' locker room, the battered Giant snarled, "Shut the damn door."

Tittle remembered the Giants' post-game locker room as an "awful scene." New York was a team of great pride, Tittle said, and to have been crushed as they were was a terrible blow. Everyone on the club showed the emotional strain of such an embarrassing defeat; head coach Allie Sherman's eyes were moist, and he was flushed with anger and humiliation.

Now, the Giants geared for their chance at revenge. They had been hoping for a second shot at Green Bay, Tittle said, "and now we had it." New York was gripped with championship fever. There was talk of little else during the days leading up to the game. Between periods of a New York Rangers' game at Madison Square Garden, ice hockey fans began the chant, "Beat Green Bay." Tittle recalled the chorus being picked up all over town. Every time he turned on the radio, the balding, 35-year-old quarterback heard disc jockeys repeating the phrase. Store windows in Manhattan were filled with Christmas decorations and signs that read "Beat Green Bay." Fans stopped Giant players on the streets, in restaurants, or Christmas shopping in the stores, and implored them to "Let's go, beat Green Bay."

The Packers were the pick of oddsmakers to repeat as NFL champions. Green Bay had the best record in the league at 13–1; New York was second at 12–2. The Packers led the league in points scored with 415; the Giants were second with 398. Green Bay also led in defense, allowing the fewest points with 148, but New York had Tittle, who took over as the Giants' offensive leader following the retirement of quarterback Charlie Conerly.

Tittle highlighted the Giants' season in Week Seven, when he threw for 505 yards and seven touchdowns in a 49–34 win over the Washington Redskins. Though his aging appearance sometimes led to mistakes off the field—an airline stewardess had stopped him from getting on the team's chartered plane with the statement, "I'm sorry, sir, this flight is only for the football players"—there was no mistaking Tittle on the field.

Middle-aged among NFL players, Tittle would retreat into the protective pocket and, denying the furious rush of the defense, survey the field for a receiver. If he wasn't firing bombs to split end Del Shofner or flanker Frank Gifford, who had returned from a one-year retirement following the concussive hit by Philadelphia linebacker Chuck Bednarik, Tittle was backpedaling before onrushing defenders and beating blitzes with screen passes to fullback Alex Webster. Near the goal line, Tittle crossed up defenses by bootlegging his way to the end zone, his black high top cleats carrying his thin legs to paydirt.

Tittle's emergence at quarterback and the return of Gifford had made the Giants a more dangerous offense than they had been the year before, and they were confident they could score points on the Packer defense. Gifford was a charismatic veteran, a hero of Giant victories of the past, and he spoke for the team when he said everyone on the club "wanted revenge for the clobbering [the Packers] handed us the year before."

While the Giants were sky-high for the rematch, practices in Green Bay that week lacked the intensity Lombardi was looking for, and he pulled Nitschke aside on the Wednesday prior to the game.

"Hit those guys, Ray," Lombardi said. "Hit those guys like they're Giants."

Nitschke nodded, and when he looked at the members of the Packer offense in practice that day, he saw the Giants instead. Green Bay center Jim Ringo became New York center Ray Wietecha, and in a scrimmage, Nitschke drilled him with his huge forearms, leaving Ringo with a severely pinched muscle in his neck.

Ringo's nerve problem reached deep into his right arm, which grew numb from the force of Nitschke's hit. When he found he had trouble centering the ball, Ringo didn't think he'd be able to play against New York. He didn't want to hurt the team by trying to do something he was physically unable to. The Packers arrived in New York on Friday, and following a workout at Yankee Stadium, *Newark Star-Ledger* sportswriter Dave Klein was in the visitors' locker room looking to interview some of the Packers. The room had been mostly cleared, but on the other side of the lockers, Klein could hear a conversation between Ringo and Lombardi.

"How's the arm?"

"I can't feel it at all, coach."

When Lombardi saw Klein in the room, he exploded in rage. Ringo was a bit more calm. He explained to Klein that if the Giants knew about his injured arm, they might take shots at it, and then he ran a risk of permanent injury. Ringo promised Klein that if he didn't write about the injury beforehand, he would give him an exclusive afterward. Klein agreed, and when the Packers took the field on game day, Klein could see that Ringo's right arm at times hung limply at his side.

Ringo's injury soon became secondary to the game-day conditions. The night before the game brought wet but mild conditions, but early-morning churchgoers on Sunday were blasted by icy winds that gusted up to 40 and 50 miles an hour. By kickoff, the temperature was 14 degrees and dropping. Hot coffee froze just minutes after it was poured at stadium concession stands. The field was hard-packed and full of pebbles, and the grass had been eroded by a season's worth of games. Coleman did, however, point out one plus to his NBC listeners.

The sun keeps peeking in and out from behind the clouds of the east end of this great stadium. . . .

Among those seeking warmth down on the field was Packers' photographer Vern Biever. He started covering the Packers in 1941 as an 18-year-old stringer for the *Milwaukee Sentinel.* Two years later, he was an army photographer with the 100th Infantry Division, rolling into France and then Germany. When Biever returned to Green Bay following the end of World War II, he looked up Jug Earpe, the Packers' public relations director, and proposed a deal.

"You want a record of your games?" Biever asked. "Give me a field pass and I'll give you some pictures."

Biever became the NFL's first team photographer, and since then has provided a visual record of Packer legends—Don Hutson, Tony Canadeo, and Curly Lambeau; Lombardi, Starr, and Nitschke; Mike Holmgren, Bret Favre, and Reggie White. Biever has photographed 16 NFL championship teams, 15 Hall of Famers, and every Super Bowl game.

When he started covering the Packers, Biever would be accompanied by a maximum of three or four other photographers doing the game for the various wire services. He soon gained a reputation among the players as being quick on his feet and wily. Though he was positioned close to the action on the sidelines, he never got "rolled up," the players' term for being knocked off his feet by plays along the sideline. With his 4X5 Speed Graphics camera, Biever captured the game as it was played, using tight, focused shots and portrait-style close-ups.

Through the early years, Biever always wished there were more sideline photographers at each game, if for no other reason than to cut the wind that came howling through the old stadiums. His wish was never more fervent than in the 1962 championship game, when the wind gusted through Yankee Stadium with vicious intent.

"I always say this, they talk about the Ice Bowl being cold, but I felt colder at the 1962 championship game than I did at the Ice Bowl," Biever said. "That wind was dominating and more penetrating than the Ice Bowl. The Ice Bowl was cold, but this game here, the wind was such a factor."

The Giants won the toss and elected to receive, and as the two teams tried to loosen up on the sidelines, Lombardi sought out Nitschke.

"Give us some hits right away, Ray," he said. "Get the boys started hitting."

Nitschke started the hitting, teaming with left tackle Dave Hanner to stop halfback Phil King for a two-yard gain on the game's first play from scrimmage. On NBC Radio, Coleman made the first of what would be many mentions of Nitschke's name that day:

The ball is spotted down at the 32 for New York and it is first down, ten yards to go for the Giants as Ray Wietecha leads them out. Webster and King are set in behind Y. A. Tittle and Shofner comes out wide on the left side. . . . Tittle takes and he gives it to (King), driving straight on and digging out a couple of yards. Ray Nitschke, the middle linebacker, and Dave Hanner, the defensive left tackle, are in there to make the play. . . .

Coleman's reference to Nitschke as the "middle linebacker" was unique that day. At that time, the position was still referred to in many circles as the "middle guard," and on Coleman's next two references to Nitschke, he called him Green Bay's middle guard. Two plays later, Nitschke was fronting the Green Bay defense again, and game films show him spinning King to the ground after an 8-yard gain on a draw play. Packers' defensive coordinator Phil Bengston always told his team that the first five to ten plays were pivotal in determining how the opposition was going to play Green Bay on a given day, and Nitschke had gone out for that first series intent on showing the Giants he was going to be coming after them all day, hitting hard on every down.

New York stalled on their own 42-yard line, and following Chandler's punt, the Packers took over on their 20. On the sideline, Nitschke shivered amid the icy conditions. The bitter gales slapped exposed skin like a barber's blade on a strop. It pierced every fibre of Nitschke's being; he could feel it whipping through his uniform and heavy pads. It even seemed to find its way under his skin, he said later, and rattle the bones beneath. Nitschke had played in cold weather in Green Bay, but this day in New York was colder than any he had ever experienced. It was so cold that even Nitschke couldn't find any fun in being in Yankee Stadium that day.

Bundled against the cold with a fur collar pulled up around his ears, Lombardi thought the game-time conditions were the worse he had ever encountered. "It was the worst day I can ever remember for a football game," he said later. "I was half sorry to ask people to play in those conditions."

To compensate for a field as hard and frozen as the Russian steppes, Nitschke joined with Packer backs and ends in wearing ripple-soled coaching shoes. Packer linemen wore cleats, and right guard Jerry Kramer, who would be called on to replace a hobbled Paul Hornung and handle the place-kicking duties, wore a cleat on his right foot and a ripple-soled shoe on his left, or plant, foot.

As hard as Nitschke had hit the Giants on their first offensive series of the game, New York's defense hit just as hard on the Packers' initial drive. The memory of the embarrassment in Green Bay the year before had been burned into their brains, as had pregame talk of the Packers being a superior team.

"Bullshit," Giant defensive end Andy Robustelli snapped at a reporter before the game. "I've never been as anxious to play a game as this one. We will absolutely kill the bastards. It's the only way I'll be able to forget the one out there last year.

"It won't be enough to just win this game. We have to destroy the Packers and Lombardi. It's the only way we can atone for what happened to us last year."

Giants middle linebacker Sam Huff set the tone early. On the Packers' fourth play from scrimmage, fullback Jimmy Taylor took Starr's handoff and headed right for a pickup of 14 yards. As Huff chased him down, the two neared the New York sideline. Drawing a bead on Taylor, Huff thought, "Okay. It's live or die right now."

Mustering every ounce of his 230 pounds, Huff hit Taylor so hard he dented his own helmet. Both fullback and linebacker went sprawling out of bounds, and the die had been cast. New York had been humiliated the year before by Green Bay, Huff said. They were not going to let it happen again. The Giants, Huff said, went into the game with blood in their eyes, and they were going to let Taylor know from the start that they were going to knock him down, and knock him down hard.

Green Bay Press-Gazette sportswriter Lee Remmel thought Huff's fierce play was motivated in part by an Associated Press wire photo from the title game year before. The picture showed Huff lying on the ground and Packer linemen figuratively dusting off their hands. "That picture ran all over the country," Remmel remembered, "and as a result, Sam was hitting Taylor in bounds and out of bounds, before the whistle, after the whistle, you name it."

Green Bay drove 60 yards in 11 plays and capped its first series with a 26-yard field goal by Kramer. Initially, Kramer had thought his kick had gone wide, and he cursed under his breath. When he saw the referee signalling the kick good, Kramer turned to Starr.

"What the hell's he doing?" he shouted.

"Shut up," Starr barked, "and get off the field."

The Packers maintained their 3–0 lead through a viciously fought first quarter. Taylor engaged in a running exchange with New York's defense, challenging them. "Hit me harder," he would say, then gouge out a four-yard gain. "I only got four this time," he would tell Huff and Robustelli. "Next time I'm going to get more."

To Huff, Taylor was a maniacal competitor who would do whatever it took to win. "He'd kick you, gouge you, spit at you, whatever it took," Huff said. "It was a street fight."

Taylor ran low to the ground, and all Huff and the Giants saw of him was his lowered helmet and high knees. More than any other Packer, Taylor took to heart Lombardi's belief that a football player had to direct all his anger toward his opponent during the game. "I hated them, from the opening whistle to the final gun," Taylor said. "I loved to take the battle to them, to sting them, to go right at them and pick up the extra yard. I figured I couldn't out-cute them, so I just ran over them."

From the Packer sideline, Nitschke watched in fascination as Taylor took the battle to the Giants. Nitschke figured the Packers had gained their three-point lead on the strength of Taylor's determination. "Early in the game," Nitschke said, "Taylor set the tone."

Nitschke had seen that first sideline collision between Taylor and Huff, had watched Huff drive Taylor out of bounds, and as the two men skidded across the ice, had seen Huff using his knees and elbows on Taylor as they tumbled out of bounds.

When the Giants got the ball back, Nitschke returned the favor. He stuffed King for a one-yard gain on a draw play, then short-circuited the

Giants' drive. Defying both the gusting wind and the Green Bay defense, Tittle had completed three passes for a combined 38 yards to move New York deep into Packer territory. On a second-and-nine at the 15, Nitschke stared across the line at Tittle. As Nitschke and Tittle matched wits, a banner flapping from the railing at Yankee Stadium read "O.K. Y.A., Make Green Bay Pay."

Nitschke knew the Giants had done the bulk of their scoring through the air, and though Green Bay wasn't a blitzing team, Nitschke figured it was a good time to gamble. With Giant fans rocking the stadium with a breathless "Go! Go! Go!" chant, Tittle retreated into the swirling dust of the pocket. Nitschke waited for a second, then looped behind Hanner at left tackle on a delayed blitz. King cut over from his left halfback slot to pick up Nitschke, who was by now two yards deep in the Giant backfield, but he was too late. With his arms raised, Nitschke tipped Tittle's pass, and the deflected ball fell into the arms of left linebacker Dan Currie, who returned it to the 39 before his left knee buckled and he was downed.

Green Bay took over and drove to the New York 30. Taylor carried four times on the march, grunting and growling his way to short pickups on power sweeps and off-tackle slants. On the next-to-last play of the first quarter, game films show Taylor was going down when Huff plowed into him. The violent collision caused Taylor to bite his tongue. Swallowing blood and spitting ice, the Packer fullback climbed groggily to his feet. He was jack-knifed in pain, and Nitschke watched as Taylor steadied himself by grabbing Starr's arm. Taylor, who said later that Huff "is a great one for piling on," left the game for a play as Kramer's 36-yard field goal on the final play of the first quarter fell short in the swirling wind.

"That was a nasty game," Currie remembered. "Geez, Jimmy Taylor split his elbow and still played. The Giants were really up for that game, and there were almost some altercations there a few times. That was the nastiest game I've ever been involved in."

While Taylor continued his constant battle with the Giant defense, Nitschke engaged in his own war with the New York offense. Whether it was wrestling Webster to the rock-hard turf, colliding with King, or blitzing his way into the Giant backfield, Nitschke went after the Giants with a fury.

From the Giants' sideline, Huff watched as Nitschke blitzed Tittle, "blitzed almost at will," the Giants' linebacker said. The Giants became incensed when they claimed King was a full four yards out of bounds when Nitschke plowed into him. But it was that kind of a day in New York, and Huff admired the intensity Nitschke brought to the position.

"He was a great, great linebacker," Huff said. "A great hitter, and the intensity was there. I admired the great ballplayers. Sometimes ballplayers are jealous of one another. But I don't think Ray Nitschke was ever jealous of me and I was never jealous of him."

As the second quarter wore on, Yankee Stadium took on the look and feel of Siberia. The skies grew dark with clouds, and the stadium lights had to be turned on even though it was still early afternoon. Violent winds ripped dirt from the grassless field and funneled it into mini tornadoes. Strong gusts blew the passes of Tittle and Starr back into their faces and wreaked havoc with the passing game. Gifford remembered passes thrown by Tittle landing in front of him and behind him, and at times seemed to be aimed at anyone but him.

By the second quarter, Tittle's fingers were frozen and he had trouble gripping the ball. The wind was clocked at 50 miles per hour on the field, and Kramer noticed the currents were doing crazy things that day; it would blow one way at field level; then blow in the opposite direction just above the ground. The same was true depending on which end of the field the teams were at. The wind would gust in one direction at one end, and Kramer would look down the field and see the dust swirling in a completely different direction at the opposite end zone.

"That was a difficult game to play in because of the weather conditions," Green Bay cornerback Herb Adderley said. "It was extremely cold with the wind-chill factor."

Blizzards of torn paper littered the darkening field during play, and once, a sideline bench that was unoccupied was lifted by a gale and tossed 10 feet onto the field. On the sideline, Bengston thought the combination of the whipping wind and the chants of close to 65,000 Giant fans threatened to sweep the Packers out of Yankee Stadium.

Nitschke, however, provided a second turning point when he recovered a King fumble at the New York 28 with 3:06 remaining in the half. Currie, who was having a big game at outside linebacker, forced the turnover with a jarring hit on King, and Nitschke covered the loose ball.

On NBC Radio, Coleman made the call on a play many considered to be the game's turning point:

Second-and-five at the 34 of New York. Y. A. Tittle, on a draw play, gives to King again. . . . Fumble . . . scramble . . . and it is grabbed by the Packers! The Green Bay Packers have come up with the ball and Ray Nitschke is the man who fell on it at the 28-yard line. . . . "

Nitschke's fumble recovery paid immediate dividends for the Packers. On first down, Hornung headed right on what looked to be a power sweep, then stopped and lofted a long pass that flanker Boyd Dowler gathered in on the 7. One play later, Starr kneeled in the huddle and called "Blue Right 37." The play was designed for Taylor to go off right tackle, and Giants left tackle Dick Modzelewski saw something in Taylor's stance that tipped where the play was going. At the snap, Taylor took Starr's handoff and veered right. Modzelewski followed, but when Kramer drove "Little Mo" further outside, Taylor read his block and cut back across the grain, through the middle. The game film shows Taylor eluding the diving grasp of Rosey Grier at the 5 and skating into the end zone for the score. A play that had been designed to hit the "7" hole off right tackle had actually hit the "0" hole over center. Huff, who knew Taylor was a great option runner, had been trapped out of position, and Taylor hit the end zone untouched and standing up.

"It was the only play of the game they didn't touch me," Taylor said later. "But they sure made up for it the rest of the time."

Up to that play, Huff had been telling Taylor in pile-ups that the Packers fullback "stunk." When Taylor crossed the goal line, he turned his head in Huff's direction. "Hey Sam," he yelled. "How do I smell from here?"

"He was that type of guy," Huff said. "He'd tell me, 'Yeah, you're just a big talker.' He brought the best out in you. He was an unusual player; a great player, but an agitator."

Kramer's extra point made it 10–0 Green Bay, and the score stuck there through the rest of the first half. As the cold intensified, so did the hitting. Nitschke watched as Taylor continued his personal war with Huff and the New York defense. Nitschke compared Taylor to a bull moose who knocked Giant defenders down, trampled them into the icy ground, and kept going. Several times, Nitschke saw Taylor pull himself up from a vicious hit, then turn and snarl at the Giants. "Is that as hard as you can hit?" Taylor would snap. To Nitschke, Taylor was defying the Giants, defying them even though he was getting smashed to the frozen ground and getting piled on by half of the New York defense.

"He was always shooting his mouth off on the field," Huff said of Taylor, and the verbal battle heightened with the hitting. On the films, Taylor can be seen screaming at Huff, and he later accused the Giants' middle linebacker of trying to cripple him by using his knees and elbows on him when Taylor was on the ground. Nitschke thought Huff played a game that bordered on being dirty, and recalled one play where Huff seemed to be twisting Taylor's head in a viselike grip even though the play was over. Taylor's battles weren't with Huff alone. Films of the game show him exchanging words and near punches with Robustelli, and Modzelewski claimed Taylor bit him in a pileup.

"They were beating on us," Packers wide receiver Boyd Dowler recalled, "and we were beating on them."

The hitting was so fierce the Packers fumbled five times; the Giants twice. Taylor put the ball on the ground three times, courtesy of a defense that Tittle thought was delivering some of the hardest tackles he had ever seen. Huff, Robustelli, and the rest were giving Taylor the same treatment they reserved for Cleveland fullback Jim Brown—maximum effort on every play. They were driving into Taylor, Tittle thought as he watched from the sidelines, and flattening him on the frozen ground.

"The ground was like concrete," Hornung said, "and I remember one time Taylor wanted to leave the game. I said, 'Bullshit, you get back in here.'"

Starr would hand off to Taylor, then watch as his fullback would fight for yards before being gang-tackled. It was terrible, Starr thought. The huddle would form and Starr would watch Taylor come back after run-ins with Huff and left end Jim Katcavage, would see his fullback bent over and holding his insides together. "I never saw a back get such a beating," Starr said.

"Taylor was really banged up," Remmel said. "He was bleeding from the mouth, he had a cut tongue, he had bruises all over his arms and I'm sure all over his body. The intensity of Taylor and Huff kind of matched the weather; it was a raw, very frigid day."

The half ended with Green Bay leading 10–0, and as the Packers ran for the locker room, Nitschke could hear them panting hard, trying to catch their breath in the cold. Once inside, the players lined up to get hot coffee or bouillon, and as the team separated into offense and defense to discuss strategy, the words of Lombardi and Bengston were interrupted by a loud yell from the back room. It was Taylor, whose elbows were scraped raw and whose forearm bore a wide gash. Team doctors were sewing him up, and Taylor was screaming in pain, the kind of scream, Nitschke said later, that a player makes when he's in agony. When the doctors finished, they taped his arm, but all Nitschke could think was that the Packers might have to play the second half without Taylor, who in Nitschke's opinion was the toughest guy on the team and maybe the toughest guy in the league.

"How are we going to go out there," Nitschke thought, "and play two more quarters?"

The third quarter resembled the first two. Nitschke continued to battle Webster and King, and Taylor continued his battles with Huff and the Giant defense. Klein thought the game had become one of "ground thrusts and vicious tackles." It was primeval football, he wrote. Taylor would hurl his pain-wracked body at the Giants defense, and they would hurl him back. When New York had the ball, King and Webster, two of the biggest and toughest backs in the NFL, would plunge into the line to be met by Nitschke, Jordan, and Willie Davis. From his right tackle position, Grier thought the game had dissolved into a "bone-crushing defensive duel." High above the stadium field, Coleman called the game "a bruising defensive battle." Taylor continued to spit barbs at the Giants defense, but by the second half, even the members of the Packers' offensive line were telling their fullback to "shut up." Huff said that the Packers realized that the more Taylor talked, the angrier the New York defense became.

"I hit him so hard I don't how the hell he got up," Huff said. "I didn't think I could get up either but I had too much pride to stay down. Most guys, rather than get hit, would run out of bounds. But I knew Taylor wasn't going to do it. I knew he was going to turn back into me and bury me. And I thought, 'One of us is going to die.' "

The Giants finally broke through when Erich Barnes blocked Max McGee's punt on the 15-yard line and Jim Collier covered the loose ball just across the goal line. Don Chandler's point-after cut New York's deficit to 10–7, but again, Nitschke helped regain the momentum for Green Bay. After the Giant defense dug in and forced Green Bay to punt on its next series, return man Sam Horner tracked the flight of McGee's punt against the steel-gray sky and then saw the spiral slip from his numb hands at the New York 35. A scramble ensued, and both Nitschke and Green Bay tackle Forrest Gregg dove for the ball. They were fighting for it under the pile at the Giants' 42 when Gregg shouted, "Who is it?"

"It's Nitschke."

On NBC Radio, Packer broadcaster Ted Moore, who was sharing duties with Coleman and had taken over the play-by-play for the second half, made the call:

> The line of scrimmage is the Packers' 30-yard line. McGee standing on his 15. Ringo over the ball. There's the snap. McGee gets the kick away, a low one, coming down to Horner, who fumbles the ball. . . . Recovered, I believe, by the Packers. . . . There's a tremendous pileup down on the Giants' 41-yard line. . . . And the Green Bay Packers did recover. I believe it was Ray Nitschke. Nitschke coming up with the football finally for the Green Bay Packers down on the Giants' 42-yard line.

Gregg released the ball, and Nitschke gained credit for the fumble recovery, his second of the game. With Taylor doing the bulk of the running, the Packers fought their way to the 22, where Kramer hit a 29-yard field goal to give Green Bay a 13–7 lead. Both sides suffered amid the brutal cold and equally brutal hitting throughout the second half. Taylor carried 31 times for 85 yards despite swallowing his own blood for much of the game, and Huff played with what was later diagnosed as a slight concussion. Hornung was knocked out of the game in the fourth quarter after colliding with the ground and the Giant defense on a power sweep, and Green Bay safety Willie Wood was ejected from the game after knocking down an official during a disputed pass inteference call.

Nitschke and the Packer defense matched the heightened emotion by ratcheting up their own intensity. For the second straight year, they prevented the Giants' record-setting offense from producing any points, and when Kramer lined up for another field goal attempt, a 30-yarder with two minutes remaining, he thought, "If you make it, it's all over. We've got the game won." Keeping his head down and allowing for the wind, Kramer's kick cleared the uprights. When he turned toward the Green Bay sideline, Kramer saw Lombardi with a clenched fist in the air. Green Bay now led 16–7, and Lombardi's clenched fist was the Packers' victory sign.

The talk in both locker rooms afterward focused on what remains some of the hardest hitting in NFL championship game history. Since then, there have been several great defensive duels, notably the Baltimore–Tennessee matchup in the 2000 AFC playoffs when Ravens middle linebacker Ray Lewis matched up against Titan running back Eddie George, but even that showdown failed to live up to the intense conditions of the '62 NFL title game.

The Giants defended their play against Taylor afterward. Cornerback Dick Lynch said Taylor "never stops defying you." Modzelewski called Taylor "a crazy runner," and Huff said that Taylor was a back who would do anything to gain an extra couple of inches; he would crawl on his hands and knees if he had to. Since a runner isn't officially downed in the NFL until the whistle blows, Huff figured that if Taylor was down in the frozen dirt fighting for extra inches, the Giants would be down there fighting just as hard to prevent him from getting them.

Nitschke had been fighting just as hard on the Packers' side, and a review of the original radio broadcast reveals he finished the game with 10 tackles to go along with his three forced turnovers. For his dominant play, Nitschke was named the player of the game by *Sport* magazine. Tittle said later that Nitschke had played an alert defensive game, recovering two fumbles and creating a third turnover when he deflected a pass for an interception, a pass Tittle thought would have been a sure touchdown since tight end Joe Walton was so alone in the end zone he was waving for the pass.

Nitschke was both surprised and pleased by being named MVP, which earned him a new Corvette, as well as recognition as the first defensive player in NFL history to win the award. Nitschke was most pleased, however, by the fact Green Bay had earned a second straight NFL championship, and the game's highlight film shows him standing in front of his locker talking reflectively to reporters.

High above the dark and now deserted playing field, league officials were scanning a play-by-play account of the game. It had been so cold in Yankee Stadium that the ink in the duplicating machine had frozen in the second quarter. Today, the play-by-play account of the second quarter can barely be read, and among all the dim lines, one seems dimmer than the rest:

King fumbled, Nitschke recovered on the Giant 28.

As New York writer Harold Rosenthal later noted, that single line might serve best to sum up the story of the '62 title game.

SEVEN

MR. NITSCHKE, are you connected with the government?"
Just hours after being named the Most Valuable Player of the
1962 NFL championship game, Ray Nitschke appeared on the CBS
prime time game show *What's My Line?* A Mark Goodson-Bill Todman production, *What's My Line?* was a primetime fixture from 1950 to 1967.
Hosted by John Daly, the show was filmed in CBS Studios in New York and
included arguably the wittiest panel of celebrities in game-show history:
Arlene Francis, Dorothy Kilgallen, and Bennett Cerf. Mystery guests were
brought on the show, and with Daly serving as the suave moderator, the
show's panelists would probe for their guest's occupation one question at a
time. In a testament to the innocence of the times, guests received the
grand sum of $5 for every "no" answer, and among the notables who
appeared on the show and were asked by Daly to "Enter and sign in
please . . . " were future presidents Jimmy Carter, Gerald Ford, and Ronald
Reagan. It was on *What's My Line?* that panelist Steve Allen first uttered the
now-famous query, "Is it bigger than a breadbox?"

Kilgallen opened the panel's line of questioning to Nitschke by asking if
he was connected with the government, and Nitschke answered with a flat
"no." Looking very businesslike in his dark-framed glasses and conservative
suit and tie, he remained a mystery to the panel through the first two questions.

"He's very quiet and reserved," Francis said finally, "which would lead
one to believe he'd be with the Giants, but I believe he's with the Green Bay
Packers."

"We were really having some fun," Daly told his audience. "We thought
with the glasses and Ray's very quiet nature that we might get away with it
for awhile and we did actually. Well, Ray, needless to say we congratulate
you and all your colleagues. It was a great game, we're sorry . . . to see our
Giants lose but if they had to lose they certainly lost to a great team and to
the greatest middle linebacker in the league."

Nitschke's performance on national television in the '62 title game elevated his status at a time when the NFL was dominated by Hall of Fame-cal-
iber middle linebackers and fullbacks. In Chicago, Bill George is remembered as the first man to play the middle linebacker position on a regular

basis. An All-America tackle at Wake Forest, the 6-foot-2, 230-pound George joined the Bears in 1952. At the time, most NFL teams were still running a defensive alignment of five down linemen, two linebackers and four defensive backs. As the middle guard in the five-two, George's responsibility on pass plays was to bump the opposing center and then backpedal into coverage. George played the position well enough to earn all-pro honors in both 1952 and '53. In a 1955 game against Philadelphia, however, George was being beaten regularly on passes over the middle. To compensate, the Bears changed tactics. Rather than have George bump the center before dropping into coverage, George would stand up and take a quick step back. The strategy worked immediately. On first down, he knocked down an Eagles' pass over the middle. On second down, he picked off the first of his 18 career interceptions. Four years earlier, Giants' head coach Steve Owen and defensive captain Tom Landry had developed the Umbrella Defense in response to the problems presented by the Cleveland Browns' offense. The position of an every-down middle linebacker was born in Chicago that December 11 against the Eagles, and by 1957, the NFL replaced middle guard with middle linebacker on its annual all-pro teams.

A strong, intelligent player, George was responsible for molding the middle linebacker position into one of field generalship; the counterpart to the quarterback. In 1956, when the Bears were running various defensive alignments under head coach George Halas, George was given the responsibility of learning them all. Bears' defensive coordinator George Allen, who went on to coach strong defensive units in Los Angeles and Washington, called Bill George the smartest defensive player he ever coached. "He called defensive signals for the Bears when they were at their best," Allen said. "He made as few mistakes as any player I've ever seen."

George's strength of mind and body—he wrestled running backs to the ground with techniques he learned as a wrestler at Wake Forest—provided a role model for future linebackers to follow. From 1955 to 1962, George was named to eight consecutive Pro Bowls and led the Bears to two Western Conference titles and one NFL championship.

While George is generally regarded as the game's first pure middle linebacker, Detroit's Joe Schmidt proved instrumental in making middle linebacker the most important position on defense. Relatively small for his position at 6-foot, 220, Schmidt used speed and intelligence to help lead the Lions to Western Conference championships in 1953, '54, and '57, and NFL titles in '53 and '57. A product of the University of Pittsburgh, Schmidt was drafted by the Lions in 1953. Because he had suffered through an injury-plagued career with the Panthers, Schmidt's arrival in Detroit was treated with indifference. But when injuries depleted Detroit's linebacking corps, Schmidt stepped in and became a starter. The Lions had won NFL championships in 1952 and '53 with a five-two defense anchored by 350-pound middle guard Les Bingaman. But in 1955, head coach Buddy Parker dropped the five-two alignment the Lions had been using and instituted the modern four-three. Moving from left linebacker to the middle, Schmidt flourished in the new formation, and was named to the Pro Bowl 10 straight seasons from 1955 to 1964. Like Bill George, Schmidt combined strength with strategy. "He's a great tackler and a strong leader," Lombardi said at the time. "He can diagnose a play in an instant."

Schmidt's heady style may have been most evident in his pass defense. He recorded 24 career interceptions and according to Parker, helped revolutionize modern defenses.

"His style of play brought about the zone defense," Parker said, "and the modern defensive look of pro football."

Pioneered by George and Schmidt, the four-three was popularized in 1956 with the emergence in New York of Sam Huff. Committing to the four-three as their base alignment, the Giants drafted Huff out of West Virginia in '56 for the specific purpose of patrolling the middle. But when head coach Jim Lee Howell hesitated on where to play the 6-foot-1, 230-pound rookie, Huff grew discouraged and walked out of camp. He was persuaded to return by Lombardi, the Giants' offensive coordinator at the time, and Huff took over at middle linebacker when starter Ray Beck was sidelined with an injury. Huff's emergence as a starter coincided with Landry's development of what he called his "Recognition Defense." Rather than following the rule of the day which saw defenses swarm to the ball carrier, Landry taught his players to recognize the play and avoid the blocking schemes before committing to the play.

Landry's restrained style reflected both his analytical mind and reserved manner, and it ushered in a new era of defensive play. The Giant defense of the late 1950s became the forerunner of the "Flex" style Landry would later introduce in Dallas, and because Landry's style was suited to freeing the middle linebacker to flow to the ball, it made Huff a national hero. He became the NFL's first glamour player on defense, was featured on the cover of *Time* magazine in 1959, and in 1960 was the subject of a CBS documentary titled "The Violent World of Sam Huff."

As the focal point of the defense, middle linebackers like Huff, George, and Schmidt became the defensive equivalent of quarterback. They were responsible for knowing the formations and responsibilities of each defensive play, called out signals, and countered quarterbacks by engaging in mental gymnastics in the seconds before each snap of the ball. Landry aided Huff by sliding his down linemen to the center-guard gaps, thereby freeing his middle linebacker to flow to the ball.

For five years, from 1954 to 1958, Lombardi worked alongside Landry in

New York, and when Lombardi moved to Green Bay in 1959, he took Landry's four-three principles with him. Just as Paul Hornung would become Lombardi's Green Bay version of versatile Giants' offensive star Frank Gifford, Nitschke became the Packers' defensive answer to Huff. Green Bay's success in winning three straight Western Conference crowns from 1960 to 1962 gave Nitschke the recognition usually reserved for Huff, George, and Schmidt. From 1962 to 1967, Nitschke earned nominations to at least one of the five all-pro teams of the time—Associated Press, United Press, Newspaper Enterprise Association, *New York Daily News*, or *The Sporting News*.

The increased responsibilities of the middle linebacker position brought increased study time for Nitschke, and he worked closely with defensive coordinator Phil Bengston to master his position. Green Bay at the time ran a base four-three defense with man-to-man coverage. Out of the four-three, they could shift to a four-three Over, where the down linemen slid one position over toward the strength of the offensive formation, and the four-three Under, an undershift away from the strong side. It was a simplified system, but the Packers also employed "pinch" and "stack" principles that were innovative for their time. To keep the center and guards off of Nitschke, Bengston positioned his tackles in the center-guard gaps and instructed them to "pinch" inside, thereby rendering a blocker helpless. The stack would become a staple of the AFL, and Green Bay used it as a mixer in their base defense by stacking either of their tackles head-up on the center, thereby preventing the cutoff blocks aimed at eliminating Nitschke. Green Bay also ran an array of blitzes that Bengston had formulated during his days as the defensive coordinator in San Francisco. Nitschke's middle linebacker blitz was usually coordinated with one of his defensive tackles. If Nitschke blitzed to the strong side of the offense, the strong side tackle would take an inside route and Nitschke would loop behind him. If Nitschke was blitzing to the weak side, the weak side tackle charged inside. A third blitzing scheme required Nitschke to charge straight up the middle, and both defensive tackles to take outside routes. Occasionally, the Packers also ran a double blitz, with Nitschke coordinating his charge with one of his outside linebackers.

In the Packers' system, Nitschke had four keys to follow on each play. His initial key was the movement of the center, followed by the fullback and two guards. The coordinated movement of those four players at the snap of the ball revealed to Nitschke what play the offense was running. Film study during the week preceding each game saw Nitschke learning the habits of the opposing offense in general and his four keys in particular as he searched for clues and tip-offs. Green Bay's film study was so meticulous that during the off-season, Lombardi and his offensive coaches would scout the Packer defense while Bengston and his defensive coaches scouted the offense. What each side was doing was searching for the smallest clue, the smallest tip-off to what the offensive or defensive call was. If Lombardi saw a Packer defenseman tipping the call, the information was noted and given to Bengston for correction in the next summer camp. If Bengston saw a Green Bay lineman leaning one way or the other and tipping the play, he would inform Lombardi.

On the field, Green Bay defensive tackles Dave Hanner and Henry Jordan helped by pointing out to Nitschke certain tips on what to look for from the opposition. The tips were usually of the smallest nature; if a linemen or back leaned ever so slightly to his right or left, Nitschke could count on the play going in that direction. If a linemen's knuckles were showing white from the pressure of his weight leaning forward, Nitschke knew the offense was getting ready to fire out on a running play. If the linemen was leaning lightly on his down hand and was back on his haunches, the Packers figured he was getting ready to retreat and pass-block, and would set their defense accordingly.

Green Bay's defensive plays were relayed from Bengston via hand signals. During his first few years in Green Bay, Bengston would wigwag his fingers, signaling either a change in formation or a blitz. In time, opponents began picking up on Bengston's hand signals and he adjusted by changing his signs from game to game. One week would find Bengston signaling plays in by adjusting the brim of his fedora; the next week the signs were relayed by the straightening of his tie or the toss of a tuft of grass in the air as if to check wind direction. Linebacker Bill Forester would relay the call in the huddle, and Nitschke would shout the offense's formations once they lined up. Because Green Bay's defensive plays were automatic depending on what formation the offense was in, Nitschke had to be certain his split-second diagnosis was correct. Offensive formations at the time included "Red" or "Split" in which the running backs are split to either side of the quarterback; "Brown" or "Opposite" where the fullback is behind the quarterback and the halfback splits slightly to the weak side; "Blue" or "Near" where the fullback is behind the quarterback and the halfback splits slightly to the strong-side.

NFL teams in the sixties also used early versions of the Shotgun, the Slot, the I, the Double Wing, and even a Triple Wing. Nitschke would study the formation just before the snap, and his call depended on where the tight end was lined up, since that indicated the strong side of the offense. If both backs were split behind the quarterback and the tight end was lined up next to the right tackle, Nitschke's call would be "Red Right." If the backs were in a Brown formation and the tight end lined up left, he would shout call out "Brown Left."

Because the Packers' defensive calls were prearranged, Nitschke knew once he went through his progression of keys what his responsibilities were. He knew instantly whether he should follow the fullback, blitz the quarterback, or drop into coverage. By 1962, Nitschke's study habits had him firmly entrenched as Green Bay's starting middle linebacker, the leader of a Packer defense that was the NFL's best. On the verge just two years before of being run out of town by his head coach, Nitschke impressed Lombardi so much the Packer boss was completely passing over middle linebackers in the annual draft. Nitschke still irritated his coach with mistakes made on the practice field, but Lombardi was resigning himself to the fact that at the very least, Nitschke was able to eliminate his own errors. Lombardi told writer W. C. Heinz that when he chewed Nitschke out, Ray took it like a child in the sense that he was repentant and didn't argue, but he would turn around and make the same mistake again. Criticism rolled off Nitschke so much that even Lombardi, the master motivator, wondered if he was getting through.

"You don't improve him," Lombardi told Heinz, "but happily he improves himself."

To Nitschke, Lombardi was an amazing man. As a player, Nitschke had found that he needed to pace himself emotionally as well as physically in preparing for a game. Lombardi, however, was always "up" emotionally. "He had extraordinary emotional drive," Nitschke said, and while Lombardi yelled a lot at practice, Nitschke thought it was, at times, an act for the benefit of the player he was yelling at. Lombardi had yelled a lot at him their first few years together, Nitschke said, because he was wild and he needed to be kept in line. Lombardi's demand for perfection and dedication had infected the Packers as a team, and even though Nitschke could see that his coach's rage was an act at times, he bought it anyway.

Nitschke's observation was an astute one. Lombardi did have to work to get himself emotionally ready for every practice, every film session. He worked himself into frenzies in the coaches' room beforehand, then announced to his assistants, "I'm just going to give these guys complete hell today. . . . Today is going to be one of those days."

"He really stayed on us," Nitschke said, and at the end of the day, Lombardi would wipe the sweat from his forehead with a handkerchief like a stage actor wiping off greasepaint and announce, "I really gave it to them today, didn't I?"

Lombardi's outbursts became predictable; he would cuss the team early in the week, guard Jerry Kramer said, and kiss them as game day approached. Nitschke was Lombardi's whipping boy, and he often took the public lashings with a grin. "He gave Nitschke a lot of hell," safety Emlen Tunnell said at the time. "He was trying to help the guy and he did. . . . Vinnie knew the guy was going to be a football player. He *knew*. He handled Ray just right."

Mike Manuche, a friend of Lombardi's, agreed. "Vinnie really did a job on him," Manuche said. Lombardi would tell Nitschke, "We don't need you!" but in reality he saw something in his tough middle linebacker that made him want to work to straighten his life out.

"He helped turn my life around as a person," Nitschke said later.

Nitschke's improvement as a middle linebacker came under Bengston's quiet tutelage, and the two men struck up a warm working relationship. Lombardi's occasional rage was tempered by Bengston's reserved approach; if one of his defensive players felt Lombardi's verbal lash, Bengston would soothe the player's hurt feelings with quiet words of encouragement. To Nitschke, Bengston was a cool customer, a quiet, dedicated man whom he admired. "There is no man I respect more," he said. Unlike Lombardi, Bengston was able to maintain his poise; when he did get angry, however, his players knew it because his voice level would go up. "When he yells, you jump," Nitschke said, "because you know he is really mad." As quiet as his defensive coach was, Nitschke felt that Bengston could still be just as tough as Lombardi.

Quarterback Bart Starr saw firsthand the interaction between Bengston and the members of his defense. "Coach Bengston was an astute coach," Starr said. "He was a great teacher and I think he was a very compassionate and understanding person as well. He had a sense and feel for different individuals, and I believe he had a great feel for Ray and how to work with him."

Bengston was a sound defensive strategist, and Nitschke benefited from his teachings. "He simplifies the defense and explains it better than any coach I ever saw," Nitschke said. Under Bengston, Nitschke learned more than ever how to study the game, how to apply himself. Nitschke learned to study not only the moves of his opponent but also his personality, and Bengston also taught Ray how to study his own moves. The two would watch Green Bay game films together, and Bengston would quietly show Nitschke what he was doing right and what mistakes he was making. He taught Nitschke how to react to a certain blocking pattern in a way that would allow him to get to the runner quicker. He saw things that Nitschke overlooked and made Ray aware of his role in the overall context of the game. By learning the fine points of his position, Nitschke became as much a heady player as he was a heavy hitter.

Defensive end Willie Davis said Bengston was instrumental in saving Nitschke's NFL career. "Phil simplified Ray's assignments, and Ray had enough talent to play through some of his mistakes," Davis said. "Phil was a very methodical guy and he really prepared you very well to play the game. And after Ray was in the starting lineup for a couple of years, the mistakes went away and he became a great linebacker."

Bengston referred to Nitschke as a "dynamic manifestation of the anti-quarterback." If an observer wanted a lightning review of the plays and formations an opponent would use against the Packers, Bengston suggested they first check with the enemy quarterback. If he's not available, Bengston said, then ask Nitschke. Film study allowed Nitschke to match wits with opposing quarterbacks, and Bengston would watch from the sidelines as Nitschke would follow the opposing quarterback's audibles with signal changes of his own. When both arrived at the same call, Bengston said, the result was a victory for his fast-guessing anti-quarterback.

Out on the Packers' practice field, Nitschke's victories were sometimes greeted with less enthusiasm by Lombardi. In 1962, Lombardi had installed a special series of tight end reverses out of a double-wing formation in preparation for a key early-season contest against Western Conference rival Detroit. As Starr led the offense to the line of scrimmage, Nitschke's raspy voice cut through the gray, wet air.

"Double-wing!" Nitschke shouted. "Double-wing!"

Lombardi, aware there may be Detroit scouts watching the practice, cringed. "Not so loud," he said, admonishing Nitschke.

While Lombardi would run the Packer offense in practices, he gave Bengston full control of the defense. To Nitschke and the other members of the Green Bay defense, Bengston was as much a student of the game as Lombardi.

"Phil Bengston always said, 'It's not the defenses that we call, it's the men implementing the defenses,'" left cornerback Herb Adderley said. "All we did was basic defense, believe me. We had ten pages in our playbook. When I went to Dallas (in 1970) their playbook was like the Yellow Pages. Bengston had the players, and we were a basic defensive team. It was just a matter of going out there and playing like we practiced."

Bengston's approach was to get his players to practice hard during the week to gain the confidence necessary to do their jobs on game days. To Nitschke, football knowledge seemed to just flow from Bengston. Later, Nitschke would say that he learned more about the game from Bengston than from any other coach he'd ever had.

"Phil was our coach," remembered Dan Currie, who played left line-backer for the Packers from 1958 to 1964. "Vince coached the offense. He'd come into the defensive meeting, start hollering, and then slam the door, just to let you know that he was the boss. But Phil manned the defense. He did the teaching and he was very good at it."

While Lombardi was more offense-oriented, his early years with the

Packers saw him concentrate on building a championship defense. Nitschke knew the offense was Lombardi's pride and joy, but he also knew that his head coach realized that if the defense didn't get the offense the ball often enough, the Packers weren't going to win. Since the team that gets the ball the most is going to win, Nitschke figured the job of the defense was a fundamental one. "To get that ball," he said.

The emergence of great middle linebackers like Nitschke, Bill George, Joe Schmidt, and Sam Huff paralleled the rise of power backs like Jim Brown, Jim Taylor, Alan Ameche, and Joe Perry. The NFL in the early sixties was a game of power, and there was a sense of moral balance to the game because winning teams were not only considered superior skill-wise but also superior in courage, character, and desire. In the early 1950s, the game's moral balance had been altered by point-a-minute passing games that cheapened the game with long bombs and quick scores. The man-to-man power game was being phased out in favor of finesse blocks and free-and-easy offenses. Defenses reacted by dropping their passive play in favor of an aggressive attitude. Coaches like George Allen, Chuck Drulis, and Clark Shaughnessy put their defenses on the offensive, and the result was a smashing array of blitzes and formations. A defensive coordinator for the Bears in the late '50s, Shaughnessy developed a dizzying system of combination blitzes and coverages. Drulis, who handled the St. Louis Cardinals' defense, sent wildman safety Larry Wilson crashing after quarterbacks as the eighth man in a terrifying eight-man blitz. In Los Angeles, Allen fielded a football-grabbing unit that gained fame as "The Fearsome Foursome."

"We want the ball," Ram linebacker Maxie Baughan said, "and we have more than 300 defenses we can use to get it."

By the early '60s, the ball-hawking monsters of the defense had helped restore the balance that had been missing from the game for almost a full decade. Bigger, faster defensive specialists were shutting down the end runs and long bombs, and when offenses found themselves faced with a shrinking field, the game was forced back into an elemental confrontation, back into a moral balance where winners were judged superior not only by their physical strength but by their strength of character, commitment, and desire.

Power struggles were waged along the lines of scrimmage, and at the forefront were the middle linebackers and fullbacks. Because they played in the same conference, Nitschke went helmet-to-helmet twice a season with Baltimore's Alan Ameche and San Francisco's Joe Perry. A 6-foot, 220-pound product of Wisconsin, Ameche was nicknamed "The Horse," and he galloped through NFL defenses in helping lead the Colts to consecutive world championships in 1958 and '59. He climaxed the famous '58 title game when he lowered his helmet and drove in from a yard out to give Baltimore a 23–17 overtime win against the Giants.

At 6-foot, 206 pounds, Perry wasn't as big as Ameche, but his power was undeniable. He was called "The Jet" for his explosive 9.5 speed in the 100-yard dash, but former 49ers' coach Frankie Albert had another, more apt description of his star back.

"Perry is like a bowling ball fired from a Howitzer," Albert said. "It whistles down the middle of the alley and sends the pins flying in every direction."

Perry's head-down, head-first plunges into the line didn't always pay off. In a game against the Giants, Perry lowered his helmeted head and plowed into the end zone, an irresistible force about to meet an immovable object. The collision caused Perry to stagger to his feet, where he saw Jimmy Patton, the Giants' little 183-pound safety, snarling at him.

"Run past me again," Patton said, "and I'll cold-cock you again."

Perry headed to the sidelines, still shaking the cobwebs from his head, and told coach Red Strader, "Did you see that little sumbitch hit me? He's murder."

Strader laughed. "It was the goal post, you dummy," he said. "Good thing you hit it with your head."

Nitschke responded to the challenges posed by the fullbacks of his day with a snarling, forearm-throwing intensity. To him, football was an instinctive game, and his instinct was to follow the man with the ball. "And then," he said, "you make them sorry they took the damned thing from the quarterback."

Nitschke's play was fierce but also fundamentally sound. Rams' linebacker Les Richter said at the time that it wasn't Nitschke's speed or his quickness in getting to a play that was most amazing. "It's a desire to make the play," Richter said, "an ability to get to the right spot ahead of everybody else."

Green Bay opened the 1963 preseason on a down note. Halfback Paul Hornung was suspended by NFL commissioner Pete Rozelle for violating the league rule that prohibits players from betting on the outcomes of games. Nitschke was injured in practice prior to the annual College All-Star Game, and was in traction at home when the Packers played the All-Stars on August 2 at Soldier Field, Chicago. The game would have represented a homecoming for Nitschke, but he settled for watching the game on television. To compensate for the absence of Hornung and Nitschke, Lombardi started Tom Moore at halfback and switched backup center Ken Iman to middle linebacker. Coached by Otto Graham, the All-Stars featured future Pro starters in tackle Bob Vogel and guard Ed Budde, defensive linemen Jim

Dunaway and Fred Miller, safety Kermit Alexander, and a linebacking corps of Bobby Bell, Lee Roy Jordan, and Packer draft pick Dave Robinson. "Greatest collection of talent ever assembled on a football field," Lombardi said.

Fueled by a fourth-quarter touchdown pass from Ron VanderKelen to Pat Richter, the All-Stars scored 10 points in the final 15 minutes to stun Green Bay, 20–17. The win was the All-Stars' first since 1958, and it left the Packers embarrassed. Lombardi was mortified, and Nitschke always believed that if he had been able to play, Green Bay would have won.

The Packers won the rest of their preseason games, then hosted the Bears in the regular season opener on September 15. Brilliant sunshine and temperatures in the mid-70s greeted a Green Bay crowd of 42,327 as they jammed into Lambeau Field. The Packers–Bears rivalry was an ancient one, dating back to their first meeting in 1921. The coaching matchup was classic sixties—Lombardi versus Halas. The Packers had won five straight over the Bears, including final scores of 49–0 and 38–7 in 1962. They had won 13 straight at home, and their roster featured 13 players who had been named All-Pro in 1962 or would be in '63; 10 of those players would eventually be inducted into the Pro Football Hall of Fame.

In addition, the Packers entered the game with what appeared to be a huge advantage on the right side of their now-famous offensive line. Right guard Jerry Kramer and right tackle Forrest Gregg were all-pro players. Across the line, the Bears had moved offensive lineman Stan Jones to left defensive tackle to replace Fred Williams, and put Bob Kilcullen at left end as a substitute for the injured Ed O'Bradovich. It was expected that the Packers would pound away at the left side of the Bear line with Taylor and Moore, and *Chicago American* columnist Bill Gleason picked up on the theme in the days leading up to the game. Jones was a schoolteacher in the off-season and Kilcullen was an artist, and Gleason in his column wrote the Chicago defense looked solid except for the schoolteacher and the artist on the left side.

Whatever perceived shortcomings the Chicago defense may have had were offset by two off-season developments. George Allen had been named the Bears' defensive coordinator and he immediately began charting the tendencies of opposing offenses by meticulously breaking down their game films. Bears' linebacker Joe Fortunato said that Allen realized that Green Bay had tremendous tendencies. One such tendency was picked up when the Packers ran the power sweep. Allen's attention to detail revealed that when Green Bay was planning a sweep left, Gregg would cheat out some six inches from his normal position in order to get a better blocking angle. The Bears picked up on it, and Allen planned to adjust his defense accordingly.

Described by writer Murray Olderman as owning "the grimacing mien of a coal mine paymaster and the devotion to detail of an old maid librarian," Allen spent the summer poring over Packer game films. He realized that since Green Bay's well-schooled blocking schemes were based on instant recognition of defenses, the Bears would seek to confuse them by playing odd-man fronts with a man over center Jim Ringo. Since Bart Starr was an excellent audible quarterback, Allen planned to disguise Chicago's coverage schemes by dropping his linebackers—Fortunato, Bill George, and Larry Morris—into short zones.

Allen's intense preparation was aided by an unlikely source. Linebacker Tom Bettis, whom Nitschke had replaced as Green Bay's starter back in 1960, had been traded to Pittsburgh after having words with Lombardi in 1962. The Bears picked Bettis up prior to the '63 season, and the former Packer proved more than eager to help Halas and the Bears prepare for Green Bay. "Halas picked my brains, for sure," said Bettis, who cooperated by giving the Bears a rundown on the Packers' player personnel, their plays, and their system.

From the day the Bears arrived in training camp in the summer of '63, Halas had them pointing toward the season-opener against the Packers. Bears' running back Ronnie Bull remembered Halas repeatedly telling his team, "If we win that game, we have a chance to go all the way."

A gentle, southerly breeze wafted through Lambeau Field as the game got underway, and the Chicago defense, primed for its confrontation with the Packers' precision offense, forced an early turnover when safety Richie Petitbon covered a Taylor fumble at the Green Bay 33-yard line. Three plays later Bob Jencks booted a 32-yard field goal to give the Bears a 3–0 lead, but the Packers tied the game on their next possession on a 41-yard field goal by Kramer.

For the remainder of the first half, the game settled into a defensive struggle. Game films show Nitschke battling Chicago guards Ted Karras and Roger Davis. To Karras, the way Nitschke played his position was different than the other middle linebackers of his day. Karras found that Nitschke always took his blocks head-on; he seemed to especially enjoy taking on the linemen, and he played tough, hitting and holding his ground. To Karras, Nitschke played the game with power, as opposed to a player like the Giants' Sam Huff, whom Karras thought was quick in trying to shed his blocker. Nitschke, Karras thought, tried to punish offensive linemen, which Karras said only served to make him more hated around the league.

"Ray was a tenacious competitor," Cleveland center John Morrow said. "He was a son of a bitch. But that's a center talking about a linebacker."

Minnesota center Mick Tingelhoff said Nitschke was a loud, intimidating presence when he hovered over the ball just before the snap.

"He'd be out there yelling," Tingelhoff said, "and he would try to intimidate you. He was very, very intense, a big, rawboned, tough guy. He'd knock your head off with that great forearm."

Nitschke had a stated desire to manhandle the opposition. In a conversation with Currie, he talked about the physical contact, the man-to-man challenge of playing pro football.

"That's what I like about this game," Nitschke said.

Currie countered by telling how he enjoyed the artistic, scientific side of the game. "With me," Currie said, "it's the tackle instead of just belting the other guy."

"Not with me," Nitschke responded.

Opponents may have hated Nitschke, but they also respected him. Bears' Hall of Fame tight end Mike Ditka, whose career lasted from 1961 to 1972 said Nitschke was the best middle linebacker he played against. As a rookie, Ditka made an immediate impression on Nitschke when they met in the 1961 Midwest Shrine Game, an exhibition played in Milwaukee. Ditka was running across the middle of the field when the whistle blew to end the play. In an attempt to pull up, the rookie put his arms out and ended up pushing Nitschke from behind. Ditka said Nitschke took the contact the wrong way, and after the game, the two met accidentally in a Milwaukee bar where members of both teams had congregated.

"You're a dirty player," Nitschke said.

"Fine," Ditka responded, and within moments the two had to be restrained by teammates. They continued their feud on the field the next two games, and carried it over into the '63 season opener. In the second quarter, Ditka got the better of it when he executed a perfect peel-back block that violently upended Nitschke and put him out of the game. If it had been another linebacker, Ditka said, he would have hit him high, but since it was Nitschke, he went low.

Films show Nitschke flying head-over-heels, but his stay on the sidelines was short. Not long after, Ditka watched in amazement as Nitschke came hobbling back into the game, the knees of his yellow-gold pants taped up.

Joe Marconi's one-yard touchdown run in the third quarter gave the Bears a 10-3 lead, and Chicago's defense made it stand up the rest of the way. Starr, who had thrown just nine interceptions in the entire '62 season, was picked off four times in one afternoon by the Bears. Allen's shifting fronts and zone coverages helped confuse the Green Bay quarterback, and the Packers' proud ground game ground to a halt. Taylor was limited to 53 yards rushing, Green Bay's offense gained just 150 yards total, and the Packers never advanced beyond the Bears' 33. Bettis' information on the Packer defense allowed Bears' QB Bill Wade to continually frustrate Green Bay's blitzing schemes. A Wade-to-Marconi pass on the Bears' touchdown drive came when Wade had caught Nitschke and the Packers in a blitz and beaten them with a short pass that went for a long gain.

Ditka said later that Nitschke had played a great game, but Ray didn't agree. His knee had been injured on Ditka's block, and he had been caught offsides—a rare occurrence for him—when Chicago center Mike Pyle saw Nitschke jump the line of scrimmage on a blitz and quickly snapped the ball before Nitschke could jump back. It was smart football on Pyle's part, Nitschke said, and as the referee counted off the penalty yards, Nitschke stood there, angry at himself.

Despite the disappointing defeat, the Packers responded by reeling off eight straight wins. The Bears had dropped a Week Six decision to San Francisco, and when the Packers arrived at Wrigley Field on November 17, the two teams were 8–1 and sitting atop the Western Conference. It was a hugely anticipated matchup; tickets priced at $2.50 were being scalped for $100. Because NFL games at the time were blacked out within a 75-mile radius, Bears' fans wanting to watch the dramatic showdown on television began a mass exodus the morning of the game to watch it in bars and motels outside the city's limits. Wrigley Field pulsated with a full-house crowd of 49,166, and as the Packers took the field they radiated confidence. Even though Green Bay entered the game minus Hornung and Starr, the latter having suffered a broken hand against the St. Louis Cardinals, the Packers were loose. *Sports Illustrated* artist and photographer Robert Riger had spent time with Kramer and Fuzzy Thurston two days before the game, and Riger told Bears' defensive end Bob Kilcullen there was no way the Packers thought they were going to lose this game.

Nitschke was confident as well. Privately, many members of the Green Bay defense just didn't think Wade was a championship-type quarterback. Nitschke felt that since the Packers had been able to get themselves up for big games the past three seasons, there was no reason to think they couldn't do it again.

George Allen had other ideas. Having held Starr and Co. to three points in their season opener, the Bears' defensive coordinator planned to welcome Packer backups John Roach and Zeke Bratkowski by adding yet another defensive wrinkle. Green Bay center Jim Ringo was a master of the cutoff block on the middle linebacker, and in the season opener, Allen had shifted his down linemen, Stan Jones and Earl Leggett in "Over" and "Under" sets to keep Ringo off middle linebacker Bill George. For the

November rematch, Allen instructed Jones and Leggett to line up in an "Over" defense at the start, then shift just before the snap.

"We were in an overshifted defense to the left," Allen said; "Before the snap of the ball we'd move into an undershifted defense to the right."

Allen had never been a big proponent of the odd-front defense, but in that November game against Green Bay, the Bears continually shifted from one odd-front to another. Chicago players came back to the sidelines and told Allen the shifting confused the Packers. Offensively, the Bears planned to attack Green Bay's right side, where rookie defensive end Lionel Aldridge had taken over after Lombardi had dealt Bill Quinlan following the '62 championship. The word out of Green Bay was that Lombardi had traded Quinlan because the two men didn't get along. Lombardi's decision thrilled the Bears, especially assistant coach Chuck Mather. Quinlan was a veteran player, and he had given the Chicago offense problems in the past. With Quinlan gone, Mather said the Bears planned their ground game to run at Green Bay's right side. The plan paid dividends in the second quarter, when halfback Willie Galimore took a handoff and veered left. With Nitschke caught blitzing, the Bears sprung Galimore, and his 27-yard touchdown gave Chicago a 13–0 lead.

"A lot of times Nitschke would guess and take a chance," Adderley said. "Most of the times he was right, but when he was wrong, look out. When Galimore broke one for a touchdown that helped Chicago beat us in '63, Nitschke played a hunch and went to the wrong hole. Galimore went to the other side and once he broke it, that was it."

The Bears continued to pound away at the Packers' right side, and Nitschke said later that it seemed throughout the day that he had no sooner reached the sideline following a tough defensive series when he would have to take the field again. The Bears built a 26–0 lead before settling for a 26–7 victory, and they finished with 248 yards rushing. Later, Mather said the Bears had success running to their left because Lombardi had traded Quinlan. "That was one time," Mather said, "when the Italian outsmarted himself."

The defeat dropped Green Bay a game behind the Bears in the conference standings, and the Packers followed with a win in San Francisco. When Chicago tied Pittsburgh 17–17, the Packers were just a half-game behind the Bears in the Western Conference. Nitschke knew that if Green Bay continued to win and someone could knock off the Bears, the Packers could take over first place. Nitschke's season, however, would end sooner than he had anticipated. Playing the Lions in Detroit on Thanksgiving Day, Nitschke was fighting off a block by halfback Tom Watkins when his right forearm collided with Watkins' silver-and-blue helmet. Nitschke heard a sickening cracking sound, then felt a sharp pain shivering up his right arm.

"My arm's broken, guys," he told his defensive mates. "I'm taking myself out."

Currie wouldn't hear of it. "Oh no, you aren't," he snapped. "Wait until this series is over."

Nitschke stayed in and tried to disguise the injury from the Lions. He had no feeling in his broken arm, but he still managed to get in on the next couple of plays. He broke his nose on the second play when he stopped 225-pound Lions' fullback Nick Pietrosante on a running play at the Packer 36.

That was all for Nitschke. Green Bay's defense had made its stand, and Nitschke headed off the field with a broken arm and broken nose.

"The guy had a lot of mental toughness," Adderley said of Nitschke, "and mental toughness to Lombardi was playing injured. Don't complain about it and don't go into the trainer's room laying up there on the table and getting all kinds of treatment. Because football, Lombardi always said, was not a contact sport. 'If you want contact,' he always said, 'go to Arthur Murray's.' Football is a collision sport, so you have to expect bumps and bruises. So mental toughness was playing injured.

"I saw Nitschke play with a broken arm in Detroit. He hit Tom Watkins with a forearm, like a clothesline shot, and he broke his forearm. And the guy was in a lot of pain but he played. He came out, and they didn't have x-ray machinery in the locker room, so the doctor looked at him and said, 'Well, you got pain here?' and he said 'Yeah,' and they wrapped it up, put some gauze on it and he went right back out there. It was snowing and cold in Detroit that day and he went out and played. I saw him play with pulled muscles where he could hardly get around, but he didn't miss any games.

"He was, no question, the toughest guy on our defense. Without a doubt. And it was inspiring to other guys to see him play that way. Other guys would get hurt and say, 'Hey, he's doing it, we've got to do it too.'"

Green Bay led 13–6 when Nitschke left the field for good, but Detroit rallied to tie the game. He remained on the sidelines as the Packers won their final two games to finish 11–2–1, but they remained a half-game behind the Bears, who went 11–1–2 and defeated the Giants 14–10 in the NFL title game at frozen Wrigley Field.

Lombardi said later that the '63 Packers were the best team he ever coached, and Green Bay defensive end Willie Davis thought the '63 squad was at least as good as the '62 and '66 teams that are generally considered the best of the Lombardi era.

Out of the championship game for the first time since 1960, Nitschke spent the off-season with his wife Jackie and their young son, John. In past years, Nitschke had always spent his winter months killing time and getting into trouble. As he looked at his young son, Nitschke knew his life had been changed forever. He was now a husband and a father, and just as John would soon be taking his first steps toward walking, Nitschke was taking steps of his own—steps on the road to maturity.

Nitschke had ended the season in much the same way he had begun it, sidelined by an injury. As frustrating as the 1963 season had been for him, the '64 season was even more so. Hornung had returned from his suspension, but the year away dulled the luster of Green Bay's Golden Boy. After opening the regular season with a 23–12 win over Chicago, the Packers lost three of their next five games because of missed kicks by Hornung. The offensive line had been weakened by the trade of all-pro center Jim Ringo to Philadelphia, a trade that despite the stories passed down through the years, had actually been requested by Ringo so he could be closer to his home.

With Ringo gone, left tackle Bob Skoronski was shifted to center, but the line became a shambles when Thurston was injured and Kramer was hospitalized due to stomach surgery. A 27–17 loss to Los Angeles in Week Seven dropped the Packers' record to 3–4, far behind the streaking Baltimore Colts. While the Green Bay offense struggled, the defense stepped to the fore. They led the NFL against the pass and were second behind the Colts in points allowed. Nitschke, Davis, Henry Jordan, and Willie Wood were named to the NFL's All-Pro defensive unit, but it proved small consolation to finishing in second place for a second straight year. Green Bay's 8–5–1 record was their worst since a 7–5 finish in 1959, Lombardi's first year. The Colts ran away with the Western title, fashioning a 12–2 record before being stunned by the underdog Cleveland Browns 27–0 in the NFL championship game. The Packers suffered a final jolt when they lost the Playoff Bowl to St. Louis, 24–17, just the second post-season loss for Green Bay during the Lombardi era. The game was played January 3 in Miami, and one week later Nitschke made his first and only appearance in the NFL's Pro Bowl game. Held January 10 in Los Angeles, Nitschke sparked a dominating defensive performance from the West squad when he returned an interception 42 yards for a score in a 34–14 victory. A film of the play shows Nitschke dropping into coverage, making the interception, and then veering to his right, where he displayed the running style that had marked his fullback days at Illinois.

Teaming with Merlin Olsen, Roger Brown, and Gino Marchetti, along with Packer mates Davis and Wood, Nitschke helped hold an East team lineup of Jim Brown, Bobby Mitchell, Charley Taylor, and Paul Warfield to just 47 yards in the first half.

Being named to the All-Pro team and playing in the Pro Bowl gave Nitschke added ammunition when he headed to Lombardi's office to talk contract. By 1964 Lombardi's negotiating skills were legendary. He sweet-talked some players; harshly criticized others. Most players, like Davis, signed whatever offer sheet Lombardi gave them. When Davis once approached Lombardi with an aggressive case for a substantial raise, Lombardi listened quietly, then interjected one thought.

"Willie," he said, "you forgot just one thing."

"What's that, Coach?"

"Willie," Lombardi said, "I made you."

After that, Davis would go into Lombardi's office at contract time, make some small talk, and accept Lombardi's salary offer.

Nitschke, however, would not. He and Jim Taylor were two Packers who argued loudly with their coach over contracts. Nitschke actually looked forward to the impending argument, but the women in the Packers' front office did not. When Nitschke arrived for negotiations, the secretaries would sit back and listen to the loud, angry shouting match between Nitschke and Lombardi.

"He'd start roaring and I would too," Nitschke said, and with that the office secretaries would leave their desks and head for the hallway. "Between us, we scared them out of their socks."

Nitschke's contract dispute remained unsettled as the Packers prepared for the '65 campaign. He had been voted the NFL's best middle linebacker by both the Associated Press and United Press International, and was put off by Lombardi's salary offer.

"They're paying the rookies too much and forgetting the veterans," Nitschke told a reporter. "I'm worth more money."

Nitschke told Lombardi he was going to play out his option, but when a reporter called to verify Nitschke's contract status, Lombardi brushed the controversy aside.

"Nobody on this ball club," he said, "plays out his option unless he's talked to me for the last time."

Nitschke eventually signed, then put together another All-Pro season. He was named to the UPI All-Pro team, along with Davis, Adderley, and Wood. As a unit, the Packers allowed a league-low 224 points and for the third time in four years led the NFL in pass defense. At the forefront of the great Green Bay defense was Nitschke, the team's spiritual leader and leading hit man.

Highlights from the Packers' season show Nitschke making numerous big plays:

- Blitzing Steeler quarterback Bill Nelsen off his feet in the season opener in Pittsburgh, then picking off a Nelsen pass to set up a score in a 41–9 win;
- Blocking *two* Colts while clearing a path for Adderley to score on an interception return of a John Unitas pass in the home opener against Baltimore, a 20–17 Packer win;
- Recovering a fourth-quarter fumble by Minnesota's Bill Brown to set up a touchdown in a 38–13 comeback victory over the Vikings;
- Escorting linebacker Dave Robinson through the Baltimore fog on a game-turning interception in Green Bay's eventual 42–27 win.

The Packers' win over the Colts came in the penultimate game of the regular season and gave Green Bay sole ownership of first place in the Western Conference. But when the 49ers rallied to tie the Packers 24–24 in Week 14 and the Colts defeated the Rams 20–17 in the L.A. Coliseum, Green Bay and Baltimore finished tied atop the conference standings. A special one-game playoff was scheduled for Lambeau Field on the day after Christmas, and a crowd of 50,484 ignored the 10 inches of snow on the ground and the cold, gray air to witness a game that Nitschke said no one would want to miss. After missing the title game for two straight seasons, this was a game Nitschke believed would decide whether the Green Bay dynasty was indeed dead, as was being written in some circles.

The Colts entered the contest short of quarterbacks—both Unitas and backup Gary Cuozzo were injured, so head coach Don Shula went with halfback Tom Matte. Armed with a plastic wristband listing play calls and a simplified offense relying on quarterback draws, sweeps, and rollouts, Matte had guided Baltimore to victory over the Rams the past week. Matte had been a rollout quarterback under Woody Hayes at Ohio State, and when Shula contacted Hayes to inquire about Matte's ability to play the position at the pro level, Hayes assured him he could. Hayes went on to say that NFL teams featuring a four-three defense couldn't stop a rollout or bootlegging quarterback. The reason, Hayes said, was defenses had to spread their ends wide to stop a scrambling quarterback, and that the best defense to stop an option offense was the five-two that college teams used. Bengston and Lombardi had met with Hayes in coaching clinics and were aware of his thoughts on the four-three. Bengston, however, decided to stay with his standard defense, and not make special adjustments for the Colts' newest quarterback.

The quarterback shortage grew more desperate on the game's first play from scrimmage. After faking a draw to Taylor, Starr found tight end Bill

Anderson for a short completion. But a crunching hit by cornerback Lenny Lyles forced a fumble and linebacker Don Shinnick scooped the ball up at the 25. Trying to make a stop on Shinnick along the sideline, Starr took a heavy blow to his right shoulder from cornerback Jimmy Welch and had to be helped off the field. He was sidelined for the rest of the game with a broken rib and replaced by Bratkowski. With just 21 seconds of time elapsed from the scoreboard clock, the Packers had not only spotted the Colts a 7–0 lead but also their starting quarterback as well.

"We evened things up for them," Lombardi said.

Shula, however, didn't quite see it that way.

"There was a big difference," he said. "Bratkowski had about ten years' experience. My guy had two weeks."

Lou Michaels' 15-yard field goal in the second quarter increased the Colts' lead to 10–0 at the half and Lombardi blistered the locker room walls at halftime. "If you go down today after coming so close," he said, "how hard do you think it will be to climb this high again?"

Green Bay battled back in the third quarter. A high snap from center Buzz Nutter prevented Baltimore's Tom Gilburg from getting off a punt early in the second half, and the Packers took over on the Colts' 35. Bratkowski found flanker Carroll Dale deep for a 33-yard pickup, and Hornung hammered in from the 1. With nine minutes left in the game, Green Bay began a 15-play march that ended with Don Chandler taking aim from a severe angle on a 22-yard field goal attempt. As soon as he kicked the ball, Chandler threw his head back in disgust, and Colt end Ordell Braase clapped his taped hands together in celebration. But Baltimore's joy turned to outrage when field judge Jim Tunney raised his arms to signal the kick good with 1:58 remaining in regulation.

Nitschke acknowledged later that Chandler's field goal, which appears on the game film to sail above the left upright, was a controversial call. Nitschke had watched the kick wobble toward the goal posts, which in 1965 consisted of the old, white double uprights. What happened after that, he said, depended on which team you were rooting for. On the field, Nitschke could hear the Colts cursing the call, claiming that the ball didn't go through the uprights. All Nitschke knew was that the officials had ruled it good, the game was tied, and Green Bay had new life.

For months following the game, NFL owners and coaches studied the game film of Chandler's field goal and sought suggestions on how to avoid such a situation in the future. One idea was to place a net between the uprights to catch the ball, but the rules committee decided instead to extend the height of the posts to 20 fee and paint them bright yellow rather than white.

The playoff ended in a 10–10 tie, and the two teams prepared for overtime. As he awaited the extra period, Nitschke could feel the combined
effects of the game and the weather. It had been a bruising, physical battle,
played out amid darkening skies and crackling cold weather. The field was
frozen, and for Nitschke and the Packers, the game had been an uphill
battle from the start. Lombardi called it a "street fight," and Gregg thought
it was one of the toughest games he had ever played in. "They just kept
coming," he said of the Colts. "You have to give them a lot of credit for the
way they played."

As overtime raged on, it appeared as if Green Bay was on the verge of
being beaten. Behind the hard running of Matte and halfback Lenny Moore,
Baltimore drove to the Green Bay 37. The Colts were in field goal range, and
to inch the ball closer they ran first Moore and then Matte into the guts of
the Green Bay defense. Nitschke and the Packers responded, hurling Moore
back for a one-yard loss and then stopping Matte two yards behind the line
of scrimmage. In two plays, the Colts had been pushed back three yards to
the Green Bay 40. Unwilling to risk losing any more yardage, Shula sent
Michaels in on third down to attempt a 47-yard field goal.

Michaels had beaten the Packers the year before with a long field goal,
and Nitschke knew that the Colts' left-footed kicker had the range to make
it from 47 yards out. Desperate to prevent a Baltimore victory, Nitschke
positioned himself over Colts' center Buzz Nutter. At the snap of the ball,
Nitschke provided an extra push that he hoped would disrupt the timing of
Nutter's snap. Michaels' kick was short, and Nitschke felt later that his push
might have prevented the Colts from winning the game.

Packers' broadcaster Ted Moore called the pivotal play on WTMJ Radio:

*The ball is on the hashmarks at the far side of the field. It is fourth down
and five yards to go for the Baltimore Colts. Lou Michaels will attempt a
47-yard field goal. The angle is to the left. Bob Boyd will hold. . . . There's
the snap, the ball is booted, it's in the air and it's going to be . . . short and
wide to the right! It is no good. . . .*

Eight minutes of overtime had elapsed when the Packers took over on
their own 20 following Michaels' missed kick. Moore commented later that
"sheer tension was riding on every play." Bratkowski, who would finish the
game with 248 yards passing, jump-started Green Bay's drive to victory
with an 18-yard completion to Anderson on a crossing pattern. Two plays
later, Bratkowski threaded a pass through a crack in the Colts' zone, and
Dale gathered it in for another 18-yard gain. With the ball on the Baltimore
26, Taylor and halfback Elijah Pitts carried three times for eight yards.
Chandler trotted back on the field, and with 13 minutes and 39

seconds having elapsed in sudden-death overtime, ended what was at the time the longest NFL game in history when his 25-yard field goal sailed cleanly through the uprights.

On WTMJ Radio, Moore made the historic call:

Now the Green Bay Packers have a shot at it. They will be kicking from about the 25-yard line. The ball is slightly to the right side of the field. There will be a very slight angle to the left. The ball is on the 18-yard line. Bill Curry gets over the ball at center. Bart Starr will kneel at the 25-yard line. It's all up to Bart Starr and Don Chandler now. Starr stretches out the hand, there's the snap, the boot. The ball is in the air . . . it is good! The Green Bay Packers are the Western Division champions by a score of 13–10 over the Baltimore Colts.

Green Bay's win clinched the Western Conference title, and amid the post-game celebration Nitschke's thoughts turned to the impending title game matchup with the reigning NFL champions, the Cleveland Browns. His thoughts turned, too, to the man who would be his personal responsibility, a man Lombardi believed to be the greatest player of all time.

Jim Brown.

EIGHT

F OR RAY NITSCHKE, the days leading up to the NFL championship game left him preoccupied with one primary concern—containing Jim Brown.

The Cleveland fullback was a phenomenon, a 6-foot-2, 232-pound power back gifted with sprinter's speed. His running style—a loose, shuffling gait that seemed to leave him gliding over the grass fields—is one of the more powerful images of the NFL in the 1960s. Content to run past opponents, Brown when cornered could punish defenders as well. His big shoulders would shrug free from an opponent's grasp; the tapered, 32-inch waist would twist away; and his thigh and calf muscles would drive him forward for additional yardage. At the end of each run, Brown would rise from the mountain of men who had brought him down, walk slowly back to the huddle in a manner that deceptively implied injury, then explode into the defense again on the following play.

Through it all, he maintained a stoic, Spartan approach to the game. His face reflected neither defeat nor victory, and in later years he scoffed at a writer's notion that he was "thrilled" when the Browns won the 1964 NFL championship by blanking the heavily favored Baltimore Colts, 27–0.

"I was a warrior," he said. "I didn't go around getting 'thrilled.'"

So how did he feel at the time?

"Potent," Brown said.

In a nine-year career that began in 1957, Brown posted numbers that were not only potent, they were without parallel in league history. His numbers were not only beyond comparison; they were beyond comprehension. There had been great NFL backs before him—Red Grange, Bronko Nagurski, Ernie Nevers, Steve Van Buren, Marion Motley—but Brown embodied the best of each of them. He was strength, speed, grace, and intelligence personified. He had all the makings of a fictional superhero, but to the defenses of his day, he was concrete fact, not comic-book fiction.

"I always thought Superman was white and wore a cape," one NFL defender said. "Then I found out he was black, wore Number 32, and played for the Cleveland Browns."

Brown led the NFL in rushing five consecutive seasons and in eight of the nine years he played. In 1963 he ran for a league-record 1,863 yards, a 14-game average of 133 yards per game. He rushed for more than 100 yards in a game 58 times and more than 200 yards four times. His 12,312 career rushing yards were nearly 4,000 more than his closest pursuer, and his 5.22 yards per carry average remains a record to this day.

"He was the most devastating ball carrier in the history of the NFL," Browns' radio announcer Ken Coleman said, and Brown did seem invincible. For nine seasons, he was a marked man on the field, the target of every defensive player he faced. He carried the ball a league record 2,359 times, and films from Cleveland's 1965 campaign show Brown enduring multiple hits every time he touched the ball.

Against Dallas, he took eight hits on a seven-yard gain.

Against St. Louis, seven hits on a 19-yard run.

Against Philadelphia, six hits on a 15-yard pickup.

Every defender in the NFL, Coleman said, was committing his body to an all-out war against Jimmy Brown. Eagles' linebacker Chuck Bednarik agreed, then remarked that even with five members of the Philadelphia defense converging on him, Brown would somehow still get the first down. Despite being the focal point of every defense, he never missed a game due to injury in his nine-year NFL career, and he always came back on the next play, sweeping the flank with that signature loping style, gliding through the line on ground-eating runs and warding off tacklers with a forearm whose power Mike Tyson would have envied.

New York Giants middle linebacker Sam Huff, who engaged in several memorable Eastern Conference duels with Brown, said the Cleveland fullback lulled defenders to sleep with his slow retreat to the huddle, then attacked them the next down with the speed and power of a freight train. Running full steam into Brown, Huff said, was like running full steam into an oak tree. Huff had the fillings knocked from his teeth on one attempted tackle against Brown, and Steeler cornerback Brady Keys was another victim, suffering a bruised sternum and broken ribs after Brown had run over him.

Green Bay cornerback Bobby Jeter felt Brown's power in a 1965 exhibition game. "He busted four of my ribs," Jeter recalled. "I was trying to tackle him and he dropped that big forearm—it looked like a tree trunk—and put it in my ribs and that was it. The next time I opened my eyes I was in the dressing room."

Hall of Fame halfback Bobby Mitchell lined up next to Brown in the Cleveland backfield for four straight seasons from 1958 to 1961. "Forty-eight straight games," Mitchell said, "and I watched this man in every type of weather, every type of situation, and he always came through. I saw him play football in a way that I never saw anybody else play. There's something about every runner that's exciting and tells you that he's a great runner, but they just don't step out on the field and everybody knows that the boss is there. But that's the way it was with Jim. He would pull on his pants and everyone would get excited, you know, 'The big man's ready to run.'"

Run in a manner never seen before or since. He combined the abilities of the all-time greats—the power of an Earl Campbell, the fluid motion of a Gale Sayers.

"He would run inside and turn it loose on the defense," Mitchell said. "And then once he started popping you good inside and got you set up, he'd pop outside and go 70 yards. He'd hit up in there, and he'd meet somebody like Bednarik and you'd hear that sound—*whack!*—and both of them would be standing there and all of a sudden Jim would take off again. Everything would be stopped, and in the next second Jim would be gone."

Coached by Blanton Collier, the Browns had displayed remarkable balance offensively in winning the '64 championship. Brown was still the ultimate ball carrier, but halfback Ernie Green and rookie Leroy Kelly lent variety to the running game. The offense was spiced by a passing attack that featured quarterback Frank Ryan firing to Gary Collins on the post and rookie Paul Warfield on the corner. Brown led the NFL with 1,446 yards and a 5.2 average, but when injuries crippled the Cleveland attack in '65, leaving Ryan nursing a severe shoulder injury and Warfield a broken shoulder, Brown's workload increased again.

Carrying the ball a league-high 289 times, Brown carried Cleveland to a second straight Eastern Conference title. He led the NFL with 1,554 yards rushing and rushed for 17 touchdowns in just 14 games. He was named the league MVP, and in the week prior to the '65 title game, he became the primary concern of the Packers' defense in general, and Nitschke in particular.

Studying film of Cleveland, Nitschke could see that Brown was a gifted athlete. Since he was the key to Cleveland's offense, Nitschke knew Brown had to be stopped and that it was his responsibility to stop him. Brown was a triple-threat back. Nitschke would watch the film and see Brown soaring for a short-yardage score against the Eagles in Week Three; swinging out of the backfield and spinning his way through the secondary against the Giants in Week Six; then pulling up on a sweep to spiral a 39-yard scoring pass to Collins against New York.

There were other highlights as well. Brown, hurdling one Eagles' defender and gliding past another; knifing through four Dallas defenders to score on a weak side sweep; ripping off the NFL's longest run of the season, a 67-yarder against Pittsburgh, and scoring four TDs in a 42–21 win over the Steelers that clinched the Eastern Conference three weeks before the end of the regular season.

As he watched the films, Nitschke could see that Brown was unique in that he played the fullback position like a halfback. Like Packer power back Jim Taylor, Brown could bend the defensive line with straight-ahead thrusts, but the Browns also featured him on wide running plays that required a halfback's speed. To Nitschke, Brown was a fullback with finesse. He ran with speed and read his blocks; he knew where his teammates were on the field and where his downfield help was coming from.

All those elements came together on the Browns' number one running play, the toss sweep. Run from a double-wing set, the play was designated as "Flip-8" in the Cleveland playbook when run to the right side; "Flip-9" when run to the left. Brown would take Ryan's pitch left or right, read the blocks of pulling guards Gene Hickerson and John Wooten, and glide through the defense.

"We only needed to give him a crack—18 inches—and he would be in the secondary," center John Morrow recalled. "But one way or another, he'd get the yards. Jim got the job done."

The Cleveland offense worked tirelessly perfecting the toss sweep. "The trick was to get the ball to Jim when he was in full speed," Ryan remembered. "Jim was so fast and so quick that if we could get the ball to him and he could get around end, he could be effective."

Brown loved the toss sweep because it gave him room to create, to perform freely in open space. Once he was in the other team's secondary, he was on his own, and he could take defenders on one-on-one.

"That's when I'd go into my bag of stuff," Brown said at the time. "They're in trouble now—I'm in their territory, 55 things happening at once. I'm moving, evaluating their possible moves, trying to outthink and outmaneuver them, using my speed, quickness, and balance."

In the open field, Brown would limber-leg one opponent, offering the leg then jerking it away when somebody grabbed at it, then high-step past another. Brown called it "instinctive football," but there were times when he took on the defense with strength and brute force. On those occasions, Brown battered defenders by using the straight-arm, the forearm, or a lowered shoulder.

Nitschke watched Brown and saw that he knew how each defensive player was going to attack him. For some defenders, he'd lower that shoulder and run over them. Against others he'd call upon quickness and finesse to outrun them. On almost every occasion, Brown would use his forearm to protect his legs. Film study convinced Nitschke that Brown had a sixth sense that allowed him to read on the run the reactions of the defense. Brown was an artist, Nitschke thought, a player who ran with a purpose, an aim, and defeated opponents not only physically but mentally as well.

One story previewing the game praised Brown as a "smooth, strong, sophisticated superstar," but Nitschke and the Packers were prepared to respond with a defense that was the NFL's toughest to score against. Green Bay's 224 points allowed were more than 50 fewer than the second-ranked Chicago Bears, and four members of Packer defense—Nitschke, end Willie Davis, left corner Herb Adderley, and free safety Willie Wood—had been named to various NFL All-Pro teams in 1965.

"We had a total team effort," Adderley remembered, "and Ray Nitschke was the leader of that team. The fullback was his responsibility, and whether it was Jim Brown or Bill Brown of Minnesota, it didn't matter. That was his responsibility as the middle linebacker and he took the challenge."

Nitschke and the Green Bay defense game-planned for Brown in film study and on the frozen practice field. Defensive coordinator Phil Bengston found it amazing that this late in the season, during the week between Christmas and New Year's, the Packers were still out on the same spot where training camp had opened the previous July, still working hard on fundamentals. His defense had just put together one of its finest seasons, and they were still out in the dark cold, drilling, working and adjusting as if it were summer again. But Bengston realized that consistent preparation and practice had taken the Packers to where they were in 1965, and only a constant and rigorous attention to detail could carry them past Cleveland in the championship game.

As the practice week drew to a close, Bengston pulled Nitschke aside. They met in a conference room adjoining the dressing area, and together worked on revising their defensive play numbers and signals. Bengston knew from watching film of the Browns' offense that Cleveland could do severe damage to the Green Bay defense if Brown was able to make his cuts into alleys created by the Packer linemen being drawn too far to the strong side and their onside cornerback being too far over as well. The way the Browns ran their sweeps, out of the double-wing, presented unique problems, and Bengston recognized what those problems were. He also recognized that this time, it wasn't going to be enough for the Packers to rely on experience and past reputation. Green Bay would have to prevent Brown from breaking free on the strong-side sweeps by having Davis combine with left outside linebacker Dave Robinson to turn Brown in so that Nitschke could catch up with him. Bengston told Nitschke to watch for his signals from the sideline; the finger wigwags and hat-brim touches Bengston made would indicate what adjustments Nitschke would call for whenever Cleveland lined up in its double-wing set. Those adjustments, Bengston told Nitschke, could make the difference in stopping Brown before he swung out and away.

Nitschke loved the challenge of facing Brown, and wished he could play every game during the regular season against a superior player like that. He also loved the fact that Lombardi had told him earlier in the week that Brown was his responsibility. Knowing that Brown could embarrass a defense heightened Nitschke's intensity. To stop him, Nitschke knew he was going to have to play his position at the highest level possible. In the days leading up to the game, he gave himself pep talks, asking if he was up to the challenge of taking on Jim Brown. "Brown's your responsibility," Nitschke would say to himself. "Are you big enough to handle it? Are you a big enough man to stop him?"

Members of the Packer offense looked forward to the showdown between Nitschke and Brown as well. "The structure of our defense was basically the same as the New York Giants at that time," Boyd Dowler recalled. "When the Giants played the Browns it was always Sam Huff against Jimmy Brown. And our defense was structured the same way as the Giants. The linemen would keep the blockers off the middle linebacker, and the middle linebacker either tackles Jimmy Brown or he doesn't. If he does, we win. If he doesn't, we lose. That's about what it amounts to.

"That's the kind of challenge that Ray, with his personality and every-thing, would really get up for. And he had Jimmy Taylor riding him all week, because Taylor was always scrambling to be the top fullback in the league. Ray knew what he was up against and what he had to do."

Davis could see Nitschke readying himself for the meeting with Brown, and the Packers' defensive captain could see too the impending collisions between two men considered at the time best in the game at their respec-tive positions.

"We went into that game thinking we had to stop Jimmy Brown," Davis remembered. "He was their running offense. And because of that fullback–middle linebacker matchup, I could envision some occasions when those two guys—Jimmy and Ray—would go at it."

As Nitschke geared for the confrontation with Brown, Lombardi reem-phasized to his team that just as the running game is the heart of offensive football, stopping the run is the heart of defensive football. The team that can force the offense to throw more than it runs the ball, Lombardi said, will win more often than not. In four previous playoff games, the Green Bay defense had allowed just one rushing touchdown, Eagle halfback Ted Dean's five-yard score amid the Franklin Field mud back in 1960. And that score, Lombardi reminded his team, was the one that gave Philadelphia the title.

Dean's run had been a sweep around left end, and the Packers made it a point through the years to clamp down on wide running plays. A team that cannot keep its opponent from running wide to the outside, Lombardi would say, is a team that has lost the control on which the defense of the

Receivers who ran over the middle and into Ray Nitschke's territory paid a heavy price. In a sight familiar to NFL fans of the 1960s, Nitschke towers over Washington Redskins end and fellow future Hall of Famer Charley Taylor after delivering a crushing hit.

COPYRIGHT © JOHN E. BIEVER.

Ray Nitschke and Packers head coach Vince Lombardi had a sometimes
tumultuous relationship during their ten years together in Green Bay. But the
two men respected each other, as shown here with Nitschke helping Lombardi
maintain his balance following an out-of-bounds play.

COPYRIGHT © VERNON J. BIEVER.

The face that frightened a generation of NFL ball carriers. Nitschke's toothless, menacing visage symbolized the fierce Green Bay defense as coached by coordinator Phil Bengston.

COPYRIGHT © VERNON J. BIEVER.

Ray Nitschke receives a handshake from Packers trainer Bud Jorgenson
following a Green Bay defensive stand.

COPYRIGHT © VERNON J. BIEVER.

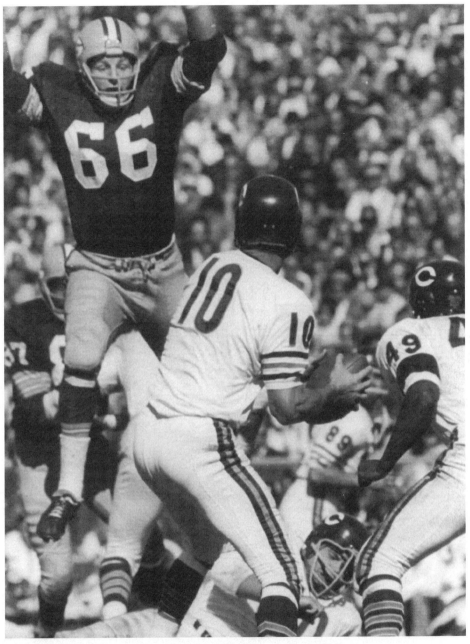

The Packers didn't blitz much under defensive coordinator Phil Bengston, but when they did, Nitschke proved to be a most able pass rusher. Here, the Packers' middle linebacker leaps high to block the passing lanes of Chicago Bears QB Rudy Bukich.

COPYRIGHT © VERNON J. BIEVER.

Even in the twilight of his career, Ray Nitschke (66)
remained the focal point of the Green Bay defense.
COPYRIGHT © VERNON J. BIEVER.

Ray Nitschke Day at Lambeau Field. Ray and wife Jackie join with daughter Amy and son John in a ceremony retiring Nitschke's Number 66 jersey. To this day, Nitschke's jersey is one of just four retired by the Packers organization.

COPYRIGHT © VERNON J. BIEVER.

Always a doting father, Nitschke and son Richard enjoy a laugh together in 1968.

COPYRIGHT © VERNON J. BIEVER.

Whether it was hauling in one of his 25 career interceptions or recovering a fumble, Nitschke was known for his ball-hawking skills.

COPYRIGHT © VERNON J. BIEVER.

running game is founded. "The defense," he said, "must demolish every end run." As the end run was basically a power play off-tackle, if the ball carrier turned the corner cleanly the angle of pursuit was so great the defense could not hold the play down. The Packers' plan to stop the sweep was to turn the end run back to the pursuit men, and to turn it back early. Green Bay employed several different schemes to defense the sweep: the halfback force, in which the onside defensive back is responsible for stepping up and containing the play; the safety force, where the onside safety cheats and forces the sweep inside; the linebacker force, in which the strong side linebacker fights off the block of the tight end and takes a wide angle of pursuit; and the "tango" maneuver, in which the strong side defensive end and linebacker exchange responsibilities and rush lanes, with the linebacker charging inside and the end looping to the outside.

Since the left side of the Green Bay defense was so strong—Davis at end, Robinson at outside linebacker, and Adderley at the corner—the Packers dictated to the offenses of their day the direction their plays had to be run.

"We shut down the left side of the field," Adderley said. "We made the offense play on half a field. We helped (right linebacker) Lee Roy Caffey and (right cornerback) Bob Jeter make All-Pro and get to the Pro Bowl because we sent the business their way. Even Nitschke didn't make too many tackles on the left side of the field because by the time he got there he was yelling, 'Hold 'em up, hold 'em up! Let me get to 'em!' Too late, man, because Willie Davis had made the tackle and Dave Robinson and I came in to clean up. We'd tell Ray, 'We need you on the other side, man, stay away from this side of the field.' No team we played in the sixties could say 'We had success running the ball, we had success throwing the ball against the Packers' left side.' Uh-uh. Not against our left side, man. No indeed. They had no success. So Ray would cheat over to the right side."

Still, the Packers knew Cleveland was going to attempt to sweep both flanks, and because Brown was such an intelligent runner, Bengston planned to use each of those schemes in an effort to keep him from reading the Green Bay defense on the run. Nitschke figured Brown had his own theories about playing the Packers, and about playing Nitschke. No two men played their positions exactly the same; Nitschke played off his blocks differently than the middle linebackers Brown saw in the Eastern Conference, Sam Huff and Lee Roy Jordan for instance. So Nitschke knew Brown was studying the Packers' film to see how he played a certain defense, how he reacted to sweeps and traps. Since Nitschke had never been overpowered at the point of attack, he figured Brown wasn't going to try and run over him. He believed Brown would analyze him, then combine that knowledge with his natural ability once the game began.

"We played team defense and Ray was our leader," Jeter said. "Everybody knew what they had to do to stop Jimmy Brown, and Nitschke was the key ingredient."

By the eve of the game, Nitschke had sufficiently psyched himself for the challenge. Brown would get some yards, Nitschke thought, but he wasn't going to get as many against him as he did against other middle linebackers. Lombardi added one more bit of incentive for Nitschke, posting a sign in the locker room that read "Pursuit is the shortest course to the ball carrier."

Quarterback Bart Starr watched Nitschke pump himself up for the coming showdown with Brown and thought it was an indication of Nitschke's desire to succeed. "The man was a fierce competitor," Starr said.

Huff could relate to Nitschke's feelings as the Packers prepared to face Cleveland. From 1957 to 1965 Huff faced Brown twice every season because their teams were neighbors in the Eastern Conference. Like Nitschke, Huff saw the game as a personal challenge.

"My only fear was that if Jimmy Brown had a big day, everybody would say I was terrible," Huff said. "When you're playing Jim Brown, you don't sleep before the game. I couldn't wait for them to kick it off because I knew Jim Brown was my man. If he had the ball, I was going to tackle him. Hell, there wasn't any use in looking at anybody else. Just look at him. He was going to get the ball and I was going to have to get him.

"Jimmy Brown was so good he made you change your defense. Any other back, if he flared out for a pass, the outside linebacker would take him and you would take your regular pass drop, you cover inside and 10 to 12 yards deep. And if they throw that little flare pass out to the back, the outside linebacker comes up from the outside and I come up from the inside and we got 'em. Not with Jim Brown. When Brown came down that line I was right with him. And if the quarterback threw to him out there, I was isolated one-on-one with Jim Brown. And that was something you did not want to do. So you would get up close on him so the quarterback would see you and wouldn't throw the ball to Brown. You gave Cleveland the turn-in (pattern) so they wouldn't throw to Jimmy Brown."

The Browns spent the Saturday before the game, New Year's Day, working out at Lambeau Field. The turf was frozen and fast, and Morrow was confident the fast track would help the Browns' ground game. Game day, however, saw a bone-chilling wind whip from Lake Michigan through Green Bay. Swirling snow shut down Austin Straubel Airport in Green Bay and blanketed morning churchgoers in white. Governor Warren Knowles of Wisconsin had flown up from the capital in Madison to attend the game, but his plane couldn't land in the blinding storm. The governor returned to Madison and settled for watching the game on CBS. Packer fans, however, turned out by the thousands. A crowd of 50,852 made its way to Lambeau Field, and long lines of cars backed up traffic for miles around the stadium. The huge traffic jam frustrated the Browns, who were quartered in a Holiday Inn in Appleton, some 40 minutes from the stadium.

Collier had wanted his team to stay away from Green Bay to avoid being caught up in the city's frenzied activity that went with preparing for an NFL championship game and for the new year. When the Browns boarded their buses Sunday morning to head to the game, they were caught in the congested traffic. Cars were moving slowly because of the heavy snow, and because the highway crews that should have plowed the north-bound lanes had instead only cleared the south-bound lanes. The Browns' buses would creep forward, stop, then creep forward again along the 30-mile stretch of highway. The long line of snarled traffic inched its way toward Green Bay, so slowly that by the time the Browns made it to the stadium, some of their players were unnerved at having their pregame rituals upset. As the players left the bus, Cleveland sportswriter Hal Lebovitz noted that only Jim Brown seemed to have his game face on. Inside the stadium, Ryan watched as helicopters hovered just a few feet above the surface, blowing four inches of fresh snow off of the seats. Two bulldozers from the city's sanitation department were brought out just to find the field; within minutes they were pushing mounds of snow to the sidelines and piling it into large banks. Earlier that morning, a thick field cover of straw had been removed by men with pitchforks, and another crew had been busy rolling up the tarpaulin.

The snow had abated, and to Ryan, the playing surface looked lush and green. But when the Browns finally took the field, they were disgusted with the conditions. The snow had started up again, and it was now mixed with freezing rain. The mix of snow and sleet turned the once frozen field into a mud bowl. Ryan stepped on the field and thought it felt like mush. Brown, wearing a white Cleveland warmup jacket, ran gingerly for a few steps and then slid in the snow. His face was solemn; to sportswriter Jack Hand, Brown's look was one of disgust.

"The mud was coming up over our shoelaces," Morrow said. "That was a terrible day. Our running game was central to our offense, and their field was a quagmire, like soup."

Across the field, the Packers were grinning. Fullback Jim Taylor told guards Jerry Kramer and Fuzzy Thurston, "It's Packer weather." Green Bay fans agreed. They swept the wet snow from the seats, ignored the gray chill and filled every corner of Lambeau Field. Packer backers showed their fortitude throughout; one woman who slipped on the ice and broke her leg refused to go to the hospital until the game was over. Down on the field, the heavy snow was obliterating the yard lines, making it impossible to see the first down markers on the sidelines. So Mark Duncan, the supervisor of officials, began placing small red flags five yards apart along each sideline.

In the press box high above the field, Arthur Daley of the *New York Times* studied the muck below and thought no championship game should be decided under such conditions. Inclement weather had interrupted both the World Series and major golf tournaments in years past, Daley wrote, but only in pro football must the show go on.

"It was cold as hell and it was muddy," Hornung remembered. "But that was our kind of field."

Just to be perverse, the Packers opened the game by putting the ball in the air. Showing once again why he was one of the best big-game quarterbacks ever, Starr theorized that since the Browns had only arrived at the stadium a short time ago and had to get dressed quickly and get in a brief workout, he would keep them off-balance by throwing early in the elements. "We knew it had to be bad for them psychologically," Starr said after the game, "so we hit them right away."

Short passes to Taylor and Hornung led to a pair of first downs, and when Cleveland became conscious of Starr using his backs as primary pass targets, he drew the Browns in with a play-fake to Hornung and threw a towering pass to flanker Carroll Dale. Hampered by a heavily taped broken rib under his throwing arm, Starr's pass was underthrown, but when Dale stopped and came back for the ball, right cornerback Walter Beach and strong safety Ross Fichtner both slipped and fell to their knees. Dale skipped through an attempted tackle by right linebacker Galen Fiss, sidestepped free safety Larry Benz and raced into the end zone to complete a 47-yard scoring play.

Trailing 7–0, the Browns came out throwing on their initial series. Ignoring the wet snow and heavy ball, Ryan flared a first down pass to Brown. This was the same flare pass that had kept Huff awake at nights before facing Brown, and the big fullback wrestled the ball away from Robinson and turned upfield before being ridden out of bounds by Nitschke at the Green Bay 36. With a white hand towel draped from the back of his yellow-gold football pants, Nitschke rose from the sideline mush with the feeling that since the field wasn't in great shape, the poor footing might slow Brown down.

Following a game plan designed to emphasize the pass, Ryan found Warfield for a completion that carried to the Green Bay 17. Ryan followed with another pass, a 17-yard out pattern to Collins, who beat Adderley to the right corner of the end zone for the score. Bobby Franklin's bobbling of the center snap, however, prevented Cleveland kicker Lou Groza from attempting the extra point, and Green Bay maintained its lead, 7–6.

Cleveland engineered another first-quarter drive that eventually stalled when Ryan, scrambling from the pocket and skirting right end, tripped and was downed two yards shy of a first down by Nitschke. Groza's 24-yard field goal gave the Browns a 9–7 lead at the close of the first quarter, but Green Bay regained the lead in the second quarter when Don Chandler drilled a 15-yard field goal to put the Packers up 10–9. Another Chandler field goal, this time from 23 yards away, made it 13–9 Packers. With the heavy mud hampering the footing and making it difficult for receivers to run their patterns, both teams switched to their ground games. Game films show Brown taking handoffs from Ryan, then churning through the sleet and slush and into the heart of the Packer defense. Awaiting Brown amid the freezing muck and the meshing lines was Nitschke, who was trying to claw his way past Morrow to get to the Cleveland back.

"Ray won some battles and I won some battles," Morrow remembered. "He was trying not to get tied up too much in the line and I was trying to cut him off. On one play, we were going to pass and he knocked the crap out of me with his right elbow. I guess he just wanted to vent himself a little bit."

After each carry, Brown would rise from the slippery bog and head slowly back to the huddle. His white uniform, trimmed in orange and brown, was daubed with frozen mud. On the other side of the scrimmage line, Nitschke would adjust his half-cage facemask, then look to the sideline for Bengston's defensive signal. Future post-season games would feature other classic middle linebacker–running back duels—Jack Lambert and Earl Campbell in the 1978 and '79 AFC title games in Pittsburgh; Mike Singletary and Eric Dickerson in the '85 NFC championship in Chicago; Ray Lewis and Eddie George in the 2000 AFC semifinal in Tennessee—but Nitschke versus Brown was a confrontation carried out on a grander scale. In 1969, the Hall of Fame Selection Committee selected both Nitschke and Brown for the All-Decade team, and also named Brown the best fullback and Nitschke the best middle linebacker of the NFL's first 50 years. In 1965, both men were all-pros, both were in their prime, and both were the best in the game at their respective positions.

"The Packers pretty much freed Ray up to get to Jimmy," Ryan said, recalling the matchup. "Their defensive line allowed Ray to get to the point of contact against Jimmy."

On Cleveland's next series, Brown carried three consecutive times. Running a power sweep left, he picked up nine yards when Nitschke, taking an inside route on the linebacker force, was cut down by Hickerson. Wood and Henry Jordan combined to make the stop, and Brown followed by sweeping right, outrunning Nitschke to the corner and picking up 14 yards before Adderley and Wood jolted him out of bounds. On the next play,

Cleveland switched into the double-wing formation the Packers were most concerned about, and Brown ran a toss sweep to his left. Nitschke, bumped off stride by Hickerson, was taken out of the play and it was left to Jordan and Wood to once again bring Brown down, this time after an eight-yard gain.

Nitschke and the Packers were seeing first-hand the Browns' famed ground game. In three plays, Brown had run for a combined 31 yards, and CBS-TV sportscaster Ray Scott remarked that Brown was still "the big gun" in the Cleveland attack. Across the line of scrimmage, the Packer defense studied the movements of a man who had run for more yards and scored more touchdowns than anyone in pro football history, a man Scott said set a new record with every yard gained.

"We'd put a good hit on Jimmy, and he'd get up real slow like he was hurt," Jeter said. "Then the next play, here he comes again."

The success of the Browns' sweep relied on the quickness of its pulling guards. "On our sweep," Brown explained at the time, "we try to get our guards out front. If they get to the corner, you're going to make a gain."

On two of the previous three plays, Hickerson had pulled and taken Nitschke out of the play. Bengston's linebacker force was designed for Nitschke to chase the sweep from behind and cut into the backfield through the hole vacated by the pulling guard. With the Browns having success against the linebacker force, Bengston signaled to Nitschke to switch to a safety force play. When Brown swept right on a third-and-two, strong safety Tom Brown came up and forced Brown inside, where the pursuit was waiting. Robinson and left tackle Ron Kostelnik combined to stop Brown for a one-yard loss, and Cleveland ended a key series with a punt.

With less than two minutes to go in the half and the Packers clinging to a four-point lead, Bengston called for a linebacker blitz. Stacked behind Jordan, Nitschke looped around his right tackle, who took an inside charge and pressured Ryan. The Cleveland quarterback shook free from Nitschke but was sacked by Robinson for a five-yard loss. On third-and-15 from the Green Bay 35, Ryan flared a pass to Brown in the left flat. Nitschke chased from behind, then combined with Jeter to stop Brown one yard shy of a first down. The 14-yard gain set up a Groza field goal 53 seconds before the half, and his 28-yard conversion cut Cleveland's deficit to 13–12 at halftime.

Despite leading by a point at the break, there was cause for concern in the Packer locker room. Starr's ribs were aching, and several times in the first half Nitschke had winced on the sidelines when he saw Starr taking hits from the Cleveland defenders. Taylor was playing with a severe muscle pull and swollen ankle, Hornung was hampered by nagging injuries, and Dowler was starting despite a bad ankle and two damaged shoulders. Green

Bay's injury situation worsened when starting right cornerback Doug Hart left the game with an injury and was replaced by Jeter.

Defensively, Nitschke and the Packers were concerned about containing Brown. He had outmaneuvered the Green Bay defense on two pass plays in the first half, and the result was nine Cleveland points. Brown was having success sweeping the flanks and appeared on his way to duplicating his championship game performance from '64, when he barged through a Baltimore defense designed specifically to stop him for 114 yards rushing and another 37 yards receiving.

To keep Brown off the field, Lombardi made some hard decisions. Realizing the slick field was slowing the speed of their running backs to the hole, the Packers would go with straight running plays that would get Taylor and Hornung to the hole quicker. The Browns had taken away the power sweep in the first half by sending defensive ends Paul Wiggin and Bill Glass on wide rushes. Starr noted that Cleveland seemed willing to give the Packers the inside, and Lombardi ordered a steady diet of off-tackle slants and quick counters off a simulated sweep.

"The snow and mud were our allies," Lombardi said later. "When you have conditions like these, it's best to be basic, not fancy. And we're the most basic offensive team there is."

The Packers' second-half plan, Starr said, was to inch the Browns to death inside, and they put their plan into motion midway through the third quarter. Taking over on their own 10-yard line, the Packers put together a drive whose power would have made Patton's Third Army proud. Taylor, the toy tank, bulldozed his way to short but important gains. With Taylor running off-tackle slants to the weak side and Hornung hitting the strong side at a controlled trot, Green Bay took out a land claim on the football. Driving 90 yards, the Packers melted seven minutes off the clock and put seven more points on the board when Hornung swept left behind Kramer and scored from 13 yards out.

Packers' radio broadcaster Ted Moore called the game-turning drive on WTMJ Radio:

Starr is moving the club very well at this point. . . . Handoff to Hornung, slash over the right side and Hornung scampers across the 25, the 20, and down to the 15-yard line. The big hole was there on the right side. Beautiful blocking by Jerry Kramer and Forrest Gregg and Hornung drove through it. . . .

Starr fakes, hands to Taylor up the middle, across the 15 to the 13-yard line on a straight-ahead smash. . . .

Starr takes the ball, hands off to Hornung, sweep to the left side, he gets a block, he's inside the 10, at the five, cuts into the end zone for the touch-

down! And there you saw the Green Bay Packer power sweep as in days of yore. Forrest Gregg cleared the way with a beautiful block, the two guards, Jerry Kramer and Fuzzy Thurston, doing a great job at the line of scrimmage. . . .

Trailing 20–12, the Browns looked to catch up quickly. From the Green Bay 40, Ryan sent Brown circling out of the backfield on a deep route down the middle of the field. Nitschke, his muddied white towel flapping from the back of his pants, gave chase. Brown was two steps ahead of Nitschke when he crossed the goal line, and had Ryan's pass in his hands for a moment. The touchdown would have pulled the Browns back into the game, and left them trailing by just 20–19. But Nitschke dove at the last second and dislodged the slippery ball from Brown's hands. It was a touchdown-saving play—and one of the key turning points of the game.

Nitschke said later that as he chased Brown down the field, all he could think of was that Brown was his responsibility, and that he couldn't let him make a touchdown. Nitschke knew Brown was faster than he was, but he had shadowed him down the field and felt he had a good angle on the ball. When he threw his arms up in the end zone, Nitschke felt the weight of the heavy ball hit as he batted it free.

From his position on the sideline, offensive tackle Bob Skoronski had seen the play, had seen Brown drop the ball in the end zone, and knew why he had failed to hold on to Ryan's pass. "Nitschke was all over him," Skoronski said, "hustling and hollering and screaming."

Dowler had watched along with Skoronski, had seen Nitschke hustling after Brown amid the freezing rain and slippery field. "They sent Jimmy Brown up the gap on a seam pass, and Brown could run awful fast," Dowler said. "Brown got a little behind him, and Ray was coming hard to knock the ball down in the end zone. They were both 30 yards downfield, and you know, that's a middle linebacker running with Jimmy Brown, who was one of the faster players in those years. Brown was awful big, but he was also awful fast, and Ray went right with him. Ray made a good play on the ball, and at the time, it would have been a big swing if they had scored there."

Knowing Nitschke and the Packers would gang up to stop Cleveland's ground game, Ryan said the Browns had entered the game looking to attack the Green Bay defense through the air.

"Ray was great against the run, and they really counted on him to plug holes," Ryan recalled. "We wanted to take him on by throwing the ball. It was not easy to find a weakness in their defense. They were just superb. They had very standard setups but they had such great defensive players. Their players were always where they were supposed to be."

Nitschke followed up on his great play against Brown by teaming with end Lionel Aldridge to wrestle a scrambling Ryan to the mud at the line of scrimmage, then joined with Jordan to thwart a Groza field goal that would have pulled the Browns to within five points. Just as he had disrupted the crucial center snap by Baltimore's Buzz Nutter on Lou Michael's overtime field goal in the Western Conference playoff the week before, Nitschke helped foul the Browns' attempt as well. Rather than line up directly over center, Nitschke got down in his stance in the gap between the center and massive Walter Johnson, Cleveland's rookie defensive tackle who was playing left guard on special teams. Nitschke shot the center-guard gap, and his charge caused Johnson, who should have blocked Jordan, to take a half-step to his right to block Nitschke. That small movement gave Jordan just enough of a crease to slip through the line, and he penetrated deep enough to get his right hand up and deflect Groza's field goal.

For the rest of the game, the Packers stuck with their simplified ground game, gouging out one grimy yard after another. Green Bay's line would knock the Cleveland defense back a yard or two, Taylor or Hornung would plow in behind them, and they would return to the huddle hitching their pants and shifting their shoulder pads. In his radio broadcast, Moore referred to Taylor and Hornung as "the thunder and lightning of the Green Bay backfield," foreshadowing by some 35 years the term used to describe the New York Giants' "Thunder and Lighting" tandem of Ron Dayne and Kiki Barber in the 2000 season. For the purists who loved power football, the Packers were putting forth a clinic in ball control. In the Green Bay huddle, second-year center Ken Bowman listened as his mud-caked team-mates shouted, "Just like 1962."

"I guess," Bowman thought, "this is how they used to do it."

As the snow and sleet intensified, a heavy fog shrouded Lambeau Field. The stadium lights, which had been on all day, flared brightly in the bog, and amid a setting that seemed more suited to a filming of *The Hound of the Baskervilles,* the Packers put the finishing touches on their muddy, 23–12 masterpiece. Brown watched solemnly from the sidelines as Taylor, his competitive rival at fullback, ignored a badly swollen ankle and slanted and blasted his way through the Cleveland defense. When Cleveland had the ball, Taylor watched as Brown and Nitschke engaged in numerous colli-sions amid the dark mud.

"Our defense, Nitschke and them, always played tough against Jim Brown," Taylor said later. "They always rose to the occasion."

Davis said that once the Packers shut down the passing game, they could turn their full attention to stopping Brown. "Every time we played against Cleveland, Jimmy always presented that kind of a challenge," he said. "Everybody on our defense had the notion that Jimmy was the guy we had to stop."

Like Jordan, Davis was a former member of the Browns, and the duo always put forth an extra effort whenever Green Bay played Cleveland in those years. "We wanted to make the Browns regret having traded us," Davis said.

Against Cleveland in the '65 title game, Davis and Jordan were spurred on by Nitschke's chatter behind them. Every time Brown swept wide on the toss sweep, Davis could hear Nitschke yelling. "Here they come," Nitschke would yell. "Here they come!"

"He was our rah-rah guy, our chatterbox, and he was directing us where to go," said Davis, who was called "Dr. Feelgood" by his teammates. "It was always in the direction of winning the game, but he'd just start hollering at you. 'Hey, Dr. Feelgood, you gotta get in there! You gotta get to that passer.' I'd look at him like, 'Hey, what the—*You* get in there!'"

On one play, Brown veered outside and Davis gave chase. When Brown turned and headed into the hole, Davis realized he was suddenly in a one-on-one situation with the Cleveland fullback.

"Anytime you found yourself one-on-one with Jimmy Brown, you immediately looked for help," Davis recalled. "On this play, I was one of the first ones there to meet him and it was just Jimmy and me, and the one thing on my mind was, 'I've gotta stop this guy.' "

Davis did stop Brown; then heard the voice of Nitschke behind him. "Hey Doctor," Nitschke rasped. "That's the way to go."

Nitschke, his green-and-gold uniform splattered with gray mud, drew compliments for his play that day. Bill Curry, a rookie center for the Packers that season, recalled the game, recalled Nitschke having "a big afternoon" against Brown. Covering the game for *Sports Illustrated*, Tex Maule wrote that the Green Bay defense "read the Browns sweeps as though Nitschke were a party to their huddles."

Davis told Maule after the game that when the Browns came out in their double-wing set with Brown the lone back and tight end Jim Brewer and halfback Ernie Green set to the strong side, Cleveland was planning to sweep right. "So we flew out of there to turn Brown in," Davis said. "If we could turn him in, then he would run into Nitschke. . . . "

Peeling off his Cleveland uniform for the final time, Brown praised the Packer defense.

"Willie Davis is their leader in the line and they've got two great defensive backs in Herb Adderley and Willie Wood," Brown said. "As for Ray Nitschke at middle linebacker, well, he seems to know where I'm going before I know myself."

Jeter had the feeling that Brown, great as he was, hated to play against Nitschke. "Ray always brought his game up to another level when he played against Jimmy," Jeter said. "And I was glad about that, because it meant I wouldn't have to tackle Brown as much."

Brown had been held to 50 yards rushing and finished with less than 100 yards of total offense (94). In the second half, Nitschke and the Packer defense limited Brown to just nine yards rushing.

"When you can hold Jimmy Brown to less than 100 yards," Hornung said, "the middle linebacker has to be a big part of it."

Taylor, who for years had played in the considerable shadow cast by Brown, was named the game's MVP after finish with 96 yards on 27 carries. Hornung added 105 yards on 18 carries, and slogged through the slippery turf for one score.

In the somber Cleveland dressing room, Brown talked to reporters about the man who had been his most persistent pursuer. "I noticed that Ray Nitschke was keying on me," Brown said. "He's as tough as anybody."

Nitschke and the Packer defense, Brown said, were rough and skilled. But, he added, he thought they had received an assist from the elements. The field was ice and mud and left him bumping into defenders, Brown said, that he would normally have avoided.

When Nitschke read Brown's comments later, he smiled. He figured Brown was referring to a certain bald-headed defender that he had been running into all afternoon. Nitschke's meeting that day with Brown had been his fourth since becoming a starter. In 1961, Nitschke and the Packers held Brown to 72 yards on 16 carries in a 49–17 victory in Cleveland. In 1963, Brown gained just 56 yards on 11 carries in a 40–23 loss in the Miami Playoff Bowl. In 1964, Cleveland's championship season, Brown finished with 74 yards on 20 carries as Green Bay won again, 28–21, in Milwaukee.

Brown averaged an NFL-record 104 yards rushing per game in his career, but he never rushed for 100 yards against Nitschke and the Green Bay defense. Bengston's unit is the only NFL team that can claim that distinction against arguably the greatest running back in NFL history.

"That was because of Ray," Jeter said. "Ray Nitschke was Jimmy Brown's nemesis."

NINE

BEING NAMED to the NFL All-Pro team for the second straight season in 1965 helped further establish Ray Nitschke as one of the leaders of the NFL champion Green Bay Packers. But as the new year of 1966 dawned, Nitschke was becoming increasingly more interested in being a leader not only on his team but in the town as well.

Ray and Jackie adopted their second child, Richard, who was just 10 days old when the Nitschkes brought him home in 1966. John was three years old, and his growing family gave Nitschke a fulfillment he hadn't known since early in his own childhood. At Christmas, Nitschke would dress up in a full Santa Claus outfit, complete with red-and-white fur cap, and play Santa Claus for his young sons. Jackie decorated their house in a festive style and always arranged a miniature Christmas village complete with blinking lights and fake snow. She would then invite neighborhood children by to see the village and spend time at the house.

Nitschke didn't always have the time to spend with his family that he would have liked, especially since the Packers' seasons always ran long because of their annual appearances in the post-season. From 1960 to 1967, Green Bay played a post-season game every year for eight straight seasons. But Nitschke made up for lost time once the season was over, and family photos show him smiling broadly as he poses for photos with Jackie and plays with his children.

Getting married and settling down, Nitschke said, made him more concerned with being a man. "The responsibilities of family life turned me on," he said. "No matter what profession you have in life, you have to have happiness at home. I've had a happy family life, and I think it has helped me to go about my job in a better way."

The former street tough from suburban Chicago considered himself blessed to have what he described as "a wonderful wife and wonderful children." The man who once believed that everyone in the world was against him now looked to his family as his main source of strength.

"The family," he said, "is the single most important thing to me because of not having a very sound family life in my youth."

Nitschke became famous for his hugs, and one of the enduring memories that his children have of him is the strength of his embrace. John

Nitschke once recalled his father's bearhuglike hug as "pretty neat stuff." Green Bay defensive coordinator Phil Bengston said Nitschke and free safety Willie Wood were the biggest huggers on the team. Every time the Green Bay defense made a successful goal-line stand or forced a turnover, Bengston would brace himself for what he described as the "huge bearhugs" he was sure to receive as soon as Nitschke and Wood returned to the sideline.

By 1966, Nitschke had not only adopted two sons, he had adopted Green Bay as his hometown. Packer teammate Carroll Dale, who roomed with Nitschke on road trips, said that Packer team buses often sat idling curbside because Nitschke remained outside, signing autographs for children. "He never turned anyone down that wanted an autograph," Dale said, and Nitschke would take so much time signing that when he eventually did climb aboard the bus his teammates would kid him. "Ray, hey Ray, what are you doing, running for office?" someone would shout. Boyd Dowler began referring to Nitschke as "the People's Choice."

Thomas Content of the *Green Bay Press-Gazette* thought Nitschke had an "unfailing ease" with autograph seekers. One of the reasons Nitschke took so long to sign his autograph was because he made sure he signed items in a clear and legible fashion. Vern Biever, who has been the Packers' official photographer for the past half-century, said Nitschke took his time when signing to ensure his signature came across as being very neat. Unlike many in the public eye, Nitschke never scrawled his name in a hurried or haphazard fashion. Biever never saw Nitschke turn anyone down for an autograph, and the nicest thing about it, Biever said, was that a person could *read* Nitschke's signature. "It was his trademark," Biever said of Nitschke's neat signature, "and it never varied."

Nitschke owned a zest for life that extended beyond the football field. He would talk football with anyone at any time, and while he comforted children with a wide-mouth grin and some kind words, he intimidated adults with a menacing look and a voice that could stop traffic.

John Bankert, the director of the Pro Football Hall of Fame, said Nitschke scared him the first time they met. Nitschke's handshake was uncommonly strong, Bankert thought, but he didn't think Ray realized it. Bankert was intimidated by the piercing glare of Nitschke's blue eyes and his clenched jaw. Nitschke looked hard, but Bankert quickly realized that Ray didn't mean to scare him. Within a moment, Nitschke loosened his grip, his eyes twinkled, and the clenched jaw gave way to a mischievous smile. When that happened, Bankert said, "you knew that he liked you."

Tommy Nobis wasn't sure what to make of Nitschke the first time he met him. The heralded rookie linebacker from Texas was the number-one draft choice of the expansion Atlanta Falcons in 1966, and as a Maxwell

Award winner, was at a banquet with Nitschke during the off-season.

"I certainly knew of Ray when I came into the league," Nobis said. "I knew he was one of the standard-setters at middle linebacker. He had that gruff look, that voice, and he'd look at you and say, "What're ya starin' at, rookie?' He'd scare the shit out of you.

"We were at a banquet at the Washington (D.C.) Touchdown Club in 1966, and we both get into an elevator and he looks over at me and says, 'So you're that rookie who thinks he can play in this league?'

"I didn't know if he was playing with me or not. It was the first time I was ever face-to-face with him, and every time he talked it looked like the durned tie was going to burst off his neck. I'm looking at him and thinking, 'Should I swing at 'em? Should I shove 'em? Should I run?' But then I got to know him, and we would talk whenever we saw each other. Even in a sports coat and suit, if Nitschke walked into the room, you knew there was something special about him. He just radiated that feeling. That's the way Ray was."

Theresa Starkey, Ray and Jackie's niece, remembered the day during the Green Bay glory years when she brought her "Uncle Ray" to her seventh grade class for show-and-tell. The jaws of her classmates, Starkey said, dropped when Nitschke walked into the classroom.

Jack Camp, a nephew of Nitschke's, was there the day Ray was in a parade and police tried to push the fans away from him. Nitschke stopped the police and proceeded to sign autographs for the fans.

Nitschke's attitude toward signing autographs was refreshingly old-school, particularly in light of the attitudes exhibited by latter-day athletes.

"When people ask me for my autograph," he said, "I'm very thrilled that they do ask. I think it's a responsibility a ball player should have to the game. My philosophy is that it's a privilege to play."

It was even more of a privilege, he said, to play in Green Bay. He and Jackie and the kids grew to love the people, the area, and the state of Wisconsin. "There's no place like Green Bay," he said on more than one occasion, and to Nitschke, there was no NFL team like the Packers. He admired the organization and thought the story of the team's growth from a meat-packing company–sponsored town team to an NFL dynasty was special. "It's a beautiful sports story," Nitschke said, "and to be part of the tradition is just a fabulous thing."

Football was a way of life in Green Bay. Everyone, it seemed, was a fan—the middle-aged woman filling her grocery cart at the supermarket who told an interviewer, "Goodness, I haven't missed a game in 15 years;" the butcher who told a camera crew, "Our boys are really going to clobber those Bears this Sunday;" the group of small boys wearing youth-sized Packer helmets and imitating their heroes in the park.

Nitschke loved talking with them all, and to the people of Green Bay, he became a pied piper who went around doing good. Margaret Nitschke of Mayville, Wisconsin, said her husband Frank was a distant cousin of Ray's. "Frank had the Nitschke nose, the receding Nitschke hairline, the big shoulders," she said. Margaret was moved once to contact Ray by mail during the mid-sixties. Her daughter Charon was in the sixth grade at the time and, because she was big for her age, classmates at St. Margaret's school teased her by calling her "Ray." The taunts upset Charon, and her mother sent a letter to Nitschke at the Packer offices. He responded by writing a letter back to Charon and enclosed along with it one of his Green Bay jerseys and two tickets to a Packers game. When the kids at her school found out Nitschke had written her a letter and sent her a Green Bay jersey, Charon became the envy of the sixth grade.

"He made her feel a whole lot better," Margaret said. "He was very generous, a super guy. But that had to come, too. For a while, he had his ups and downs. But then he put it all together, and he became very personable."

Teammate Willie Davis, who played alongside Nitschke on the Green Bay defense, felt no individual ever made a greater transition from the football field to the community than Nitschke. Leo Waldschmidt of Howards Grove, Wisconsin, recalled how Nitschke ended conversations not with a "good-bye" or "so long" but with a "sayonara."

The man who once made the rounds at Green Bay bars now made the rounds of his community. Former Packer team president Judge Robert Parins first met Nitschke in Ray's rookie season of 1958. Nitschke was getting in trouble off the field and Parins, an attorney at the time, had occasion to help him out on a few matters. He remained friends with Nitschke through the years and came to admire the way Nitschke went from raising hell to raising a family.

"It took a great person to do that," Parins said.

Mike Horn, who played for the original Green Bay Bobcats ice hockey team, met Nitschke in 1958. They had frequented bars together during Nitschke's early years in Green Bay, and Horn was one of those outside the Packer organization who witnessed Nitschke's transformation from street fighter to family man.

"He changed after he met Jackie," Horn said. Nitschke had a fascination with ice hockey, and along with some of his Packer teammates was a regular at Bobcat games. Though Nitschke was considered by some to be a madman on the field, it was hockey players Nitschke thought were the maniacs.

"You guys are nuts," he would tell Horn. "I play once a week and I wear a helmet. You guys play twice a week and you don't even wear helmets."

Nitschke would laugh, the blue eyes would lighten, and an easy smile would crease his face. It was a look that changed dramatically once the season began. The eyes would become squints, the smile would harden into a grin, and the light countenance would revert to its craggy, hawkish features. "He had those eyes, that grin," Chicago Bears' Hall of Fame tight end Mike Ditka said. "He kept me focused out there. If you'd ever let up, he'd kill you."

Nitschke never let up, on game days or in practices. "He performed during practices," Biever said. "He put his heart into everything." Teammates called Nitschke the "Bald Eagle" because of his gleaming dome, and on occasion conspired against him to settle him down. Bill Curry, who joined the Packers as a rookie center in 1965, thought Nitschke was one of those men, like Packer boss Vince Lombardi, who harnessed and used rage. They had an aura on the field that Curry found both unique and scary. It was a feeling, he thought, that old-time hitters must have felt whenever they dug in against someone like Sal Maglie, a fearsome pitcher for the Brooklyn Dodgers in the 1950s who earned the nickname "The Barber" for the close shaves he gave to hitters leaning too far out over the plate.

Curry had first become aware of Nitschke when he watched the 1962 NFL championship game between the Packers and Giants on TV. Curry had never heard of Nitschke before that awesomely cold day in Yankee Stadium, but he soon became aware of the man in the white-and-yellow uniform with the green number 66 on his jersey. Curry was fascinated by Nitschke's play, the quick, crablike shuffle across the frozen field, the smashing hits on Giant ballcarriers. Curry's fascination increased when he saw Nitschke that same night on the TV game show *What's My Line?* He could hardly believe his eyes. There was Nitschke, appearing gentlemanly in his dark-rimmed glasses and conservative business suit. To Curry, Nitschke seemed to have a professorial demeanor.

Two years later, Curry signed with the Packers and was in awe when he met Nitschke. The sheer mass and power exuded by the Packers middle linebacker kept Curry's eyes riveted on him all day. When Curry arrived in Green Bay in the spring of 1965 for the Packers' training camp, his awe of Nitschke turned to hatred. Nitschke would show up on the practice field fully padded. "Padded to the hilt," Curry said later. "Forearms, hands, everything." The sight of Nitschke in full pads left every member on the offensive line knowing it was going to be a long, tough scrimmage. Nitschke would run around the field, yelling and shouting in a voice that to Curry sounded rough and nagging, with a streets-of-Chicago accent:

"Come on, let's have some ent'usiasm . . . "

Curry called it a constant stream of chatter that irritated everyone, but

Nitschke would just stand there grinning, then wait a play or two before he'd be running around and screaming out the plays again.

Curry said Nitschke ran through scrimmages clotheslining his teammates, crashing into them. Tired of being brutalized, the Packer offense would police the field themselves. Curry said there were times when Green Bay's linemen—Jerry Kramer and Fuzzy Thurston, Forrest Gregg and Bob Skoronski—ganged up on Nitschke. "Just to slow him up," Curry said. In September 1966, Kramer was running a dummy scrimmage drill that required him to block Nitschke. Kramer was going through the motions, and as he positioned himself in front of Nitschke, not planning to hit or block him, Nitschke brought one of his padded forearms up and smashed Kramer in the face. Stung by the blow, Kramer returned to the huddle and told backup quarterback Zeke Bratkowski to run the same play again. Bratkowski did, and Kramer went after Nitschke, pushing him down and driving him into the ground. "He got the message," said Kramer.

Nitschke was given free reign in scrimmages, Curry said, because Lombardi used him as an instrument to instill fear in his teammates. Fear in the sense that as proud professionals, they would raise their level of play to avoid being humiliated by Nitschke. Curry didn't understand Lombardi's methods at first, until one day during his rookie camp when Lombardi gathered the team together for the blitz drill. Curry had been involved in such drills during his college days at Georgia Tech, and the drill was pretty simple. The middle linebacker would rush on a mock blitz, the center would drop straight back for three yards, then hit and recoil to shield the blitzing linebacker away from the quarterback.

But when Lombardi called for the blitz drill, Curry caught starting center Ken Bowman looking at him out of the corner of his eye. The unsuspecting Curry got down in his stance against Nitschke, and at the snap was knocked off his feet. Curry was shocked; it was the hardest hit he had ever taken. He got up, thinking, "I'll hit *him* that way next time." He tried, but Nitschke decked him again. As a veteran, Nitschke had distinct advantages over the rookie. He knew the drill, had been a professional for seven years and an All-Pro, and knew the snap count. Curry was convinced Nitschke was jumping the count, was crowding the line of scrimmage and moving a split-second before the snap. Nitschke cracked Curry's helmet with the sheer force of his forearm, then snapped the rookie's chin strap with another hammer blow. With every play, Nitschke seemed to hit harder. He was literally running over Curry, scattering the backs and messing up the play. Curry couldn't get to him, and because Nitschke had bad knees and was scrimmaging without knee pads, he couldn't cut block him low either.

Every time Curry missed Nitschke, Lombardi would go into a tantrum. "Dammit, Curry! Can't you move? Can't you do anything?"

Suddenly, Curry realized what Lombardi had been talking about when he spoke of the fear of humiliation. Curry began dreading the drill, and as the Packer offense regrouped, Lombardi stuck his head in the huddle.

"Curry," he said. "I want you to cut Nitschke."

Curry was stunned. "What?"

"I want you to cut Nitschke."

Curry couldn't believe what Lombardi was saying. He looked over at Nitschke, saw the huge shoulders and arms, the bad knees. Nitschke was drilling without knee *and* thigh pads. Still, he couldn't question his coach's orders, so on the next play Curry fired out and cut Nitschke down. He half-expected Nitschke to kick him in the face, but Ray didn't say a word. Offensive players tired of watching Nitschke knocking everyone around actually cheered.

"Hey, good block," they shouted. "That-a-way to git 'em."

Curry went back to the huddle feeling rather proud of himself, until Lombardi stuck his head in the huddle again.

"Hit him *again*."

Curry went pale, then started to stammer. "Oh no, what?"

At the snap, he cut Nitschke again, and Lombardi, with that big, jack-o-lantern grin, said, "See there? You got him."

On other occasions, Curry wasn't so fortunate. Nitschke would physically punish him so much that Curry would grow frustrated and start pushing after the drill was over. Nitschke never retaliated; he wouldn't deign to fight a rookie. All he would say was, "Kid, what the hell's wrong with you?"

It was humiliating, Curry said, Nitschke brushing him off as if he was flicking away a mosquito.

Bobby Jeter shared an experience similar to Curry's. After joining the Packers in 1963, Jeter spent his first two seasons at wide receiver before becoming an All-Pro at right cornerback. The first time he attempted to block Nitschke, Jeter was jolted back into the backfield.

"Coach Lombardi told me to get my butt back in there," Jeter said. "I had all kinds of things going through my mind. And then I thought, 'Well, hell, I know the snap count and Nitschke doesn't, so I can use that to my advantage.' So the next time I drove out there, I got 'em, I moved 'em back a couple of yards. And he got up, hit me on the back, and said, 'Good block, Jeter. That's the way to attack.'"

Nitschke could, on occasion, show pity on his teammates. The Packers ran a drill called the "nutcracker" in which a defensive player positioned himself between two huge bags filled with foam rubber. The bags formed a chute, and the defender would take on an offensive blocker in order to get to the ball carrier. Many of the Packers hated the nutcracker drill, hated it for the helmet-rattling collisions that often led to the offensive and defensive players ramming each other's necks down into the chests. Kramer said the primary idea was to pave a path for the runner; the secondary idea was to draw blood.

During one nutcracker drill in 1967, Red Mack, a reserve flanker who stood 5-feet-10 and weighed 185 pounds, lined up against Nitschke. Players gathered around for the expected bloodletting. Nitschke weighed 240 pounds, and Kramer considered him to be the strongest 240-pounder in the NFL. Nitschke also used his forearm better than anyone in the game, and Kramer said that when Ray brought his forearm to the head of a lineman, it was a lethal weapon. Nitschke was not only used to beating people's heads in during the drill, Kramer said, he enjoyed it.

Looking at Mack lined up against him, however, Nitschke showed a sudden reticence.

"Oh, no," he said. "I can't go against this guy."

Mack, who may have been the toughest 185-pounder in the league, glared at Nitschke.

"Get in here you son of a bitch," Mack growled, "and let's go."

The two men lined up, Mack fired out, and Nitschke clubbed him to his knees with a forearm.

When guard Gale Gillingham joined the Packers in 1966 as a first-round draft choice out of the University of Minnesota, it didn't take him long to become acquainted with Nitschke. "He was always easy to find," remembered Gillingham, who played alongside Nitschke through the 1972 season. "He was always yelling. Ray played the consummate hard ass, but if he saw somebody needed some help, he'd give them the shirt off his back. If someone needed a pat on the back, Ray would go out of his way to find that kid and help him along. At the same time, if he thought someone was slacking off, he could be unmerciful."

Gillingham realized quickly that the Packer veterans accepted the rookies quickly if they sought to blend in. "They would be the hardest team to join if you thought you were a hot shit and something special," Gillingham said. "But if you went in there and kept your mouth shut and had some ability, they adopted you pretty quick.

"I had Bow (center Ken Bowman) on one side and (tackle) Bob Skoronski on the other, and I said, 'If I have any questions, I'm just going to ask.' And they said, 'Okay.' But people who came in there with a chip on their shoulders, there was no way they were ever going to fit in."

Like Curry had before him, Gillingham learned to scrimmage hard against Nitschke. "He was always taking shots at guys, no question,"

Gillingham said. "I just think that was Ray's way. He was a winner and he just wanted to keep guys awake. But I've seen him get his ass kicked plenty of times too, and he never squawked about it."

Gillingham recalled a scrimmage where Nitschke took a shot at guard Bill Lueck. "Lueck just beat the hell out of him," Gillingham said. "In fact, he took Ray's helmet off and hit him over the head with it. Before the helmet hit the ground, the knot on Ray's head was up about three inches."

Even in non-scrimmage situations, Nitschke couldn't resist giving a teammate a little nudge if they invaded his turf. Even if that teammate was quarterback Bart Starr.

"I can recall jogging past him after a practice session or something and he'd hit you with his elbow, hit you in the backside, and kind of push you off-stride," Starr said, laughing at the memory. "He'd say, 'Sorry, didn't mean to do it,' and you knew darn well he meant to do it."

Starr said Nitschke "energized" the practice field with his intensity, and as hard as Nitschke could be on his teammates in scrimmages, he was just as protective of them on Sundays. The first time Curry played against the Bears, in the 1965 Shrine Game in Milwaukee, Nitschke approached him during warm-ups.

"If you happen to make a play near the Bears' bench today," Nitschke said, "just get up and hurry back to the huddle."

Curry politely nodded, then asked why.

"There's a short, fat coach on this bench," Nitschke said, "who's got a real loud mouth and you shouldn't hear that kind of stuff."

Curry searched Nitschke's face for any slight tremors that might indicate he was joking. There wasn't any. Nitschke was staring him straight in the eye, and his voice was flat and calm.

"I don't want you exposed to that kind of filth," Nitschke said.

On another occasion, Nitschke was sidelined for a game against the Detroit Lions in the 1965 regular season. Lee Roy Caffey, who started at right outside linebacker, was moved to the middle in Nitschke's absence. The Lions took immediate advantage of Caffey's inexperience at his new position and scored three touchdowns to take a 21–3 lead at halftime. As players and coaches filed toward the locker rooms at the break, some of the Packers heard Lions' defensive tackle Alex Karras taunting Lombardi.

"Hey, how you like that, ya fat wop!"

In the Green Bay dressing room, while Lombardi calmly went over subtle changes in strategy for his offense, Nitschke visited a despondent Caffey. "Now Lee Roy," Nitschke said quietly, "here's what you did wrong." Nitschke proceeded to give Caffey a crash course in the art of middle linebacking. Nitschke's reassuring talk perked Caffey up; he played a solid second half, helping Green Bay shut Detroit out the rest of the way in an eventual 31–21 win.

The Lions and Bears were two teams who figured to challenge the Packers in 1966, but the biggest challenge came from the Baltimore Colts. NFL schedule-makers had indulged their sense of drama by rematching the Western Conference playoff participants from 1965 in the '66 regular season opener. The game was played Saturday night, September 10, before a crowd of 48,650 at County Stadium in Milwaukee. Because of the controversy stemming from their last meeting, the Colts–Packers game was set up to kick off the NFL season. It was also one of the most anticipated season-openers of the 1960s.

The Colts had waited all winter and summer for another shot at the Packers, and no one on the team was more ready than Unitas, who had missed the playoff game because of an injury. "This time," he said, "I was going to be able to play."

Just as Unitas was eager to take on the Green Bay defense, Nitschke was looking forward to going up against the man many still consider the greatest quarterback of all time. Like the Colts, Nitschke had been waiting all summer for the rematch. He had grown tired of Baltimore fans chirping that their team had been robbed of the conference title. To Nitschke, the '66 season opener provided an opportunity for the Packers to show that not only could they beat the Colts, they could beat them with their All-Pro quarterback on the field.

Nitschke had played against other great quarterbacks in his career— Norm Van Brocklin, Y. A. Tittle, Sonny Jurgensen—but to him, Unitas was the best. His ability to call the right plays, his poise, the way he coordinated the Colts passing attack allowed him to take control of a game. Unitas could pick a defense apart, and he could wear defenders out by consistently coming up with the right play in crucial situations. Nitschke knew that if the defense made even one mistake, Unitas would make them pay for it. Nitschke also knew that because of Unitas's poise, the game was never really over as long as he had the ball in his hand.

Nitschke thought that the coordination between Unitas and his primary receiver, Raymond Berry, was hard to believe at times. Unitas-to-Berry had been pro football's most famous pass-catch combination since 1958, and their execution of the sideline pattern was nearly perfect.

Green Bay defensive coordinator Phil Bengston game-planned the Colt offense with a design to break down the precision timing between Unitas and his receivers. The early minutes of the season opener saw Unitas having success against Nitschke and the Packers; he guided Baltimore to a 3–0 lead. But late in the second quarter, Packer planning paid off. Caffey snared a Unitas pass and returned it for a score, and moments later, Jeter picked off another pass and ran it in from 46 yards out for a touchdown and a 14–3 lead at the break.

Nitschke and the Packer defense shut Unitas down the rest of the way, and Green Bay won 24–3. The Packers ran their record to 4–0 before losing 21–20 in San Francisco, then won eight of their final nine games to finish 12–2 and clinch their second straight Western Conference title. Along the way, they had defeated Chicago twice, including a November 20 meeting made memorable by the fierce hitting on both sides. The game marked the 96th meeting between the midwest rivals, and the matchups quickened the pulse of NFL fans—Nitschke against halfback Gale Sayers; Jim Taylor against middle linebacker Dick Butkus. Sayers and Butkus were second-year stars, and they impressed Nitschke and the rest of Green Bay's veteran squad. Lombardi said Sayers might have been the best "pure" runner he had ever seen, and Nitschke looked on Sayers as the finest instinctive runner he had ever played against. Nitschke compared Sayers' running style to that of a rabbit; he had a rabbit's quickness and ability to change pace. Watching film of Sayers left Nitschke wondering at times how it was humanly possible for Gale to make a certain move. "How can the guy do those things?" Nitschke would ask himself. As great as Sayers was, Nitschke knew it was impossible for one man alone to stop him. The Packers learned that the first time they met Sayers in '65. Green Bay had taken an aggressive approach, and paid for it when Sayers gained ground on cutbacks against the pursuit. At the time, the game against the Packers was just Sayers' second start in the NFL, and he was given a quick introduction to the Green Bay defense. On a sweep to the right, Sayers saw Nitschke and left end Willie Davis shedding blockers and pounding across the Lambeau Field turf after him. The double hit lifted Sayers off the ground, and as the trio landed, Nitschke had hold of Sayers' left leg, and Davis had the right. "Okay, Ray," Sayers heard Davis say, "make a wish, baby."

Trailing 20–0 in the third quarter, Sayers scored the first of his two touchdowns that day when films show him heading off-tackle from the Green Bay 6-yard line. He saw the hole plugged, then slid wide laterally across the line, lowered his helmet, and dragged four defenders into the end zone for the score. Later, Sayers curled inside of Caffey on a pass play, took a pass from quarterback Rudy Bukich, and ran 65 yards untouched for the score. It was one of five catches Sayers made that day, and he finished with 80 yards on 17 carries in a 23–14 loss.

In the rematch at Wrigley Field, a 31–10 Bears victory, Sayers gained 62 yards on 16 carries, and scored a 10-yard touchdown. In '66, the Packers blanked the Bears 17–0 in a Week Six game in Chicago, and Sayers was limited to just 19 yards rushing. Bengston had fine-tuned his defense for the Bears star, developing what he called "a moving perimeter" in which each defender was to guard a certain area whenever Sayers had the ball. To Nitschke, the idea was to keep Sayers in the middle of that moving perimeter, keep him contained until the pursuit could arrive. Nitschke was willing to give Sayers inside yardage as long as the Packers could prevent him from getting outside.

"Keep him in a moving perimeter," Bengston told his defense the week before the Bear game, and Nitschke and the Packers had responded. The second meeting was more of the same. On a cold, gray Sunday, the Packers and Bears slugged it out in the annual renewal of pro football's oldest and longest rivalry. With Lombardi and Bears patriarch George Halas watching from opposing sidelines, the Packers and Bears engaged in a contest CBS sportscaster Ray Scott described as a "raw, mean, old-fashioned football game. . . . There were no heroes, there was no glory. It was trench warfare."

From the time he had entered the NFL in 1965, Sayers had been told by Halas that the Packers were the team to beat. Before Packers–Bears games, Halas would tell Sayers, "These are the people you measure how good you are by."

Films of the game show Nitschke and the Pack defense gang-tackling Sayers, and Butkus drawing a bead on Taylor. When it was over, Sayers had been held to 68 yards on 20 carries, and Green Bay earned a hard-fought, 14–6 win.

The penultimate game of the regular season rematched the Colts and Packers in Baltimore. A drenching rain muddied the field, and late in the game the Packers were clinging to a 14–10 lead when Unitas began the type of late-game drive Nitschke had been concerned about. Forced to scramble, Unitas was slammed from behind by Davis. Nitschke arrived a split-second later, and as Davis's hit forced the ball free, left linebacker Dave Robinson recovered the fumble for Green Bay.

The Packers' 12 victories in '66 gave them their second-highest total in the Lombardi era, and they had come within four points of a perfect season. There is a debate to this day inside the organization which team was Green Bay's greatest—the '62 squad or the '66 version. The 163 points allowed by the defense in '66 ranked behind the '62 squad's total of 148 as the best in franchise history, and Bengston's unit led the NFL for the second straight year in scoring defense and for the third straight year in pass defense. Nitschke was named all-league for the third straight season, joining Davis, Herb Adderley, and Willie Wood as all-pros on the Packer defense.

If the defense provided the Packers a team personality, as Ray Scott said at the time, then it was Nitschke whose personality loomed largest. "Ray was the backbone of that defense," Ditka said, "the glue that held it all together."

Fran Tarkenton, who quarterbacked the Vikings against the Packers in '66, always felt that Nitschke was the hub of the Green Bay defense. The other Packers were afraid of Nitschke, Tarkenton said, afraid of not playing well with him looking on. Sideline cameras caught Nitschke exhorting his teammates on, and in one particular game, calling for halfback Paul Hornung to put the ball in the end zone in a goal-line situation.

"Git it in there, Paul, git in in," he yelled, and punctuated his shouts by pumping his padded right fist into the air. "Stick it in there!"

Scott called Nitschke the one player Green Bay opponents loved to hate, and opponents hated him because he was an intimidator. "He intimidated you physically," NFL Films president Steve Sabol said, "and he intimidated you mentally."

Highlights of the '66 season show Nitschke at his ball-hawking best. In Detroit, he lifted a Lions receiver off his feet with a blind-side hit, then scooped the loose ball off the turf with his huge right hand and shook it in the face of an official to indicate a fumble recovery. Nitschke could intimidate players and officials alike. Colts tight end Jim Mutscheller compared Nitschke to Butkus and to Bears' old-time defensive end Ed Sprinkle, nicknamed "The Claw" for his clothesline hits on quarterbacks, as the most intimidating players he had ever seen.

NFL referee Jim Tunney understood Nitschke's nature. To Tunney, Nitschke was cut from the same cloth as intimidators past and future like Bill George and Jack Lambert, rock-and-sock middle linebackers who knew that football was not a contact sport, it was a collision sport. And as the spearheads of their respective defenses, it was their job to knock somebody down.

"Football is a violent sport," Nitschke said, "and you can't feel too much for the other guy. That's one of the great things about it, the basic premise of man dealing with man."

Lee Remmel, the Packers' executive director of public relations, covered Nitschke's career for the *Green Bay Press-Gazette*. To him, Nitschke was an intense, all-out performer. "That certainly endeared him to our fans, who have a great respect for that," Remmel said.

Opponents respected it but didn't always like it. Ditka once recalled the Bears' 31–10 win over the Packers in 1965, when players on both sides were content to run out the clock in the game's waning moments. It's common for even the most intense players to throttle back in the final seconds when the outcome is no longer in doubt. Merlin Olsen, the great defensive tackle for the Los Angeles Rams, would extend a hand to help the opposition up;

Pittsburgh's Joe Greene, whose nickname was "Mean," would engage opposing linemen in small talk.

"What it is, brother man," Greene would say. "How's the wife?"

Nitschke, however, refused to accept defeat and even on the last play of a losing effort against Chicago, was like a wild man, shouting at Ditka in his gravelly voice.

"Hey you, yeah you," Nitschke yelled. "I got ya! I'm gonna bite you back."

The moment impressed Ditka, who thought that everyone on the Packers was resigned to the defeat. "Everyone," he noted, "except Ray."

"I hated to play against Nitschke," wide receiver Tommy McDonald said. "You knew he was an individual who was going to give not a hundred percent but two hundred percent out there on that field. He was the number-one instigator in getting that defense to play the way that would satisfy Vince Lombardi. Ray's the type of guy that you may not want his opinion, but dad-gummit, he's going to give it to you. He talked out there, but it was a motivation-type thing, trying to get other people up, keep them up and get them going. He was a foreman on the job, and you have to have individuals like that on the field. You know, Lombardi could only go up to the little white line, so you have to have guys like Nitschke to be your focal point, you sergeant-at-arms out there on that field."

If Nitschke was the one Packer opponents hated to play against, he was also the one they game-planned the most for. Matched up against the Eastern Conference champions, the Dallas Cowboys, Nitschke became the focal point of Coach Tom Landry's offensive game plan. Led by quarterback Don Meredith, backs Don Perkins and Dan Reeves, and game-breaking split end Bob Hayes, the Cowboys featured a flashy I-formation offense that had rolled up an NFL-best 445 points in 1966. When the Dallas offense gathered to discuss the Green Bay defense, the first question they addressed was, "How do we handle Nitschke?" It was the same question offenses would ask in future years as they game-planned for a Joe Greene, a Lawrence Taylor.

"Any time we played the Packers, our number-one priority was blocking Ray Nitschke," Cowboy tackle Ralph Neely said. "We knew if we were going to be successful, we had to block Nitschke."

Because the Packers shielded blockers away from Nitschke so well, Reeves said it was difficult to find ways to reach him. "They did a great job of keeping people off of him and allowing him to get to the football," he said. "He could make tackles from one side to the other. He was a great football player in a great scheme.

"You had to account for him, you had to have someone assigned to him. They had a lot of good football players but he was the key to their defense, he was in control of everything. He was the guy that knew formations, he was the guy that got everybody in the right position, where to be, what the coverage was, and what defense they were playing. He was not only a tough guy, he was an extremely bright football player. You could see that when you were competing against him. You weren't going to be successful against Green Bay if you didn't account for Ray."

Guided by Landry and triggered by Meredith, the Cowboy offense was the most complex in the NFL. "We had 18 to 20 formations," Neely said, "and 18 to 20 plays out of each formation." This at a time when most NFL offenses used just six formations. The Cowboys also employed a variety of blocking combinations, and varied their technique on each.

The Packers' philosophy for dealing with Landry's multiple offense was to remain as basic as possible. Football is blocking and tackling, Lombardi said, and the team that blocks and tackles the best will win. In preparation for the Cowboys, Bengston kept his defensive plan simple and relied on fundamentals and execution so his players would have confidence in what they were doing. Each player was given the freedom to make small adjustments that he deemed necessary, but the basic Packer plan for the '66 title game was to hold their ground against the Cowboys' shifting formations and bracket the explosive Hayes short and long with Adderley and safety Tom Brown.

Nitschke said that by 1966 it had become harder to prepare a defense for Dallas than for any other team in the league. Landry was a fine coach, and Nitschke knew there was more to the man than the stoic image he portrayed on the sideline every Sunday. On one occasion, Landry had driven to the Cowboys' practice facility amid a morning rain only to find his parking spot occupied by rookie linebacker Steve Kiner. When Landry entered the locker room several minutes later soaking wet, he walked over to where Kiner was sitting and said, "I admire a man with courage."

Because of the high number of offensive sets Landry's Cowboys used, defenders not only had to be able to recognize each set but also be in the right place to stop them. Nitschke thought that while Landry didn't expect to beat defenses with formations alone, he did want to create a moment of doubt, a moment of confusion in the defense. Once that happened, Nitschke said, the situation would snowball.

"It was a good test," Nitschke recalled years later. "That was a well-coached Landry team. They had it all. But we were prepared for anything they did. Bengston was a real perfectionist, just like Lombardi. He ran the defense and Lombardi ran the offense, but Phil never got the credit he deserved. He kept it simple for us.

"We knew Dallas was going to have to line up somewhere eventually, and what we had to do was line up in the right place and execute. We had a

lot of experience on our defense, so we weren't going to get rattled by anything."

"We emphasized the basics," Bengston recalled once. "I always empha-sized that it's not the plays, it's the players."

Amid near-perfect temperatures in the Cotton Bowl in Dallas on New Year's Day 1967, the Packers and Cowboys took the field for the late-after-noon kickoff. The NFL title game was the second half of a Sunday double-header featuring the AFL and NFL championship games. Earlier in the day, the Kansas City Chiefs had beaten the two-time defending AFL champion Buffalo Bills, 31–7, in the frozen mud of Buffalo's War Memorial Stadium. The victory advanced the powerful Chiefs, who featured the AFL's best record, to the first AFL–NFL World Championship Game, scheduled for Jan-uary 15 in the Los Angeles Coliseum.

A trip to the Super Bowl awaited the winner of the Green Bay–Dallas game, and the Packers sprinted to an early lead on a 17-yard touchdown pass from Bart Starr to halfback Elijah Pitts, and Jim Grabowski's 17-yard score on a fumble return on the ensuing kickoff.

Privately, some of the Packers thought the game was going to be a rout. Especially the members of their defensive unit, like Adderley, who said that whenever Green Bay got the lead in a championship game, they did what Lombardi asked them to do. Which, Adderley said, was to rise to the occa-sion and shut the opponent out.

The Cowboys, however, came back, and showed why they were one of the exciting young teams in pro football. Perkins picked up huge gains out of the Cowboys' shifting sets, and the Packer defense was suddenly on its heels. Reeves scored from three yards out, and Perkins capped the Cow-boys' next drive with a 17-yard scoring burst that tied the game at 14. A review of the play shows Nitschke being faked out of position by Reeves, who ran right on a simulated sweep. Nitschke followed and was caught flat-footed when Perkins took Meredith's handoff on a counter and exploded through a wide-open gap in the Green Bay line.

To Adderley, the source of Dallas's success was simple. The Cowboys were running traps and misdirections inside, confusing Nitschke with false keys and reads. "And when you get the middle linebacker confused and going the wrong way," Adderley said, "that makes it real tough on the defensive backs to come up and make the play."

Sideline cameras show Nitschke and the defense looking stunned. They had given up 14 points in the first 15 minutes, more points than they had allowed in a championship or playoff game since the 1960 loss in Philadel-phia. Landry had added formations Nitschke and the Packers hadn't seen before. Green Bay was being caught off-guard by the new plays and was trying to read and react on the run. From his middle linebacker position, Nitschke could see what the Cowboys were doing. Landry was running Perkins out of the I-formation on quick openers and cross bucks against the flow of the play.

"That was all Coach Landry," Reeves remembered. "He and Coach Lombardi had coached on the same staff in New York and they kind of knew how their defenses were constructed, how their offenses were constructed. They were playing a chess match.

"Landry's theory on beating any defense was to use a lot of mis-direction, a lot of formations so that people didn't know exactly where you were coming from. We weren't the type of team like the Packers, where they said, 'Okay, here comes the sweep. Try and stop us.' We used more formations and misdirections trying to counter those things."

On the sidelines, Lombardi sought out Bengston. "Hey, Phil," he shouted. "Shake up those linebackers!"

Nitschke and the defense were already shaken, and they came off the field in an angry, agitated state. Seeing this, offensive guard Fuzzy Thurston ran over to calm them down.

"Hey, don't worry about it," Thurston told them. "We'll get it back. Don't worry about it."

Green Bay did get it back, Starr connecting with Carroll Dale on a 51-yard TD pass. Lombardi's offensive game-planning caught the Cowboy defense off-guard. Plays that had been run from one set all season were now being run from another. Dallas's well-schooled defenders were suddenly dizzy; Green Bay's game plan left them feeling as if they were trying to watch a movie being run in reverse.

Once again the Cowboys rallied, and Dallas cut its deficit to 21–17 at halftime on an 11-yard field goal by Danny Villanueva. Nitschke knew the Packer defense had been outplayed in the first half, but he also knew they could stay in the game if they adjusted their defense to what the Cowboys were doing. All they had to do, he felt, was play the way they knew how to play, the way they had played during the regular season. The Cowboys may outcute them, Nitschke thought, but if the Packers maintained their poise, they would win.

Ironically, Green Bay's defense was aided by the Cowboys coaching staff, which decided to go away from the game plan that had been confusing the Packers—the inside traps and misdirection runs by Perkins—in favor of a passing game. Perkins had been running the ball with great success, Adderley said, but just when it seemed he was unstoppable this day, the Cowboys switched to another phase of their game plan.

The result was that after scoring 14 points in the first quarter, Dallas managed just three points in both the second and third periods. Starr, meanwhile, was having a big day passing. In the third quarter he gave Green Bay a 28–20 lead with a 16-yard scoring pass to flanker Boyd Dowler, then made it 34–20 in the fourth with a 28-yard TD pass to split end Max McGee. On a day in which the Green Bay defense and running game were not at their best, Starr proved to be the difference, decimating the Dallas secondary for 304 yards passing and four TDs.

When the Cowboys blocked Don Chandler's extra-point attempt, the Cotton Bowl came alive. Down by 14, Dallas rallied again. When Brown fell in the secondary covering tight end Frank Clarke, Meredith found the wide-open Clarke for a 68-yard score. In the game's final minutes, the Cowboys drove toward a game-tying touchdown and overtime. On the sidelines, McGee nudged a teammate and said if the Cowboys forced overtime, the Packers were in trouble. "We're dead," McGee said.

On the field, Nitschke and the Packer defense stayed patient, stayed with the game plan. Dallas drove to the 2-yard line, but just as Nitschke thought they eventually would, the Cowboy computer crossed itself up. Dallas jumped offside, a crucial penalty that cost the Cowboys five yards. It took them two plays to get back to the 2, and now it was fourth down. Since a field goal would do Dallas no good, the Packer defense dug in for the goal-line stand. As the Cotton Bowl crowd roared, Nitschke shouted to his teammates.

"We gotta hold 'em," he yelled.

In the Dallas huddle, Meredith called Fire 90, Quarterback Roll Right. It was an option roll-out by Meredith, a play the Cowboys had used with success throughout the season. At the snap, left linebacker Dave Robinson recognized the play from the films and made a hard, inside move to grab hold of Meredith. The Cowboys quarterback made an outstanding effort to get the ball away despite being draped by Robinson's 245 pounds, but he was trying to throw across his body. The result was a weak floater that hung in the night air for a few moments before settling into Tom Brown's arms in the back of the end zone.

On WTMJ Radio, Packers' announced Ted Moore called the decisive play:

The clock is running with 52 seconds remaining. If the Cowboys go in here and kick the extra point, we're going into overtime. They've got one play to travel two yards. . . . Meredith takes the ball, rolls out to the right, he's going to be nailed. . . . He gets a pass away and it's intercepted in the end zone by Tom Brown! And the Packers have just taken the championship!

The Packers won the game, 34–27, and while Caffey acknowledged that Green Bay didn't played particularly well on defense, they had won because of team togetherness. "Down there, man, it was love, pure love," Caffey said of the goal-line stand. "We knew we could stop them."

To Nitschke, who finished the game with eight tackles, the Packers had stopped Dallas because they had maintained their poise, maintained their patience. Green Bay had won its second straight NFL championship, its fourth in six years. But now, for the first time, there was one more game to be played, one more challenge to be met.

A game that, for Nitschke and the Packers, represented the most important challenge they had ever faced.

TEN

IN THE LONG history of the National Football League, it's unlikely that any team has felt as much pressure to win a game as the Green Bay Packers did in preparing for that historic first meeting between the NFL and AFL.

The two leagues had been warring since August 22, 1959, when 27-year-old Texas millionaire Lamar Hunt announced the formation of the fledgling American Football League. Like millions of other Americans, Hunt had been fascinated by the drama of the 1958 NFL championship classic between the Baltimore Colts and New York Giants, and he petitioned the NFL to purchase the struggling Chicago Cardinals franchise. Unsuccessful in his attempt, Hunt joined with a group of seven other owners—the original "Foolish Club"—to form a league that would begin play in 1960. The NFL responded to Hunt's announcement by extending to the new league an iron first gloved in velvet. While NFL commissioner Bert Bell went before a Senate sub-committee and pledged to befriend the AFL, old-guard owners like George Halas recalled the bloody financial battles with the All-America Football Conference that raged from 1946–49 and recoiled at the thought of yet another new rival. AFL plans to put a franchise in Minnesota were scuttled when the NFL wooed the Minneapolis-based investing group headed by Bill Boyer and Max Winter, who had previously been rebuffed in their attempts to join the NFL, away from the AFL with a promise to field an expansion team in Minnesota in 1961. The NFL dropped another bombshell when it announced it would expand into Dallas, where Hunt had located his team, with a club that eventually became known as the Cowboys.

To stunned AFL owners, the NFL's back-door dealings had a Yalta-like deception about them. Territory became a premium, and both leagues viewed marketable outlets as spheres of influence to win over the sporting public. The war between the leagues raged from 1960–66, growing more uncivil each year as NFL and AFL owners battled for blue-chip college players, assigned "baby-sitting" scouts to sneak sought-after senior players away from the rival league, and opened their checkbooks in an all-out signing spree. The war spread to the courtrooms, where the AFL brought an antitrust suit against the NFL, and the older league responded in turn with a court case against the young rival's signing of Louisiana All-America Billy Cannon. Some members of the AFL openly campaigned for a season-ending showdown between the champions of the two leagues, a "World Series" of pro football as *Sports Illustrated* titled it in a December 1963 issue that featured the explosive San Diego Chargers, the standard-bearers of the AFL's wide-open game, as the coverpiece of a story examining the prospects of such an encounter. New York Titans' owner Harry Wismer openly campaigned for an AFL–NFL championship game, and AFL veterans like George Blanda, who had quarterbacked the Chicago Bears before taking over in Houston and leading the Oilers to the first two AFL titles in 1960 and '61 were certain the young league could hold its own against the NFL's best.

"That first year, the Houston Oilers or Los Angeles Chargers could have beaten—repeat *beaten*—the NFL champion (Philadelphia Eagles) in a Super Bowl," Blanda said later. "I just regret we didn't get the chance to prove it."

The rebels had fired the first shot over the port bow, and Halas, who had numerous personality conflicts with Blanda in Chicago, fired back for the Establishment. "The AFL can't be anything but a Mickey Mouse league," the Bears patriarch snorted. "How can it be anything else? Isn't George Blanda a first-string quarterback over there?"

Throughout the AFL's early years, Wismer became the AFL's front-man in the push for a season-ending showdown. In 1960, he claimed the Chargers–Oilers AFL title game was "far better" than the Packers–Eagles championship. From 1960 to 1962, Wismer maintained a public persistence that the AFL's best—the Oilers and Chargers—could "easily" beat the NFL's lesser teams, the Rams, Redskins, and Cowboys, and play a "representative game" against the Packers, Eagles, and Giants.

Tex Maule, who covered the NFL for *Sports Illustrated,* scoffed at Wismer's claims of equality. He denigrated the AFL in print, claiming that not a single member of the two-time league champion Oilers could start for any of the NFL's top four teams, and only one or two Houston players could start for the weaker teams in the NFL. In words that left the AFL seething, Maule compared the Oilers to a semi-pro team, one step ahead of the college boys.

"The question," Maule wrote, "is 'How good are the Oilers?' Unquestionably, they are better than Missouri or Minnesota or Mississippi. They are smarter and more versatile than these college teams; but they are not as good as the Dallas Cowboys, the newest and weakest team in the National Football League. The Cowboys, who are smarter and more versatile than the Oilers, would beat them, and easily."

Publicly, the AFL railed against Maule and what they perceived as his elitist opinions. Privately, however, AFL people like league commissioner

Joe Foss agreed with Maule, albeit reluctantly. Foss was hoping that AFL teams would have a few more years to gather strength before taking on the NFL. "If the NFL had paid attention to Harry's cries for a championship those first couple of years, we'd never have lived to see the day of the merger," Foss said. Shuddering at the thought of the Oilers or league champion Dallas Texans playing the Packers in 1961 or '62, Foss was blunt in his feelings about what an early Super Bowl against Green Bay would have yielded. "They'd have handed us our heads," he remarked.

Public opinion about an NFL–AFL championship game shifted at the end of the 1963 season, and the exact date can be traced to January 5, 1964. Amid balmy, 71-degree temperatures in sun-bleached Balboa Stadium, the San Diego Chargers stunned the football world with a 51–10 rout of the Boston Patriots. The Chargers' lightning attack, symbolized by the jagged bolts that adorned their helmets and uniforms, was electrifying. Head coach Sid Gillman had amassed an offensive armada—wide receiver Lance Alworth, quarterbacks Tobin Rote and John Hadl, backs Keith Lincoln and Paul Lowe, tackle Ron Mix, guard Walt Sweeney—and turned them loose with a state-of-the-art passing game that became the forerunner of the West Coast offense.

No one had seen anything quite like it before. San Diego's attack was based on the big play, and it emphasized explosive quickness. The running game featured quick traps and toss sweeps, the passing game was all precision routes aimed at gaining separation from befuddled defenders. Gillman's game plans were so innovative that even NFL people like former Cleveland Browns quarterback Otto Graham were impressed with "El Sid" and his high-tech offense.

"If the Chargers could play the best in the NFL," Graham said in '63, "I'd have to pick the Chargers."

San Diego became the first AFL club to invite serious comparisons with the NFL's top teams, but when Buffalo physically dominated the Chargers in the 1964 AFL championship game, Bills fans in old War Memorial Stadium held op a sign that read, "Bring on the NFL." Through the winter of '64 and '65, hot-stove debates on the merits of the two leagues intensified. Outside the Buffalo Rust Belt, the AFL was basketball on stripes, finesse football played on fast tracks amid soft sunshine. The NFL was old-fashioned football, power backs sweeping the flanks behind pulling guards under darkening, snow-filled clouds.

When the NFL–AFL war began raging out of control in 1966, cooler heads realized that the escalating cost of signing free agents threatened to bankrupt owners in both leagues. Just as the AFL launched an all-out raiding of NFL rosters to sign star quarterbacks, NFL Commissioner Pete Rozelle joined with AFL founder Lamar Hunt on June 8, 1966, to announce a merger of the two leagues. A yearly championship game would be played, and while Hunt coined the term "Super Bowl" after the "Super Ball" that his young daughter Sharon was playing with, the long-awaited first meeting between the two leagues was officially titled the "AFL–NFL World Championship Game."

Fittingly, it was Hunt's team, the Kansas City Chiefs, that would represent the rebels in this historic game. Utilizing an I-formation offense complete with multiple shifts, "moving pockets," and double tight end alignments, the Chiefs were following in the footsteps of the Chargers as practitioners of flashy, AFL-style football. Kansas City head coach Hank Stram succeeded Gillman as the league's most innovative coach. Just as Gillman had attracted attention by appearing professorial on the sidelines with his pipe, buttoned-up collar and bowtie, the short, stocky Stram was easily distinguishable in his black blazer, bright red vest and gray checked pants.

To Stram, a football team should reflect the personality of its coach. Since Stram thought of himself as a varied man, he liked to express himself through the abilities of his players. He liked the idea of seeing himself in the Chiefs' stack defense, tight-I offense, and rolling pocket. The Chiefs had 18 different offensive sets and could run 350 plays off of those sets.

"We present the same face with different makeup each play," Stram said, "and I'm a good makeup man with an excellent makeup kit."

If Stram's Chiefs were fitting representatives of the break-the-mold AFL, the Packers were perfect standard-bearers for the establishment. Green Bay was one of the old guard's original franchises and the last of the town teams that had made up the early NFL. Just as Stram's varied personality was reflected in the Chiefs' strategic variations, the Packers' tough, disciplined approach had been drilled into them by Lombardi, the inspirational leader who had built them into a hard-hitting, precision machine.

"They were pure vanilla," Stram remembered. "No nuts, no chocolate, just plain vanilla. Preparing for that game was so simple it was amazing. We saw everything in the AFL, and here we were, preparing for a team that defensively used one just one alignment and one coverage. It was unbelievable, but they were good enough to get by with it."

Nitschke recognized from the start that there was more to this game than any other he had ever played in. He had followed the Bears when they had Nagurski and Luckman; he knew the NFL's tradition. He also knew that tradition would be on the line when the Packers took the field against the upstart Chiefs. The hype surrounding the game grew, and the Packers felt it. Nitschke and his teammates were reminded daily of the Chiefs' great physical size and strength, were reminded too of the awesome responsibility they had in representing the NFL in this game. It wasn't only Packer prestige that was on the line against Kansas City, Lombardi told his team; the whole NFL was on the line as well. In the two weeks before the game, the Packers received phone calls or telegrams from every one of the NFL's owners impressing upon them the importance of beating the AFL. Lombardi trembled as he read the team telegrams from Halas and Giants owner Wellington Mara urging the Packers to victory, and the Green Bay boss grew increasingly anxious as the publicity buildup began in earnest. When a photographer from a national magazine called to ask if he could photograph him praying in church, Lombardi, the devout Catholic, ran out of patience. "No way," he shouted into the phone at the man.

To Nitschke, the game was being blown out of proportion. He knew the Chiefs must have a pretty good team. But he didn't feel they were in the Packers' class. Green Bay had already beaten Baltimore, Cleveland, and Dallas during the regular season, so why couldn't they beat the Chiefs, he wondered. Two weeks of film study did little to change Nitschke's opinion of the AFL champions. Defensive coordinator Phil Bengston broke down the Chiefs' offense, which mirrored Dallas in many ways. Like the Cowboys, the Chiefs looked to confuse defenses with shifting I-formation sets that disguised their formation until the last second. Against the Bills in the AFL championship game, the Chiefs had used 12 variations of the I-formation alone. The Packers, however, weren't overly concerned with K.C.'s pre-snap shifts and movement.

"We had an exchange of films with the Chiefs and we went about our normal preparation," Bengston recalled once. "The Chiefs had some fine personnel and they were well-prepared, but preparing for their style of offense wasn't that difficult. Dallas used more formations than the Chiefs did."

What was difficult was judging just how good the Chiefs were. Since the Packers had never played against AFL teams, they had trouble gauging the quality of Kansas City's competition. The Packers had seen Chiefs quarterback Len Dawson when he played in the NFL with Pittsburgh and Cleveland. But Otis Taylor? Mike Garrett? Buck Buchanan? Clearly they were talented enough to play in the NFL, but just how talented would remain a mystery until game time.

"It was real difficult," Nitschke said once about preparing for the Chiefs. "We didn't know how good their opponents were, so it was pretty hard to judge them. I know that was a big concern for Coach Lombardi."

The Chiefs were slick, quick, and knew how to trick, and Bengston alleviated concerns among his players by devising a defensive game plan that was not much different than what the Packers had used all year. Green Bay wasn't overly concerned with Kansas City's multiple formations or "moving pocket," which featured Dawson rolling left or right behind a wall of blockers. Bengston was concerned, however, with the Chiefs' play-action game, which if successful could freeze Nitschke and the Green Bay linebackers in place. Film study revealed that the Chiefs' play-action style was vulnerable to a linebacker blitz, but Bengston advised Lombardi he wouldn't call for a blitz during the first half. The idea was to build up in Dawson a false sense of security, and to save the surprise of the blitz until a critical moment presented itself.

While the Packers went quietly about their business, Kansas City cornerback Fred Williamson held court for reporters. Nicknamed "The Hammer," for the tremendous forearm blows he used to floor AFL receivers, Williamson was a big, physical cornerback who had knocked Buffalo receiver Glenn Bass out of a game with a high hit. Williamson padded his forearms and described his clotheslinelike hits to a *New York Times* reporter as "a karate blow having great velocity and delivered perpendicular to the earth's latitude." To teammates, he described it as "a lethal muthah," and promised to level it on the NFL champions.

"The Packers, sheeit, Taylor, sheeit, Lombardi, sheeit," Williamson said. "We're going to whip their asses, all of them, and if Boyd Dowler and Carroll Dale or any of those other guys have the nerve to catch a pass in my territory they're going to pay the price, man."

Starr said the Packers were more amused than riled up by Williamson's tough talk. "You accept people for what they are," Starr remarked. "We took it in stride."

Super Sunday dawned sunny and bright over the greater Los Angeles area. By game time, a thin layer of California smog hung over the Los Angeles Coliseum, which was only two-thirds full for the game. League allegiances were vividly on display throughout the stadium. The game was being broadcast by both CBS, which covered the NFL, and NBC, which had been broadcasting the AFL since 1964. Ray Scott and Frank Gifford were the lead announcers for CBS; Curt Gowdy and Paul Christman for NBC. Viewers found league loyalties on display in the commercial slots as well. CBS viewers were treated to a steady diet of Ford automotive commercials; NBC viewers to Chrysler ads. The Packers and Chiefs were not only represented by their own networks and corporate sponsors, they were also using their own footballs as well. When Green Bay was on offense, the Packers used the NFL ball "The Duke." When Kansas City went on offense, the Chiefs used the Spalding J5-V, which was longer and thinner than "The Duke" and was said to be easier to throw.

"Is it easier to intercept too?" Lombardi quipped to reporters before the game, and went on to compare the AFL ball's shape to "a Long Island frankfurter."

As the Chiefs massed in the tunnel before taking the painted Coliseum field, some Kansas City players suddenly realized what they were up against. The AFL had never produced a fullback with the ferocity of Jim Taylor, a middle linebacker as violent and well-schooled as Nitschke. Chiefs linebacker E. J. Holub looked around and saw some of his teammates had wet their pants and were throwing up.

Finally, after seven years of a war that had been fought in the courtrooms and newspapers, the champions of the two leagues were on the same field. It was strange for viewers to see the Packers in their green-and-gold going against the Chiefs in their road white uniforms with the bright red and yellow trim. Strange for the two teams as well, and they spent the opening minutes of the game probing one another to find strengths and weaknesses.

After Green Bay's initial series ended in a Don Chandler punt, Kansas City went on offense for the first time. With the ball resting on the Chiefs' 37-yard line, Dawson approached the line of scrimmage, and the first Packer defender he laid eyes on was Nitschke.

With his cheekbones streaked with black shoe polish to cut the sun's glare, with his craggy face covered by his half-cage facemask, Nitschke stared back at the Chief quarterback and began barking out defensive signals. Dawson saw the Packer middle linebacker shifting back and forth, saw what he believed to be foam coming out of Nitschke's mouth as he shouted signals in that loud, raucous voice, and thought to himself, "This is the meanest, ugliest man I have ever seen."

Both teams gained one first down on their initial series, and then the Packers struck. Facing a third-and-three from the Kansas City 37-yard line with 6:04 left in the first quarter, Starr beat a linebacker blitz by connecting with split end Max McGee on a quick post for the first score in Super Bowl history. McGee had entered the game for Boyd Dowler, who had reinjured his left shoulder on the third play of the game, and the 34-year-old veteran turned in a circus catch by reaching back for the ball and making a one-handed grab en route to the gold-painted end zone.

Nitschke made his presence felt on the first play of the Chiefs' next series, when he stopped a scrambling Dawson after a 7-yard gain. On NBC Radio, play-by-play sportscaster Jim Simpson made the call on Nitschke's first stop in the Super Bowl:

Two minutes and 55 seconds to go in this, the first quarter of the AFL–NFL championship, the Super Bowl, from the Coliseum in Los Angeles under sunny skies, little or no wind. . . . It is second down and inches to go for Kansas City. Burford goes out as a flanker to the left, I-formation now, and Garrett steps over to the right. . . . Dawson is back to pass, lots of time, now in trouble, looking gets past one man and has his own first down across the 40-yard line and is driven back across the 41. Dawson, looking for running room, did get enough for the first down, and Ray Nitschke, the middle linebacker, came up very quickly and threw him back across the 40.

Five plays later, Nitschke dragged Dawson down again, this time on a two-yard pickup, then dropped end Reg Carolan four yards short of a first down on a third-and-11 play at the Green Bay 33. Nitschke's tackle forced the Chiefs into a 40-yard field goal attempt, and Mike Mercer's kick sailed wide right with 34 seconds remaining in the first quarter.

The AFL champions got on the board early in the second quarter. Employing the play-action passing game that had caused Bengston concern, the Chiefs drove 66 yards in six plays. Dawson capped the march with a 7-yard scoring pass to fullback Curtis McClinton and Mercer's kick tied the game 7–7.

Nitschke grew angry on the point-after attempt when a Kansas City player gave him the elbow on Mercer's kick. Nitschke's anger wasn't with the Chiefs player but with himself. Nitschke had used his elbows on opposing players during the regular season, but since most PAT attempts are automatic, NFL players rarely went all-out during the kick. That the Chiefs player had elbowed Nitschke on the PAT indicated to the Packer veteran that the AFL champs had come to play, and it made him mad that he was the one getting hit and not doing the hitting.

The Packers responded to Kansas City's score with a drive that Bengston said later could have come straight out of a 1962 newsreel. After an illegal procedure penalty nullified Starr's 64-yard touchdown pass to Carroll Dale, the Green Bay quarterback began picking the Kansas City secondary apart with an assortment of short and medium-range passes. On third-and-five, Starr found McGee for 10 yards. On third-and-10, he hit Dale for 15. On third-and-five, he connected with tight end Marv Fleming for 11. On third-and-seven, Starr passed to halfback Elijah Pitts for 20. The play carried to the Kansas City 14, and Taylor followed by sweeping left behind pulling guards Jerry Kramer and Fuzzy Thurston and dragging two Chief defenders into the end zone for a 14–7 lead.

Surprising the Packers with their ability to counterpunch, Kansas City answered Green Bay's scoring drive with one of their own. Dawson was holding Nitschke and the linebackers in check with his play-action fakes to Garrett and McClinton, and buying time on passing downs by rolling out in the floating pocket. On second down, Nitschke hauled down tight end Fred Arbanas following a 12-yard gain, and two plays later stopped Garrett following a two-yard run up the middle. With time running out in the half, Mercer's 31-yard field goal with 54 seconds to play brought the Chiefs to within 14–10 at halftime, and brought nervous looks from both the Packers and NFL partisans during the break.

Buddy Young, an NFL man, told press box companions, "Old age and heat will get the Packers in the second half." AFL writers, who had feared a Green Bay blowout, found themselves smiling at the sight of Tex Maule fidgeting nervously at the half.

"Tex was very worried," recalled Jerry Magee, who covered the AFL for the *San Diego Tribune*. "He kept stalking up and down in the press box."

Nitschke was worried as well. He had realized early in the game that despite their great physical size, the Chiefs' offense was a finesse unit. Whether it was following the movements of Dawson's moving pocket or the darting, waterbug runs of Garrett, Nitschke could see that the Chiefs were another team like the Cowboys, a team that tried to outcute the defense rather than outhit them.

Leading by just four points at the half didn't fill the Packers with a lot of pride or confidence. In the Green Bay locker room, someone had written the words *Know Thyself* on the chalkboard. Gathering his team around him, Lombardi let loose with a few choice words.

"Hey, you guys better wake up," he snapped. "The game will be over and you'll be on the short end. What the hell's going on out there?"

Nitschke listened as Lombardi told his players that they were not only representing themselves but every player in the National Football League. Looking hard at his veteran team, Lombardi left them with one final thought.

"Are you the world champion Green Bay Packers?" he asked. "Go out on the field and give me your answer."

Reemerging into the sunshine for the second half, Nitschke knew he had played the first half uptight. The pressure of the game was thick enough to slice; he had felt it and played conservatively. If the Packers could get back to playing football the way they knew how, Nitschke was confident they could put the game away. As tight as Green Bay was, the Chiefs were wound just as tight. Garrett remembered the team being uncommonly tired at halftime. The combination of the game's emotional buildup as well as the grueling two weeks of practice were taking a toll. "We were on dead legs in the second half," Garrett remembered.

Four plays into the Chiefs' first series of the third quarter, Green Bay got the break it was looking for. With Kansas City facing a third-and-five from its own 49, Bengston signaled in the first blitz of the game. The Chiefs' tendency chart on Green Bay indicated that the Packers had blitzed only five percent of the time—three times in two years to be exact—in third-and-five situations. Bengston crossed up Kansas City with a surprise linebacker blitz, sending Dave Robinson and Lee Roy Caffey shooting in from the corners. Right tackle Henry Jordan provided an extra push up the middle, and when Jordan tipped Dawson's passing arm, the pass intended for Arbanas fluttered weakly. Free safety Willie Wood stepped in front of Arbanas at the Green Bay 45 and returned it 50 yards before Garrett dragged him down from behind at the Kansas City 5-yard line. One play later, Pitts took Starr's handoff and plunged in off the left side, and the Packers' lead was pushed to 21–10.

Wood's interception proved to be the turning point in the game. Starr launched two more time-consuming scoring drives, and the Packers scored on a 13-yard pass to McGee, who made a juggling catch in the end zone late in the third quarter, and a 1-yard run by Pitts, again off the left side behind tackle Bob Skoronski. On the sideline, Nitschke found irony in the performance by McGee, who had a game-high seven catches after finishing the entire regular season with just four receptions.

"Way to go, McGoo," Nitschke said, calling McGee by his nickname.

Leading 35–10, the Packers took care of one final bit of unfinished business. Running the power sweep to Williamson's side, Green Bay watched as the Kansas City cornerback barreled low into pulling guard Gale Gillingham and halfback Donny Anderson, caught Gillingham's knee flush on the helmet, and was knocked cold. As the Chiefs carried the prone Williamson off the field on a stretcher, the Packer sideline reverberated with calls of "The Hammer got it!" Thurston whistled the tune, "If I had a hammer . . . "

Nitschke, who had five first-half tackles, registered two more in the second, including a 7-yard sack of backup quarterback Pete Beathard on the Chiefs' final series. When the final gun sounded, Green Bay had given the NFL a convincing 35–10 win over the AFL, and a grass-stained Nitschke walked off the field with seven tackles and an appreciation for AFL-style football.

"We came away with a lot of respect for Kansas City," he remembered. "They were a quality team with a lot of talent."

Amid the joyous Green Bay locker room, Lombardi stood holding a game ball in his hard hands. "An NFL ball," he joked to reporters. At first, he refused to be drawn into comparing the Chiefs to NFL teams. "I have nothing to say about it," he said. Finally, he relented.

"That's a good football team," he said of Kansas City. "But it is not as good as the top teams in our league." He paused. "That's what you wanted me to say, and now I've said it. It took me a long time to get that out."

Later, Lombardi deeply regretted the remark. "I came off as an ungracious winner," he told a friend, "and it was lousy."

Not far from where Lombardi was holding court for the media, Starr stood at his locker talking with reporters. He had been named the game's Most Valuable Player after completing 16 of 23 passes for 250 yards and two touchdowns. Starr had picked apart the AFL's best defense with his heady play-calling and precise passing. He converted 11 of 15 third-down plays and six of seven third-down passes, lending weight to his reputation as the best clutch quarterback of his era. He had come a long way from the unheralded, 17th-round draft pick who had joined the Packers in 1956, two seasons before Nitschke. Starr was entering his third season when Nitschke joined the team in 1958, but the Alabama native was so quiet and unassuming that Nitschke soon realized that no one on the team was paying any attention to Starr. It didn't seem likely, Nitschke thought at the time, that Starr had much of a future in the NFL.

It was an opinion shared by Lombardi, who took over the Packers in 1959. He immediately identified the quarterback position as one of Green Bay's glaring weaknesses, and even after Starr had helped guide the Packers to the 1960 Western Conference championship and title game appearance against Philadelphia, Lombardi spent the off-season trying to engineer a trade for Dallas rookie quarterback Don Meredith.

"Some guys see them and some don't," Lombardi grumbled after Starr missed a wide-open receiver in the Packers' 17–13 loss to the Eagles. "I'd like to get that guy, Meredith."

Lombardi offered Dallas head coach Tom Landry any two players on the Packers' roster for Meredith. Landry refused, and beginning in 1961, Starr's emergence as the leader of Lombardi's offense paralleled Nitschke's rise as the leader of Bengston's defense.

As different as they were in background and personality—Starr, the soft-spoken Southern gentleman; Nitschke, the volcanic and violent Chicago street tough—they shared similarities that linked them together, on and off the field. Both had preceded Lombardi to Green Bay, and both spent the early years of their pro careers as frustrated bench-warmers. Starr wore a Green Bay uniform for 16 years, from 1956 to 1971; Nitschke's career with the Packers lasted 15 years, from 1958 to 1972. They're just two of four Packer players who have had their jersey numbers permanently retired by the club. In Packer history, Starr and Nitschke rank first and second, respectively, in years played with the team. Both were honored with special days at Lambeau Field, and Starr and Nitschke were once voted the two most recognizable faces in Wisconsin. Starr was named to the Pro Football Hall of Fame in 1977; Nitschke followed one year later. Both also had an interest in coaching. Starr was an assistant coach with the Packers in 1972 and coached the team from 1975 to 1983. Nitschke would have liked to have coached, but as he said once, "nobody ever asked."

To Packers' trainer Domenic Gentile, Starr and Nitschke symbolized the

Packers of that era. Both in their own way became extensions of Lombardi. Starr epitomized Lombardi's calculating perfectionism; Nitschke embodied his coach's fierce, competitive fire.

Like Nitschke, Starr became a student of the game, endlessly studying films for the smallest advantage. Gary Knafelc, a tight end with Green Bay from 1954 to 1962, roomed with Starr for six years on Green Bay road trips. The two spent hours reviewing different plays. Lombardi had installed an advanced passing system based on breakoff patterns and optional reads. When Starr called a play in the huddle, he wasn't calling it for one receiver; he was going to throw to the open man based on the coverage. Starr would read the defense and knew who would be open regardless of whether he was facing a blitz, man coverage, or a zone rotation. Lombardi's system required intelligence and instant recognition of defenses, not only by Starr but by Green Bay's backs and receivers as well. The Packers' passing game appeared to fans and opponents to involve basic routes, but as Dowler said, it was made to look easy by the hours of practice the players put in every June and July. In games, Green Bay's seemingly uncomplicated passing game carved up coverages, and on more than one occasion frustrated defenders would tell Dowler, "I don't know what you guys are doing. Doesn't look like you're doing anything but the ball keeps moving down the field."

"That's the way it's supposed to look," Dowler would respond. "That's the way it's planned."

It worked because the Packers were students of the game. Center Ken Bowman said that Starr's greatest asset wasn't his throwing arm, it was his brain. Halfback Paul Hornung said Starr never made mental mistakes, and the reason for that, Knafelc said, was thorough preparation. Knafelc would quiz Starr on game situations, giving him the down, the distance, the field position, and asking "What would you call?" Starr would consistently come up with the right play, and the two men repeated the process constantly. By game time, Starr was so confident in his ability to call the right play that he never got rattled, regardless of what the defense was showing him.

Like Nitschke, Starr wasn't as publicized as other players at his position, and just as Nitschke was often overlooked in favor of Joe Schmidt, Bill George, and Dick Butkus, Starr was often overshadowed by John Unitas, Sonny Jurgensen, and Y. A. Tittle. From 1960 to 1965, the Green Bay offense was geared to the twin thrusts of power backs Jim Taylor and Paul Hornung operating behind a smoothly meshing line. Critics overlooked his league passing titles in 1962 and '64 and labeled Starr a robot whose sole responsibility was to implement Lombardi's basic game plan. When the Green Bay ground attack began to slow in 1966, Starr proved his critics wrong. Throwing an NFL record-low three interceptions in 251 attempts, he led the league by completing 62 percent of his passes and averaged 9 yards per pass. In the post-season, Starr ravaged the Dallas and Kansas City pass defenses, completing 35 of 51 passes for 554 yards and six scores. He had gone from a man who had leaned on his teammates to one who could lead them. Over the course of the 1964–1965 seasons, Starr set an NFL record by throwing 294 consecutive passes without an interception, a mark that stood for two decades. He was named league MVP in 1966, and led the NFL four times in percentage of passes completed.

As with Nitschke, Starr's chance at playing regularly stemmed in part from a teammate's falling out with Lombardi. In Nitschke's case, it was starting middle linebacker Tom Bettis. For Starr, it was quarterback Lamar McHan. The turning point in Starr's career can be traced in part to Sunday, October 30, 1960. The Packers were trailing the Steelers in Pittsburgh, and Lombardi made the decision at halftime to bench McHan in favor of Starr. The Steelers had been playing an overshifted zone to the strong side, and McHan had struggled against it throughout the first half. Starr went in during the third quarter and began picking the Steelers apart. He hit Knafelc on two turn-in patterns of 15 yards each to put the Packers in scoring position. Realizing the safety was responsible for the tight end, Starr pump-faked another turn-in pattern to Knafelc to draw the safety up, then threw deep to Dowler for a 20-yard score. Green Bay won 19–13, but on the plane ride home Knafelc heard McHan say he was going to tell Lombardi off for benching him. McHan was later traded, and Starr began playing regularly.

Kramer said that while Starr was rarely the best quarterback in the league from a statistical standpoint, for three hours each Sunday Starr was almost always the best quarterback in the game he was playing.

Unitas, the quarterback to whom Starr was most often compared in the sixties, expressed his admiration for Starr's abilities. To Unitas, Starr was arguably the best short passer in the NFL. To his Packer teammates, Starr was not only a great passer, but a great leader as well. Thurston said that every time Starr stepped into the huddle, the Packer offense assumed something good was going to happen. "That's just the way he was," Thurston said, "the feeling he inspired in everybody."

Like Nitschke, Starr played hurt. During the 1961 season he played despite a painful torn stomach muscle. In 1965, he took the field against the Browns in the NFL title game with his ribs broken and corseted in tape. In 1967, a rigorous preseason schedule left Starr battered and bruised. A sprained thumb prevented him from gripping the ball properly, and a pulled thigh muscle hampered his movement dropping back. With Hornung having retired because of a pinched nerve in his neck and Taylor having played out his option and joined the expansion New Orleans Saints, the success of the Packer offense rested squarely on Starr's shoulders. Green Bay struggled to a 17–17 tie in the season opener, then beat Chicago 13–10 in Week Two. Against Atlanta the following week, Starr took a blow to his right armpit by blitzing linebacker Tommy Nobis and was sidelined. With Starr out, Green Bay's drive to the newly formed Central Division title now came down to the success or failure of its great defense.

In Week Four, Nitschke keyed a 27–17 Green Bay victory over the Lions in Detroit by returning a tipped pass 20 yards for a score. It was Nitschke's first touchdown since 1960 and came courtesy of a double blitz by Nitschke and Robinson. When Lions quarterback Milt Plum tried to beat the blitz with a short pass, Robinson jumped and tipped the ball. Nitschke hauled it on the run, and with his left leg aching, limped his way into the end zone for the game-breaking touchdown.

Nitschke's all-out effort against the Lions summed up his 1967 season. Whether it was running down Colts halfback Lenny Moore on a sweep, dropping Rams back Dick Bass in the backfield, or hitting a Browns receiver so hard he dropped a Frank Ryan pass, Nitschke was a leader who carried the rest of the defense with him.

Of all the members of Green Bay's walking wounded, Starr thought Nitschke played through more injuries than anyone. Defensive captain Willie Davis saw Nitschke's atrophied leg, saw the mass of deep purple bruises covering his lower body from hip to knee, and drew inspiration from his teammate.

"Ray was a guy who was almost oblivious to pain," Davis remembered. "I saw the guy play with almost every injury imaginable. As a middle linebacker that's almost a prerequisite, to play with some pain, because they're after you all day. Every guy along that offensive line, and the tight end, is after that middle linebacker at one time or another by assignment. And Ray paid some prices for that. He was in the hot tub probably more than the rest of us."

With Nitschke as its hobbling ringleader, Green Bay limited Chicago to just six first downs and held superstar halfback Gale Sayers to 68 yards on 20 carries in Week Two in Lambeau Field. Sayers was frustrated by a sore knee and by a defensive alignments that lined up ends Davis and Lionel Aldridge across from the Bears' tackles and slanted them inside. Green Bay tackles Henry Jordan and Ron Kostelnik also pinched in, and the result was that the scheme knocked off the Bears' pulling guards, leaving Sayers alone against Nitschke and the Packer pursuit.

Nitschke and the Packers limited the Falcons to 58 yards on 50 plays en route to a 23–0 shutout in Week Three, then earned their second shutout of the season in Week 10 with a 13–0 win over San Francisco. One week later, Sayers galloped through the Green Bay defense for a 43–yard touchdown run and 117 yards rushing, but the Packers held the Bears to 13 points, and won 17–13 to clinch the Central Division title.

Lombardi was relentless in his drive for a third straight NFL championship, and he drove himself and his team through a grueling campaign. He pounced on sloppy plays, and sideline cameras caught him in mid-rant.

"What the hell's goin' on out here?" he shouted, shoving his clenched fists deep into the pockets of his beige, camel-hair overcoat. "Everybody grabbin', nobody tacklin'. Grab. Grab. Grab. Nobody tacklin'. Put your shoulders into it out there!"

Starr's return from injury in Week Six had spurred the Packers to a 48–21 win over the Giants in New York, but plagued by injuries that wiped out their first- and second-string backfields, Green Bay limped through the final weeks of the regular season and finished 9–4–1. The Packers had won largely on the strength of their defense, a unit that saw eight of its 11 members named to various All-Pro teams in their careers.

In time, a record five members of the Green Bay defense would be voted into the Pro Football Hall of Fame, but both Bengston and his players are often overlooked when talk turns to the great defenses of all time. When the Baltimore Ravens were drawing comparisons to the great defensive units of all time during their record-breaking run to the Super Bowl in 2000, the Packers of the sixties were rarely mentioned. Unlike the "Fearsome Foursome," "Doomsday," the "Purple People Eaters," or the "Steel Curtain," Green Bay's defense was never glamorized by a gimmick nickname. But Cowboys All-Pro offensive tackle Ralph Neely, who played against the best defenses of the sixties and seventies, believes the Packers of the sixties were the best unit he ever faced. Pittsburgh and Miami had great defenses in the seventies, Neely said, but for a complete defense, from front line to linebackers to defensive backs, he ranked the Packers ahead of everyone.

Neely's point is well-taken. Some of the NFL's legendary defenses— the Rams' "Fearsome Foursome" and the Vikings' "Purple Gang"— offered great front fours but not necessarily great defenses overall. Pittsburgh featured Hall of Famers on each of the three lines of defense in tackle Joe Greene, linebackers Jack Lambert and Jack Ham, and cornerback Mel Blount. To date, the '85 Bears list two Hall of Famers on their famous unit, middle linebacker Mike Singletary and end Dan Hampton.

Of all the great years the Packers' defense put together, the '62 season was arguably their best. And in a comparison of seven of the greatest defensive seasons in NFL history, the '62 Packers ranked higher in more categories than the '48 Eagles, the '56 Giants, the '75 Steelers, the '85 Bears, the '90 Giants, and the '00 Ravens.

By 1967, Green Bay's defense was aging. Four of their starters were age 31 or older, and the media began writing them off as "old men." Battered and bloodied, the Packers fought off challengers to their throne with the grim defiance of the defenders of Bastogne. The '67 season was the year of "the big push," as Lombardi called it, and the Packers entered the Western Conference championship game heavy underdogs to the Los Angeles Rams. L.A. had rallied to beat Green Bay 27–24 in a Week 13 game in the Coliseum, and the Rams boasted afterward that they had broken the Packers' magic. The week of the playoff game, Lombardi spurred his team with bulletin-board remarks made by the Rams, and on the Tuesday before the game, gave his team a speech and a slogan.

"Everything you do this week, you run to win," Lombardi said. "On or off the field, run to win."

The words, borrowed from St. Paul, burned into Nitschke's brain, and as he ran through practice that week, he kept reminding himself, "I'm running to win." On Saturday, December 23, Nitschke and the Packers took the field in Milwaukee's County Stadium under cold, overcast skies. The Rams scored first, quarterback Roman Gabriel throwing a 29-yard touchdown pass to flanker Bernie Casey in the first quarter. L.A. threatened again, but when Robinson blocked Bruce Gossett's 24-yard field goal attempt, Green Bay grabbed the momentum.

Tom Brown's 39-yard punt return in the second quarter set up the Packers' first score, a 47-yard sprint off right tackle by halfback Travis Williams. On WTMJ Radio in Milwaukee, Packers' announcer Ted Moore provided the call on a play that ignited Green Bay's comeback:

> Starr checks the defense, the handoff goes to Travis Williams, slant over the right side, goes to the outside, he's at the 40, 35, 30, 25, 20, and he's gonna go in! Travis Williams slanted over the right tackle spot and goes 47 yards for the touchdown! And there's the 'Roadrunner' really turning on that speed. . . . The daylight was there, as Jerry Kramer, Forrest Gregg, and Marv Fleming opened the way.

Starr followed shortly thereafter with a 17-yard touchdown pass to flanker Carroll Dale. Leading 14–7 at halftime, the Packers' punishing defense took physical control of the game. Gabriel was sacked five times by Jordan, and Nitschke played a particularly reckless game. "But it was all right," he said later, "because I was running to win."

In the Packers' defensive huddles, Jordan was popping Nitschke on the shoulder pads and shouting, "Come on, let's get 'em." Nitschke was hitting the Rams so hard he was hoping to see them bounce off the thick, winter-brown turf with each hit. He hated to leave the field that day, hated to see the Green Bay offense coming off the sideline.

In the press box, Red Smith of the *New York Times* described Nitschke as "a living flame." Nitschke's competitive fire had been fanned into a burning incandescence, and even Rams head coach George Allen was impressed. Allen thought so much of Nitschke that when he was defensive coach of the Bears, he named one of his defenses the "47 Nitschke" after the way Ray played a certain situation. Allen said once that when Nitschke got wound up "he could take apart an offense all by himself." Nitschke, Allen said, seemed to go a little crazy at times; he was a wild man who was almost impossible to contain.

Wood used to tell Davis that while he could hear Nitschke hollering during the game, he couldn't understand half the time what Nitschke was hollering about. Jeter recalled Nitschke's yelling too, and remembered when the other members of the defense would have to calm him down.

"He was a very aggressive player who liked to win," Jeter said. "Once he was out there on that field, he was something else. He did a lot of talking, and sometimes we'd have to talk to him to settle him down."

The Rams had entered the game with the number-one ranked offense in the NFL, but Nitschke and the Packer defense held them to one touchdown and 75 yards rushing. When Green Bay had the ball, Nitschke crowded the sideline, hollering encouragement. He watched as Gregg and tight end Marv Fleming carried out Lombardi's game plan to neutralize Ram defensive end Deacon Jones.

"Coach Lombardi has a theory that if you beat a team at its strength you win the game," Nitschke said at the time. "So we set out to whip Deacon Jones."

The Packers had opened the game by running right at Jones, double-teaming him with blocks by Fleming and Gregg. In time, Nitschke said, Jones became so conscious of the double-team he began looking for it. The result was that he was hesitating rather than rushing into the backfield, and Gregg was beating him on his blocks. With the source of their strength taken away, the "Fearsome Foursome" was filled with confusion. The rest of the Ram defense, Nitschke thought, was wondering what had happened to Jones and why wasn't he getting to Starr? "They began to hesitate and wait," Nitschke said, "and then they were getting whipped as bad as Jones was."

Fullback Chuck Mercein's six-yard plunge on a draw play gave Green Bay a 21–7 lead in the third quarter. Starr, who completed 74 percent of his passes and threw for 222 yards, burned the Rams one final time in the fourth quarter when he found Dale for a 48-yard completion that carried to the L.A. 2-yard line. Williams blasted the final two yards for the touchdown, and Green Bay stunned the Rams with a 28–7 win.

"That was a big game," Nitschke recalled once. "The Rams had a great defense, the 'Fearsome Foursome,' and they had beaten us in the next-to-last game of the season. Before the game Lombardi quoted the Bible and told us to 'Run to win.' That was our motivation. 'Run to win.' And we ran away with the game."

Kramer said later that the Packer defense had played a fantastic game, and that Nitschke and Jordan, in particular, were incredible. Both had been left off the NFL's All-Pro defensive team, and since both Nitschke and Jordan have tremendous pride, Kramer thought they set out to prove that they were still the best in the league at their respective positions. Nitschke stopped Ram runners at the line of scrimmage, Kramer said, stopped them whether they tried to run left, right, or through the middle.

In the locker room, the team knelt to say the Lord's Prayer, and Nitschke followed by walking around, hugging and kissing his teammates. "Thank you, Jerry," he told Kramer, then turned to Gregg and remarked, "Thank you, Forrest." To no one in particular, Nitschke muttered, "I just wish the game hadn't ended."

On Christmas Eve day, the Packers settled back to watch the Cowboys beat the Browns, 52–14, in the Eastern Conference championship. That night, members of the team gathered in Nitschke's house. Jackie had invited them to stop by, and as his living room filled up Nitschke couldn't figure out why everyone was still hanging around. In time, he ran out of chairs, and teammates and their wives took to sitting on the floor. Around 9 P.M., Jackie told Ray to look out the front window. She had heard a noise, she said, and wanted Ray to see if anyone was there. When he looked out, Nitschke saw a new 1968 Lincoln Continental sitting on his front lawn. It was Jackie's Christmas present to him, and Ray was so thrilled that tears came to his eyes.

"He was like a little boy," Kramer said later. "He had to take the car out for a spin right away."

When he returned, Nitschke told Kramer that when he was small, someone had once given him a ride in a Lincoln. "Ever since then, I've dreamed of owning one," Nitschke said. "I never thought I would."

Kramer looked at Nitschke and thought he was ready to bawl. He also thought that there wasn't a running back in the NFL who would have believed that Ray Nitschke was capable of crying.

One week to the day later, Nitschke and the Packers took the field for the 1967 NFL championship game against Dallas. An overnight cold spell carried in on Canadian winds had plummeted temperatures in Green Bay from 20 degrees Fahrenheit late Saturday afternoon to minus-13 at kickoff. Winds clocked at 15 miles per hours dropped the wind-chill temperature to minus-38. The mass of arctic air caused Lambeau Field to flash-freeze, turning the stadium turf as hard and slick as glazed pavement.

Years later, Nitschke recalled the Packers' intensity on that New Year's Eve afternoon, at that time the coldest day in the long, cold history of Green Bay.

"The elements? That's all part of the mental toughness that Lombardi always talked about," he said, "When you go out there, you go out there with the idea of winning. We knew we were kind of at the end. We were getting older, and some of the guys, like Taylor and Hornung, weren't around anymore.

"But that particular team and that particular year, we committed ourselves to winning that third championship in a row. That's something no one else has ever done. We knew we were playing against a young, strong Cowboys team, but when we went out there, we went out there with that idea that we were going to win. We believed that."

Running onto the field, Nitschke was struck less by the frozen field than by the frozen fans, a standing room only crowd of 50,861 who ignored the sub-zero temperatures and rocked the historic stadium with their cheers. Squinting through the bright sun, Nitschke scanned the stands and realized he could barely see any faces. Thousands of fans, seeking protecting from the dangerous cold, had covered every inch of exposed skin, layering themselves with hats, coats, jackets, and blankets. As Bengston gathered his defensive team around him for last-minute instructions, he was struck by the red halo surrounding the field. In September, the coloration of the stands at Lambeau was usually white and light, reflecting the late summer clothing of the fans. By October, Lambeau took on the look of late autumn, muted browns and oranges of men's jackets and hats and women's coats and scarves. On the day of the Ice Bowl, the stands took on a bright reddish-orange tinge thanks to the thousands of hunting jackets, lap robes, and helmet-masks worn by fans.

When the Cowboys scanned the stands, they were struck by a large sign that read "Cold enough for you?" A few Dallas players silently cursed Lombardi, whom they thought had deliberately turned off his famous underground heating unit that was supposed to keep Lambeau field soft and playable in wintry conditions. The underground blanket of heating coils had been working all morning, but when stadium workers removed the tarpaulin covering the field, the moisture generated by the heat froze instantly when exposed to the intense cold. As the Cowboys grimly searched for some semblance of footing in the pregame "warm-ups," they became aware of an overwhelming smell of peppermint schnapps. Looking up, Ralph Neely saw fans swigging from small metal flasks. "Wish I had some," he thought.

Across the ice-slick field, Nitschke looked up in the stands, saw the clouds of condensed air pouring forth from thousands of faces, and thought the least the Packers could do was win the game for them and send them off to the pneumonia ward happy.

More acclimated to cold-weather games than the Cowboys, Green Bay jumped to a 14–0 lead in the second quarter. The first time the Packers had the ball, Starr engineered a 16-play, 82-yard drive that ended with an 8-yard touchdown pass to Dowler. In the second quarter, Starr outfoxed the Doomsday defense by drawing them in on a play-action fake and lofting a 46-yard scoring strike to Dowler.

Blaring horns trumpeted the Packers' 14–0 lead, but the Cowboys came back late in the half to score 10 points on two Green Bay turnovers. Defensive end George Andrie's recovery of a Starr fumble and 7-yard return for a score halved the Dallas deficit, and Willie Wood's fumble of a Cowboy punt led to Danny Villanueva's 21-yard field goal. As the halftime gun sounded, the brittle air over Lambeau Field was filled less with the cheers of Packer fans than the rumble of hollow-throated gas heaters that were blowing into the tarpaulins that formed makeshift shelters on both sidelines.

The game had settled into a grim defensive struggle, and Nitschke, who had five tackles in the first half, felt that on this day, the Packers' four-point lead might be enough to pull out the win.

Green Bay maintained its slim lead through a scoreless third quarter, and by the start of the fourth the game had settled into what pro football historians David Neft and Richard Cohen described as "a titanic struggle under nightmarish conditions." No professional football game had ever been played in conditions to match what has become known in NFL lore as the "Ice Bowl." Players on both sides breathed steam and spit ice, and officials were forced to call the game without whistles because the small wooden peas inside their whistles had frozen. When umpire Joe Connell attempted to use his whistle at the start of the game, he pulled half of his lower lip off. He had forgotten to cover the whistle with a rubber mouthpiece, and the metal had frozen fast to his lips. When Connell pulled the whistle from his mouth, his lips tore and blood flowed out; within seconds the blood froze fast on his chin. For the rest of the game, referee Norm Schachter's crew regulated the action by shouting at players, "Stay away!" and "Keep off him!"

As the sun began to set behind the scoreboard, taking with it the last remaining remnants of heat, fans built small fires in the stands and huddled around them. One spectator died from the intense cold, and players on both sides were feeling the effects of frostbite.

The Cowboys stunned Nitschke and the Packer defense on the first play of the fourth quarter. Halfback Dan Reeves ran left on an apparent sweep, then pulled up and lofted a long pass to flanker Lance Rentzel. The Dallas flanker had slipped behind the surprised Green Bay defense and was all alone downfield, and the 50-yard scoring pass put the Cowboys up, 17–14, eight seconds into the final quarter.

As the clock wound down, neither team could mount much of a sustained offense. The icy conditions and skill levels of two of the greatest defenses of their era were proving dominant. Tempers began to flare on both sides, and Reeves angrily accused Nitschke of kicking at Dallas fullback Don Perkins.

"He went wild after we had gone ahead," Reeves said after the game. "He actually kicked at Don Perkins after Don had gained five yards. He's an animal. It made all of us mad when he took a kick at Don like that, right in front of everyone, and no one called it."

Nitschke resented Reeves' statement, resented being called a dirty player. Perkins had run wild on Nitschke and the Packer defense in the 1966 championship game in Dallas, and the fact that he became the first and only back to run for more than 100 yards against Bengston's defense in a post-season game insulted the Packers' middle linebacker. Nitschke made up his mind before the '67 title game that Perkins, as good a back as Nitschke knew he was, wasn't going to get anywhere near 100 yards in the rematch at Lambeau Field. On the play in question, a short pickup by Perkins in the fourth quarter, the film shows Nitschke wrapping Perkins up, driving him back toward the line of scrimmage, and after releasing him with a shove, kicking at the frozen ground close to where Perkins was.

"I kicked the ground because I was disgusted with myself," Nitschke said. "I didn't have anything against Perkins."

Nitschke insisted through the years that he wasn't mad at Perkins for picking up the yardage, he was mad at himself for failing to make a tackle that would have stopped the play for no gain.

Years later, Reeves couldn't recall the incident. "All I know is Ray was one of the all-time great competitors," he said. "He was one of those unique people who loved to hit, and did it often."

With 4:50 left in the game, the Packers took the ball for perhaps the final time of the '67 title game. Starr had been dumped by the Dallas defense eight times for a loss of 76 yards, and the Green Bay offense, which looked so strong in the first half, had ground to a halt. On the Packer sideline, Nitschke stood shivering, trying to ignore the frostbite that would afflict six of his toes. "We're losing," he thought, "but we have the ball. And we have Starr."

In the Packers' huddle, Starr stared into the frozen faces of his teammates and said, "Let's get it done."

Over the next three minutes, Starr pried apart the Doomsday defense with short passes. On the sidelines, Nitschke thrust his padded right fist into the gray, icy air and shouted, "Don't let me down! Don't let me down!" At the 11, Starr crossed up the Cowboys with "65-Give," an influence play aimed at All-Pro tackle Bob Lilly. As Lilly chased a simulated Green Bay sweep, Mercein galloped through the gaping hole for an eight-yard pickup. Nitschke knew about the "give" play, knew Starr had it in his game plan. He had wondered when Starr would call it, and smiled as he saw the play develop, saw Lilly, whom Nitschke regarded as a great defensive player, chase the sweep, saw Mercein running right up the gut. It was beautiful, Nitschke thought, the best play he had ever seen Starr call.

"It was a great call, man," Nitschke recalled. "Bart saved it for the right moment, the right time."

From the three, halfback Donny Anderson plunged to the one to give Green Bay a first-and-goal with 30 seconds remaining. "We're close," Nitschke thought. "How are they going to stop us?"

Starr sent Anderson driving into the Dallas line two more times, but the slick field and the stubborn Dallas defense stopped him shy of the gold-painted goal line each time. With 16 seconds remaining, Starr called his final timeout and headed to the sideline.

The wind-chill factor had dropped to an estimated minus-70 degrees. Nitschke's feet were so numb they felt detached from his body. He had never been so cold in his life, but as he stared at the stadium clock, he shoved the weather conditions from his mind. "Who cares about that?" he thought.

What Nitschke cared about was Lombardi's decision during the timeout to ignore the potential game-tying field goal and gamble everything by going for the win. To Nitschke, Lombardi's decision to go for broke and settle the game one way or the other was based on the coach's love and respect for his veterans. Eleven members of the team that day—Nitschke, Starr, Kramer, Thurston, Gregg, Skoronski, Dowler, McGee, Davis, Jordan, and Wood—had been there in 1960 when the Packers had played in their first championship under Lombardi. Through the years they had endured the torturous grass drills in the summer, endured the bitter wind of the '62 title game against the Giants in Yankee Stadium, the icy mud against the Browns in '65. They had played with pride and won, they'd made mistakes and lost. They'd put in peak performances, they'd played hurt, and through it all, they had become Lombardi's extended family, his adopted sons.

"When you get that close, if you can't make a foot you shouldn't be out there," Nitschke said. "The field was getting worse, but we had it right there, in our hands. That's what it's all about."

As Lombardi and Starr conferred on the sidelines, Nitschke felt that if placekicker Don Chandler was sent out there, it would have meant that his coach no longer had the confidence in his veterans to take that last step, to win a game that would decide not only a berth in Super Bowl II, but also Green Bay's drive to an historic third straight NFL championship.

As Starr returned to the field, some Packers heard Lombardi mutter, "If we can't score from the 1, we don't deserve to be champions."

In the huddle, Starr called "Brown Right, 31-Wedge," a drive play between Kramer and Bowman, then amid a cloud of frost, told his team, "We're going in from here."

As fans in Lambeau Field held their collective breath, Moore made the call in clipped tones WTMJ Radio:

Here are the Packers. . . . Third down, inches to go to paydirt . . . 17-to-14, Cowboys out in front. Packers trying for the go-ahead score. Starr begins the count, takes the snap, he's got the quarterback sneak and he's in for the touchdown and the Packers are out in front! There's 13 seconds showing on the clock and the Green Bay Packers are going to be world champions, NFL champions, for the third straight year. . . .

Moments later, as Nitschke ran off the field amid the post-game celebration, he experienced feelings he had never felt before. The Ice Bowl was an instant classic, and the drama and circumstances surrounding the game left Nitschke shook emotionally. When he reached the Packers' crowded locker room, he saw that many of his teammates were in tears. As he made the rounds crying and embracing his teammates in his trademark bearhugs, Nitschke savored the moments as among the greatest in his life.

Amid the celebrations in the Green Bay locker room, CBS sportscaster Tom Brookshier was conducting interviews with various Packers. When he saw Nitschke approaching, Brookshier announced, "Here's Green Bay's madman, Ray Nitschke."

Brookshier was smiling when he said it, but the smile faded when he saw Nitschke fixing him with a glare usually reserved for opposing ballcarriers.

"I'm not a madman," Nitschke snapped. "I just enjoy football."

In his earplug, Brookshier heard director Bob Dailey say, "If Nitschke hits Brookshier, let's cut to a commercial."

A former Philadelphia cornerback, Brookshier had played against Nitschke in the 1960 NFL title game. As a CBS sportscaster, he had seen Nitschke play on several occasions, but even Brookshier was surprised to see Nitschke kicking the air viciously after the Perkins gain. "I thought, 'Wow, this guy's wild,' " Brookshier said.

When he introduced Nitschke to the national television audience of more than 50 million people as "Green Bay's madman," Brookshier said he thought he was being cute. He soon realized his mistake when he looked over and saw Nitschke standing there, red-faced.

"He was a behemoth," Brookshier said. "And he was furious."

Nitschke was angry, he said later, because all he could think of was that he was being insulted in front of his family, in front of his friends. He was concerned how they would take it to hear Nitschke being called a dirty football player. He was no madman, he told Brookshier, he was just trying to play the game as hard and as well as he could.

Chicago Bears' middle linebacker Dick Butkus defended Nitschke's play against the Cowboys in the Ice Bowl, defended his icy response to Brookshier. "Nitschke is just rough and tough," Butkus said. "I nearly fell over when Brookshier said that to him."

Bears guard Mike Pyle watched Nitschke's ferocious play against the Rams in the Western Conference playoff, against the Cowboys in the NFL championship game, and said he had never seen Nitschke play so aggressively.

"He must have been seeing nothing but dollar signs," Pyle said.

For Nitschke and the Packers, there was one big payday remaining. For the second straight year, Green Bay would represent the NFL in the Super Bowl against the champions of the AFL. Oakland had supplanted Kansas City as the league's dominant team, winning the Western Conference with a 13–1 record that ranked as the best in AFL history, and the Raiders had overrun Houston 40–7 in the title game.

Nitschke wasn't worried. Leaving the warmth of the locker room, he limped through the minus-20 degree darkness and climbed into his new Lincoln Continental. He had frost-bite in his toes and was fighting a cold, and when he returned to his home in Oneida for New Year's Eve he put his feet up and thought about what Kramer had told a TV reporter after the game.

Glancing around at his teammates hugging and weeping together, Kramer remarked that there was a great deal of love amongst the Packers. "Maybe," he mused, "we're living in Camelot."

Nitschke thought about that, thought too about the man whose career with the Packers was so closely paralleling his own. The man whom no one, including Nitschke, thought would make it in the NFL. The man who had just scored the winning touchdown in arguably the most memorable game ever played.

"Bart Starr utilized everything God gave him," Nitschke said. "He rose to the challenge. His best games were in the big games."

For the Packers, there was one more big game to play. Having already played 22 games that season, Green Bay's "big push" was finally nearing its end.

ELEVEN

T **HREE DAYS** after Green Bay's 21–17 win over Dallas in the epic Ice Bowl game, Ray Nitschke sat on a trainer's table in the Packers' locker room having the big toes on both feet bandaged by trainers. The daytime temperature in Green Bay on Wednesday, January 3, 1968, had warmed up to five degrees above zero, and as he sat on the trainer's table getting treatment for frostbite, a team trainer advised him that the only way to keep the condition from worsening was to avoid going out in the cold again.

"How the hell do you do that," Nitschke asked, "and go out and practice in five degrees?"

At that moment, head coach Vince Lombardi walked in. Hearing Nitschke's complaint, Lombardi offered some advice to his middle linebacker. "Just go out," he said, "and get up a good sweat."

Green Bay guard Jerry Kramer, who was nearby weighing himself, saw Nitschke begin to ask his coach how he could work up a sweat in five degree cold, then watched as Ray resigned himself to the fact that he was in an argument he couldn't win.

"Aw, forget it, man," Nitschke said.

Nitschke and the Packers went out and practiced, and when the temperature the next day was six degrees below zero with 15-mile per hour winds whipping across the practice field, Nitschke remarked in the locker room that he wasn't going outside. The Packers seemed close to revolt, particularly when defensive end Willie Davis asked Lombardi what the temperature was in Miami that Thursday.

"About 78 degrees," Lombardi answered. "Why?"

Davis just shook his head. "Oh, nothing," he answered. "Just wondering."

All the Packers were wondering why they were still in Green Bay, why they hadn't headed to Florida to prepare for the Oakland Raiders and Super Bowl II. The Packers were suffering; Nitschke had frostbite on his feet, Starr on his fingers. Nitschke was also suffering a debilitating head cold; so too, was Kramer, whose cold reached down into his bronchial tubes and stomach. Nitschke limped noticeably; Kramer wondered if his lungs had frostbite.

The Packers practiced for 45 minutes amid the subzero cold and bitter winds before even Lombardi had enough. With a half dozen of his players exhibiting flu symptoms, he cut practice short by 15 minutes. "The hell with it," he suddenly announced. "Let's go in."

Three days later, on January 7, Nitschke and the Packers whisked themselves through minus-seven degree temperatures as they boarded a 727 for the trip to Florida. When they arrived, the temperature was 75 degrees. As he settled into his room amid the Packers' headquarters at the Galt Ocean Mile Hotel in Fort Lauderdale, Nitschke realized he wasn't physically ready to play in the Super Bowl. The intense cold from the Ice Bowl game had caused his toes to turn purple and his toenails to fall off. "I damn near froze my toes off," he said. He had dropped eight pounds due to the flu, and he was still limping with frostbite. Limping everywhere, that is, except in the presence of Lombardi.

Amid an interview session with reporters at the hotel, Lombardi was answering questions when a reporter asked about the physical effects of the Ice Bowl on his team. Nitschke's ears, toes, and fingers were whitened by frostbite, and Packers' publicist Chuck Lane said the skin was falling off Green Bay players by the yards. Fixing reporters with a glare, Lombardi remarked that only the Dallas players had been hobbled by the cold.

"The Dallas Cowboys got frostbite," he said. "Ray Nitschke just had a blister. Only a blister. That's all it was. A blister."

Nitschke, who was limping by at that precise moment, immediately stopped limping when he heard his coach's remark. Writer Mickey Herskowitz saw Nitschke's sudden recovery and attributed it to what he described as Lombardi's "Throw-Away-Your-Crutch-And-Walk School of Coaching." When reporters pressed him for a response on going from playing in subfreezing temperatures in Green Bay to playing in the Miami heat, Lombardi brushed off their questions.

"Weather," he said emphatically, "is a state of mind."

The Packers were headquartered at the same Fort Lauderdale training complex the New York Yankees had used every spring during their glory years. When a reporter pointed out that Nitschke was now dressing where Mantle and DiMaggio had dressed before him, the big linebacker shrugged. "It might have meant something a few years ago," he said.

The Raiders rode into Super Bowl II with a reputation for intimidation. Oakland had overrun AFL defenses by scoring a league-high 468 points during the regular season. Quarterback Daryle Lamonica led both leagues by throwing for 30 touchdowns, and thick-legged Raider backs rushed for an AFL-best 19 touchdowns. Coached by John Rauch, Oakland popularized the use of the fullback as a deep pass receiver, and 220-pound fullback Hewritt Dixon, a converted tight end, led the team with 59 receptions.

Game films reveal the Raiders' offensive firepower—halfback Clem Daniels sweeping left for a long gain against defending AFL champion Kansas City in Oakland; Dixon breaking five tackles on a flare pass against Buffalo in old War Memorial Stadium; Fred Biletnikoff outfighting Chiefs cornerback Fred Williamson to gather in a Lamonica bomb on Thanksgiving Day in Kansas City; a massive, 17-play drive in the rain against the Oilers in Houston's Rice Stadium; halfback Pete Banaszak bowling over New York Jets cornerback Randy Beverly on an off-tackle run in the penultimate game of the regular season.

The Raiders ravaged the AFL with a 13–1 record that ranked as the best in AFL history, and matched Green Bay's 13–1 finish in 1962 as the best of the decade to that point. As Nitschke and the Green Bay defense watched the three game tapes provided by Raiders—victories over Kansas City, Buffalo, and the Jets—they made notes on each of Oakland's key offensive players:

Lamonica: "Likes to work from play-action . . . rollouts, bootlegs; can drop back and throw;"

Dixon: "Strong runner, big and powerful. Heavier than press book indicates;"

Banaszak: "Not impressive in size or moves, but churns out yards. Watch him if he gets an opening;"

Biletnikoff: "One of the best in his league. Other ends, (Bill) Miller and (Billy) Cannon, are hot, too. All are heavy guys;"

Gene Upshaw, offensive lineman: "A rookie, but he sure doesn't look like it. Treat him like a veteran;"

Jim Otto, All-Star lineman: "One of the great ones."

As Green Bay's chief scout, Wally Cruice, ran down the rest of the Raider offense, including speedy end Warren Wells and the Oakland offensive line, he again emphasized that the AFL champions were big, strong, physical players. Comparing the listed size of the Raiders' players to what he was seeing on film, Cruice told Packers' defensive coordinator Phil Bengston, "The last time they weighed these guys was in high school."

Cruice reminded Nitschke and the Packer defense that the Raiders had ties to the Green Bay and greater Wisconsin area. Lamonica had been the Packers' 12th round draft pick in 1963, and Raider defenders Ben Davidson and Howie Williams were members of Green Bay's 1961 and '62 NFL championship teams, respectively. Placekicker George Blanda had played against the Packers while with the Chicago Bears in the 1950s; Banaszak was from Crivitz, Wisconsin, and Otto, in whom Lombardi had shown interest during the NFL–AFL wars, was from Wausau. While Cruice remarked that the great many ties several Raiders had to the Packers and Wisconsin would undoubtedly provide emotional fuel, Nitschke was unimpressed.

"I don't care if they come blowing Chinese bugles, riding horses, and waving sabers," he said.

Nitschke's attitude toward the AFL champions reflected the Packers' approach to the game. This was their second straight Super Bowl, and they weren't as excited for the game as they had been the year before. They weren't taking the Raiders lightly, but when it came to big games, losing was not in the Packers' lexicon. They had played together so long that individually they were able to pick up very quickly on what the opposition was trying to do. They would spend the first half deciphering the opponent's game plan, then spend the second half prying them apart.

Over the course of their second championship run of the sixties, the Packers had become a second-half team. The reason for that, Nitschke said, was that the team they played on Sundays was invariably not the same team they had studied in movies the week before. Lombardi had warned his team on several occasions that they were marked men. Opponents, he said, had read the papers and seen the stories asking, "Who can beat the Packers? Can anyone beat them?" The response, he said, was that teams were now saying "We can do it, we can beat the Packers." This was the price of winning, Lombardi said. It was the price that came with being five-time champions, and the Packers were paying it because everyone in the NFL wanted to beat them.

"They're giving it their maximum supreme effort," Lombardi said. "There's no loafing, no halfway, against the Green Bay Packers."

Nitschke saw the worth of Lombardi's words firsthand on the field. Even the NFL's worst teams were bringing a special effort and dedication to bear against Green Bay. They would give their all in the first half, play the Packers to a standstill, but then, realizing that they couldn't dominate Green Bay even with a peak performance, endured a letdown in the second half. Nitschke watched as opponents slowly but steadily lost their poise and character. Since the Packers played hard the whole game, they almost always took advantage of the opponent's second half meltdown and gradually pulled away.

That's what Green Bay had done to Kansas City the year before, and of the three game films the Raiders provided, Nitschke and the Packers gleaned the most from Oakland's victory over the Chiefs. Since the Packers were familiar with the Chiefs' personnel, the Oakland–Kansas City reel provided a point of reference from which Green Bay could work. To Nitschke, the Raiders provided a vastly different challenge than Kansas City had in Super Bowl I. With their shifting alignments and multiple offense, the Chiefs were a flashy team that played fancy football, the kind of team, Nitschke said, that the Packers liked to enlighten in the ways of fundamental football.

Oakland, on the other hand, was a team that resembled Green Bay in its approach to the game. Unlike Kansas City cornerback Fred Williamson, who had belittled Green Bay before Super Bowl I, the Raiders spoke highly of the NFL champions. Their tone was set by their general managing partner, Al Davis.

"Imagine," Davis said with a syrupy smile, "the li'l' ol' Raiders on the same field with the Green Bay Packers. *Imagine . . .* "

Rauch called the Packers "the very best team in all of football," and Lamonica's locker contained a 1966 hardcover book titled *Quarterbacking*, written by Bart Starr. "I admire Starr," Lamonica said. "I consider it a real privilege to play against the man who is rated tops in the business." One of the Raiders compared playing against the Packers to "playing against our fathers," and massive defensive end Ben Davidson told AFL reporters, "I hope we don't get run off the field."

As the Raiders watched the three Packer game films supplied by Lombardi, Otto studied Nitschke's play at middle linebacker. "Nitschke was someone you had to handle," Otto remembered. "This was the first time I was going to be playing against him, and I liked his style of play. I liked his toughness because that was basically my game too. The Green Bay Packers had a tremendous defense, there's no doubt about it, and Nitschke was the leader of that group. He was always aggressive, always where the play was."

Otto could see from the films that the Packers pinched and slanted their tackles, Henry Jordan and Ron Kostelnik, to shield Nitschke from the center's blocks. "If you were quick enough you could get to Nitschke," Otto said, "but that was a formidable threesome they had inside, with Jordan, Kostelnik, and Nitschke."

Oakland would look to counter with an offense that Nitschke felt was similar to the Packers in that it could nickel-and-dime defenses to death all day. Nitschke studied Lamonica, studied how the All-AFL QB liked to throw to his backs. Nitschke also studied Dixon, and saw that he was a strong, aggressive runner, and since he had led the Raiders in receptions, Nitschke prepared himself to slow Dixon down from the start.

At the same time the Packers were preparing for Super Bowl II, they were also preparing to play what many of them believed would be their final game for Lombardi. Nitschke could see the strain the long season was having on his head coach. Lombardi didn't appear to be the same man he had been just a few years earlier; to Nitschke, he didn't look as healthy as he should have. Lombardi had always demanded that his teams win, and to win as consistently as Green Bay did in the 1960s, a price had to be paid. The Packers paid that price, and their bruised bodies were testament to that. But to Nitschke, Lombardi had paid the heaviest price of all. Kramer once figured out that on an average, the Green Bay coaching staff headed by Lombardi made less money at the time than a Green Bay garbageman. Nitschke wanted to see Lombardi on the sidelines for the '68 season, wanted to be driven through the summer drills toward yet another title. But when he saw his head coach's condition, saw his hands shaking and the toll nine years of demanding perfection had taken on him, Nitschke knew Lombardi was ready to step down.

Nitschke's beliefs were confirmed the Thursday before Super Sunday. Standing up to address his team, Lombardi began rubbing his hands together.

"Okay, boys," he began. "This may be the last time we'll be together, so . . . uh . . . "

Players could see their coach's lips quivering, his body trembling. Nitschke thought Lombardi was ready to start crying. With that, the man *Newark Star-Ledger* sports writer Jerry Izenberg referred to as "Invincible Vince" turned his back to his team and sat down in a chair. "Let's break up," he said.

On the morning of Super Sunday, the Packers gathered at 10:45 A.M. for a pregame meal, then boarded chartered buses for their ride to the Orange Bowl and the 3 P.M. kickoff. The stadium was sold out, and the crowd of 75,546 guaranteed that this would be the first football game to gross more than $3 million dollars. Combined with the $2.5 million CBS paid for the rights to broadcast the game to a record viewing audience of 70 million people—more than one-third of the entire population of the U.S.—Super Bowl II became the richest single athletic event to that time.

Taking the field amid sunny, 68-degree temperatures, Nitschke saw the palm trees swaying beyond the open end of the Orange Bowl, saw that the decorated field had been dyed green to look good on color TV. Testing the footing, Nitschke found that the closed end of the stadium was sandy, and that the yard stripes up and down the field were gullies. The Orange Bowl had become an AFL stadium in 1966 to accommodate the arrival of the expansion Miami Dolphins, but Nitschke and the Packers had played there before. In 1963 and '64, the Orange Bowl had hosted the NFL Playoff Bowl, the post-season game between the runners-up in the Eastern and Western Conferences. Green Bay had finished second in the West in both 1963 and '64, and was familiar with the nuances of the stadium, the sudden wind shifts and the grass sod that covered the sandy turf underneath. Nitschke watched the pregame festivities, saw the two giant, 30-foot high figures on floats—one trimmed in Packer white and yellow-gold, the other in Raider silver and black—square off at midfield and puff smoke at one another through three-foot wide nostrils.

In the Green Bay locker room before the game, Nitschke dressed in his road white jersey with the green-and-gold trim, streaked shiny black shoe polish on his cheekbones to cut the sun's glare, then listened as the pregame speeches began.

Offensive captain Bob Skoronski stood up first and said that if the Packer lost this game, they would lose everything they worked for all season. "I don't have any damn intention of losing this ballgame," he said, "and I don't think anybody else here does."

Defensive captain Willie Davis followed and said the next 60 minutes would determine what would be said about the Packers the next day. Offensive tackle Forrest Gregg implored his teammates to go out and take the game to the Raiders right away. Oakland, Gregg said, is a little bit afraid of Green Bay, and the Packers could gain the early edge by putting it to the AFL champions from the first play on.

Max McGee followed, said it would be a tough thing to live the rest of their lives having lost this game, then he yielded the floor to Nitschke. Nitschke's message mirrored his style of play—no-frills and direct.

"Let's play with our hearts," he said.

Nitschke set the tone for Super Bowl II on the game's first play from scrimmage. Reading a Raiders' sweep at the Oakland 28-yard line, he shot through a gap in the line, lowered his left shoulder into Dixon's right knee, and flipped him. Flipped him, in the words of a *Time* magazine reporter, "cleats over clavicle."

In the press box, *Detroit News* columnist Jerry Green saw the hulking Dixon, a player he knew was a home-bred AFL star, take Lamonica's handoff and start left. "Nitschke, fangs flashing, met Dixon at the line of scrimmage," Green wrote. "The collision was terrifying. Dixon was bowled over, bounced backwards, and set down in a heap."

In what he later acknowledged as smart-aleck fashion, Green turned to his NFL colleagues and in a voice loud enough for AFL writers to hear, remarked, "Well, this game's over."

Nitschke's hit on Dixon remains most vivid in the mind of Lee Remmel, who covered the Packers for the *Green Bay Press-Gazette* for more than 29 years. To Remmel, Nitschke's hit on Dixon remains one of the signature plays of Ray's long career.

On CBS Radio, play-by-play announcer Jack Drees made the call on a play that set the tone for the entire afternoon:

First-and-10 for Oakland, Banaszak, and Dixon the running backs . . . Lamonica is snug under center. He gives the ball to Dixon and . . . Dixon is stopped! Coming in there was Nitschke as Dixon tried the left side of the line, was upended at the line of scrimmage by Nitschke, and dropped down on the 28.

Lamonica had called "69 Boom Man"—a fullback sweep to the weak side that had been the Raiders' number one running play all season. Banaszak, who was starting at halfback in place of the injured Clem Daniels, recalled coming out of the huddle on that first play, looking across the line and seeing Nitschke, Jordan, Davis, and Adderley, all of whom were players he had once collected bubble-gum cards of when he was younger. Banaszak's responsibility on the play was to block left linebacker Dave Robinson, but he never touched him. Films show Nitschke flying past the fallen Banaszak to drop Dixon.

"Nitschke came over me to get Dixon for no gain," Banaszak said. "I had his cleat marks all over my back."

Seeing Nitschke and the rest of the Packers up close and in person left Lamonica as impressed as his counterpart on the Chiefs, Lenny Dawson, had been the year before.

"We were a very young ballclub," Lamonica remembered, "and we were facing some old warhorses who could really put the leather to you. Nitschke, Dave Robinson . . . those guys were solid. We weren't in awe of the Packers, but they had that mystique."

Throughout the game, Nitschke battled Otto, nicknamed "Double-Zero" for the silver uniform number he wore on his black jersey. Otto had been an All-AFL center from 1960 to 1967, and would become the last of the pro football linemen to wear a double-bar facemask instead of the half- or fullcage masks that were coming into favor. Like Nitschke, Otto's rough features, usually accompanied by a trickle of blood running down his face, unsettled opposing players.

Nitschke was unmoved. He had given Oakland what he later called, "a pretty good introduction to the NFL brand of defensive football," and proved instrumental in upending the wide running game. Oakland had overwhelmed the AFL's best defensive team, the Oilers, in the league championship game two weeks earlier with sweeps. In that game, Dixon gave the Raiders their first touchdown when he swept left and thundered 69 yards behind Banaszak and Upshaw on the first play of the second quarter. Throughout the game, Dixon and Banaszak continued to pound away at the Oilers behind a fired-up offensive line, and by day's end, Dixon had 144 yards rushing and a 6.9 yards per carry average, and Banaszak had 116 yards on the ground and averaged 7.7 yards per attempt. As a team, the Raiders ran 48 times for an AFL championship game record 263 yards. Oakland's power sweeps battered Houston's right side, and in the film of the game, Banaszak and Dixon can be seen dancing through the Oilers defense to set up four Blanda field goals.

Bengston knew all about the AFL title game, about Blanda's shrinking the field with kicks that ranged from 36 to 42 yards, and knew the Raiders' ageless kicker represented a serious threat any time Oakland penetrated Packer territory. Nitschke knew it too, and helped shut down the Raiders' ground-eating sweeps by firing through the gaps left by Oakland's pulling guards and hauling Dixon and Banaszak down from behind.

Nitschke's success against the Raiders stemmed in part from Oakland's difficulties in dealing with the quickness of right defensive tackle Henry Jordan. Otto said that one reason the Raiders' wide running game failed was because they could only pull one guard rather than two. Upshaw had to stay back and take care of Jordan, Otto said, because the Packer tackle was so quick off the ball.

"Maybe," Otto mused, "we should've run right at 'em."

With Nitschke heading a mobile linebacking corps that prevented Raider backs from turning upfield, the Packers took physical control of the game. Lombardi told his defense that anytime they can take away an opponent's number one play, they could force them into trying something they're not as effective in doing. With the Oakland offense providing no pressure, Green Bay engineered time-consuming drives. Playing with what one wire-service reporter described as "the effervescence of overworked morticians," the Packers drove 34 yards in 11 plays on their first possession and took a 3–0 lead on Don Chandler's 39-yard field goal.

The next time Green Bay had the ball, Bart Starr pried apart Oakland's unconventional three-four defense with a 17-play, 84-yard drive that consumed almost nine minutes off the white-on-green scoreboard clock. Chandler's 20-yard field goal gave the Packers a 6–0 lead, and as Izenberg watched Chandler, not Blanda, provide the early points, the thought occurred to him that no team in football had ever been more cruel than the Packers. They delighted, he wrote later, in beating teams at their own game.

Having lulled the Raiders to sleep with two long drives, Starr struck quickly on the Packers' next possession, when he found flanker Boyd Dowler for a 62-yard touchdown and a 13–0 lead.

The Raiders finally responded with a scoring drive of their own, Lamonica hitting end Bill Miller for a 23-yard touchdown. But Chandler's third field goal of the first half, a 43-yarder, gave Green Bay a 16–7 lead at the break.

Nitschke had played an active first half, and sideline cameras showed him taking deep inhalations from an oxygen mask on the sideline. "I had lost 10, 15 pounds from the flu," he recalled. "But I was going to be there if I had to be there on a stretcher. We played every game for 60 minutes; we let it all hang out. There was no tomorrow for us. We got the adrenaline flowing, and we let it go, man."

At halftime, Nitschke joined with some of the team's aging veterans—Starr, Kramer, Gregg, Skoronski, Davis, Jordan, Fuzzy Thurston, and Max McGee—and pledged to play the last 30 minutes for Lombardi.

"Knowing that Lombardi was going to retire gave us an edge," Nitschke said. "That was extra motivation for us. We weren't going to get beaten by anybody that day."

Starr's mastery of the Raiders' shifting defense continued throughout the second half. On Green Bay's second series of the third quarter, he beat an Oakland blitz by sending fullback Ben Wilson up the middle on a draw play that gained 13 yards, then drew the Raiders in with a play-fake to Wilson on a third-and-1 from his own 40 and lofted a 35-yard completion to McGee. Starr followed with an 11-yard pass to split end Carroll Dale, a 12-yard comeback pass to halfback Donny Anderson, and then handed off to Anderson for a two-yard run over the right side for a 23–7 lead.

Lamonica had enjoyed some success in the first half by rolling out and throwing, but Nitschke and the defense adjusted by widening the splits in their line to shorten the room on Lamonica's rollouts and blitzing more. As the Packers widened their lead and the gloaming settled over the Orange Bowl, Nitschke could see the Raiders suffering the same kind of second-half letdown the Chiefs had the year before.

Lamonica was stunned at the deep drops taken by Green Bay's linebackers—Nitschke, Robinson, and Lee Roy Caffey. "They closed up my passing lane," he said. "On my first touchdown I had to throw the ball over Robinson's head. Here's a guy who's 6-4 and 250 pounds and he's 30 yards downfield with the receivers.

"On our sweeps, the linebackers ran 45 degrees and they really got out there. I found out too late that the sweeps weren't working."

A 31-yard field goal by Chandler on Green Bay's next series made it 26–7 and marked the sixth time in their first nine possessions that the Packers had put points on the board against the AFL's most feared defense. Chandler's field goal was his fourth of the game, and Nitschke remarked later that while Blanda was the kicker getting all the pregame attention, it was Chandler who was piling up the points.

As the final seconds ticked off on Green Bay's 33–14 win, Nitschke's legs were covered with welts. Dried blood stained his knee bandages. But he was still out on the spongy Orange Bowl field, still smashing into any Raider who violated his turf. He finished the game with nine tackles and impressed the Orange Bowl audience with his play. One writer noted that Nitschke played with "joyous abandon," and San Francisco quarterback George Mira remarked in a column he was writing for the *Miami Herald* that the Raiders had made a mistake trying to run sweeps against Nitschke.

"You don't run outside on Ray Nitschke," Mira said. "He's tough and reads plays a lot."

When Steve Sabol of NFL Films recalls Super Bowl II, the thing he remembers most about Nitschke is how many times the Packers middle man stopped the powerful Dixon on short-yardage plays. "Nitschke played to win," Sabol said. "He didn't need the media or television, he didn't need the billboards and all the publicity. He would've played the game in a parking lot."

Afterward, reporters crowded around Nitschke's locker. He was kind in his comments. The Raiders, he said, were "a real sound football team" that compared favorably with the previous AFL champion, Kansas City. But when *Green Bay Press-Gazette* sportswriter Lee Remmel asked if he was concerned when Oakland had halved the Packers' lead in the second quarter, Nitschke shook his head.

"No," he said. "There was no way they were going to beat us. Phil had us well prepared. It was just a matter of executing."

The Raider running game that ravaged the AFL was limited to a total of 107 yards. Dixon and Banaszak, who had combined for 260 yards rushing in the AFL title game, were held to a combined 70 yards by the Packers.

"We knew going into those games that those teams may have scored a lot of points in their league," cornerback Bob Jeter recalled, "but they weren't going to score a lot of points against us."

The Packer defense had done its job but paid a heavy price. The backs of Nitschke's legs were completely black-and-blue, and Jackie noticed that it took her husband longer to recover from the bruises than it had in earlier years. Asked how much longer he might play before retiring, Jackie said that the way her husband looked at the end of the '67 season, he would likely stay in the NFL "only more year."

That was good news for NFL ball carriers, who had engaged in brutal man-to-man warfare with Nitschke during the season. Though he was left off the NFL's All-Pro team, Nitschke's status among his peers continued to grow. In a *Sport* magazine article, five former All-Pro linebackers were asked to name the best middle linebacker in the game. Bill George voted for Chicago's Dick Butkus, and Chuck Bednarik picked Atlanta's Tommy Nobis, but Nitschke was the choice of Bill Pellington, Joe Schmidt, and Pat Richter. Pellington and Richter cited Nitschke's leadership ability, and Schmidt spoke of Nitschke's amazing lateral mobility and quickness. The magazine also asked Colts quarterback John Unitas his opinion on who the best middle linebacker was, and Unitas didn't hedge. They had all hit him hard, he said, and all were close in ability. But what set Nitschke apart in Unitas's eyes was his experience.

"He just seems to get the job done more consistently," Unitas said. "Nitschke was the toughest one I played against last year."

The toughest the Raiders had played against too. Even in defeat, Otto and Lamonica considered it an honor to have played in Super Bowl II against Nitschke and the Packers. "I had grown up in the Wisconsin area," Otto said, "and going up against a team from the great Vince Lombardi era was very exciting for me."

Exciting too, for a 30-year-old Oakland assistant coach named John Madden. Several times during the game, Madden had stolen quick glances across the field at the Packers' sideline, and at the man who had become his coaching idol. Madden stared at Lombardi and took it all in: the black blazer, white shirt and red-and-blue striped tie; the gray slacks and the black football shoes with the white laces. As linebackers coach for the Raiders, Madden's responsibility was to try and stop Lombardi's offense.

"I'm on this sideline and Vince Lombardi's on the other sideline," Madden said to himself. "I'm telling my linebackers how to stop Lombardi's plays." To Madden, who had followed Lombardi around the coaching lecture circuit since 1963, that was like trying to stop God's plays.

Madden wasn't alone in his assessment of Lombardi. A joke making the rounds at the time focused on a football player who had died and gone to heaven. When he arrives he sees a team of angels scrimmaging while a short man screams at them from the sidelines. When the player asks St. Peter who that fellow on the sideline is, St. Peter replies, "Oh, that's God. He thinks he's Vince Lombardi."

Nitschke thought Green Bay's second straight Super Bowl victory had elevated the Packers' head coach to folk hero status. *Sports Illustrated*'s cover story on Super Bowl II carried a picture of Lombardi being carried off the field on the shoulders of Kramer and Gregg and a headline titled, "The Super Champion—Lombardi of Green Bay."

Like his coach and many of his teammates, Nitschke was alarmed at what was going on in the country around him—the protests and riots in Watts and Newark, the political assassinations, the clash between the establishment and the counterculture. The Packers themselves were well-ordered and disciplined; big band music in the age of Aquarius. Younger, hipper AFL fans at the Orange Bowl had booed every time Starr led his team out of the huddle in the fourth quarter. The two generations, Nitschke thought, had discovered a big gap between them.

The old ways were changing, and Nitschke felt that a lot of Americans were worried and uptight about what their future would hold. Already, the American public had lost a popular president, and would lose a civil rights leader and a future presidential candidate to assassin's bullets. Cities were being set on fire, streets and campuses were filled with protesters. The times, they were a-changin', and not just for Bob Dylan. Nitschke thought that many Americans had lost track of what was going on, had lost track of whether they were winning or losing in their everyday lives. Football helped clarify matters, he thought, if only for three hours on a Sunday afternoon. Fans could see what was happening down on the field and knew whether their side was winning or losing.

Because the Packers were winners, because they had become the dominant team in professional sports, people outside of the NFL seeking clarity amid the social confusion suddenly wanted Lombardi's opinion on more than just the power sweep; they wanted his views on the changes sweeping the country. People may have been changing, Nitschke thought, but one thing still remained the same. The American public still respected a winner.

On February 1, 1968, Lombardi officially announced his retirement as head coach of the Packers. He would remain as Green Bay's general manager, but would turn the day-to-day coaching activities over to Bengston. Nitschke knew the difficulties Bengston would be facing. If the Packers repeated in 1968, it would be because it was Lombardi's team. If the Packers failed to repeat, it would be because it was Bengston's team. Still, Nitschke thought Green Bay was good enough to win without Lombardi. In a *Sports Illustrated* cover story headlined "Green Bay's Greatest Team," Nitschke, who had been named the team's MVP by Green Bay fans in a radio poll taken by WNFL, said the '68 Packers should be the best Green Bay team of all time.

"With Starr healthy for a full season, Grabowski and Pitts back in the lineup, Marv Fleming at full speed, and with Anderson and Williams carrying another year's experience, we should be more explosive offensively," he told *SI*'s Tex Maule. "I don't anticipate much change in the defense, although we do have some fine young players."

There were reasons for the Packers to play with passion in 1968. Some members of the team had grown tired of the publicity paid to their head coach and were anxious to prove they could win without him. It was a situation similar to the 49ers of 1989, when members of that team were resentful of the praise being heaped upon their head coach, Bill Walsh, and were determined to prove they were as much a reason for San Francisco's great success as the man writers dubbed "the Genius." Just as the Packers replaced an offense-minded head coach in Lombardi with his chief lieutenant and defensive coordinator, the 49ers replaced Walsh with their assistant head coach and defensive coordinator, George Seifert.

The difference between the '68 Packers and '89 49ers, however, was that while San Francisco returned its star cast intact under Seifert, the Packers were forced to deal with the dual retirements of Chandler and McGee. The loss of McGee hurt because he was a big-game player whose laid-back attitude kept the locker room loose. Chandler's departure hurt even more because Lombardi, as GM, never found a suitable replacement. In 1967, Chandler had made 19 of 26 field goal attempts, and had personally provided the difference between victory and defeat in three games. Without Chandler, the Packers might well have finished 7–5–2 rather than 9–4–1. In '68, the Packers started fast, beating Philadelphia 30–13 in the regular season opener. But kicking problems led to Bengston scrambling for reliable field goal kickers during the season. By season's end, he had tried four different kickers, including fullback Chuck Mercein, to no avail. The Packers as a team made just 13 of 29 field goal attempts, and lost or tied four games that could have been wins. Instead of a 10–4 finish that would have allowed the Packers to repeat as Central Division champions, Green Bay finished 6–7–1 and in third place behind Minnesota, which won the division with a mediocre 8–6 mark.

Halfback Paul Hornung said once that Lombardi alone accounted for at least three victories a season for the Packers. In 1968, three victories would have given Green Bay a berth in the NFL playoffs.

"That's an interesting thought," Kramer said. "We missed Vince's fire, his strength, motivation, and presence. In some of the games we lost, you'd have to believe he would have made the difference. Whether or not we could have dug deep once again when the playoffs started is another question."

In the end, the Packers were doomed by the lack of a reliable placekicker, by Starr missing almost half the season with a bad arm, by a defense stripped of its depth due to injuries that crippled tackles Jordan, Ron Kostelnik, and Jim Weatherwax and hampered ends Davis, Lionel Aldridge, and Bob Brown. Playing without the protection of his front line forced Nitschke to fight his way through waves of blockers in every game. He suffered severe pain in both shoulders and a chronic neck injury, and would sit in the trainer's room getting taped and bandaged before taking the field. Nitschke played hurt throughout the '68 season, playing against the Vikings with pinched nerves in *both* shoulders, and getting ejected from a game against New Orleans in Week 10 for forearming tight end Monty Stickles after the play had ended. Nitschke and Stickles had been feuding for years; Nitschke thought Stickles was a dirty player who blocked in the back and hit opponents in the back of the head. Stickles thought Nitschke approached football not as a game but as a gung-ho marine storming the beach.

"Ray and I would have one or two fights every time we played," Stickles said. "To me, it was a game. To him, it was war and destruction."

"That was a classic matchup of two guys not liking one another," said Tommy Nobis, who as a middle linebacker for the Atlanta Falcons watched films of Packers–49ers games every season. "We used to laugh, it was such a show to watch those two. Ray would line up over him on extra points and they would get after it. What would happen is, Stickles would take a shot at Ray's knees and try to cut him. If it was a sweep to his side of the field and Ray was in pursuit, Stickles would do something that would tick Nitschke off. And you can just bet that the next time Stickles came running over the middle on a pass route, Nitschke would clothesline him. We watched the 49ers on film because we played them twice a year, and there was one game that was just absolutely brutal for both of them, because they were both getting leveled by the other."

Nitschke's temper finally boiled over in '68 when Stickles was with the Saints, and though he admitted he could have gone after Stickles' head, he forearmed him in the chest instead. It was enough to get him ejected from the game, and to enhance his reputation as an intimidator. "There were probably some offensive guys who didn't like Nitschke," Nobis said, "because he was going to do whatever to get a guy down and maybe they didn't appreciate his techniques." Indeed, at season's end, Nitschke joined Butkus, Deacon Jones of the Rams, Alex Karras of the Lions, and Dave Wilcox of the 49ers on *The Sporting News'* list of the five meanest men in football.

Nitschke's hard play inspired his teammates, inspired Bengston, and at season's end, he was named team MVP for the second straight year.

Nitschke was disappointed in the Packers' season, and his disappointment deepened as he watched Super Bowl III and saw Joe Namath and the New York Jets defeat the favored Baltimore Colts to give the AFL its first championship game win over the NFL. The Jets' victory came on the same Orange Bowl field that the Packers had established NFL superiority on the year before against the Raiders, and Nitschke thought the Colts had let the league down. What made it worse for Nitschke was that the AFL's first victory had been engineered by Namath. As a quarterback, Nitschke thought Namath was outstanding, but he didn't appreciate the way the flamboyant Jets star carried himself off the field. Just as Namath had guaranteed a win over the Colts, Nitschke guaranteed that if it had been the Packers playing the Jets in Super Bowl III, Green Bay would have given the NFL three wins in a row over the AFL.

Having endured his first losing season since 1958, Nitschke looked to rebound in 1969. Lombardi, missing what he called "the fire on Sundays," left the Packers' organization on February 5 to become head coach and general manager of the Washington Redskins. His departure saddened Nitschke, whose sometimes volatile relationship with his head coach had softened in recent years. In a surprising display of emotion, Lombardi had kissed Nitschke on the cheek following a big win in the difficult 1967 season, and had gone out of his way to express his thanks to Nitschke for his play during the championship years. Lombardi told Nitschke he had always liked and admired him, but had realized that he was a player who didn't constantly need a pat on the back. To Lombardi, Nitschke was a player who always had to be ridden, always had to be critiqued.

"There were times when I didn't want to do it," Lombardi told him, "but it was for your own good."

In time, Nitschke came to accept Lombardi's coaching methods. Nitschke thought Lombardi had handled him just right, had gotten the most out of him. And his coach's constant demand for excellence—"There's a right way to do things and a wrong way," Lombardi would say. "Which way are going to do it, *mister*?"—impressed Nitschke.

"He helped to turn me around as a person," Nitschke said. "He inspired me by his determination in what he did."

Marie Lombardi said once that her husband had turned some men into football players and some football players into men. Of the two, she said, her husband had always been most proud of the latter. Nitschke, the ex-rowdy, was one of those football players that Lombardi had helped turn into a man.

"He set a standard," Nitschke said, "that I chose to follow."

Later, Nitschke would tell Vince Jr. how much his father had meant to him.

"He was most appreciative about what my father had done for him," he said.

At the start of the 1969 season, Lombardi was gone, Kramer and Skoronski retired, and age was creeping up on the team's heroes of the past—Nitschke, Starr, Davis, and Jordan. Once again, placekicking was a problem. Green Bay kickers converted a league-low 6 of 22 attempts, costing the team at least two wins. The Packers again finished in third place in the Central Division, albeit with a winning record at 8–6. They were still a tough team, but their greatness was fading. They had been replaced by the Vikings as the most physical team in the NFL, and Minnesota had ridden the hard-edged performances of Joe Kapp, Bill Brown, Alan Page, and Carl Eller to a second consecutive Central Division championship, this time with a 12–2 record that was the best in the league.

As the luster of Green Bay's glory years gradually wore thin, so too did the cool veneer that had always polished their performances in the Lombardi years. Opposing players like Alex Karras of Detroit could hear Packer linebackers cursing out other members of the defense when games started going bad. It was sweet, Karras said, because he had never heard anything like that before when playing Green Bay. Under Lombardi, the Packers had always played with what Karras called "a superior aloofness." To Karras, the

Packers had carried themselves during their title days as if they had all been born in some great palace somewhere and that losing wasn't worth considering. "They were elite," Karras said.

Even in defeat, Nitschke maintained that elite status, and in 1969 was named the greatest linebacker of the NFL's first 50 years. In choosing Nitschke as the best ever at his position, the editors of the book *The First 50 Years: The Story of the National Football League* wrote that as the field leader of one of football's greatest defensive units, Nitschke suffered the problems of recognition that sometimes plague teams blessed with numerous All-Pro players. In an age of Packer dominance, it was impossible to give credit to every Green Bay player, so Nitschke was frequently passed over when it came time to choose players for the Pro Bowl.

But in an era ruled by great middle linebackers, the editors wrote, Nitschke deserved his reputation as the best ever. "In the emotional cauldron of professional football," the editors wrote, "the big linebacker from Green Bay brings the game down to its most elemental form—man against man. In the final analysis, this is football's criterion of excellence."

The honor was one of the highest of Nitschke's career to that point, and he joined 12 of his Packer teammates in being named to the NFL's All-1960s team. For Nitschke, it was an appropriate climax to a decade that saw him go from second-string in 1960 to second-to-none in NFL history. The 1970 season, however, saw the realignment of the two leagues under the NFL umbrella, and also saw the final breakup of the Lombardi Packers. Davis, Jordan, and Dowler retired, and Adderley, Pitts, Caffey, and Fleming were traded. Of the starters that remained, Starr suffered through another sore-armed season and Robinson was sidelined by a torn Achilles tendon. In the realigned National Football Conference, the Packers finished 6–8 and in last place in the Central Division.

Bengston resigned at the end of the 1970 season, victimized by both injuries and the success of his famous predecessor. For Nitschke, the dawning of a new decade brought changes in both his personal and professional lives. In 1972, Ray and Jackie added to their family by adopting a baby girl, Amy. Around the house in Oneida, Nitschke was a much different person than he was on autumn Sundays. Jackie told a reporter once that her husband was very tenderhearted, never used any harsh or mean words toward the family, and was always willing to help around the house, be it cleaning up, doing the dishes, baby-sitting, or changing diapers. When it came to disciplining the children, Jackie said, she was the one who had to administer an occasional spanking.

"It just breaks Raymond's heart," she said, acknowledging that her husband would much rather get down on the floor and roll around with the kids than be stern with them. John said later that while many words had been used to describe his father—a player, leader, winner, a champion—to his children he was simply "Dad." And, he added, they could not have asked for a better father.

As a child, Richard was impressed by his father's dedication to his football career, even as he entered the twilight years of his playing career. On game days in Lambeau Field, Richard would watch as his father would remain behind late into the day, lifting weights after the locker room had emptied. Then, he and his father would help team trainer Domenic Gentile and equipment manager Dad Braisher clean up. "We would fold towels, do whatever," Richard remembered.

Being adopted by his parents, John said, was the most significant, most blessed day of his life. Amy, who never knew her father as a football player, said the legacy he provided for her was of a giving, loving man, a man of compassion and respect for others.

To his teammates, Nitschke's transformation from wild man to family man never ceased to amazed them. Kramer kiddingly remarked once that Nitschke had turned into a monk—"no drinking, no carousing, no nothing," Kramer said. When Nitschke's teammate, linebacker Dan Currie, asked him once what it was like not drinking anymore, Nitschke looked at him and smiled.

"Quiet, man," he said. "Real quiet."

Nitschke lived for his children; Kramer called him the most devoted father he had ever seen. In an era when NFL players were still modestly paid in relation to today's salaries, Nitschke was one of the few Packers who didn't take an off-season job. He was approached once in the mid-sixties by representatives of the Everseal Industrial Glue Company, who were looking for a salesman in the Wisconsin area. Nitschke didn't want the job and turned it down, so the company reps approached backup offensive tackle Steve Wright. After Wright took the job, he laughed when he heard that Nitschke had been the company's first choice.

"If you can imagine the least likely salesman in the world," Wright said later, "it would be Ray Nitschke." To Wright, Nitschke was the kind of guy who would walk into an executive's office, throw down a hunk of glue in front of him, and say, "You want some glue? Here. Buy it."

Nitschke turned down dozens of other job offers during his playing career, preferring instead to stay home and spend time with his family. He had a treehouse built in the family's backyard, and teammates thought it was so elaborate the only thing it lacked was a color television. When John saw a fishing program on television one day in 1966, he approached his father and asked why he had never taken him fishing. The following off-season, Nitschke took John to Florida on a month-long fishing trip.

The addition of Amy to the family followed the Packers' hiring of Dan Devine as Green Bay's new head coach and general manager. For the first time since his rookie season in 1958, Nitschke would be playing for someone other than Lombardi or Bengston. Nitschke had played the first seven games of the 1970 season hampered by a sore back, and like many of his teammates, he was preoccupied with thoughts of Lombardi, who had passed away from cancer on September 3. Bald and battered at age 33, Nitschke rebounded to play a strong second half. When Devine took over as head coach, he studied films of the Packers' 1970 season and saw the aging, hurting Nitschke moving slower than usual. Convinced Green Bay had to go with a youth movement, Devine played Jim Carter, a third-round pick from the 1970 draft out of the University of Minnesota, ahead of Nitschke throughout the exhibition season.

Nitschke started the regular season opener against the Giants, a 42–40 loss in Green Bay, and when the Packers hosted the Denver Broncos in Milwaukee's County Stadium the following week, he rode the bench for the first time since 1960. Leading 34–13 in the fourth quarter, Green Bay coaches motioned for Nitschke to go into the game. The great linebacker balked; hurt and angry, his pride stung, he felt for the first time in his life that he didn't want to get into a game. The feeling passed, and Nitschke pulled his helmet on. As he ran onto the field with those short, mincing steps, Packer fans rose and applauded. Hearing the ovation, Nitschke wiped his face, wiped away the tears streaming down behind his full-cage facemask. In a matter of an instant, Nitschke had gone from being angry with Devine to feeling tremendous love for Packer fans.

"It was unbelievable how I felt at that moment," Nitschke told Gentile. "It was one of the great moments of my career."

The relationship between Carter and Nitschke became strained. Carter had grown up in St. Paul, Minnesota, a six-hour drive west of Green Bay, and the thought of playing alongside legends like Nitschke and Starr was glamorous to him. Yet Packer fans turned on Carter when he was given Nitschke's starting role in 1971. The two regarded each other warily. In a biting comment, Nitschke said once that if he was going to be replaced at middle linebacker, it should only be by someone who had more talent than he did. Carter went around telling teammates he *was* better than Nitschke. The rivalry escalated in 1972, when Carter hurt his knee in a Week Six game against Atlanta in Milwaukee and had to leave the County Stadium field. The fans who had previously booed him now cheered, and Carter took it as a derisive cheer for his leaving the game. Nitschke, however, saw it as cheers not for Carter being injured, but for his entering the game.

Carter made the Pro Bowl in 1973, but he forever felt distanced from Packer fans. When a woman asked him once during a live call-in show from

Fuzzy Thurston's Left Guard restaurant if he would ever fill Nitschke's shoes, Carter cussed her out. "Go to hell," he said.

On December 12, in the 100th Bears–Packers game, Green Bay honored Nitschke with his own special day. The only Packer player who had been so honored previously was Starr. Bill King, a retired Green Bay police sergeant and civic leader, had contacted Nitschke to tell him that the Packers and their fans wanted to organize a Ray Nitschke Day. Nitschke agreed, and for weeks before the game the town was filled with bumper stickers and buttons that read "We Love Ray." Some 50,000 stickers and buttons were sold, and became so well-received that Nitschke's young nephew, Frank, wouldn't go to bed at night unless he had a Nitschke button pinned to his pajamas. King asked Nitschke what gifts he'd like to be presented with and suggested a new car. Nitschke declined. He had a car, a house, everything he really needed. Declining any expensive gifts, Nitschke asked King to take money raised for Ray Nitschke Day and establish a college scholarship fund. Nitschke knew that if it hadn't been for his own athletic scholarship, he would never have even gone to college, never become a pro football player. To Nitschke, establishing a college fund in his name would prove more satisfying than having another car in his garage. Nitschke insisted too, that the fund be open to all needy students, not just athletes.

Devine told Nitschke he would start against the Bears. Carter was moved to outside linebacker for the game, and as Nitschke printed the words "Beat the Bears" inside his knee pads, he thought of all the previous games he had played against the team that had been his boyhood favorite. Thought of his first game against Chicago, when as a member of the Chicago All-Stars he had traveled to Rensselaer, Indiana, to scrimmage the Bears. As he warmed up he caught sight of 6-foot-8 defensive end Doug Atkins. To the 21-year-old Nitschke, Atkins was huge and built like a Greek god. Once the game started, Nitschke grew comfortable after the first couple of plays, and after barreling into the Bears' big fullback, Rick Casares, along the Chicago sideline, was stunned to hear Bears' coach George Halas screaming at him.

"Here was my boyhood idol, cussing me out," Nitschke said later. From that point on, Nitschke developed an intense rivalry with Halas and the Bears. The intensity grew with Nitschke's first visit to Wrigley Field as a member of the Packers. Since he was from Chicago, Nitschke thought he'd get a few cheers from the fans when his name was announced. Instead, all he heard was Bear fans cursing him.

Through the 1960s, Nitschke saved some of his best games for the Bears. Lombardi stoked his club's competitive fire by declaring the week before each game with Chicago "Bear Week." Willie Davis said that while Nitschke got up for every game, the Packers' middle linebacker would psyche himself to another level for the Bears. Nitschke had interceptions against the Bears in 1962 and '66, and in '68 he preserved a 28–27 Packer victory by picking off a Jack Concannon pass with 1:07 left. The loss kept Chicago from clinching the Central Division title, and the Bears finished the season one game behind Minnesota and out of the NFL playoffs.

Nitschke punished the Bears at every opportunity. In 1964, he slammed tight end Mike Ditka so hard following a reception over the middle he could see Ditka's eyes roll over white before he spun to the ground. For a moment, Nitschke was scared. He thought he had killed Ditka. Knocked cold, Ditka was carried off the field by Chicago team trainers.

Chicago center Mike Pyle recalled Nitschke's interception that cost the Bears a shot at the Central Division title, but said once that the memory that lingered longest and strongest in his memory was of teammate George Seals going down with a blown knee. Seals was a power lineman, a 6-foot-2, 260-pound guard who ran the field like a marauder. Opposing defenses feared and hated Seals, and when he went down against the Packers, Pyle saw Nitschke standing over Seals, yelling at him, taunting him.

The Bears respected Nitschke, respected his hard hits, his approach to the game. Halas called Nitschke "a hard hitter but never a cheap-shot artist."

When Butkus joined the Bears in 1965, pro football writers at the time began comparing him to Nitschke. Butkus was probably a better defender in the short pass zone, Nitschke in the medium-range zone. The big difference was in how they played off their blocks. Nitschke broke up blocking schemes with his huge, punishing forearms; Butkus shed offensive linemen with his quickness and balance. Even the Lombardi Packers, drilled in precision angle blocking and owning the best offensive line of the 1960s, found it difficult to get a clear shot at Butkus. Forrest Gregg said when the Packers tried to cut Butkus, he'd jump over them. If they went too far upfield in their blocks, he'd slip inside them. If they waited too long trying to negate his inside move, Butkus would go over the top of them. Kramer recalled Butkus's great strength, his great hustle.

Nitschke and Butkus had a warrior's respect for one another. What Nitschke liked about Butkus was his tenacity as a player. To Nitschke, Butkus played every down with everything he had. "That's the way you're supposed to play the game," Nitschke said.

Butkus was incensed when the Bears lost to the Packers in '68. He argued with teammate Lloyd Phillips and nearly shoved him off the field for not taking the game seriously enough. When the Bears lost on Nitschke's interception, Butkus was enraged. "I was so damn mad," he said later, "I could have bit the goal posts."

Sunday, December 12, found Butkus standing in the tunnel waiting to take the field on Ray Nitschke Day. Game programs featured a three-page tribute to Nitschke. Under a heading that read "The Packers' 66" the tribute began with the words "Ray Nitschke is an internal contradiction, the kind of split personality that can be found only in a sport like professional football." The words were accompanied by a 12-photo collage of Nitschke's career, along with an insert from Marie Lombardi, Vince's widow:

Dear Ray and Jackie, Congratulations! There is a very happy coach in Heaven today who is very proud of you and all the Packers and the City of Green Bay for honoring one of its finest. You are a credit to the game, the Packers and Green Bay. God bless.

Amid frozen sunshine, Lambeau Filled was filled with 56,263 fans. It was cold and muddy, and Butkus noticed that everyone on the Packers was wearing warmup jackets; everyone that is, except Number 66. As Butkus watched Nitschke, he thought first how fortunate Nitschke was to have played for Lombardi.

Like Butkus, Nitschke was a graduate of the University of Illinois, and Butkus had always admired him more than any other player. They had first met in November 1962 when Butkus was a sophomore at Illinois. Nitschke had arrived at the university for a visit, and the two men were introduced by Dick's older brother Ronnie, who played defensive tackle and was a teammate of Ray's for a brief time. They made small talk, and Butkus struggled years later to recall what Nitschke had told him. Keep your head up? Wash behind your ears at night? Butkus couldn't remember, but it hardly mattered. He was quiet and self-conscious at the time, and what mattered most to him was that Nitschke, a man who was doing what he wanted to do with his life, had taken the time to talk with him.

A month later, Butkus sat in front of television and watched Nitschke dominate the 1962 NFL championship game against the Giants in Yankee Stadium. As he watched the game, Butkus felt he was out there helping Nitschke make every tackle. When Nitschke was named the game's MVP, Butkus was thrilled. If Nitschke had asked him, Butkus said, he would have gladly chauffeured Ray around in the new sports car Nitschke received as the MVP.

Seven years had passed, and Butkus and Nitschke hadn't spoken much since. They had become on-field rivals for the role of the best middle linebacker in the game in the late 1960s, and as Butkus watched Nitschke moving around out on the field he knew that the comparisons would continue this day as well. Nitschke headed toward the microphones positioned at midfield. He was accompanied by Jackie and his two sons, all bundled against the cold. John, the older of the two boys, carried his father's huge helmet by the facemask with both hands. Nitschke cut a familiar figure as he stood before the mikes—the bald head, the heavily padded forearms, the green-and-gold Packer uniform—but he had left off the black shoe polish beneath the eyes, and left in the partial plate he'd worn since his front teeth had been knocked into the dirt against Ohio State.

Three of Nitschke's former coaches—Elmer Johnson, Andy Puplis, and Ray Eliot—were introduced, and King announced the establishment of the college fund established in Nitschke's name. A token, he said, of the respect, admiration, and esteem the Packers and their fans held for Nitschke.

"You are more than a football player," King announced. "You are more than a professional athlete. You are a symbol of how all of God's children should live."

Stepping to the microphone, Nitschke told the cheering throng, "This is finest day of my life." He had been gifted by God, he said, to be an athlete, and he thanked all the people who had helped make his life something his children could respect. With his eyes misting up, Nitschke told the crowd, "Words can't express how I feel." With that, the aging warrior turned and joined his family as they walked toward the tunnel.

Seeing Nitschke in the tunnel, Butkus had an urge to walk up to him, stick out his hand and say, "Congratulations, Ray. You deserve it." He didn't, the moment passed, and Butkus regretted it for years. Moments later, they were both running out into the bright sunshine, playing on the same field together for the final time.

Willie Wood said later that the Packers were trying to win that day as much for Nitschke as for the team, and Green Bay set the tone on the game's first play from scrimmage when quarterback Scott Hunter threw a 77-yard touchdown to Carroll Dale. By game's end, Green Bay had gained a 31–10 win, and as Nitschke walked off the field, he was approached by Chicago defensive end Ed O'Bradovich, who gripped him in a friendly bearhug.

Asked later how he had played on Ray Nitschke Day, Nitschke shrugged.

"I could've played better," he said.

From Proviso High to the University of Illinois to the Green Bay Packers, the man voted the best linebacker in the NFL's first 50 years never left a football field believing he couldn't have played a better game.

TWELVE

OFFICIALLY, Ray Nitschke pulled his Green Bay Packers uniform off for the final time in the gathering dusk of Christmas Eve, 1972, following a 16–3 loss to the Washington Redskins in an NFC Divisional playoff game. He helped lead the team out of the tunnel onto the spongy RFK Stadium turf, and though he didn't start the game, Nitschke represented the Packers at midfield for the ceremonial coin toss prior to the game. He had been named a team co-captain prior to the season, and though he spent much of the year blocking for field goals and extra points on special teams and donning a headset on the sidelines to help with defensive signals, he remained an intimidating presence. Prior to an exhibition game against Houston, Nitschke's intensity frightened Oilers quarterback Dan Pastorini when they met at midfield.

"All right, dammit! C'mon ref, toss the damn coin," Nitschke said, jawing at the referee in his loud, nagging voice. "Let's get it over with . . . I want the hell out of here! Let's get this game going!"

Under Vince Lombardi, the Packers had learned to always call "heads" at the coin flip and always take the ball if heads came up. Someone told Lombardi once that heads was a better percentage call because the eagle side of the coin weighed more. Lombardi believed the idea, believed too that when the Packers won the toss, they should take the ball. "Vince always wanted to drive the ball down somebody's throat before they drove it down ours," offensive captain Bob Skoronski said.

Skoronski and defensive captain Willie Davis would gauge the other team's strength by the strength of their captain's handshake. Skoronski figured that if a captain on the other team had a handshake like a dead fish, then he had to be a pushover and so did his team. Skoronski and Davis always gave out the most brutal handshakes they could. They would grab the opposing captain's hand and submerge it in their own. "Then we'd squeeze like hell," Skoronski said. Skoronski and Davis believed if they could intimidate a player at the coin flip, it was one less guy Lombardi had to worry about during the game.

As a team captain, Nitschke picked up where Skoronski and Davis left off. He intimidated Pastorini at the coin flip, to the point that the Oilers quarterback later told a teammate that he was frightened by Nitschke's intensity. Though he spent much of the 1972 season on the sidelines, Nitschke was pleased that Green Bay was back on top in the Central Division, pleased that with a 10–4 record, the Pack was indeed back, as bumper stickers throughout Wisconsin proclaimed. He was not pleased with his lack of playing time, however, telling former teammate Bill Curry before a 1973 exhibition game, "I can play, man, I can go. I can still do it."

In the final days of his playing career, Nitschke would sit in hotels on game day, and to observers like Curry, who ran into him at the Pfister Hotel in Milwaukee, Nitschke's presence created an impression of being caught in a time warp. To Curry, it was almost eerie, seeing the Packer legend sitting there in a lobby chair, his bald head gleaming in the lights. The old warrior had a regal presence about him; Curry thought Nitschke could have passed for a sultan or a potentate of ancient times, surveying all that had once been his. Prior to one of his last games, Nitschke was in the lobby of the Pfister Hotel when he spotted Curry.

"If I do play," Nitschke told him, "you better buckle it up."

When Curry remarked that he always had to buckle it up against him, Nitschke remarked, "Yeah, but I'm fighting for my life this time."

Nitschke never got in the game. With five minutes left and the Packers leading by some 20 points, fans in County Stadium began chanting "We want Nitschke!" Nitschke didn't move, and as he stood there, straight as a statue, it struck Curry that Packer coach Dan Devine was trying to turn Nitschke into a monument before Ray was ready to become one. Curry was reminded of his former teammate in Baltimore, John Unitas, and how he had been treated at the end of his career. Colt lineman Dan Sullivan once said, only half-jokingly, that Unitas was the only guy whose number they tried to retire while he was still in uniform.

Curry thought Nitschke's situation was just as sad, and as the final minutes ticked off the stadium clock, Curry was drawn closer to the Packer bench, which in County Stadium was on the same sideline as the visiting team's. At the final gun, Curry ran over to thank Nitschke for all he had done for him, and as he watched the big Number 66 shuffle off the field in that familiar gait, Curry realized he had just touched a living legend. As Nitschke left the County Stadium field for the final time, it appeared to Curry that the Packer great had, like so many others, been brought down in the end by the very sport he had helped so much to build.

Packers trainer Domenic Gentile watched Nitschke struggle, physically and emotionally, in his final days. In the 1972 season, Nitschke tore his right hamstring prior to a game against Detroit, and the back of his leg from his groin to his knee turned black from the hemorrhaged muscle.

Since he was already playing with a left leg that had atrophied early in his career, Nitschke by Gentile's account played against the Lions on one-half of one good leg.

Though his body was wearing down, Nitschke remained an intimidating figure, a physical enforcer from the old days. On Sunday, September 24, he stood on the sidelines as the Packers struggled against the Oakland Raiders at Lambeau Field. As Green Bay fell behind 20–14 in the fourth quarter, Oakland center Jim Otto could hear Nitschke yelling at middle linebacker Jim Carter from the sideline.

"I was having a very good game against Carter and the interior linemen," Otto recalled. "It was a tough day, but we were moving the ball and doing the things we had to do. And Ray was on the sidelines, screaming and yelling at Carter not to let Otto block him.

"Finally, Ray came into the game, and he came in with the intent of not doing anything but destroying me physically. And he darn near did. He was screaming and hollering; he'd scream out the signals and directions for his linemen and then scream out the player's name that he was going after, you know, 'I'm gonna git you, Otto.'

"He hit me with his fists, forearms, and everything, broke my helmet, broke my cheekbone, broke my nose, and detached the retina in my left eye. It was a very brutal attack. But I kept right on playing, kept right on hitting, and eventually my face swelled up. I couldn't see out of my left eye and wouldn't see out of it for the next six months.

"I looked the worse for wear after that game, I'll guarantee it. My folks were over from Wassau and they went to the airport with us and they couldn't believe it. The whole left side of my face was swelled up, my eye was closed. And I said, 'Well, Mr. Nitschke did that, mom.' "

Unlike other athletes of his era—Jim Brown, Sandy Koufax, Bill Russell—Nitschke hung on to the game he loved despite the slow but steady erosion of his skills from age and injury. Hung on, he said, to prove he could survive 15 years in a sport that challenged him not just physically but mentally and emotionally as well.

Nitschke survived, and when it finally came time for him to make his retirement official, he at last seemed at peace with his decision.

"I guess the time has arrived," he said. "It comes for everybody. It has happened before and will happen again. . . . For the benefit of myself and the Green Bay Packers, I feel it's the right thing to retire. Every good thing must come to an end someday and so must my football playing days."

For close to 15 years, Nitschke had starred in Packer game films. Starting in 1975, he would go on a 13-year run as a prominent part of a series of 128 national television commercials. He had done some acting before. In 1968 he appeared in *Head,* an unusual motion picture starring the TV rock group

The Monkees. The picture proves a satire of several movie genres, and Nitschke's role occurs in a vignette on war movies. Nitschke plays the part of "Private One," a shell-shocked soldier who is wearing a blue-and-gold Notre Dame-style football uniform with the number one on it. When Monkee Peter Tork is sent out during a battle to get extra ammunition, he takes momentary cover from the exploding shells in a bunker, where he meets up with Private One. Nitschke repeats the mantra, "We're number one!" to a wary Tork, then slams helmet first into the side of the bunker. Interpretation of the scene is left to the viewer, but at a time when Lombardi's "Winning isn't everything, it's the only thing" slogan was being chiseled into stone, it was ironic that The Monkees chose one of the more famous Packers to play the role of Private One. The movie was written and produced by Jack Nicholson, and featured appearances by Terri Garr and Frank Zappa, along with another famous sports personality, former heavyweight champion Sonny Liston.

Nitschke appeared in his second movie in 1974, playing the part of Bogdanski, a hard-edged prison guard and member of the prison's semi-pro football squad in *The Longest Yard*. The film starred Burt Reynolds as Paul "Wrecking" Crewe, a former All-Pro player who leads the prison's team of inmates. Crewe is at odds with the warden, played by Eddie Albert, and just before the climactic game at film's end, Bogdanski appears in the prisoner's locker room. Looking to intimidate the inmates, Bogdanski punches a hole in the locker room wall, then takes up his role as the warden's enforcer during the game. Bogdanski inflicts physical pain on the prisoners before the inmates get even at the end and win the game.

Nitschke always negotiated his own business deals, and shrugged off advice that he could get rich if he hired a business agent. "I'd rather handle that stuff myself," he said, and proceeded to do so. He became a spokesman for Oldsmobile and joined Dick Butkus in a series of Midwest regional TV commercials. One commercial found Nitschke dressed as a woman and appearing as his fictionalized sister. He did good-will work for a major Wisconsin dairy and public relations work for Clairmont, a trucking firm.

His most remembered part, however, was as one of the ex-athletes on the Miller Lite beer commercials. His first Miller Lite commercial teamed him with Rosey Grier and Ben Davidson and showed the three big men doing needlepoint. Another spot had the balding Nitschke surrounded by chrome-domed look-alikes.

Nitschke took his TV appearances seriously and was proud of the fact that the Miller Lite series had become the most successful advertising campaign in the history of commercial television. To a generation of younger viewers, Nitschke was recognized not for his Hall of Fame career with Lombardi's legendary Packers, but for his appearances in beer commercials. He was comfortable with that, comfortable with the fact that people saw him as more than just a frightening specter on the football field but as someone they could approach and talk to.

"I think I'm a pretty nice guy," he said. Nitschke enjoyed people, enjoyed meeting them and getting along with them. He told Warren Gerds of the *Green Bay Press-Gazette* in a 1987 interview that people related to him because they knew he was trying to be a good guy and was striving to improve himself as a human being.

"I treat everybody like I want to be treated," Nitschke said. "That's kind of been my philosophy."

Nitschke's business trips sometimes took him away from home for as much as two weeks at a time. "He traveled a lot, and did a lot of speeches for different companies, a lot of motivational speeches," his daughter Amy remembered. "He did a lot of autograph shows too, but when he was home, he was really there for us. He was always very loving, very caring, but he was kind of comedic too. He could be a real jokester."

Once he retired, Nitschke didn't speak to his children much of his NFL career. But there were times when his memory was prodded, and he would open up to them about what it was like to have played in such a special era.

"We'd go to the games together and that would trigger some memories," Amy said. "He would compare life then to what it was later. But there were other times I would say something to him and I would have to prod him, you know. There were times when he didn't seem comfortable talking about it."

Amy's earliest memories of her father date back to 1975, when he was already three years out of football. The stories she's heard since of his playing days, the video clips she's seen, she said, are hard to relate to the man she knew as her father growing up.

"I didn't really see that part of him," she said, "and I'm sure it was probably very different for my brothers because they're older than I am. They were around when he was still playing, when he was getting ready for the game, getting his mindset ready to play. But he was so out of football when I was young, I can't relate him to that at all."

On July 29, 1978, Nitschke took his place among the game's immortals when he was inducted into the Pro Football Hall of Fame. Other inductees that day in Canton, Ohio, included Lance Alworth, Weeb Ewbank, Alphonse "Tuffy" Leemans, and Larry Wilson. When Nitschke's bust was unveiled, the words inscribed on it provide a terse description of his career:

First Green Bay defender from 1960s to be enshrined . . . Exceptional team leader, tough, strong, fast . . . Savage defender on rushes, cat-like quick against passes . . . Named NFL's all-time top linebacker, 1969 . . . All-NFL three years . . . Intercepted pass for TD in 1964 Pro Bowl . . . Had 25 *career interceptions . . . MVP in 1962 NFL title game.*

207

Dressed in the beige sports jacket that all new inductees wear, with a white shirt and brown-and-tan patterned tie, Nitschke stepped to the podium to address the sun-splashed audience. He spoke with passion and feeling, pausing at times only to check his notes and adjust his dark-rimmed glasses.

"Football gave me a chance to express myself, to get recognition, and to do something well," he told his audience. "I was committed to the game of football, and I'll never forget the great game that it is. It's given Ray Nitschke the chance for an education, to better himself, to be a better human being."

He had been enshrined the previous February in the Packer Hall of Fame, and in 1981 was inducted along with Bart Starr into the Wisconsin Hall of Fame. His number 66 was retired by the Packers in 1983, and in 1997 one of the team's practice fields was named after him. In 1994, Nitschke was named by writers and historians to the NFL's 75th Anniversary Team and to the Team of the Sixties.

Surprisingly, he is not listed among the distinguished graduates of Proviso, a list that includes NASA astronaut Eugene Cernan, a 1952 graduate; actor Dennis Franz ('62) and actress Carol Lawrence ('50); Olympians Gerald Holan ('49) and Blanche Kloss ('55); and 13 pro athletes, including major league pitcher Lee Stange ('54), NBA players Glen "Doc" Rivers ('80) and Michael Finley ('91); and NFL defensive back Ray Buchanon ('87). Nitschke's glaring omission rankles some of his former teammates at Proviso, but the school has at times honored him with a display of various Nitschke mementos, including the plaque he received on Ray Nitschke Day at Lambeau Field.

Nitschke accepted each honor with a humble grace, because he knew, as Paul Hornung said, how much the game had given him.

"I've always said that pro football did more for Ray Nitschke than anyone else," Hornung remarked. "There was a time when he was headed out of the league and down, until he stopped and turned it around."

As he aged, Nitschke cut back on his traveling, and when at home would settle in and watch sporting events on his big-screen TV. The TV fronted the north wall of his family room, which also housed a large oil painting of him in uniform at Lambeau Field. He watched a variety of sports, but had the greatest interest in football and baseball, the two sports he had starred in at Proviso and had received pro offers for. In his later years, his interest in football other than the Packers was confined largely to the college game. He could see the passion in the college players, and as

Amy heard him say, many of the kids who were playing college football were still playing for the love of the game.

When he wasn't watching sports, he tuned in The History Channel or took in an occasional war movie if he happened to catch one while channel-surfing. He enjoyed movies about World War II, but not about Vietnam. One of his favorite war movies was Patton, starring George C. Scott. Scott's portrayal of the all-conquering general was such that several members of the Lombardi Packers said they're always reminded of their former coach when watching the film.

Though he was a fan of the old movies, Nitschke rarely rented them on his own. He would sit down and watch a movie with his children if one of them brought a video to his house, but he rarely went out of his way to visit the video store.

His taste in reading materials was just as selective. He read newspapers every day, and enjoyed *Golf Digest* and *Time*. After Jackie passed away, he made it a point to read an AA daily devotional. "He liked motivational books," Amy said, "something where he could read a page every day."

He continued to do various commercial and charitable causes. His name adorned the weekly *Ray Nitschke's Packer Report*, which began in 1970. For nine years, Al Pahl was a ghost-writer for Nitschke's column. Pahl would call Nitschke after every Packer game, interview him, then write Nitschke's column, which appeared on the inside cover of the publication.

"Ray couldn't write a lick," Pahl said, "so some time Sunday night I would get a hold of Ray, wherever he was. Might be Orlando, Anaheim, or Chicago. If Ray hadn't seen the game, I actually had to tell him the highlights. Then he would give me his thoughts. Then we'd get off the phone and I would go back and dress it up. But Ray took this very seriously, so he always made sure I could contact him."

Nitschke was a spokesman for Norwegian Cruise Lines, and he and Jackie liked the cruise ships and would take one or two trips a year. On one occasion, when Ray and Jackie were on a cruise during a Packer game, Pahl had to set up a ship-to-shore connection to conduct the interview.

Pahl was impressed by Nitschke's dedication to his publication, and impressed too by the sheer physicality of the man. Nitschke, Pahl said, had huge hands and shoulders, but Pahl was more taken with what he described as Nitschke's "huge heart." The two men became friends, and in their nine years working together, Pahl said Nitschke never refused to sign an autograph with a smile, never refused to stop and talk to strangers. At the request of a friend, Nitschke once telephoned a man who was dying of cancer to offer words of encouragement; on another occasion, he helped smooth a difficult relationship between a father and his stepchildren by talking the man up in front of the kids during a chance meeting at the mall.

Nitschke made friends far and wide. Terry Ainsworth, who lives in Birmingham, England, telephoned Nitschke regularly and even opened his own Packers Hall of Fame overseas. Nitschke was close to many of the Packers of the mid-1990s, and Reggie White, for one, was always appreciative of his support. "Ray was always there for us," White said.

White said many of the Packers from that era were awed by Nitschke and the other legends of the Lombardi years. As the years went by, Nitschke became a source of inspiration for many of the people he came in contact with. Whether it was signing an autograph for 4-year-old Steven Golla— "To Steve, always try hard, do well in school, and never give up. . . . Ray Nitschke"—or handing over a perspiration-soaked Packer hat to Wisconsin governor Tommy Thompson at a game in Dallas, he seemed to loom larger than life.

"His indomitable spirit embodied the Packers," the governor said. "I had great respect for the man. Just being with him was a thrill."

Nitschke could startle people with his cement-mixer voice, as he did Carla Dionne of Marinette, Wisconsin. She was in the pet supply aisle at the Wal-Mart in Green Bay, struggling to lift a 50-pound bag of dog food from the bottom shelf when she heard a graveled voice behind her:

"Either you need to stop feeding your dog so much or you need to get smaller dogs."

She spun around and was greeted by the sight of the massive Nitschke, grinning at her. He bent over, picked up the 50-pound bag and with what she described as the ease of a man tossing a pillow, tossed the heavy bag into her cart.

He routinely took off his 1967 Super Bowl ring to allow others to try it on for size—"It was so big I could fit three of my fingers in it," longtime friend Tony Fiovani said—and delighted showing it to children. "Hey, kid," he'd say, pulling the diamond-encrusted ring off his finger. "How'd you like to see something special?"

He never turned anyone down for an autograph or a posed photo, and he didn't just sign autographs, he personalized them:

"Congratulations to my good friend, Cliff Kinabrew, from old #66";

"To Gabe Yandoli, a big-time Packer fan, Best wishes always, keep happy and well";

"To my friend Billy Toogood . . . You're a real fine young man. . . . Hit 'em hard";

"To Karen, a beautiful football fan . . . Love ya and God bless."

Anticipating autograph requests, Nitschke carried extra copies of his 8x10-inch black-and-white glossies and Hall of Fame pictures with him. When Jim Kardoskee of Oconto Falls, Wisconsin, asked him once for autographs for himself and his uncle, Nitschke willingly obliged. When

Kardoskee asked for a third autograph, Nitschke winked at the boy's mother.

"Kind of pushing a good thing, aren't you?" he asked. "Who's it for?"

When Kardoskee told him it was for his brother—"He'd kill me if I got one for my uncle and not him," he said—Nitschke signed it without delay. He would muss the hair of little ones with his bearlike paw, then lean over and in a stage whisper, say, "Take care of your parents."

When friends asked how he could always be so accommodating, Nitschke would issue a quick smile.

"I'm a has-been football player," he would say. "This is good for my ego."

He talked to strangers about commitment, about giving all they had to give in work and in life. He touched people with his grace and dignity, a gentle giant with a fondness for overpowering hugs and oversized cigars.

He was standing in the lobby of a Chicago hotel, smoking his cigar when he was mistaken by a couple as a part of the staff. He had been hired as a greeter for a local business, and was wearing a dark tuxedo and red bow tie. As the couple approached with their bags, he tried to hide the cigar by placing it behind his back. When the couple dropped their bags at his feet, he brought the huge cigar slowly around from his back, took a long draw, and told them, "Nitschke don't do bags."

What he did do was charitable causes. Ray and Jackie spent 22 years as co-chairpersons of the Cerebral Palsy Telethon, and Ray supported his wife's involvement in The Bridge, Inc., an organization dedicated to helping recovering alcoholics and their families. Nitschke also served on the board of the Green Bay Boys Club and as chairman of the Kinney Kidney Foundation of Minneapolis.

Marianne Oates, a communications coordinator for Schreiber Foods in Green Bay, worked with Ray and Jackie on the Cerebral Palsy Telethon from 1977 to 1985. She remembered Nitschke personally signing hundreds of donor letters every year, and recalled the couple making numerous appearances at fund-raising events, visiting the centers to chat with clients and participating in countless photo sessions.

Nitschke's involvement with his wife's causes impressed those who knew the couple. Jackie was a recovering alcoholic, and when the Jackie Nitschke Center was dedicated in April of 1997 to honor her for having spent the last 16 years of her life helping others battle the addiction, Nitschke stood in a stairwell at the center introducing himself to those who had come to the dedication.

"Hi," he told each person. "I'm Jackie Nitschke's husband."

Al Guldan, Nitschke's accountant, watched Ray that day and had seen the gruff man's sincerity.

"He was so proud of her," Guldan said.

Jim Temp, a former teammate of Nitschke's on the Packers and now a member of the Packers Executive Committee, remembered once how Jackie always called her husband by his full name, "Raymond," and how her voice seemed to brighten his face.

Guldan once related to Ray and Jackie the story of their first meeting with Nitschke in the summer of 1972. The Packers training camp had opened and Guldan, then 11 years old, and his nine-year-old brother Buzz biked from their house in Ashwaubenon to Green Bay. Knowing that Packer team trainers sometimes threw away rolls of tape with a few feet left on them, the brothers began rummaging through garbage cans at the camp for tape to use on their hockey sticks. When Buzz, who was wearing sandals, cut his foot and began crying, Al bent down to inspect the damage. At that moment, the brothers heard a raspy voice behind them.

"Hey! What're you guys doin' there?"

Turning around, they were startled to see Nitschke towering over them. He took the two boys into the locker room, where a team trainer took care of Buzz's bloodied foot. A call was placed to Al's older brother, and Nitschke waited with the boys until they were picked up.

When Guldan finished his story, Jackie smiled. "That's my husband," she said.

As the couple's accountant, Guldan saw how much money Ray turned down in endorsements, and the amount of non-profit work he and Jackie did.

Jackie's influence on Ray extended to one of his favorite hobbies, golf. He played at the Oneida Golf & Riding Club, which was located just five miles from his home, and despite an unorthodox swing, eventually got his game down to a 1-handicap. Art Daley, a member of the Oneida Club and the former sports editor of the *Press-Gazette*, said Nitschke's swing was strictly homemade, but he made up for it with physical strength.

"He really crushed the ball," Daley said.

Still highly competitive, Nitschke enjoyed playing golf with friends at Oneida. The game served as an outlet for his aggression. As he grew older, tightness in his back limited him to a three-quarters swing and deprived him of remaining a consistent long-ball hitter, but he loved the game too much to stop playing. He played for personal pride and played for money— small side-bets with his golfing partners. There was one Saturday morning, however, when Nitschke's golf game was unexpectedly cut short. Nitschke had already played 18 holes that morning and had joined playing partner

Jock Seals and two others for another round. The foursome was on the first tee when they saw Jackie coming down from the ninth hole.

"Raymond, are you playing 18?"

"Yeah."

"Oh no, you're not."

Nitschke left the group after the ninth hole. "She really ran the roost," Seals said of Jackie.

On another occasion, Guldan was on the course with his young stepson when they saw Nitschke on a nearby practice green. Guldan wanted to take the boy over to meet the Packer great but was reluctant to interrupt his practice. Jackie, however, didn't think it would be an intrusion at all.

"Raymond," she called.

"Yeah?"

Moments later, Nitschke went over to Guldan and his stepson, visited with them, and signed an autograph for the boy.

The Nitschke children watched the dynamics of their parents' relationship with a sense of fascination. "It was very interesting," Amy said. "They had fun together, they loved doing things together. They loved playing golf and they had their interests, but they both had their tempers too; neither one minded voicing their opinion. There was a point where they just couldn't take each other and they needed a break. So that was a nice thing about my dad traveling a little bit. They really appreciated each other when they were together."

Richard recalled days when his parents, like all parents, would argue. "Mother was in AA," he said, "and there were times before she quit drinking that they would have fights. But it was never anything serious. They were together, and that was it."

Ray and Jackie were friendly with quite a few couples, and would go on golfing outings locally or to Florida or Arizona. The children went along at times too, and were always subject more to their mother's words than their father's.

"She was more of a disciplinarian, as far as us kids go," Amy said. "She could really put her foot down with my dad."

When she did, and called him "Raymond," the kids knew their dad had done something wrong. "He was in trouble," Amy laughed.

Temp thought Jackie was Ray's entire life, and when she passed away from cancer in the summer of 1996, the loss hit him particularly hard. She had struggled with cancer for years. In May 1995, she had a cancerous lung removed; in April 1996, a cancerous brain tumor was taken out. When she passed, Rev. Arni Jacobson, the pastor of the Bayside Christian Fellowship Church in Green Bay that Ray and Jackie attended, said Jackie's illness had profoundly impacted Ray's life. He replaced Sunday morning golf with church and began living a Christ-centered life.

Jacobson observed Nitschke's conversion to religion first-hand. He first met Nitschke in 1992, when Jackie invited the Reverend and his wife to attend a Packers preseason game. Jackie had been a church-going member of the congregation for years, and when Ray and the Reverend met for the first time at the game, Nitschke let his feelings on church be known immediately.

"The first thing he said to me was, 'My wife likes you, I'm going to like you, just don't talk to me about church,'" Jacobson recalled. "His mom died and his dad had been killed by a street car, and he kind of felt God had dealt him (a harsh blow). We saw each other at quite a few social functions, and then his wife became quite ill."

Jacobson said that during the time of Jackie's illness Nitschke really embraced a close relationship with the Lord. When friends called to inquire about Jackie's health, Nitschke would tell them, "It's in God's hands."

Amy said that her father's conversion was many years in the making. The death of his parents, she said, had left him bitter and angry. "It was very hard for him to cope with that," she said.

Jackie had been raised Catholic, and while she observed her religion, Amy remembered her going through stages where she would alternately lose and then regain interest. Because Jackie had to get an annulment from her first marriage, she found it difficult to go to Mass with her parents when they visited. "That left a bad taste in her mouth," Amy remembered. "There was a period of eight years or so where she wasn't very religious."

Jackie would go to church on occasion, but her involvement in it wasn't very strong. "She went mostly for the kids," Amy said. "Dad would go sometimes. If he didn't go, we would ask mom, 'If Dad's not going, why do I have to?' And then here would come Dad, in his suit."

Friends invited Jackie to non-denominational services, and she soon began attending Bayside Christian Fellowship.

"It took some time, but Dad started coming around too," Amy said. "When my mom got sick, he started looking around for answers, trying to understand. And his faith in God became a very big thing for him."

Kay San Miguel remembered seeing Nitschke in church when Jackie was ill, and seeing him weeping so that tears were dripping off his nose. Jackie was dying, he told San Miguel, and he was taking care of her. She had always taken of him, Nitschke said, and now he was taking care of her. He gave San Miguel a hug, and as he walked away, San Miguel said she saw in this giant of a man a hero.

When Jackie passed, a part of her husband went with her. When friends visited him Nitschke after Jackie's death, they got the impression that the spark that once ignited Ray's life had been reduced to a flicker. Nitschke began thinking more about heaven and the after-life, and talked with his children about his own eventual funeral arrangements.

He filled the void left by Jackie's passing by spending more time with his children and grandchildren. Nitschke would take Amy and his one-year-old granddaughter, Jacqueline Rae, to the Oneida Club and show the baby off to his friends. "He was really proud of that granddaughter," Temp said.

He walked three miles a day, rousing the Siberian husky he named Butkus from his plastic, igloolike home in the yard to accompany him. He spent increased time at Skip's Place, a coffee shop located on Holmgren Way near Lambeau Field. Skip's became an automatic stop for Nitschke, and he indulged in blueberry pancakes and trading small talk and good-natured insults with the hired help and customers. Nitschke always sat on the same stool—second from the end at the counter. Rob Heinz, co-owner of Skip's, remembered Nitschke's gruff bantering with the customers, remembered too the time Ray stood to have his picture taken with some women, only to find out later his zipper had been down for the photograph.

"There were a couple of places he would hit," Richard remembered. "Skip's Place, a little Greek restaurant called the Golden Basket. He used to go in and give the waitresses some shit once in a while. He didn't mean anything by it, he just liked picking on some of them, just for the hell of it. He would get a kick out of it when some of them would argue with him. He was funny that way."

Nitschke's personality could be overpowering, and he drew a crowd wherever he went. When the Packers returned to the Super Bowl in January 1997 for the first time since the Lombardi era, Nitschke spent part of the week in New Orleans, the host city. Despite the number of celebrities and football greats in town, Nitschke was surrounded by fans every time he visited Bourbon Street.

"I'm bigger now than when I was playing," Nitschke would tell his family, and Amy knew why. Her father loved being with fans, she said, and fans loved being with him. When people would stop and tell him he was their favorite player in the 1960s, Nitschke would grin. "Aw, you're kidding," he would say, then shake their hand and make small talk. Hardly a day went by when someone wasn't bringing up his playing days under Lombardi. "I think I'll always be 'Number 66,'" Nitschke said. And he continued to add to his legend by becoming a spokesman for America's Pack Fan Club, making appearances at hardware shows for "Easy Painter" products and endorsing clothing for NFL Throwbacks and Champion sportswear.

Nitschke saw his dealings with the public as a way of repaying the debt he felt he owed to football. He saw himself as someone who had been lucky enough to make a living doing exactly what he wanted to do, and felt the game of football had been so good to him that he wanted to give back to the game by treating people in the same manner he wanted to be treated.

At times, the attitudes of modern athletes disturbed him. Dick Butkus remembered being with Nitschke at an NFL Properties luncheon prior to one of the Super Bowl games. Butkus had arrived first, and was sitting in a chair by himself when Nitschke arrived. Butkus watched as the Packer great went around the room, renewing acquaintances with players from his own era and introducing himself to others. There were two current NFL stars slouched on a couch, and when Nitschke introduced himself to them, their response was indifferent. From his chair, Butkus saw Nitschke turn and approach him.

"I'm watching him, and he comes up to me," Butkus said. "He'd always hit you on your shoulder, and he comes up and says, 'When someone older than you comes up and introduces himself, you get your ass up.'"

Every summer, Nitschke would attend the Pro Football Hall of Fame induction ceremonies in Canton, Ohio, and he made it a point to impress upon the new inductees at the formal luncheon how special it was to be a part of the Hall. Joe Horrigan, the Hall of Fame's historian, recalled Nitschke's passion during the luncheon that has since been renamed in his honor.

"He would read the new guys the riot act," Horrigan said. Gale Sayers said the luncheon was Nitschke's time to shine, and Frank Gifford recalled once how Nitschke would rant and rave, in a style that seemed Lombardi-like, and remind each Hall of Famer how much it means to be part of such a select group. St. Louis Cardinals Hall of Fame safety Larry Wilson said the intensity from one of Nitschke's speeches stayed with him for three or four years. "It pumped you up," Wilson said.

Nitschke's circle of friends wasn't limited to football players. Vern Biever recalled a day when he and Nitschke were walking around the grounds at Canton when they spotted former Speaker of the House Tip O'Neill.

"Hi, Ray," O'Neill said.

"Hi, Tip," Nitschke answered.

Biever laughed at the memory of the exchange. "Ray knew everybody," he said, "and everybody knew Ray."

Don Smith, who served as the Hall's vice president of public relations from 1968 to 1997, thought Nitschke epitomized what Canton was all about. Smith first met him in 1978, when Nitschke was inducted into the Hall. To Smith, Nitschke felt more strongly about his induction in Canton than any other Hall of Famer he had ever known. So strongly in fact, that in 1996, when Jackie was dying of cancer, she insisted her husband attend the induction ceremonies without her. Nitschke did, and he delivered a passionate speech about the honor the Hall of Famers share, and that it was important enough that his dying wife had insisted he make the trip. Three days later, Jackie died, and not long after, his health began to suffer as well.

The flame that had brightened Ray's life for so long had been extinguished, and Richard could see that his father was no longer the same man, physically or mentally. "We were at the (1998) Super Bowl and he was complaining about stomach problems," Richard said. "And without my mom to drag his ass to the hospital or to the doctor . . . And that's what it would have taken for him to go."

In early March 1998, just before he left for a trip to Naples, Florida, to visit Amy and his granddaughter, Nitschke's favorite stool at Skip's Place collapsed suddenly and fell apart. Just days later, on Sunday, March 8, Nitschke was traveling with his daughter and granddaughter to visit friends in Venice, Florida, when he began experiencing chest pains at around 12:30 P.M. Amy pulled in to a Venice convenience store to get water, and when she returned to the car, she realized her father had suffered a heart attack. She performed CPR, and he was rushed to Venice Hospital. At 1:30 P.M., Ray Nitschke was pronounced dead. He was 61 years old.

Nitschke's memorial service was held at Bayside Christian Fellowship at 2 P.M. on Saturday, March 14. It was the first public event at the new facility, a fact that struck Rev. Jacobson. "Ray was so excited to see it finished," he said, "and to be part of it."

Nitschke's Hall of Fame bust, his 75th Anniversary All-NFL team trophy, a portrait and several photos were displayed at the service. In attendance were numerous former teammates—Bart Starr, Willie Davis, Carroll Dale, Jim Taylor. The ceremony drew in excess of the church's capacity of 1,250, and was carried live on WBAY-TV Channel 12. A videotape shows Mary Smits and Bill Jartz guiding viewers through the service with a minimum amount of conversation and commentary. The setting outside seemed reminiscent of so many of those big games Nitschke had played in during the Green Bay glory years—the air was clear and cold, the winter-brown grass covered with patches of ice and snow. Some Packer fans attended the ceremony wearing a replica of Nitschke's forest green jersey with the gold and white piping on the sleeves and the big number 66 in white on the front and back. One of those wearing the green-and-gold was John McMahon, who traveled from Milwaukee to attend the ceremony. His Nitschke jersey had been signed by Ray in 1997, and he said the funeral would mark the last time McMahon would wear the jersey. He was going home to have it framed for hanging on his wall.

Nitschke's remains were cremated, and he was buried in Green Bay. A Ray Nitschke Memorial Fund was established at Northwest Bank in Green Bay, with funds being distributed to several charities. Just as he had in life, Nitschke was continuing to give to others even in death.

Praise for Nitschke as a person and a player poured forth from numerous sources.

Amy thanked God for bringing her into his life 26 years ago. "He is the best father I could have ever had," she said. "I will miss him deeply."

"You could never ask for a better father," John said. "Richard, Amy, and I are going to miss our father. We are going to miss those big hugs."

Rev. Jacobson thought Nitschke squeezed more out of life in his 61 years than some of the oldest people that have ever lived. "I haven't seen Ray for the last time," he said. "In my spirit, I can hear him say, 'Pastor, I am having a wonderful time, wish you were here. Jackie sends her love.' "

The list of those offering their memories of Nitschke as a player and a person was long and impressive.

Vern Biever: "He came to play . . . you could tell by the expression on his face, even on the sidelines. . . . Off the field, Ray was a very kind gentleman, a very quiet man."

Carroll Dale: "Ray was a man that in my memory always loved people genuinely."

Lee Remmel: "He was loved by thousands and thousands of Packers fans, because he always had time for them. I remember sitting in the hotel lobbies when we were on the road and he obligingly posed for many photos and signed hundreds of autographs."

Former Bears tight end and head coach Mike Ditka: "There's no one I went against who I respected more than Ray. There was no love lost between us, but that's the way he wanted it. He left everything he had on that field. . . . There aren't many like him anymore."

Willie Davis stood and spoke of Nitschke's life as a journey, a journey that began in Chicago and ended in Green Bay. Along the way, Davis said, Nitschke created a love affair with Packer fans, and with the city itself.

"There will be a lot of people that will play middle linebacker for Green Bay and in the National Football League," Davis concluded. "In my opinion, there will never be another Ray Nitschke."

EPILOGUE

FRIDAY, **OCTOBER 2, 1998,** dawned cool and partly cloudy over greater Green Bay. Downtown, a crowd of some 500 people gathered to dedicate the new Main Street Bridge that spans the Fox River. The $22 million steel-and-concrete structure was built to stand as a link between east and west Green Bay, to serve the needs of not only those who travel by car but walkers and bicyclists as well.

In short, the sturdy bridge symbolizes the name of the man who served the needs of the people of Green Bay for so many years, the man to whom the bridge was dedicated that cool autumn day.

"Not only now is my father part of the Green Bay Packers history, now he's part of the Green Bay city history," Amy Klaas told the gathering at the dedication of the Ray Nitschke Memorial Bridge. She choked back tears as she saw a dozen or so people wearing Packer jerseys with uniform number 66 on them. Three city workers were also wearing Nitschke replica jerseys as well.

Wisconsin Governor Tommy Thompson told the crowd that the sturdy bridge was a fitting tribute to a sturdy man. "To me," Thompson said, "there was no greater Packer than Ray. I tell you, we've all got Ray in our hearts and minds today."

Amy and her brother Richard tossed a bright green memorial wreath with their father's name on it from the side of the bridge into the Fox River, and 66 white doves were released into the air. Toward the end of the ceremony, a bronze plaque bearing a sculpture of Nitschke was unveiled, and as people stood in line waiting to have their picture taken with Nitschke's likeness, some wondered if the plaque looked mean enough. Sue Wilde, who together with her husband Bob Antolec own the De Pere Foundry where the plaque was cast, wasn't worried.

"He looks plenty mean enough," she said.

Shirley Knaus, whose family was acquainted with Nitschke, told *Green Bay Press-Gazette* writer Tom Cioni she just had to be at the dedication. "I wouldn't miss this for the world," she said.

LaVerne Webster, who lived near Nitschke in Oneida and talked with him at times, was glad the day had finally arrived when the people of Green Bay could give something back to the man they admired. "He is so deserving," she said at the ceremony. "It's a wonderful day, a long-awaited day."

Today, the Ray Nitschke Memorial Bridge supports traffic of all kinds—business men and women in cars, mothers pushing strollers, cyclists, walkers. That a bridge bearing Nitschke's name and likeness serves the needs of his community and links east and west Green Bay is fitting, since Nitschke himself gave so much to the people of his area during his lifetime and served as a bridge between Green Bay's past and present.

"We all loved Ray Nitschke," Willie Davis said. "In Wisconsin, there was no player more revered than Ray."

Nitschke not only linked Packer history, he bridged the history of two generations of great middle linebackers. He was drafted by the Packers in 1958, at a time when the position was being pioneered by Bill George, Joe Schmidt, and Sam Huff, a time when NFL announcers like Ray Scott and Jack Drees were still referring to middle linebackers as middle guards. Nitschke learned from the greats, learned the angles they took, the drops, the way they played the pass. He would study them up close or on film to see how they played sweeps and attacked blockers, then incorporated their finer points into his play.

"I took parts from every one of them," he said once. "You pick out each player's things they did well."

By 1969, Nitschke was widely regarded as the greatest middle linebacker in the NFL's first 50 years. He was the centerpiece of a championship defense that featured nine all-pros and five future Hall of Famers, and served as a link between those who had pioneered his position in the late fifties—Huff, Schmidt, and George—and a generation of middle men who were rising stars by the mid- to late sixties—Dick Butkus and Nick Buoniconti, Tommy Nobis, Willie Lanier, and Mike Curtis.

"Nitschke was a serious run-stuffer, as they all were in those days," said Paul Zimmerman, a pro football historian and senior writer for *Sports Illustrated*. "He could cover sideline-to-sideline and get in a frenzy and play dynamically as far as his range goes. It didn't seem like he played in a system sometimes because I saw him in some sort of crazy pursuits."

Offenses struggled to find ways to cope with Nitschke's ferocious play. "He'd run through a stone wall to get you," remembered former Chicago fullback Ronnie Bull. "He wouldn't let anything stop him. And he tried to intimidate you. He'd let you hit him, and then just shed you. It was like he was saying, 'I'm not going to let you block me.' "

Chicago assistant coach Jim Dooley spent hours breaking down Green Bay's defense down on film, and what he discovered was what the Bears had believed for years—the entire Packer defense was coordinated to the movements of two men, Nitschke and free safety Willie Wood. Bull compared it to pulling strings—where Nitschke and Wood lined up and where they moved at the snap of the ball dictated the movements of the other Packer defenders.

"They were the guys their defense was built around," Bull said. "Those were your two keys. Where they lined up told you exactly where they were going."

NFL offenses countered in a variety of ways. In Dallas, Tom Landry tried to get Nitschke to take himself out of the play by giving him false keys—misdirections and counters that got him moving in one direction while Cowboy backs Don Perkins and Dan Reeves flowed against the grain. In Los Angeles, George Allen took a more basic approach. Recognizing Nitschke as the focal point of the Packer defense, Allen instructed quarterback Roman Gabriel to occupy Nitschke early by running Les Josephson and Dick Bass right up the middle. It wasn't the easiest way to make yards, Gabriel said at the time, but it was worth it.

"If he has to think about the middle," Gabriel said of Nitschke, "he can't go flying all over the place and mess up everything else."

Allen always thought of Nitschke as one of those special players who could do things others couldn't. "He was big and strong," Allen said once, "yet quick and agile." To Allen, Nitschke was smart and alert, as good in pass coverage as he was against the run. Impressed as he was with Nitschke's hard hits, Allen was just as impressed with his clutch play. "He always seemed to make a big play or two in a big game," Allen said. "He was a money player on a team that always had the stakes piled high on the table."

Nitschke built a reputation as a savage run-stopper, but his mobility and lateral quickness for a man his size—6-foot-3, 235 pounds—made him one of the great middle linebackers of all time. Where he ranks among the all-time greats is a debate for NFL historians.

"How would he rate against Butkus? Not as good," Zimmerman said. "How would he rate against Tommy Nobis? Better. Mike Curtis? Better. Willie Lanier? Not as good. Joe Schmidt? Tough to say. Schmidt was underrated, a very precise player, not quite the fire and dynamite of Nitschke but very effective. Probably a tie.

"How would he rate against Jack Lambert? Difficult to say because Lambert had so many good people around him. Of course, Nitschke did too. Probably just a shade below Lambert because of speed. Mike Singletary? It's a wash. Nitschke was probably a little bit better because Singletary in that ("46") scheme had a lot of things helping him.

"How would he rate against Ray Lewis? Not as good. Ray Lewis moved his game to another dimension at the end of the (2000–2001) season. His coverage was just knock 'em dead."

Zimmerman, who has studied on film or covered in person all of the great players in NFL history, graded Nitschke higher than two of his Hall of Fame predecessors—Bill George and Sam Huff—and overall rated him as one of the top five all-time at his position.

Nitschke was a classic, straight-up style middle linebacker, and the images of him that are frozen in Zimmerman's memory stem from his performance in the brutal 1962 NFL championship game against the Giants in Yankee Stadium.

"I was young and sitting in the stands and it was so cold that day, the coldest I've ever been at a football game," he said. "I remember him going from sideline to sideline making tackles. Shit, the guy was in another dimension. What a game. But that was when the position meant something. It wasn't a guy who played just one or two downs out of the three."

Fritz Shurmur, who was the Packers defensive coordinator for their Super Bowl teams of the nineties, said once that the guy who stood in the middle of your defense back in the sixties was a symbol of what you were as a defensive team. If a team had a Nitschke or a Butkus, Shurmur said, they were a good defense. If not, they were just another team.

"I don't think you find guys like that anymore, with that kind of persona," Shurmur said then. "Those guys had a special temperament. Ray brought a special, competitive temperament to the game."

Joe Horrigan, the Pro Football Hall of Fame's historian, rated the all-time middle men and said perhaps the only difference between Nitschke and Butkus was that the Bears great called his own signals. But Horrigan felt that Nitschke probably hit harder than Butkus. "He threw more people than Butkus," Horrigan said. "Ray truly enjoyed hitting people. He had a personality trait that made him that much more aggressive. He clobbered people."

Dave Manders, a center for the Dallas Cowboys from 1964 to 1974, remembered being impressed most by Nitschke's quickness and intelligence. "Nitschke seemed liked a combination of Butkus and Huff," Manders said. "He was strong like Butkus and quick like Huff."

Steve Sabol ranks Butkus as one of the game's elite players—along with Jim Brown and Jerry Rice. "Butkus to me is the greatest linebacker," the president of NFL Films said, "but he didn't have the effect on his teammates that Nitschke did. Nitschke lifted the play of his teammates, and he left an impression on offenses that they were going to have to play a superhuman game to win.

"When you're comparing middle linebackers like that, sometimes it's like comparing saints. Is Saint Mark better than Saint Matthew? The thing about Nitschke is that he was always in position, and he never missed a tackle. They keep a stat now, Yards After Contact, that measures how many yards a runner gets after he's hit. If they had kept that stat back when Nitschke played, I bet Ray's number would be lower than anyone's. He was a deadly tackler. He would wrap his arms around the runner's back, the hands would lock. . . . He was very sound technically."

Red Cochran, who served as an assistant coach with the Lombardi Packers and has been an NFL scout since the fifties, said Nitschke was such a good all-around athlete he would have excelled in today's more specialized game. "Nitschke with his speed would have still been a three-down player," Cochran said.

Pro football came of age in the sixties, and the game's rise paralleled that of television. This was the electronic generation, and TV ratings at the time showed that pro football was becoming a major part of America's leisure time. For those who watched the game intently on TV, the images that remain from the sixties are lasting; they are, as The Supremes sang in their Motown classic, reflections of the way life used to be.

The game then was John Unitas, in his bristlebrush haircut and hightop cleats, and Joe Namath, with his long, black mane and white leather shoes. It was the passion of Vince Lombardi; the professorial approach of Sid Gillman. It was the NFL versus the AFL, CBS versus NBC; Ray Scott and Pat Summerall, Curt Gowdy and Al DeRogatis. It was "31-Wedge" in the Ice Bowl and "65 Toss Power Trap" in Super Bowl IV. It was Jim Brown following his blockers in the November mud and it was Lance Alworth soaring to snare a pass in the soft San Diego sunshine.

And it was Nitschke, hunched over center, breathing steam in some icy December classic, covered in Packer green and gold; covered in pads and tape stained with blood and mud.

"You'd see him," Oakland center Jim Otto remembered, "and any wraps on his hands were coming apart. There was no care for the wear. He just kept right on going."

"I can close my eyes," Zimmerman said, "and see him going sideline to sideline. He could get outside, and he always took great angles. Some of them don't know how to play the angles, but he was always on the money with those angles, gauging them right."

Nitschke played his position with a warrior spirit, and Packer photographer Vern Biever loved his intensity. To him, Nitschke's hawkish features and emotional style made him a picture-perfect subject. "He gave you that feeling of intenseness," Biever said.

Nitschke's rise to prominence in the sixties paralleled that of NFL Films, and whenever the fledgling company needed an expressive closeup, they would focus in on Number 66.

"I was a young cameraman at that time," remembered Sabol, "and anytime we wanted a compelling shot we went to Nitschke. The way he looked, that voice of his—he personified that era of great middle line-backers."

In his own way, Nitschke symbolized the NFL of the sixties, and for that, he remains a beloved figure. Long into his retirement years, fans would look him up in the Green Bay White Pages, would travel to 410 Peppermint Court in Oneida, where his two-story brick home with its four white pillars out front sat in a cul de sac. The west side of Nitschke's home was flanked by a wooded area; the south side by a two-car attached garage and two large, leafy trees.

For Al Pahl, the driveway that led to the garage provided the setting for one of his lasting memories of Ray. Pahl had made his way through a deep snow to visit Nitschke, and he had pulled his SUV into Ray's driveway. When he tried to back out of the driveway, Pahl's tires began spinning in the snow. Nitschke came out to lend a hand, and began pushing on the front of Pahl's truck. From his seat behind the wheel Pahl could see Nitschke's huge hands bending the plastic shield that rose above the hood of his truck as protection against stones and debris from the highway. Rolling down his driver's side window, Pahl leaned over, stuck his head out and began yelling at Nitschke to stop pushing.

Later, Pahl considered the course of his actions.

"I was probably the only guy," he said, "who ever yelled at Ray Nitschke and got away with it."

Be it Pahl or any fan who was interested in spending time with a living legend, the harsh Green Bay winters did not deter them from traveling to Nitschke's house. Near the end of a phone conversation in the winter of 1997, Nitschke excused himself for a moment to answer the doorbell. He returned several minutes later, and apologized for the interruption.

"Sorry, man," he said. "We're havin' a blizzard here and some guy drives out to have a helmet autographed for his kid."

Nitschke laughed, a short, raspy bark.

"Packer fans are nuts, man," he said.

Ray and Jackie's house was always open to friends and fans, and visitors were greeted by the strong stench of Ray's oversized cigars. To Pahl, the smell of cigar is the overwhelming memory he has of the house. Once, Ray and Jackie gave an oversized, two-foot stuffed koala bear to Pahl's youngest daughter. The bear smelled so strongly of cigar that Pahl had to keep him on the patio by day and in the garage by night. "He lived outside for about two months," Pahl said.

For Pahl, for all of the people who came in contact with Ray Nitschke during his lifetime, the impact he left on their lives is still strongly felt. People related to his life struggles, his fight to make himself worthy, and drew inspiration from the sudden and dramatic conversion he underwent.

"It was like a curtain had been drawn," Vince Lombardi Jr. said. "You read and you hear about those kinds of things, but you rarely see them."

People saw it in Nitschke, and were impressed. Dave Robinson said that as great a player as Nitschke was, he was an even better person. To Ray Scott, Nitschke's real talent—brightening the lives of everyone around him—was most evident once his playing career ended. When Willie Davis thinks of his old teammate, he thinks of the special bond between them, a bond that surpassed all racial and social barriers, a bond strong enough to link a white man from urban Chicago with a black man from rural Arkansas.

"Everyone talks about the love those old Lombardi teams had," Davis said. "Well, I can tell you, I loved Ray Nitschke. I loved the man."

Wisconsin governor Tommy Thompson said at the time of Nitschke's passing that to live in the hearts of those left behind is not to die. "Ray Nitschke," he said, "certainly lives in the hearts of millions of people in Wisconsin and across America."

Perhaps it is less an impact than an imprint that Nitschke left behind, and it can be felt not only by those who knew him, but by those who wished they had.

When Ronnie Lott was inducted into the Pro Football Hall of Fame in 2000, he listened to Joe Greene tell him how emotional Nitschke would get every year at the luncheon. "He was always the guy who was enthusiastically welcoming the new group in," Greene told Lott. Later, Lott looked for Nitschke's bust in the Hall, and lingered before it for awhile.

"You know what? He spoke to me," Lott said later. "He spoke to me about the game. He represented what football is all about. He was a true warrior, a true man."

And because he was, Nitschke left his mark off the field as well as on, and his passing left a void in the lives of those he came in contact with.

"That's why so many people were affected by his death," Sabol said. "His heart was as warm as it was strong. When you'd see him he'd talk to you in that voice of his—'Hey, how ya doin'?' He was the last warrior, and there was a certain grandeur about him.

"When he left that field for the last time, something left with him that will never return."

INDEX

112; middle linebacker, recognizing importance of, 81; missed during 1968 season, 192; 1960 NFL championship game, comments after, 59; 1962 NFL championship game, 85–86, 88, 95; 1962 season, 78; 1963 Packers best team coached, 112; 1963 season opener, 107; 1965 NFL championship game, 124–25, 131; 1965 Western conference playoff, strategy for, 115; 1967 season, 169, 170, 172; Nitschke, appreciation for, 193–94; Nitschke, desire to trade, 52–53; Nitschke, impressions of, 46–47, 102–3; Nitschke used as instrument of fear in practices, 141–42; offense, focus on, 39; Packers' cool style of play under, 194; Packers' hiring of, 38, 40–42; Packers' initial attitude toward, 47–49; Packers' veterans playing Super Bowl II for, 188; passing system, 166; as player, 38–39; promoting Nitschke to starting linebacker, 51; racial inclusiveness, 48–49; respect for, 191; response to Landry's complex offense, 150; retirement from head coaching job, 191; role in Nitschke's settling down, 64; on Sayers, 146; Starr, initial impressions of, 165; Starr and Nitschke as extensions of, 165–66; Super Bowl I, 158–59, 163, 164; Super Bowl II, 179–80, 187; taking Landry's principles in move from New York to Green Bay, 99–100; team rule against standing at public bars, 52–53; training camps, toughness of, 43; with Washington Redskins, 193; wearing down, 183–84; "winning" slogan, 205

Lombardi, Vince, Jr., xi, 47, 53, 194, 224
Lombardi sweep, 79–80
Los Angeles Chargers, 156
Los Angeles Rams, xiii–xiv, 35, 50, 52, 53, 115, 156, 170–72, 220
Lott, Ronnie, 224
Louisiana State University, 70
Lowe, Paul, 157
Luckman, Sid, 6, 32, 38, 158
Lueck, Bill, 144
Lujack, Johnny, 6
Lyles, Lenny, 116
Lynch, Dick, 95

Mack, Red, 143
Madden, John, 190
Magee, Jerry, 163
Maglie, Sal, 140

Manders, Dave, xvii, 221
Man-in-Motion-T, 39
Mantle, Mickey, 180
Manuche, Mike, 61, 101
Mara, Wellington, 54, 159
Marchetti, Gino, 113
Marciano, Rocky, 70–71
Marconi, Joe, 109, 110
Masters, Norm, 72
Mather, Chuck, 111
Matte, Tom, 115, 117
Matuszak, Marv, 39
Maule, Tex, 134, 156, 163, 191
McCafferty, Don, 80
McCoy, Mike, xix
McDonald, Tommy, xii, 54, 57, 149
McElhenny, Hugh, 51
McGee, Max, 42–43, 48, 58, 74, 82, 94, 153, 161, 162, 164, 176, 185, 188, 191–92
McHan, Lamar, 44, 167
McLean, Ray "Scooter," xi, 35, 36, 37, 48
McMahon, John, 216
McNally, Vince, 54
Meihlan, Jack, 8, 10, 14
Mercein, Chuck, 171, 176, 192
Mercer, Mike, 162–63
Meredith, Don, 149, 150, 151, 153, 165
Miami Dolphins, 80, 169, 184
Michaels, Lou, 31, 116, 117, 133
Michigan State University, 25, 29
middle guard, 87, 219
middle linebacker, 36, 97–100, 219
Midwest Shrine Game (1961), 109
Miller, Bill, 187
Miller, Fred, 107
Miller Lite commercials, xiv, 204, 205–6
Mills, John, 1
Milwaukee Sentinel, 86
Minnesota Vikings, 115, 192, 194
Mira, George, 188–89
Mitchell, Bobby, xviii–xix, 17, 18, 20–21, 26–28, 31, 114, 120–21
Mix, Ron, 157
Modzelewski, Dick, 92, 95
Monsters of the Midway, 6, 32
Moore, Lenny, 80, 117, 168
Moore, Ted, 94, 117, 118, 131–32, 133, 153, 170, 177
Moore, Tom, 49, 106, 107
Morrall, Earl, 25
Morris, Larry, 108
Morris, Mercury, 80
Morrison, Joe, 76
Morrow, John, 108–9, 122, 126, 129

ACKNOWLEDGMENTS

AS WITH ANY PROJECT OF THIS SIZE, there are many people involved who helped bring the final work to completion.

First, I would like to thank my family for their continued support and encouragement. Without their patience and understanding of the time demands involved in writing a book, I would not have undertaken such a project. So thanks to Michelle, Patty, and Katie, as well as my mother, Roberta, and my sisters, Kathie and Patrice, and their children.

Thanks also to Ross Plotkin, Ginger Strader. and Barbara Werden, for their work in the editorial process; to Packers photographer Vernon Biever, for the excellent photos that comprise the book's insert; to Burt Wilson, for his help in the editing process; and to Deb Grove, for taking the time to take the author's photo.

Of course, this book could not have been completed without the contributions of the Nitschke family. Years ago, Ray Nitschke took time to speak with me on the phone for extended, long-distance interviews. His warmth and strength of character were evident during those interviews, and I will forever be grateful for the kindness he showed me. Two of his children, Richard and Amy, were also very gracious in passing along to me memories of their famous father. Unfortunately, Ray's wife Jackie had already passed from cancer before this project had even began, and Ray's son John was not available for interviews at the time for personal reasons.

The list of those whose personal interviews past and present contributed to this book is a lengthy one, more than seventy-five names in all, and chief among those are many of Ray's contemporaries from the NFL: Bart Starr, Paul Hornung, Jerry Kramer, Boyd Dowler, Gale Gillingham, Willie Davis, Herb Adderley, Bob Jeter, Dan Currie, Bobby Dillon, Phil Bengston, Dick Butkus, Frank Ryan, John Morrow, Dan Reeves, Ralph Neely, Bob Lilly, Ronnie Bull, Mick Tingelhoff, Sam Huff, Tommy Nobis, Chuck Bednarik, Tommy McDonald, Bobby Mitchell, Jim Otto, Daryle Lamonica, Len Dawson, Mike Garrett, Otis Taylor, Bobby Bell, Jerry Mays, Hank Stram, former Green Bay sportswriters Lee Remmel and Art Daley, Packers former play-by-play announcer Ted Moore, Sports Illustrated senior writer Paul Zimmerman, NFL Films historian Steve Sabol, and Pro Football Hall of Fame historian Joe Horrigan. To all of the above, and to all the friends and relatives who took the time to recall their personal memories of Ray Nitschke, thank you.

ED GRUVER, *April 2002*

Lincoln Christian College

W9-AHG-133

CLINICAL BEHAVIOR THERAPY

Clinical Behavior Therapy

Edited by

ARNOLD A. LAZARUS, Ph.D.

Professor of Psychology, University College, Rutgers University
1970-72 Visiting Professor and Director of Clinical Training
Department of Psychology, Yale University

BRUNNER/MAZEL • NEW YORK
BUTTERWORTHS • LONDON

Copyright © 1972 by Brunner/Mazel, Inc.

published by
BRUNNER/MAZEL, INC.
64 University Place
New York, N. Y. 10003

All rights reserved. No part of this book may be reproduced
by any process whatsoever, without the written permission
of the copyright owner.

Library of Congress Catalogue Card No. 70-184151
SBN 87630-051-4

MANUFACTURED IN THE UNITED STATES OF AMERICA

616.891
L43

Preface

IT IS EVIDENT that the publication explosion has not yielded a parallel increase in useful information. Those interested in psychological treatment often deplore the fact that very few books can actually enhance their therapeutic skills. It is hoped that readers of this book will emerge with several new and different notions and techniques, thus enriching their own clinical repertoires. The book is addressed to service-oriented individuals who are especially interested in efficient psychotherapy.

In the field of behavior therapy (as may be the case in most other areas of scientific endeavor) researchers and academicians have both the time and incentive to publish their findings, whereas practitioners less often have the opportunity or inclination to share their ideas in writing. Of course, there are those who claim that only controlled laboratory studies are worthy of note and that the biased nature of most clinical impressions and observations renders them quite worthless. For a rebuttal

47916

of this viewpoint see Lazarus and Davison (1971) who underscore the fact that practitioners "may discover important individual nuances that remain hidden from the laboratory scientist simply because the tight environment of the experimental testing ground makes it impossible for certain behaviors to occur or for certain observations to be made" (p. 196).

The efforts of experimental psychologists and their burgeoning literature on behavioral procedures have resulted in a persistent view of behavior therapy as superficial and mechanistic. As a practitioner of behavior therapy, I have found that my treatment strategies and understanding of the field have consistently differed from those who espouse a "pure" experimental outlook (e.g., Eysenck, 1971). In the practical details of my day to day work with clients, I have found it necessary to broaden the base of conventional behavior therapy (Lazarus, 1971). Is this an idiosyncratic reaction, or in their daily work, do most (if not all) practicing behavior therapists find it essential to transcend laboratory derived principles and techniques which constitute the core of behavior therapy? This book grew out of the foregoing question.

The doctrine of *technical eclecticism* (Lazarus, 1967) has enabled me to learn from and work productively with therapists whose theoretical orientations differ widely from my own. The chapter by Akhter Ahsen and myself bears further testimony to this point of view. But what of other people who consider themselves "behavior therapists" and who work with patients rather than subjects? Do they employ assessment and/or treatment methods that do not easily fall within the conventional boundaries of behavior therapy? Do they find it necessary to modify, extend and revise existing procedures within their practices?

Accordingly, the following invitation was sent to ten of my colleagues: "It has occurred to me to edit a book entitled CLINICAL BEHAVIOR THERAPY. The idea is to provide practitioners (rather than researchers or academicians) with an opportunity to air their own views and experiences concerning the active ingredients of effective therapy. The behavior therapy literature is flooded by the writings of individuals who seem to work with ideas rather than with people. The same names in the field (usually theoreticians rather than true clinicians) appear with monotonous regularity in journals and books. Hopefully, the proposed volume will allow some much-desired "new blood" to enter the field.

The aim of the intended book is to examine whether practitioners often transcend techniques derived from "modern learning theory" when called upon to make clinical decisions, and whether innovations in method and technique usually ensue. The scope of the book is bound up with the procedures, theories, methods, techniques, etc., which each contributor finds especially useful in aiding diagnostic and/or therapeutic processes.

The main thrust of the book is intended to be practical rather than speculative. I am inviting you to contribute a chapter outlining those methods and ideas which "turn you on" because of their productivity and effectiveness.

I truly hope that you will be able to contribute to what I hope will be a really exciting and much-needed publication."

My major editorial prerogatives were wielded in excising gross stylistic incongruities from initial drafts. The chapters contain several points of emphasis and various biases with which I do not agree, but in my view, an edited book of this kind should disseminate divergent "behavioral" opinions, rather than be forced to fit the constraints of one particular outlook. Personally, I found that the chapters refreshed my perspective and enriched my clinical repertoire. If most readers derive similar stimulation from this volume, its aims will most admirably be met.

ARNOLD A. LAZARUS

REFERENCES

EYSENCK, H. J. A mish-mash of theories. *International Journal of Psychiatry*, 1971, 9, 140-146.

LAZARUS, A. A. In support of technical eclecticism. *Psychological Reports*, 1967, 21, 415-416.

LAZARUS, A. A. *Behavior Therapy and Beyond*. New York: McGraw-Hill, 1971.

LAZARUS, A. A. & DAVISON, G. C. Clinical innovation in research and practice. In A. E. Bergin & S. L. Garfield (Eds.), *Handbook of Psychotherapy and Behavior Change: An Empirical Analysis*. New York: Wiley, 1971.

Contents

Contributors

AKHTER AHSEN, PH.D.: Private Practice, Yonkers, New York; former president, Institute of Eidetic Psychotherapy, Philadelphia, Pa.

BARRY M. BROWN, M.D.: Private Practice, Houston, Texas.

EDWARD DENGROVE, M.D.: Diplomate of the American Board of Psychiatry and Neurology. Private Practice, West Allenhurst, New Jersey.

HERBERT FENSTERHEIM, PH.D.: Clinical Associate Professor of Psychiatry, New York Medical College, New York. Private Practice.

PHILIP H. FRIEDMAN, PH.D.: Family Psychiatry Division, Eastern Pennsylvania Psychiatric Institute, Philadelphia, Pa.

MAX JACOBS, M.A., LL.B.: Private Practice, Johannesburg, South Africa.

THOMAS KRAFT, M.B., CH.B., D.P.M.: Private Practice, London, England.

ARNOLD A. LAZARUS, PH.D.: Professor of Psychology, University College, Rutgers University.

JOHN MARQUIS, PH.D.: Chief Psychologist, Mental Hygiene Clinic, V.A. Hospital, Palo Alto, California.

GERALD W. PIAGET, PH.D.: Behavior Therapy Associates, Los Altos, California; Staff Psychologist, Santa Clara County Mental Health Services, Palo Alto, California.

1

The Use of Behavior Therapy in a Psychotherapeutic Context

THOMAS KRAFT, M.B., D.P.M.

WHEN READING ARTICLES on patients who have been successfully treated by behavior therapy, one usually finds that the author has divided the material into several sections: after an introduction, in which he draws attention to previous work in this field, he then goes on to give a short résumé of the case history, followed by the treatment, results, discussion and a summary. While this makes for a neat article which is acceptable for publication, it does not give the reader a clear idea of what happened during the treatment. The case history of the patient cannot be divorced from the remainder of the treatment as it forms an integral part of the whole treatment process. History-taking is not a mere collecting of facts but is an important interaction between patient and therapist. During the first interview, the patient will discover some of the qualities of the therapist, and also to what extent he will be allowed to discuss his problems or whether the treatment will be restricted to symptoms only.

3

The literature in behavior therapy gives the reader the impression that most psychiatric patients come to the therapist requesting treatment for their phobia or sexual disturbance, but while this does apply to a few, most psychiatric patients have no idea, except that they are in a muddle and need "sorting out." The therapist may have to spend several sessions with the patient in order to determine the precise nature of his problem. In the first interview, the patient may wish to talk about marital problems, difficulties at work, or inferiority feelings, and he may not know which areas require therapeutic intervention. These points are rarely discussed in articles on behavior therapy, possibly because behavior therapists are often given a selected group of patients, or because it is thought to be irrelevant. The object of writing this chapter is to highlight the interaction between patient and therapist during a course of treatment which is behavior-oriented, and to show that a great deal happens during the treatment other than that reported in the behavior therapy literature.

THE ART OF HISTORY-TAKING

While it is important to obtain factual data about the patient's background, emphasis should be placed on the patient's feelings about events in his life rather than their precise nature. He should feel free to elaborate where he feels a need to do so, and should not be pressurized into giving certain replies. It is important that the therapist have no preconceived ideas of what he expects to hear from the patient and that history-taking be a flexible process moulded by the patient's replies.

After giving the age of his father, the patient may wish to talk about certain aspects of their relationship, either at the present time or in the past, and he should be allowed to do so, as this may give valuable information about his problem. It is not sufficient to know that his father is a solicitor, but more important to find out whether this had a bearing on the choice of his own career. When inquiring about the physical health of the father, it is more important to find out the effect this had on the patient than the exact nature of the illness. The patient might volunteer certain information about his father—for example, that he was keen for him to play football even though he was not keen on the game. This may lead to a discussion about the significance of the game in relation to his other symptoms and why this should be a source of conflict between father and son. He may wish to talk about his father's drinking behavior, how this affected him or his mother, or the relationship between his parents, and all this information should be recorded at the time of the interview.

After obtaining information about the father, the therapist asks the patient about his mother, brothers and sisters, in much the same way, and any other members of the family who seem important to the patient. He may have been brought up by his grandparents, or he may wish to talk about a favorite uncle or some more distant relative.

After obtaining details of the family history, the therapist asks the patient for date and place of birth. While this may not lead to any further discussion, this may be very relevant to immigrants or patients whose parents were born in other countries.

The therapist then asks the patient about his childhood and often the patient will be able to remember important events and may inquire whether these are relevant to his present state. For example, a patient who had difficulty in swallowing remembered that during his childhood he had "choked" while learning to swim, and feared that he might not reach the side of the swimming pool. Later, this symptom was reactivated after the death of his father, who also had difficulty in swallowing. Immediately the therapist can show the patient how these are interrelated.

When asking about academic achievements, it is more important to know what significance these had for the patient than the actual level of achievement, though this should be recorded too. Academic ability may have been a large factor in the production of symptoms in the patient who failed intentionally because he did not wish to compete with a brilliant older sister. Neurotic symptoms can often be traced back to early childhood and early neurotic traits should be recorded.

When discussing his occupation since leaving school, the patient is asked whether he likes his present job, whether there have been frequent changes of employment, and if so, the reasons for this, also his relationship with fellow employees and staff. If there have been frequent clashes with members of staff, this will lead on to a discussion about problems with authority figures in general. The type of occupation selected is important in relation to his other symptoms, so that if a ladies' hairdresser seeks treatment for his homosexuality, it is pointed out to him at this stage that altering his sexual adjustment may well lead to a change in his employment too. The author feels that it is only fair to make this point early in treatment so that the patient is not disappointed at a later stage.

The next stage in history-taking is to make an assessment of the patient's sexual adjustment, taking note of overt sexual behavior as well as masturbation fantasies, whether the patient is married or single, and whether he has extra-marital ties, and their nature. In the case of the phobic patient, attention should be focused on her sexual adjustment before marriage and changes which occurred subsequent to the marriage, and the exact time of onset of phobic symptoms. It is frequently found that before marriage the patient made important relationships with two or more men and that phobic symptoms emerged when she attempted to make a relationship with one man only. The nature of the relationship between the agoraphobic wife and her husband needs to be thoroughly investigated, especially if she can go out only when accompanied by him, since it is usually found that the patient at the same time is dependent upon and wants to get away from him, and this is a central feature of the phobic situation.

The male homosexual patient is asked whether he usually takes the active or passive role, and whether he identifies with the male sex. It is also worth inquiring about intimate physical contact with important female figures early in life. It is pointed out that it is easier to treat those patients who have had some heterosexual contact than those who are exclusively homosexual, and that failure to identify with the male sex is a more complicated problem.

When asking about past physical illnesses, attention should be paid to the psychosomatic group, such as psoriasis, eczema, asthma, colitis, and whether these preceded the psychiatric symptoms. The patient is now asked about psychiatric treatment which he has received in the past, the type of treatment involved and the improvement obtained. This may lead on to a discussion about behavior therapy and its aims.

Having obtained information about the patient's background, the next stage in treatment is to obtain a history of the illness. A good way of starting here is to ask the patient when he last felt perfectly well and to continue from there. If the patient has already seen several doctors he may be able to give a coherent account, but if he has not had any previous treatment, he may be quite vague and say that he feels unwell, that he has a headache, lacks energy and feels tired for no reason. In this case one can help the patient by asking questions such as: "Do you have difficulty in social situations?" "Do you have difficulty traveling?" "When did you last go to the theatre?" In this way it is possible to work out with the patient the areas of difficulty and throughout the treatment emphasis should be placed on working things out together rather than the usual practice of the doctor administering treatment to his patient.

If the patient has difficulty in traveling, an attempt should be made to trace the early origins of this symptom and, if possible, to localize a particular traumatic incident. A patient may well recall a particular journey during which the train stopped for twenty minutes between stations and he became panic-stricken, developing symptoms from that time. Further inquiry may lead to important information about personal problems at that time. One patient recalled that this occurred after the death of her first husband, and recognized that this was related to the onset of her symptoms. During history-taking, the patient is asked whether she has difficulty with all forms of transport or only on public transport. Many patients find that while they cannot travel by bus, train or Underground, they can still travel in their own car, possibly because they feel that the car is an extension of the home. Some patients can travel only when accompanied by a husband or a relative, and here it is important to investigate the nature of the relationship between the patient and the person who accompanies her. During the discussion, the patient may wish to talk about other aspects of the phobic situation, and it is important to let the patient talk about these. It will soon become apparent that there are many factors in the patient's life situation which support the phobia and it is important to establish these maintaining factors. The patient is asked to describe the sequence of events in particular situations and the husband's reactions. It is usually found that the husband colludes with his wife in her phobic illness despite his outcries to the contrary. For this reason many therapists feel that it is important to see the husband of phobic patients.

If the patient has a drinking problem, he is asked when he began drinking, the type of drink involved, the quantity drunk, and whether he needs to carry a hip flask. Also whether he enjoys drinking or whether he just wants to rapidly increase his alcohol level. A guide to this will be found by asking the patient about the rate of his drinking and whether he gulps it down. Some patients are aware of the reasons why they need to drink to excess, while others just say: "I enjoy drinking!" In either case, it is important to determine the degree of social anxiety present. One patient may admit that he finds talking to other people extremely difficult unless he has had some alcohol first, while other patients flatly deny this. At this point in the discussion the author points out that the need for alcohol is related to social anxiety and that once patients have become socially competent they no longer need to drink to excess. Many patients accept this argument, but others remain unconvinced at this stage. After establishing the patient's need for alcohol, it is necessary to ask about drug-taking in general. Some may admit to smoking marijuana, but one must always ask specifically about the use of amphetamines, barbiturates and other drugs. For those patients who rely on alcohol or drugs for their support, one should always inquire about anti-social conduct.

After detailed history-taking of this kind, the therapist will have a good idea of the patient's problems and is in a good position to start developing a treatment program best suited for his patient. A sample of a history-taking interview will now be given as an illustration.

Therapist: How old is your father?
Patient: 72.
Therapist: I suppose he has retired.
Patient: No, he is still working two days a week. He works in a Delicatessen. He used to have a shop of his own, which he sold, and he now works for a friend of his.
Therapist: Has he had any illnesses?
Patient: In 1953 he had a serious illness and there was the question of amputation of both legs. They did some sort of by-pass operation. I think it was one of the main arteries. I was 16 at the time.
Therapist: What was your relationship with your father?
Patient: We never had much of a relationship all my life. When mother could not handle me, she threatened me with father. He never represented too much of a father figure to me. We never did anything together, as father and son. I wanted desperately to be part of "Smith and Son,"* but whenever representatives called, father sent me out. I felt rejected by my father.
Therapist: And your mother? How old is she?
Patient: She is a lot younger than father. She is 63. The business revolved around her rather than him (referring to father). She was the dominant figure—always has been and always will be. All she would have to do is to turn on the tears. . . .
Therapist: In order to get her own way with father?
Patient: Yes, that's right. She's extremely emotional and insecure.
Therapist: What do you mean by "insecure"?
Patient: Well, she is continually seeking praise for things which she has done in the past. (Pause). Little things. (He did not elaborate further on this point).
Therapist: Has she had any illnesses?
Patient: Yes, she had a spot on the lung. She was on anticoagulants in the past year, but she is off them now.
Therapist: Anything else?

---

* The name has been changed.

Patient: Yes, she has varicose veins in the legs. Otherwise she is quite healthy.

Therapist: How many brothers and sisters have you got?

Patient: I have one sister. She is older than I am. She is 37, married with one child. A son.

Therapist: Does she go out to work?

Patient: No, she is a housewife.

Therapist: Has she had any physical illnesses?

Patient: Yes, she had "colitis," but it ended up as appendectomy!

Therapist: What is your relationship with your sister?

Patient: Childhood relationship pretty bad. She took great delight in getting me into trouble. I took a more protective role towards her when I was 16 or 17. She is a tremendously educated person. When she came to visit me in America, my friends asked me not to bring her again. She had 7 Honors in Matriculation, including French and Latin. She was Head Wages Clerk for a company in television and films. She was pretty bright. She would get 100's or 98 at school and I would get much lower. Mother used to say: "You can't let your sister beat you," but I had no desire to compete with my sister.

Therapist: When were you born?

Patient: In 1937 in Tottenham. At my grandmother's place.

Therapist: Any bed wetting as a child?

Patient: No.

Therapist: Nail biting?

Patient: No.

Therapist: Thumb sucking?

Patient: No.

Therapist: Afraid of the dark?

Patient: No, it was always dark during the War.

Therapist: Tell me about your childhood.

Patient: I was sensitive about being Jewish. I had many fights with other children about this. There was a lot of antisemitic feeling at school. I was leader of one half of the class with my lieutenant and there was another boy who was leader of the other side with his lieutenant.

Therapist: What age were you when you went to school?

Patient: Five.

Therapist: And you left at 15. (The therapist remembered that he had already told him this at a previous interview.)

Patient: Yes, I was fighting against it. If I had tried to make it work . . . I regret now that I did not make much of school. I did not take School Certificate. To size it all up, I regret my education. I intentionally tried not to succeed.

(End of Interview.)

During an interview of this type, one obtains a lot of information about the patient, the nature of his relationship with his parents, his feelings of inferiority towards his sister and his intentionally failing at school. The patient also gives some indication that his choice of friends has been dictated by his educational level and that his friends rejected his sister because they did not reach her level. The patient felt rejected by his father and felt that his mother, though the dominant figure in the household, threatened him with father if she could not handle him.

CONSTRUCTING THE HIERARCHY FOR SYSTEMATIC DESENSITIZATION

It is unwise to use a standardized hierarchy for all patients even though they may be suffering from a similar type of disorder, and it is recommended that a hierarchy should be specially constructed to meet the needs of each individual patient.

Some patients find it quite easy to construct a hierarchy of their own and know which situations cause little distress and which are extremely anxiety-provoking, but this is certainly not true of all. The author has found that many patients are prepared to begin treatment using an easy item at a time when a hierarchy has not yet been developed, and then to progress towards more difficult situations, offering helpful suggestions to the therapist as treatment proceeds. This allows the patient to participate in the treatment program rather than being a passive agent to whom treatment is administered. This is extremely important because eventually the patient must learn to conduct his own affairs without the assistance of a therapist.

A patient who has a fear of heights may be able to construct a suitable hierarchy of increasing height quite easily. He has a ladder at home and feels that he can climb a little higher each day. On the other hand, many patients find it very difficult or even impossible to construct any sort of hierarchy, and need a lot of assistance from the therapist. One patient who had a severe dog phobia could not think of any situation involving dogs which would not provoke maximum anxiety, so it was suggested that she look at a picture of a dog in a children's picture book, which was quite acceptable to her. Soon she was able to hug a toy dog, and gradually she learned to cope with dogs in the street. A neighbor who owned a dog was very helpful in her treatment in that she gave her a graded series of situations, first when the dog sat still, then walking away from her, towards her, cuddling and feeding the dog. Another patient who had a fear of water learned to swim and later dive with the assistance of a life guard who happened to be an in-patient in the same ward at that time.

It may be necessary to construct two hierarchies and these can often be offered to the patient concurrently. For example, a male homosexual patient who had difficulty passing urine in public toilets was given one hierarchy involving heterosexual situations leading to sexual intercourse, and a second hierarchy for using urinals in public toilets.

It might be helpful at this stage to give some examples of hierarchies used in particular patients. The first patient was absolutely terrified of dogs, a fear which developed at the age of five when she was running down an alley and an Alsatian dog grabbed her by the hair and dragged her along the alley, though finally she managed to get away. Her friends called her mother, but she was reluctant to come and fetch her as she too was frightened of dogs. The hierarchy was very carefully constructed and the patient has made a very good recovery.

Dog Phobia

1. Looking at a picture of a dog in a children's picture book.
2. Cuddling the children's toy dog.
3. Seeing a poodle on a lead a) 10 yards away.
                                                b) 5 yards away.
                                                c) A woman passing by her.
4. Touching a puppy behind a wire mesh in the market.
5. Looking at the neighbor's spaniel, Kim, held in the arms of its mistress.
6. Touching Kim when the dog is quiet, held in the arms of its mistress.
7. Touching Kim when the dog is quiet.
8. Stroking Kim.
9. Kim putting up her paws.
10. Looking at an Alsatian dog.
11. Watching Kim jumping on the road when she is indoors and the windows are closed.
12. Watching Kim walk round the room.
13. Feeding Kim with a biscuit.
14. Kim held by its mistress, and then jumping on the ground.
15. Kim running.
16. Kim jumping from a chair onto the floor.
17. Kim jumping on the floor and then putting up her paw.

18. Kim wagging her tail.
19. Kim wagging her tail and then putting her paw up.
20. Kim running down the corridor.
21. Kim running away from her.
22. Kim running towards her.
23. Kim roaming round the house without a lead.
24. Knocking on the door of the neighbor, and Kim running towards her, barking.
25. Dogs fighting.

This hierarchy was completed in 21 sessions.

The second patient was a 38-year-old docker who became phobic to water and heights after a serious accident at his work. He often stepped on and off ships without the safety precaution of a gangplank, but on this occasion, he missed the quay, fell onto a wooden fender and then dropped into the water below. Once in the water, he knew that the tide here was strong and that he could drown or be crushed to death between the ship and the quay. He was given two hierarchies and the first of these will be given in full.

Fear of Water and Heights

1. Taking a bath at home.
2. Taking a shower at home.
3. Going into the shallow end of the swimming pool.
4. Starting to swim at the shallow end of the swimming pool, breast stroke only.
5. Swimming at the shallow end, doing the crawl.
6. Jumping into the swimming pool at the shallow end.
7. Jumping into the pool and then doing the crawl.
8. Swimming at the shallow end, first breast stroke, then the crawl.
9. Pushing himself away from the bars and causing a splash.
10. Swimming in the middle of the pool at a depth of 5 ft. 3 ins.
11. Swimming at the shallow end and then at the deep end (10 ft. 3 ins.).
12. Going into the deep end of the swimming pool.
13. Watching people jump from the diving boards.
14. Standing on a step at the deep end of the pool and making a "little jump" into the water.
15. Backstroke at the shallow end of the pool.

16. Jumping into the water at the shallow end of the pool ("belly flop dive").
17. "Belly flop dive" at the deep end of the pool.
18. Racing dive at shallow end of the pool.
19. Racing dive at the deep end of the pool.
20. Swimming three times across the deep end of the pool without stopping a) breast stroke
          b) crawl
          c) backstroke
21. Jumping into the pool at a depth of:
          a) 5 ft. 3 ins.
          b) 6 ft.
          c) 7 ft.
22. Several jumps at 6 ft., 7 ft., alternating these, and then remaining at the 7 feet depth.
23. Going onto the 1st diving board and jumping into the water.
24. Jumping off the 1st diving board, then diving from the 1st board.
25. Diving off the 1st diving board.
26. Jumping from the 1st diving board, jumping from the 2nd diving board, then diving from the 1st diving board.
27. Jumping off the 1st, 2nd, and 3rd diving boards, then diving from the 1st diving board.
28. Jumping off the 1st, 2nd, and 3rd diving boards, then diving from the 1st, and then the 2nd diving board.
29. Jumping off the 4th diving board, then diving off the 2nd diving board.
30. Jumping off the 5th diving board, then diving off the 3rd diving board.
31. Jumping off the 5th diving board, then diving off the 4th diving board.
32. Jumping off the top board, then diving off the 4th diving board.
33. Jumping off the top board, then diving off the 5th diving board.
34. Diving off the top diving board.
35. Random stimuli.
36. Looking round before jumping off the 3rd diving board.
37. Looking round before jumping off the 4th board.
38. Looking round before jumping off the 5th diving board.
39. Diving from the 5th diving board and looking round before diving.
40. Diving from the top board and looking round before diving.

This hierarchy was completed in 40 sessions, each lasting half an hour. He then started the second part of the desensitization program which involved standing near a lake, rowing on a lake, and crossing viaducts, bridges, canals, rivers, and finally going down the vertical ladder to the water's edge at the original site of the accident. This patient received 107 treatment sessions in all, and he has made a complete recovery, which has been maintained for over three years.

SYSTEMATIC DESENSITIZATION UNDER CONDITIONS OF RELAXATION

Most patients who are given systematic desensitization are given some form of relaxation, but little is said about this aspect of the treatment situation in the articles which are published. The author offers two forms of relaxation, either hypnosis or intravenous injections of Methohexital sodium, but in the case of drug addicts they are only offered hypnosis, since it is felt that injections should not be encouraged by the treatment. Other patients are given the choice, and some prefer hypnosis, particularly if they are afraid of injections, while others prefer injections which they regard as more "medical."

The patient is asked to lie on a bed, but if he feels very threatened by this, he can be hypnotized sitting in a comfortable chair. Intravenous injections of Methohexital sodium must not be given to a patient in the sitting position as this may prove dangerous.

For those patients who receive hypnosis, the author tends to use the hand levitation technique, which will be described in detail at the end of this section. Some patients, particularly adolescents, respond to a very quiet voice, while others respond better to loud instructions, and this varies from one patient to another. When the patient is hypnotized, he is given the first item on the hierarchy. A patient who is being treated for her frigidity might be asked to imagine being in the kitchen at home, talking to her husband. At first, she may find it difficult to imagine this scene and here the therapist helps to produce visual images. He can assist her in this by additional cues such as seeing the kettle boil, making a cup of tea, asking the patient to describe the clothes worn by her husband, and sooner or later the patient will say that she can see her husband quite clearly. The patient may say that she feels perfectly alright provided that her husband is two feet away from her. The scene is then withdrawn and the patient is told to stop thinking about it and relax. The second scene to be presented might be sitting with her husband watching television, and the third, saying goodnight to him, without any physical contact. The therapist suggests that she will reach a deeper level of relaxation next time, and that with practice, she will obtain stronger visual images as the treatment proceeds. Unfortunately, not all patients have the capacity to form visual images, but desensitization can occur in the absence of either visual or auditory imagery, providing there is the appropriate emotional component. Some patients find it helpful to be given a relief response between items, and this aids anxiety-relief. One patient might like to think of roses, another of strawberries, and young people often like to think of a favorite pop record.

If the patient is presented with a scene which she finds very disturbing, it may be necessary to withdraw it, because if the patient comes out of the hypnotic state at this point, she may refuse to be hypnotized again, either on this or on a subsequent occasion.

As each scene is presented, it is quite easy to see from the facial expression whether the patient feels comfortable in this situation. On the first presentation, the patient may bite his lip, or furrow his brow or show a pained expression, and the therapist may have to present the scene several times before he remains perfectly calm and relaxed when visualizing it. Although it is quite satisfactory to present the next scene when the patient shows no evidence of anxiety, the author continues to present it until the patient is so happy with it that he can smile and dismiss it as though it had never been a problem at all. This is based on the principle of over-learning. At the beginning of each session, patients find it very helpful to start with a scene which has been well rehearsed, as this increases their confidence, but this is not essential.

Before bringing the patient out of the hypnotic state, it is important to give a strong counter-suggestion that he will be able to open his eyes, be wide awake, and perfectly fresh, because otherwise he may remain in a semi-hypnotized state for the rest of the day. One patient could not understand why he was not fully awake and said that he felt confused and as if walking through clouds, and further counter-suggestions were given later. It has been the author's experience that drug-addicted adolescents are particularly resistant to the counter-suggestion, and this may be due to a reluctance to come out of the hypnotic state, which they say is somewhat similar to the drug-induced state.

When patients are hypnotized frequently, it will be found that the induction will become quicker on each occasion, so that eventually a deep trance state can be induced by a signal such as a click of the fingers.

Here it is important to emphasize that it will only happen in the treatment situation when the therapist clicks his fingers and in no other situation, as this might prove embarrassing elsewhere, for example, in a crowded department store.

For those patients who have Methohexital sodium-induced relaxation, the author usually uses a 2½% solution by adding 4 mls. of distilled water to 100 mg. of the powder. The 4 mls. (100 mg.) are drawn up into the syringe, and a fine needle is used, so that the drug can be injected slowly. The drug is given intravenously, and after an initial loading dose of up to 1 ml. (25 mg.), the patient becomes very relaxed. This level of relaxation can be maintained throughout the treatment session by keeping the needle in the vein and injecting a little more of the drug at regular intervals. The quantity of Methohexital sodium used varies considerably from one patient to another, and in the first treatment session, it is wise to start with a very small quantity, in case the patient is very sensitive to the drug. One patient was nearly asleep (this is not the aim of treatment) after injecting less than 0.5 mls. of the 2½% solution, and in this case it is wiser to use a weaker solution. Very tense patients often require quite large doses to obtain adequate relaxation, but this may vary from one treatment session to another.

Although Methohexital sodium is a relatively safe drug, especially in the dosage employed, one must not forget that this is an anesthetic agent and may only be given by medical practitioners.

During the treatment session using Methohexital sodium, scenes are presented to the patient in much the same way as under hypnosis. Towards the end of the session, the needle is withdrawn from the vein, and a few minutes later, the patient is ready to get up from the bed. No counter-suggestions are necessary in drug-induced relaxation.

Although the author likes to use hypnosis or intravenous injections of Methohexital sodium to induce relaxation, neither of these is essential for the desensitization process to take place, and many behavior therapists use simple muscle relaxation techniques. Recent work would suggest that it is quite sufficient to present a graded series of images, even in the absence of specific relaxation procedures.

After each treatment session, the patient is told to practice the situations which were rehearsed during the session, preferably on the same day as the treatment, or as soon after this as possible. Sometimes a patient finds that although he felt perfectly happy *imagining* the situation in treatment, he feels much less happy when putting it into practice. In this case, the patient should be reassured that this is frequently seen in clinical practice and all that is necessary is to repeat the situation in the next treatment session.

In the first session, the patient might be given the following instructions: "Would you like to lie on the bed? You can cover yourself with a blanket if you wish. Make yourself perfectly comfortable. Now, hypnosis is just a method of relaxation. All I want you to do is to concentrate your thoughts on your right hand. As you begin to relax, you will find that the right hand becomes light, and later, the hand will begin to rise. This is perfectly natural, so there is nothing to worry about, just concentrate your thoughts on the right hand, and soon you will find that it starts to rise. You may close your eyes if you wish." As soon as the therapist sees a movement occurring in the right hand, this is immediately reinforced: "The hand has started to rise, soon it will rise more and more; as you relax more deeply, the hand will get lighter and lighter, and it will rise more and more." The patient may now feel his hand rising and may start to laugh. The therapist now reassures the patient: "That's perfectly alright. Patients often find this rather funny on the first occasion. Yes, you can laugh if you like, it doesn't matter at all. And breathe slowly and deeply and relax." (The author has found this comment particularly helpful to patients.)

As the hand starts to rise from the bed, the therapist gives further suggestions that the hand is rising: "The hand is rising quite quickly now. It has already left the bed, and soon it will rise more and more." Suggestions are also given that the hand feels light. "The hand is beginning to feel really light now, it is getting lighter and lighter, it is floating upwards, it is rising, moving upwards, it is as light as a feather, like a cloud drifting upwards, it is rising up and up and up." Here the therapist's voice gets quieter to create the impression of floating. When the hand has risen several inches from the bed (this varies from one patient to another), the therapist may now say: "Now that you are nice and deeply relaxed, you can put your hand down. I will now give you a "count-down" for ten. I shall count slowly from one to ten, and with each number you will find that you become more and more relaxed. One . . . two. . . ." The therapist counts from one to ten, each number coinciding with a breath out. It will be observed that the patient's breathing becomes slower during the hypnotic procedure. When the therapist has reached ten, he may now say: "Now that you are perfectly calm, relaxed and peaceful, we can begin." The first scene to be introduced is usually a "neutral scene" which does not cause any anxiety to the patient. After this, the therapist can introduce the first scene from the hierarchy.

THE COUNTER-SUGGESTION

Towards the end of the hypnosis session, the therapist must give a strong counter-suggestion. He might say to the patient: "I am now going to count from one to ten. With each number you will find that your relaxed state will become lighter and lighter, so that by the time I reach ten, you will be able to open your eyes, you will be wide awake and perfectly fresh. Your hand will be perfectly normal in all respects." It is probably a good idea to repeat this and say to the patient: "I repeat, by the time. . . ." Usually the patient opens his eyes when he hears the word "ten," but if not, it may be necessary to count again from one to ten, and give further counter-suggestions. It is important that the therapist is in perfect command of the situation and knows exactly what to do, as this transmits to the patient.*

COMBINED BEHAVIOR THERAPY AND PSYCHOTHERAPY

In the majority of patients treated so far, the author has found that after a few treatment sessions of the type described in the previous section, patients find that a lot of unexpected things are happening, which they would like to discuss with the therapist. For this reason it was decided to divide each treatment session into two parts, the first for psychotherapy and the second for behavior therapy. The content of the first part of each session depends entirely on the material which the patient chooses to bring into the treatment situation. Usually there are many problems arising out of the treatment which he is keen to discuss, and the patient should be given the opportunity to do so.

1. Responses of Family and Friends

It has been the author's experience that, as the patient improves, he meets strong opposition from his family and friends, who object most

---

* Editor's note: It is usually useful to count *backwards* from 10 to 1 when dehypnotizing patients whose hypnotic state had been increased by counting from 1 to 10.

strongly to any change, however small, in his behavior. The environment would appear to be extremely sensitive to these changes, and as soon as they are detected, (often before the patient has become aware of them), counter pressures are exerted onto the patient, to try and force him back into his former behavior. This may be formulated in the following way: *"There is a state of dynamic equilibrium between the patient and his environment and any attempt to change this will lead to opposing forces being set into motion to try and recreate the former state."* The patient in behavior therapy usually manages to survive these counter forces and makes a recovery, but if he fails to do so, he will return to his former state. The second point is that once the patient's behavior has changed, if the environment fails to exert sufficient counter pressure to reverse the treatment, then there is a change in the nature of the relationship between the patient and the people in his environment. This may be formulated as follows: *"If the state of dynamic equilibrium between the patient and his environment is upset, and the opposing forces cannot survive the alterations in the patient's behavior, then this leads to an alteration in the environment."*

These two formulations may be illustrated by the case of a 22-year-old male homosexual patient who was receiving treatment from the author. As he was being desensitized to heterosexual situations, he soon learned that his male companions did not approve of any alteration in his sexual adjustment. When he started dating girls, his friends did not encourage him in this; on the contrary, they told him that he had no right to do this, especially on a Saturday night, and that his first responsibility was with them. This caused considerable conflict in the patient and he began to wonder whether he was doing the right thing after all. He was being given one set of instructions from the therapist and another from his friends. Up to now he was experiencing the opposing forces which were set in motion in an attempt to force him back into the homosexual position. This is in keeping with the first formulation. Later in treatment, when his friends realized that they could not achieve their aims, they began to show changes themselves in the direction of heterosexuality, and found that they were dating girls too, and dancing more. This is in line with the second formulation. The patient met similar problems in relation to members of his family.

The successfully treated alcoholic patient who can drink socially without the need to drink to excess finds that his friends do not appreciate his altered attitude towards drinking. They expect him to drink as much as before, and when he does not do so, they cannot understand it. At first, they think this is of a temporary nature and "cannot last," but later, they realize that this is a new pattern of behavior which will be maintained. One patient who had just completed a course of treatment reported that his mother had warned him that she had detected his finger prints on the wardrobe where she had hidden a large supply of whiskey. Presumably she had hoped to sabotage the treatment and encourage further drinking in her son, but she failed to achieve this, for he no longer wished to drink to excess.

The successfully treated drug addict meets fierce opposition from his friends. If he tells them that he no longer needs to take the addictive drug, they become so angry that they may use physical violence and injure the patient. The sister of one successfully treated addict became extremely hostile and accused the therapist of brainwashing him.

A frigid patient who was treated by behavior therapy thought that her husband would be delighted if she could show more interest, but when this happened, he felt less inclined to make love to her, and became impotent. Her husband said that he did not like his wife to show sexual interest (this is the reverse of his original attitude) and that frigid women were "more sexy." He resented her more feminine approach, found it strange when she started preparing elaborate meals for him, and was alarmed when she dismissed her maid because she was not satisfied with her standard of cleaning. Later, the husband readjusted to his wife's improvement, though this took a long time, and several joint sessions were needed where husband and wife were interviewed together.

2. Relationship with the Therapist

When the patient has received intensive treatment of any kind over a prolonged period, whether this is behavior-oriented or not, he develops an attachment to the therapist who is treating him. Behavior therapists tend to deny the importance of this, though some recognize that it may be a useful adjunct to treatment.

After a few sessions of behavior therapy using hypnosis, the author has found that the patient develops feeling for the therapist. This may be quite strong and the patient finds himself thinking about the therapist when he is working or at other times, and he may wonder why he is thinking about the therapist at all. Sooner or later, the patient may develop complex thoughts relating to the therapist. On the one hand, he may look forward to the next treatment session when he can see the therapist again; on the other hand, he may consider the possibility that the therapist has come to some harm which will prevent him from seeing him. One patient feared that the therapist might be killed on the road and wanted to ensure his safety by escorting him across the road. The author interprets these comments and tells the patient that his ambivalent feelings towards the therapist are a reflection of emotions which were felt by him at an earlier stage in relation to important figures in his life and that these are not in fact intended for the therapist. The fear of death of the therapist is interpreted in terms of death wishes, and the patient may remember harboring death wishes for his father.

Though the exact nature of the relationship which the patient makes with the therapist during a course of treatment varies from one patient to another, all patients who recover in treatment make a strong attachment to their therapist. One female patient who was treated for frigidity and housebound syndrome wanted the therapist to make love to her, and when this was refused, she was very angry and cried bitterly, saying that if she had known that treatment would produce such an emotional turmoil she would rather not have had the treatment at all. Later, she was pleased that the therapist had not been influenced by her demands and that these had been interpreted to her in the light of earlier emotional experiences.

CONCLUSION

It is hoped that the author has been able to convey that, during a course of treatment which is essentially behavior-oriented, there are many important changes other than the target symptom being treated. Treatment of a frigid woman brings about an alteration in the relationship with her husband, and altering the sexual adjustment of a homosexual leads to severe repercussions in his immediate environment. A few examples are given in the text to illustrate the magnitude of the reaction in the environment to changes occurring in the patient. An attempt has also been made to show the importance of the relationship with the therapist during a course of intensive treatment. It is felt that psychotherapy is necessary for all patients receiving behavior therapy, and a broad spectrum approach to treatment would seem to offer the best help to our patients.

2

The Initial Interview

HERBERT FENSTERHEIM, Ph.D.

BEHAVIOR THERAPY TENDS to focus upon specific target symptoms and has a wide array of treatment techniques at its disposal. It differs from the more traditional psychotherapies in a number of ways that bring diagnostic considerations closer to the "blueprint for action" (Cameron, 1953) ideal than is true of the more traditional settings. Behavior therapy requires a series of meaningful decisions on the part of the therapist from the very first contact with the patient. Hence, the initial interview in behavior therapy takes on a special importance.

The problems presented from the very first contact with the patient are accentuated in the private practice of behavior therapy. In an institutional setting, at the very least, the patient has been filtered through a screening process which minimizes the chance of a completely inappropriate referral. The patient may be preceded by a chart containing the results of an intake interview which will include a description of the problem, a brief history and a mental status examination. There may also be an extensive social work case history, an intensive psychological examination, a medication chart, and, perhaps, voluminous notes of previous treatment.

In a private practice all one usually knows is that there is a voice on the telephone asking for an appointment. At this point two major decisions have to be made: should any appointment be given at all and, if so, how quickly should the patient be seen.

PROBLEMS IN THE FIRST CONTACT

Because it is novel and holds the promise of more effective results, many patients while undergoing more traditional forms of treatment decide to change to behavior therapy. Many times such a change is appropriate and beneficial to the patient. There are times, however, when the change of treatment may be inappropriate (as when the patient is misinformed about the nature of behavior therapy or expects a magical solution to rather complex problems). There are other times when such a change may actually be harmful to the patient as when a change of therapies is an avoidance of making necessary changes in behavior during the course of an otherwise successful ongoing treatment. Hence, every new patient should be asked whether he is currently in treatment and whether he has discussed the change with his therapist. The therapist should always be contacted prior to giving the first appointment.

CASE 1: The case of Mr. A. illustrates some of the ethical problems involved with patients under treatment. He had been in psychoanalytic treatment for about three years with the presenting problem of sexual impotency. At the time of his first contact he was still in treatment and there had been no improvement in the symptom. He had discussed behavior therapy with his therapist who was very much opposed to it. No appointment was given until his therapist had been contacted.

The therapist involved had a good professional reputation and, in my discussions with him, appeared to be competent, sensitive and mature. He was not against the use of behavior therapy for the treatment of sexual impotence either in principle or for the specific patient. His concern was with the timing of such intervention. The patient, he stated, was a general underachiever in all areas of his life, vocational, social, and personal. He was given to periodic temper outbursts and was unable to form close emotional relationships with anyone. Motivated mainly by his desire to overcome his sexual symptom, he had been working well analytically. Recently he had made some major behavioral changes and had achieved some important insights. He appeared to be at the point of a major analytic breakthrough. This possibility carried a good deal of anxiety in its wake and, to avoid this anxiety and still relieve the symptom, he had sought out behavior therapy. To treat the symptom behaviorially *at this point* could very well distract him from a potential growth experience of major importance to all areas of his life and, in that sense, would be destructive. This formulation, supported by many details, seemed quite credible.

Under these conditions should I see the patient? I described his therapist's formulation to him over the telephone to make certain that he understood it. I also told him that so far as I could determine this formulation was most reasonable. When he still insisted on the behavioral approach, I followed the principle that he had a right to choose the form of treatment he was to receive and I accepted him for treatment. As he could not afford the cost of both treatments simultaneously, he stopped the analytically oriented therapy.

A combination of systematic desensitization through imagery and graded sexual tasks in life yielded complete symptom relief in fourteen sessions. His other problems (difficulty in achieving emotional closeness and irrational temper outbursts) appeared to remain unchanged nor did he desire to work on these problems. The fourteenth session was therefore the terminal session with me. He did not return to his previous therapist nor did he continue any treatment at all. He remained quite satisfied with his "symptomatic gains."

It may be noted in this case that it was not only the fact that the patient was currently in treatment that posed the problem. Part of the problem stemmed from the fact that behavioral techniques can be used to modify specific symptoms while leaving others unchanged. This, too, can bring about certain ethical problems.

CASE 2: During his first telephone contact with me, Mr. B. stated that he had a problem of sexual potency. He was a homosexual, his difficulty occurred in his homosexual relationships and he did not want treatment for homosexuality. In fact, he would enter treatment only if I agreed to confine my treatment attempts to the specific problem of sexual potency and to avoid completely any attempt to influence the homosexuality. He did recognize that there could be no guarantee that the homosexuality would be unchanged but he insisted that there be no deliberate attempts to change it.

Consultation with colleagues yielded three distinct sets of opinions concerning the propriety of accepting these limited treatment goals. One group claimed that it would be like treating a diabetic ulcer without treating the underlying diabetes and so would be unethical. The people holding this point of view also held the basic belief that the homosexuality and the impotency were merely expressions of the same underlying pathology and their conclusions stemmed logically from this conceptual position. Several of them also held the belief that it would be impossible to treat the impotency without also treating the homosexuality. (This is untrue for I have now treated six such patients with a simple systematic desensitization and all have responded successfully in from two to seven sessions.)

A second group of colleagues was more practical. They held that I should agree to the conditions imposed since the patient himself may come to change the goals. They argued that the only reason the patient did not want the homosexuality treated was because he felt hopeless about it, he did not believe treatment would work. If, through the treatment of the impotency, it could be demonstrated that the behavioral techniques were effective, he would gain hope and decide on further treatment. This position was not supported by any evidence. In fact, of the six such patients I have treated only one showed any desire to give up an exclusively homosexual mode and that one patient wanted "the best of both worlds."

A third group of colleagues, mainly people involved in the behavioral, hypnotic or psychopharmacologic approaches (i.e., those approaches directed towards target symptoms), held a different view. There was no reason to believe, they argued, that the two conditions were directly related. It might be assumed that the patient had two separate and distinct sexual problems. They felt that he had the undeniable right to seek treatment for one condition and to reject it for the second. The important point was that the patient should be aware that available techniques do exist which may modify the homosexual pattern should he so desire.

This last approach is the one I adopted for Mr. B. and for all such patients. I do agree to confine the treatment to the specific target symptoms as best as I can. However I also state that I will present for their consideration a plan for the treatment of homosexuality. All I ask is that

I be permitted a brief time to present a possible treatment plan and that the patient listen to it. When I do present such a treatment plan I do so as objectively as possible with no attempt to "sell" it to the patient. During the terminal session I once again refer to the possibility of modifying the homosexual behavior. In this way I accept the patient's right to seek treatment for one condition and to reject treatment for the other while knowing what treatment is available.

Beyond the problem of ethics, there is the problem of the urgency of the appointment. As with any form of therapy, the content and the affect must be assessed during the initial contact to determine the acuteness of the condition. If there is intense distress the patient should be seen within forty-eight hours or even sooner. If this cannot be done, he should be referred to a colleague who may be able to see him at once. There are patients who, having taken the important step of calling for an appointment, are impatient or manipulative and demand to be seen immediately. Such patients usually can wait for a convenient appointment time and should not be confused with the more acutely disturbed people who do need to be seen immediately. As mentioned, the clinical decision to be made here is essentially the same no matter what type of psychotherapy is practiced.

There is a difference between behavior therapists and other therapists concerning patients who do have to wait a week or longer for a first appointment. Behavior therapists, probably more as a matter of style than of conceptual differences, tend to rely more on questionnaires than do other practitioners. Hence, while a patient is waiting for an appointment I often mail him a life history form, a fear inventory, an assertion questionnaire and an MMPI. The patient completes these and brings them to the first interview or mails them back prior to that interview. This procedure helps to make the initial interview more efficient and also provides a supportive function while the patient awaits the appointment date.

The last point about initial contact, unique to a private practice, concerns fees. Fees should be clearly stated before making the first appointment. Unlike most other forms of treatment, because behavior therapy is so new, few low cost treatment facilities exist at present and the problem of the patient with limited financial resources is a major one. I have attempted to meet this problem to a small extent through the use of a therapeutic assistant to perform certain of the routine treatment procedures, through the use of small groups for desensitization and through the use of "mini-groups" for assertive training. In this way there is some lowering of fees but the major problem remains and will be overcome only when many more trained behavior therapists are available.

FORMAL DIAGNOSTIC CONSIDERATIONS

The initial interview for behavioral treatment is closely allied to therapeutic action. In actuality there are two major types of initial interview, each with a different goal. For patients not in acute distress the major purposes of this interview are to obtain a clear statement of the most important problems, to form some working hypothesis concerning these problems, and to develop a beginning approach to treatment. For the person in acute distress, the goal of the first interview is to furnish some measure of relief even if it means a delay in the systematic gathering of information.

Formal diagnostic considerations do play some role. Although it has been well established that the major diagnostic categories tend to be unreliable and often unrelated to treatment, certain diagnoses are indeed related to behavioral treatment. This area has not been well researched and what follows are clinical impressions.

A differential diagnosis between a character disorder and a neurosis is often important. Neurotics tend to have anxiety and guilt connected with crucial problem areas and the treatment of choice usually centers around some form of desensitization and tension reduction. Character disorders, when they do show anxiety, usually experience it as a consequence of the symptom rather than as a cause of the symptom. Desensitization may be difficult because of the inability to experience anxiety when picturing scenes or even in the actual situation. At best, the desensitization procedures lead only to peripheral changes in that the patient becomes more comfortable with an inadequate mode of life. The treatments of choice for character disorder usually center around a combination of operant methods, aversive techniques, assertive training, education and guidance.

Another important differential diagnosis is between hysterical neuroses and obsessive-compulsive neuroses. The obsessive tends to be intellectualized, rigid and to have a shallow affect. The hysteric tends to be impulsive, given to strong feelings and is often described as childish and immature. Witkin and his colleagues (1954, 1962) have found that obsessives tend to be field independent whereas hysterics tend to be field dependent; that the perceptual fields of obsessives tend to be highly differentiated while those of hysterics tend to be global and undifferentiated.

In general, my clinical impression is that there usually are fewer problems in relaxation among hysterics. Also hysterics seem to require simple hierarchies, with relatively few steps, and in all, fewer hierarchies are required for a given behavioral change. Obsessives, probably because of their highly differentiated thought and perceptual processes, usually require more steps in the hierarchies than do the hysterics and may require a number of hierarchies to be applied to a given problem.

A comparison of two young men, one generally hysteric and the other decidedly obsessive, with anxieties in social situations may illustrate this difference. With both patients systematic desensitization to images of being at a party were used. The scenes used for the hysterical young man included speaking to a friend, to a stranger, to a girl he had dated, to a strange girl, asking for a telephone number, etc. In all, a fourteen step hierarchy was used with successful symptom relief. The obsessive young man required four different hierarchies of twelve to twenty-one steps each. These hierarchies concerned rejection, disapproval, doing something "gauche" and expressing anger. The symptom was not completely alleviated until the desensitization was supplemented by some assertive training in a group situation.

Perhaps the most important differential diagnosis to be made concerns the distinction between "neurotic" and "psychotic" conditions. With the overt psychotic, the significance of this diagnosis is obvious and will not be considered here. It is the borderline or the pseudoneurotic schizophrenic where the differential diagnosis may become difficult yet crucial.

The relation of such a differential diagnosis to behavior treatment may be illustrated by considering pervasive anxiety and pananxiety. Although both types of anxiety are generally chronic and at a high level, there is a qualitative difference between them. As used here, pervasive anxiety is a neurotic reaction to a large number of different stimuli. Pananxiety is an expression of a psychotic process and may even be due primarily to an organic dysfunction within the central nervous system. The differential diagnosis between a neurotic and a psychotic condition is crucial in making the distinction. Neurotic patients with pervasive anxiety often respond to a treatment plan of intensive relaxation training and nonsystematic desensitization (to be described later) followed by systematic desensitization and assertive training as the general level of anxiety decreases. Such patients should be seen initially two to three times a week and definite changes may be expected to occur during the first month of treatment. Initial treatment of psychotic patients with pan-anxiety involves the use of proper medication supplemented by relaxation training, and, eventually, by guidance concerning life situations. The relaxation exercises I use take about twenty minutes to perform and are tape-recorded for the patient. He is instructed to play them once a day. Extremely tense patients also receive half-hour relaxation sessions in my office. Generally, though, I see such patients on a once-a-week basis, progress is slow, beset by unpredictable panic outbursts, and goals are limited. I have found that after long periods of relaxation training, which consists of playing the relaxation tape every day for a period of well over a year, marked changes in pananxiety may occur, panic reactions may become less frequent, but the basic inadequate life style may show only minimal improvement.

One final caution must be made about the formal diagnosis. A problem oriented approach may sometimes underestimate pathology; problems which initially appear to be rather simple may turn out to be most com-plicated. To guard against this underestimation I always try to make a formal diagnosis and to supplement it with the scores from an MMPI. The information needed for the making of such a diagnosis often alerts me to pathology I may otherwise have missed.

PROBLEM FORMULATION

It has already been noted that with patients who are not in acute distress the initial interview should attempt to gain a clear definition of the problem. Very often (but far from always) the patient is able to state exactly what is wrong: he has a sexual problem or he is frightened of flying or he cannot sleep at night. Sometimes, however, the complaint is more general and vague: he cannot form close emotional ties, or he is in trouble with his work, or he is generally depressed. Both of these sets of problems can be handled in the same manner although the more general set of questions may take somewhat longer to explore and to formulate into working terms.

To investigate the problems in a systematic manner I attempt to answer the following questions:

1. What is the basic problem? How intense is it? To what extent is it disruptive?
2. When did it start? What was going on in the patient's life at that time? What were the exact circumstances under which it first occurred?
3. When is the problem greatest? When is it least disturbing?
4. Is there a specific fear, or some other feeling or thought connected with the problem? What is the worst that can happen?

The answers to these questions, combined with other information about the patient, may provide the basis for a behavioral therapy diagnosis and a tentative treatment plan. However, it would be premature to formulate such a plan until one further evaluation is made.

At this point we are attempting to deal with a problem of greater or lesser specificity presented by the patient and refined by the interview procedure described. However, all problems, all disrupted behavior, all disturbed emotions, do not stem from incorrect learning, psychopathology, or the characteristics of the person. If only for the sake of parsimony certain other variables must be investigated. Among these variables are:

Environment: A nonoptimal environment may often lead to psychological disruption. While this may be a particularly common variable among poor people (cf. Normand, Fensterheim and Schrenzel, 1967), it may influence people at all socio-economic levels. The approach to these problems usually does not involve psychotherapy but rather social casework to help solve the reality problems.

Stress: Life itself holds many stressful situations. People under such stress may become quite upset but their reactions may be completely appropriate to the situation. When people seek help under such circumstances, all that is usually required is reassurance that they are not going crazy, plus emotional support. The latter is often best provided by close friends and family rather than by a professional therapist.

Misconceptions: Some people become concerned with behaviors that are not really problems simply because they have incorrect concepts of the nature of "normality." The following illustration is an unusually clear example of this:

CASE 3: A 22-year-old man stated that he had a "sexual problem." Whenever he went to bed with a girl whom he did not like or whom he found unattractive, he had difficulty in obtaining an erection. When he did like the girl or when he did find her sexually attractive, he had no such problems. In all other areas of his life he appeared to be functioning normally.

His misconceptions were twofold: he believed that he should jump into bed at every possible opportunity whether he wanted to or not and he believed that a "real man" obtains and maintains an erection at any time or place or under any circumstance. These misconceptions were discussed with him and he left much relieved. A three-month and a six-month follow-up (I myself found it hard to believe it was quite that simple) showed a more discriminating pattern of sexual behavior and no further doubts of his manliness.

Style: People sometimes find the wrong approach for themselves in work or in social life. They try to fit into a pattern that runs counter to their own intellectual or temperamental style. Thus introverts try to become salesmen and extroverts try to become bookkeepers. This may be particularly common among students who, for a variety of reasons, attempt to major in subjects not really suited to their mode of function. These people would be most helped by the techniques of counseling and guidance rather than by psychotherapy.

While still other variables could be noted, the major point has been made. All problems presented by patients do not require psychotherapy and a careful evaluation may actually contraindicate a formal behavioral approach.

However, most problems presented to the therapist will require psychotherapy. The major behavioral approaches would tend to formulate the problems in terms of (a) phobias, (b) assertion problems, (c) absence of desirable habits, and (d) presence of undesirable habits. Although these are stated in simple form, let it be noted that "habit" may refer to a rather complicated series of behaviors, overt or covert. Because I have little that is new to offer about the last two sets of problems, this discussion will center around the diagnosis of phobias and assertive difficulties.

DIAGNOSTIC CLASSIFICATION OF PHOBIAS

In the behavior therapy lexicon, a phobia is any disturbed feeling elicited by a given class of stimuli. Although the published literature yields the impression that all phobias are basically the same, any good behavioral clinician is aware that there are different kinds of phobias requiring different kinds of treatment approaches.

1. *Direct Phobias:* These phobias tend to be the most simple and straightforward, with the much studied snake phobia as the paradigm. Cooper and his colleagues (1969) notwithstanding, the clinician does see many of these problems in an office practice. The usual, but not exclusive, form of treatment is systematic desensitization using relaxation and imagery. Even when the fear is intense and long hierarchies are needed, signs of progress are often evident from the very beginning.

A variant of this direct phobic condition concerns those fears that are present simply because the person does not know how to behave in certain situations. Fear of dating among adolescents and young adults is one example. Although systematic desensitization may be used here, the main approach involves education, fact giving and behavior rehearsal. Again, signs of progress are usually evident from the beginning of treatment.

2. *Direct Generalizations*: This is probably the most common type of phobia. Some fears do not stand alone but are generalizations of other fears. Thus, a fear of riding in subways may be a generalization of the fear of being trapped. The importance of this distinction is that without using the correct variables the results of desensitization may be most limited or may fail altogether. All behavior therapists are aware of the importance of this type of phobia, although it sometimes is difficult to determine the correct core fear.

3. *Indirect Generalizations:* This type of phobia is less well recognized by behavior therapists. Direct generalizations appear to make sense, to bear directly on the problem situation. It is easy to understand how the fear of being trapped may lead to a fear of riding in subways. However, some generalizations are not quite so obvious. As this type of indirect generalization has not been extensively considered, I will cite two examples.

CASE 4: Miss C. was a woman in her late twenties who was being treated for her difficulties in relating to men. A crucial point appeared to be her tension concerning a rejecting father and a desensitization to this was attempted. At the beginning of the desensitization session the patient casually mentioned that at some time we ought do something about her fear of heights; prior to the session she had become upset while looking out of a sixth floor window. There was no discussion of this and the desensitization concerning her rejecting father proceeded. The very next day (she reported) she was at a cocktail party and suddenly was made aware that she had been looking down from a twenty-first floor terrace with no anxiety at all. The fear of heights was completely gone and stayed gone. Upon questioning, no evidence was obtained to suggest that during the desensitization there had been intrusions of scenes concerning heights. Although there are a number of possible interpretations of this event, one reasonable interpretation is that in some way the fear of heights was a generalization of the fear of a rejecting father. When the latter was removed (as it was during that one session), the former also disappeared.

CASE 5: The patient was a former airline stewardess who had become terrified of flying. The treatment was a straightforward desensitization to flying and to airplane crashes. Towards the end of treatment she brought up the fact that her fear of tough-looking men in the street, a fear not previously elicited, had completely disappeared. No evidence of intrusion of tough-looking men into the flying images could be elicited.

The connection between a rejecting father and the fear of heights, or between airplane crashes and the fear of tough-looking men, is not quite as evident as those in the direct generalization category. These indirect generalizations become important when such a fear as agoraphobia is considered. Several colleagues and myself, based upon clinical experience, have come to consider many cases of agoraphobia as an indirect generalization of the fear of the loss of a significant person by an otherwise dependent person. With a married person it most often is the fear of losing the spouse. With such people I tend to get best results not through a desensitization to outdoor excursions, but through working on the marriage relationship.

4. *Excessive Inhibition:* People who lack assertive or excitatory behavior (Salter, 1949) tend to develop many different symptoms. Specific fears or phobias may be one such set of symptoms. My own clinical experience suggests that most hypochondriacal fears, as well as certain sexual fears, stem from an excess of inhibition. The desensitization procedures do not work with fears of this type and assertive and excitatory training is the treatment of choice.

Thus, I diagnose four different kinds of phobias, each requiring a different treatment. However, it must be noted that there is no diagnostic method presently available that will predict with certainty which treatment approach should be used. I have unsuccessfully attempted to treat hypochondriasis with assertive training only to find that it responded to a simple desensitization. I have improved the marital relationship of an agoraphobic woman with no change in the major symptom only to find that it did respond to an *in vivo* desensitization to going outside. I have unsuccessfully attempted to treat an airplane phobia as both a direct phobia and as a direct generalization only to find that it disappeared with assertive training.

At present, unless there are strong indications to the contrary, I always use the most simple therapeutic approach first. If I diagnose a phobic condition, I first treat it as a direct phobia or a direct generalization. Unless technical problems such as difficulty in relaxation or difficulty in visualizing scenes intervene, changes should be noted rather quickly. If changes in the symptom are not forthcoming, I then investigate one of the other approaches.

DIAGNOSTIC CLASSIFICATION OF ASSERTIVE PROBLEMS

Disturbed psychological functioning is usually intimately bound up with disturbed interpersonal relations. These disturbed interpersonal relations are often due to problems in assertion. These types of psychological disturbances almost invariably include a low self-esteem and an inadequate mastery of life situations, and often include depression, rages, apathy or withdrawal. Since phobias, psychosomatic disorders and other symptoms may also be included, a differential diagnosis must decide which aspects of the psychological disturbance and the disturbed interpersonal functioning are primary. If the primary focus is upon person-to-person interactions the area of assertion must be carefully investigated.

A working definition of assertion is "an open and direct, honest, and appropriate expression of what a person feels and thinks." Before a treatment plan can be prepared to remedy dysfunctions in this area, several different aspects of these behaviors must be formulated.

1. *Area of involvement.* The Casper Milquetoast who is unassertive in all areas is easily identified. However, in most cases the lack of assertion seldom generalizes into all areas of life. A man may be assertive at work, in his social life, and with his children, and yet be unassertive in his relations with his wife. A man may be direct and open about his tender feelings and uncommunicative about his angry feelings, and vice versa. Whenever the presenting problem is one of a mood disturbance, even though the patient may indicate a generally assertive life style, particular care should be given to the search for meaningful areas where unassertive

behavior may dominate. In those areas where assertive difficulties are encountered, discussion and behavior rehearsal usually bring about marked and rapid change. The more general the lack of assertion, the more complex the treatment usually must be.

2. *Type of difficulty.* Some people do not act assertively because they have never learned how to do so; others know what to do but cannot bring themselves to do it. These latter are usually phobic patients. They fear scrutiny, or rejection, or aggression or any number of other consequences of assertion. Once the fears are identified and mitigated or removed, assertive behavior usually emerges quite spontaneously. The former type, the people who had never learned to be assertive, may be typified by the young adult who has never dated. With these persons education, modeling, and structured experiences (often preceded by tension reduction as with a direct phobia) are usually the treatment of choice.

3. *Type of Behavior:* As assertion has been defined it has three behavioral characteristics: (1) openness and directness, (2) honesty, and (3) appropriateness. People with assertive difficulties may be deficient in any or all three areas. However, it is not uncommon to see people who are deficient in only one area. It is possible for people to appear to be open and direct and yet to be dishonest in what they express. To be inappropriately honest and so to create a distance between themselves and others is not an uncommon technique used by those who fear closeness.

3a. OPEN AND DIRECT. People whose assertive problems are limited to this area tend to be wordy. This often is accompanied by shallowness of feeling, difficulty with close relationships and lack of clear-cut desires. I have often found them to be related to circumscribed work difficulties such as report writing. Practice and exercises in the use of the pronoun "I" and in making simple direct statements often change this entire pattern. Group therapy may be particularly helpful because other group members can model the desired behaviors and can provide immediate feedback when necessary.

3b. HONESTY. These are the people who appear to be open and direct, generally appropriate, often extraverted, but who are dishonest in what they express. They appear to be assertive but, because of the lack of honesty, are not genuinely so; hence the label of "pseudo-assertive." They are the hail-well-met salesmen or politicians. Many alcoholics and drug addicts would fall into this category. Those who are not alcoholics or addicts usually come with a presenting problem concerning closeness ("I can't make up my mind to marry her."), lack of satisfaction in life ("Nothing turns me on."), or mood difficulties. I have been generally unsuccessful in treating these conditions and therefore I shall make no recommendations for treatment.

3c. APPROPRIATENESS. This is the most rare of the specific behavioral deficiencies. These are the people who are open and honest in their behavior but, because they are often inappropriate in these expressions, they usually encounter numerous interpersonal difficulties. Such people are often naive and immature and are often at the extremes of an exploitation continuum, being highly exploiting or highly exploited. They tend to have rapid and fairly great (but not extreme) mood changes. They have not learned the realities of social relations within our complex society nor have they learned the appropriate expression of feelings. Education and behavior rehearsal, particularly in a group setting, often work well. Those who do not respond to role-playing techniques may respond well when desensitized to a fear of closeness, followed by some training in assertive behavior.

One last caution must be presented when dealing with problems of assertion. The patient's subculture is of great importance and the therapist must have a genuine understanding of the social patterns and modes of function within these subcultures before diagnosing and planning treatment for an assertive difficulty. That subcultural atmosphere, ideology and values tend to select and to reinforce certain patterns of social behavior is well known and has been illustrated many years ago by Fensterheim and Birch (1950) in their analysis of the behavior of Displaced Persons in an UNRRA camp following World War II. The subcultural group sets the type of social pattern a person may encounter, influences the patterns of confrontation with and relations to other people and, above all, defines what is considered to be appropriate interpersonal behavior. The role of physical combat in different social groups is but one obvious example of this. The therapist must take all these into account in planning his treatment for an assertive problem.

THE ACUTELY DISTRESSED PATIENT

The foregoing emphasis has centered around the usual initial interview where the patient comes in with a problem, where a first formulation of the nature of the problem can be made, where a tentative treatment plan can be drawn up, and where the patient leaves with homework to do, (i.e. questionnaires, tests to complete or assignments to perform). With most patients all this can usually be accomplished in one session although, at times, two or three interviews may be necessary. The formulations are of course subject to modification as more data concerning the patient becomes available.

Some patients, however, come for the initial interview in a state of acute distress. They may be in a panic, have a severe depression, be suicidal, or suffer from a mild psychotic break (the more violent or florid psychotic episodes will not be discussed here). Under these conditions the goal of the initial interview must shift from one of a systematic problem formulation to one of bringing immediate relief to the patient.

The interview with the severely disturbed patient begins with a discussion of the symptom, its content and its origin. At some point, based upon the clinical judgment of the therapist, this inquiry is abandoned and energies are directed towards bringing relief to the patient.

There are a series of traditional tension reduction methods available to the therapist. These include reassurance and support, making a human contact with the patient and so breaking through the isolation, and allowing opportunity for catharsis. There are also several behavioral techniques which are helpful for this purpose:

1. *Relaxation.* This is usually used where tension and anxiety are general and where a secondary reaction to the tension has been set off. These secondary reactions are usually a fear of loss of control, a fear of the anxiety itself or an overwhelming feeling of helplessness in face of the tension. Almost invariably relaxation procedures bring about at least a slight and temporary reduction of the tension level and this I draw to the patient's attention. I point out that *we* reduced the anxiety by about 12% or 20% or 30%, as the case may be. Often the anxiety quickly spikes to its former level and it is necessary for the therapist to reflect this too with some statement that as the patient practices it may last for longer periods of time. Sometimes the relaxation exercises reduce the tension level quite considerably and the patient leaves feeling much better. At other times the patient leaves just as tense as when he came but with a knowledge that he is not completely helpless in the face of the disturbance. At all times I tape record the relaxation exercises and the patient leaves with the tape and with the homework assignment of using the relaxation tape at least once daily. This provides both structure and

support to the patient as well as the potential anxiety reduction of the exercises themselves.

Some patients are too agitated to perform the lengthy relaxation exercises or even some shortened version of them. Yet it may be necessary to bring about some tension reduction. I use a very brief relaxing exercise with these patients. While they are talking I can see the tension build up. At some point I stop them and tell them to take a deep breath, to hold it, to slowly let it out, to picture the word or image of "calm" and to relax their muscles. The entire exercise takes about ten seconds. It often results in a very temporary and slight, yet a definitely noticeable, reduction in tension. After doing this several times, the patient often appreciates the fact that there is some simple way of controlling tension and may even begin to do it himself. This can be an extremely supportive procedure.

2. Non-systematic Desensitization (NSD). This method has not been published although I have reported on it at a meeting of the New York Chapter of the Association for Advancement of Behavior Therapy. Basically, it fits within a counterconditioning paradigm where the anti-anxiety aspects are a task orientation and the attempts to relax, rather than relaxation itself. The patient is instructed to think about or to picture whatever is disturbing him, the very worst aspects of it. He is to signal at the very first sign of tension. Upon signalling, the patient receives instructions and help in picturing a pleasant scene and in attempting to relax. It is hard work for the patient, boring for the therapist (the disturbed scene should be repeated fifteen to twenty-five times) but fairly successful in cases of extreme anxiety or depression in well over 50% of the time.

This method is indicated during an initial interview when the disturbance is fairly extreme and centers around a relatively specific content area. It is contraindicated in psychotic conditions where at best it is usually ineffective and where it may actually increase the disturbance. A decision to use this method during an initial interview must be made early in the session, for close to a half hour must be allowed. When it does work, the major relief often comes about several hours after the session or even during the next day.

Other behavioral methods may also be used to bring relief to the acutely disturbed patient during the very first interview. Thought stopping (on occasion even covert sensitization) may be used to stop these and other obsessive thoughts and the shocker may be given the patient to take home.

Any other behavioral technique, when used with sound clinical judgment combined with a good understanding of the basis of the technique itself, may be used to ameliorate the acute distress during the first interview.

At the close of an initial interview, three important questions must be answered. Unfortunately, the professional literature provides few guidelines that will be of help and the therapist must rely on his own clinical judgment.

1. *Is behavior therapy the treatment of choice?* Perhaps some other form of treatment would be best for the patient. The guideline I usually use is that if I can formulate a reasonably precise therapeutic program with which to approach the major problems, a behavioral approach is worth trying.

There are patients, however, where it becomes obvious that the major therapeutic thrust must be non-behavioral. One such type is the patient who requires closely supervised medication as the core of treatment. Another type of patient is the one who is so isolated, so in need for "working through" some kind of relationship with another human being, that the usual symptom relief and behavior modification, while necessary, is not sufficient. Finally there is the person who is so immersed in the psychoanalytic mode of thinking that he really cannot understand the behavioral perspective, does not really want it and could not tolerate it for more than a few sessions.

2. *Can I work with this patient?* All therapists find certain problems or certain people difficult to treat. I have already noted in this paper that I get poor results with the pseudo-assertive patient. There are other patients with whom I have difficulty. The identification of such patients is as important in behavior therapy as it is in any other form of psychotherapy. It is important for both patient and therapist that this judgment be made during the initial interview so that it can be tactfully explained to the patient, and so that he be referred to a colleague for treatment.

3. *How fast should treatment proceed?* There have been no studies of drop-outs from behavior therapy. Recently I have surveyed my own patients who have dropped out early in treatment. The largest group of these patients appeared to have dropped out because I moved too fast in treatment. These are people to whom I had explained the treatment plan but who did not truly accept it. They are people who needed the feeling

of being understood, of being able to trust the therapist and his judgment, before specific behavioral techniques could be used.

With such patients it is necessary to spend several sessions establishing rapport and a feeling relationship as a context for treatment. A smaller group of patients appeared to drop-out because of their magical expectations; when they were not "cured" in two or three or four sessions, they became angry or bitter and left treatment. To attempt to work too fast is to reinforce these magical expectations. The initial part of the treatment should temper the patient's unrealistic demands and help him gain a more realistic expectation. Again, a proper context for treatment must be established.

SUMMARY

The behavior therapist must be primarily a clinician. The application of an effective behavior therapy program calls for a meaningful relation between diagnosis and treatment. Hence, the initial interview takes on a special significance. During this interview the therapist must take into consideration certain aspects of formal diagnosis, make a behavioral formulation and confront several ethical and clinical judgments, all of which are directly influential in determining the most productive course of treatment. However, because he has behavioral techniques at his disposal, he may attempt to bring relief to the patient even before making his basic formulations.

REFERENCES

CAMERON, E., A theory of diagnosis. In H. Hoch and J. Zubin (Eds.), *Current problems in psychiatric diagnosis.* New York: Grune & Stratton, 1953.

COOPER, A., FURST, J. B., & BRIDGER, W. H., A brief commentary on the usefulness of studying fears of snakes. *Journal of Abnormal Psychology,* 1969, 74, 413-414.

FENSTERHEIM, H. & BIRCH, H. G., A case study of group ideology and individual adjustment, *Journal of Abnormal and Social Psychology,* 1950, 45, 710-720.

NORMAND, W. C., FENSTERHEIM, H., SCHRENZEL, S., A systematic approach to brief therapy for patients from a low socioeconomic community, *Community Mental Health Journal,* 1967, 3, 349-354.

SALTER, A., *Conditioned reflex therapy,* New York: Creative Age, 1949.

WITKIN, H. A., *et al., Personality through perception,* New York: Harper & Brothers, 1954.

WITKIN, H. A., *et al., Psychological differentiation,* New York: John Wiley & Sons, 1962.

3

An Expedient Model for Behavior
Therapy

JOHN N. MARQUIS, Ph.D.

WHEN I WAS IN HIGH SCHOOL I had a friend who was interesting to talk
to because he spent a lot of time in the library reading strange and
wonderful things about philosophy and psychology. The ideas that he
talked about were heady and quite alien to the things discussed in high
school in a small midwestern town in those days. Such ideas were almost
categorically relegated to the college curriculum. I was overwhelmed with
the multiplicity of ideas that he expressed, and asked him where would
be a good place to start reading in order to gain an understanding of
psychology. He suggested that I read William James' *Principles of Psychology*, (1890), Watson's *Behaviorism*, (1924), and Freud's *General
Introduction to Psychoanalysis*, (1917).

The following year as a freshman in college I was taking too many
courses to be able to do my homework anyway, so I found time to follow
his advice. I returned home from Christmas vacation full of enthusiasm

about the new world that I had discovered and told him about my decision to seek a career in psychology. His answer set a very good goal for me: "That's nice. Maybe you can help get psychology out of the witch doctor stage."

The three books he recommended still strike me as being very well chosen. The perspective of seeing the three giants exemplifying, first, the finest of general academic psychology struggling to free itself from philosophy, a position which James represented so well; second, the vigor and rigor of Watson's scepticism and his strong emphasis upon an objective scientific approach; and third, the subjective, individual approach of Freud with his willingness to pursue counter-intuitive hypotheses, enabled me to see in perspective the works of men who followed them. In particular, their criticisms of one another were enlightening. James was a little too preachy for my taste, but I was fascinated by his approach of specifying concrete things to be done in order to modify habits. Freud's hypotheses were untestable and untested, and Watson's almost complete rejection of mental content seemed too limiting and austere. Watson's accusation that James made rhetorical geese that laid golden eggs has left me with an unremitting suspicion of any pat analysis as being arbitrary, especially if it forms an acronym or has three basic points. Each approach held considerable appeal but left me with a high level of uneasiness.

In the late Forties I met with a seminar led by Arthur Broadbeck at the University of Illinois which tried to cast psychoanalytic hypotheses in empirically testable forms. By 1955 I was very much the behaviorist and was attempting to get group members to talk in eclectic psychotherapy groups by passing them the M&M's. (This, of course, backfired, since the alcoholic patient saw the procedure as "Kid stuff" and negatively reinforced members for speaking and for accepting candy (see Buehler, Patterson and Furniss, 1966). Nevertheless, I was always impressed with the early, isolated instances of behavior treatment. That movement, as I see it now, was considerably thrown off the track by the work of Dollard and Miller (1950) who translated psychoanalysis into learning theory terms. (See Marquis, 1970.)

Thus paradoxes persisted throughout my graduate studies until one day in the spring of 1960, at about the time that I finished my dissertation, Joseph Wolpe gave a colloquium at the University of Michigan. I was more intrigued by what he said than by anything I had ever heard, and spent the evening eagerly questioning him about his new psychotherapy. I was intrigued by the realization that one can use behavioral treatment methods and at the same time see a human being as being able to imagine, and thereby provide himself with his own stimulus material for deconditioning. Furthermore, I immediately appreciated the value of using a person's complex past conditioning and learning history, and then rehearsing behaviors in order to learn new modes of action rather than in order to gain insight into repressed complexes.

I read everything about behavior therapy I could get my hands on and, as I moved to Palo Alto, began trying to apply what I had learned. For some time I had been instructing patients in a behavioral view of life combined with the use of some psychoanalytic techniques and some confrontational techniques which I construed as extinguishing maladaptive behavior patterns by withdrawing from them the reinforcement of success in deceit and manipulation. Intellectually I felt that a very broad learning model was sufficiently complex to account for all human behavior with certain physiological and structural characteristics taken into consideration. However, I had difficulty in construing old diagnostic concepts in behavioral terms. How to account for feelings of inferiority and inadequacy, of depression, withdrawal, schizoid characteristics, and manipulative behavior? No one seemed to have the specific phobias that would lend themselves to desensitization. The severity of this problem is exemplified by my long search for an initial patient who would be suitable for behavioral treatment, and, conversely, the large number of people who fell between the cracks in my new-found theory. I have since found this to be the most serious problem of students learning how to do behavior therapy. A great step forward came when Arnold A. Lazarus came to Stanford for a year and later when he returned to the Behavior Therapy Institute in Sausalito for a year, giving many of us in the San Francisco Bay Area a chance to place behavior therapy in a broader theoretical and practical perspective. With experience, behavioral methods resulted in improvement of patients and other methods dropped out as they were not reinforced. At the same time more and more problems were easily construed in behavioral terms.

Traditional methods of psychotherapy are not only inefficient, they are also hostile. A classical psychoanalyst may go for six months without doing anything but instructing the analysand in the techniques of free association, and interpreting his resistances. Almost everything that the patient says is considered as being wrong. At best it represents some sort of derivative of his unmentionable impulses filtered through ego-mechanisms whose primary function is to deceive the patient and others about him. At worst it is a deliberate attempt to evade and subvert efforts to help him. The analyst is the expert on everything, including how the patient feels. Non-directive therapy is perhaps more respectful and certainly there is much to be learned from Carl Rogers (1951) about respecting our fellow human beings, no matter how troubled they may be. Nevertheless, it is an extremely hostile act to refuse to answer a direct and reasonable request or to withhold information from patients instead of providing the data that they need in the form of expert help in solving life's problems.

Perhaps the benign approach of the behavior therapist is made most clear in Patterson and Reid's (1967) *Reciprocity vs. Coercion.* The essence of their position is that people can control one another's behavior either by coercive demands or threats, or by reciprocal positive reinforcement. Surely a better understanding of these principles would do much to bring peace and love to the world.

Wesley G. Morgan of the University of Tennessee deserves credit for a model which is useful in construing all kinds of behavior change, but the writer takes full responsibility for discussing it in its present form. In my opinion, when the approach of a behavior modifier approximates this model, his methods become more effective and are perceived as being more benign. To the extent that the approach deviates from this model it tends to become more ineffective, or more judgmental and hostile. The model is really very simple and there is nothing really new about it. It divides therapeutic transactions into three parts. First the client and the behavior modifier must come to a clear understanding of the service that is to be performed. Behavior change has a starting point and a goal, and it is important at the outset to come to as clear an understanding of both of these as possible. A careful diagnosis is made of the patient's present state of affairs in relation to the behaviors he wishes to change. Then a careful analysis is made of the terminal behavior desired. This may involve the patient's doing something that he was not able to do formerly. It may involve his learning how to do comfortably something that he currently can do, but with considerable suffering and loss of effectiveness. He may need to learn how to be comfortable without doing something that he currently does and would rather not do.

After a careful diagnosis and analysis of the client's present condition and the desired terminal behavior have been made, the second step is to analyze the paths that can be taken to get from one to the other. Often several courses of action must be taken in order to produce the desired results. Also there are frequently several alternative courses of action which would lead the client from his present state to the terminal behavior. The third step is to construct a program, usually based on small incremental steps leading from the starting point to the goal.

Figure one gives an example of how the model might be applied to a hypothetical case. Treatment planning would also include orchestration of the several programs with proper timing. David Fisher *(Personal Commun.)* reports the results in treating a homosexual of getting an *in vivo* program ahead of a desensitization to women, which resulted in the following midnight phone call: Client, *"Hey Doc, I kissed her."* Dr. Fisher, *"Gee, Charlie that's great!"* Client, *"and then I went out in the alley and heaved."*

Although difficulty in changing behavior can result from the client's providing inaccurate information, a usual problem is a faulty analysis by the therapist, or even more likely, a programmatic mistake which usually consists of making the steps too big. If one has one hundred thousand dollars to develop a programmed text in mathematics, he can do a pretty good job of avoiding this difficulty. In working with an individual client on personal problems, precise programming is almost impossible. Therefore, the important thing is to be patient, constructive, and goal-oriented when the difficulty occurs.

It is easy at such times to become frustrated and blame the client for being unable to accomplish the task which we have set for him. Probably all of us have had a good deal of this kind of behavior modeled for us as children, and I doubt if there exists a human being so saintly that he does not at times feel angry when his attempts to influence the behavior of another person are not going ahead according to schedule. But we should keep in mind that anytime we blame another person for anything that he does, and when we claim that he ought to have done something else, we take leave of the reality of psychological determinism. Realistically we all know, as Andrew Salter (1949) says, that people do not do what they ought to do, they do what they have learned to do. They can do no other. When the client fails to do something that we think he should be able to do, we have made a wrong prediction. There is much to be said for George Kelly's (1955) formulation of hostility which points out that when a person makes a wrong prediction about another's behavior, he often attempts to coerce him into behaving in such a way as to validate

Clinical Behavior Therapy

FIGURE 1

Diagnosis	Problem	Treatment	Incremental Step	Terminal Behavior
Homosexuality	Afraid of criticism from women	Desensitization[1]	Increasing stimulus intensity with no anxiety	Comfortable with critical women
	Afraid of control by women	Behavior rehearsal[2]	Increasing assertiveness, less anxiety with assertiveness	Able to handle dominant women
	Not attracted to women	Orgasmic[3] reconditioning	Picturing women earlier in masturbation	Attracted to women
	Ignorant about how to give pleasure to women	Instruction	Increasing information about female sexual responses and elicitation of useful feedback	Confident of being a good lover
	Afraid of "nice girls" who are seen as like mother	Implosion[4]	Decreasing anxiety on picturing sex with mother	Able to be intimate with "nice girls"
	Attracted to men	Covert[5] sensitization	Increasing anxiety to men as sex objects	Not attracted to men
	Unable to relate intimately with women	In-vivo program	Increasing intimacy with women with little anxiety	Good heterosexual relationships

[1] Marquis, Morgan and Piaget (1971)
[2] Lazarus (1966)
[3] Marquis (1970)
[4] Stampfl & Levis (1967)
[5] Anant (1969)

the theory instead of accepting the validational evidence that the other person's behavior presents him with.

I do not mean to imply that all attempts to change behavior need to be done in tiny steps or even that social censure is not effective in changing people's behavior. Mowrer (1950) discusses the problem of reconciling determinism and responsibility very cogently. When a person is punished for being irresponsible, the point is not that he can logically be held responsible for his behavior in a moral sense. Rather it is that, having acted irresponsibly, if he is held responsible, he will hopefully act more responsibly in the future. The question then becomes the empirical one of whether punishment will be effective in changing his behavior.

Of course one of the nice things about a behavioral model is that the hypotheses used as a basis of treatment are tested in every case. Not only are we made aware of the places where we have erred in the microstructure of programming, but we also get feedback that makes it possible to see areas of anxiety which have been neglected and faulty hypotheses which may have been used in setting up treatment. To the extent that behavioral methods are effective in eliminating anxieties we are enabled to see what remains to be eliminated. As the client becomes more and more relaxed and fewer things bother him, the remaining hang-ups stand out dramatically against the background of relaxation and disinhibition.

This process of utilizing feedback to correct the treatment program and to eliminate remaining problem areas is of particular importance in helping the client to the highest possible level of functioning. Most practicing clinicians, in contrast to the academic experimenter, are eager to ferret out and eliminate all unadaptive responses. Experimental psychologists are usually interested in demonstrating a reliable result from a treatment method. The results of seeking a statistically significant difference on one variable are quite different from those obtained when seeking an optimal level of functioning for the human being who happens to be one's client.

I have had the experience a number of times of referring patients to colleagues whom I know to be skilled in behavioral methods only to have them treated by somewhat less effective methods based on somewhat less parsimonious theories, primarily therapeutic approaches around the periphery of behavior therapy such as Gestalt therapy or other existential approaches, neo-Reichian techniques, or family therapy based on communications theory. Although there are certainly times when these therapies are useful, patients usually learn to be aware of their feelings and to communicate more clearly with very little time and trouble when their basic anxieties and behavioral deficits are removed. Relaxation training, hierarchy construction, desensitization, and, in particular, shock aversion and anxiety relief conditioning can be meticulous, exacting tasks which can become very dull and boring. Nevertheless, I feel that it is the responsibility of the therapist to use the most effective techniques in dealing with patients, rather than the most enjoyable. It is natural enough when faced with immediately non-reinforcing consequences to drop down the habit family hierarchy to the next most salient response, but I think we should try to avoid it when it is not in the patient's best interest. When I first started doing behavior therapy, I would drop back to an analytic approach to the problem and search for some secret key to the patient's behavior. Such efforts almost universally met with failure.

This points to an interesting phenomenon which tends toward conservatism. Some clients are eager, able, and ripe for improvement. Others have difficulties which are rigidly ingrained and are highly resistant to change. Therapists try their favorite techniques first and reserve innovations for those clients where the favorite techniques have failed. These are usually the people who are less likely to respond well to any technique. Thus the usual techniques are tested under much more favorable conditions.

What kind of relationship develops from a learning model of human behavior? If, indeed, the client's behavior is the result of the experiences he has had, it is irrational to blame him for being what he is. If the therapist had had the same experiences as the client and vice versa, each would be sitting on the other side of the desk. Therefore, there is no justification whatsoever for the therapist to look down his nose at the client. The relationship is as direct and straightforward as that of the therapist consulting his attorney about a legal matter, or his accountant about his income tax. The expert is supplied with data, and a request for help with a specific problem, although the expert may also be called upon to formulate the problem more precisely. Perhaps a better example would be the more personal and complex relationship of the architect using his technical skills to design and build for the client a house which matches his needs and his lifestyle.

Armed with effective means of building self-reliance and independence in the client, the therapist need not worry about the client becoming dependent upon him for answers, or even for sympathy. The resulting relationship is one in which I have felt quite comfortable having good friends as clients and good clients as friends. If the therapist can succeed in teaching the client to construe the world of his own behavior and that of other people in terms of learning and psychological determinism, a number of benefits can accrue. Most of our clients—indeed most of us—have been reared by moralistic Christians and Jews. Even those of us whose parents have not been too moralistic and judgmental have grown up in a society whose institutions march to the beat of a moralistic drum. Until recently, teachers meted out rewards and punishments on the basis of the child's guilt or virtue, rather than in a specific attempt to increase or decrease the frequencies of certain behaviors. Most still do. Crime and punishment, guilt, innocence, and the categorical imperative run through the warp and woof of all our mass media. Even the basic ritual of the institution of divorce is an adversarial process in which one of the unfortunate parties must be blamed, found guilty, and treated punitively in terms of the settlement of the practical problems involved in dissolving the marriage.

Many patients find it a great relief to lay down the burden of obsessively adjudicating every action which they or those about them perform in terms of guilt or innocence. For many it is a real revelation to realize that it is not necessary to find someone to convict and hang every time things go wrong.

Therapists from other schools often see behavior therapy as a useful way of dealing with very specific symptomatic problems, but find it hard to understand how it can be used to deal with problems of existential despair, alienation, feelings of inferiority and inadequacy, etc. I feel that such highly generalized problems are usually the result of an inadequate diagnosis of the specific areas of anxiety and lack of skill. Usually a few minutes of careful questioning of a person who claims no specific areas of anxiety, but generalized depression or philosophical ennui, will suffice to reveal a number of very discrete and specific problems, often of considerable severity. Certainly a careful analysis of a fear survey schedule will provide reason enough for the feelings of generalized despair or inadequacy. A careful behavior analysis often reveals dozens of specific subjective fears. Indeed, such a person can often be found to have an area in his body which is in a chronic state of such intense tension as to cause excruciating pain. Conversely when those persons who are seeking philosophical solutions to difficulties construed in over-generalized terms have found basic solutions to their specific problems such as fear of criticism, rejection, disapproval; fear of being the center of attention; inability to reinforce others, or to accept affection or kindness without anxiety; and when they have become relaxed and effective in dealing with other people through shedding the burdens of anxiety and acquiring necessary interpersonal skills, then one can look in vain for the existential problems which brought them to the consulting room.

I do not mean by this to deny the reality of existential problems. All of us live in a world where there is gross injustice and where innocent people suffer, starve and die. Indeed, if you believe in determinism, only innocent people can suffer. We all must grow old and someday die. Alone among the species of the earth our breed of ape knows it. And each man in his own way must deal with these unpleasant facts. It is a bearable burden for people who are relatively free from morbid anxieties and have the skills necessary to cope with the daily problems of life with relative equanimity. It is probably also of considerable help to see the world in terms as realistic as possible in order to avoid the confrontations with false attitudes and discrepant data which plague the lives of people whose views of the world involve too much self-deception and romanticism. It is also of help to be involved in working to solve the problems of the world and increase the quality of human life. I am not prevented by any scientific snobbishness from discussing these problems with my clients on a philosophical level.

There are some situations which the incremental programming model as previously described does not seem to handle very well. One example is those situations in which the client or clients come to an agreement with the therapist and promise to do certain things or refrain from doing certain things, usually until the following interview. For example, a set of parents may agree with each other and with the therapist to ignore some noxious behavior on the part of the child. In other situations a contract is negotiated in which a husband and wife agree that each will behave in certain ways or refrain from doing certain things in return for reciprocal concessions on the part of the other spouse. Also a client may resolve and promise not to engage in some behavior which has been very gratifying for him. For example, a transvestite may promise not to dress up or an alcoholic will resolve not to drink during the week. Such agreements are sometimes effective in changing behavior for the short run or even permanently, which gives the appearance of a discontinuous behavior change involving no incremental steps.

In such cases, advantage is taken of the fact that many clients are made quite anxious by the prospect of violating a promise because of their past conditionings. By tying the promise to specific behaviors, one changes the reinforcing consequences of alternative behaviors. Such agreements are effective only when the client has more anxiety about breaking his promise than he has about following the course of action to which he has committed himself. Meanwhile, two forces are operating in the direction of a permanent change in the client's habits. First of all, if the course of action is a realistic one, the natural reinforcers in the environment will take over and permanently support the new behavior. (The parents are rewarded by a decrease in frequency in the child's whining; the alcoholic is rewarded with a clear head which does not ache in return for refraining from drinking. The assertiveness which the client shows in acting on his promise to ask for a raise is often rewarded with a raise.) The increase in strength of the new response is thus incremental, if not programmed specifically by the therapist. The other process can be variously construed in terms of extinction or implosion. Initially, following the agreed upon pattern of behavior, the client's anxiety level may rise, but as the feared consequences do not occur—again if the therapist has been realistic in his assignment—the anxiety response diminishes incrementally, and relatively permanent, stable change is achieved.

Another situation takes a metaposition to any therapeutic model. It is difficult to help a client who is not being honest with the therapist. The most common examples include the client's motive for therapy consisting of the desire for a pleasant hour of conversation and understanding. The therapist is trying to bring about more permanent change. The client may be interested in making a good impression on the therapist and therefore may simulate improvement rather than achieve real improvement. The danger of this is lessened by the therapist convincing the client that he is not being judged or condemned. The situation is less likely to develop when the therapist has independent information as to the client's behavior between sessions, as in a hospital setting, or when the spouse is included in therapy sessions.

CASE HISTORIES

The first two following cases have been chosen to illustrate the strategy and tactics of broad-spectrum behavior therapy (Lazarus, 1966 A) applying the model proposed above. It is often the custom to report dramatic and exceptional cases. Instead of selecting unusual cases, I have chosen two who represent the most common types of problems dealt with in a usual suburban private practice. Thereafter two other cases will be described broadly and one aspect will be discussed in detail. Some identifying data have been changed in each case in order to protect the identity of the clients.

CASE #1. Jane was an attractive 22-year-old graduate student whose chief complaint was frequent tension headaches and severe neck pain due to muscular tension. She had been treated with tranquilizers and physical therapy with slight relief. Her father was a retired Air Force sergeant and she had lived in many places around the United States and in Europe, largely growing up on air bases. She had difficulty in asserting herself and in expressing either displeasure or positive feelings. This led to a number of difficulties.

Jane had recently effected a reconciliation with her parents after an open break of some two years' duration occasioned by telling her mother about an affair she had had. Her mother was quite upset about this and Jane had become too upset to go to school and had dropped out for a semester. At that time her headaches started. She disagreed with her parents on a number of things and had been unable to come to terms with them.

She had felt comfortable with her original boy friend and only one of the six men she had gone with since then. In the year previous to beginning treatment, she had been living with a boy friend. A friend of his moved in for the summer in order to share the rent. She went to bed with the roommate (said she didn't know why), and her boy friend was furious with her. At his insistence she told off the roommate, although she was not really angry with him. After that, she and the boy friend went on a back-packing trip which turned out to be a terrible ordeal for her because of the cold and the dust. They argued and he broke up with her, but they completed the month living together because the rent was paid on the apartment. She cried most of the time.

Careful questioning revealed that Jane was extremely submissive, although capable of bitter arguments involving considerable self recrimination. She had great difficulty in saying no, whether to a boy's sexual advances or her mother's request for information. She was quite sensitive to criticism and rejection, anxious about being the center of attention, and worried about papers and examinations.

Because Jane was bright and well motivated, because she had considerable sophistication and social skills, because her anxieties were moderate, and because she had limited financial resources, it was decided to use *in vivo* relaxation and behavior rehearsal as the primary therapeutic tools rather than desensitization treatment. Plans are outlined in Figure 2.

After the second diagnostic session she was given a tape of relaxation instructions. The procedure was adapted from that used by Wolpe and Lazarus (1966, pp. 177-180), but with special emphasis on relaxing the eyes and the vocal apparatus. At the third session she reported that she had listened to the tape twice. It had not gone very well the first time, but by the end of the second time she had been completely relaxed. She was in a psychodrama group at school. One of the other members of the group was a boy who had told the group of some of his sexual exploits. She was afraid to go out with him for fear of being seduced when she did not want to. He had asked her out and she was very proud of refusing him. Meanwhile, she was going with another boy a year younger than she who had had no sexual experience. She was very fond of him and wanted to have intercourse with him, but he said that he did not believe in sex before marriage.

She was told that both of these situations presented her with an opportunity to learn that she did not have to be a passive victim of circumstances. She was given the homework assignment of calling the boy from her group, going out with him, and not allowing herself to be seduced. We then rehearsed several ways of saying no and she was given the information that he would not likely be insulted by her refusal. In the second case she was told that she should see the situation as one in which her boy friend had anxieties about sex which she could desensitize by engaging in sexual behavior that he felt comfortable with for longer periods of time and moving very gradually toward the goal of intercourse. It was predicted that after intercourse his rationalizations would disappear and he would be proud of having made it.

Jane came into the fourth session very happy and excited. She had called the boy in her group, gone out with him, had no trouble in not being seduced, and had decided she was not interested in him anyway. He had called her several times since, in spite of her refusing to go out with him again. She succeeded rather easily in seducing the boy she liked. His response was to tell her that he had been considering it seriously for the past couple of weeks and had decided that his ideas on the sub-

FIGURE 2—JANE

Diagnosis	Problem	Treatment	Incremental Step	Terminal Behavior	
Psychophysiological reaction	Tension (Headaches and stiff trapezius muscles)	Relaxation	More deeply relaxed. Relax in wider range of stimulus conditions	Relaxed in most circumstances. No headaches or stiff shoulders.	2.
	Can't assert self with others. Difficulty speaking in class. Difficulty expressing feelings. Sensitive to criticism and center of attention	Behavior rehearsal followed with homework assignments	Assertive in wider range of circumstances, more comfortable being assertive, more able to express feelings	Able to avoid being dominated. Able to speak in groups. Able to express positive feelings.	2.
	Infrequent orgasms	Instruction. Homework assignments	More knowledge of female sexual response. Reinforcement for applying knowledge	Usual orgasms	1.
	Worry	Relaxing vocal apparatus. Discussion	More able to control. See worry as unnecessary	Infrequent worry. Constructive planning	2.

1. Apparently cured
2. Much improved

ject were in error. The episode had led to a great improvement in their relationship and she now felt comfortable in being silly with him.

She had listened to the tape twice and realized that she was not succeeding in relaxing her eyes. Her headaches were unchanged. She was asked to bring in a list of her various daily activities arranged in hierarchical order according to how tense they made her. In addition, she was offered a reduction in fee if she spent a half hour relaxing on six of the seven days before her next appointment.

The following week she reported having relaxed six times as specified and also at a folk music concert on Saturday night. Things were going well with her younger boy friend and she had broken relations with a former boy friend whom she had been seeing once a week. We rehearsed class speeches on dress codes and women's rights.

A program of *in vivo* relaxation was set up which consisted of three parts. My notes do not reflect the first part in detail, but the general procedure is as follows. The inital skill in the program consists of being able to relax completely with the help of relaxation instructions from the therapist, either in person or by means of a recording. The depth of relaxation is tested carefully by observing the client visually and by manipulating the extremities.[1] The arms are checked by putting one hand around the wrist and grasping the elbow with the other. The arm is then shaken and rotated and will move with complete ease if the muscles of the arm and shoulder girdle are completely relaxed. Similarly the leg is supported with one hand at the knee and one just above the ankle. Again, if the foot flops, the knee swings easily and the hip joint rotates freely, we know that the pelvic girdle and leg are completely relaxed. The head is rotated to determine if the neck muscles are relaxed. In this procedure it is advisable to introduce rapid and unexpected changes of direction to make sure that the client is not moving in response to pressure, a response which is often learned in helping the dentist or barber.

Relaxation is practiced initially in conditions of reduced stimulation, on an easy chair or bed, and in a quiet place with little chance of interruption. These conditions are kept constant while the client first practices relaxing without verbal instructions, usually before going to sleep at night. This practice is begun only after several successful attempts to relax deeply with instructions and is usually continued for a week before

---

[1] Psychologists and social workers are often reluctant to touch a client, but even most clients with phobias about being touched accept the procedure easily.

moving on to the following program, although athletes and dancers can often move very rapidly because of their familiarity with muscular control.

The client is encouraged at all times to program his relaxation by kinesthetic cues rather than by using a verbal or visual program. This makes possible deep relaxation of the eyes and vocal apparatus and also makes it possible to use these structures for some other activity while relaxing. Kinesthetic cues also allow for more efficient increase in the speed of relaxing and facilitate development of an automatic and unconscious motor skill. Witness the dancer who is forever tied to the verbal program learned in dancing class and therefore cannot converse with his partner because his head is full of "one-two-three."

When the client can relax without verbal instructions with some efficiency, he is asked to time how long it takes to get from an average level of tension to a state of moderately deep relaxation. This is recorded and he then performs some everyday activity for a few minutes and then returns to relax again. The time is recorded and the process is continued until he can relax in a few seconds.

The rest of the first phase consists of moving from the conditions of low stimulation to more usual situations. First the task is to stay relaxed during the new situation, usually in the consulting room, and he is given homework of relaxing in the new situation. Whenever difficulty is encountered, the process is broken into smaller steps.

The client is relaxed deeply and asked to open his eyes while trying to stay relaxed. If difficulty is experienced it may be necessary to start by opening the eyes for a few seconds and gradually increasing the amount of time. Others cannot stay relaxed with their eyes shut and the process is reversed. The client is asked to sit up and stay relaxed. At this point differential relaxation is introduced since some tension is needed to hold oneself loosely erect. Then he stands, leaning over with head and arms hanging and gradually rises to an erect position, using only the minimum amount of tension necessary to maintain his posture. Then he flops around the office, imitating a drunk, and subsequently adds enough tension to walk without flopping, but with no unnecessary tension.

At this point he may practice some simple task, such as passing a pencil from one hand to another. Most people have trouble staying relaxed while working fast and the next step involves starting with some simple task, such as sanding or polishing something, or doing writing exercises such as making cursive ovals or push-pulls. This is done very slowly at first and the speed is gradually increased until the movement is at maximum speed. Most of my clients end up with a shiny automobile at this point.

At this stage the basic components of most activities have been practiced while staying relaxed. The second part of the program consists of working on staying relaxed during increasingly difficult, naturally occurring activities. Here the procedure followed is the one developed by Haugen, Dixon and Dickel (1958). Basically it consists of setting up one's entire life as an anxiety hierarchy and desensitizing the hierarchy by staying relaxed during the easiest activities or times and gradually adding more difficult ones.

The third phase consists of finding recurrent stimuli to nag the client to check his muscles. This control is particularly effective if the stimulus occurs as the client begins to tighten up. The list is endless, but things I have found most useful are reaching for a cigarette, looking at one's watch, recognizing a worried thought, biting one's fingernails, or any nervous habit, the telephone ringing, the dog barking, and commercials on radio or television. I often send a client out with a parking meter timer set to go off every fifteen minutes. When he begins to find himself relaxed when the alarm sounds, he increases the interval.

Let us return to the sessions with Jane. We discussed her hierarchy of activities and decided that she would attempt to stay relaxed while showering, reading and listening to the radio. We also rehearsed sending back an order of food in a restaurant.

In the next interview, Jane reported that she was relaxing much better and proved it by relaxing in the office in thirty seconds. Her boy friend had challenged her ideas about "The Feminine Mystique," and she had given in too easily. She had made progress in interrupting herself when she started to worry, and managed to relax her vocal apparatus. We reheased a couple of scenes from the previous list. For homework she was to ask questions she would like to ask in class while observing herself in the mirror in order to eliminate a phony smile which she displayed when self conscious. She was instructed in the physiology of sexual responses and agreed to tell her boy friend precisely what she found most stimulating and to continue foreplay into the high plateau phase (Masters and Johnson, 1966), in order to insure her orgasmic response. Staying relaxed during meals was added to the existing list of activities.

In the ninth interview she reported that she had not been relaxing as she should and her headaches were still not improved. She had seen herself making funny faces in the mirror but had finally been able to relax her mouth and yet be comfortable while talking aloud. She had some concerns about what kind of job to look for and this was discussed. She was quite concerned about meeting her boy friend's mother whose social status was considerably higher than that of her own parents. She was encouraged to consider her own status in the future as the holder of an advanced degree and as an attractive and articulate person. Talking to other people and walking were added to the list of times she was to stay relaxed and she was once again offered an incentive for remaining relaxed at least one-half hour a day and asking a question in one class. She was to keep a schedule of her activities and record how relaxed she had been. She reported difficulty in concentrating on her studies and was assigned a program described by Ljndberg Fox (1966). She was to break her work into pieces that should take approximately five minutes to complete. She was then to study until she began to feel restless and then do one more piece. The n-1 pieces would be done quickly and easily because she was within the limits of her concentration and the nth piece because she would follow it with some pleasant activity. She was to put the onset of study under the control of some appropriate stimulus by beginning immediately upon entering her apartment or putting her dishes in the sink in order to avoid procrastination.

In her tenth and last interview she reported that the study technique was working and she was now studying effectively for thirty minutes with a five minute break. Stimulus control for initiation of studying was working well. She was remembering to relax better and more frequently. Her headaches were somewhat improved and she was becoming quite effective in relaxing her neck. She had been comfortable with her boy friend's mother. During sexual intercourse, orgasms were usual and often multiple. She was speaking freely in class.

At this point it was decided to terminate therapy in spite of her continuing headaches and arrangements were made for Jane to send me a schedule indicating how much of the time she was relaxed for the following eight weeks. She reported increasing success and by the end of the time reported that she had headaches rarely and only when she forgot to relax. She was on vacation from school and was working as a receptionist, which required considerable social contact. A year later she sent me a check for her treatment. She reported that she had continued to improve and that the same boy friend she had seduced was paying all of her bills as a wedding present.

One day after writing up this case and a year and a half after terminating therapy, a letter from Jane arrived. In the last few months she had been increasingly tense and her headaches were again increasing in frequency. Therefore she requested referral to a behavior therapist near her new home.*

CASE #2. Bob, a 32-year-old unemployed truck driver was seen for thirty hours over a period of two years. He had eight children ranging from four to seventeen but had had a vasectomy four years before starting treatment. He was of stocky build and was warm, direct and confident in his social relations. Three years previously he had been well established, owning a tavern and two trucks in a town in northern California. He had found the temptations of a tavern-keeper's life too great and had gotten into a pattern of drinking too much, gambling and chasing women. He sold his tavern and trucks, moved to a town on the coast south of San Francisco and took a job as a long-line truck driver.

He traced his anxieties to his father's death at age twenty-nine of a coronary occlusion. At the time Bob, who was seven years old, became afraid of death. When Bob was nine years old, while on a picnic he was playing with the other children and fell on his head. He heard his neck pop and thought that he had broken his neck and was dying. He experienced an extreme panic and was taken to the doctor who reassured him that he was only suffering from a sprain. Since that time he had been afraid of dying and saw anxiety attacks as threatening imminent death. He had been somewhat afraid of being trapped away from help but his anxiety attacks had been infrequent until one day about a year before treatment, when he had been crawling up a hill in his semi-trailer truck and it occurred to him that he could have an attack and die before he could get to town to seek medical attention. He took one more trip in his truck in a constant state of severe anxiety.

He had then retreated to his house, spent the last of his savings and had gone on welfare. He could venture out on short trips with his wife, a practical nurse, but was severely agoraphobic and claustrophobic. It was only because of his great faith in the psychiatrist who referred him that he was able to make the fifty-mile trip over the mountains to see

---

* *Editor's note:* In my experience, relapses of this kind usually respond well to a second course of behavior therapy. During "booster therapy," hitherto unsuspected factors responsible for the deviant behavior emerge and lend themselves to direct treatment.

me. He worried constantly about how to get to the nearest doctor and about his car breaking down. He was afraid of any physical exertion leading to rapid breathing which he saw as a symptom of a heart attack. He was afraid of having anyone know about his neurosis but was otherwise confident socially.

His anxieties were often greater in anticipation than in actuality. If he had only one car in running condition (he liked to have two or three), he would change one spark plug at a time. However he sometimes changed a tire on the highway with less anxiety than he experienced in contemplating the possibility of such an event. He usually dreaded his trip over the mountains to see me early in treatment but often experienced little anxiety on the road.

At the end of the first interview the client was given a brief talk about the nature of behavior therapy and was encouraged to think of his problems as solvable in a reasonable amount of time. At the second interview Bob reported that he had felt elated at the prospect of solving his problems and had enjoyed the ride home and felt better all week. A tentative plan of treatment was set forth which included most of the features of the final plan described in Figure 3. Relaxation training was begun and anxieties about death were explored in preparation for the construction of a hierarchy. Interestingly, Bob was not afraid of accidents or injuries in the least. He was bothered by doctors, hospitals, funerals, sickness, sirens, obituaries and high blood pressure.

Because of vacations, inclement weather, occasional anxiety too severe to make the trip and crises of various kinds with the eight children, the first thirteen hours spanned a period of six months. Bob learned to relax well and began to use it erratically *in vivo*. Hierarchies of his two major anxiety areas were constructed and desensitization commenced. When feasible Bob was to follow desensitization of an item by going through it *in vivo* before the following session. He did so about half the time. At the sixth session he reported that he was eating with the family for the first time in five years, much to their delight. He was relaxing each night and sleeping better. By the eighth hour he was able to remove three spark plugs at a time from his car and take a son to the hospital without anxiety.

At one point Bob was worried about his mother being killed while driving back to Oregon after a visit. I showed him how to estimate the probability roughly. We guessed one fatal accident in a thousand years of driving, one chance in three that it would be his mother who was

FIGURE 3

Diagnosis	Problem	Treatment	Incremental Step	Terminal Behavior	
Agoraphobia	Fear of being trapped away from help	Desensitization in vivo program	Increasing distance from home or car with little or no anxiety	Able to travel freely or repair car without anxiety.	2.
	Fear of death (shortness of breath, doctors, hospitals, funerals, illness, sirens, obituaries)	Desensitization	Increasing stimulus intensity with no anxiety.	Able to tolerate stimuli listed under 1 without anxiety.	1.
		Hyperventilation training	Increasing realization that dizziness does not portend death, ability to control dizziness.	Able to catch himself starting to hyperventilate. Anxiety therefore less regenerative.	1.
	General anxiety	Relaxation in vivo	Stay relaxed in increasingly difficult situations	Relaxed most of the time.	2.
		Stop smoking	Decreasing anxiety without smoking	Stopped	
		Exercise program	Increasing ability to tolerate vigorous exercise	Perception of decreased probability of coronary.	1.
		Weight reduction diet	Decreasing weight	Slim and keep weight off	
	Mediocre relationship with wife, wife anorgasmic, client chasing women. Premature ejaculation	In vivo desensitization of wife's sexual anxieties. Facilitation of communication, Seman's method.[1]	Wife's increasing sexual arousal without anxiety. Increasing awareness of wife's needs, increasing freedom of communication. Increased time to ejaculation	Wife orgasmic, client faithful, greatly improved relationship, client reasonable time to ejaculate.	1.
	Fear of having an anxiety attack	Anxiety relief conditioning[2]	Increased anxiety relief conditioned to word calm	Able to reduce anxiety by saying "calm."	2.
		Pocket shocker	Less likely to obsess about possibility of an attack	Less worried	

[1] Semans, 1960
[2] Wolpe and Lazarus, 1966

1. Apparently cured
2. Much improved

killed, one chance in 365 that an accident this year would fall on a particular day. 1,000 $\times$ 365 $\times$ 3 is one chance in more than 1,000,000. He was thereafter able to assess probabilities of feared events more accurately and found it comforting.

After a month's hiatus between the eighth and ninth hours, Bob reported that he had not been going much of any place, but that he was relaxing well at home. He had seen a surfer wiped out and was right there with the rest of the nosy people. He had ridden in a friend's car to the next city down the coast, which was an accomplishment since it was a situation in which he was not in control. In the tenth session he was given a pocket shocker with instructions to shock himself when he started to obsess about getting stranded. The correlation of smoking, obesity and lack of exercise with coronary disease was discussed and Bob agreed to start a diet which ultimately took him from 214 pounds down to 185.

The following week he reported that he had only had to use the shocker twice, but had found it a great comfort. He keeps the battery fresh and carries it in his glove compartment to this day, although he never uses it now. He forgot it while riding down the coast to the next city with a friend, but comforted himself with the thought that he could pretend to hear a miss in his friend's car, get under the hood, ostensibly to check the spark plugs, and shock himself with the plug wires. In this hour (number 11) the death hierarchy was completed and he pictured walking 490 yards away from his car down the beach (item 5.5 on the Loss of Mobility hierarchy, a parametric item, Marquis, Morgan and Piaget, 1971).

In the twelfth session Bob reported that he had suffered three flat tires and run out of gas, with considerable anxiety (up to 60 suds) but no panic. He was feeling better about riding in other people's cars and had been as far as forty miles. At this point an *in vivo* relaxation program beyond relaxing in his bed or easy chair was begun. He was given homework of relaxing with eyes open, relaxing in the shower, and walking down the beach.

In the thirteenth hour he reported walking a block and a half from his car and feeling comfortable in heavy traffic. He reported that things were not going well sexually and agreed to have his wife join us during the next session to discuss it.

This was not done because shortly after the thirteenth hour Bob slipped on his wet front porch and fell through the window, cutting his arm to the bone. He remained calm through emergency surgery but panicked when settled in his room at the hospital. He got his wife to bring him his clothes and some money and had her park his car outside the window where he could see it, giving him the keys. Then he was able to relax somewhat for his three weeks stay in the hospital.

LOSS OF MOBILITY

1. You and your wife have won a trip to Tahiti and you are on deck looking off the fantail while the coast disappears.
2. You are one-half way up El Capitan pounding in a peton and rigging a rope to it.
3. On a flight to Hawaii the pilot says, "Ladies and Gentlemen, we have now reached the point of no return."
3.5 Landing at airport, Honolulu.
4. You are pulling out of Salinas on a train non-stop to Los Angeles.
5. You are on a bus going up Highway 1 to San Francisco.
5.5 Gradually walk one mile from car.
6. You are driving a Porsche across the Bay Bridge.
7. Take a bus from your house down to the beach.
8. Drive down by the beach, pick up density of traffic by degrees.
9. You are riding downtown with Bill for coffee.
10. Drive from summit to here.
11. You are in the car, ready to go to the store and the car doesn't start.
12. Your wife takes the car down to the store.
13. You come out to find a flat on your car in the driveway. Change it.
14. You're putting in a new spark plug.

Pleasant scene: Relax in a boat fishing on the reservoir.

FEAR OF DEATH

1. You are seven years old looking at father lying in the coffin.
2. You are nine years old, at a picnic, and fall on your head. Your neck pops and feels kind of stretched and you wonder whether it is broken.
2.5 The doctor says your blood pressure is dangerously high and that you need to lose weight.
3. You are at Bill Clausens' funeral, A) thinking about how they were killed, B) looking into the coffin.

4. You visit your wife at Star Lodge and she says, "just a minute, honey, this woman just died and I have to wait until the coroner comes."

5. You are driving down the street and come upon an accident. A woman has broken her arm, a compound fracture, and you put on a tourniquet.

6. The doctor says your wife has a strep throat and a temperature of 104°.

7. You're having a beer with Stan and he's explaining how they embalm a body.

8. You are at the hospital to visit someone with a broken leg and look in and see a man, pale, tube down his nose, tube in his arm, bottles, etc.

9. You hear on the radio that Lloyd Gandy has been shot.

10. The doctor says, "Bill, this is a little skin cancer. I'm going to send you to a dermatologist—99 times out of 100 no more trouble."

11. You are at home reading funnies and a siren sounds outside.

12. You read an obit in the paper that Bill Finley of Finley's store died at 45 of an apparent heart attack.

13. You read in the paper that Grandma Moses died at 102.

A week after being discharged from the hospital, Bob reported that he had gone four hundred yards from his car in a wrecking yard, panicked for a moment, and then relaxed. Otherwise he was close to normal and much more relaxed around town. His wife joined us and I outlined a sexual program of doing only what she could do comfortably with her directing him at every step. Foreplay was to continue until she felt that she was just short of having an orgasm before starting intercourse.

The following week they reported having intercourse three times during which she experienced prolonged orgasms. Bob reported doing better at relaxing in the car and increased his mobility. He was given twenty-five trials of anxiety relief conditioning (Wolpe and Lazarus, 1966) and then deeply relaxed and instructed to say the talisman word, "calm control," each time he exhaled for ten minutes, a technique for which Gordon Paul deserves credit.

The following (eighteenth) session, Bob reported feeling great. The "calm control" was working well, he had filed for bankruptcy, and was off to a good start with an automotive specialty business. In the nineteenth session we set up an exercise program which he followed for a while and then dropped, but his work required considerable exercise and kept him in fairly good condition. We bypassed item 5.5 on the loss of mobility hierarchy and proceeded without completing it. The last I heard Bob had still not made it a mile from his car. On the sixteenth session things were still slowly improving.

Bob did not come in for two months. At that time we finished the Loss of Mobility hierarchy and pictured taking a trip to Oregon where Bob's aunt was dying of cancer. The following week he returned on the eve of his trip to Oregon, the aunt having died. He was anxious at the prospect and his wife and I reassured him and we discussed ways of handling his anxiety.

In the next session (twenty-four) we discussed his trip to Oregon. He had been scared when he left—a little shaky, concerned and worried—but relaxed as the trip progressed and did not panic once. He took one town at a time by reassuring himself that there was a doctor in each one. He handled three flat tires with minimal anxiety. At the funeral he was sad but not anxious. He drank only one beer on the trip and enjoyed the drive and the scenery. He had since gone six blocks from his car with slight discomfort.

In the twenty-ninth session Bob reported that he had been in a very good mood. "Nothing bothers me." His wife sat in and they said that their sexual problem had returned. More careful questioning revealed that he suffered from premature ejaculation. They were instructed in the Semans method (see Masters and Johnson, 1970, although it had not been published at the time). In addition they were to practice scratching each others backs. He was to reward her for any expression of bodily sensations in order to facilitate feedback. He was to concentrate on his sensations when thoughts of inadequacy arose. If either masturbated they were to picture having intercourse with each other (both had been picturing other people). Then they were to re-introduce the program of *in vivo* desensitization (see Wolpe and Lazarus, 1966).

Four months later I visited them at home. Bob's business was thriving and he was working very hard. He and his wife had completely solved their sexual problem and were communicating freely with each other and were enjoying each other as never before. The weather had been bad and he had been too busy to go anywhere. Although his fear of death was completely gone, his fear of being stranded away from help had returned—not so much within fifty miles of home, but at the prospect of a trip. He had taken on the responsibility of a business trip down the coast and was quite upset at the prospect.

Bob came over two months later. His trip had gone badly and he was almost back where we started as far as his fear of loss of mobility was concerned. We started desensitization over at the beginning of the hierarchy and he was once more encouraged to exercise and to relax. He also reported that he had quit smoking after nineteen years. He had been smoking three packs a day. He has not smoked since.

He returned for two more sessions the following month. He had been exercising and his wind was better. He was feeling more comfortable with not smoking and by the second interview was able to drink without a strong desire to smoke.

In the second interview he said that he was still afraid of going crazy and I started out to contrast his classically neurotic problems with some psychotic symptoms in order to reassure him. In the process I mentioned the delusion that people were going to poison him and he had a panic attack because when he was a boy his mother had been so mean and irritable that he had developed a fear that she would put poison in his food. This was my first opportunity to see one of his anxiety attacks and I expressed surprise at how mild his anxiety seemed to me. I told him that I knew a famous behavior therapist who went around more anxious than that all the time. I had him tip the recliner back and in fifteen minutes he was deeply relaxed and cheerful again.

I saw him again a month later and we progressed to item 5 on the loss of mobility hierarchy. His business was prospering and he was once more able to move about comfortably within fifty miles of home as long as he didn't get too far from his car. Several months later he did some work on my car and at that time his gains had persisted. He was enjoying life and his wife reported that he was a pleasure to live with. He still was reluctant to travel to San Francisco.

CASE #3. Rutherford. This case is chosen to illustrate what can happen to an intellectualizer who learns to relax and stop obsessing. Many people have the conviction that if they can only find the right philosophy of life it will hold the key to all of their problems. It is certainly possible for people to be inspired by a philosophy to fulfilling patterns of behavior or led by a philosophy into self defeating patterns, especially if the philosophy is taught by a powerful model. Nevertheless, most human problems result from the individual having learned to feel anxious in harmless circumstances or from not having learned the necessary skills to deal with the situations in which he finds himself.

Skills Rutherford had in ample supply. He was a twenty-five-year-old space scientist who had risen from a deprived childhood to excel in almost everything. He was keenly intelligent, handsome, and very well coordinated. Having fought his way up from the bottom, at first by his fists and later by his intelligence, he was fiercely competitive and preferred being hated to being ignored. He was afraid of being second in anything and of being laughed at, but his response to either threat was aggressive.

He came to me in a state of frenzied anxiety occasioned by the impending breakup of a very mediocre marriage. He was seriously contemplating suicide. Probably the greatest threat occasioned by the breakup of his marriage was that it meant losing to a professor of his wife's with whom she was probably having an affair eight hundred miles away. He had read countless books in the areas of philosophy and psychology and was glib but frantic in his pursuit of new ways of construing his life. In spite of his unusually good intellectual grasp of the content of these theories all it amounted to was constant worry.

The first hour was taken up by giving an account of his life and his present predicament which was surprisingly lucid considering his extremely high level of anxiety. He was extremely cynical and saw everything as being absurd. During the second hour he volunteered the information that he had noticed that he had been "squeezing his toes up." I took this as the occasion to ask him to consider a new view of himself and a possible road to salvation.

I suggested to him that he was not likely to find philosophical solutions to his problems since the source of his discomfort was physiological, i.e., the fact that he kept his muscles tight all the time. "Worry is an activity that consists of saying anxious things to yourself and tightening up your muscles." Although he saw this activity as an attempt to solve his problems, in fact it *was* his problem. Many people go through life worrying about improbable eventualities and are reinforced by the belief that the worry has prevented their occurrences. They feel that they would be unable to survive if they stopped worrying.

This is simply not true. Man alone among the species on the earth is capable of worry. The elephant lives for a hundred and twenty years, rears his young through a long helpless period in a land full of lions, and provides himself daily with huge quantities of food and water—all without worrying.

Perhaps some external stimulus starts the process. Either it is conditioned to elicit tension or reminds the person of something that does. Being in a state of tension the person reaches into his hippocampus for a tape that is appropriate to that level of tension. Soon an idea comes that arouses a higher level of tension and the process escalates.

As Jacobson (1938) long ago pointed out, there is a simple way to break this vicious circle. The tape of worried thoughts is played by the vocal apparatus. If these muscles are relaxed, the tape stops. So all that needs to be done is to watch for the first sign of a worry. The process is usually quite distinct from constructive planning or creative thought, and is usually inimical to such thinking, so nothing is lost by interrupting the worry without even finishing the phrase. The only value of worry is to indicate that you have some tight muscles somewhere. Then you relax your vocal apparatus and proceed to check the rest of your muscles and relax any you find to be tense.

Rutherford eagerly took up the idea. Here was a new philosophy and a new obsession. He listened to the relaxation tape I gave him two and a half times before his next session four days later and found that "When everything is relaxed, everything is OK." He had been working on staying relaxed on his own initiative. The next few weeks were very stormy with the marriage off-again-on-again, the wife coming and going, threatening suicide, Rutherford being unable to reach her by phone for days at a time. At such times he was unable to relax but between crises he made it his full time occupation to relax and between discussing crises we worked in the hour on perfecting his skills at relaxing.

At the eighth hour, which followed the first by three weeks, Rutherford reported that he was reconciled to the fact that his marriage was through. At the end of the hour we decided that during the following meeting we would set up hierarchies for desensitization. The next day he was in an automobile accident and suffered a concussion and a broken arm.

He returned a month later with his arm in a cast saying that he had lost the ability to relax and was being driven wild by the itching. He had trouble relaxing in the hour and found that he was trying to support his broken arm and was picturing the broken ends of the bone which he had seen in the X-ray. We discussed the fact that the cast and sling would support the arm without effort on his part and worked on differentiating between tension and the strain and fatigue in the arm. I had him picture being injected with novocaine by the dentist and when he could make his jaw numb quickly and easily, we transferred it to the arm with considerable relief in the itching.

The next week he had mastered relaxing again. Things were so much better that he decided he could handle his remaining anxieties just by relaxing and we terminated without ever getting around to desensitization. His parting statement was to the effect that as his efficiency at relaxing goes up his need for omnipotence goes down. He now sees nothing to panic about. If someone says something threatening he considers his motives and finds that it becomes the other person's problem and not his.

I invited Rutherford to my house for a drink a month or two later and he had almost completely eliminated his remaining hangups. His gains persisted when I stopped by his apartment a few months later.

Two years after treatment he came to my office once more. He had been happy and relaxed in the meantime. He had married a much more satisfactory wife and was doing outstanding work in a very difficult doctoral program at Stanford University. He was planning to take a preliminary exam ahead of schedule just for practice. He became afraid of failing the exam even though he could do so without prejudice.

I told him that I had failed my major prelim once and survived* and reminded him of some of the things we had discussed. He relaxed well in the office and went out resolved to work on staying relaxed. He called in a couple of days to say that he had been successful in staying relaxed and was no longer worried about the exam.

CASE #4. Carl was a twenty-two-year-old man whose phobias were extremely difficult to treat. The main reason for this was that the keystone of his anxiety response was severe stomach tension of rapid onset. Each time this response occurred it took five or six minutes for his stomach to relax, which made desensitization very slow. I have generally had poor luck with such persons and Carl was no exception. He was seen for 144 hours before a successful conclusion. Discussion will be limited to one interesting sequence in this very complex case.

By the 106th interview, Carl had become quite proficient at relaxing *in vivo*. His most severe phobia had to do with his parents leaving town. During the few periods when they were not planning a trip Carl was by now able to spend much of the time relaxed. However, he noted two things which were not related to any of his anxieties. He would be

---

* There were some psychoanalytic people on the committee.

driving to work, checking his muscles faithfully and feeling fine when suddenly for no reason he would be up to 50 suds. Also, he had noticed that he would become extremely tense when doing bench work. Coincidentally I had noticed that his eyes were often the first part of his body to become tense and the last to relax. I determined to work intensively on teaching him to relax his eyes.

To this end I asked him to look hard to the left as the first step in studying the eye muscles. He rose up in the chair as though he had been stuck with a pin and reported that his stomach had tightened up. I asked him to fixate upon the eraser of a pencil and moved it back and forth before his eyes while he reported anxiety responses. By this means it was determined that he began to tense if he moved his eyes beyond approximately 30 degrees from the straight ahead position in any direction. This included anxiety when the pencil was moved closer to his eyes than would permit remaining within the 60 degree cones.

He was instructed to try turning his head instead of his eyes when he had to look in the rear view mirror when driving and to drop his head instead of his eyes when working with something below his line of vision on the bench.

He returned the next session to say that the tactic had been successful. He no longer suddenly found himself tense for no apparent reason when driving and was able to stay relaxed while doing bench work. He was asked to relax deeply and then to fixate the pencil once more. I moved it back and forth, up and down and closer and closer to his eyes, going slowly enough not to arouse tension. Gradually the response-produced stimuli were desensitized and in twenty minutes he was able to look as far as his anatomy permitted, including the closest convergence, without anxiety. I have since encountered two other similar cases and many others in which response-produced stimuli from tension in certain muscles caused tension in other muscles.

I believe in a behavioral approach to life as an effective and comprehensive philosophy. I try to organize my life and see the behavior of my fellow human beings in behavioral terms and certainly encourage my clients to do the same. On a more philosophical level I believe in working to better the lot of mankind and feel that it contributes to the mental health of my clients if I can convince them to join me in the endeavor. I believe that a man should be himself and do what he feels like and say what he thinks as long as it doesn't harm anyone. Then you know who you are and who your friends are. They like you as you are instead of for some custom-made act you put on for their benefit. Again I encourage my clients to try this philosophy.

There is nothing unscientific about this and there are indeed good behavior principles which predict that a more uninhibited and genuine person will be more free of anxiety. Honesty can be the best principle as well as the best policy.

REFERENCES

ANANT, S. S., (Ed.) *Readings in Behavior Therapies.* New York: MSS Educational Publishing Co., 1969.

BUEHLER, R. E., PATTERSON, G. R., & FURNESS, J. M. The reinforcement of behavior. In Institutional Settings *Beh. Res. and Therapy,* 1966, 4, 157-167.

DOLLARD, J., & MILLER, N. F. *Personality and psychotherapy.* New York: McGraw Hill, 1950.

FOX, L. Effecting the use of efficient study habits. In Ulrich, R., Stachnik, T., and Maybry, J. (Eds.) *Control of Human Behavior.* Glenview, Illinois: Scott, Foresman and Co., 1966. Pp. 85-90.

FREUD, S. *A General Introduction to Psychoanalysis.* Garden City, N. Y.: Garden City Publishing Co., 1917.

HAUGEN, G. B., DIXON, H. H., & DICKEL, H. A. *A therapy for anxiety tension reactions.* New York: Macmillan, 1958.

JACOBSON, E. *Progressive Relaxation.* Chicago: U. of Chicago Press, 1938.

JAMES, WILLIAM. *Principles of psychology.* New York: Henry Holt, 1890.

KELLY, G. A. *The psychology of personal constructs.* New York: Norton, 1955.

LAZARUS, A. A. Broad-spectrum behavior therapy and the treatment of agoraphobia. *Behavior Research and Therapy,* 1966, 4, 95-97. A.

LAZARUS, A. A. Behavior rehearsal vs. non-directive therapy vs. advice in effecting behavior change. *Behavior Research and Therapy,* 1966, 4:3, 209-212.

MARQUIS, J. N. Orgasmic reconditioning: changing sexual object choice through controlling masturbation fantasies. *Journal of Behavior Therapy and Experimental Psychiatry,* 1970, Vol. 1. Pp. 277-285.

MARQUIS, J. N., MORGAN, W. G., & PIAGET, G. W. *A guidebook for systematic desensitization.* Palo Alto: Veteran's workshop, Veterans Administration, 1971 (2nd Edition).

MASTERS, W. H., & JOHNSON, V. E. *Human sexual response.* Boston: Little, Brown, 1966.

MASTERS, W. H., & JOHNSON, V. E. *Human sexual inadequacy.* Boston: Little, Brown, 1970.

MOWRER, O. H. In Jon, M. R. (Ed.) *Nebraska symposium on motivation.* Lincoln: University of Nebraska Press, 1950.

PATTERSON, G. R., & REID, J. Reciprocity and coercion: two facets of social systems. Paper prepared for the Ninth Annual Institute for Research in Clinical Psychology, sponsored by the University of Kansas, Dept. of Psychology, *Behavior modification for clinical psychologists.* Lawrence, Kansas, April, 1967.

ROGERS, C. R. *Client centered therapy.* Boston: Houghton Mifflin, 1951.

SALTER, A. *Conditioned reflex therapy.* New York: Creative Age Press, 1949.

SEMANS, J. H. Premature ejaculation: a new approach. *Southern Medical Journal,* 1956, 4a, 353-357.

STAMPFL, T. G.. & LEVIS, D. J. Essentials of implosive therapy: a learning-theory-based psychodynamic behavior therapy. *Journal of Abnormal Psychology,* 1967, 72, 6, Pp. 496-502.

WATSON, J. B. *Behaviorism.* New York: Peoples Institute, 1924.

WOLPE, J., & LAZARUS, A. A. *Behavior therapy techniques.* Oxford: Pergamon Press, 1966.

4

Practical Behavioral Diagnosis

EDWARD DENGROVE, M.D.

ALL BEHAVIORAL THERAPIES must be preceded by a proper behavioral diagnosis. The application of behavioral principles is so precise that without a proper delineation of the "target" symptoms one can go astray. It is worth emphasizing that target behaviors involve the identification of "emotional habits" and faulty cognitions. "Symptoms" merely denote the patient's awareness of the reactions that go on within him.

I recently treated a young, married woman who worked as a waitress. Her presenting complaints were the usual phobic ones: fear of shopping, fear in church, fear of crowds, and other interpersonal tensions. In addition, she presented three rather unusual features: difficulty with vision in that things seemed small (micropsia), a tendency for her voice to sound far off, and a feeling that she was fading away, all indicative of a need to avoid facing her problems directly. Asked what she could not face, she described her fears again. I proceeded with systematic desensitization. At

73

first she made excellent progress and returned to her job. Then she struck a plateau and I discovered that she was not fully relaxed, though she had so indicated. Simultaneously she was having problems with her mother, daughter, and husband. It took a longer period to relax her sufficiently for further progress to ensue. She then left her job because she did not want to get involved in her boss's personal problems.

She had resolved her external problems with her husband, daughter and mother, but in other areas of her life progress was lacking and she complained bitterly of not feeling well. By this time she had lost the specific fears which had brought her into treatment initially and now addressed herself to the fact that she could not find another job and feared she could not keep it if she had one. I faced her with her fear of work and she replied that people at work—and at no other place—made her nervous. I was not happy with this answer, so I injected Methedrine intravenously to lighten her mood and increase her ability to talk. She then confessed that it was not concern for the people at her job that made her nervous but the fact that if she went to work her family would suffer. If she worked the morning shift, her daughter would have no way of getting to school two miles away; her mother, whom she visited daily, would not have her comfort and help in shopping. If she went on the evening shift, her daughter would not have a hot meal, nor would her husband. She felt that she had to do the right, good, and expected thing. On the other hand she complained that she was not doing what she wanted to do: go to work, and have time to go out with her girl friend. She feared her husband would beat her as her first husband had done. Though they were not getting along well, this was not true. The therapeutic focus was now far removed from her original fears. A different approach involving marital counselling and assertive techniques seemed strongly indicated.

If this conflict had been disclosed earlier in treatment, much time would have been saved and treatment results would have been more certain. How can a therapist determine these events sooner? A simple listing of fears is insufficient for diagnostic purposes. As Wolpe (personal communication) remarked, "Without correct identification of the relevant stimulus elements, one may expend a great deal of time and effort without result." One can form conclusions about important hierarchical items through skillful interrogation, the use of fear surveys or other questionnaires, autobiographical notes, the letter association technique (Dengrove 1962), and various psychophysiological measurements. Unfortunately patience and luck still play an important role. More of this later.

Stevenson and Hain (1967) decry the failure to identify with sufficient precision the exact stimuli of the patient's neurotic responses, declaring that the therapist can waste valuable time by tackling the wrong elements in the patient's neurotic reactions. They illustrate their point by analyzing the barber shop phobia, and insisting that one does not merely settle for the general environment in which it occurs, e.g. the barber shop as a whole. There may be a fear of scrutiny by others, a rebelliousness against social customs, impatience with delays, fear of confinement, fear of mutilation, anxiety-arousing experiences with chairs resembling barber chairs, sexual arousal, issues of seniority, and other explanations for the phobia; a multiplicity of stimuli which touch off the phobic response.

A stutterer I had been treating stuttered more while dictating to his stenographers. He changed stenographers without effect, and desensitization to these girls produced no reduction in his affliction. Further diagnostic probing indicated that he was not bothered by individual stenographers but by the fact that what he was dictating was being made a matter of public record and he would be held accountable for it. A change to assertive techniques helped overcome this complication. Similarly an agoraphobic who feared walking away from her home was really afraid of encountering dogs, and desensitization to these animals enabled her to walk freely again.

According to Meyer and Crisp (1966) the presence of historically earlier sources of anxiety may complicate recovery. Thus, the presenting symptom may be the result of higher order conditioning or secondary generalization, yet the basic source of the symptoms may still be present, acting upon the individual and influencing the course of the presenting complaints. Consequently, it too must be ferreted out and dealt with in addition to the secondary complaints. I have not found this to be much of an obstacle, particularly if I utilize the letter association technique. (Details of this technique are outlined in the section dealing with diagnostic procedures.)

Davis (1958) points out that memory images are perceptions, just as those caused by current people or objects, and we respond to the stimuli in memories just as we do to those in other perceptions. The recall of a scene once painful can then evoke anxiety *not* as an old de-repressed emotion, but in response to the stimulus for anxiety occurring in the *immediate* perception. Thus *memory* of the cruel mother may stimulate *present* anxiety rather than release old anxiety.

Clarke (1968) concluded that the permanence of early learning will depend not only upon the age of the child and the duration and intensity of the experience, but more particularly upon its later reinforcement. Early learning will fade if not reinforced. Similarly, Montenegro (1968) suggests that rather than concern ourselves with the past history, we should become more involved in the present conditions that are maintaining and reinforcing the patient's symptomatology. Behavior therapy is directed primarily to removing or counteracting the circumstances that are perpetuating the given behavior problem. Yet it is important to stress the fact that when treating higher order learning and bypassing the original learning situation, relapse is likely to be the net result.

Lazarus (1966) emphasizes the part played by others in the continuance of a symptom. In one instance he had to call in the patient's husband and mother and inform them how they were reinforcing the patient's dependency by displaying concern and expressing reassurance whenever she complained of minor somatic discomforts. They were requested not to pay attention to these negative statements, but to reward by attention, encouragement and approval all positive self-references and independent responses. He states that it is presumably impossible to become an agoraphobic without the aid of others who will submit to the inevitable demands imposed upon them by the sufferer, who play a vital role in sustaining and maintaining the agoraphobic behavior and making lasting therapeutic changes unlikely without treating them concurrently.

One needs to desensitize not only to the act, but to anticipation of the act, as a separate hierarchy. Sometimes the anticipation takes on an obsessive quality, at which time we must revert to thought blocking procedures. Furthermore, it is not merely the anticipation of the act per se which must concern us, but also the general anticipation of the future. As one patient told me, "I can do the little things, like drive around the block, then I think ahead to what will be expected of me, and I fall apart and don't even want to do the little things." We must—in some way—convince the patient to look at the scene, one portion at a time. Particularization prevents or reduces feelings of overwhelming anticipatory anxiety.

Wolpe (1964) writes of pervasive aspects of anxiety which may be difficult to ferret out, such as space, time, one's own body, light verticality, light-shade contrasts. I recall treating a woman who developed a phobic state after a car had rammed into her home in the dark. She became sensitized to the dark and to outside car noises and was not aware of these specific irritants, complaining only of general nervousness with tension headaches.

Lang (1964) writes of the pressure of partially digested food against the wall of the intestine, or a phase of peristalsis itself as interoceptive conditioned stimuli for anxiety, such as might follow family arguments during or following a meal. Gantt (1964) notes that the Russians have successfully conducted conditioning experiments employing many subtle internal cues such as urinary secretions, thyroid endocrine secretions, metabolic changes, etc. He adds that it may be very difficult to extinguish these, and certainly that the individual himself would be unconscious of what is producing the changes in his visceral system.

The emphasis thus far is upon the need to distill basic and primary problem areas in endeavoring to diagnose the covert and overt factors responsible for the patient's presenting complaints.

Lazarus and Serber (1968) point out that in making a behavioral diagnosis one should carefully separate deficits from basic anxiety responses. For instance, it is important to keep in mind that a male patient's inability to approach eligible females may not be a function of anxiety toward women but rather a reflection of inadequate learning, simple naïvete, and poor verbal skills; that phobic complaints may be secondary to a psychotic process requiring antipsychotic medication; that with some phobic reactions, depression may be the predominant illness and need anti-depressive medication, environmental manipulation and assertive training; that other phobic cases may warrant re-education and direct instruction, modeling and practice, plus rational discussions of ethics and morality.

Lazarus (in Abramovitz 1970) further points out that one of the chief limitations of behavior therapy is the application of specific techniques which ignore the patient's values, attitudes and beliefs and do not define the particular goals of the patient and orient therapy toward their attainment. Individual therapy, he (Lazarus, 1970) states, obviously imposes limitations upon the person-to-person exploration of these specific behaviors, and adds, "Many facets of a problem which may elude the scrutiny of even the most perspicacious therapist often become clearly delineated during or after an intensive group discussion." All in all, the clinician should strive to obtain information about his patients from many sources—observation, measurement, inquiry, outside opinion and above all, a detailed exploration of stimulus antecedents and behavioral consequences.

PROCEDURES FOR DIAGNOSTIC EXPLORATION

A systematic approach to history taking (Table A) leads to a practical

TABLE A

HISTORY-TAKING

How do you feel? What are your complaints?
Headaches—Any other aches or pains?
    Ascertain: Where do you feel the pain? Does it stay there or go to any other place? What is it like: aching, pressing, throbbing, etc.? How often do you get it? How long does it last? What brings it on? What relieves it? Do you suffer nausea or vomiting with it, visual difficulty, dizziness? Other accompaniments?
Nervousness: Are you tense, restless, irritable or impatient, jittery or jumpy, tire readily, shaky?
Appetite and weight loss.
Sleep difficulty: Trouble falling asleep, interrupted sleep, restless sleep, early waking? Do you have nightmares or bad dreams of any kind?
Memory—concentration.
Sweating—hot flushes—faint feelings or fainting spells—dizziness—weakness—noises in the ears.
Trouble with stomach: indigestion, nausea or vomiting, diarrhea or constipation, pains in abdomen, heartburn.
Trouble with heart: palpitations, double beats or skipped beats, pains in chest.
Trouble with lungs: tightness in chest, shortness of breath, coughing, choking feelings, things sticking in throat, hard to swallow.
Trouble with bladder: difficulty holding or passing water, go too often during day or night.
Any fears: delineate and detail, circumstances, onset, etc.
Depression, crying spells, suicidal thoughts.
Trouble with sexual life: detail.
Trouble with social life: detail.
Smoking habits—drinking habits—drug habits—taking medications at all.
Worries of any kind: health—future—ability to work—finances.

PAST and PERSONAL HISTORY: Any serious illnesses, operations or injuries in past: details. Any nervousness: detail, treatments previously.
    Married or single. Children. How get along with spouse. Details of marriage relationship.
Family history: Mother and father, siblings. Details. How get along, etc.
Work history.
Any police record, juvenile or adult.
Military service: details, including type of discharge and hospitalizations.
Education.
Hobbies: other interests.

DRAW-A-PERSON PRODUCTION

THREE WISHES

WHAT KIND OF PERSON ARE YOU (Self-evaluation)

REQUEST: AUTOBIOGRAPHY
    LIST OF FEARS. LIST OF ANGERS.
    LIST OF WHAT HE/SHE WOULD LIKE TO SEE DIFFERENT
    ABOUT SELF

OPTIONAL: FEAR SURVEY (Wolpe and Lang)
    REINFORCEMENT SURVEY (Cautela and Kastenbaum)
    Specific questionnaires: re alcoholic habits, etc.
    Other psychological tests: Maudsley Personality Inventory
                        MMPI
                        Others.

LETTER ASSOCIATION technique for pinpointing etiology.

diagnostic evaluation within the first half-hour of the first session; the latter half of the initial interview can then be devoted toward initiating treatment. I like to see the patient leave, after the first visit, feeling considerably better and more hopeful for the future.

The questions asked in Table A cover fairly completely the complaints of most patients. Simultaneously the patient's mode of dress, speech and comportment are observed: whether anxious or depressed, restless or apathetic, intelligent, responsive, and the like. First impressions, though fleeting, are valuable. One can tell much of a patient's inner feelings by the facial expression, particularly about the eyes. Telling the patient one's impressions in a conversational and interested voice often puts him at ease.

The Draw-A-Person production is a favorite addition of mine because of the wealth of information it gives about the patient in a very short time. I offer the patient a pad and pencil and ask him to draw a picture of a person from head to toe, not just a head, and not a stick figure. Interpretation of these drawings is beyond the scope of this paper but there is much literature on the subject. There is nothing like experience, however, to give one the feel of the response, particularly when every patient seen and treated is given the test.

I also use the Three Wishes test as a matter of routine. For those unfamiliar with it, one simply asks the patient, "If you had three wishes, what would you wish for?" The information derived assists in helping the patient to establish goals of treatment.

The patient's self-evaluation is often helpful, and may tend to corroborate or refute your own evaluation of him. Sometimes added data are thereby obtained for hierarchy building.

The patient is requested to bring in a list of fears, as complete as possible, in order to add to the facts and impressions already secured during the first session. It is highly important to "target in" upon the symptoms and to be certain that what the patient claims he fears is truly the "target." Detailed interrogation will usually supply the items needed for setting up of hierarchies, emphasizing the people, places, objects, and situations that engender anxiety.

I ask the patient to prepare an autobiography (Annis 1967). The length of the manuscript is left to the discretion of the patient but should be at least several pages long. The purpose is to fill in possible gaps in the history secured at the first session, in hopes that further material for therapy will be supplied. It also has the effect of making the patient participate more actively in therapy.

Requesting the patient to list, at his leisure, those traits he would like to see different about himself adds to the determination of treatment goals. It is also helpful to add all the things that irritate and make him angry, and the times he may have wished to be more aggressive but failed to assert himself.

Useful information may sometimes be obtained from the addition of a Fear Survey Schedule (Wolpe and Lang, 1964, Lanyon and Manosevitz, 1966, Rubin, B. M., 1968, Scherer and Nakamura, 1968, Rubin, S. E. 1969, Bernstein and Allen, 1969), of a Reinforcement Survey Schedule (Cautela and Kastenbaum, 1967), and other specific questionnaires, or psychological tests.

The Letter Association technique (Dengrove, 1962) was devised some years ago and has proven most useful to me in pinpointing targets. It shortens the necessary time immeasurably and is used in each treatment session for ongoing diagnosis. In essence, the mood of the patient is set by asking him to close his eyes and to relax as much as possible. He is to think of a particular symptom, to relate it to the last setting or event in which it was felt, and to attempt to relive or reconstruct—to whatever extent is possible—the feeling tone of the complaint. As a rule only a few seconds are required for this phase.

Then he is asked to give the very first letter that comes to mind— not the second or third, but the very first one. This is necessary since there are times when the patient will toy around with the alphabet.

The letter is noted, and the patient is then asked to give the very next letter that comes to mind. In all, five letters of the alphabet are obtained. If any letter that follows is sequentially related to the one given before it, the patient may be instructed to scatter the next one, to pick it out from any other place in the alphabet. The initial letter, A, and difficult letters, such as Q, X, Z are most often used to resist the process and may be disregarded.

There will be occasions when the patient will insist that he cannot think of a letter. In this case, one urges the patient to make some attempt. After all, who does not know the alphabet? Remind the patient that there are only 26 letters. If there is still resistance, one need only point out the letters of the alphabet in written form and ask the patient to look at the list and to choose one. I prefer to ask him to think of all the letters as printed on bits of paper, placed in a hat, and then thrown into the air; he is to choose the one that he grasps as the pack comes down in a shower.

When five letters are taken—the number is arbitrary and could be only one—they are listed vertically in order. The patient is then allowed to open his eyes and requested to give the first word—again only the first one—that comes to mind and which begins with each of the letters previously chosen.

In this way we have five words listed. The patient is asked to make a sentence using each word, or to free associate with each word, i.e. saying what it brings to mind, how it connects up with the symptom. Almost always the words form a battery of information related to the original difficulty and no word is without meaning in relation to the person's difficulty, no matter how far-fetched it may seem at the time. The information so derived is often dramatically related to the patient's difficulties; often the patient himself sees the connection.

Timing is important. When the patient delays in giving a letter, he should be urged to do it as quickly as he can. It is essential to prevent the patient from mulling over the alphabet, particularly during second or subsequent experiences with this method. Thinking about the subject is not desired; the more quickly the letter is pulled out of the air, the more useful it is for our purpose. Tell him not to think about it, just to say it. Nor is one to be distracted by a patient's desire to give a full word, since the word may only be a "red herring." One wants only the letter. Associations may be given afterwards.

As an example of this approach, a 37-year-old housewife presented complaints of "ungodly thoughts going through my head. I sit and cry and cry and cry, and I don't know why." Asked to give five letters, she produced the following and their associations:

> F-free-the boat won't let me be free financially.
> G-good-it's good for my husband. He enjoys it.
> P-poor-it's making us broke.
> B-boat-the same thing.
> B-Bob-my husband.

This led into the precipitating event of her depressed state, which was the purchase of a boat by her husband, with the consequent strain upon their finances. Further exploration led to her other conflicts and underscored the way she used the purchase of the boat as a means of expressing antagonism toward her husband.

As another example, a 16-year-old high school youth was found in a neighbor's house, dressed in feminine attire, doing his homework on a bed. He declared that he felt like a girl at times. There was no psychotic material. Asked to give five letters, he presented the following:

> B-boy-body build, most usually masculine, and I'm not. I'm so weak. I can't do things like other kids can, like play sports.
> F-failure-I'm afraid I'll be a failure in life. Be a bum.
> N-Neal-myself.
> O-open-open the box-any kind of box-you put something in or pull something out of it.
> T-top-top of a mountain-above sea level-usually forests and woods around there.

I was able to follow the first three associations into his relationship with his father; the last two were not pursued, since they presented material he would not be ready to cope with.

I find the technique interesting, rich in profusion of material, and direct in approach. Its use is not limited to initial contacts with the patient but may be applied at any time in therapy. It is a time-saver. The patient cannot claim that nothing comes to mind, since all that he has to do is to give a letter of the alphabet.

Following the end of the interview, I ask the patient—now that I am aware of the information he has given me—what he wants me to do for him: a therapeutic goal is set. It is surprising how often the goals set by the patient will differ from those presupposed by the therapist.

General personality attributes are important when arriving at a differential diagnosis. For example, if one separates those phobic conditions associated with post-traumatic states and schizoid disorders, one is left almost entirely with patients who display a basic compulsive personality pattern—perfectionism—in varying degrees. These people are, for the most part, neat, systematic, orderly, conscientious, and concerned that everything should be in its right place and that there is indeed a right place for everything. They want to do the good thing and be the good person, to please everyone (except their spouses). They range from the woman—and 15 to 1 it is a woman—who will pick up the ash tray to empty it the moment someone drops a cigarette into it, to the much less frequently seen artist whose studio may be messy but whose concept of her work must be perfection.

All of these people have one thing in common: a highly developed conscience which sits heavily upon them. The majority have a mother, or much less frequently a father, who is compulsive and perfectionistic also, and who has dominated them, often to the point of distress.

The phobic symptom is precipitated at a particular time in their lives when they are undergoing a stressful situation and feel particularly helpless. It is important not only to delineate the basic compulsive character structure but to pinpoint the original stressful situation, and, if necessary, to desensitize to it; it may have been continually reinforced to the present time.

The compulsivity and perfectionism call for a broad array of techniques in order to help the patient to cope with a stressful environment. These patients often need to be desensitized to feared authoritative figures, and have the burden of their compulsivity lessened. An important feature of therapy is to help them to a point of not caring so much about what others think of them.

Diagnosis is not limited to the first session but is an ongoing process. Each time the patient comes for therapy, he is asked, "What has occurred since the previous session?" Any symptom, old or new, is immediately elaborated upon and its time and setting specifically described, often with the patient closing his eyes and attempting to relive the situation as in the present. Then, if the patient cannot state why the symptom occurred at a particular moment in a particular setting, in its special way, the letter association technique is often able to determine these details.

The source of the reinforcement of the symptom must be dealt with on each occasion. There may only be a repetition of material previously unearthed but it is important to make the patient aware of what it is that keeps him ill. As noted previously, there is extinction of the symptom unless something or someone is keeping it alive, much as a hoop will run down if not given a push from time to time.

Each patient is asked to relate both the good and bad things that have happened since the previous session. When a patient speaks of several anxiety attacks, each is traced back to its original time of onset, the setting in which it occurred, and if the patient cannot discuss the origin of the attack, the letter association technique is used, quickly pinpointing the source. As an example, a patient opened the session with, "Why do I get nervous whenever I think of coming here?" She was asked to sit back in the chair, close her eyes and become aware of the feeling of nervousness. When she indicated that this was present, she was told to give the first letter that came to mind. In this instance it was the letter, F. The first word she connected with it was "fear." She was then asked to give a letter after thinking, "Fear of what?" This turned out to be "Y-you." Asked to think of the word, "because," she said, "Because I don't know what you're going to do." Further discussion of this point allayed her anxieties.

Ongoing diagnosis is important where there is delay or inability to transfer improvement from office to real life, and directs attention to motivation in particular. For example, a 20-year-old woman was doing well—in the office—with systematic desensitization to her fears of walking and driving from her home, but actually had made no progress at all in the actual situations. Asked to attempt movement in real life situations, she produced only excuse after excuse during each session as to why it had been impossible throughout that week. She had an anticipatory fear response but she would not make the slightest attempt, even with proffered help. Further diagnostic exploration revealed the reason for her lack of progress to be her fear that if she would be free to come and go as she pleased, she would simply go and not return. She had no respect for her immature husband, yet feared giving up the kind of life that she was leading.

Similarly, a 34-year-old housewife had been doing quite well with her fear of driving away from her home when her infant child died suddenly under circumstances for which she blamed her pediatrician. Immediately she relapsed and no coaxing could get her to drive again, until diagnostic exploration revealed her fear that if she could drive on her own, she might drive to the doctor's office and commit mayhem there. She dreamed of it, and was protected against these effects of her hostility by her inability to drive at all.

Finally, it is worth noting that some patients may appear to suffer a relapse (i.e. the return of initial symptoms) when in fact new organic or different environmental forces are operative. For example, one of the first patients whom I treated with systematic desensitization was a woman in her early forties. She had suffered a phobic state for about 12 years. With systematic desensitization she progressed to a point where she could travel, not only from her home but for great distances. She was a most grateful patient because her husband always wanted to travel with her and she had held him back. One day she phoned for an appointment. She was frightened; her symptoms had returned. Diagnostic exploration, however, proved her alarm to be unfounded. She was suffering from some of the symptoms of her menopause, had mistaken them for the return of her previous illness and developed an anxiety over them. Reassurance and estrogens limited her visits to one, and thereafter she phoned to say that she was her renewed self again. Another woman who returned for further treatment had developed symptoms about a fear that had not shown itself before because she had had no occasion to encounter similar situations previously. Treatment of this item through desensitization quickly returned her to her previous symptom-free state.

Behavioral diagnosis requires versatility, together with a sharp, inquiring mind. Properly done, its end results enhance therapeutic progress.

REFERENCES

ABRAMOVITZ, C. M. Personalistic psychotherapy and the role of technical eclecticism. *Psychological Reports*, 1970, 26, 255-263.

ANNIS, A. P. The autobiography: its use and value in professional psychology. *Journal of Counseling Psychology*, 1967, 14, 9-17.

BERNSTEIN, D. A. & ALLEN, G. J. Fear survey schedule (II). *Behavior Research and Therapy*, 1969, 7, 403-407.

CAUTELA, J. R. & KASTENBAUM, R. A reinforcement survey schedule for use in therapy, training, and research. *Psychological Reports*, 1967, 20, 1115-1130.

CLARKE, A. D. B. Learning and human development. *British Journal of Psychiatry*, 1968, 114, 1061-1077.

DAVIS, R. D. *British Journal of Medical Psychology*, 1958, 31, 74.

DENGROVE, E. A new letter association technique. *Diseases of the Nervous System*, 1962, 23, 25-26.

GANTT, W. H. Autonomic conditioning. In J. Wolpe, et al (Eds.) *The Conditioning Therapies*. New York: Holt, Rinehart, and Winston, 1964, Pp. 117, 125.

LANG, P. J. Experimental studies of desensitization psychotherapy. In J. Wolpe, et al (Eds.) *The Conditioning Therapies*. New York: Holt, Rinehart, and Winston, 1964, Pp. 51-52.

LANYON, R. I. & MANOSEVITZ, M. Validity of self-reported fear. *Behavior Research and Therapy*, 1966, 4, 259-263.

LAZARUS, A. A. Broad spectrum behavior therapy and the treatment of agoraphobia. *Behavior Research and Therapy*, 1966, 4, 95-97.

LAZARUS, A. A. Behavior therapy in groups. In G. M. Gazda (Ed.) *Theories and Methods of Group Psychotherapy and Counseling*. Springfield: C. C. Thomas, 1970.

LAZARUS, A. A. & SERBER, M. Is systematic desensitization being misapplied? *Psychological Reports*, 1968, 23, 215-218.

MEYER, V. & CRISP, A. H. Some problems in behavior therapy. *British Journal of Psychiatry*, 1966, 112, 367-381.

RUBIN, B. M., et al. Factor analysis of a fear survey schedule. *Behavior Research and Therapy*, 1968, 6, 65-75.

RUBIN, S. E., et al. Factor analysis of the 122 item fear survey schedule. *Behavior Research and Therapy*, 1969, 7, 381-386.

SCHERER, M. W. & NAKAMURA, C. Y. A fear survey schedule for children (FSS-FC). *Behavior Research and Therapy*, 1968, 6, 173-182.

STEVENSON, I. & HAIN, J. H. On the different meanings of apparently similar symptoms; illustrated by varieties of barber shop phobia. *American Journal of Psychiatry*, 1967, 124, 399-403.

WOLPE, J. Behavior therapy in complex neurotic states. *British Journal of Psychiatry*, 1964, 110, 28-34.

WOLPE, J. & LANG, P. J. A fear survey schedule for use in behavior therapy. *Behavior Research and Therapy*, 1964, 2, 27-30.

5

Eidetics: An Internal Behavior Approach

AKHTER AHSEN, Ph.D.
and ARNOLD A. LAZARUS, Ph.D.

IT SEEMS WIDELY AGREED that most problem behaviors are learned in some manner and that psychotherapy is a relearning and unlearning process. Behavior Therapy has given explicit direction to the basic thrust of learning adaptive habits while unlearning maladaptive responses, but unfortunately the S-R formulation of learning adopted by some behavior therapists is too limited to account for the realities of life (Lazarus, 1971). This limitation inherent in the theory is also generally apparent in the techniques developed within the counter-conditioning framework.

"Learning" in its widest sense of acquiring a "pattern" is a meaningless term and it should properly include insights, images, symbolic materials, ideas and cognitive-affective interchanges that stretch between all these. A proper theory of behavior in our view will only emerge as a result of the interaction of clinical theories and experimental psychology in which clinical data will be obtained primarily from controlled studies

87

of patients rather than subjects. One can see that such a scientific approach in psychology would not be particularly restricted to "learning theory."

Our main objection to non-cognitive learning theory is that it does not aim at understanding what generally passes between the patient and the therapist and it has no means available which can help us in so doing.

In an endeavor to emphasize the need to extend therapy beyond the narrow boundaries of conventional behavior therapy, Lazarus (1971) described the case of Mrs. D, a housebound lady stricken with anxiety. If she ventured further than her front porch, she would become faint and panicky. When Mrs. D consulted Lazarus, his first therapeutic objective was to enable her to come on her own to the clinic, which was achieved by hypnotizing her and asking her to picture herself accomplishing this feat without undue disturbance. After this followed a period of extensive history-taking and more hypnosis in which she was repeatedly asked to picture herself travelling unaccompanied to and from the clinic. Then came the evidence that her husband was subtly attempting to undermine her progress by encouraging her extreme dependency. Her husband admitted a sense of security in knowing that his wife was always at home and was dependent on him and felt that if she were mobile and self-sufficient, she would leave him for another man. This fear on his part was traced to his own sexual ineptitude. After this revelation the husband and wife were seen together and discussions were devoted to ways and means of improving their relationship. She was encouraged to stand up for her rights through goal-directed role-playing which subsequently made it easier for her to contemplate standing up to her father. After enacting several role-playing sequences, Mrs. D improved further and now enjoyed taking long walks alone and was able to go shopping and visiting without distress. However, she continued to consider herself a worthless person and was not able to overcome her negative self-evaluation during therapy. Some time after she had terminated therapy, she became active and established an organization of a charitable nature and, as its president and founder, discovered self-worth and meaning. The last act of healing carried out by Mrs. D was totally self-initiated but what had been done prior to the final goal (self-worth) was considered a necessary turning point.

Follow-up studies of cases treated by behavior therapy indicate that durable outcomes usually require philosophical as well as behavioral changes (Lazarus, 1971). This leads to the open question of the possible advantages of combining external behavioral and internal behavioral treatment strategies. Of course, in the sense that our only access to clinical data is through some form of behavior (verbal and non-verbal), all therapy is behavioral. Nonetheless, it is useful to separate therapies that deal mainly with external observable behavior from those that concentrate on internal experiential phenomena. Basically, the question then is whether there are specific advantages in combining eidetic therapy (Ahsen, 1968) with behavioral techniques. What follows is an important case in which both methods (eidetic analysis and behavior therapy) were employed.

The circumstances which made the demonstration of this case possible were very interesting. Mrs. Jay, aged forty-one, had been treated at the Eastern Pennsylvania Psychiatric Institute by a group of behavior therapists for more than a year, during which time she had initially showed improvement and finally surprised everybody by relapsing and developing her symptoms all over again. Mrs. Jay was still visiting the Institute but had completely regressed to her pretreatment symptoms, namely, severe irrational anxiety which made her homebound, chest pains, palpitations, nausea, pins and needles, dizziness, extreme feelings of personal unworthiness, etc.

At this time, one of the therapists who had treated Mrs. Jay happened to meet Akhter Ahsen and a somewhat heated debate ensued regarding their respective theoretical and technical differences. The meeting culminated in a challenge to Ahsen to demonstrate his methods of eidetic analysis before a group of professionals. Ahsen had stressed that his theories of eidetic symbolism (Ahsen, 1965) would enable him to select appropriate therapeutic strategies at various stages of therapy and to predict the specific consequences of each intervention. Before the meeting ended, it was decided that Ahsen would treat a case at Eastern Pennsylvania Psychiatric Institute in the presence of the staff and that he would utilize short steps and demonstrate each step through a definite causal link and predict beforehand what results were expected and how they would be achieved.

The use of eidetics provides testable predictions and deductions and the methods of treatment they employ often eliminate surmise, hunch and intuition. They replace oversimplifications with realities about subjective phenomena, and the complexities of these realities are, in turn, testable and demonstrable.

These assertions will become more clear when we describe eidetic methods of treatment in respect to Mrs. Jay. The description of Ahsen's treatment will be discussed in detail to provide an idea of how eidetics actually appear to an outside observer and how they seem to work internally. Ahsen's demonstration suggested that where narrow behavior therapy failed to provide a valid change inside the patient, the eidetic approach succeeded in swiftly eliminating what appeared to be psychotic states, proving them to be memories of important events which formal behavior therapy had completely ignored.

CASE HISTORY OF MRS. JAY

Mrs. Jay, a forty-one-year-old white, married female of Jewish extraction, was suffering from symptoms of pain located in the upper left abdomen, chest and left breast, excessive irrational anxiety involving fear of death and numerous other manifestations of anxiety, such as palpitations, dizziness, nausea, pins and needles, fainting spells, as well as strong uncertainties and feelings of personal unworthiness, so much so that she was finding it impossible to perform daily chores and was unable to go places, especially crowded places. The treatment under behavior therapy was started in the regular way as a typical laboratory model involving principles of extinction, counter-conditioning, positive and negative reinforcement, including aversive conditioning and punishment with a small electrical gadget which she was expected to carry with her all the time and to shock herself if she entertained a negative idea involving a maladaptive approach to a life problem. Her symptoms were being treated in isolation from their origin and background because all the behavioral questionnaires and case history procedures had failed to bring out any causal link between the symptoms and her developmental past.

The previous formal behavioral approach had initially succeeded in reducing Mrs. Jay's anxiety for a short time but the symptoms returned in full blast one day when the patient came to the clinic and found nobody there. She reacted so badly to the incident that her condition deteriorated below pretreatment levels. The situation grew from bad to worse. After many more attempts, she was finally pronounced a borderline schizophrenic. It is obvious that formal behavior therapy had proved ineffective in ridding the patient of her maladaptive fears. All along she had shown a difficulty in absorbing behavioral treatment and in the end she threw all the training and conditioning overboard, making scores of hours just another negative experience in her life. Nothing much was known about her real emotional life. All said and done, the patient now stood at the threshold of no hope. Her original behavior therapist had described this case as the "acid test" for any other system of therapy.

At the commencement of eidetic analysis which took place early in 1967, Mrs. Jay was acutely disturbed. She was panting for breath and perspiring and complaining about dizziness and palpitations. She wanted the windows to be opened wide so that she could breathe cool, fresh air. Ahsen had already explained to the small group of observers that he would first assemble the character of her symptoms and then give her what he called the Age Projection Test* (Ahsen, 1968, Pp. 253-261) to see if the symptoms were "hysterical" and to determine whether any particular event in her past was connected with them. This, he said, would be possible to establish through an eidetic (self-image) which she would see during the Age Projection Test. Ahsen stated: "If the symptoms are in any way directly connected with specific past events, this self-image will provide us with the ability to exacerbate or to ameliorate her symptoms."

After Ahsen had noted down the main features of the symptoms, namely, how Mrs. Jay tended to describe them, how they tended to reflect in various parts of her body in the form of somatic feelings, and how they tended to get particularly localized in a certain area, a graphic picture of the symptoms emerged. These were noted down in the actual words which Mrs. Jay used to report them, including her elaborations. The chest pain and palpitations were thus localized around the region of the heart. Her other symptoms, like nausea, dizziness, needles, etc., emerged as secondary responses which described generally the feeling side of the main symptoms of chest pain. During this phase Mrs. Jay was lucid and described things very well. Ahsen passed the word among the main observers by writing on a piece of paper, "When I repeat the actual symptom descriptions to Mrs. Jay, she will react to my constant repetition by developing acute symptoms. When they reach an intolerable pitch, I will suddenly start talking about the opposite, of relief, of absence of pain, of, in fact, pleasant sensations and feelings in the same areas of the body. Then I will suddenly request her to see herself in the form of an image somewhere in the past. This image will shed light upon the etiology of her somatic symptoms."

After circulating this message, Ahsen started repeating the symptoms back to Mrs. Jay in her own words and, as he had predicted, her symptoms gradually became so acute that she begged him to stop repeating them to her. At this point, Ahsen reversed his procedure by repeating pleasant

---

* Editor's note: Ahsen now refers to this as the "Symptom Oscillation Test." For complete details, the reader is referred to Ahsen, 1972.

opposite descriptions (e.g., calmness, no pain, no discomfort, etc.). The patient showed clear signs of relaxation and relief. When asked to project herself into the past, she reported a self-image around age twenty-six while wearing a red blouse and black skirt. As to the memories around age twenty-five, *she recollected the death of her father during that year.*

The circumstances surrounding Mrs. Jay's father's death were found to be particularly traumatic upon inquiry. The father, who was a coronary patient, had suffered a heart attack and was brought back to life temporarily through cardiac massage by the attending doctors. The patient had been present throughout the procedure and for her to see the father returning to life and then dying again all within a few minutes was extremely distressing. She recalled begging the doctors not to massage the heart and to let the father die peacefully. The doctors, however, did not listen and performed what they considered their duty, not minding Mrs. Jay's reaction to it. She stated that she had felt extremely traumatized at this point and had an experience of choked hysteria inside.

At this point, Ahsen circulated another written message to the observers: "Her symptoms of pain in the upper left abdomen, left breast and part of the chest are probably related to this traumatic memory of cardiac massage. If the hypothesis is correct, we should be able to ameliorate her symptoms as well as make them acute if we repeat images of the two opposed ends of the event, namely, (i) massage of the heart and (ii) death of the father immediately after cardiac massage. Symptoms should react to (i) by becoming more acute and will decrease and even disappear when the image belonging to (ii) is concentrated upon by the patient. Images belonging to these two opposed areas are of the eidetic nature."

After circulating this note, Ahsen proceeded to develop (i) and (ii) eidetic images. By the end of this inquiry, it was found that the two lucid images had been clearly arrived at and Mrs. Jay showed a clear tendency to react to them: to (i) by developing the acute symptoms and to (ii) by becoming relaxed, though not without some symptoms. Ahsen then circulated another piece of paper saying, "My hypothesis is that just as the doctors wanted to actively revive the father, Mrs. Jay wanted to actively let the father die, amounting to images of aggressively rendering the father to death, a form of 'murder fantasy.' If the hypothesis is correct, the symptoms should disappear if Mrs. Jay is encouraged to discover her need to actively render the father to death in images."

Ahsen proceeded to arrive at further images pertaining to Mrs. Jay's hidden feelings toward the father. As questions and answers proceeded, we saw an unusual phenomenon, namely, that Mrs. Jay did, in fact, on her own see images in which she suffocated her father with a pillow and put him to death on the hospital bed. As she did so, she bitterly cried and then became completely peaceful, as if the storm had passed. After she "killed" the father with the help of the pillows, her somatic symptoms disappeared.

All the observers were examining the proceedings closely and saw that Ahsen was not feeding ideas or images to her and that eidetics were somehow emerging and expanding her awareness as she came to recognize that her symptoms were linked with the death of the father and that somehow or other she wanted her father to die. She was reproducing her needs and fantasies as far back as ten years. Her previous Behavior Therapy had never explored this area and there was no hint of any of this material in the history-taking when Mrs. Jay gave her extensive history in the initial stages. The eidetic procedures moved with a sure foot and showed no looseness in this direction and were able to lay open the probable causal link in the very first session. One could only say that the extensive stimulus analysis previously carried out was rudimentary, vague and indeterminate and clearly lacked the ability to unearth basic elements, at least in this area.

The eidetic approach disclosed that, to start with, Mrs. Jay's symptoms were of a hysterical nature and that her subjective states tended to split up into two distinct, significant image configurations—cardiac massage and death after the cardiac massage—and concentration on the image of the cardiac massage produced chest pain, profuse sweating, shortening of breath, feelings of giddiness and nausea, whereas concentration on the father's death released feelings of relaxation and comfort in the patient. Subsequent to repeated testing and oscillation of the symptoms through the two image states, Ahsen suggested that the patient now consciously repeat the images pertaining to the death of the father and concentrate only on this end of the image and drop the other side altogether. In reaction to these instructions, Mrs. Jay related further material involving how much her father loved her and how he used to take her out on long walks and sing songs for her on the way when she was a little girl. Now she seemed to be preoccupied with the father's two previous heart attacks.

After Mrs. Jay had overcome her main debilitating symptoms through a single session, she was able to cooperate more with psychotherapy. Now started further unfolding of her past as well as her fantasy life in relation to her symptoms. The theme of her father's cardiac attack seemed to be a continuous one and connected to two previous heart attacks, especially the first one when the father suddenly developed a heart attack when the mother was boiling water. The image pertaining to the boiling water appeared to be laden with powerful affect which threw the patient again into an experience of symptoms around the region of her heart. This image, however, proved "cathartic" instead and left the patient stronger in the end. The memory passed like a cloud, bringing to the surface other memories in which their house was robbed and a thief mugged her father inside the store which was directly below their living apartment. The memory pertaining to the mugging brought out other hidden fears concerning strangers and her own feelings of aggression. She experienced an image of herself attacking a thief in the store which helped her in mastering the memory. After this came memories of her stealing candy from the store and her concern about her weight and the father's insistence that she should try to hide herself behind the counter because she was too fat. As a result of this memory, she saw herself clobbering the father on the head and the image was similar to the thief attacking the father.

The patient showed keen understanding of the symbolism involved and also developed a clearer realization of why she wanted her father to die during the cardiac massage. However, the eidetics did not merely demonstrate the negative side of her wishes because there was also a jolly father in her mind and the images pertaining to the jolly father brought tears and sorrow to the patient. In the images, the two of them sang together on the footpath while going to school or just going for a walk. The profound experience of this jolly father restored a feeling of worth in her. She immensely enjoyed picturing these images.

The images then moved in the direction of her fears at the school when her classmates ridiculed her for being fat. She remembered some of these classmates and saw their images and repeated the visual experience and understood why she had grown to be so passive in respect to others. These children had cruelly persecuted her. After this came images pertaining to her growing up and her first menstruation. The eidetics in this area gradually led to her fears concerning conception and problems of miscarriage, a theme which had also appeared in the second part of the Age Projection Test.

She described her miscarriage experience and the fear that she could not have another baby. The doctor had told her that he could not hear the baby's heart and that "dead babies don't grow." This had been extremely traumatic for her. She remembered experiencing severe anxiety and uncertainty and horror at what she was facing. It appeared that her desire not to have a child was offset by an equally strong wish to have a child. She remembered thinking on those contradictory lines but was unable to resolve the conflict. A range of additional images (Ahsen, 1968, Pp. 258-261) enabled her to work through this conflict and led to various realizations that many problem areas were connected with her rejecting mother.*

Mrs. Jay's mother seemed to lack warmth, understanding and tolerance for the patient. She emerged as an impatient and critical person who did not hide how disappointed she was in her daughter. Her main concern seemed to be her daughter's being overweight. She was a martyr who had dominated her husband and had a loud voice without any comforting words in it. The father on the other hand had been an understanding person in her life. The mother was ashamed of her daughter and the daughter knew how she felt about her. She had infused her daughter with her feelings of worthlessness and guilt.

She began questioning whether her mother had normal attitudes toward life and whether her feelings of martyrdom were directly responsible for creating feelings of guilt in Mrs. Jay. By understanding the source of her guilt and by knowing in an experiential manner how it affected her, Mrs. Jay then drew a parallel between herself and her mother, suggesting that perhaps she was acting in the same manner toward her own family. The feelings of worthlessness and guilt had been engendered by the mother and were now being reinforced by her, and Mrs. Jay felt that she might even be punishing her mother in this manner. At this point she understood images of her mother as they appeared in the Eidetic Parents Test (Ahsen, 1968, Pp. 262-288) as the images of a martyred individual. She experienced feelings of tension and rage inside her and felt that she really wanted to punish her mother. At this point she

---

* Editor's note: While the psychoanalytic undertones reflect Ahsen's orientation, it should be understood that his *active* use of imagery departs radically from the passive and indirect stance of psychoanalytic therapy. Upon reading this chapter, one may not be aware that Ahsen is, in fact, very directive in selecting images, identifying their polarities, exploring them with the patient, and in assigning "homework" for the patient in the form of rehearsed images and fantasies.

expressed many images of anger against her mother. The Eidetic Parents Test brought a decisive awareness in Mrs. Jay and created an ability on her part to understand some important psychological interactions. Mrs. Jay made further progress through this test when she expressed concern as to whether she was doing the same thing to her own family. Her mother worked hard and was good, but was also a martyr. Mrs. Jay did not work hard, was "bad" and was a martyr.

As a next step in therapy, Mrs. Jay continued to experience a series of images in respect to the mother, covering situations of extreme frustration from the mother and her reactions to those situations involving the discharge of anger, etc. It was through these images that she gradually came to feel that she needed to separate herself from the mother. All along she had been bringing her mother to the clinic as an escort but now she decided to try and come alone. She understood that by being passive and afraid she was allowing herself to be destroyed by the mother. Her mother's support and her feeling of martyrdom were serving her own needs in making the patient feel worthless.

The realization that Mrs. Jay was also identifying with the mother and doing the same to her own family was naturally the next step in the therapy. These feelings of identification became more obvious when she reported that her son had recently complained of heart symptoms somewhat similar to her own and she had felt frightened on that account. She was consciously fantasizing that her son had suffered a heart attack, or an epileptic attack or had symptoms of high blood sugar because her own father had diabetes before he died. This is how she expressed her concern in respect to her son:

"Yesterday my son had mowed the lawn and he was fixing the lawnmower. After he was done he came in and said that for a few minutes his circulation went fast. I think he meant his pulse was rapid and his heart pounded. He did not seem frightened. He said he thought it may have happened once before, a few years ago.

"I get petrified inside when he is sick. He once had a staph infection that wouldn't clear up. I felt that yesterday he may have had an epileptic attack. I thought the doctor should check his blood sugar level for diabetes. My father had diabetes before he died. I also thought maybe he had a sort of allergy attack, as he is allergic to many plants."

Ahsen pointed out that Mrs. Jay had been reading physical symptoms into her son and because she had been doing it for so long, she had made him invent many illnesses. In a nonjudgmental way she was told that she had encouraged him to be shy, had given him the thought that many people were unkind to him, and had also given him the idea that probably he might even die.

The above-mentioned factors were all elicited through the eidetics and each time a point was raised for Mrs. Jay's consideration, an eidetic image was evoked to bring evidence to her and give her time to make up her own mind. As Ahsen demonstrated, any discussions held with Mrs. Jay which did not involve direct evidence from images tended to bog down in verbal controversy and led Mrs. Jay to sidetrack her emotional issues.

Following the above-mentioned eidetic procedures, Mrs. Jay was abe to go shopping, visiting places alone and without distress. The astonishing progress which she had made in the very first session had resulted in her overcoming the symptoms of chest pain, dizziness and severe palpitations. Symptoms of nausea, pins, and needles and fear of other people similarly had been overcome along the way. Her treatment had centered around the initial overcoming of her main debilitating symptoms, followed by a series of progressive experiential "peak experiences" which permitted a new and different perspective and outlook to emerge. The insights which she had lacked due to adverse developmental conditions were clearly engendered in her through demonstrating an emotional causation within her own mind. It was not a treatment directed toward her overt behavior, which was never brought into discussion, but of purely subjective images and associated affects and it emphasized emotive and cognitive variables and other internal events, like her fantasy life. It was the case of a person riddled with subjective experiences involving guilt and self-doubt. This had resulted in her self-defeating attitudes generating overt symptoms.

A criticism of many subjective approaches is that overt behavior changes seldom ensue. In the case of Mrs. Jay, this criticism is certainly not upheld. It should be remembered that traditional behavior therapy had failed to make any significant inroads and that consequently the case was dismissed as "schizophrenic" and unamenable to psychotherapy. Furthermore, the patient's rich and significant fantasies had eluded all behavioral forms of inquiry. While Lazarus does not hold with many of Ahsen's theoretical points of emphasis, he must concede that the usual life-history, fear-checklist, Willoughby Personality Inventory and behavior analysis could not possibly have elicited the crucial data described above. In cases similar to the above he now makes use of imagery in the various ways and means described in this chapter. The net result is an increased therapeutic repertoire which enhances treatment outcome in many cases considered intractable by strict behavior therapists.

It is noteworthy that when, for technical reasons at Eastern Pennsylvania Psychiatric Institute, Mrs. Jay was transferred to Lazarus for therapy (six months after Ahsen had commenced treating her), the patient was most amenable and receptive to behavioral procedures. Now that the major internal sources of her anxiety had been ameliorated, the external factors maintaining various deviant responses were open to correction. This does not imply that all cases require a progression of treatment from "internal" to "external." In a broad spectrum therapeutic approach there is no reason why both approaches cannot be employed concurrently.

While Ahsen's use of imagery and fantasy techniques had almost entirely eliminated Mrs. Jay's somatic complaints and had rendered her less dependent and more mobile, she remained somewhat claustrophobic, socially reticent, unassertive, and afraid of travelling more than a few miles from home. She was also still deficient in feelings of self-worth. Furthermore, she tended to interact with her husband in a passive-aggressive manner and thereby triggered unnecessary tensions in the home.* Methods of assertive training, behavior rehearsal, desensitization, and a variety of rational techniques were all productive in achieving further gains. Several interviews with Mrs. Jay and her husband successfully modified the tension-producing elements in their home. It became obvious, after these joint interviews, that Mrs. Jay was deriving secondary gains from her husband's attention and over-concern. The couple was given a broad outline of operant principles of reinforcement, and the patient's husband agreed to reward a range of constructive behaviors that were pinpointed and listed during the interview.

Significant gains in Mrs. Jay's remaining areas of tension and uncertainty accrued soon after she weaned herself away from home several days a week and obtained employment as a part-time secretary.

A follow-up inquiry after one year revealed Mrs. Jay's progress had not only been maintained but had advanced beyond the point where therapy had been terminated. She has a full-time job, has taken several

---

* Editor's note: In fairness to Ahsen, it should be emphasized that he did not regard his own therapy as "complete" when he transferred the case to Lazarus.

long car journeys and two ocean voyages without any distress, and she is a generally more confident, relaxed and happy person. A second follow-up inquiry, two years later, revealed still further gains.

REFERENCES

AHSEN, A. *A Short Introduction to Eidetic Psychotherapy.* Published in India by Lahore Nai Matbuaat, 1965.

AHSEN, A. *Basic Concepts in Eidetic Psychotherapy*, New York, Eidetic Publishing House, 1968.

AHSEN, A. *Symptom Oscillation Test for Hysterias and Phobias*, New York, Brandon House, 1972.

LAZARUS, A. A. *Behavior Therapy and Beyond*, New York, McGraw-Hill, 1971.

6

An Holistic Approach to Behavior Therapy

MAX JACOBS, M.A. (Clin. Psych.), LL.B.

EYSENCK (1964) WRITES, "The most successful behavior therapists are likely to be those who have a wide grasp of the whole literature, and owe no allegiance to any particular school; the weapons in our armamentarium are not so numerous that we can afford to neglect any that may be there." It is the theme of this paper that effective behavior therapy depends upon the flexible and full use of the available techniques.

However, a perusal of the literature reinforces the point of view that behavior therapy is often mechanistic, concerned with specific techniques, rather than a "total" therapy, as if most patients suffered merely from monosymptomatic neurosis, which can be dealt with by a single procedure. Books on behavior therapy are often descriptions of various techniques, without any attempt to integrate these into a total therapy. We thus have books with such titles as *Behavior Therapy Techniques* (Wolpe and Lazarus, 1966) and *Conditioning Techniques* (Franks, 1964).

47916

The writer in no way wishes to denigrate these excellent books, but only to point out the apparent stress on technique which is associated with behavior therapy.

Not only are monosymptomatic problems, in the writer's experience, rarely encountered, but even the most simple phobia can be viewed in terms of "classically conditioned" autonomic anxiety responses (intervening variables), "operantly conditioned" avoidance behavior and "catastrophic" cognitions about the phobic situation. It follows from this analysis that all three aspects should be dealt with by the behavior therapist. But Wolpe's (1958) technique of systematic desensitization which is most often used in the treatment of phobic conditions (a Classical Conditioning Paradigm) concentrates treatment only on the first aspect. The Skinnerians stress instrumental learning, employ extinction techniques and treat the second aspect, whereas, Ellis (1962) devotes his efforts to cognitive reorganization.

The writer's approach to behavior therapy, which he has arbitrarily labelled "holistic," is to treat, wherever possible, simultaneously the autonomic anxiety, the overt motor responses and the cognitions which go to make up the patient's neurosis. These may be paraphrased as the way the patient "feels, acts and thinks." The patient's anxiety is treated by procedures such as desensitization or deep relaxation; operant techniques are used to modify or condition new motor responses; and the patient's cognitions are modified by such cognitive reorganization techniques as Ellis' Rational Therapy (Ellis, 1962) and Frankl's Logotherapy (Frankl, 1970).

A monistic view of neurosis and its treatment, e.g. the treatment of only one of the above aspects of a phobia, cannot be justified by recourse to learning theory, and behavior therapy techniques are far from adequate and often tenuous (Buchwald and Young, 1969, Lazarus, 1971).

In addition, many behavior therapy techniques cannot be said to be clearly based on any particular theory at all. Rachman and Teasdale (1969) discussing aversion therapy write: "The connections among aversion therapy, psychological theory and verified experimental data are tenuous." Feldman (1966) comes to a similar conclusion. Buchwald and Young (1969) point out that an adequate explanation of how reciprocal inhibition works is nonexistent.

Therefore, if the behavior therapist cannot rely entirely on "learning theory" to justify his choice of technique in treatment, he should base his treatment on the test of effectiveness. This implies that the behavior

Lincoln Christian College

therapist should not confine himself to a narrow range of treatment methods, but should make use of all methods of behavior modification which have been found effective.

It has been submitted that total treatment requires the modification of autonomic anxiety, motor responses and cognitions. This 3-factor model can be usefully employed to analyze most of the problems dealt with by the therapist, particularly phobias, obsessive behavior, and homosexuality. The use of this model will be described below.

Not only should all three aspects be dealt with, but as many techniques as possible should be brought to bear on the problem. The writer in an earlier publication (Jacobs, 1969) discussed the use of emotive imagery (Lazarus and Abramovitz, 1962) concomitantly with the usual desensitization paradigm in order to strengthen the anxiety inhibitory effects of the procedure. Instead of having items of the hierarchy presented in the usual way, emotive images are produced, e.g., the following two items from a claustrophobic's hierarchy:

"Picture yourself standing in the center of a crowded room at a cocktail party; you are talking animatedly to a very attractive, interested female; you have a drink in your hand and are enjoying yourself." (The emotive images are the attractive female, the drink and the fact that he is enjoying himself.)

or

"Picture yourself in the elevator, going up to the fifth floor. You have just met an old friend in the elevator, whom you are very pleased to see. You are leaning against the elevator and are feeling calm and relaxed." (Emotive images of excitement and pleasure at seeing an old friend, relaxed posture and feeling.)

This method was used with 29 phobics and the results appear, although tentatively, to indicate the increased effectiveness of this approach over that of the usual desensitization procedure.

CASE 1. *Phobic.* Mrs. K. a married woman, in her late thirties. Her presenting problems, of at least 15 years standing, manifested as severe claustrophobia. The phobia extended to flying in aircraft, travelling in elevators, being in trains, buses, cinemas, restaurants, theatres, department stores and other closed, confined spaces. She was even unable to wear jewelry or close-fitting clothes around her neck. She attempted to avoid the above situations whenever possible, but if she was compelled to be in any of them she would panic, severely hyperventilate, feel swollen, develop tachycardia, severe stomach cramps, and tension headaches. Her phobias became exacerbated after the death of her mother in a foreign country three years prior to treatment when she had to fly to her mother's funeral. The problem was particularly debilitating since Mrs. K., who lived in Britain, was an actress and was often required to fly abroad in order to act on stage and television. Further, her aged father resided in South Africa and she wished to visit him from time to time and would have to fly to see him. The patient presented herself for treatment eight days before being due to leave South Africa, where she was holidaying, to return to Britain. She had recurring nightmares of being buried alive and during the first case-history taking interview, it emerged that in the phobic situations she feared she would choke or die (since she felt both short of breath and dizzy as a result of hyperventilation). Another area of difficulty for the patient was that she became very tense when about to appear on stage, lest she forget her lines (needless to say, she had never done so in many years of acting).

Now, if phobic anxiety is to be viewed simply as conditioned anxiety responses to specific situations and stimuli, I would have treated the patient by Wolpe's method of desensitization. Carefully calibrated hierarchies would have been drawn up to desensitize the patient and she might have been admonished not to expose herself too hastily to real life phobic situations unless she could handle them, lest she resensitize herself. Such an approach would deal with the "autonomically conditioned" anxiety, but would pay little attention to the patient's "voluntary" avoidance behavior and cognitions. Furthermore, it became immediately apparent, during the taking of the case history, that the patient reacted in an all-or-none manner to all phobic situations and that it would be impossible to construct hierarchies.

The course of treatment is detailed below and, as can be seen, therapy was directed particularly at the behavioral and cognitive aspects of the phobia.

1st session: The case history was taken. Patient's husband was present during the whole interview. The patient was told that the shortness of breath and giddiness she experienced in the phobic situations were due to overbreathing and she was reassured that no physical harm could befall her in the phobic situations. She was shown how to control hyperventilation by breathing into a paper bag or holding her breath. She was then made to hyperventilate, whereupon she began to panic and weep. She was immediately told to hold her breath. The symptoms ceased after she had done so. Her reaction was one of amazement and delight at discovering that these sensations which had so terrified her were due only to overbreathing and that she could control them. She stated, "Why has no one told me before that it was only my breathing? I actually thought I was physically sick." It was again stressed to her that she could from now onwards control those symptoms and that since she now knew what it was (overbreathing, not a terrible disease) she had no cause to fear them. A learning theory model for the acquisition and maintenance of her phobias was discussed with the patient and her husband (at which stage she remembered that she thought her phobia had started when, as a child of about 6 years of age, she had often been locked up in a cupboard as punishment by a nursemaid). She was told that if she became anxious in a situation and then ran away from it, and subsequently avoided it, she would develop a phobia. Conversely, she was told that if she would expose herself to her phobic situations and make herself remain in them (no matter how bad she felt initially) until she became calm, she would soon overcome her fear. Thus, during this first session the patient was reassured, given a new response to diminish the hyperventilation symptoms, was shown that these symptoms were non-dangerous but controllable (a cognitive reorganization), and instructed not to avoid phobic situations, but, with her husband's help, to seek them out and remain in them for as long as it took for her to become absolutely calm in them. (This might be called *in vivo* desensitization, but the writer feels that the crucial element is the elimination of avoidance behavior habits by non-reinforcement and the learning of new non-avoidance patterns, which will be reinforced by the mere sense of achievement). The patient was also told that if she succeeded in placing herself in and remaining in a phobic situation, she ought to boast of it to as many people as possible. It is clear that this approach is very different from the use of gradual, careful exposures to the phobic stimuli which is the approach usually adopted.

2nd session (the following day): The patient came without her husband and reported feeling much more confident. She had already been in an elevator with her husband and had had little difficulty. She was praised for this by the therapist. The first half of the session was devoted to a Rational Therapy approach in attempting to effect a cognitive reorganization. The patient was made to logically examine her "catastrophic" ideas, i.e. she had for all the years of her phobia thought, "It

is awful and terrible to be in an aircraft elevator, cinema, etc., I hate it."
She was made to replace these thoughts with, "So what if I am in an
aircraft, elevator, etc., it can do me no harm," "It's fun to travel by air,"
"So what if I forget a line on stage, I've never done so yet, nothing will
happen, why should I be perfect?" She was then taught thought stopping
(Wolpe and Lazarus, 1966) and told to use this to block out any
"catastrophic thoughts." Frankl's (1970) technique of paradoxical intention was then brought in to further attack her cognitions and behavioral
responses to the phobias. She was told that whenever she began to feel
anxious in any of the phobic situations, instead of trying to fight and
suppress the symptoms and thoughts which troubled her (e.g. feelings
of dizziness, loss of control, thoughts of death and suffocation), she was
to say to herself, "I know there is nothing physically wrong with me,
I'm only tense and hyperventilating, in fact I want to prove this to myself
by letting these symptoms become as bad as possible." She was told to
try to suffocate or die "right on the spot" and to try to exaggerate her
physical symptoms.

She was then taught a brief modified form of Jacobson's (1938) progressive relaxation. She was told to practice it and to apply it in the
phobic situations to remain calm, but it was stressed that she should
not try too hard to relax or fight the tension. While under relaxation,
desensitization was begun. She was asked to imagine flying back to
Britain. Lazarus and Abramovitz's (1962) technique of emotive imagery
was used simultaneously as part of the scene in order to increase the
anxiety inhibition effects. Thus, the scene was presented as follows:

"You are in the aircraft, you are completely relaxed, you are having
a drink, smoking and having an interesting conversation with your husband. You're sitting back in your seat and looking forward to the delicious
meal which the air hostess is about to serve." The patient was attached
to a GSR monitoring machine. At the third presentation, the machine
showed no response and the patient reported no anxiety. During the first
two presentations, the patient was not asked to stop imagining the scene
as soon as she reported anxiety or when autonomic reactions were shown
on the machine; but she was asked to continue imagining the scene
(while continuously being given suggestions of relaxation) until both the
machine and the patient indicated that the anxiety was becoming easier.
The rapidity of desensitization is attributed to the therapy carried out
prior to desensitization, in particular the teaching of new responses and

cognitions to the patient and the feeling that she could both understand and control the anxiety.

I feel that it is of the greatest importance that the patient realize that he is in control; that he perceive that he is not subject to mysterious uncontrollable forces, but that he has a choice and can choose his reactions to situations, circumstances and stimuli. In this respect my thinking has been particularly influenced by such "existential" writers as Frankl (1970), Sartre (1966), Vizinczey (1969), and by the work of Ellis (1962). Therefore, my patients are taught that it is not situations themselves which are "bad" or "catastrophic," rather it is the way they are perceived and reacted to that usually causes difficulty. For example: a patient with a panic reaction to tachycardia, because he fears dying of a heart attack, would be shown that it is his misperception of the tachycardia as dangerous and awful that is his problem and he can choose to react differently.

Before the patient left the consulting room, she was instructed to seek out all the previous phobic situations, such as elevators, crowded stores, cinemas, restaurants, initially with her husband, then alone; place herself in them and to do the following: to relax as taught, hold her breath if she hyperventilated, to tell herself to let it come, "I don't care, I can handle it, let it do its damndest I want to prove that nothing happens." Perhaps most important of all she was to remain in the situations until completely calm.

3rd session: She was seen two days later and reported that she had carried out her instructions, that she had been in a cinema and restaurant, had travelled innumerable times in elevators alone, and had been in several buses and crowded stores. Although there had been some initial anxiety in the bus and store situations, this had soon dissipated. She expressed disappointment that the cinema was not more crowded, but she had made a point of taking a seat in the middle of a row, not on the aisle. The husband confirmed her improvement. She was again praised for her determination. The session was devoted to further training in relaxation and desensitization to the aircraft phobia, which had been her major fear. During desensitization presentations, no anxiety to the scenes was reported by the patient or indicated on the GSR machine.

4th session: The patient was seen four days later, just prior to her departure, by plane, for Britain. She had maintained her improvement and was feeling no anticipatory anxiety whatsoever regarding the flight she was about to undertake. She reported, and her husband confirmed, that she had been in elevators, buses, crowded stores, in a restaurant and cinema, etc. without any anxiety or fear. She had had none of the psychosomatic symptoms, tension headaches, stomach cramps, tachycardia, had not hyperventilated or swollen up. The rest of the session was spent discussing the lessons she had been taught.

The patient wrote to me, the letter being received two weeks after she had left South Africa. She reported that she had had no difficulty at all during the flight home and that she had been completely free of her phobias. She had also been travelling on London subway trains—which she had not done for many years. Her latest report—now some four months after treatment—indicates that she is maintaining her improvement.

CASE 2. Mr. T., 39 years old, was referred for the treatment of an extremely debilitating obsessive-compulsive neurosis. His neurosis was of 12 years standing. He had undergone various treatments, such as psychoanalytically oriented therapy and E.C.T., both to no avail. He had been spending at least 50% of his waking time in carrying out various ritualistic and checking behaviors so that he was finally unable to work and had to resign his job as an advertising manager. These rituals consisted of (to mention a few): counting all his clothes in his cupboard, (shirts, socks, suits etc.) at least 12 times every morning and evening; constantly examining the clothes he wore in case they were stained or marked (this would take up to half an hour at a time); checking the walls and furniture of his house to see whether they were marked or dirty; checking his car before he could drive it to make sure that it was absolutely clean and that the tools in the trunk were arranged in a certain order; inventing elaborate codes to remind himself not to forget to check; he would have to check through his wallet at least twice a day (for at least 20 minutes at a time) to see and count that it contained all that it was supposed to; checking and arranging the contents of the drawers of his office desk in a certain order. He was unable to tear himself away from light switches, door handles etc.; he felt compelled to constantly remind himself of all outstanding debts he owed and kept repeating certain codes to himself in order not to forget. In addition, he felt compelled to write down every single task he had to do, no matter how minor, and to keep constantly referring to this list. He then constructed a second identical list to check on the first. When the task was completed, it had to be deleted in a particular manner. He also suffered from obsessive-compulsive ruminations such as thinking he would do ridiculous things in public. He had also over the previous 7 years developed an obsession and fear about choking, so that he found it difficult to eat or drink as he became extremely anxious and in trying to force himself to swallow had produced a state of globus hystericus. He found it difficult to cross a road as he thought he might choke when halfway across it. His only help lay in alcohol.

According to an holistic theory, the obsessive behavior would be conceptualized as a learned habit, reinforced because it reduced basic autonomically conditioned fear and also anxieties caused by "catastrophic" cognitions. Most writers (Walton and Mather, 1963; Eysenck, 1960; Haslam, 1965; Wolpe, 1964) stress treatment of "underlying anxiety or autonomic drive"—but this appears too narrow a view (Jacobs, 1967). It would in this case have meant desensitization to innumerable hierarchies (dirt on walls, untidyness, forgetting to pay bills, drinking, eating, crossing roads etc.). Since the patient's compulsive behavior was making life intolerable for himself and his wife and was preventing him from working, it was decided first to concentrate attention on the elimination of these compulsive habits.

The first session was devoted to case history and the giving of reassurance. The next two sessions were devoted largely to discussing the various obsessions, which were listed by the therapist. The patient was then (during the third session) instructed to cease carrying out all the obsessive behavior. He was told that it would be difficult at first, but that if he resisted the desire to carry out the obsessive behavior, it would weaken as the habits weakened (the paradigm of extinction through nonreinforcement had been explained to him). Each obsession which had been listed was dealt with and he was given very specific instructions as to what to do, e.g. obsession 1 on the list was "counting shirts in my cupboard every morning and evening"—he was told to go to his cupboard only to take a shirt out and never to count. His attitude was, "I will do it if you tell me to."

When he came for the next treatment session, he reported that he had been able to desist from carrying out his obsessive acts although sorely tempted to and initially made anxious by nonperformance. He had, however, rapidly found a diminution in the desire to carry them out and was already feeling much better. He delivered over to the therapist all the lists and codes he had previously so carefully made and which governed his life. These were destroyed in front of him. He was then instructed to deliberately set about doing the very things he had so feared and which his obsessions were meant to obviate, until they no longer bothered him. Thus he was instructed to mark the walls or furniture, to deliberately make small stains on some of his clothes, to untidy his desk and car. It was felt that this would be *in vivo* desensitization of the anxiety caused by these stimuli.

The next session was devoted to cognitive reorganization. In particular it was felt important to correct his "internalized sentences," which themselves were a major cause of anxiety maintaining his obsessive behavior. Thus he was asked, "So what if your suit has a stain on it, or you forget to pay a bill, etc."? His "catastrophic sentences" were constantly challenged until he was made to state that it did not matter that the wall had a small mark on it, that it was not the end of the world if he lost a shirt, etc. He was also taught thought stopping to control his obsessive-compulsive ruminations.

At the next session he reported a very strong diminution in all the obsessive behavior, save that of his choking obsession, in spite of the fact that he had not been avoiding crossing roads or eating and drinking. He had, in fact, found it very difficult to eat and (as he had done for many years) he had avoided lunch and taken a great deal of time over breakfast and dinner (which he was only able to consume after vast quantities of beer). He was relaxed and desensitization was begun.

It should be noted that finely calibrated hierarchies were not drawn up. Instead the situations in which the choking response was present were listed (there were six such situations) and the patient desensitized to these. The GSR monitoring apparatus was also used as described above. It would have been extremely difficult to construct hierarchies as the patient tended to react in an all-or-none manner and the amplitude of his choking responses seemed to be equally intense, whenever it occurred. Further, it has been my practice to commence desensitization to situations as high up on the hierarchy as possible. This means that desensitization is begun not with the item of lowest anxiety evocation, but rather to the item of highest anxiety tolerable to the patient. Of course, cognizance is taken of the possibility that if the anxiety is too overwhelming desensitization might not be possible (but cf. Stampfl's Implosion Therapy). However, using the GSR machine and the patient's subjective reports, it is usually possible to assess, after a few presentations, whether the anxiety response to the particular visualization is being reduced. If not, a lower item is presented. In this way, desensitization can be both speeded up and simplified.

The patient was also instructed to practice relaxation whenever eating, drinking or crossing roads. Using the technique of paradoxical intention, he was (after the desensitization) given a glass of water to drink and told to try as hard as possible to make himself choke—which he was quite unable to do. He was instructed to try to choke at least 3 times a day. It can be seen that although the autonomic anxiety factors in this "choking obsession" were particularly strong and had been treated by desensitization, the behavioral aspect was also treated (he was instructed not to avoid eating, etc., as he had done, and by carrying out paradoxical intention thrice daily he was indeed changing his behavior). In addition the paradoxical intention implies a different attitude of "let it happen." He was, of course, reassured that it was impossible for him to choke.

The next few sessions were devoted to further anxiety reduction techniques and the use of paradoxical intention. The patient was also invited to lunch with the therapist on each visit as an *in vivo* desensitization. By the 12th session the patient was able to report the complete disappearance of his former obsessions. He no longer had difficulty in eating, swallowing, drinking, crossing roads, had no desire to carry out any of his rituals, checking, etc., and was not troubled by his obsessive compulsive behaviors. The patient subsequently began work again and at present, after a three-month follow up, has remained completely well.

CASE 3. Mr. N., 37 years of age, desired to overcome homosexuality. He had been receiving psychoanalytically oriented psychotherapy for some years without apparent change. He had been married for 12 years, was the father of three children but had no desire for sexual relations with his wife. He most often avoided this, and only had physical contact "out of duty" to her. He was otherwise happy with her as a person. He had married in order "to cure himself." He was a school teacher and obsessed with thoughts of indulging in mutual masturbation with his male pupils. He would very frequently have homosexual relations with males whom he picked up in bars and at parties. He also frequently masturbated with homosexual fantasies. He had two years previously declared his homosexuality to his wife and the marriage was in the process of breaking up (the wife had promised to remain with him for as long as he was receiving therapy).

An holistic approach is particularly useful in the treatment of homosexuality. A perusal of most reports in the literature, describing the use of various aversion therapies, indicates that the therapists are conditioning aversion or avoidance to only the external manifestations, behavior and stimuli associated with the homosexuality, but that the internal homosexual drive or desire is left untouched, as is the patient's attitude to women and his thoughts and fantasies about hetero- and homosexuality. This comes from seeing homosexual behavior as a conditioned response or habit to external stimuli, rather than as a response to an inner need, desire or tension. It is much the same as forgetting the fact that a conditioned salivary response to a bell can only occur if the experimental animal is hungry or wants food.

An holistic theory would propound that there are three aspects of homosexual behavior: the first an autonomic drive or desire, the second homosexual acts and habits, and thirdly the homosexual fantasies. If only the second aspect is treated, e.g., an avoidance response conditioned to certain classes of men and specific sexual acts, it is quite possible that the patient may still become aroused by other classes of men or male sexual stimuli as his basic drive or desire remains strong. It is noteworthy that aversion therapists have generally obtained poor results in treating homosexuality (Feldman, 1966).

Using a 3-factor approach, the writer adopted the following aversion/avoidance conditioning procedure for treating homosexuality. At each therapy session the patient is given 10 conditioning trials (using a classical conditioning paradigm to "suppress" the autonomic drive), 10 trials (using an operant avoidance conditioning technique, as described by Feldman and McCullough [1965], to condition an avoidance/aversion response to the external homosexual acts and stimuli) and 10 conditioning trials (using the patient's fantasies as the CS) to deal with the cognitive aspect of the problem. In the first instance, the electrodes of the transfaradic unit having been attached to his forearm, the patient is asked to visualize homosexual acts (which for him are most arousing) and may be shown pictures of naked men, whom he finds to be arousing. When and only if the patient becomes aroused, excited, "worked up" or reacts to his visualizations, he signals to the therapist, whereupon an unpleasant shock is delivered to his forearm and maintained until the patient signals a complete disappearance of the arousal or desire. The procedure is repeated 10 times. Then, with an approach based on Feldman and McCullough (Jacobs, 1969b) the patient is given 10 conditioned avoidance trials. Briefly a picture of naked men or even the words "think of homosexual sex" are projected onto a screen, which the patient is observing. Exactly 8 seconds thereafter, a shock is delivered to the patient's forearm if he does not attempt to avoid the shock by pushing the switch on a control box in front of him. If the patient receives shock, by pushing the switch he removes the picture from the screen and terminates the shock. If he pushes it before the 8 seconds have elapsed, he is allowed to avoid 40% of the time (i.e. as soon as he switches off, the picture disappears and he knows he will not receive shock), he is delayed 40% of the trials (i.e. the picture does not disappear immediately, but after 4 seconds, although he does receive a shock) and on 20% of the trials he is not allowed to avoid and is shocked (i.e. in spite of his switching off, the picture remains illuminated and he is shocked 4 seconds after attempting to avoid). In order to treat the "cognitive" aspect (the patient's usual homosexual fantasies), a stimulus card with the word "fantasy" is used as the CS in the apparatus instead of the pictures of naked men. On being presented with this stimulus, the patient is instructed to bring to mind his usual homosexual fantasies and is shocked until the fantasy disappears.

Mr. N. was treated as follows:

Session 1: Devoted to case history. N. seemed well motivated and was given reassurance.

Session 2: N. and his wife were counselled as regards improving their sexual relationship. In particular it was stressed to Mrs. N. that she should try to understand her husband's problem and that she could help him overcome it by reassuring him that she did not demand any particular criterion of sexual performance from him. Mr. N. had always been tense when love-making with his wife as he had felt that he had to prove his masculinity to her and at least satisfy her. Wolpe's (1958) method of *in vivo* desensitization for impotence was explained to them and they were encouraged to have some form of sexual contact as often as possible. They were told to have long love-play periods and that Mr. N. should only do what gave him pleasure; they were to experiment sexually and not to have intercourse unless N. had a strong desire for it. Mrs. N. agreed to cooperate, to make no demands on her husband and to "let her hair down." N. was told not to try to do well. They were both reassured that the patient was merely suffering from a strong "bad" sexual habit rather than a disease and that with mutual help and understanding he would be able to overcome it. The wife was told that she had to help him learn to like sex with her.

Mr. N. was very strongly instructed not to masturbate (he masturbated at irregular intervals) with male-homosexual images and fantasies;
but was told to force heterosexual fantasies into his mind whenever he
masturbated. He was also taught thought stopping in order to block out
homosexual fantasies whenever he thought of them. The writer feels
that unless these steps are taken the patient will merely re-establish his
homosexuality in the real life situation in spite of any treatment procedures. The elimination of homosexual thoughts and the substitution of
female thoughts is considered essential in the successful treatment of the
problem. This is regarded by the writer as part of the cognitive aspect
of the problem.

The following 4 sessions (at weekly intervals) were spent in carrying
out aversion and avoidance conditioning, as described above. After 2
such sessions, the patient reported a "complete loss of interest in my
own sex." He and his wife had been carrying out the instructions given
to them and he was able to report a great improvement in his sexual relationships with his wife (confirmed by her); in particular he was both
discussing and enjoying sex with her much more than he had ever done.
By the 4th session he stated that he felt "completely cured." There was
no desire for homosexual activities, he no longer felt attracted to men
(he was able to walk in the street without being attracted to any of the
male passers-by) and he no longer had homosexual thoughts, fantasies
or dreams. His sexual life with his wife was "good." They were having
intercourse 3-4 times a week and he was obtaining full satisfaction.
Therapy was terminated at this point. The patient was last seen, some
7 months after this date, for a follow-up visit with his wife, when they
both stated that he had maintained his improvement.

The rapidity of treatment in the three above cases is attributed to
the application of the "holistic" approach. Effective therapy should be
rapid; slow improvement, as typified by psychoanalysis, is slow precisely
because it is inefficient. For illustrative purposes I have selected three
cases with a traditionally negative prognosis who nevertheless responded
to direct therapeutic retraining quite spectacularly. The reader should
not be misled into assuming that the writer claims such dramatic results
for all of his cases. The point at issue is that a direct (and, in the writer's
opinion, total) attack on target symptoms employing the "holistic"
notion that feelings, thoughts and specific behaviors require specific attention is often extremely rapid and effective. One element in accounting
for such rapid and seemingly straightforward gains in the three cases

was their respective readiness for change. They had each reached a stage of life where they genuinely desired to effect fundamental changes. Nevertheless, it is my belief that a narrow behavioral approach or a purely interpretive therapy could not have achieved similar results despite the patients' apparent readiness for change. A further possible factor was the stress conveyed to the patients that they themselves could control, or choose to control, their symptoms by a change in their reactions, both motor and cognitive, to their problems.

Many therapists, when confronted by seemingly intractable phobic patients, obsessive-compulsive neurotics or homosexuals, convey an attitude of semi-hopelessness. Perhaps the writer's very firm belief that change (often rapid change) may be expected is a major contributing factor to his therapeutic results. It is hoped that this chapter will lend other therapists the temerity to apply direct, frontal and holistic behavioral methods to some of their more refractory cases.

More recent follow-up data is available for each of the three cases described. Case 1: I saw Mrs. K. and her husband (on a visit to London) 15 months after the termination of treatment. Both confirm that she has remained completely free of her previous symptoms. Case 2: Four months after cessation of treatment Mr. T. became depressed and was diagnosed as suffering from "endogenous depression." He did not respond to anti-depressant medication and was hospitalized. I saw him in hospital and he reported that he had remained free of his previous obsessions until he became depressed. As his depression deepened, he developed a host of debilitating obsessions, different from those for which he had been treated by me. In addition, his previous phobias had remained absent. Case 3: Twenty-two months after termination of treatment, Mr. N. reported that he had had no homosexual desire or fantasy whatsoever. His wife confirmed that intercourse was taking place frequently and "very satisfactorily."

REFERENCES

BUCHWALD, A. M., & YOUNG, R. D. (1969) Some Comments on the Foundations of Behavior Therapy, in Franks, C. M., *Behavior Therapy Appraisal and Status*, New York, McGraw-Hill.

ELLIS, A. (1962) *Reason and Emotion in Psychotherapy*, New York, Lyle Stuart.

EYSENCK, H. J. (1960) *Behaviour Therapy and the Neuroses*, Oxford, Pergamon Press.

EYSENCK, H. J .(1964) *Experiments in Behaviour Therapy*, Oxford, Pergamon Press.
FELDMAN, M. P. (1966) Aversion Therapy for Sexual Deviations: A Critical Review, *Psychol. Bull.* 65:65.
FELDMAN, M. P., & McCULLOUGH, M. J. (1965) The Application of Anticipatory Avoidance Learning to the Treatment of Homosexuality. 1. Theory, technique and preliminary results, *Behav. Res. Ther.* 2:165.
FRANKL, V. E. (1970) *Psychotherapy and Existentialism*, London, Souvenir Press.
FRANKS, C. M. (1964) *Conditioning Techniques in Clinical Practice and Research*, New York, Springer.
HASLAM, M. T. (1965) The treatment of an obsessional patient by reciprocal inhibition, *Behav. Res. Ther.* 2:213.
JACOBS, M. (1967) The Treatment of Obsessive-Compulsive Neuroses by Behaviour Therapy, *S. Afr. Med. J.*, 41:328.
JACOBS, M. (1969) Possible Aids in the Practice of Reciprocal Inhibition, *Medical Proceedings*, Vol. 15:365.
JACOBS, M. (1969b) The Treatment of Homosexuality, *S. Afr. Med. J.*, 43:1123.
JACOBSON, E. (1938) *Progressive Relaxation*, Chicago, Chicago University Press.
LAZARUS, A. A. (1971) *Behavior Therapy and Beyond*, New York, McGraw-Hill.
LAZARUS, A. A., & ABRAMOVITZ, A. (1962) The use of "emotive imagery" in the treatment of children's phobias, *J. Ment. Sci.* 108:191.
SARTRE, J. P. (1966) *Existential Psychoanalysis*, Chicago, Henry Regnery Company.
VIZINCZEY, S. (1969) *The Rules of Chaos*, London, Macmillan.
WALTON, D., & MATHER, M. (1963) The application of learning principles to the treatment of obsessive-compulsive states in the acute and chronic phases of illness, *Behav. Res. Ther.*, 1:163.
WOLPE, J. (1958) *Psychotherapy by Reciprocal Inhibition*, Stanford, Stanford University Press.
WOLPE, J. (1964) Behaviour therapy in complex neurotic states, *Brit. J. Psychiat.* 110:28.
WOLPE, J., & LAZARUS, A. A. (1966) *Behavior Therapy Techniques*, Oxford, Pergamon Press.

7

Personalistic Family and Marital Therapy

PHILIP H. FRIEDMAN, Ph.D.

THE LITERATURE ON BEHAVIORAL APPROACHES to family and marital therapy has been primarily confined to discussions of behavioral problems with children (Bernal, 1969; Hawkins et al., 1967; Lindsley, 1966; O'Leary, et al., 1967; Patterson, et al., 1968, 1970; Tharp and Wetzel, 1969; Wahler, 1969; Wahler, et al., 1965; Werry and Wollersheim, 1967) or between married couples (Knox and Madsen, 1969; Lazarus, 1968; Liberman, 1970). The approach has mainly consisted of attempts to modify behavior patterns in dyads with only occasional limited attempts to see the family as a complex social system composed of triads, tetrads, etc., with each component of the family system interacting with each other and having continuous feedback effects on the other components of the family system. The theoretical orientation for selecting techniques and conceptualizing problems has been predominantly learning theory and, more narrowly, operant learning theory. Consequently, a relatively restricted range of available interventions in families has been used. Depending upon the referral problem, the concern of the behavior therapist has usually been the deviant behavior of the child, or the disturbed or maladaptive behavior of one or both spouses. The major exception to the above statements has been the recent articles and book by Arnold Lazarus (1967, 1971).

The orientation of the present author is somewhat different from most of the above authors. A broad and flexible approach to intervention techniques is espoused. Therefore, a wide variety of behavioral interventions are used drawn from therapists of many different theoretical orientations. The conceptualization of family and marital problems is an evolving one based empirically on the author's observation of families and also on the groundwork provided by many other observers of family malfunction (Ackerman, 1966; Beels and Ferber, 1970; Framo, 1970; Haley, 1963; Minuchin et al., 1967; Nagy and Framo, 1965; Satir, 1964; Watzlawick, Beavin and Jackson, 1967; Zuk, 1966, 1969). The author, for example, has observed the maladaptive influence of members of three generations of one family toward the disturbed behavior of a child, a spouse or a grandparent. Moreover, the author has observed that, when one member of a family is referred for a behavior problem, between 60% and 80% of the family members demonstrate behavioral problems of their own within two family interaction sessions. This means, for example, that when a family of five is referred for treatment because of a depressed wife or a highly aggressive son, an additional two or three family members are observed to have behavioral difficulties within two sessions, such as underachievement in school, psychosomatic problems, (ulcers, stomach pains, muscle spasms, asthma) impotence or frigidity, suicidal thoughts and feelings, alcoholism, poor peer relationships, difficulty in holding a job, inability to give affection or assert oneself, etc. This suggests, furthermore, an orientation which shows concern for the problems, worries, and dysfunctional or maladaptive behavior of all family members. An attempt is made to improve the behavioral relationships of all members of the nuclear and extended family with each other and often with friends, work associates and neighbors.

The personalistic family therapist uses not only a broad spectrum of behavioral interventions, and a system oriented three generational conceptualization of family problems (Bowen, 1966; Haley, 1967) but also tries to develop a personal relationship with each family member which respects his individual behavioral style, values, beliefs, and cognitions.

He may try to modify each family member's attitudes and the family based attitudes and myths but he does so with compassion and empathy. He considers it an asset to reveal many of his beliefs, desires, feelings, strengths and weaknesses to the family. His purpose is both to serve as a model to the family and to share his role in his own family with them.

WHAT IS THE FAMILY PURCHASING? WHAT IS THE THERAPIST SELLING?

The most obvious answer to the first part of the question is that the family is purchasing a contract with the family therapist to alleviate the symptoms, behavior problems or malfunctions of the person labelled by the family as the patient. Some parents will indicate that no one besides the labelled patient has problems, or dysfunctional or annoying behaviors. However, the therapist and his assistants, if he has any, make observations of their own as to the problems, concerns and interpersonal maladaptive behavior patterns in the family. In many cases the perceptions of the family members and the therapist differ when it comes to defining the basic difficulties in the family. For example, in Family A the parents indicated that their 15-year-old son was frequently truant from school and underachieving but that there were no difficulties with their youngest son or themselves. The therapist, with the help of the 15-year-old son, observed that the parents fought constantly, that the husband ignored his wife's complaints for more affection, a different house and greater occupational efforts by her husband. In addition, the wife had frequent stomach distress and appeared notably depressed. The therapist perceived a marital struggle in these parents in which the mother and father were mutually disappointed that their respective spouse hadn't lived up to their expectations. Also, Mrs. A felt extremely competitive with her brothers who lived nearby but ignored her and Mr. A felt abandoned by his father.

In Family B, the parents also identified the children as the problem. The 12-year-old boy was depressed, confused and underachieving in school while the 11-year-old was having temper tantrums, hitting children at home and in school and threatening to throw himself out the window. These two boys fought constantly with their three brothers and one sister, ranging in age from 4 to 13. The parents spoke with outrage about their own parents but denied any difficulty between them, which the children initially agreed with. The therapist perceived, however, that Mr. B was deeply hurt that his wife failed to appreciate the highly skilled and theoretical nature of his job and that he was blamed for being aloof and uninvolved in family life. Mrs. B was resentful of the lack of affection she received from her husband and of being constantly misunderstood by him.

In Families A and B the family may want to purchase less than the therapist wants to sell them. The therapist may want to sell the parents an improved marital relationship, a different set of interpersonal behaviors with their own parents and a new pattern of behaving with their children. The therapist must first decide whether to adhere to a "limited contract intervention" such as selling the family only behavioral changes in the children. It is the author's belief that it is advantageous to the family members in the long run for the family therapist to be concerned about and try to sell all the family members a comprehensive regimen aimed at alleviating their own problems and modifying their broader behavior patterns even if the family members do not acknowledge that they have problems in these other areas. Moreover, even if the family therapist were to accept a more limited goal, he might believe from empirical observation that change in the labelled patient will not be as effective, rapid or as durable unless parts or all of the three generational system of family behavior patterns are modified.

Whom does the family therapist see during therapy sessions? What constellations of family members are seen during family treatment? Broadly speaking, the family therapist will see children, parents, grandparents, unmarried siblings living away from home, married siblings and their spouses, relatives, boy friends or girl friends, neighbors, school teachers, counselors, principals, theologians, and welfare workers at various times with different families. He may see an individual, the married couple, the siblings, the nuclear family, and the three-generational family including children, parents and grandparents. He may see any of these constellations of family members alone or with other couples or family groups. For example, while the author may see two or three families simultaneously, including parents and children, Patterson (1970) sees couple groups and Lindsley (1966) sees parent groups, i.e. fathers. Moreover, various combinations of family members may be seen at different times. For example, in Family C, the 28-year-old divorced daughter was seen alone for several months, then she and her sister were seen together, and then she was seen with her mother and father for a few months. In family D, the wife was seen alone for six sessions and then the wife and husband were seen for 14 sessions with a child included on occasion.

In Family E the husband was seen alone once. Then the husband, wife and two children were seen twice and finally the husband, wife, two children and grandmother (who lived with them) were seen for 15 sessions. In most cases, however, the nuclear family consisting of mother, father and children are seen regularly in family sessions.

The decision as to who should attend family sessions and when and where they should take place is a complex one. The personalistic approach respects the desires of family members. However, family members may not only differ as to the problems they perceive in the family, they may also differ as to who should be present in family sessions, and when and where they ought to take place. The therapist may agree with one, two, all or none of the family members concerning these decisions, depending on his assessment of the family difficulties. In addition, grandparents, relatives, friends, neighbors, school counselors, teachers, welfare workers, judges and other professionals may all have their own views as to which family members should attend meetings. Moreover, a grandmother may be willing to meet with the family and therapist in the parent's home but not in the therapist's office.

The only rule that can be given is that the family therapist must decide for himself as to what seems most likely to help a particular family and then negotiate with the family members and other members of their ecological environment. The personalistic family therapist respects the differing views of the family members, their ecological network and his own professional judgment and competence. Eventually, through negotiation, persuasion and discussion, a contract is made between family members and the therapist as to who should attend sessions, when, where and how frequently. This negotiated contract between therapist and family is similar in many ways to the contracts between teachers and children and parents and children discussed by Homme (1969), Patterson et al. (1968) and Tharp and Wetzel (1969).

PERSONAL RELATIONSHIP WITH EACH FAMILY MEMBER

Although a personal relationship with the labelled patient is taken for granted, it is just as important for the family therapist to show concern and empathy for other family members because they also may be in emotional distress and may exhibit maladaptive family behavior patterns. Even if other family members do not demonstrate these difficulties, the therapist nevertheless displays compassion and concern to the entire family. It is particularly important that he do so in the initial interviews because later he may want to confront a family member with the consequences of his behavior on another family member. This confrontation is likely to be perceived as moderately aversive to the family member unless the therapist has preceded it with empathic statements that are reacted to in a positive way. For example, in one family a 30-year-old Negro mother came in with her three children. The 17-year-old daughter had just been released from the hospital after attempting suicide by taking an overdose of sleeping pills. The 15-year-old daughter was roaming around the room, ignoring the conversation, complaining about coming, and writing on the blackboard. The mother revealed that she had been pregnant at age 12 and 14, never married, put herself through high school and 2 years of college while working at a bar and worked 16 hours a day. Her urgent tone of voice, and tense facial expression indicated that she was overburdened and under tremendous stress herself. These nonverbal behaviors as well as the frowns and grimaces she made to her 15-year-old daughter were used by the therapist as cues that the mother was depressed and needed some relief from family pressures herself. When this was pointed out to her in a quiet reassuring tone of voice, the mother cried and reached over to touch the therapist's arm. After crying, her facial expression and verbalization indicated that she felt considerable relief.

In the second interview the therapist pointed out to this mother that due to her resentments she never really listened to what her 17-year-old daughter had to say, and that her 15-year-old daughter appeared to be no less defiant and distressing to her than the 17-year-old. Moreover, the therapist noted that the mother herself failed to speak up and tell her own sister, who was older than she and lived upstairs, that she was annoyed with her or that she wanted her sister to stop interfering in her family's affairs. It was pointed out to the mother that she presented a poor model to her daughters if she wanted them to communicate frank and open feelings to her. When the consequences of the mother's behavior were pointed out to her, she initially reacted as if she had been presented with a mildly aversive stimulus. However, if the therapist had not preceded these statements with some empathic and positively reassuring ones she would most likely have perceived them as moderately to extremely aversive and might have withdrawn emotionally and behaviorally from any constructive interaction with her daughters.

The personalistic family therapist uses a wide variety of therapeutic approaches, techniques and strategies with families. Moreover, he tailors the techniques to meet the unique needs of each family.

Relabeling, Cognitive Restructuring and Reconceptualizing Family Behavior Patterns

The family therapist tries to be a perceptive observer of family interaction. He uses a wide range of cues, both verbal and nonverbal, of all family members to organize what he observes into a coherent pattern. Through his previous empirical observation of many other families and the observation of other therapists, he skillfully learns to elicit behavior patterns and affects that would ordinarily be unobservable in the clinical setting. He is particularly attuned to sequences of behavior patterns between three or more family members that occur repetitively.

Eventually the family therapist labels the interactional sequence for the family. His goal is to help the family members to focus on the sequential patterns of behavior occurring in the family. Through repeated labeling by the therapist and other procedures such as charting, graphing and audio and videotape playback, the family members learn to discriminate what is happening in their family from a random series of events. In many families they develop a more accurate, less distorted set of perceptions of family interaction. This new capacity to discriminate more accurately enables them to begin to engage in a new set of behaviors in reaction to the behavioral cues put forward by other family members. In doing so they also emit a new set of behavioral cues. This is the beginning of a more adaptive and satisfying pattern of behaving in the family for all members.

For example, in one family a fairly typical sequence of family interaction occurred whenever the mother was talking about something of concern to her. Then the father would interrupt her. The mother would look irritated and tell him to stay out of the conversation because she had not finished talking. The husband would show a hurt and resentful expression on his face, and turn away from her. He would then look at the 11-year-old "aggressive son" referred for treatment, snap his fingers at him and in a harsh tone of voice demand that the son stop what he was doing and move rapidly over to the couch and sit near his 13-year-old brother. The 11-year-old son would sulk and resentfully comply. Then he would look at his 13-year-old brother scornfully, and lightly hit him on the arm. This provocation would set off the 13-year-old who would hit his brother back. Within 30 seconds the two brothers would be hitting, clawing and screaming at each other. The parents would then temporarily unite. The mother would get very upset and turn to her husband to discipline the boys. He would scream at them and harshly punish one or both of them. The mother would turn on her husband and criticize and insult him for being so ineffective and punitive with the boys. This sequence would occur with minor variations many times. After this sequence was pointed out to the family, the 13-year-old mentioned that at home his mother often insulted his father, who "buries his anger toward her and then takes it out on us." By labelling this sequence on a number of occasions, the therapist taught the parents that the disruptive, aggressive behavior of their sons was a consequence of their own maladaptive behavioral patterns. The next step was for the parents to learn how to resolve their own marital problems so that their anger at each other was not directed at their children.

In another family the grandmother would criticize her 29-year-old married son, who lived with her, for being irresponsible, that is, not working regularly. Whenever the son expressed hurt or annoyance at his dead father, his mother started blaming her son for his irresponsibility, and heavy drinking. He in turn criticized his wife for being inadequate as a mother because she was always so tired, didn't help out around the house and let his mother discipline and comfort their one- and three-year-old children. The son's wife would then meekly criticize the grandmother for being too domineering with her and disapproving of her son. As the sequence continued the grandmother would defensively state that her son, who was adopted, was given the best home environment anyone could reasonably expect. The son would point out that his mother wasn't very affectionate or approving of him and that his father drank heavily as far back as he could recall. This would be denied vigorously by his mother. She would then withdraw all affection from her son, nonverbally as well as verbally, calling him ungrateful and a liar. The son, would become increasingly infuriated at his mother and wife, and would withdraw and pout. Subsequently he would drink heavily and be criticized by his mother and wife for it. He would then drink even more heavily and go out and smash up the car. This repetitive behavioral sequence was described and labelled by the therapist, and the behavioral pattern leading to the son's heavy drinking and car accidents were reconceptualized for the family. In this way the family therapist helped the family members re-construct the chain of behavioral events leading to extremely maladaptive behavior in one or more members. This cognitive reconstruction permitted the therapist, and later the family members, to constructively intervene into the dysfunctional chain of events at an early stage.

Sometimes what appears to the family to be maladaptive or annoying behavior is labelled by the therapist as adaptive or considerate behavior. For example, in one family, whenever the mother talked about the struggle between her husband and herself for attention and the right to make decisions, the 17-year-old daughter and later the 14-year-old daughter would interrupt, make loud noises, say something mean to her siblings or parents, or hit someone. When the parents were alone they could openly disclose to one another how they each felt threatened by any assertive behavior exhibited by either one of them toward the other or with their children. The parents could also discuss how they retaliated or withdrew in response to it. They were obviously somewhat uncomfortable discussing this area of their marital relationship when alone with the therapist and even more so when the 3 children, 2 girls and a 6-year-old boy, were present. However, whenever the parents began to seriously discuss their behavior and feelings toward each other in front of the children, the annoying, disruptive behavior of the children would intercede and distract the therapist and parents from continuing to discuss the marital problems. The so-called maladaptive behavior of the two children was labelled as considerate of the wishes of the parents not to discuss their marital prob-lems. Consequently, it was pointed out that the alarming behavior of their children served to reduce anxiety in the parents. Although the parents initially protested against the therapist's formulation, in ensuing weeks they reported that on numerous occasions they noticed that they did not have to confront each other with their feelings because of the disruptive behavior of one of their children. Although they felt relieved when this happened, because a marital struggle was avoided, they became pro-gressively aware that this was an unsatisfactory way to resolve their difficulties with each other.

In another family, the 50-year-old husband's vulgar language, temper tantrums and abusive behavior at home were labelled bizarre, dangerous, and almost psychotic by his 45-year-old wife who wondered whether he should be hospitalized. The therapist, however, observing that the wife was silently angry at recent events in the family and markedly depressed, labelled the husband's behavior as considerate and adaptive to his wife's need not to express her anger or to openly face up to her depression because of the anxiety it would generate in her. The husband became noticeably less tense and the wife more uncomfortable when this reconceptualization was presented to the couple. Placing the husband's behavior in a new frame of reference (Haley, 1963) in itself helped to reduce his abusiveness and vulgarity. Also the marital couple's new cognitive set toward the husband's behavior permitted them to explore further their behavior and feelings toward each other and to experiment with more effective ways to deal with marital stresses.

Behavioral Feedback and Interpersonal Consequences

The personalistic family therapist uses a variety of methods to give family members feedback on how they interact with each other. He attempts to help each family member perceive the consequences of his own behavior on the other family members as well as the effects that other family members have upon him. Furthermore, it is also useful for family members to learn to evaluate their reactions, internally and externally, to the ongoing interaction between two or more other family members. The therapist can provide his own verbal and affective feedback to the family by his comments, gestures and facial expressions. Moreover, he can arrange for feedback to be presented via roleplaying, audiotape, videotape or frequency charts.

In order to provide feedback, the therapist may not have to relabel a behavior sequence, but just point out to a mother that although she says she wants her daughter to speak up more, her tone of voice when she says it is harsh and aversive. Or a husband may be told that the way he verbally expresses affection to his wife is unconvincing because of the frown on his face, the sarcastic tone of voice and indirect body posture. Thus, one major area of feedback occurs when the therapist points out the discrepancy between a family member's verbal statements and his non-verbal behavior.

Another opportunity for the therapist to provide feedback occurs when one family member behaves inconsistently toward another family member. For example, a father may comment on how attractive his daughter's dress is but ignore the talented art work which is more important to her than her dress. A wife may approve of her husband's occupational endeavors but criticize his sexual performance even though she says she always says positive things about her husband. A mother may request that her daughter express her feelings and opinions but change the topic or disagree with her as soon as she does. In addition the therapist may give feedback to any family member who inaccurately labels his own behavior or affect. Thus, in one family a mother talked about her own father whom she visited over the weekend. She said she enjoyed the visit and felt good about her talk with her father. However, her facial expression looked very sad and unhappy. When she was provided with this feedback, she initially denied being sad. Later she admitted that she felt like screaming at her father because she was so mad at him for criticizing her children, although she could never tell him this. Interestingly, the 7-year-old daughter had asked for permission to scream at the beginning of the session.

The goal of providing feedback of this sort is to increase the congruence between a family member's verbal and non-verbal behavior and between his verbal behaviors toward a family member at two different times or in two different situations. Lack of congruence in a family member's behaviors decreases his ability to be perceived as predictable by other family members. This causes confusion and conflict for other family members and elicits stressful reactions in them. Furthermore, it makes it almost impossible for them to respond consistently in return.

Feedback can also be given via roleplaying procedures. In one family, for example, the children were asked to play the roles of their parents while the parents played the roles of the children. In their new role the children screamed at their parents, chided them and hit them for misbehaving. The parents perceived for the first time how punitive they appeared to their children and how intensely their children felt about it. By playing the role of their children, the parents could see themselves withdrawing and not wanting to speak up, just as their children did when they screamed at them. The children also learned how difficult it was for their parents to put them to bed at night when they giggled and fought with each other. In this case, both the parents and children learned something about the consequences of their behavior on each other. Also the parents and children learned something about the consequences of each other's behavior on themselves. When each played his own role, the parents discovered that the children's foolishness in the bedroom could easily get them irritated at each other and provoke a fight between them. The children learned how exasperating it was to them to have their parents make such indecisive, sporadic attempts to back up their requests for a change in behavior by the children.

Feedback can also be administered by audio or videotapes. In one family a 37-year-old mother saw herself in the videotape and responded with disgust. "I look just like my mother and hate it," she remarked. In another family, the father saw himself on videotape and said that he never realized before just how timid, frightened and withdrawn he looked when amongst his family. After seeing himself, he became extremely motivated to change his behavior. Roleplaying and videotape feedback can be combined. In one family the father was seen alone for a session and a scene was roleplayed in which the 50-year-old father had a conversation with his own father, a 92-year-old man who would be visiting him that weekend. The father was attempting to express his desire to have his own father refrain from constantly prescribing medical remedies for his son's walking difficulty. When the taperecording of the roleplayed sequence was played back to the father, he remarked that he was much more hesitant and ineffective when talking to his father than he had imagined.*

Feedback can also be provided by charting or graphing the number of times a parent engages in a certain behavior to a child or to a spouse. In one family, for example, the 13-, 12-, 11- and 9-year-old children were asked to keep individual records of the number of times each parent praised them or said something positive or reassuring to them for some behavior they did. The four boys were also asked to count the number of times each parent praised the other parent. The data a week later indicated that for the first two days the boys received no more than three compliments apiece from their father and one to six from their mother. They also indicated, (by writing it down), however, that most of the compliments were bribes or had been said sarcastically. The boys were so discouraged by the minimally positive feedback that they stopped recording after two days. However, they did report unanimously that they saw no instance of their parents complimenting each other except when their father told their mother that he liked her cooking. This information from the boys led to a discussion of the parents' inability to express affection and praise to each other or to their children and how they might try to change their behaviors.

In other situations the therapist may keep a record of how many times a mother praises her son when he behaves properly, or how many times she ignores his temper tantrums, or hits him or screams at him

---

* Editor's note: For a comprehensive treatment of the use of videotape, see, *Videotape Techniques in Psychiatric Training and Treatment*, M. M. Berger, Editor, New York: Brunner/Mazel, 1970.

for misbehaving. The therapist then shows her the frequency chart or graph, which serves as feedback to her of her behaviors in certain situations. The information received from the feedback can later serve as a cognitive cue to the parent to behave differently.

One difficulty that can occur when a family member counts the behaviors of another family member in response to them is that the recorded frequency of positive feedback may be so low that it is aversive to the family member recording, and he may engage in some withdrawal or retaliatory behavior before the next session with the therapist. For example, a 29-year-old husband agreed to stop drinking if his wife recorded every day that she did not smell alcohol on his breath, and his mother (who lived with him) and his wife gave him some praise each day for not drinking. The husband was going to record the number of times his mother praised him. This contract was agreed to by the husband, wife and mother and negotiated by the therapist. The contract broke down when the wife failed to record the number of days the husband did not drink and the mother failed to praise him. When the husband recorded no checks for praise from his mother, he was extremely upset, and angry at her. He left home, got drunk and got in trouble with the law, all before the next meeting with the therapist. This was a considerable setback to the progress which had already been achieved in this family. It was not until after the husband was released from jail that the meaning of the mother's and wife's neglect was able to be discussed with the family.

Feedback can also be given to other families in multiple family therapy and, of course, by one family member to another. For example, a mother upon observing a mother from another family screaming at her 7-year-old son when he fell backward off a chair said to her, "I scream and holler at my children when I'm frightened, too." Not only did this statement provide feedback to the mother who screamed and to all members of her family that she was really scared and not angry, but it also provided feedback in a way that could be easily accepted.

DIRECT INTERVENTIONS

The family therapist directly intervenes into the ongoing maladaptive family behavior patterns in a number of ways. One way he does so is by interrupting a sequential chain of family behaviors at an early stage and by indicating the insidious ways in which repetitive behaviors can become self-defeating. He may ask the family members to change the pattern by engaging in a new set of behaviors. He may change the sequence himself by redirecting the conversation to another family member or back to the family members who are the initial links in the chain. For example, in one family the husband was angrily telling his wife that he wanted to be number one in the family when it came to receiving the attention and companionship of his wife. He felt his two daughters were favored by his wife. His wife complained that he was "nasty" to her and to her daughters and she did not like the way he treated them. The 28-year-old depressed daughter, who often asserted that her parents were incapable of changing, burst into the conversation by blaming her mother for not being sufficiently devoted to her father. Typically, mother and daughter would start a verbal battle at this point and the father would be ignored. The therapist intervened by stopping the daughter from continuing, pointing out that the present battle was between her parents, that she was taking attention away from her father, and that the parents should continue the conversation in order to work out their marital problem. As it turned out, the father indicated that he was nasty to his wife and daughters because he felt neglected by his wife. Since the daughter's depression was partly based upon her feeling that it was hopeless to imagine her parents changing in any way and her marked irritation at her father's nastiness, the successful resolution of the parents' marital problem was beneficial not only to them but eventually to the daughter as well.

In another family, the mother would constantly talk about the inability of her husband to communicate with their 15-year-old daughter. However, on the numerous occasions when the therapist would ask the father to talk to his daughter, the mother would not even permit the father to say one word before she would start talking for her husband or for her daughter. It was necessary to stop the mother from continuing in order to permit the father to talk to his daughter. In another family, the 17-year-old wife would constantly criticize her 18-year-old husband from whom she was separated because she objected to his using drugs, to his going out with the boys all the time, and to his not wanting to take back their three-week-old child from a foster home. The therapist intervened by interrupting the wife when she started her attack again and by asking her to list all the positive qualities she saw in her "hippie" husband. She stated that he was a hard worker and economically dependable, sexually exciting and capable, and affectionate with her and with most children.

The therapist then asked her to give reasons why her husband might be reluctant to keep the baby and why he might prefer to give it up for adoption. She was able to say that her husband might be scared of the responsibility of having a child and unsure of whether he could be a good father. As a result of the wife being helped to focus on what she liked about her husband and upon what he might be afraid of instead of blaming him and condemning him, this young couple was able to reexpress the warmth and affection they felt for each other. Three weeks later they had reunited, and retrieved the baby from the foster home. Additional therapy taught the wife how to become even more perceptive and empathic concerning her husband's feelings and emotions.

In one family, a mother would frequently attack her 11-year-old daughter for being an irresponsible liar and thief and constantly starting fights. The mother usually labelled her daughter the "bad one" after the mother completed a long vitriolic harangue against her own punitive, irresponsible father. Her father had always ignored his daughter. Moreover, the mother's outbursts usually followed a visit to her own parents who lived nearby. It was necessary to interrupt the mother when she started castigating her 11-year-old daughter in order to redirect her back to talking about her intense anger toward her own father (the maternal grandfather). Later it became apparent that the maternal grandmother was an accomplice to the maternal grandfather's physically abusive behavior. When this became evident, the therapist intervened by redirecting the mother's comments toward her own mother. The stored-up anger that the mother felt toward her own mother (the maternal grandmother) was then expressed but with considerable anxiety. The mother was then encouraged to express her feelings directly toward her own mother and father rather than taking it out on her 11-year-old daughter.

In another family, a 55-year-old, overweight, mildly depressed mother on social security complained that there was no communication between her and her three sons, ages 23, 18 and 13. The mother's husband had died 10 years earlier and the mother appeared overburdened trying to raise and guide her active, highly talented and intelligent sons. In the initial sessions, however, the mother talked constantly and rapidly, hardly permitting any of her sons to talk. The therapist consistently stopped her and gently reminded her that her sons had something to say. The mother became easily upset, however, when any of her sons spoke up and complained that she was overprotecting them by restricting their hours out, fussing too much about what and when they ate, and with whom they associated. The mother would then complain about not having a husband around to guide her sons. Eventually, through the therapist's intervention, the 13-year-old would start talking about how he missed his father, whom he had hardly known, and about how rough it was for his mother without a husband. He would talk so rapidly and emotionally that it soon became almost impossible for his older brothers to talk. Consequently, the 13-year-old had to be stopped from talking so that his 23-year-old brother could talk. His 23-year-old brother would then talk resentfully about the way in which his mother held him responsible for his father's death. His mother and younger brother became upset when he expressed these feelings and attempted to cut off his communication to them. The therapist had to intervene on these occasions to maintain an open flow of communications among all the family members. It was not until the 23-year-old was absent for a few meetings, beginning with the tenth session, to coach the track team, that the 18-year-old son spoke up and expressed a range of opinions and feelings about various family members.

The foregoing examples illustrate the need for the therapist to intervene not only in the parent-grandparent subsystem, the marital subsystem, or the parent-child subsystem, but also in the sibling subsystem. Moreover, the therapist should be alert to the fact that family members can get anxious when other family members openly communicate their feelings and beliefs. When this occurs, family members will often try to reduce their own anxiety by cutting off the direct, forthright communications they verbally proclaim to desire. The therapist's judicious interventions help open these channels of communication, thereby fostering confrontations that lead to open, honest and more authentic relationships.

INDIRECT INTERVENTIONS

Assertive Training, Emotional Freedom, Sexual Liberation and Family Relationships

The family therapist can employ an indirect intervention when the behavior to be changed cannot be directly observed. This may occur for ethical or practical reasons. Sexual problems are one area where this is prominent. For example, a husband complained that, in addition to other marital and family problems, his wife was often frigid and he experienced premature ejaculation. Further exploration of this couple's sexual difficulty revealed that the previously observed maladaptive marital interactions had affected the couple's sex life as well. Both spouses vied for control over each other. When either spouse asserted himself by making a decision for the family or couple, the other became threatened. This applied to vacations, weekend activities, meals, and activities with the children, as well as sexual relations. The husband indicated that he did not like his wife reading in bed when he was sexually interested in her. He was afraid to do anything, however, because he felt that "she has a right to read if she wants." Moreover, on the few occasions that he meekly complained about her reading, she would get upset and say that she was tired and just wanted to read and go to sleep. The husband rarely told his wife that he was sexually excited and desirous of having sexual intercourse with her on these occasions. The wife, on the other hand, would tend to read in bed at night whenever the husband had asserted himself during the day with her or the children. She felt threatened by the control she perceived he had over her and the children and she withdrew from him. She then asserted herself in retaliation by stubbornly reading and refusing to get sexually involved. The husband felt resentful when she read because he could not satisfy his sexual desires. This pattern would occur for three to four weeks at a time. When the couple would finally have sexual relations, the wife stated that she felt obligated to first satisfy her husband. It was her "duty as a wife and woman." Consequently her husband would become highly sexually aroused when she manipulated his penis, while she remained relatively unaroused. They would then have intercourse and the husband would naturally ejaculate quickly. His wife indicated she did not relax until her husband had an orgasm. Then she was able to relax and let her husband masturbate her to orgasm.

In this situation the wife, who was involved in women's liberation activities, felt extremely guilty when asking her husband to engage in sexual foreplay with her for an extended period of time until she could become sexually aroused. Politically and socially this woman sought liberation for females. Sexually, however, she was afraid to liberate herself from oppressive sexual attitudes. The therapist pointed this out to the couple and openly disclosed his own values and attitudes toward sex. He indicated his belief that the wife had a right to request or strongly urge her husband to engage in considerable sexual foreplay with her. He pointed out that a woman has no obligation to satisfy her husband's sex drive first even if in her family women were expected to serve a domineering father. He told the husband that he should tell his wife when he was sexually interested in her and should take the book away from her if necessary. (Interestingly, the 17-year-old daughter had previously frustrated the father in monthly meetings with the three children by reading a book and not participating in the family discussion). He told the wife to discuss with her husband the behaviors he engaged in that were threatening to her. Moreover, he suggested that the wife should stimulate her husband less during foreplay activities so that he would not be as likely to ejaculate as rapidly during intercourse. The result was a remission of the premature ejaculation, an increased frequency of sexual intercourse, an increased number of orgasms by the wife during intercourse, a greater ability to discuss intimate problems, and a raise in self-esteem and pleasure by both husband and wife. Moreover, the wife said she became sexually aroused when her husband would take the book away from her even if it did make her slightly anxious. "He's more of a man when he does that," she said. She respected her husband more for being sexually more assertive. He, in turn, was pleased that she got sexually aroused more often and more intensely.

Since the therapist obviously could not observe the couple having sexual relations, the suggestions and instructions he gave them served as indirect interventions. He could intervene directly on the values and beliefs that the couple expressed toward sex but only indirectly on their sexual practice. The therapist had at an earlier meeting successfully encouraged the husband to take a book away from his daughter, and had successfully encouraged both the husband and wife to openly discuss other behaviors that threatened each of them. These direct interventions served a useful function in augmenting the execution of the indirect interventions.

In another family, a direct intervention was followed by a crucial indirect intervention. In this Negro family, the wife was seen five times individually for hypochondriacal complaints and depression. She had received hypnotic relaxation instructions for three sessions when she came to her next meeting extremely overwrought. While deeply relaxed she was asked to state at the count of ten what she was upset about. She said she was angry at her 6-year-old son's school teacher. After listening to her account, the therapist advised her to talk to the boy's teacher. Two days later she frantically called up to ask if her husband could be hospitalized. A conjoint appointment was scheduled during which the wife expressed considerable frustration with and resentment toward her husband. Over the course of a few weeks the husband in turn had numerous complaints to make about his wife, the most prominent of which revolved around her sexual inhibitions and unwillingness to sexually approach him. The wife wanted more help around the house, more time alone with her husband, outings together at the movies or weekend trips, and an unequivocal statement from her husband that he was faithful to her.

Over the course of 15 sessions the therapist engaged in numerous direct interventions to increase self-expression in both the husband and wife. He openly discussed sexual attitudes and values with the wife in the husband's presence and helped the couple negotiate for desirable behaviors from their spouse. The key intervention, however, was indirect since the wife had to be willing to sexually approach her husband, and engage in intense vocal sounds and rhythmic body movements before and during sexual intercourse. As the wife began to receive the attention and help she wanted from her husband, she started to become sexually less inhibited. He then paid more attention to his wife and was more helpful. Her sexual inhibitions were further reduced and her anger toward her husband abated. In addition, her depression lifted and she stopped having hypochondriacal complaints. Thereafter, the wife spoke proudly of her husband and he was delighted with his wife's sexual freedom.

THE USE OF TASKS AND ASSIGNMENTS

The personalistic family therapist assigns tasks to family members to help them assert themselves in family interactions, free themselves from emotional conflicts and develop improved interpersonal relationships with family members. In the two previous families discussed, this was done by assigning tasks centering around sexual problems and affection. Task assignments, however, can center around almost any conflict area. Often tasks are assigned that require one or more phone calls, letters or personal visits between family members, especially between parents and grandparents. Thus, a 50-year-old married man was encouraged to write a letter to his elderly father expressing hurt and annoyance at the constant demanding comments made by his father. A 45-year-old depressed woman was persuaded to write a letter to her mother inquiring about the problems encountered by her mother in her life. She was surprised to receive a letter, in return, particularly one that stated that perhaps the mother's mother hadn't given her daughter enough affection when she was a child.

A 30-year-old man and his wife were both assigned the tasks of making telephone calls and personal visits to their parents who lived within an hour's ride. The husband had never told his mother how much he cared about his stepfather whom she constantly berated, and his wife had never told her father to stop disciplining her own children harshly, and criticizing her for expressing her own beliefs. Both spouses successfully completed their assigned tasks with increased feelings of self-esteem. The wife, however, was unable to tell her father that she knew she was adopted even though he had never told her.

Frequently, a husband is assigned a task that a wife ordinarily does. For example, the husband is told to put the children to bed at night, to spend weekends playing baseball or working with the teenage boy, or to make a phone call to the child's teacher. In these cases the wife's task is to let her husband take the lead. This is often as difficult for the wife as being the leader is for the man. At other times, the couple may be assigned the task of going out alone together for dinner or a movie. A woman might be assigned the task of taking a vacation, or getting a job, or cooking dinner a certain way, or enrolling in an art appreciation course. After extensive discussion a husband might even be assigned the task of buying a new house long desired by his wife or a wife might be encouraged to get her tubes tied to prevent pregnancy.

Other assignments that can be made are reading certain books such as *The Intimate Enemy,* (Bach and Wyden, 1969) *Between Parent and Child* (Ginott, 1965) or *Living With Children* (Patterson and Gullion, 1968). These books give numerous examples of marital and parent-child problems and many clear-cut behavioral prescriptions on how to deal with them. In this sense they serve as verbal models for family members. One father, for example, after reading *Between Parent and Child* stated, "I never knew you could tell your children you were angry with them. I'd like to try that." A mother, after reading *Living With Children,* said she did not realize one should reward children for good behavior. She always thought children should just behave a certain way because they were supposed to. A young divorcée, after reading *The Intimate Enemy,* indicated that she would never have thought of talking about sexual conflicts with her husband, let alone having constructive fights for more sexual enjoyment. Other books that can be assigned include *The Angry Book,* (Rubin, 1969) or any of the various books by Albert Ellis such as *Sex Without Guilt,* (1965).

PERSONALISTIC ASPECT OF TECHNIQUES AND INTERVENTIONS

No technique nor intervention is administered in a vacuum. Every time the family therapist engages in the cognitive restructuring of a family behavior sequence, or provides feedback to family members, or directly intervenes into an interaction pattern or assigns a task to a family, the family members react in very personal and highly idiosyncratic ways. Many of the reactions of the family members to the therapist on these occasions replicate long standing patterns of behavior in the nuclear or extended family (as previously observed by the family therapist). Other reactions of the family members to the therapist's interventions reflect their own uniqueness. Moreover, the family members sometimes react as a family unit, sometimes as individual family members and sometimes as family subgroups. The personalistic family therapist tries to deal with the family's reactions in a number of different ways and his behavior serves as a model for the family.

One family was given feedback by the therapist on the role of the children in protecting the parents from focusing on their marital problems. As previously mentioned, whenever the parents started talking about their difficulties, first the 17-year-old girl and later the 4-year-old girl started interrupting, making noises, screaming or hitting. The week following the session in which these interactions were identified, the mother entered the room with a particularly sullen expression on her face. Although only her husband was present she was noticeably reluctant to talk. Her husband, who was usually the less talkative of the two, started discussing at some length the outburst by his 4-year-old girl before, during and after the previous week's session. He said she had been acting up for 2½ weeks. He was puzzled since his 17-year-old daughter had been much calmer for the past month.

After mentioning how upset and guilty she was that her 4-year-old daughter was being so vindictive, the mother said that she blamed herself for being a bad parent. She said she was mad at herself and at her daughter. When she was asked if she was mad at anyone else, she said in a soft, methodical voice that she was furious at the therapist for having told her and her husband the previous week that their daughters were being considerate of their needs by protecting them from discussing their marital problems. She said she had thought a great deal about that statement during the week and realized how true it was. However, she was angry at the therapist for confronting her with this information.

"All these years I tried so hard" she related. When asked why she had not said something the previous week, she stated that it was very difficult for her to tell anyone she was angry, especially men such as her husband or father. The therapist had observed in earlier sessions that this woman had difficulty in expressing both hurtful and angry feelings toward her husband. Naturally, this had been one of the focuses of family sessions. Her husband, who had an equal or greater difficulty in expressing angry feelings, then volunteered that he, too, was mad at the therapist because family therapy was making him aware of problems that had not previously been evident (i.e. in his 4-year-old daughter).

On other occasions, the therapist might have only supported their expression of strong feelings and pointed out how uncomfortable they felt about telling the therapist, as well as each other, their parents, friends, and coworkers that they were angry and upset with them. This time, however, the therapist chose, in addition, to tell the couple that since he cared a great deal about them he did not want them to blame themselves, since they were doing the best they could to resolve the family problems. Moreover, the therapist indicated that his feelings would also have been hurt if he had received the same feedback about his own family. In this way the therapist tried to convey that he had emotions too, in relation to the couple, and that he could talk openly about them. He thus tried to serve as a model for the open communication of feelings. He did, however, also discuss with the parents the fact that this aspect of their interpersonal problem, i.e. their failure to openly express feelings, extended into their behaviors toward the therapist. They were encouraged to express strong feelings to the therapist when they experienced them, even at the risk of hurting his feelings. He indicated that he "could take it." In subsequent weeks the parents made noticeable progress in openly communicating hurtful and angry feelings with each other and the therapist.

In another family, the therapist had seen a young female divorcée individually for some months and in the course of therapy felt progressively provoked and irritated by her subtle, sarcastic jibes, and demands for more and more specific advice and therapeutic time. Every specific program planned for her she dismissed in a wailing tone of voice as inadequate and as not benefiting her. Eventually, the therapist gave her feedback on these behaviors and indicated how they were irritating him and making him very angry. It was also mentioned that similar behaviors seemed to be responsible for the fact that she had difficulty in maintaining a satisfactory heterosexual relationship.

When her parents and sister were included in the therapy sessions, it became obvious that many of these behaviors also irritated them. However, although her parents and sister had many charming, positive qualities, it soon became apparent that they also made excessive demands for attention on each other and the therapist. They would make subtle but nevertheless sarcastic comments to the therapist, and would insist on specific suggestions which were then not followed. In the early family sessions the therapist pointed out how the family members engaged in these behaviors with each other and how it created angry and hurt feelings among them which often led to an outburst or resulted in depression. After the eighth family session, the therapist told the parents that they were irritating him with their provoking, sarcastic, demanding behaviors. He was explicit in what bothered him. Previously, he had joked and laughed with them, and referred on a number of occasions to the enjoyable aspects of their family. In many ways they were a very likable family. Consequently, the therapist's very personal feedback to the family was cushioned by his prior positive and empathic statements. The therapist's intention was both to reveal something about his own feelings in relation to the family and to convey the seriousness with which he thought this family behavior pattern was disturbing to others and maladaptive as a manner of getting along within or outside of the family system. Eventually the family members learned to be less demanding and sarcastic with each other and the therapist and more concerned with and empathic to each other's needs.

In a third family, the therapist was so emotionally moved by the sorrow of the father and sons that he openly cried on two occasions. On the first occasion the father was talking in a roleplayed situation to his father (played by his son) about his natural mother who had died six weeks after he was born. His longing for her was so great that the father started crying for the first time in 30 years. Three of his sons, ages 11 to 13, then started crying. On the second occasion, a week later, the 12-year-old depressed son started talking about how upset he was that his father had experienced so many painful feelings during the week as a result of talking about his dead mother. The son cried profusely over the fact that his father had been so depressed and blamed himself for bringing his family into therapy. The father displayed more physical affection to his sons at the end of each session than the therapist had ever seen him show. Moreover, the father indicated that he saw the therapist crying. A discussion followed in which the father indicated that he never knew that anyone cared about him or his children so much. Until those two meetings the father had doubts as to whether the therapist only cared about him in the usual way a professional is concerned about his client or whether he was concerned about him as a person. The fact that the therapist was moved to tears proved to be an important ingredient in the build up of the therapeutic trust with this particular family.

When a family therapist assigns a task to a family, the task may or may not be readily accepted by one or all family members. The therapist may feel strongly that the task is an important one for the family member or members to carry out. However, family members may openly refuse to carry out the task or may verbally accept the task but still not carry it out. The reactions of the family therapist to this set of circumstances can be dealt with effectively in a personalistic way.

In one family the therapist suggested that a 50-year-old man, who was being seen with his wife and children, write a letter to his father telling him how he had always felt neglected by his father who had paid more attention to his younger sister when they were teenagers. In particular, his father used to take long walks with his sister while sending him on errands. His symptom, an hysterical limp, made it impossible for him to walk adequately, and had developed during his teens. He had always felt hurt by his father's neglect and sibling favoritism and resented both his father and sister for it. He had never told his father about these feelings, particularly since his sister died in a tragic car accident. He felt both guilty and relieved at her death; he had never cried over her death.

When the task to write to his father was assigned to this man, he initially agreed, saying that it was a good idea. In the following weeks it turned out that he resisted complying with the task, particularly since he perceived it as a demand by the therapist. He said he did not like to do anything under pressure because his father had always made demands on him and he had always complied like an obedient child. He was encouraged to tell the therapist openly and directly when he disliked any of his suggestions and particularly to state if he was annoyed at the task assigned. In the following weeks the man was able to state more directly his annoyance at suggestions made by the therapist. The therapist made no further mention of the letter. Two months later, however, the man indicated that maybe it would be beneficial for him to write a letter to his father as previously discussed. His wife volunteered to help him write the letter. It was necessary in this case to allow a sufficient amount of time to pass so that the initiative for the task came from the client. This was especially important for this man whose usual style of asserting himself was by resisting the desires or requests of other people. If the therapist had insisted on his writing the letter, he would not have done it and therapy progress would have been retarded by the resentment accruing from the client toward the therapist. It is also important to note that many suggestions made or tasks assigned by the therapist will be complied with only after a delay of from a few weeks to several months.

It is of some interest how the information about this man, his father, sister and symptom development was obtained. The mother was talking about the death of her mother at the age of three and how she had never seen her father cry when her mother died. The therapist then described a personal experience that had recently had a profound impact on him, the memory of which had been elicited by the wife's comments. He discussed a recent conversation he had with his father who told him about the tragic death in an automobile accident of his younger brother when he was 22 years old and his brother was 7 years old. The therapist's father, who by family reputation never showed his emotions, cried profusely on that occasion, and his son, the therapist cried with him. The only other time the therapist had ever seen his father cry was when his grandfather had died.

The therapist was looking at the mother while telling the story but he noticed that the father became very emotional while the story was being told. When the father was asked what was upsetting him, he stated for the first time how upsetting his sister's death and his feelings toward her had been to him. Previous interviewing had revealed only minimal information about his sister, his father and himself and the affect attached to this triangular family involvement. The personal self-disclosure by the therapist had positive ramifications well beyond the intended goal, which was to share a related experience with the mother. It released in the father some strong affects and some important information about his past life which still bothered him in the present. This led to the assignment of a task, writing a letter, designed to eventually establish a new set of constructive emotional communications between this man and his father.

In another family, the therapist assigned an overweight, depressed, widowed mother of three sons the task of taking a vacation for herself and getting involved in more activities from which she would derive personal pleasure. The mother, who spent almost all her time around the house or in the community doing things for others, constantly complained about being overworked but resisted complying with the therapist's suggestion. She insisted that her sons, ages 13, 18 and 23, should do more to help her around the house but all indications, including actual charts of their work, showed that the boys helped a great deal. In this case, the therapist persisted and for almost two months he urged her to get involved in some activities for her own enjoyment. She did make an occasional trip to the swimming pool and spent one evening out with some woman friends, but she always found some reason or other for not taking that long-desired vacation.

The therapist inquired about the mother's own family and found out that her parents placed a high value on dutiful, constant work on behalf of the family. Thus, to take a vacation would, in the eyes of this woman, have been disloyal to the family's values. After acquiring this information, the therapist switched tactics somewhat and put pressure on the sons to encourage their mother to go on a vacation and to verbally and physically express affection to the mother so that she would not have to work constantly to feel loved. Again the therapist persisted in his approach with only minimal success for a few weeks. The 18-year-old son did express some affection to his mother which initially embarrassed her. However, it was only after the 23-year-old son entered the service and the 18-year-old son went to work in Maine that the seeds of the therapist's efforts began to bear fruit. The two oldest sons wrote their mother frequently and comprehensively about their activities and showed obvious concern for their mother's wishes in making important decisions. The 13-year-old son agreed to go on a 10-day vacation to the shore with his mother, accompanied by a friend and his parents. The mother seemed very pleased by these events, was no longer depressed and looked much more attractive and cheerful.

In another family, the mother appeared to be markedly depressed over the fact that she did not feel loved by her parents. She was an adopted child but her parents had never told her that she was adopted. She had accidentally found out about this when she was 13 years old. Her own daughter also complained that she felt unloved. The mother complained that her daughters would not talk to her when things bothered them. It was pointed out to the mother that she did not serve as a good model for her daughters since she never told her parents, whom she frequently visited, her true feelings. The mother was assigned the task of telling her parents that she knew she was adopted, felt unloved by them and bewildered as to why she had never been told of her adoption. The mother was very reluctant to carry out this assignment and resisted doing so for the next two weeks. The therapist initially employed verbal persuasion. However, in subsequent weeks the mother still did not respond to these pressures and was getting obviously annoyed at the therapist for inquiring about it. The therapist then asked the mother if she felt that he was picking on her, since she looked so perturbed. She admitted feeling irritated by the therapist's insistence since she did not wish to tell her parents about the adoption. The therapist agreed not to mention it anymore. The therapist's empathy with the mother's irritation and willingness not to pressure her further appeared to facilitate the mother's openly revealing for the first time that she was extremely angry at her husband because of the arbitrary demands he placed upon her. A very important series of discussions between the mother and her husband followed, centering around their marital problems. Sometimes a task assignment will not be acted upon by the family member, but will catalyze change in an important area that is related to the one focused on by the task. This is more likely to occur if the therapist will empathize with the family member's emotional reactions to carrying out a difficult task.

The personalistic approach to task assignment implies that sometimes the therapist needs to persist in his endeavors to assign a task and sometimes to desist. Furthermore, it implies that sometimes the therapist needs to switch tactics and to use other family members as levers of task assignments. Each family is unique and the type of task, timing of the task and reactions to the task must be carefully tailored to each different family.

FAMILY THERAPIST AS LEADER, ADMINISTRATOR, NEGOTIATOR,
DEMONSTRATOR, EXPERIMENTER, COACH AND PARENT

The family therapist often temporarily becomes the leader of the family while they explore new territories in family relationships. He lets parents know that it is alright to talk about most emotional conflicts in the presence of their children. He asks questions that will elicit these conflicts and reassures the parents that the family, including the children, will benefit by openly discussing and resolving family problems. Thus, in one family which was very overcontrolled in their emotional and physical expressions, except for the 11-year-old son's uncontrolled bowel movements, the therapist prodded the parents to talk about their marital and family difficulties in the presence of the children. The parents protested that this would be harmful to the children which included a 17-year-old son, and 4- and 8-year-old girls. They did not want to bring the children to family sessions and even attacked the therapist for firmly stating he would not see them alone.

Since this family had had previous therapy in which the mother, father and oldest son had been seen in their own group or individual sessions, the therapist perceived that the family needed to work on problems as a family. He admitted to the family that it would be difficult for them but that he would lead the way for awhile. By the third session the father began talking about his inability to be sympathetic to his wife and children and his wife started talking about her inability to express direct anger to her husband or her own mother who lived nearby. The oldest son complained that he only got through to his father after constant arguing with him, and the 11-year-old son said that he was scared when he heard his parents fighting because they might hurt each other. The mother, moreover, admitted that she and her husband could never reach agreement on any decision. These open revelations enhanced communication among and between family members.

There are times when the personalistic family therapist must demonstrate to the parents how to express affection, verbally and physically, to their spouse or children, and how to control or enforce limits on aggressive or disruptive behavior when it occurs. In this sense he serves as a model to the parents (Friedman, 1968, 1971, 1972; Liberman, 1970; Patterson, et al. 1970). In one family the father indicated that he had never received praise or physical affection from his father, so he found it almost impossible to give affection and praise to his sons. The therapist would spontaneously put his arm around one of the sons, rub his hair or compliment him. Soon after, the father would tentatively reach over and touch his son. Eventually, the father could put his arm around his son or rub his hair affectionately or compliment him on helping around the house. However, the father needed to receive some affection and praise himself since he had never received any as a child from his father. When the therapist complimented him for being affectionate to his sons, being considerate of his wife's needs, or completing assigned tasks, he was being like a "good parent" to this father. The personalistic family therapist tries to recognize the needs of each family member and is not reluctant to be a "parent" when it is necessary. In the case of this family the therapist also demonstrated how the father could compliment the mother when she stopped criticizing him or the children. Not only did the wife receive praise from the therapist which she had rarely received from her parents, but the husband had a model to observe for giving compliments to his wife. The husband gradually became better able to express affection and praise to his wife.

Although it is difficult to define, it is important for the family therapist to demonstrate ways and means for family members to display empathy, compassion and concern for each other. Praise and affection are usually not enough to maintain a cooperative, emotionally gratifying family system. An ability to know what each family member feels in various situations and an ability to communicate that knowledge is an important ingredient of family relationships. Furthermore, the capacity to enhance positive feelings or to reduce negative feelings is often more important than giving praise and affection. Thus, in the previously mentioned family the therapist modeled compassion and empathy for both the husband and wife. He did this by the questions he asked, the statements he made about their feelings and the tone of voice and facial expression with which he made them. Eventually, the wife learned that when she complained that her kitchen was too small and ranted and raved about it, her husband's feelings were hurt. He considered himself as the family provider, and perceived his wife's criticism of the kitchen as an indication that he had inadequately provided for his wife's needs. When the wife realized that by "letting off steam" she was hurting her husband's feelings, she found other ways of venting her emotions. The husband also learned that his wife felt neglected when he listened to music through earphones and worked late at night. He not only learned to identify his wife's needs but to care about them by spending more time with her.

The personalistic family therapist models empathic concern for each spouse's feelings towards their children and towards each other, and for their feelings towards their own family of origin. The events which disturb or concern each person in relation to his own parents may have occurred in the past or in the present, but one's feelings exist in the *present* and consequently are contemporary experiences. It is this therapist's belief that some degree of compassion or empathy by one spouse for the other spouse's feelings toward his own parents is necessary for a successful marriage. Moreover, the children will perceive the compassion one parent has for the other parent's feelings and learn how to show empathy and compassion themselves.

In one family the mother constantly blamed the family's problems on her husband's "neurotic" family who caused her husband to be so "mixed up." The husband, on the other hand, blamed many of the problems on the wife's family for not having been considerate of his wife or children. Both parents had strong feelings of despair, rage and guilt toward their parents, but rather than receiving empathy for their feelings from their respective spouse they each gave and received condemnation. "Because of your parents, you hate and despise them, which messes up our children and causes me grief," was a fairly typical paraphrase of their statements. The family therapist replaces condemnation with compassion. He demonstrates how each parent can help his spouse to show concern and respect for the other's feelings. The children in turn learn to appreciate and show compassion for their parent's problems not only with each other but also with their family of origin.

Roleplaying scenes can sometimes be used to elicit intense feelings that otherwise stay submerged. When these feelings do emerge, the personalistic family therapist models empathic concern. Naturally, he must himself experience these emotions before he can demonstrate to others how he feels. For example, in the M. family the husband was asked to have a conversation with his natural mother, Carol, who died when he was 6 weeks old. The wife played the role of Carol while two chairs were placed back to back. Mr. M. quickly became very emotional and said that he simply could not do it. The therapist encouraged him to do so, after which Mr. M. said the feelings he had were very painful. The therapist then played the role of Mr. M.'s father. A long conversation ensued in which Mr. M. spoke to his "father" about his natural mother and his step-mother. Again Mr. M. said it was very painful for him to talk about his feelings towards his two mothers. He told his father that he thought life would have been very different for him if his natural mother, Carol, had lived. He wanted to know what she was like as a person and what her desires were. Mr. M. indicated how much resentment he had to his step-mother for putting him down all the time and to his father for supporting his step-mother and not wishing to talk about his natural mother. The therapist empathized with his feelings of hurt, sadness and anger while at the same time trying to convey in the role of "father" how upset he felt when his "wife" died.

In the most emotionally moving sequence of this role enactment, Mr. M. started crying because of his sadness over never having met his natural mother. He had not cried in 30 years. His 11-year-old son, referred for hyperaggressiveness, became restless at this point and looked as though he wanted to participate. The therapist asked him to play the role of Mr. M.'s father. He did so and responded to Mr. M. in an extremely soft, concerned tone of voice. Mr. M. then reached out for his son and pulled him toward him. His son started crying profusely and Mr. M. wrapped his arms around his son and continued to talk to him about how painful and distressing life had been for him for 30 years of his life. At the same time, Mr. M. was very reassuring to his son who indicated he wanted to spend more time with his father. As Mr. M.'s other two sons began to cry, the therapist also felt tears streaming down his face. He had never seen the sons express concern and care for their father in this way.

In another family the therapist demonstrated how to enforce limits on disruptive and aggressive behavior in 4-, 6- and 9-year-old boys. The young mother of these boys, who was divorced, was noticeably affectionate with her children, at least with the two youngest ones, but she was unable to restrict them when they ran around inappropriately, hit each other, talked incessantly or threw temper tantrums. The therapist demonstrated both time-out and incentive procedures for controlling her children's behavior. The children were told specifically during a family session that if they got out of their seats during a five (later ten and fifteen) minute period, or if they hit each other, interrupted the ensuing discussion or threw a temper tantrum, they would be put across the hall in an empty room for five minutes. Whenever these behaviors occurred, the therapist promptly put the disruptive child or children in the "time-out" room for five minutes. If the child stayed quiet for specified lengths of time, he would receive M and M's, praise and later earned time as "keeper of the clock" (kitchen timer). After watching the therapist demonstrate this procedure a few times in the clinic and once in the home, using the bedroom as time-out room, the mother gradually became fairly adept at administering the contingencies herself. In fact she improvised upon them by substituting toys and television time for "good behavior." At first, it was somewhat difficult for this mother to deprive her children even briefly, because of her very deprived background. The therapist empathized with her feelings about her past and by modeling "time-out" procedures reassured her that she would still be a "good" mother if she deprived her children of attention and toys for disruptive behavior as long as she continued being affectionate with her sons when they were not disruptive.

The family therapist serves as a negotiator among family members.

He helps them bargain amongst each other for behavioral changes that are most meaningful to each person and to the family as a whole. His job is to aid family members in evaluating what changes in other family members they desire most, how intensely they feel about these behavioral changes and what changes in their own behavior they are willing to make in exchange for behavioral changes in the other family member or members. The family therapist encourages family members to engage in this "exchange process" on their own but coaches them in the bargaining process when they appear to need guidance or support. In many ways the personalistic family therapist does what Zuk (1966) calls the "go-between" process, while aiding family members to learn what Bach calls bargaining or constructive fighting (Bach and Wyden, 1969).

In one family, for example, a 15-year-old son referred for effeminate behavior and two homosexual episodes wanted his mother to stop babying him by constantly asking him if he had cleaned up his room, brushed his teeth, finished his homework, eaten his vegetables, etc. The mother, in turn, wanted her son to start participating in teenage male activities instead of spending all his time engaged in feminine activities with girls. The therapist supported both mother and son by affirming that these were legitimate requests for behavioral changes and every effort should be made by both parties to exchange one desired behavioral change for another. This twosome needed to be prompted in subsequent weeks to keep their end of the bargain, but eventually they succeeded. In a married couple, the therapist mediated a bargain between husband and wife for more affection expressed verbally and physically by the husband and more uninhibited sexual involvement by the wife. This meant that the wife would engage in more physical movements and vocal sounds during sex and the husband would put his arm around his wife, kiss her, compliment her and smile at her more frequently. For the first few weeks this couple complained bitterly that each spouse was not keeping to the bargain, but by the fifth week the husband was not only showing more affection but he was also taking his wife out to shows and movies more often and the wife in turn was willingly initiating sexual activities in an uninhibited way for the first time in their marriage.

Sometimes a family member may wish to exchange some behavior that the therapist does not consider especially relevant or important. For example, in one family the mother was willing to exchange television time with her sons for cleaning up the living room and bedroom every day. In the process of negotiating an agreement between the mother and her sons, the therapist was aware that the mother was not completely satisfied with this arrangement and was bothered by something else despite her harangues against her sons. Further questioning revealed that she wanted her husband to supervise her sons' cleaning up since she claimed that he almost never helped her out with the children. She was, however, afraid that he would get very angry at her for mentioning this. The therapist then started to mediate a behavior exchange between husband and wife. This led to further complaints by the wife about something which she felt more intensely than the fact that her husband failed to supervise their sons' house-cleaning activities. She wanted her husband to pay more attention to her even when the children were not involved. He wanted more respect from her and fewer attacks on him as a father, a husband and a provider. The bargain that was finally negotiated was for the husband to spend at least two hours twice a week talking to his wife about things that bothered her, and for the wife to stop attacking the husband for not making enough money and for being a poor father. The therapist's task was to elicit the strongest concerns of each person, support each person in bargaining for those concerns, and try to keep the discussion from becoming a vicious battle rather than a negotiated exchange of desired behaviors. In subsequent weeks, the sons in this family asked their father to spend more time with them by going bowling, going to the museum and taking rides in the car. The implicit contract agreed upon between father and sons was for the boys to help their mother more in exchange for more time with their father.

Another area in which the family therapist often has to aid families is in negotiating conflicts between spouses and in-laws. Wives frequently complain that their mothers-in-law are the first to hear about a promotion or an argument on the job, or that their husbands speak to their mothers when they want comfort and not to them. Husbands complain that their wives spend endless hours neglecting them while talking to their mothers on the telephone and taking advice from their mothers and not from them. The therapist mediates these conflicts by trying to establish what bothers each person the most and negotiating with the couple for the desired behavioral changes.

The family therapist serves both as an administrator and negotiator when arrangements are being made with school principals, teachers and counselors to change a child's behavior. Thus, when one school felt extremely harassed by the destructive behavior of an 11-year-old boy, arrangements were made with the principal to restrict the boy's school day to afternoons and to eliminate all free play periods and lunch hours when the hitting, kicking and screaming were most prevalent. This administrative decision was arrived at by the principal in consultation with the therapist and imposed on the family as a precondition of family therapy. The family was told that when the boy's behavior became less disruptive he would gradually be allowed to come to school for a longer part of the school day. At first the boy was delighted to be out of school for half a day, but his mother did not like it very much. Moreover, after a week this boy felt lonesome and left out of school activities since all of his friends were in school. In addition, the boy's father made a contract with his son that helped to eliminate the disruptive behavior. He offered his son five dollars if he did not get any bad conduct marks on his next report card. However, one bad conduct mark, that is an F in conduct, would cost the boy ten dollars. When the boy was abusive in school, the teacher sent a note home to his parents. The father reminded him of the potential ten-dollar penalty. The son reported later that after this occurred he became scared that he would lose two months allowance if he was not careful. The aggressive behavior in the school situation ceased rapidly after the principal's time-out from school contract and the father's reward-penalty contract were put into effect.

The personalistic family therapist is continually trying out new approaches to family therapy in order to increase his effectiveness. Some of these new approaches will eventually be incorporated into his repertoire and others will be discarded. For example, encounter group and psychomotor techniques appear to offer promising methods of enhancing family therapy. Family members have been instructed to yell at the top of their lungs together, hug each other, arm wrestle with each other, or hit pillows held by each other while indicating how angry they are at the other person. They can also be asked to mimic another person, to physically suppress another person or to caress a family member. These and other non-verbal encounter techniques may eventually expand many of the approaches currently being used. The personalistic family therapist espouses an atheoretical orientation to the methods he employs. He is always experimenting and searching for ways to be more effective with more families. If he is willing to learn and grow, his only limitations are his own abilities and ethical restrictions.

OVERVIEW OF PROBLEMS SEEN, BACKGROUND AND RESULTS

Of the twenty families seen between January 1969 and June 1970 which did not involve a psychotic family member, six were seen exclusively for marital problems. In fifteen of these families one or more family members was markedly depressed or suicidal. In five of these families separation or divorce was seriously contemplated. In six of these families there were sexual problems. Three families were headed by a mother only. In over half the families, at least one family member was withdrawn or noticeably unassertive. In seven families one person was excessively aggressive. There were major psychosomatic or hypochondriacal complaints in two families, underachievement in four, excessive alcoholic drinking in three, theft and lying in two, and overweight in two. As previously mentioned, symptoms were evident in an average of 60% to 80% of family members. Different symptoms existed in different family members, although it was not unusual for depression to exist in more than one family member or for one family member to be depressed while another one was overly aggressive. Based on the occupation of the father, or of the mother if there was no father living, eight families were of middle class background and twelve were of working class background. Eighteen families were white and two were black. Depending on how stringent the criteria for success one employs, between 70% and 80% of the families were successfully treated and between 45 and 50 people in these families benefitted from the treatment. These figures are based on the therapist's estimate of behavioral changes in the family and the family's reports of decreases in symptomatic complaints. Whenever possible, follow-up questionnaires and phone calls were employed. The length of treatment ranged from three hours to sixty hours. Eight families had ten hours or less of family therapy, four had between ten and twenty hours, three had between twenty and thirty hours, and five had between thirty and sixty hours of therapy. Even in the families receiving from thirty to sixty hours of therapy per family, the amount of therapy time was only between eight and twenty therapy hours per person helped. Since the possibility of bias always exists when a therapist evaluates his own cases, additional independent, objective research is needed to adequately determine the effectiveness of the personalistic approach to family and marital therapy. It is expected, however, in keeping with the personalistic emphasis, that as this approach is applied to a wider range of families, particularly the lower socioeconomic, disadvantaged families, some variations of the present approach will have to be made.

SUMMARY

The personalistic approach to family and marital therapy is an outgrowth of a broad-spectrum behavioral approach to therapeutic interventions, a system-oriented three-generational approach to conceptualizing family and marital problems, and a humanistic concern for the uniqueness and worth of each family. The personalistic family therapist respects the values, attitudes and behavior of each family member as well as the interrelationships among the values, attitudes and behaviors of family members. He tries to establish a personal relationship with each family member and empathizes with each individual family member's distress. However, he also engages in the relabeling, cognitive restructuring and reconceptualizing of maladaptive family behavior patterns for the family in order to clarify the sequence of events leading to disturbed or dysfunctional behavior. This is a preliminary intervention which, along with giving behavioral feedback to family members and pointing out the interpersonal consequences of each family member's behavior, sets the stage for the therapist's direct and indirect interventions.

Direct interventions consist of having family members stop engaging in maladaptive behavior patterns and engage in more constructive behaviors in the therapist's presence. The therapist redirects behavioral sequences, instructs family members in new behaviors, elicits suppressed behaviors, and uses modeling and roleplaying techniques. In addition, he uses his own affect to facilitate behavioral changes in the family. Indirect interventions center around the tasks and assignments the therapist gives to a family between therapy sessions. These interventions are designed to increase assertiveness and affection while decreasing destructiveness, reduce sexual inhibitions, fears and guilt, produce emotional release, and generally improve family relationships. The personalistic approach to task assignment recognizes that family members often carry out difficult tasks only after considerable emotional turmoil and delayed compliance with the tasks. Consequently, the therapist deals with the family's reactions to assigned tasks in a variety of ways designed to maximally facilitate change.

The personalistic family therapist tailors his interventions to meet the specific needs of each family. Moreover, he willingly reveals something about himself as a person to the family in order to serve as a model for intimate relating. He tries to demonstrate to the family ways to express affection, anger, disappointment, sadness, and delight. Finally, the personalistic family therapist realizes that to be effective with families he will often have to adopt at different times a variety of roles, such as leader, administrator, negotiator, demonstrator, experimenter, coach and parent.

REFERENCES

ACKERMAN, N. W. *Treating the Troubled Family.* New York: Basic Books, 1966.

BACH, G. & WYDEN, P. *The Intimate Enemy.* New York: Morrow and Co., 1969.

BEELS, C. C. & FERBER, A. Family therapy: a view. *Family Process,* 1969, 8, 280-332.

BERNAL, M. "Behavioral feedback in the modification of brat behaviors" *J. of Nervous Mental Disease.* 1969, 148, 375-385.

BOWEN, M. The use of family theory in clinical practice. *Comprehensive Psychiatry.* 1966, 7, 345-374.

ELLIS, A. *Sex Without Guilt.* New York: Grove Press, 1965.

FRAMO, J. L. Symptoms from the viewpoint of the family therapist. In N. Ackerman (Ed.) *Family Therapy in Transition.* Boston: Little, Brown & Co., 1970.

FRIEDMAN, P. The effects of modeling and roleplaying on assertive behavior. Unpublished doctoral dissertation. Univ. of Wisconsin, Madison, 1968.

FRIEDMAN, P. The effects of modeling and roleplaying on assertive behavior. *Advances in Behavior Therapy,* Vol. II., New York: Academic Press, 1970.

FRIEDMAN, P. The effects of modeling, roleplaying and participation on behavior change. In B. Maher (Ed.) *Progress in Experimental Personality Research.* Vol. VI. New York: Academic Press, 1972.

GINOTT, H. *Between Parents and Child.* New York: Macmillan, 1965.

HALEY, J. Toward a theory of pathological systems. In Zuk, G. and Nagy, I. (Eds.) *Family Therapy and Disturbed Families.* Palo Alto: Science and Behavior Books, 1967.

HALEY, J. Marriage therapy. *Archives of General Psychiatry,* 1963, 8, 213-234.

HAWKINS, R., PETERSON, R., SCHWEID, E., & BIJOU, S. Behavior therapy in the home: amelioration of problem parent-child relationships with the parent in a therapeutic role. *J. of Experimental Child Psychology,* 1967. 4, 99-107.

HOMME, L. *How to Use Contingency Contracting in the Classroom.* Champaign, Illinois: Research Press, 1969.

KNOX, D. & MADSEN, C. Behavior therapy and marriage problems. Unpublished manuscript. East Carolina University and Florida State University respectively.

LAZARUS, A. Behavior therapy and group marriage counseling. *Journal of American Society of Psychosomatic Dentistry and Medicine,* 1968, 15, 49-56.

LAZARUS, A. In support of technical eclecticism. *Psychological Reports,* 1967, 21, 415-416.

LAZARUS, A. *Behavior Therapy and Beyond.* New York: McGraw-Hill, 1971.

LIBERMAN, R. Behavioral approaches to family and couple therapy. *American J. of Orthopsychiatry,* 1970, 40, 106-118.

LINDSLEY, O. R. An experiment with parents handling behavior at home. *Johnstone Bulletin,* 1966, 9, 27-36.

MINUCHIN, S., MONTALVO, B., GUERNING, B., ROSMAN, B., & SCHUMAN, F., *Families of the Slums,* New York: Basic Books, 1967.

NAGY, I. & FRAMO, J. L. *Intensive Family Therapy.* New York: Harper and Row, 1965.

O'LEARY, K. D., O'LEARY, S., & BECKER, W. C. Modification of a deviant sibling interaction pattern in the home. *Behavior Research and Therapy,* 1967, 5, 113-120.

PATTERSON, G. R., COBB, J., & RAY, R. A social engineering technology for retraining aggressive boys. In H. Adams and L. Unikel (Eds.) *Georgia Symposium in Experimental Clinical Psychology,* Vol. II, New York: Pergamon Press, 1970.

PATTERSON, G. R. & GULLION, M. E. *Living With Children: New Methods for Parents and Teachers.* Champaign, Illinois: Research Press, 1968.

PATTERSON, G. R., RAY, R. S. & SHAW, D. A. Direct intervention in families of deviant children. *Oregon Research Institute Research Bulletin,* 1968, Vol. 8, No. 9.

RUBIN, T. *The Angry Book,* Toronto: Macmillan Co., 1969.

SATIR, V. *Conjoint Family Therapy.* Palo Alto: Science and Behavior Books, 1964.

THARP, R. G. & WETZEL, R. *Behavior Modification in the Natural Environment.* New York: Academic Press, 1969.

WAHLER, R. G. Oppositional children: a quest for parental reinforcement control. *J. of Applied Behavior Analysis,* 1969, 2, 159-170.

WAHLER, R. G., WINKEL, G. H., PETERSON, R. F., & MORRISON, D. C. Mothers as behavior therapists for their own children. *Behavior Research and Therapy,* 1965, 3, 113-124.

WATZLAWICK, P., BEAVIN, J., & JACKSON, D. *Pragmatics of Human Communication.* W. W. Norton and Co., 1967.

WERRY, J. & WOLLERSHEIM, J. Behavior therapy with children: a broad overview. *Journal of the American Academy of Child Psychiatry.* 1967, 6, 346-370.

ZUK, G. The go-between process in family therapy. *Family Process,* 1966, 5, 162-178.

ZUK, G. Triadic based family therapy. *International Journal of Psychiatry,* 1969, 2, 538-549.

The author wishes to acknowledge the fact that Dr. Arnold Lazarus first introduced the term personalistic psychotherapy in his book *Behavior Therapy and Beyond,* McGraw-Hill, 1971.

The author is extremely grateful to Dr. Lazarus for the many hours he spent with him discussing the application of the personalistic approach to specific therapy clients. The extension of the personalistic approach to the family therapy field lies primarily with the present author, however.

The author would also like to thank Dr. Lazarus, Dr. Munjack, Dr. Crocco, and Margaret Olsen for their constructive comments and suggestions on the first draft of this paper. In addition, the author would like to thank his colleagues Dr. Ivan Boszormenyi-Nagy, Mrs. G. Spark, Dr. G. Zuk, Dr. L. Robinson and Dr. R. Crocco for the many hours they have spent talking with him about family therapy and for all he has learned from them. He recognizes, however, that the point of view taken in this paper is not necessarily consistent with his colleagues' frame of reference.

8

Training Patients to Communicate

GERALD W. PIAGET, Ph.D.

IT IS UNFORTUNATE that our society spends so much time teaching its members arithmetic and history, and so little time showing them how to share thoughts and feelings with one another. The result is a large group of alienated, lonely, anxious people who do not know how to communicate effectively, are not as creative, productive, or as happy as they could be, and who do not understand why they feel vaguely unfulfilled. Our consulting rooms are full of these people.

Much of the worth of traditional psychotherapeutic interaction probably results from the communication training opportunities inherent in its structure. However, these specific training benefits often become lost within some sort of subjective process orientation, and are never exploited to their fullest extent. Based on the tenets of learning theory, behavior therapy with its more technical approach is uniquely suited to optimizing the development of communication training benefits in the one-to-one setting.

Behavioral anxiety reduction procedures and communication training techniques have much in common and serve complementary needs. Anxiety reduction techniques alone provide nothing to replace the dysfunctional habits they remove. Successful desensitization creates a kind of behavioral void, one which can facilitate the recurrence of maladaptive response patterns. (In some cases, of course, the desensitized patient "fills the void" himself by learning adaptive responses to previously feared stimuli.) Most communication responses are incompatible with anxiety, and may help overcome certain fear reactions. However, communication training often generates new behavior patterns which, initially at least, are not powerful enough to counteract the mountains of anxiety experienced by severely neurotic individuals who are asked to change long-standing social habits. *Combining anxiety reduction therapy and communication training into a single, integrated program serves to minimize the problems inherent in each individual approach, while maximizing the potential benefits to be gained.*

In practice, a good many therapists successfully employ a broad spectrum therapy-training potpourri of one kind or another. This chapter describes one such program.

CHARACTERISTICS OF GOOD AND BAD COMMUNICATION

For training purposes, communication may be defined as *an ordered process of data transfer from one individual (the sender) to another (the receiver).* The sender's job is to transmit a message as clearly as possible; the receiver must accept the message without modifying it in any way, and then let the sender know that his message was received. Then the participants usually switch roles: the new sender originates a message based in part on the information he has just received, transmits it to the new receiver, and the process continues. Spontaneous, two-way communication involves the rapid and continual exchange of roles, with each party alternately functioning as sender and receiver. (This model describes dyadic peer-level communication; however, it is easily expanded to cover group interaction and other types of interpersonal behavior.)

On a behavioral level, interpersonal communication is a very complex process. The "sender Gestalt" is made up of a large number of discrete, but interrelated, movements; the power with which a message is sent is determined by the nature, quality, and pattern of these molecular behaviors. Similarly, a large number of discrete behaviors combine to generate a "receiver Gestalt" that determines the power (sensitivity) with which a message is received. *The concepts of sender power and receiver power are central to this communication training model: essentially, the patient/ trainee is taught to be a powerful sender and receiver of messages.* The powerful sender transmits messages clearly, quickly, and accurately, in a manner the listener finds easy to understand. The powerful receiver facilitates transmission, makes sure he understands what was sent, and then firmly acknowledges receipt of the message.

Several patterns of behavior which seem to characterize powerful communication have been isolated. Some are individual in nature and others involve interpersonal skills. A few require extensive training to master, but most are quite simple and can be learned with little effort. The presence of these qualities in dyadic communication promotes rewarding and successful interaction; in their absence, communication is not effective and eventually breaks down.

Some of the performance characteristics which facilitate powerful communication are described below. The list is not exhaustive, and not every item on it must be reflected in successful communication. Some are specific to particular kinds of communicative behavior and may even be contraindicated in certain situations. As communication skill can be rated in terms of the presence or absence of these characteristics, the following list can be used to advantage as a training guideline in communication courses and therapy/training sessions. It is presented in greater detail by Piaget (1971).

1. *Intention to communicate:* The sender looks and acts as if he wants to be understood, and makes sure that he is understood. The listener looks and acts as if he wants to understand, and makes sure he does understand. Communication vehicles include attention, acknowledgment, reflection, verification, vocal quality, and other nonverbal cues.

2. *Role clarity and division:* The sender sends, the receiver receives. Participants try not to do both at once or send simultaneously. Problems involving role division (how much time each party spends sending relative to how much time he spends receiving) and related expectations are handled.

3. *Verbal skill:* The sender delivers his message clearly and concisely. He speaks in concrete terms when possible. He sends the message he wants to send and not some other. Vehicles include a well-developed, topic-related vocabulary and verbal fluency.

4. *Affective skill:* Participants take responsibility for and advantage

of their ability to communicate on a feeling level. Communication vehicles include verbal and nonverbal cues, emotive expression, and the ability to employ such process skills as empathy and positive regard.

5. *Congruence:* The sender looks and sounds the way he says he feels. His verbal and nonverbal behaviors transmit similar messages. Participants send and receive only when they wish to do so. Attention and interest are never faked. Termination occurs on time.

6. *Facilitation:* The sender makes it easy for the listener to hear his message by tailoring the method and intensity of its transmission to the particular strengths and weaknesses of the receiver. The receiver makes it easy for the sender to send by creating a receptive, nonjudgmental atmosphere. Participants reinforce one another for communicating.

7. *Troubleshooting:* Participants can recognize and modify contra-communicative behavior in themselves and one another. Bad communication may involve unintentional response patterns, destructive intent, manipulative intent, or the absence of such qualities and skills as are described in this section. Successful troubleshooting depends primarily upon perceptivity, feedback, and technical skill.

8. *Personal qualities:* Intelligence, personality, sensitivity, flexibility, anxieties, tension level, self-image, energy level, and many other personal characteristics help determine an individual's ability to communicate effectively. Willingness to be trained also falls into this category.

Communication breakdowns occur when several desirable performance characteristics are absent from the dyadic interaction. These breakdowns reflect the presence of maladaptive habits and/or the absence of necessary skills. Usually, both problems are involved.

1. *The participant may possess certain response patterns which serve to inhibit, rather than facilitate, effective communication.* This category may be further subdivided:

a) When part or all of the sender's behavior is designed to produce internal gratification *directly* (bypassing the receiver), a "short circuit" develops, resulting in considerable energy drain. Short circuit reactions usually occur in the service of anxiety reduction, although other types of motivating behaviors (e.g., anger, sex drive) may be involved, as well. "Nervous" habits (such as giggling, loss of eye contact, and inappropriate anger) exemplify the kind of behavior which leads to inefficient communication. Anxiety reduction is a powerful reinforcer, and such habits are often difficult to eliminate.

b) Certain spurious reactive components may be reflections of residual habits: responses which at one time served a purpose, but are no longer necessary and have become more of a hindrance than a help. These be-haviors are maintained through a self-reinforcement mechanism: they have been a part of the sender's response pattern for so long that dropping them would introduce anxiety-producing novelty into his life. It is easier for him to go on as always, carrying the unnecessary weight of antiquated behaviors with him in spite of the long term annoyance they cause.

2. *The sender or receiver may not possess certain interpersonal skills necessary for effective, powerful communication to occur.* It may not be what the patient/trainee is doing wrong that matters as much as what he is not doing right. Consider the enterprising, young shoe salesman who arrives home from work each evening, promptly, at 5:30, heads straight for the television set, and seldom emits more than a grunt until dinner is served at 8:00. He may not *wish* to treat his wife as if she were unim-portant to him; part of the problem may be that he does not know how to implement appropriate expressions of empathy and warmth. Through the years, his lack of interpersonal skill may have led to reward patterns which extinguished behaviors involving emotional expression. Similarly, the recently terminated desensitization case who no longer fears the inter-personal setting may, yet, avoid attractive females at parties simply because he does not know how to "break the ice."

SETTING UP THE PROGRAM

The patient who stands the best chance of deriving benefit from a regimen like communication training is the one who believes that the pro-gram is in his best interest and, therefore, is well-motivated to participate actively in it. Certain individuals are surprised and somewhat threatened by the training model (communication training does not fit many people's projection of what psychotherapy is like). However, a brief description of the importance and desirability of being a potent communicator is usually sufficient to allay the patient's initial fears and give him a "com-mon sense" understanding of the approach. In addition, if the therapist tailors his discussion as closely as possible to his patient's presenting complaints and other specific needs, he should have little difficulty in presenting the concept of supplementary communication training in an appealing manner.

The amount of session time that should be spent on anxiety reduction and the amount spent on communication training vary with each patient.

Usually, the first few sessions are used to reduce anxiety. As therapy progresses and hierarchies are completed, the balance of time spent often sways toward training. Both approaches can be used in each session as long as anxiety remains a major problem. (It is not always easy to say which procedures are aimed at which goal. Several techniques provide the simultaneous benefits of training and conditioning; this is particularly true of roleplaying technologies.)

As the behavioral anxiety reduction procedures used in the program are well known (systematic desensitization, implosive therapy, and modifications thereof), the present discussion will relate itself primarily to the implementation of communication training. However, in practice the two approaches are employed together.

Data Collection

During the first few sessions the therapist attempts to experience the patient as both a sender and a receiver in order to decide how his communicative behaviors might be improved. A recommended starting point is to ask the patient what communication skills he would like to develop, and whether there are any related behaviors and/or feelings that he would like to change. Roleplaying, in its many and varied forms, is helpful—particularly in conjunction with the use of participant-observers. A behavior checklist can be used to mark target behaviors and facilitate objective comparison between observer reports. The use of standard checklists and objective rating scales yields specific information which is difficult to obtain in other ways. Occasionally, stress interview techniques are helpful. Consulting with the significant others in the patient's life often produces valuable information.

Feedback

One major problem facing the therapist/trainer is how to implement necessary training procedures without seeming critical or judgmental to his patient. The individual who begins by saying, "Well, here is a list of the things you are doing wrong," stands a good chance of limiting his future worth as a reinforcing agent. By allowing the patient to make his own decisions regarding those communicative behaviors which warrant change, it is possible to circumvent unnecessary power struggles and increase the patient's chances for positive movement. The therapist's initial task is simpler when his patient's problems revolve primarily around lack of adaptive response patterns, rather than the presence of dysfunctional habits. It is easier for most patients to entertain the possibility that they do not possess certain communication skills than it is for them to confront the idea that some of their pet mannerisms are contraproductive.

The therapist's opinions, biases, phraseology, topic selection, etc. have a decided effect on the patient, no matter how "nondirective" he tries to be. The important variable is the *skill* and *sensitivity* with which his selected experience is fed back to the patient. This phase of the operation can be initiated by saying something like, "Now, let's take a look at some of the communication techniques you, yourself, use and try to get some information about how they affect other people." Subsequently, any number of procedures may be used.

a) The participant-observer may be asked to return and give the patient feedback. (A checksheet proves valuable in this context.) This method provides the patient with outside opinion, and allows the therapist to remain somewhat neutral.

b) If equipment is available, videotape feedback of patient behavior proves uniquely valuable in that it allows the patient to respond to himself as a "third person." The therapist may facilitate the encounter by asking his patient such questions as, "How does it make you feel, when he (pointing to monitor) moves his arms like that?". Some individuals are powerfully motivated to change certain response patterns simply by seeing themselves on tape. When videotape is unavailable, verbal recordings of roleplaying situations may serve a similar, if less impressive, function.

c) In the absence of videotape equipment, the therapist may employ role reversal procedures to show the patient how he looks and acts.

d) Another valuable roleplaying device calls for a modification of the Gestalt "two-chair" procedure. The therapist has his patient play himself while sitting in one chair, and a specified third party (wife, boss, enemy, stranger, etc.) while in the other chair. While in the "other chair," he is asked to see and react to himself as he might do were he the individual whose role he is filling. He switches chairs at will to facilitate role clarity during this interaction. The patient is instructed to give himself feedback from the "other chair," regarding the quality and effect of his communicative behavior. The therapist may provide the alter-ego in either role to get his own points across. In another variation, the *therapist* roleplays with the patient's "other chair," or with a personality of his own choosing. The patient, as observer, listens passively. In this way, it may be possible for the therapist to "allow his patient to overhear" information which would be threatening to the patient if communicated directly. Variations on these themes are nearly endless.

No doubt, many feedback techniques can be devised. Again, feedback information is meant to help the patient decide which behaviors he wishes to drop from his repertoire and which interpersonal skills he wishes to develop. The therapist should reinforce those decisions with which he agrees. Obviously, he has a good deal of control over the target behavior choices his patient makes, no matter which feedback techniques he employs. The important thing is that the patient feels no one is telling him what is right or wrong, what is good behavior or bad. For optimal training results, the patient must feel that the training emphasis decisions he has made are primarily his own.

Contract

It may be helpful to draw up a written or verbal contract containing the target behavior(s) the patient has chosen to attack and the behavior change goals he has set for himself. The contract goals can be set forth in "graded structure" form for reinforcement value. (In this modification, the patient's training goals are organized into a series of progressive steps, and usually are presented to him in writing. As the training sessions proceed, he is allowed to "graduate" from one step to the next, each graduation being enthusiastically reinforced by the therapist. It is felt that the reinforcement value of this procedure provides the patient with increased motivation to change.) In some cases, a "time-limiting" clause may be added to the contract: certain goals are projected for specific dates. The contract is signed by both patient and therapist, and is kept handy for easy reference at all therapy/training sessions.

Technique Selection

The therapist/trainer is acquainted with a large number of communication training techniques; it is his job to suggest and then to implement those he feels are most suited to his patient's specific needs. As noted above, training techniques differ as to function: some are oriented toward removing maladaptive behavior, and some are intended to sharpen desirable communication skills. Cross-sectionally, they may be subdivided in terms of focus: some techniques develop sender power, some receiver power, and others facilitate both aspects of training. All good communication training techniques, however, have three qualities in common:

a) They provide a vehicle for the *modeling* and/or description of effective behaviors.

b) They provide a vehicle for the *reinforcement* of desirable behaviors.

c) They provide a vehicle for rapid and accurate *feedback control* (letting the trainee know when he is doing something right or wrong).

THERAPY/TRAINING TECHNIQUE APPLICATION

The communicative techniques described below are as diverse in theoretical origin as they are dissimilar in training function. They are fairly representative of the range of techniques which can be used to supplement anxiety reduction procedures in a therapy/training session, although many more than these are available. Most of these procedures are essentially unresearched; the data that do exist to support their effectiveness are largely empirical. In the following section, technique sources have been referenced for the reader who wishes more detailed process information than is presented here.

Elimination of Dysfunctional Behavior

Janet L. was an attractive, intelligent twenty-nine-year-old divorcée and mother of two who came to treatment seeking relief from what she described as "constant tension, nervousness, and worry." Further discussion revealed that Janet had a current boyfriend whom she "loved," but of whose affections and marital intentions she was not sure. She said that she was often the "life of the party" with friends, but wished she could feel more confident among strangers. When asked to describe herself, she mumbled such phrases as "kind of pretty" and "sort of fun to be with" in a tone of voice that screamed, "Boy, I really think I'm blah, and so will you!". These responses were directed, not at me, but at a spot on the floor three feet in front of Janet's chair. It soon became apparent that Janet planned not to look at my eyes at all unless she absolutely had to. When I suggested that she maintain eye contact while we talked, she did manage to focus on me for a short while. However, simultaneously with this new found assertion, her hand shot to a curl on her forehead and from then on she managed to hide at least one eye and half her face behind her forearm at all times.

Several additional "short circuit" behaviors became evident during that first hour. Janet "talked with her hands" excessively, and repeatedly varied the volume and tone of her voice more than was necessary to emphasize her point. She stressed words in a manner which suggested that she was not sure she could say what she wanted to say in the way she wanted, but did not quite know what else to do. Her tone of voice was vaguely apologetic and her occasional assertive verbalizations were invariably accompanied by compromising behaviors, such as: nervous laughter; shrugs; arm, leg, and hand movements; and the inevitable breaking of eye contact. While she talked, her body was turned away from me about sixty degrees. She constantly, crossed and re-crossed her legs. When not weaving in the air, her right arm was clasped tightly across her stomach, held in place by the "death grip" she maintained on her left bicep. Her left forearm, as noted earlier, was usually held in front of her face.

In reaching our therapeutic contract, procedures such as those described in the preceding section were employed with no major problems arising. As a result, Janet and I agreed to work toward the following therapeutic goals, and attempt further progress in other areas once these goals were reached.

1. *Anxiety reduction* through relaxation training and the systematic desensitization of hierarchies developed in three related areas: criticism, rejection, and expression of anger.

2. *Communication training* aimed at a) increasing assertive behavior (basically, Janet needed to learn how to stand up to people like her boyfriend) and b) decreasing the number and frequency of spurious movements and unnecessary sounds accompanying her verbal response patterns. Specific target behaviors cited were: breaking of eye contact, arm or hand in front of face, unnecessary arm and leg movements, inappropriate tonal emphasis, and unnecessary sounds (particularly, nervous laughter, clearing of the throat before speaking, and use of unnecessary antecedent words, such as "well").

Desensitization and assertive training are familiar techniques which need not be described here. However, it may be interesting to consider two of the retraining procedures used to help Janet reduce some of her communication-inhibiting patterns. They are not often applied in this context. The first involves a form of negative practice, a procedure which has been notably successful in reducing the severity of stuttering and multiple tics (e.g. Yates, 1958). It also seems to be effective in helping patients like Janet control undesirable, but semi-voluntary movement patterns.

TECHNIQUE #1: *R. I. D.* Patients who are made to imitate maladaptive habit patterns at some length and in the absence of anxiety-producing cues sometimes learn to control the habit. Proponents of the mnemonic device may introduce this technique to their patients as a means of getting R.I.D. of problem behaviors, explaining that the capital letters represent the words *recognize, imitate,* and *drop.* For negative practice to be successful, the patient must imitate precisely the maladaptive behavior he wishes to eliminate, and then repeat it many times. In this way, he either a) extinguishes the behavior via repetition *sans* reinforcement, and/ or b) brings it under more precise, conscious control, thereby acquiring the power simply to *choose* not to perform it (depending on which theoretical system one happens to prefer). Whatever the dynamics, negative practice seems to work relatively well for certain stubborn habits.

The second procedure was developed by L. Ron Hubbard (1961) to help his students practice behavior control in the face of anxiety-producing cues.

TECHNIQUE #2: *Bullbaiting.* The therapist presents his patient with a graded series of increasingly stress-producing, verbal and behavioral cues (gestures, jokes, criticisms, insults, references to embarrassing situations, etc.). The student is not permitted to respond to the therapist at all, but must continue to perform some specific communication-related task (e.g. asking a question). Any visible reaction to the therapist is noted as a mistake, and the process is begun again. Successful trials (specific periods of time during which the therapist is unable to elicit a reaction from his patient) are strongly reinforced (praise and attention are the usual rewards). This procedure bears a resemblance to *in vivo* desensitization, the major differences being that in bullbaiting no hierarchy is written out beforehand, and no counter-conditioning response, such as relaxation, is specified.

In Janet's case, R.I.D. and Bullbaiting proved quite effective in reducing the frequency of target behaviors specified in our therapeutic contract. In all, we spent seven half-sessions using these techniques. Janet was surprised at the initial difficulty she had in deliberately duplicating some of the patterns she had been performing spontaneously and perfectly for years. Incessant verbal feedback from me and visual feedback from a mirror especially positioned for the purpose soon helped her recognize and master the necessary movements. For repetition practice, we implemented a roleplaying process in which Janet held imaginary two-way conversations with a life-sized Joe Palooka punching bag. During her conversations with Joe, Janet initiated her various target behaviors, first in response to a signal from me, and later on her own. Daily homework sessions of a similar nature were assigned. During her fourth session of R.I.D., Janet reported feeling in control of most of her target behaviors and said she was bored with the technique. We initiated Bullbaiting procedures at that time. Janet acted out conversations as before, this time with me, while I applied a graded series of anxiety-producing stimuli to try to force her to react, particularly in the form of target behavior. Although Janet later reported feeling anxious occasionally during the Bullbaiting sessions, she evidenced a marked reduction in incidence of target behavior almost from the beginning, and continued to improve with each session. I soon found myself hard-pressed to come up with a Bullbaiting cue that would elicit so much as a twitch. Janet reported concurrent improvement outside of therapy as well. At that point, we switched our primary training focus from the elimination of maladaptive habits to the development of positive, assertive response patterns.

At termination three months later, Janet and I were both quite pleased at the extent of her progress with regard both to skill acquisition and anxiety reduction. Could Janet have sustained similar gains without help from the learning techniques described above? Only controlled research can provide answers to such questions. Empirically, these techniques seem to facilitate the elimination of dysfunctional habits, and help provide a solid behavioral base upon which to anchor the subsequent development of adaptive communication skills.

Training in Emotional Expression

It is commonly believed that unexpressed emotion can generate considerable physical tension which, in turn, can lead to anxiety. Several therapeutic approaches to this problem are popular today. For instance, the Reichian therapist trains his patients to scream on the assumption that the consequent tension release is intrinsically therapeutic. Alexander Lowen and other proponents of the bio-energetic movement stress the need for congruence between feeling and physical expression. Behavior therapists (e.g. Goldstein, et al., 1970) have used anger responses coupled with violent physical activity to counter-condition anxiety and facilitate subsequent assertive behavior. Encounter-oriented therapists encourage free expression of emotions for a variety of reasons.

From a communication standpoint, emotional expression is an efficient way to send certain kinds of messages: for one thing, little doubt is left in the receiver's mind as to how the sender feels. Unfortunately, many people find it difficult to express intense emotion in a congruent manner. Instead, they bottle up anger and fear until the tension becomes unbearable. The catharsis value in the resulting explosion seldom compensates for the negative social consequences and guilt reactions which usually follow.

TECHNIQUE #3: *Emotive expression.* The patient is given a book from which he is asked to read aloud into a taperecorder for approximately a minute. Then he is requested to read the same passage three additional times, donning a different *emotional role* with each repetition. On the first repetition, he is to sound as happy as possible. On the second run he is to sound very sad. During the final repetition he is to express as much anger as he possibly can. After completing these assignments, he is allowed to listen to the tape. Patients who are chosen for this kind of training usually sound pretty much the same all four times. (One effective feedback technique is to stop the tape at random during rewind and ask the patient if he can tell from the sound of his own voice which emotional role he was attempting to portray.) If the patient is unhappy with his performance and requests training in this area, the therapist may proceed as follows:

a. The therapist role-models various modes of verbal expression which communicate pleasure, and asks the patient to mimic him. When the patient can do so accurately, he is asked to reread the book passage while modeling happiness. The therapist coaches his patient, enthusiastically praising all positive gains until the patient really does sound happy while reading.

b. The procedure is repeated for sadness and anger in that order.

c. When both therapist and patient are satisfied with the latter's improvement, another session is taped. The patient is asked to compare his "before" tape with his "after" tape for additional reinforcement effect. Patients who are concerned with the artificiality of the training situation are assured that a generalization of learning will take place.

d. The patient's homework assignment is simply to try to sound happy, sad, or angry whenever he experiences these emotions. The therapist discusses with him the implications of being able to sound the way he feels.

TECHNIQUE #4: *Shout training.* This is an expressive training technique for the individual who finds it difficult to raise his voice. Basically, the patient is instructed to say a neutral sentence or phrase again and again, each time slightly louder than before, until he is yelling at the top of his lungs. If desired, the patient may be requested to pound a hassock or punching bag while he yells. Later in training, he is asked to shout appropriate material directly at the therapist, another trainee, other third party, or at an inanimate object. Gradually, the complexity, emotional content, and personal relevance of the target phrase may be increased. The training is complete when the patient no longer feels reticent to raise his voice in nonthreatening situations. The response may then be used as a counter-conditioning agent in desensitization, or as a bridge to more socially appropriate anger responses in assertive training.

Roger T. was a smallish, balding, married, thirty-five-year-old drafts-man who had received analytically-oriented therapy off and on for a period of years. Somewhere along the line, his condition had been diagnosed as endogenous depression, although he suffered from a wide range of emotional problems and maladaptive habit patterns. From a communications point of view, one of Roger's most significant characteristics was his chronic flatness of affect. He never raised his voice in anger or joy, but spoke in a constant nasal monotone. Assertive training, which was the major therapy technique used, was only moderately successful. Of the many procedures tried with Roger, emotive training was one of the few that seemed to have any lasting effect.

Roger T.'s reaction to these techniques was rather interesting. This mild, sullen, passive-aggressive individual became an accomplished shouter, and learned to express several different kinds of spontaneous emotions. His wife, for one, was delighted; evidently, Roger was becoming increasingly more bearable to live with. Even Roger seemed to be deriving more pleasure from life. Unfortunately, he moved from the area before completing treatment and no follow-up was attempted.

Training in Receiver Skills

Listening is anything but a passive art. The powerful receiver of communication is adept in at least four vital areas: he can focus much attention on the sender, he knows how to check up on the accuracy of his intake, he is good at rewarding the sender for communicating, and he can understand the feelings behind the message he receives as well as the thoughts contained in it. Learning attentional focus is a pursuit beyond the scope of this discussion. (One major requisite is the elimination of energy-draining extraneous behaviors, which has been treated earlier.) Checking intake and reinforcing communication are skills that are relatively easy to acquire. It is more difficult to train patients to receive feeling messages accurately; in most cases, previous experience accounts for more performance variation in this area than does short-term communication training.

To reinforce communication it is only necessary to 1) pay close attention to the sender and 2) communicate to him that he is receiving attention. This must be done in such a way that his sending behavior is validated without being interrupted. Patients can be trained to acknowledge the receipt of messages through a roleplaying modification.

TECHNIQUE #5: *Acknowledgment training.* Practice takes place in dyads; therapist and patient may roleplay together or a third party may be used. The participants, say Bob and Alice, engage in a discussion. Bob makes a statement. Before Alice can reply, she must acknowledge that she received and understood Bob's message. She may do this by saying, "Thank you," "OK," "I understand," or words to that effect. A non-verbal response, such as a smile or nod, may be used only if it is clearly understood by both parties to be an acknowledgment. If Alice did not understand Bob's message, she must ask for clarification: "Would you repeat that?", or "I don't understand that." Bob will then repeat his statement. If Alice now understands, she acknowledges the communication and continues with a statement of her own, which Bob must then acknowledge, or she waits for Bob to continue the discussion. If Alice is still confused, she must again request clarification; she never originates a statement until she understands the content of Bob's message. In this technique, the participants police one another, immediately calling one another's attention to missed acknowledgments. (If the therapist is role-playing, he may omit acknowledgments purposely toward the end of the session, and judge training success partly in terms of how quickly the patient calls his attention to the omission.)

> *EXAMPLE:* Wrong: Bob: "Alice, your blouse is dirty."
> Alice: "So is your shirt."
> Right: Bob: "Alice, your blouse is dirty."
> Alice: "OK," (or "Thank you," or "Yes, I see that it is.") Then, (if she still wishes to reply) "So is your shirt."

The patient should be reminded that it is the *act of communication,* and not communication content, which is being acknowledged. For instance:

> Bob: "Alice, I don't like you."
> Alice: "Thank you."

In this example, Alice is not being facetious or sarcastic, although it may seem so at first. She is not thanking Bob for his negative feelings; she is thanking him for *sharing them* with her. Honest feedback is a valuable gift. Alice may not be particularly pleased that Bob dislikes her, but now, at least, she does know how he feels. (The preceding discussion ignores the possibility that Alice may have a need to respond to negative feedback in an emotional or assertive manner. It is not being suggested that simple acknowledgment is the appropriate response in every interpersonal situation, but only that it is one good receiving technique.)

A more involved listening procedure was described by Rogers (1961). Its purpose is to facilitate the settling of disputes as well as to sharpen listening skill in general.

TECHNIQUE #6: *Intake verification.* A dyadic training setup is used, as above. Bob makes a statement. Before Alice is allowed to reply to that statement or make one of her own, she must paraphrase Bob's message and repeat it back to him. If Bob acknowledges her accuracy, she may continue. However, if she has repeated the essence of Bob's statement incorrectly, Bob tells her so, repeats himself, and Alice tries again. Alice must get Bob's message right before she can send one of her own. At that point the roles are reversed. Again, if the therapist is directly involved in the roleplaying situation, he may verify the content of his patient's message incorrectly on purpose to check training quality.

> *EXAMPLE:* Bob: "The house is always filthy when I get home from work—the dinner is never ready on time. I want you to shape up and start doing your job!"
> Alice: "You think it's my job to clean house and cook, and that I'm not doing it very well these days."
> Bob: "Right on!"
> Alice: "Well, I think you're being too hard on me; I'm human, too. The house is usually clean. Besides, why don't you ever offer to help me, like with the dishes?"
> Bob: "You think I expect too much of you and never do anything around the house myself."
> Alice: "No, I didn't say that. You do a lot to keep the house and yard up. But, you never offer to help me with anything."
> Bob: "Oh, you'd like to see more of a team effort on some things, like the dishes.
> Alice: "Yes, I would."
> Bob: "Well, I don't think that I should be expected to . . . (etc.).

Continuing in such a manner for more than a few minutes at one time would, of course, be maddening. The verification technique is primarily a troubleshooting device, used during conflict or when it is important that complicated information be received accurately. It is perfect for, say, the young married couple who profess undying love, but seemingly would rather fight than listen to one another. In addition, verification provides excellent receiver practice, in that he who uses it quickly gets into the habit of really listening to what the other person has to say. Finally, there is considerable reinforcement value in hearing one's own thoughts repeated back to one by a listener who obviously is trying to understand.

Although the training procedures are somewhat involved, patients can be taught to reinforce and facilitate the communication of feelings as well as of factual content. The basic technique they must learn is called *reflective listening*, which probably has been taught to more students in one form or another than any other single communication device (e.g. Gordon, 1971). Procedurally, *reflection* is much like *verification*, except that the primary focus is on affect feelings and not verbal content.

Three qualities of reflective listening make it a valuable communication tool. First, it catalyzes self-exploration and thus serves as a means of gathering information. The listener can induce the sender to talk about himself without "putting him on the spot" by asking a lot of questions. Second, as noted above, accurate reflective listening promotes feeling expression and reinforces constructive interpersonal behavior, in general. In new relationships, it may serve as a base from which other, more direct, forms of communication grow. Third, the dynamics of its implementation are easy to grasp; almost anyone can become an adept reflector of feelings in a relatively short time if he wishes to do so.

TECHNIQUE #7: *Reflective listening.* Patients are acquainted with the basic strategies of reflection, and then are presented with the following set of guidelines, mimeographed for home use.

a. Listen attentively to the sender's words and try to understand the meaning behind them.

b. Try to understand how the sender is feeling as he speaks, and watch for feeling implications in his words, tone, facial expression, body language, etc.

c. Repeat back to the sender, succinctly and in your on words, the essence of his message as you heard it and felt it. Your *primary* purpose here is communicating to the sender that you understand how he feels, accept his feelings without judging them as good or bad, and want to hear more about them.

d. Your secondary purpose is content verification.

e. Don't choose not to respond rather than risk being wrong. It is not mandatory that all your responses be blindingly accurate, as long as you continually check on and rectify your mistakes.

f. Respond often to the sender, even "with only a nod, to let him know you are still there with him."

Roleplaying procedures, particularly role-reversal, can be used to implement training in the office. In role-reversal, the therapist first plays himself; the patient sends feeling messages, and the therapist models reflective listening. Then they reverse roles: the therapist sends the same messages he received and the patient reflects. When the patient can imitate reflective listening in this manner, the therapist may begin sending him "unrehearsed" feeling messages, and critically evaluate the quality of his reflection. Taped sessions are valuable in that they allow the patient himself to evaluate his performance. Toward the end of training, the use of a third person in the role of interviewee provides the patient with "training under fire" and allows the therapist to check his progress.

> *EXAMPLE:* Bob: "That damn Richardson made it look like I fouled up the project again at staff meeting today."
> Alice: "He sure does annoy you with the tricks he pulls."
> Bob: "The really amazing part is how he gets the staff to buy it so easily. He comes out smelling like a rose and. . . ."
> Alice: "And you get left holding the fertilizer. . . ."
> Bob: "Yeah! I don't know how the little weasel gets away with it, but I can't handle much more of this."
> Alice: "Boy! You're damned mad at him and the whole place. It's so frustrating not to be able to do anything about it."
> Bob: "It's definitely getting me down. . . ."
> (and so on)

A trainee's ability to listen reflectively may be considerably improved by teaching him to function at high levels on certain interpersonal process dimensions. Research indicates that psychiatric inpatients, as well as outpatients and "normal" trainees, derive considerable benefit from process training. *Empathy, respect, concreteness,* and *immediacy* are a few of the more common variables which may be taught. Essentially, process training involves learning to 1) discriminate between good and bad communication in terms of specific variables, and 2) communicate at facilitative levels with regard to each variable in question. Training is conducted on the didactic and experiential level simultaneously, with the therapist functioning as role model for his patient/trainee. Elaborate criterion measures have been developed to assist the participants and insure training objectivity (Carkhuff, 1969). Implementation of process training in the therapy setting may, in some cases, be limited by practical considerations such as available training time and the therapist's own facilitative ability.

REFERENCES

CARKHUFF, R. R. *Helping and human relations: Volume I.* New York: Holt, Rinehart, and Winston, Inc., 1969.

GOLDSTEIN, A., SERBER, M., & PIAGET, G. W. Induced anger as a reciprocal inhibitor of fear. *Journal of Behavior Therapy and Experimental Psychiatry,* 1970, 1, 67.

GORDON, T. *Parent effectiveness training.* New York: Peter H. Wyden, Inc., 1971.

HUBBARD, L. R. Mimeographed communication training manual. East Grinstead, Sussex, England, 1961.

PIAGET, G. W. *Toward effective communication.* Unpublished manuscript, Palo Alto, California, 1971.

ROGERS, C. R. *On becoming a person.* Boston: Houghton Mifflin Company, 1961.

YATES, A. J. The application of learning theory to the treatment of tics. *Journal of Abnormal and Social Psychology,* 1958, 56, 175-182.

9

The Multiple Techniques of Broad
Spectrum Psychotherapy

BARRY M. BROWN, M.D.

BROAD-SPECTRUM PSYCHOTHERAPY is a technique-oriented system of psychotherapy in which all facets of the therapeutic process are considered to be composed of multiple techniques. The term "technique" will not be limited to such specific, much-discussed methods as clarification, interpretation, counterconditioning or assertive training. It will encompass, as much as possible, every way the therapist and patient interact. From the first phone call to the end of the last session, there are numerous interactions involved. Many of these are taken for granted, yet may be of great significance. For instance, the length of time a therapist spends with a patient, especially the first session, may be of great importance. Forty-five minutes may be anti-therapeutic, one and a half hours greatly therapeutic. The reverse may be true. The therapist's tone of voice, facial expression, his decisions as to when to speak or when to listen are likewise important. Again, how does he word things to the patient? Does his choice of words and their order convey blame or stimulate thinking? What techniques does he use to change the patient's concepts, beliefs and attitudes? What specific behavior therapy techniques does he use and when?

It is the premise of this chapter that every phase of Broad Spectrum Psychotherapy—RAPPORT, MANAGEMENT, BEHAVIOR THERAPY, and COGNITIVE THERAPY—is composed of multiple techniques. To be considered techniques, however, in the true sense of the word, they must be under the conscious control of the therapist and based on his working hypothesis of human behavior. Since little is proven about what is and what is not therapeutic, I am only suggesting that attention be paid to these areas and that they be given a more careful consideration in the study of psychotherapy. Hopefully, the techniques alluded to may someday be backed by experimental proof.

It is my intent to describe the techniques that I use in all phases of psychotherapy and to give my rationale for using them. Clinical material will be used widely, with emphasis on both successes and failures.

RAPPORT TECHNIQUES

Rapport is defined here as an optimal relationship between therapist and patient during the entire course of therapy. An optimal relationship is one where the patient likes the therapist, trusts him and has confidence in him. Rapport is imperative if the therapist wishes:

1. To motivate the patient to attend further therapy sessions.
2. To give the patient the feeling he is understood.
3. To enhance the patient's self-esteem.
4. To stimulate a free flow of attitudes and feelings from the patient.

Rapport techniques may vary during a session and during the course of therapy. If rapport is to exist the therapist must be constantly aware of himself and the use of his characteristics as part of his rapport regime. The following factors are important to the establishment of rapport:

1. The therapist's appearance, mannerisms and charisma.
2. The therapist's facial expressions.
3. The therapist's knowing when to talk, as well as when to listen.
4. The therapist's intensity, phrasing and general tone of voice and his choice of words.
5. The choice of subject matter.
6. The role that a therapist plays.

7. The attitude of empathy, warmth, and positive regard.
8. The therapist's ability to allow fulfillment of the patient's expectations early in therapy.
9. The occurrence of a remark by the therapist that captures the way the patient feels.
10. The use of a specific technique for relief of a troublesome symptom.
11. The educating of the patient as to what will occur in therapy and how it may work for him.

The appearance, age and charisma of the therapist can be only minimally controlled or altered. It is pointed out here because it must be considered a factor in the development of rapport. Very often, the reason for a patient leaving therapy can be explained on the basis of his not feeling any attraction for the therapist. The patient may be repelled because the therapist does not measure up to his own preconceived notions of what a therapist should be.

A therapist can be particularly skillful in the way he senses what constitutes optimal rapport with each individual patient. From the beginning of the first meeting, the therapist should note what he does that produces a favorable reaction. Does the patient seem more at ease, more open, more talkative, more intent on working on his difficulties when the therapist smiles and is friendly or when he is poker-faced and reserved? Does the patient like to do the talking or does he seem to respond better to being questioned? Does the therapist's tone of voice affect him? The therapist can speak in a very authoritarian way or can speak in a matter-of-fact way. To which does the patient seem to respond more readily? In the past, I feel that I have had a tendency to be too serious with patients, especially early in therapy, possibly from my own anxiety and possibly from wanting to "get down to business." However, I find that many patients come to therapy in an anxious state and seem more responsive when I am relaxed, warm, friendly, and spend some time discussing trivial matters.

It is also important to emphasize that a patient's personality may evoke responses in the therapist which may block effective therapy. The therapist should be aware of these responses and deal with them.

For example:

C.N. is a thirty-year-old white female, discussed in the management section. She can best be described as an obsessive-compulsive personality with tendencies toward depression, self-criticism, skepticism and an inability to enjoy life. In the early sessions, I noted how annoyed, critical and bored I felt with her. I realized my facial expression conveyed this feeling. I tried responding with a more pleasant, smiling, approving, and interested facial expression. On occasion, I started joking with her. Over our next four sessions her eye contact increased markedly, skeptical remarks about therapy decreased, and she began discussing highly personal matters more openly.

J.J. was an extremely attractive, mini-skirted twenty-two-year-old white female who talked incessantly about her "horrible" husband. Her talkativeness decreased her attractiveness. This, plus the frustration of not being able to get a word in edgewise, made me feel quite negative about her, and I am quite sure my facial expression conveyed my feelings. I decided to stop trying to interrupt her and spent the sessions looking at her "admiringly." The results were gratifying as she soon ran out of steam and not only listened to what I did have to say, but also adopted and put to use my suggestions.

In regard to actively taking a history versus letting the patient tell his own story, I have converted more to an inactive role in the early sessions and have found that giving the patient more time to talk or some gentle prods reveals much more information and is preferred by the patient. When the patient is having difficulty getting started and has no idea what is expected of him in psychotherapy or what he is to talk about, I will then help him along by asking questions.

As a therapist, as well as in my own interpersonal relations, I have felt my "vocal image" left something to be desired. I have particularly concentrated on improving my phrasing, intensity and tone of voice and my choice of words. A therapist should learn to speak in a more mellow, softer tone, to be less intense, and to watch his phrasing of sentences and choice of words. Instead of saying, "You are looking very hostile today." I might state, "Have things been annoying you?" The latter is less critical and more indirect. Rather than saying, "You are a sensitive person," one may say "You seem very alert to the environment." Words that may bear a psychological "stigma" or negative implications of any kind like "hostility," "depression" and "fear" tend to upset patients more than those with fewer psychological overtones—"sadness," "concern" and "scared." Usage of the latter increases rapport.

Often the therapist gets so engrossed in his thoughts of "What is going on here?," "What are the dynamics?," that he forgets to be the reinforcer and does not give his full attention to what the patient has said. Because of this, he may lose rapport. It must be emphasized that while rapport techniques are important throughout therapy, it is basically the first sessions that are the most crucial because early in therapy patients often need motivation, which good rapport helps establish. Later in therapy I may discuss the rapport techniques, "the way I've had to be," to demonstrate to a patient one of his characteristics. For example, in the nineteenth session with N.A. (cognitive section) I said, "Look, some days I get the feeling I have got to let you do all the talking and other days I feel you are disappointed if I don't say much." My purpose in making this remark at this time was to lay the groundwork for pointing out how his moods change, and later to relate his moods to changing predominant cognitive themes. His answer to the statement was "You're right. Today I was impatient and wanted you to talk and yet other times I am annoyed and tell you to be quiet."

I generally allow patients to discuss whatever subject they desire. Allowing certain important issues to be left unsaid may be a necessity in early sessions in order to keep anxiety low and rapport high. Once the patient has become relaxed and optimal rapport is operating, the therapist may then call attention to the issues. For example, N.A., discussed in the cognitive section, brought up little talk about girls and sex prior to the fifteenth meeting. Early attempts to encourage discussion in this area had met with resistance, so were not pursued further.

Patients tend to differ in the level of confidence they want in their therapist. Some patients prefer humility; others want certainty. The therapist should recognize early in treatment into which category the patient belongs and act accordingly. This is not necessarily constant and the therapist must "tune in" at each meeting to determine how he should act.

J.D. is a twenty-four year old white female whose father and married boyfriend are strong willed and assertive. She did not respond in the first half hour of our first session to my occasional soft-spoken statements. When I spoke louder and with more confidence, she responded more to me, i.e., had better eye contact and showed facial signs of agreement.

Then at a second session where she was overwrought about the boyfriend's loss of interest in her, she only responded after I switched from an assertive, confident role to a soft-spoken, sympathetic one.

Whereas I was originally trained in the traditional model of distance and aloofness, I find that this stance often leads to lowering of the patient's self-esteem and an increase in self-critical feelings. I have become much more prone to using techniques involving empathy, warmth, and unconditional positive regard. This approach also involves the wording of interpretations. Sentences that traditionalists use, such as "You have a need to suffer," or allusions to one's hostilities or traits in a critical light, contribute to the loss of self-esteem and also increase self-blame. An approach that views human behavior in terms of traits which are adaptive or maladaptive has been more effective for me than the traditional approach which, while disclaiming this in theory, in practice tends to see traits in "bad" or "good" terms.

Patients often have preconceived ideas as to what therapy is about and what they are supposed to say. Interrupting the patient as he is telling every detail of his past life or of a seemingly irrelevant situation may prevent him from realizing his expectation. Once the patient has told what he thinks he should tell, the therapist may then direct the session to the significant points.

A statement that is emotionally meaningful to a patient, that is, one which really "hits home," causes the patient to feel understood. This is usually evident by the response of the patient: a brightening of the eyes, nodding of the head or verbal expression of agreement.

C.M. (described in management section) showed anxiety, irritability and inappropriate affect to the point where she was considered borderline psychotic. At a marital session, my female cotherapist said to her, "I have the feeling you're protecting your husband." Her facial expression changed, her voice dropped in pitch, she couldn't speak for a moment and for the remainder of the session she was more relaxed and showed no irritability or inappropriate affect. Furthermore, she rationally discussed the statement made to her. Clearly the statement increased rapport.

Many patients have been thought to leave therapy because of the failure of the therapist to recognize at an early session the need to treat the specific symptom of the patient. I have found this particularly true regarding psychosomatic cases, specifically some headache cases. I have seen three patients referred by their physician for headaches of no known physical cause and explored their life situation, past and present, with particular emphasis on events surrounding their headaches. These patients did not see the value of this approach and therefore did not respond. A better approach for these cases would seem to be an initial treatment of the specific symptom. This may be accomplished by generalized muscle relaxation, particularly the neck and scalp muscles. This hopefully would give a therapeutic result at an early session. I feel that treating the symptom successfully will set the stage for later psychological exploration, should the relaxation treatment be unsuccessful in giving the patient complete relief. If the patient is made aware of the fact that some psychological difficulty may be contributing to his symptom, he may then be more receptive for exploratory psychotherapy. Illustrative of the effects of early symptomatic relief would be the case of a stutterer with whom I initially took a behavior therapy approach. A marked improvement in his stuttering occurred in four sessions with the use of generalized relaxation and selective relaxation of throat muscles. He then began discussing other areas of his life and a cognitive approach was used. (See Behavior Therapy, Section—D.C.)

A final technique used to develop rapport is one used with the patient who is not sure what psychotherapy is all about or what is really expected of him. This type of patient would probably respond much more readily if the first session or two were devoted to educating him in any areas of psychiatry or psychotherapy in which the therapist feels increased knowledge would relieve anxiety. Sometimes a case example may be used.

L.C. is a thirty-year-old white male who presented with a history of five panic attacks. He was most anxious at the meeting and his wife indicated he had not wanted to come at all. He revealed skepticism about therapy for "financial reasons." He had no previous contact with psychiatry and was quite unsophisticated about psychological matters. The story he gave revealed little to explain his attacks. Because of his anxiety, I limited the session to forty minutes and because of possible similarities to another case (W.B.—Cognitive Section), I described the case to him, emphasizing that certain ideas or fears always preceded the patient's anxiety attacks. I also mentioned that the patient had improved in four sessions. The patient acted most interested, and said, "That sounds just like me." He left in a more relaxed, apparently optimistic state than that in which he had entered.

MANAGEMENT TECHNIQUES

The management of patients includes six important areas: the length of therapy sessions, the frequency of sessions, the collection of fees, the use and abuse of phone calls, the involvement of parents and peers, and the role of a married patient's spouse.

Length of Sessions

It is frequently necessary for a new patient to be seen for ninety, rather than fifty minutes. I find the longer time period necessary for the patient to become sufficiently relaxed so that he can openly relate his difficulties in detail, obtain relief from catharsis, and develop a feeling that the therapist understands and can help him. The therapist needs this time to make multiple decisions involving the specific information he wishes to obtain, the meaning of information gained, the techniques to be employed to maximally lessen the patient's suffering in this initial session, and the tentative plans for future therapy.

On the other hand, I often limit the first session to thirty minutes. This is done with patients who come to a psychiatrist reluctantly and appear to be in an anxious state relative to the experience itself. Since it is my goal in these situations to lower the patient's anxiety and to increase his motivation, I concentrate on rapport techniques such as relaxed affect, warmth, and discussion of trivial matters. In addition I attempt to educate the patient about what occurs in psychotherapy and how it may help him. This use of rapport and education acts to "desensitize" the patient and, more often than not, he will return in a less anxious state, more prepared to discuss his life.

With many patients, throughout an entire course of therapy, it may take fifteen to twenty minutes to relax sufficiently to talk freely. For these people, I usually allow sixty to seventy-five minutes at early meetings and later rarely see them for less than one hour.

Frequency of Sessions

Frequency of sessions varies if there is a crisis involved. Crisis patients may be seen daily for up to four days, and may then be tapered off. Regular patients are seen more than once a week only if there is a pressing problem.

Sometimes the verbal, psychological-minded, contemplative patient feels he gains more by coming twice weekly. I never see these patients more than this as I feel no benefit is gained.

Some patients who would profit more from weekly therapy will only come biweekly or monthly because of the financial strain that weekly therapy imposes.

Fees

The handling of patients' fees varies with the type of patient with which one is dealing. Poor risk patients, such as certain character disorders and alcoholics, are told by the clinic bookkeeper, at my suggestion, that they must pay prior to each session. This promotes responsibility in the patient and avoids hostility in the therapist. Conscientious patients, known to pay their bills regularly, are allowed extended time to pay their bills should their finances be tight. Patients are not charged if they miss an appointment. Most responsible patients cancel in advance except when there is an emergency. If the patient has a poor excuse for cancelling or is absent without explanation, the therapist should look into the patient's motivation for continued treatment. Often, these are signals that the patient is dissatisfied. Calling the patient who misses an appointment and does not telephone often verifies dissatisfaction or ambivalence, is an excellent way of learning the patient's reasons for stopping therapy, and gives clues to what errors, if any, the therapist made in technique.

With patients in an explorative cognitive therapy, the implications of delayed fee payment and missed appointments may be examined in terms of life patterns.

Cotherapy, which we feel is an excellent modality for marital problems, is, unfortunately, quite expensive. Because of our interest in this, we have each decreased our fees and have tended to use combined sessions more sparingly due to their long length.

Telephone Calls

Patients conscientiously working in therapy are permitted to call for any crisis, with no fee charged or reprimand made. Patients who have avoided regular therapy and who call the therapist at home are tactfully managed by being billed at a higher rate than that of an office visit. Patients who overly concern themselves about "bothering" a therapist and who may get into difficulty, such as a severe depression in between visits, are often given specific instructions to call on a given day. I also will not hesitate calling any patient about whom I am concerned.

Involvement of Parents and Peers

In the treatment of adolescents I usually involve members of the patient's family and/or peer group in the therapy.

C.K. was a thirteen-year-old white female referred by a neurologist because of an inability to walk without falling for three months. This had been preceded by a viral illness and a facial palsy necessitating complete medical and neurological studies. There were no positive findings and because of the bizarre character of the girl's gait, the neurologist was convinced that her ataxia was functional in nature, a conversion reaction. At the initial interview, the mother revealed that the daughter might have some concern about school, but she denied family difficulties, any particular precipitating events or other potential problem areas such as menarche or boyfriends that might have catalyzed the daughter's walking difficulty. When seen individually, no obvious concerns were evident in the daughter. At this time the mother was advised to "pay less attention" to the walking problem and the daughter was told she would gradually improve in her walking. The daughter was seen individually on two further occasions where all interview techniques known to the author failed to elicit possible anxiety-producing areas for the girl. The patient and her mother were then seen by the social worker and myself so their interaction might be examined. The session was awkward, the girl being quite silent and the mother fruitlessly urging discussion. Since there were allusions to some hostility from the father and sixteen-year-old sister we decided to involve them in our next meeting. When the whole family was seen, some interesting interactions occurred which gave us an idea for a therapeutic approach. The mother was noted to be consistently understanding and protective of the patient, while the father and sister were consistently sarcastic and unsupportive toward her. Seeing these relationships and having gleaned nothing further in the areas we had continued to explore—school, boys and menarche—it was decided to instruct the family on some rules for the management of the patient. These were: only the sister and father could help the patient get to her crutches or wheel chair; the mother was to do nothing for the patient in these areas nor attend to anything she had not done before the patient "got sick." The patient was to use her crutches as her main source of ambulation, to gradually stop using the wheel chair over a one-week period and to practice walking without crutches, increasing daily the number of steps without them. The rationale was that the patient liked using the wheel chair and had complained that the crutches were most uncomfortable. The patient had always been able to take two or three faltering steps without crutches. During the entire course of therapy, suggestion had been used—"This will improve over a matter of time. The neurologist has told us that these conditions always get better. Your condition appears good enough that you should be able to increase your walking by at least one step a day."

Two weeks after this regime was started the patient walked with no abnormality and needed no assistance of any type. Her flawless walking was demonstrated at our next visit. The family was advised that we were glad of the girl's success but felt followup therapy was necessary. They were quite happy with the results and did not see the value of further therapy.

C.G. was an eighteen-year-old white female brought into my office in a catatonic-like state—staring blankly ahead, showing no spontaneous speech, laughing inappropriately and giving brief answers to all questions. The parents stated that the girl had always been a "model child," but in the past six months had been telling lies, taking illegal drugs, and had recently stayed away from home for three weeks. The family had always been most strict and in the last two months increased their strictness in response to the patient's dating a boy of a religion of which they disapproved. There were no other known objections to the boy.

It was decided to hospitalize the girl. When seen in the hospital, she was angry about being hospitalized, but otherwise her clinical picture had not changed. She was able to briefly discuss her current boyfriend and could not understand her parents reaction to him since he was not involved with drugs and was an ambitious college student. Since he had assumed such great importance in her life I thought that I would involve him in her therapy. She perked up when I suggested this. The couple was seen together for two meetings and their relationship, the patient's past problems with her parents and the current conflict were discussed. At the same time, the parents were seen by the social worker and myself. The social worker was a very warm, supportive woman and was able to establish an excellent relationship, even with the extremely rigid father. Once good rapport was established, their reasons for strictness were discussed and the fact that extreme strictness often led to rebellious behavior was pointed out. The religious issue was discussed and the boyfriend's many good traits were emphasized. The parents were able to see that the boy had been a good influence, had gotten their daughter away from drugs and had stimulated her interest in going to college. It was also pointed out that the boyfriend had excellent credentials: he was from a good family, was a conscientious premedical student and was interested in the well-being of their daughter. We brought out to the parents how they had always overreacted to many things the daughter had done and were now overreacting to the dating of a well-intentioned man on the basis of religious difference.

The parents responded well to therapy and softened their limits on the girl, allowing her to continue dating the boy. The girl showed marked clinical improvement and she and her boyfriend cancelled their plans to run away and marry. She was able to return home and the relationship with her parents went well. The truce that developed from the involvement of all family members plus the involvement of the most important person in the girl's life at that time led to a clinical remission of all her presenting symptoms as well as an understanding by the parents of what they had been doing that led to the girl's rebelliousness. At last report the boyfriend was thinking of converting to the girl's religion and the plans for secret marriage were postponed indefinitely.

Involvement of the Patient's Spouse

A married person presenting for therapy poses a challenging management problem: In what way should the mate be handled? Should the mate be ignored, the presenting spouse becoming the "designated patient"? Should the mate be an "adviser" informing the therapist of the spouse's past and present life and giving his views of the spouse's current difficulty? Should the marriage partner be a patient in his own right, needing some form of individual therapy or should he be treated as part of a marital system which then becomes the "designated patient"?

Factors involved in assessing the extent of the mate's involvement include the presenting problem: Does the presenting patient pose difficulties which do not appear related to the marriage or does the complaint involve the marriage, either some form of marital disharmony or an attitude of apathy in one or both partners? Is the patient willing for his spouse to be seen? Will the spouse come in and, if so, what aspects of his personality influence the therapist's decision as to the role he will play in the patient's treatment? These important factors in management can be demonstrated in the following cases:

D.W., discussed in the cognitive therapy section, was a twenty-eight-year-old pregnant white female with agoraphobia. Even though she indicated no marital problems, I decided, with her consent, to interview her husband. This was done to evaluate his personality, to get his views on their marriage, to elicit the meaning to both of them of her pregnancy and to learn how he responded to her phobic condition. When it became clinically evident to me that he was well adjusted, that there were no obvious marital problems, that the pregnancy was wanted by both of them and that his responses to her symptoms did not encourage secondary gain, it was decided to see her in individual cognitive therapy. Treatment on this basis was successful.

C.H., discussed in the cognitive therapy section, was a twenty-nine-year-old white female with an obsessive thought that she was going to kill her six-month-old son. Her history revealed nervousness, obsessions, compulsions and phobias dating to her teen years. She was treated with traditional psychotherapy for one year at age twenty. Even though the long history of difficulty antedated her marriage by four years and she denied marital difficulties, it was decided that the husband be seen once in order to clarify some of this patient's magnifications and distortions. She agreed to his coming and when seen he was found to be appropriate and understanding and put things in a clearer perspective than the patient had. There was no evidence from either him or his wife that there had been any worsening of her marked obsession secondary to the marital situation. He did point out that the child actually was extremely irritable and had occupied much of the wife's day and night. It was decided that her obsession to kill the child was most likely related to feelings of hostility and resentment of which she was unaware. I therefore encouraged further care of the child by the husband, relatives, friends and baby sitters, so that the patient could get some relief from the child and spend some of her time at activities she found relaxing and pleasurable. The husband cooperated fully and the decreased pressure from the care of the child and the gains made in cognitive therapy, as described in that section, led to a resolution of the obsession.

P.P. is a forty-six-year-old white male wealthy accountant. He has been married twenty-five years and has four children. He presented in a state of agitation and depression because the young married woman he had been dating and intending to marry had been wooed back by her husband after she had told him of her romance with the patient. After three weeks of supportive therapy, the patient recovered from this "loss" and began to discuss his marriage. He stated he had never felt romantic with his wife, was disappointed in her sexually, and repeatedly mentioned his resentment for her many interests and activities and the fact that she controlled the household and the children. Early in the marriage he had had one brief affair because he was "not getting enough sex" from his wife and over the years saw a prostitute on three single occasions when out of town on business. However, he states he always felt that he was looking for a "true romance." I thought it was significant that, before developing this intense relationship with the young woman, he had been transferred from a small town where he moved among the social élite and where he was a significant man in his firm's small office to a large city where he was unknown to the élite and less important to the larger office of his firm. This was felt by me to be a blow to his self-esteem and the statements relative to his wife indicated she had always reinforced this poor self-opinion. Statements concerning the girlfriend displayed a theme of how important he felt when with her.

The patient had moved out of his house prior to losing the young woman and, after the grief period, he decided to move back and "try it again." He had told his wife candidly all along of his relationship with the woman and then of her loss. She reacted sympathetically, indicated she cared for him, would take him back and never was vindictive in any way. However, the patient did not like living at home even though he felt his wife had acted favorably in every way he could ask, including her sexual reactivity toward him. He returned to the house, did not feel happy and moved out again on three occasions. With his agreement, I decided to see the wife. She was much as he described her and anxious to cooperate in any way she could. She was concerned about him and hoped he would return. It was decided, however, at that time, that the main contribution to his leaving was intrapsychic rather than interpersonal, so no marital sessions were planned. Also, I advised the wife to not allow the husband back home until I talked with her. At our next meeting, I told the patient that he was not to return home until he honestly desired his wife and until further therapy cleared up some of the issues involved. My reasoning on this matter was that this would give him time to examine possible intrapsychic causes leading to his current situation. Also, by not going home, at my suggestion, his guilt would be relieved and his positive feelings for his wife would possibly intensify. Many cases similar to this, that is a mate apathetic to his spouse and on the look for romance, were formerly handled by seeing the marital couple together with a female cotherapist present and by emphasizing examination of the communication and the ways each was being reinforcing or adversive. However, this did not meet with great success. It is my feeling that putting the couple together to treat their marriage was done too early, when motivation of the apathetic mate was low. This patient is still in individual therapy, having to date a total of fourteen meetings. He has spent most of his time recently talking of his wife; themes of his low self-esteem are quite frequent. The plan now is to continue cognitive therapy and see if the awareness that self-esteem has played a part in his "problem" leads him to return to his wife, without being vulnerable to the intensity of a new romance, particularly in regard to its esteem-building potential.

E.U. is a twenty-eight-year-old white female married ten years and having two children. She stated she has been "bored" with her husband for five years and now wants "out," "freedom." She described her husband's actions over the years as very "controlling." She has always been afraid to do anything without his approval. Her desire for freedom increased markedly when the family moved into a new home. "I felt like having a home was like going to jail for the rest of my life, as if the house had bars." The husband was seen once, did not appear especially domineering and was vaguely aware of the issues the patient had brought up. The wife during the first six sessions of therapy was intensely desirous of freedom and had obtained a job and hired a divorce attorney. Marital therapy was not suggested because of her need to avoid the husband. In individual therapy, other than mentioning marital therapy in the first session and seeing the husband once, I always acted as if I assumed she was going to get the divorce, even though I felt her dependency might prevent her. The main pattern seen and discussed in the eight meetings to date has been her continual giving into people and doing what they wanted. This was noted not only in the marriage, but also in the job she had taken. There, she had allowed herself to become the busiest secretary in the office. At our seventh meeting, one month before the husband was scheduled to move out of the home, the patient mentioned that the husband and she had had two dates, both very enjoyable and ending with satisfying sex. "When I think of myself as free from him, I can enjoy his company and the sex. But the next day when he assumes all is well and says,

'I guess we will stay together,' then I feel just as turned off by him."
Assertive training was started at the seventh session since the theme
of low assertiveness permeates her relationships with her parents and
siblings, work situation and marriage. At the eighth session she stated,
"I'm not so sure now about the divorce. C. has shaped up." It would
seem from this that she is showing more motivation toward her husband.
It is felt, however, that to maintain the good feelings she is now beginning to experience, she must continue to feel some degree of assertiveness
and independence in her marriage. Individual therapy will continue with
an emphasis on attitude exploration and assertive training.

J.T. is a thirty-five-year-old white female married twelve years and having
three children. In the past five years she has suffered recurrent severe
depressions, abused tranquilizing drugs, made at least three serious suicide
attempts and was hospitalized five times. She has been treated with drugs
and electroshock therapy. When seen by me after her last serious suicide
attempt, she was markedly depressed and appeared to be a "hopeless
case." As we talked daily, it became evident that much of her unhappiness
related to the different life styles she and her husband had and the
consequences of living in a small town. She was markedly extrovertish
while he was an introvert. Her husband was in business in a small town
and felt it was important for her to act in a more "straight-laced" way.
He was public opinion oriented, she was not. Her actions of the past few
years did not involve immoral acts of any kind; however, there was some
sexual acting out after a hysterectomy eight years ago. The husband
worked very hard and rarely took her out. Her depressions always began
with decreased attention to the children and the housework. It was my
opinion that there were no reinforcers in her life for which to work. Also,
she suffered repeated reprimanding from him for being seen with women
of the wrong race, religion or social class in the town and for outgoing
behavior at social functions. During her past illnesses the husband was
handled as the stable, "well" member of the marriage and only interviewed
by her doctors "to obtain a history." I decided that her illnesses had as
much to do with him as it did with her. This was explained to her and
drew a marked response of appreciation. She felt what I said was very
true. The husband was seen both alone and with his wife and my cotherapist. Emphasis was put on the wife's needs for attention, and his
fears concerning her friends and actions. Also, they were educated as to
their marital interaction. This was all presented in a non-blameful way,
making it fairly palatable. In the sixteen months since the patient was
first seen, she has come in every four to six weeks and he has been seen
four times. She has not been hospitalized nor has she made any suicide
attempt. She still is occasionally nervous and depressed, the marriage is
not perfect and she requires tranquilizing medication. This is a good
clinical result considering her past history. It is attributed to making the
patient and her husband aware of the causation of her illness and to both
of them recognizing the other's needs more acutely. More frequent therapy

might lead to even further lessening of the patient's symptoms and needs for medication, but financial realities have limited their attendance. The wife is seen alone until she shows signs of increased depression or anxiety, whereupon the husband is brought in and the above conditions are reemphasized.

S.H. is a twenty-six-year-old white male systems analyst married seven years and having two children. He sought help for his "troubled marriage." I saw him individually for three meetings and characterized him as bright, sensitive and persistent, with a tendency to distort and magnify things and to use multisyllabic words and detailed explanations. This made him difficult to understand, but I did not feel he was schizophrenic. His wife was then seen twice and appeared calm, intelligent, honest and motivated to improve the marriage. The focus of their conversation was on the recent arguing that had been occurring. The husband said the marriage was good until the wife had gone out to a nightclub with a divorcée who he did not feel was a good influence on her. He claimed all would be well in the marriage if she did not see this woman or go to the club again. The wife complained of the husband's lack of attention, their lack of social life and her husband's working long hours on nights and weekends. She felt they had never communicated well. I felt she was the healthier member of the marriage.

Since they had daily bitter arguments and were talking of divorce, I decided to see them together with the assistance of a female cotherapist. Our goal was to make some basic agreements to establish a truce so that we could explore with them the factors contributing to their difficulties. In the combined sessions the husband reacted quite intensively to even the most benign remarks from the wife. We attempted to point out his distortions and magnifications when they occurred. At times it appeared that he got the message and would calm down, but the next session usually revealed that he intensively goaded the wife after the session. His demands on her led to her continually going out to the nightclub, having an affair on one occasion and admitting it to him. This led to his moving out of their apartment. We supported this separation because we thought it would be good for them to avoid each other's aversive behavior. The wife was upset by the husband's leaving and at one of our sessions she agreed to stay in at night and not go out again with the divorcée. This did not satisfy the husband. He stayed apart and decided to divorce her. A three-month followup revealed he was going through with the divorce as planned. I regard this case as a failure but would like to discuss some further points not mentioned above.

1. Good rapport was established between the therapists and the patients—even though Mr. H. was exquisitely sensitive to his wife, I found I was able to relate well with him in individual and marital sessions.
2. Mr. H. was seen individually by me between marital sessions to further

point out his cognitive distortions and magnifications. I felt he got some understanding of the points made.

3. The couple was seen very frequently during acute periods to avoid a worsening of the situation.
4. Other points in the history that may be significant include:
    a. Mr. H. had always been a premature ejaculator, but the wife denied this bothered her or that she was looking for sex with other men.
    b. Mrs. H. had felt the husband was interested in affairs with other women from the way he acted at parties and spoke. Mr. H. said he appreciated looking at other women, but had always been faithful. Late in therapy when separated, Mr. H. revealed in the joint therapy meeting that he was seeing another woman. This was said in a boastful, vindictive tone of voice.
5. Our hypothesis about the precipitating event of the overt marital discord was that the wife, who had always been quite active in school, limited her activity and money spending while the husband was in college and the children were being raised. She had also spoiled her husband, waiting on him excessively and keeping the children quiet during this period. When he began his career seven months before consulting us, she was disappointed that despite having more money and less academic pressure, the husband still paid her little attention, took her nowhere, worked long hours and still demanded much from her. She stopped doing housework, and began pushing the message that she wanted more out of life. He had become accustomed to having complete control over her and could not tolerate anything like this. It is hard to explain, however, why he persisted in separating and divorcing once she acceded to his demands. It is possible that he felt inadequate about his premature ejaculation and the threatened loss of his wife may have made him feel more insecure in this respect. His leaving her, before she left him, may well have been an attempt to build his self-esteem.

M.W. is a forty-five-year-old white married female who had multiple somatic complaints, called her family physician almost daily and went through multiple physical exams, laboratory tests and x-rays. Her symptoms had developed over the last five years, but were worse in the last three after her son was killed in a skirmish with the law. She blamed herself for the son's death and the husband never denied this. Whereas she had formerly been active with the husband in camping, fishing and other activities, she became much less active over this period and the husband did not go out without her. She had also lost interest in sex. She had been hospitalized several times for her somatic complaints, marked depression and, when I first saw her, for deeply cutting both wrists. I interviewed the husband and found him to be cooperative, disappointed in the wife's apathy of recent years, and having no abnormal psychiatric signs or symptoms. Because of his apparent stability, he had never been involved in the patient's therapy except as historian. It was decided to see them together and discuss their interaction. This revealed the tendency of the wife to blame herself for the son's lawlessness and death, and the husband's tacit agreement. This assumption was challenged and the shared role in childrearing was emphasized, but put in a non-blameful perspective. That is, the fact that people's personalities may be determined by factors parents cannot control, such as genetic influences, was pointed out.

It was further emphasized that there was nothing wrong with the wife physically and that she tended to magnify aches and pains. She was encouraged to be more active with the husband again. Three combined meetings were held. Followup therapy was done one and two months after this and revealed the patient was asymptomatic physically and mentally. She was not obsessing on her son's death and was going places with her husband every weekend. He was delighted with the change in her and was taking her out to dinner during the week. The patient ceased calling her family doctor and has maintained her improvement with no further therapy. A friend of mine reading this case said it sounded too good to be true, but it is my impression that just by including a mate as part of a patient's problem, taking the onus of sickness off the patient and putting it on the marriage where it is dealt with, is a highly therapeutic maneuver.

C.M. was a forty-four-year-old white female married twenty-four years and having six children. Her husband made an appointment for her because she was irritable, continually starting arguments with him and the children and was not doing housework. She had acted similarly two years before and was treated with electroshock therapy with moderately good results, according to the husband. When I saw her, she was indeed sensitive, irritable, and appeared depressed. At times her thoughts were a bit inappropriate and she complained of feeling nervous. Diagnostically I saw her as having a depressive reaction and as possibly being borderline psychotic. Others may have seen her as an agitated depression or a schizophrenic. Her husband was seen and appeared very rational, helpful, annoyed by her condition and with no signs or symptoms of psychiatric disorder. He related that she had consulted other psychiatrists in the last ten years and if they felt it was just "her problem" and did not blame him, she did not stay with them. My initial plan was to treat her with tranquilizers and antidepressants and see her for individual psychotherapy. I felt she might well need hospitalization if she did not respond to these. In individual therapy her thinking became more logical and she related dissatisfactions in her marital life and an interest in another man. Further sessions made me feel the marital interaction was more the problem than a primary interest in romance with other men. The patient responded amazingly well to statements that captured her feelings, and became relaxed in the therapy. However, her husband would call between sessions and complain that she was "irritable, depressed and getting on everyone's nerves." I then decided that marital therapy was indicated and saw the couple with a female cotherapist. Some of the issues brought up in individual therapy were the different philosophies of raising the children and handling of finances. This woman had allowed her husband much responsibility with the children but then resented the children's dependency on him rather than on her. She also stated that she resented her husband because of his Ph.D. She had many inferior feelings and for some reason these had recently begun to dominate her thinking. She also felt a need for more stimulation than a housewife gets. As with most wives seen, she complained that the husband had an active interesting job and wanted to stay home and do nothing in the evenings. She was bored and wanted to go out. Even though her complaints centered around the marriage, she repeatedly denied wanting marital therapy. Despite this, it was decided by me to involve the husband. In two sessions of marital therapy, the patient was much more inhibited and complained little of the husband's characteristics. My cotherapist referred to Mrs. M's extremely high expectations of herself. It was also mentioned that she seemed to protect the husband in therapy. This remark seemed very meaningful to the patient. It was also pointed out that Mrs. M. got much responsibility without having the authority. As the communications between the couple were discussed, in a non-blameful way, the husband appeared more anxious and depressed. Significantly, they cancelled their next appointment one day before it was scheduled. They did not reschedule. When I called one and two weeks later I did not get either parent, left a message with an older child and the call was never returned.

One month later I learned by chance that the couple had sought out a hospital-oriented psychiatrist, told him that drugs and therapy had not helped and almost demanded electroshock treatment. This was done and the psychiatrist felt the patient showed moderate improvement.

I called Mrs. M. one month later to get some followup information for this chapter. She was very cold, did not volunteer any information about the shock therapy and simply said she was "fine."

We felt these patients left therapy because the guilt-prone wife could not tolerate seeing the husband being "blamed."

C.N. and J.N.: C.N. is a thirty-year-old white female married for seven years. She was referred by a physician because of depression. When J.N., her husband, heard this he made an appointment with me, stating to her and to me that he was her problem and that he needed treatment. When interviewed he was depressed and complained that he was not involved in his marriage, work or any activities. I agreed to see him for individual therapy. When I reported this to the referring physician, he insisted that I still see the wife as he felt she, too, needed help. The wife was seen and found to be depressed, pessimistic, perfectionistic, self-critical and tense. Individual therapy was suggested to her and she agreed. Both are now being seen in individual therapy. J.N. is discussed in the cognitive section.

He has stated, after each of them had about six sessions, that his wife is better than ever, worrying less about the housework and the kids and treating him with more respect. The emphasis in his therapy is on his fears of talking spontaneously and of involving himself in activities. Her therapy has centered around her extremes in thinking. I am treating both of them, feel they both trust me and that with this couple there is no harm in the procedure. There is no serious marital problem, though of course they are sensitive to each other's moods and acts. Marital therapy is felt not indicated at this time.

Mr. and Mrs. W.E. are in their late twenties, have been married for seven years and have two children. Mrs. E. brought her husband in because "he drinks too much and is always wanting sex." I saw the couple alone at the first meeting. The next three sessions involved my seeing the wife first, while my female social worker saw the husband. The four of us would then meet for a combined session.

In brief, the marriage had been "good" for four years but then for some reason the wife became less interested in sex and cut down its frequency. The husband, always a beer drinker, increased the number of beers he drank. At the time neither complained about the changed conditions. The wife's alcoholic father died one year ago and it was then that she got increasingly critical of her husband, mainly of his drinking (which consisted of four cans of beer in the evening), of his smoking, of his not hanging his clothes up, and of his not knowing how to manage money. In individual therapy it became evident that she was sensitized by her father's death, stating he would have lived another ten years if not for alcohol. She also revealed a premarital sex adventure with another man which she enjoyed very much, but which led to pregnancy, illegal abortion and to near death for her. She never liked sex much after that, even though she took careful birth control precautions. Whereas at first this girl presented as a hostile demanding, complaining spoiled brat, she was very responsive to both individual and marital therapy. My cotherapist saw the husband as a capable, but meek man who did well at his job, was liked by his bosses, made decisions carefully, handled his children well, both in giving attention and disciplining them, and gave his wife whatever she wanted. His chief weakness was his inability to stand up to her. His drinking was not felt to be excessive. In the combined meetings we pointed out some of the patterns we saw operating. One statement made to her was, "Despite this fighting, I get the feeling you love your husband very much. Because of this you get very scared of losing him through death at a young age. This is why it would seem it is upsetting you when he drinks and smokes." At another session, we had them list each other's good traits. Both came up with many. We then discussed the impossibility of perfection in marriage and stated that there seemed to be many things they really did like about each other. The husband's lack of assertiveness was pointed out in individual therapy and then he was urged to practice acting assertively during a combined session. We had him repeat the behavior several times until it sounded convincing. The wife, when asked about this "new way" of his acting, said she preferred him this way.

This couple was only seen four times but showed marked improvement in several respects.

1. The wife seemed to understand both the probable etiology of her sexual disinterest and the reason for her complaints about her husband, relative to her own fears of his dying, like her father, and to the fact that he never stood up to her, thus reinforcing her complaining.
2. The wife became more agreeable to sex.
3. The husband gained less insight but, according to the wife, was acting more assertively.

Unfortunately they moved from the area and no further therapy was done. Also no followup is available. We feel these people could have explored, in more detail, their personal fears—hers about sex and his about asserting himself in the marriage and other areas.

BEHAVIOR THERAPY TECHNIQUES

Muscle Relaxation

I have taught muscle relaxation much the same way Wolpe does but have emphasized specific wording and imagery to implement it. As the patient focuses attention on the various parts of his body, he is told to attend to that part only, not to let his mind wander elsewhere. He is then told the feeling he should be experiencing is a "letting go," a letting out of all tension from this part of the body. He is told he does not need to use this part for the next half hour and, therefore, can let all muscle tension out of it. Sometimes the word "paralyze" is added. "You don't need to use your arm; it feels as if it is paralyzed." If I detect a fear of loss of control, I assure the patients that this is not hypnosis. They will be fully aware of what is going on and remain in control of themselves. If a noise occurs in the room, I tell them what caused it. I then have them take frequent deep breaths and suggest that they feel more relaxed with each exhalation. I suggest all along that the relaxed feeling is a pleasurable one; all tension is going from their body and they are feeling very good. Sometimes I add pleasant imagery such as, "You are lying in a grassy field on a warm, sunny day with gentle breezes and feel very good, without a care in the world."

I have used relaxation as a modality in itself, along with other procedures such as cognitive techniques, and of course as part of counterconditioning methods. I have obtained an excellent response. Patients often spontaneously report how much better they feel just by using relaxation on a daily basis or in tense situations.

C.S. was a twenty-eight-year-old white male treated for fears of separation from his geographical home. He worked for a company that wanted to send him to a six-week training course in a distant state. On two previous occasions he had anxiety attacks when going to this course and the approaching training course would be his "last chance." The case was explored fully, revealing anxiety in many similar situations. The patient was treated mainly with a cognitive approach in which the therapist continually pointed out the patient's magnifications and challenged his ominous predictions. "Even if you were to get sick, there are doctors all over the country." He was taught muscle relaxation, but counterconditioning could not be used as he found it most difficult to imagine vividly the scenes described.

Unfortunately, it is impossible to answer whether the treatment, of twenty sessions, was a success or failure. He and his family drove to the distant state but left there after a brief stay. The patient claimed, and his wife later verified, that the living accommodations were extremely bad, and since they were unable to find better ones, they returned home. An extensive review of the happenings of the trip convinced me that anxiety factors were not prominent in their decision to come back.

The only relevant fact about this case was that the patient used simple muscle relaxation to relieve anxiety before, during and after the trip and stated that this helped him on many occasions. He gives some lip service to the cognitive aspects discussed, but there was no evidence that he magnifies conditions less or that his thinking has changed in any other way.

I have used relaxation techniques at times in relation to sexual problems. One young man whom I was treating for multiple anxieties and occasional depression told me that he also had premature ejaculation, having orgasm some thirty seconds to two minutes after penetration, always too quickly to build up his own sexual tensions and never capable of satisfying his wife. Discussion revealed an awareness of tension relative to sexual performance. A brief discussion and demonstration of muscle relaxation was given. A few weeks later the patient related how he handled this problem. Fifteen to thirty minutes before sexual relations, he tried to relax his entire body, and since shortly before sexual penetration he noted increased tension in the lower part of his body and legs, he focused on these areas and relaxed them. He stated that this had consistently and considerably increased his performance time.

Counterconditioning

Two cases with whom I have used counterconditioning techniques are as follows:

B.D. was a thirty-five-year-old sergeant in the military who was seen by me for fears concerning a fast pulse. This patient had a four-month history of taking his pulse repeatedly and if he felt it was too fast, he would rush to the emergency room, state that he thought that he was having a heart attack, and demand an EKG. When his symptoms had first begun, he had been treated with a traditional approach for two months with no improvement. A second therapist then attempted paradoxical intention—having him do ten to twenty push-ups whenever he noticed a fast pulse. This made his anxiety worse. When I began asking questions about his present and past life, as the traditionalist had done, he became somewhat annoyed and bluntly denied problems in all areas mentioned. I therefore decided to use what information I did have without pushing him for more history. First, since it was evident to me that he was overly aware of bodily processes and magnified the significance of any pain or slight increase in pulse, I pointed out to him that his pulse increase could be due to a number of things, such as exercise, heat, an exciting or upsetting thought or other phenomenon of which he might not be aware. I also told him that he seemed to get aches and pains just like other people, but he seemed to notice them more and to magnify their importance. At the same time that these cognitive processes were being discussed, I began training the patient in muscle relaxation. Imagery was added to this: "You are lying in a grassy field on a warm sunny day with gentle breezes and not a care in the world." When he was imagining this scene and in a deep state of relaxation, I had him take his pulse in the imagery. At first I had him imagine that his pulse was seventy-six. As he became more relaxed, through muscle relaxation and imagery, the pulse was raised to eighty, but I always gave him a reason for the increase. For instance, "Your pulse is now eighty since you have been lying in the sun for half an hour." "You feel like running from one area to another fifty feet away, but now you have been in the sun a half hour and even though you run slowly, you take your pulse again and it is up to eighty-four." Again, another scene was introduced such as, "You have been in the sun for an hour. You run and when you lie down again, you begin thinking of an exciting football game. You take your pulse, and it is eighty-eight." Through the use of imagery and relaxation, the patient was able to imagine his pulse at one hundred without feeling any anxiety. During the early relaxation training he had one visit to the emergency room. After he had reached a pulse of eighty-four in imagery, he did not return there again. When his pulse reached one hundred in imagery, he stopped therapy, stating that he was feeling "great." This patient has been in complete remission for over two years. The reason I emphasize the relaxation with imagery as being the more effective technique, even though cognitive techniques were used, is that the patient felt this is what helped him. He also started using relaxation techniques for other tensions that he had. He gave no credit nor mention to his tendency to magnify things. This, of course, does not rule out that the cognitive techniques contributed to his improvement.

G.L. was a twenty-eight-year-old white male first lieutenant in the military service. This man had a history of being in three tornadoes at ages sixteen, twenty-one and twenty-eight, the last one occurring one month before coming to the Psychiatry Service. He had been hurt slightly in all three of these. In the last one he was in his trailer with his wife who was pregnant and both of them were thrown around but not injured seriously. Two weeks later his wife delivered a normal baby without difficulty. However, since this last tornado the patient would become extremely nervous when going outside and seeing even a single cloud in the sky. A complete life history revealed excellent functioning in all spheres and no additional phobias or other psychiatric symptoms. Interestingly, however, he mentioned that while in college he studied tornadoes as a special project and had become somewhat of an expert on the conditions leading up to them. This knowledge did not alleviate his fears, however, and he would become anxious on hearing a weather forecast that presented conditions that could even remotely lead to a tornado.

It was felt that this was a case of pure associative learning and, therefore, would be very amenable to counterconditioning procedures. Hierarchies were constructed in three areas, the first being the actual weather conditions—one cloud, then two, then many, darker clouds, rain of increasing intensity and wind of increasing speed. A second hierarchy involved information heard on the weather report—with increasingly ominous data, and a third hierarchy involved seeing the weather map on television with increasingly threatening conditions. After the patient learned deep muscle relaxation, he was started on the hierarchy of actual weather conditions. This was the main hierarchy employed and each session was begun with it. When the patient could not advance past a particular scene, he was switched to one of the other hierarchies. This man was treated for sixteen sessions. There was no improvement. Even though he seemed capable of attaining a good degree of muscle relaxation and stated he was imagining the various scenes quite vividly, he denied any improvement in his condition.

Assertive Training

Lack of appropriate assertive behavior appears to be present in a large percentage of psychiatric patients. This would include depressives, phobics, homosexuals and passive dependent personalities—about seventy-five-percent of my practice.

The techniques that I have used to promote assertiveness include advice, education, exploration of the inhibiting factors, modeling and behavior rehearsal.

Advice merely involves telling the patient they need to be more assertive in particular situations. It is notable that few people seen in psychotherapy can respond to direct advice without being somewhat resistant. An example of a woman who did respond to direct advice and became more assertive, thus benefiting greatly, is E.W.

E.W. is a forty-eight-year-old white female seen one week following discharge from a hospital after taking an overdose of drugs. In the past six years she had experienced frequent depressions, with three drug overdoses requiring hospitalization, and had seen three psychiatrists. One treated her for a year in weekly psychotherapy. Her last doctor had placed her on multiple drugs, including major tranquilizers and antidepressants. She described her family life as chaotic, with an alcoholic, abusive father. She was the oldest of five children and was the peace mediator between the parents. She always had been the only one to assert herself with the father. As a child she felt society looked down upon her because of her father's alcoholism. She had divorced her second husband six years before, after eighteen years of a marriage in which "he let me do anything I wanted, but I was bored." She appeared nervous, moderately depressed and not very intelligent. There was no evidence of a psychosis. The diagnosis was a depressive reaction with anxiety features. As she talked, she calmed down, but I did not feel she would turn out to be a good candidate for cognitive therapy. My plan was to continue her medicine and see her for supportive therapy. During the second session, however, she began openly discussing her five-year relationship with a married man. I was much surprised that she was able to relate upsetting events to her moods. At this session I was able to markedly reduce her drugs to a low dose of anti-depressant, a mild tranquilizer and a sleeping pill. During the third session, the boyfriend was discussed in more detail and the bind the patient was in became evident. Her lover had been promising a marriage, borrowing money from her and allowing her to date no one. He continually promised her that he was going to divorce his wife. She believed him, but during the entire period she had almost constant nervousness and depression, made three suicide attempts, was hospitalized three times, and saw three psychiatrists. My therapeutic comments were along the lines of, "It seems you've put a lot of emphasis on R. and that the chances of his marrying you would appear slim. Why not develop an interest in other men?" When she came in for the fourth session, she stated that the entire week had gone better. She stated she had not heard from R., but she was not upset. She had one episode of nervousness, decided to go out dancing, and then felt better. During this session, while she discussed the money that this lover had borrowed from her and how angry she was at him, it was pointed out that during her relationship with him, she did not seem to assert herself much with him. Therapist: "Do you think there is a reason why you don't ask for the money back from R.?" Patient: "Yes, it might drive him further away." The patient was reticent about involving herself with other men and stated that she would still see R. if he called. At the next session, she stated that she had asserted herself with R., and he agreed to give back some of the money he had borrowed from her. She felt very good about this and had no guilt feelings. During this session, after a discussion of men, I pointed out that she only seemed interested in men who played hard to get. This seemed to make sense to her. This woman was very responsive all along to observations I made. She was also able to take direct advice. At this session she was advised to continue seeing other men and not to depend on any one of them for her entire social life. At the next session she reported that she was dating a new man whom she liked and who wanted to date her exclusively. She stated she would date him, but not limit her dating to him. She seemed to be feeling good. Therapy was then put on an every other week basis. At the next session she reported that she had taken steps to legally get her money back from R. She also reported an increased intensity in her new relationship. Advice was again given in this session regarding R. and the new boyfriend. At the next session, the patient revealed that she had had an anxiety attack when the boyfriend she had been going with most actively seemed to be losing interest. It was pointed out that she seemed to be searching for an intense relationship, perhaps marriage, and when she appeared to be losing a prospect she went into great panic. Her tendency to catastrophize was pointed out. At the same time, it was mentioned that considering she was forty-eight years old, she seemed quite adept at meeting men and gaining their interest. I told her that since many men were available to her, she should "keep many irons in the fire." The next session showed her to be in an excellent mood. She stated that she had been doing wonderfully the last two weeks. She had been going out and meeting new men and stated, "I've done what you told me and not gotten serious with anyone. I plan to date ten men." At this session she enthusiastically claimed that she was "doing great," had had no depressions and was feeling better than she had in the last five years. She stated that during those five years she was depressed almost continuously. She had now gone completely off all medication. "I have a new outlook. I feel free for the first time in five years." When seen five weeks later, the patient was in excellent spirits, stating that she had no depression and had not needed any medication. She stated she felt independent from men and felt that she was assertive in more areas. She stated that her friends had told her, "You're not the same person." She said to me, "No other doctor could get me over the depression or off the depression pills."

Five weeks later the patient had a slight setback. She had begun dating another man, but let herself increase her expectations of him. He was very attractive to her, and fairly wealthy. However, like the first man, he was still married and told her that while he cared very much for her, he still had to go through a divorce. Two things seemed to upset her from the weekend she had had with him. One was that the man could only be seen occasionally because business kept him moving around the country. He had asked her not to date other men and she had agreed to it, thus again putting control on her and dampening all social life. Also, for the first time in their relationship, he had gotten angry at her over a minor issue. Again, several things were pointed out to her: that she was put in an impossible situation where there would be no reinforcement from other men for possibly two or three months, that the probability of marriage to this man might not be high because of his as yet unfiled divorce, and that she had expected the man to be perfect (have no angry moods), and when he wasn't, her image of him was shattered. She improved during this session and when seen one week later was in a much better mood. She had decided that she would not be tied down by this man because of his inability to give her a guarantee of marriage and she had again begun to see other men. One week later she was back in good spirits. When she spoke with her potential fiancé, she had been more assertive with him, and while she did not tell him that she was dating other men, she did tell him that she thought he should write her more if he was as interested in her as he had said. She continued dating other men, and again she was completely asymptomatic. One month later she again experienced a rejection from a man she had been dating four weeks. However, within the session, where the old patterns were pointed out to her, that is, the high expectations and tendency to read rejection into situations, she recovered almost completely and one week later again was completely recovered. Two weeks later she was continuing at an asymptomatic level. When asked by me, "What things that we have talked about have helped you?" she replied, "Your statement, 'Don't underrate yourself.'"

Essentially then, this is a woman who was seen fifteen times in eight months and treated largely with assertive training. She is regarded as a successful case from seven points of view:

1. From the history she gave, and all other indications, she had been much more anxious, depressed and suicidal during the five years preceding therapy than in the period since.
2. Her daughter and friends told her she had been looking much better than she had in the previous five years.
3. "I told my daughter what has helped me in therapy with you. I told her you let me talk, but you will also talk back to me; you tell me things to think about and I think about these things when I leave. When I am nervous you give me medicine. I take as little as possible. I will never go back to a hospital."
4. She was acting assertively in her interpersonal relations and with me.
5. She had incorporated much of what we discussed into her thinking.
6. When she did get upset, it was quite easy to snap her out of it.

7. The therapist has a feeling of the specific events she is vulnerable to and what to emphasize in therapy.

Education about assertiveness and its importance in human interaction can serve as an indirect way to get some patients to begin developing an awareness of its role in their lives. I will educate a patient by making a general statement somewhat applicable to the patient and then amplify this by discussing another case.

"Look, in general, while being a nice guy certainly has its virtues and usually leads to one's being well liked, it also has its drawbacks in that people, unknowingly, tend to expect and demand more from agreeable people. For instance I have an extremely conscientious patient who is an excellent worker. However, his boss is never satisfied and the patient is constantly pushing himself harder to please this essentially unpleasable boss. The patient has asked for a pay raise' twice in the past year and has been turned down. He is invaluable to his boss's operation, yet he does not use his power to help himself, either by pushing himself less or demanding more money. When he decided to use his power, that is by turning in his resignation, his boss gave him everything he wanted, more assistance at work and a pay raise. Timidly asking for changes had been totally unsuccessful because it was no threat to the boss, whereas threatened loss of his prize worker brought the boss to terms. Of course, if the patient had not been a conscientious, hard worker, he would have had no power base from which he could bargain."

The technique I use most often to stimulate assertive behavior is the exploration of the inhibiting thoughts that prevent a patient from expressing himself more effectively. The inhibiting thoughts are usually some fear of loss or harm that the patient is predicting.

For example:

"If I ask the boss for a raise, he'll fire me."
"If I dispute the mark with the teacher, I'll get a poor grade next time."
"If I say the wrong thing, people will think I'm stupid."
"If I express my views, people will not like me."

There is a most important secondary implication to the harm that will be endured and that is that it will be *catastrophic* in nature.

"If I lose my job, I'll *never get another one* and *I'll starve.*"
"If she doesn't love me, *my life is ruined.*"

This second belief is usually less accessible to awareness than is the primary one. It is important, however, to stress its presence since once the intensity of the "catastrophe" is lessened, the inhibiting power of the primary fear is lessened. A patient, after gaining awareness into and learning to challenge the catastrophic remark, may say the following to himself:

"It is important that I feel less pressure and make more money at this job. I'll probably have to get fairly assertive and may have to resign to show them that I mean what I say. This may accomplish what I want, but there is a chance my resignation will be accepted. But I am a good worker and can get another job. I may miss working here and it will be disappointing to leave, but it is not the end of the world."

J.N., who is described in the cognitive section, is markedly inhibited about talking. At this point in his therapy, he is beginning to focus on the numerous times he doesn't say or do things "because people will think I'm stupid." Every time he focuses on one of these fear predictions, I add "and wouldn't that be awful." Hopefully he will begin to see that, he, too, has been adding this statement and thereby keeping himself blocked and uninvolved.

Modeling procedures are carried out on only a small scale by my speaking assertively to a nurse or secretary on the phone in the presence of a patient who would benefit from seeing or hearing this.

"Look, that report has to go out today. If you are overburdened, ask the other girl to help you." This is said in a firm but non-hostile tone.

Behavior rehearsal has sometimes been effective with dependent personalities such as W.E., discussed in the management section. W.E. was urged to repeat the same assertive statement to his wife several times. After about eight attempts he sounded convincingly assertive to his wife and the two cotherapists, and was praised for this. His wife later reported that he was maintaining this assertiveness at home and that she liked him much better this way.

An area where appropriate assertive behavior is of particular importance, but difficult to develop, is with depressive syndromes. Many depressives vacillate between sulking depressions and annoying hostility, neither of which helps them attain their goal. These people need a multifaceted approach to help them develop appropriate assertiveness. This includes education and other cognitive procedures to make them aware of the extremes of their behavior, behavior rehearsal, and modeling.

Advice rarely works with them. My results even with this multifaceted approach have had limited success in the treatment of depressives.

Imagery

I have used imagery but only to a limited degree to date. As mentioned before, I use pleasant imagery to aid muscle relaxation. I first try to find what scenes a person would find to be especially relaxing.

Imagery in the form of caricatures or animal forms, as I described in a previous article, has been used minimally by me with few worthwhile results. I have discovered that patients find it is hard to put their feelings in the form of a caricature or animal form. When they can do it, I find that it does give me clues to their fears and distortions.

With married couples, we have tried to get them to conjure up images of their early dating or early marriage scenes that were very romantic. We then have them fully describe the scene and try to put themselves back in that scene as if it were now occurring. The hope is that if we can do this, we might be able to have these emotionally divorced couples feel a bit more *"turned on"* by each other. We have even suggested that they practice these scenes several times daily. This, of course, is used in combination with other techniques we are using with marital couples which involve communication and increasing their awareness of how they reinforce and are aversive to each other. At this writing, we have attempted the imagery techniques on only two couples. However, there has been little enthusiasm on their part. During a marital session, they are unable to come up with any good description of a scene and there has been little, if any, practice. It is our feeling that their negative feelings about each other probably have to be sufficiently low to get them motivated to apply this technique.

The use of imagery as an aversive technique sounds interesting. I found that twenty-four hours after I read an article on the use of aversive imagery for the treatment of alcoholism, I went to take a drink and as I approached the liquor cabinet, I got a slightly nauseated feeling. I remembered the article but still did not take the drink. This technique appears to have much to offer.

Symptom Removal

An interesting case that involves symptom removal is as follows:

D.C. is a twenty-six-year-old married, white male who presented with a chief complaint of stuttering. Significant in the patient's history is that his father was a well-known personality in the government. The patient was conscientious and had worked hard and accomplished much in his vocation. He was motivated to rid himself of the stuttering so that he could make a better verbal presentation of his work. He had been working for someone and had planned to go into business on his own. Notable in the mental status examination was the fact that this patient was extremely polite, friendly and anxious to please. He did not talk unless spoken to and I had to watch my tendency to overtalk.

The patient was able to identify those situations where he did get nervous and stutter. The first phase of therapy was concerned with pointing out that his stuttering did not seem to be a catastrophe and that he had so many attributes that the stuttering, even if it did continue, would not ruin him. The patient accepted this but not with any great enthusiasm. Relaxation training was given, with emphasis on the muscles of his tongue, jaws, and neck. The next week he came in and said he was able to do the relaxation as taught and that he was able to relax his throat muscles. He said that when he found himself starting to stutter, he would stop talking, relax himself completely and then focus on relaxing the throat muscles. When he started talking again, he was able to proceed with great success. This patient's stuttering disappeared so quickly (in four sessions), that it had the therapist a little concerned. I was not sure if he was better or just trying to please me, or if he was not really that serious a stutterer at all. After his stuttering had improved (it had been evident only about five to ten times during any one session and at those times it was mild in nature), he started discussing other anxieties he had. His dynamics in these areas seemed to me to be related to the fact that he was a nice guy and that people pushed him to do things and that he did them without complaint. He was encouraged to be more assertive. However, in the ensuing meetings it became evident that this man was willing to accept a certain degree of subservience to please people. He assured me that he really wasn't walked on by people and knew where to draw the line. One motivation that brought him to therapy was that his brother was willing to use his father's name and rely on his father to advance him in his career. The patient said he was never like that and did not like it in his brother. He stated that he wanted to be excellent in everything so that people would not think that he had achieved on the basis of his father's connections. As a result of this, he worked very hard at not only educating himself in his career field, but in other areas as well. He picked subjects that he felt would be interesting to people and would study them in great detail. Since many of his friends were hunters and he, too, hunted, he became an expert on marksmanship and ballistics. It occurred to me during the seventh session that his coming to therapy was motivated not by a sense of an extreme disabling stuttering disorder but by some very strong need to improve himself in every area possible. Even a slight amount of stuttering, therefore, to him was an impairment and anything to improve this was necessary.

COGNITIVE THERAPY TECHNIQUES

The role of the cognitive therapist is to familiarize himself with his patient's thought content, thought processes, feelings and behavior; to note the relationships between thoughts, feelings and behavior; to organize the data from each of these areas into what appears to be recurring patterns; and to use any one of numerous techniques to add to, subtract from, or in some way change or reorganize the patient's thought content and processes. Changes in these areas, in my opinion, are basic to and precede emotional change.

Thought content is defined as the themes, concepts, attitudes and beliefs which dominate the patient's thinking. The patient may be aware of only a portion of these. Examples of thought content in different patients are as follows: The themes dominating the thinking of a depressive would be those of hopelessness, loss of interest, self-criticism and concerns about health; those of a paranoid would concern injustices done to him and dangers that await him.

Thought processes may be defined as activities postulated to occur in the mind. These would include: *magnification*—the tendency to view things as being much more important, fearful or catastrophic than they objectively are; *selective abstraction*—the tendency to take certain features out of context and emphasize them to the exclusion of others; *overgeneralization*—the tendency to make far reaching conclusions on the basis of little data; and *thinking in extremes*—the tendency to see things as absolutes, either white or black, good or bad, right or wrong. This is often exemplified by remarks such as, "I must do my job perfectly," or "The world should be fair."

The information sought varies with the therapist, and is a reflection of the model of personality he uses. For example, the traditionalist usually seeks an extensive history of early family relationships. My own tendency is to take only a brief past history initially and devote most of my efforts toward ascertaining the patient's present-day thought content, processes, feelings and behavior. I listen for what motivates or reinforces him and what discourages him or is aversive for him, as well as evaluating his ability to assert himself in different settings. If the patient is unable to give the therapist enough information to work with, either spontaneously, nonverbally or with facilitating procedures such as direct and indirect questions, comments, paraphrasing correctly (or purposely incorrectly), or repeating the last words of a sentence, the patient may be helped to talk by using several techniques. The therapist can: educate him as to the reasons that talking is necessary in psychotherapy, inform him that his remarks are confidential, and assure him that there are no right or wrong answers; use rapport techniques to decrease anxiety; or specifically focus on his inability to talk freely by exploring what fears might be involved in the therapy situation. Pinpointing and discussing these fears usually lead to the patient's talking more and may, in addition, help him with inhibitions he is having outside of therapy.

If these procedures fail to give me enough information to organize the patient's difficulties in a meaningful way, I turn to other methods to get the necessary information. These are more indirect techniques than the aforementioned and include areas more removed from the patient's here-and-now concepts. They are in a sense projective techniques.

For example:

I may ask for a more detailed history. As mentioned, with most patients I do not gather an extensive past history since I rarely find this of value; however, when I need clues to a patient's unrevealed conceptual systems, I will probe for more details of the past. "What was your parents' marriage like?" "What do you remember about your sex education?"

I rarely encourage patients to discuss dreams because if it is to be done correctly, this is a time-consuming procedure involving a complete description of the dream and the patient's associations to each detail. However, in patients where information is sparse, I urge dream description to give me additional information on the patient's governing attitudes. N.A., cognitive section, described a dream without my urging him to and without extensive associations to each detail. The dream in itself and the remarks he made about it verified some of the ideas I had about his feelings toward women. It also served to have him discuss these feelings more at this session.

I have used imagery techniques, to some extent, to increase my knowledge of the patient.

"Try and put your feelings on this matter into a picture. It can involve people or animals or caricatures."

With a man felt to have serious sexual inhibitions: "Try to imagine that your father is watching you having sex with your wife. What would his facial expression be? Would he say anything?"

Other statements used to indirectly gain information may include:

"What TV personality are you most like? Why?"
"Do other people feel the same way as you do?"
"How would your friends react if you told them you did this?"

These four ancillary information gathering techniques—detailed history, dreams, imagery and projective statements—are usually used when information gathering methods mentioned earlier are at a stalemate. The data thus far gathered from these auxiliary procedures have been minimal at best.

Just as the type of information sought reflects the therapist's concepts of human behavior, so does the organization of that information in the therapist's mind. This is demonstrated in the case of N.A. (mentioned in more detail later in this section). His traditional therapist was apparently seeing his problems as "oedipal"—his inability to work hard and become a success being caused by unresolved anxieties about the father's harming him or being angry with him should he succeed. My current working concept of the case sees his inhibitions as due to his tendency to overthink, to carefully weigh the pros and cons of everything he does so that he does it right. Only if there is certainty that he is doing the right thing (his strongest reinforcer) can he embark on any venture. Without this certainty he cannot proceed with it at all.

Once the therapist has gathered sufficient information for his own understanding and organized this into some conceptual scheme (that further information should verify), the problem is: what techniques does he use to help the patient? It is the author's opinion that one helps the patient by influencing his thinking: adding to it, subtracting from it, and reorganizing it on the basis of what the therapist has decided is maladaptive about it.

One can add to a patient's thinking by direct education. Many patients are prone to fears and misconceptions in areas in which they are least knowledgeable. When educated in these matters, misconceptions are lessened and concomitant fears are alleviated. This is well demonstrated in the cases of W.B., who was aided by education on body processes, health data and doctors' examining procedures; and J.N., who was taught about sexual norms in the United States today.

One can also add to a patient's thinking by making him more aware of his thought content, thought processes, feelings and behavior. Techniques used to do this include those already mentioned for information gathering, such as direct and indirect questions and paraphrasing, and asking him what he thinks when experiencing certain feelings (what is he telling himself, what is going through his mind). One substantially increases a patient's awareness by repeatedly pointing out recurring themes: "You always blame yourself when something goes wrong," and recurring processes: "You have a tendency to magnify things. Every time you get a pain in your chest you are certain it is a heart attack." It is felt that increasing awareness in these areas gives patients a mastery over them.

A second means of relieving patient suffering is by decreasing thoughts which are maladaptive, those which underlie unpleasant emotions. After the patient becomes aware of his current thinking, his thoughts can be challenged. I repeatedly focus on and challenge maladaptive thoughts during a therapy session and promote the patient's doing the same during the intersession period, thereby causing thoughts to lose their effect on the patient's feelings.

For example, with J.N., who was afraid to talk in many situations because he told himself he might "sound stupid," I focused repeatedly on this thought, thus bringing it more clearly into his awareness, and challenged his statements by saying, "Why would it be so awful, even if they thought what you said was stupid, which they probably won't, would that ruin your career, end your life?" Repetition usually leads to the challenging remark being incorporated into the patient's thinking. Every time the maladaptive thought occurs, the challenging remark is triggered and hopefully "defeats" the maladaptive thought. The patient is no longer anxious that a catastrophe will occur if he speaks. The maladaptive thought has become absent from, or inactive in, his thought repertoire.

While all of the techniques thus far mentioned do tend to reorganize thinking by adding to or subtracting from one's thought repertoire, other procedures may likewise reorganize the patient's thinking. The most commonly used of these would be the therapist's reduction of a large amount of data into a sentence or two. I refer to this as "making order out of chaos." This reduction to a simpler form enables the patient to understand more clearly a basic concept and to have a certain mastery over it. An example of this would be a statement of N.A. such as, "You seem to have a need for certainty." His awareness of one dominant thought motif may simplify the often confusing thought data which are processed by the human mind.

A second means of promoting the reorganization of thinking is asking the patient if there are alternative ways of looking at a situation just described. I try to get a patient to list five to ten alternatives. So when a man states that he feels uncomfortable with a girl who is quiet and gives as his interpretation of her action, "She doesn't like me," I have him list other possibilities such as, "She might be shy," "She might not have felt well," "She might have problems on her mind," or "She might feel this is the way a man wants her to act." Continually getting patients to list alternatives to the one stereotyped maladaptive thought they get in specific situations gradually increases the repertoire of explanations they have to choose from. Choosing a more adaptive thought constitutes a reorganization of thinking in the specific area involved.

During the course of cognitive therapy, I am most interested in learning if cognitive changes are occurring, and if so, is there a concomitant improvement in the patient's feeling and behavior. Many times patients in psychotherapy show complete symptom removal without the cognitive change that would be anticipated. This is demonstrated in some of the cases that follow where statements made to the patient never seemed to be incorporated into his thinking and other statements never even discussed are mentioned and sometimes credited with the patient's improvement. This is seen in the cases of W.B., D.W., and E.E. In other cases the patient begins using remarks made by the therapist earlier in therapy and attributes changes to these remarks, as did E.W. (Behavior Therapy Section). N.A., on the other hand, shows cognitive changes along the lines the therapist planned, but without the therapist ever having had the opportunity to make the remarks. In other words, the therapist and patient are in conceptual agreement without having traded specific information.

The following cases are presented to give the reader some idea of the way I employ cognitive therapy.

J.N. is a thirty-year-old white male auditor who voluntarily came to therapy after his wife was referred to me by a neurologist for depression. The patient felt he was the cause of her depression. His main concern was that he had put no effort into any area of his life for several years. There was no evidence of psychosis and he essentially presented a depressed picture, talking slowly and with no spontaneity.

Because of his lack of spontaneous information and the fact that he revealed a long-term problem, a rather complete history was taken. Briefly stated, he was the third of five children, none of whom were ever close to the others. He had a poor relationship with his father who frequently hit him on the face. "I resented him. I was never able to do what he seemed to want. My mother backed me up, even when she shouldn't have." He later said of his mother, "I used to work endlessly on my model boats, until fatigued, and hope my mother would praise me. She always did. I would push her until she said something good." As a child he described himself as a loner, having no confidence. He remembers that he could never talk in front of people even in second grade. The picture changed somewhat in high school and college where he described himself as a good student, active in clubs and holding down a job. He liked dating beautiful girls so that other people would "eat their hearts out." Since graduating from college he had been with the same company for ten years, did not like the job in general, but liked his current assignment and planned no change. The company wanted to send him for further education so he could advance, but "I had no goals in mind, so it would be worthless to go to school." He has been married for seven years and has two children. He talked little of the marriage other than, "It's O.K.," said unenthusiastically. There has been fidelity on both sides, but with his having some fantasy life about other women and his mentioning of his wife's lack of orgasm. Also significant but not mentioned specifically in relation to the marriage was that even after his active high school and college life, he maintained enthusiasm in many areas, such as model plane building and sailing. The loss of interest in activities seemed to date from one year prior to his marriage. "Over the last eight years, I have stopped many activities. I don't even sail anymore. I occasionally get overly interested in something like building cabinets. When I first moved here, I was interested in landscaping. My wife felt I was going overboard, I guess I was."

Besides his apathy about work and outside activities, he brought up two other areas for discussion. At the third meeting he stated he had better "confess" some things to me about himself, whereupon he revealed a list of thoughts and activities in the sexual area since age ten. This included masturbation, attempts to see his older sister nude and the admission that he found his mother sexually "stimulating"—"When she vacuumed the stairs, I would look up her dress." He also admitted that he now gets sexual fantasies about his wife, other women, and his wife having sex with another man. These fantasies excite him and lead to masturbation. In reality he felt his sex relations with his wife were very satisfying, except for her usual lack of orgasm. Also his wife gets upset if he looks at other girls because she feels he's not just appreciating their aesthetic qualities but looks like he wants to be in bed with them. He stated, "I guess if our relationship were better, I wouldn't look at girls in the same way."

A third area of concern came up during the fifth meeting. He revealed marked fears about what people think of him. This involved activities such as sailing and skiing, speaking in a classroom, asking a waiter to return a bad steak, and most importantly, talking in any situation where he might risk saying the wrong thing.

From a treatment standpoint this man has been quite interesting. His initial quietness was handled by active history taking. I also decided at the second session to allude to his nonspontaneity, whereupon he said, "I guess it's because you're young. Also you mentioned marital therapy and I'm not interested in that." This is when he revealed his sexual curiosities and acts over the years with much guilt. Nothing that he said sounded terribly abnormal to me and I used simple educational techniques, informing him that most of what he described was done by a large majority of boys and men and that his guilt seemed out of proportion to his thoughts and actions. He was surprised to hear what I said. My impression about this lack in his knowledge and in other areas is that it has been due to little close contact with other people where such information is usually learned. My initial thoughts about his loss of interest in things since just before his marriage were that the wife has had some role in discouraging him. This hasn't been alluded to yet, other than my saying, "It seems you've lost your spontaneity in the last seven years." In the last four sessions (fourth through seventh), each of which had shown the same pattern of no spontaneous talk, I have begun focusing on this. It has seemed to me that this is a carry over of his lack of spontaneity and lack of involvement in the outside world. It has also frustrated me. Working with this phenomenon, which is occurring in the actual therapy situation, I feel is most promising in helping the patient with his outside life and has also relieved my frustration.

Patient: Silent three minutes.
Therapist: Small talk ten minutes.
Patient: Silent three minutes.
Therapist: "Is there anything you'd like to bring up today?"
Patient: "No, we've discussed everything."
Therapist: "Are you uncomfortable coming here?"
Patient: "Yes."
Therapist: "Is it similar to talking in other situations?"
Patient: "Yes, I'm afraid that what I'd have to say isn't important."
Therapist: (I felt at this point, that the patient was sensitive to the asking of questions, the technique I was using on him. It seemed to me that when asked questions he felt he had to give a "right answer." If wrong he feared punishment, so I made the following statements.)
  "Listen, I ask you questions to get you to think about things, but I get the feeling that you feel you must give a *right* answer. However, the answers aren't necessarily right or wrong. They are just designed to learn what occurs in your thinking."
Patient: "I'm glad to hear you say that. I really feel that maybe you understand me. I feel good when you say something that relates to the way I feel."

Discussions since then have tended to center around his classroom fears of answering, fear of looking bad while skiing or sailing and current interpersonal relations. Other comments made to this patient include, "You seem to predict what's on other people's minds." He agreed and revealed he predicted they would be critical. He was later challenged on this, "How do you learn what they are thinking?" When he talked of getting an "F" in class, clarification revealed many people got "F's," and no one got above "C." When he brought up fear of answering in class "because everyone knew the right answer and I might be wrong," I challenged, "How do you know they all have the answer?" Another statement to him concerning his fear of looking stupid by making mistakes was, "You seem to have lost the ability to judge how serious or maladaptive a mistake is. Getting lost looking for a street isn't the catastrophe that driving your car into a pole is."

Remarks indicating cognitive change and general improvement are as follows:

At the fourth session—
"Recently I've felt more enthusiasm for fixing the house up."
"I felt good when you said the things I've done aren't sick."

At the sixth session—
"Things are great—the best things have been in years. My wife and I are talking more. Things don't get her down like they used to. She isn't as upset if the house isn't clean; she's not as upset with our son. She has more respect for me. We are getting along well, talking about things."

The patient's improvement so far is attributed to education and to some extent the challenging of his distortions, particularly in regard to his multiple guilts and to his fears about what others think. It is hard to assess the role his therapy plays in the improvement of the marriage because his wife, too, has responded well to individual therapy.

D.W. was a twenty-eight-year-old attractive, eight months pregnant white female who was seen in consultation in the hospital because of symptoms of depression, panic episodes and a fear of going outside. The patient had been hospitalized two years before, when not pregnant, for similar symptoms. She claims that the psychiatrist she saw two years ago did not help her. However, apparently she had improved and had functioned fairly well until two weeks prior to her admission to the hospital. On examination she was slightly nervous, agitated, emotionally labile, and showed a significant increase in anxiety when discussions of going out of the house or hospital were held. There was no evidence of schizophrenic disorder. She was diagnosed as a phobic reaction. In her early history, it was revealed that her mother died when she was seven and her father, she claims, sexually molested her at age five. This patient was treated for eight sessions in a two-week period by cognitive approach. Discussion was largely on the here and now, a description of what her current life situation was, her relationship with her husband, her feelings about her having another child and the events surrounding her panic attacks. Initially the patient was felt to be somewhat hysterical, overreacting to many things in her environment. She claimed annoyance in many situations. As details of her life were expanded and clarified, it became evident that her fear of being outside was more a fear specifically of seeing people she knew and being delayed by them. She said that everyone in their family, including herself, was always in a hurry. She experienced "sickness" when people would stop her in a store, or when waiting in line, causing her to not want to go out at all. She was afraid that if she did go out she would get sick. She discussed the fact that as a child she felt she used sickness to avoid doing things. When neighbors visited, she was quite annoyed and to get them to leave she would say she wasn't feeling well. She allowed people to be quite dependent on her and was unable to assert herself. She could never tell them that she was tired or had things to do. She could only feign illness to get rid of them. It was pointed out that she seemed to equate, from habit, annoyance with sickness and that now when she felt annoyed, she felt sick. She also catastrophized in many situations, and these were pointed out. While this woman never gave evidence that she incorporated what was being pointed out to her in the eight sessions that she was seen, there was a marked improvement. That is she stopped complaining, she catastrophized less, gained confidence, was not easily upset by disappointments or unexpected events, and began to go on her own to see her obstetrician without fear or attacks of panic. She was able to be discharged from the hospital prior to the birth of her baby and was at home and able to function, going out in public and feeling well in general. There was no problem when the baby was delivered, and a follow-up phone call one month after the patient had had her baby revealed that things were going fine and that there were no problems of any kind. The precipitating event of this severely disabling phobia was never established. Interestingly, after her treatment had been completed, her case was discussed with the therapist who had treated her two years before. The dynamics that he gave, for the first phobic reaction two years ago, concerned what he felt to be an attraction to a man at work and he stated that the phobia was an avoidance of a potentially sexual situation. When her current situation was mentioned to him, he stated dogmatically that the pregnancy was obviously the precipitating event, causing concern over her body image. While this man is a traditionally-oriented therapist and conceptualized her situation in a way that led to successful treatment two years ago, his present conceptualization was far different from the one I had formulated and used for basing my remarks to her. It would seem that his past approach and my present one had both succeeded.

W.B. is a thirty-two-year-old white male who came in with a chief complaint of feeling that he had had a heart attack, "weird feelings," and an upset stomach. The patient had been given multiple medications for his stomach and nerves in the past two months by his family physician, but none had relieved his symptoms. When put on thorazine three weeks before I saw him, his pulse got faster and his fears about heart trouble increased. The day before his first visit he had chest pains and felt that he was having a heart attack.

Present history revealed that the patient's wife had given birth to a baby six months ago and that there had been bleeding necessitating a blood transfusion. The patient had to donate a pint of blood. Even though the wife was never dangerously ill, the patient found the whole experience quite traumatic. Also at that time, the babysitter informed the patient that she knew of a girl who died from the "same thing his wife had." Later, about two months after the birth of the baby, the patient developed a severe case of the flu. One month later, about three months prior to my seeing him, he began developing some sensitivity to body processes, noticed feelings of weakness and loss of equilibrium, and became conscious of his heartbeat. The condition worsened in the past month and one day prior to being seen, he had become acutely anxious relative to the pain in the chest.

Mental status examination revealed him to be a thin, nervous, slightly suspicious man of average intelligence. There was no evidence of psychosis. I diagnosed him as an Anxiety Reaction and took him off all drugs except a minor tranquilizer and a sleeping pill.

At the first meeting, I pointed out that he seemed to magnify things greatly. The suggestion was made that he would be better in four to five visits. The therapist's attitude was firm, but friendly. The patient was seen the next day, and it was evident that any stimulus relative to health led to a panic reaction. Stimuli included TV doctor programs, reading of an auto accident in the newspaper, or hearing anything about air pollution. I decided at that session to briefly explore his past to determine the possible origin of his health concerns. He stated that he was the oldest of five boys, all of whom have always been in good health. His father has mild claustrophobia; his mother is in good health. He was raised in a strict manner. He denies that there was any emphasis on health or bodily processes in his upbringing. He had been in the military for three years and had functioned well. He had been married for ten years. There used to be fights in his marriage, but there have not been any recently. He states that he felt better when they did fight. At present there are no obvious problems in his marriage or job. At this session I told him that it appeared to me that he had always led a healthy life and seemed to have developed a feeling of invulnerability to illness. It was pointed out that perhaps the illness of his wife and the events surrounding it (his donating blood, and the babysitter's remark) and then his own serious case of the flu made him feel more vulnerable. It was also mentioned that since then he seemed to have the tendency to magnify things. The third session revealed marked improvement in his attitude and feelings. He stated that he attributed his whole improvement to the fact that his wife will "take over the bills"; also, that he was able to borrow money to pay for her hospitalization. These issues had not been discussed in the prior sessions at all. Also, he stated, "I decided to put my mind on happier thoughts like camping and doing things together and playing with the baby." He was sleeping and eating better. His medications had been tapered off by himself. On the fourth visit, two weeks after his initial visit, he stated he had an occasional "weird" feeling. This was defined as "like I can't move, like I'm moving when I shouldn't be, a pressing feeling all over my body." He also stated that when someone opened the door and warm air hit the side of his face, he would get a weird feeling and get scared. He stated that, "If the sun goes behind a cloud and the room gets dark, I think it is me blacking out." Again, the treatment was to point out his tendency to magnify and to be overly aware of bodily processes. Because of some continued nervousness and my feeling that he had a need for "magic," I decided to teach him relaxation techniques. Also, since the patient brought up financial concerns, I agreed to see him less frequently and for shorter time periods, so that he might save money. When seen one week later, he stated he was feeling the best he had in many years. There was no anxiety whatsoever. Again, when he began to magnify things, this was pointed out; the relaxation training was repeated. Two weeks later, he was off all medication, very relaxed, and he said that he had been catching up on his bills. One-month follow up revealed no exacerbation of symptoms.

E.E. was a forty-year-old married white female with no previous psychiatric history. Her chief complaint was nervousness, tension, decreased appetite, insomnia, and obsessive thoughts about her neighbors for a period of one month.

The patient dates the onset of her feelings to a mild altercation with a neighbor. This neighbor had never been friendly with any other families on the street and had recently complained to the patient about her son being a wise guy. Mrs. E. seemed fairly depressed and self-critical but, in general, from the history gleaned and the mental status examination, it was felt she was a fairly well-adjusted person. Diagnosis was depressive reaction with anxiety features.

This patient spontaneously talked of her childhood. She reported that she was the sixth of ten children, and described her father as a very critical man, especially hard on the older children, whom he physically beat up. She also remarked that he "wrecked" the oldest girl. She stated that he liked her (the patient, that is). "If he was critical of me, I kidded him back, and he laughed. He was lenient with me. I didn't give him reason to be mad at me."

When she was next seen one week later, she stated she had improved, was less tense and was sleeping better. She again began talking about her father during this session without prompting from me. She stated that between ages 5 and 12 she felt that he would beat her. Then she began talking about her neighbor, stating that he was just like her father. She said her father had tortured and shot a dog that "ate our chickens." "The neighbor beat his dog with a chain. I hate him. . . . We're Irish, and no German is any good. (That was the neighbor.) We're Democrat, and no

Republican could be any good. . . . Mainly my problem is my father. I was affected by him. I wouldn't date boys who might yell at me, even if it meant not getting married. If anyone wasn't nice to me once, that ended it." She again talked of her neighbor. I asked her what her father had predicted about Germans and Republicans. "He said that Germans were war-like and made lampshades out of humans. . . . Republicans hurt the farmers." (Her father was a farmer.) It appeared to me that she had not only compared the neighbor with her father in their strong, hostile, critical ways, but she had learned the father's attitudes, and many of these influenced her feelings toward the neighbor. At this session, I mentioned to the patient that there seemed to be a similarity between the neighbor and the father. This remark drew no response from her. Neither did a later one, "You seem to have the same concerns your father had about Germans and Republicans."

At the next session, I stated to her, "Hostile men seem to scare you." I also pointed out another characteristic she had displayed: "You seem to have a lack of assertiveness in your interpersonal relations and this makes you feel helpless and fearful." She stated, "I won't stand up for my rights. I occasionally told on my brothers to my mother."

At this next session, she talked more about her brothers, both of whom, she claimed, sexually attacked her. Her sixteen-year-old brother gave her sticks of gum when she was eight years old to allow him to try sexual relations with her; she states she didn't think he succeeded because she was too small. Her thirteen-year-old brother, she states, wasn't so bad. "He just felt me all over." This woman kept talking about her family, even though I did not promote this. It was my feeling that she had a preconceived idea that psychiatrists like one to talk about one's past and any possible sexual adventures. It was not clear as to whether these events had occurred or not. She said the referring physician had thought she was having some marital problems. She was encouraged to talk more of her marriage. She claimed her marriage was excellent. She stated she didn't enjoy sex until the fifth year of her marriage and that, since being on the birth control pill for the last four years, she has enjoyed it to a much higher degree. She stated at this visit, her third, that she was "a little less afraid of the neighbors this week."

In the fourth visit, she stated she was feeling much better. "I don't know if it is because school is starting or my sister is coming. . . . I have gone out of the house every day the last four to six days. I am not pre-occupied with the neighbors. Before, I couldn't work or fix a meal. . . . I am back to where I was eight or more months ago. . . . It's a clean break. Up until a few weeks ago there was a partial relationship between me and the neighbors. I was uncomfortable about the relationship, so I was trying to appease them. But now, I don't bother with them at all."

She was then seen one more time three weeks later and was doing excellently. She no longer had the symptoms of nervousness, tension, insomnia, poor appetite, or thoughts about the neighbors. Therapy was discontinued.

A follow-up phone call one year after the patient was seen revealed the following, "I was helped by the fact that I talked my heart out. When you said the neighbor sounds psychotic, I stopped blaming myself." Also of note is the fact that the patient's father died nine months ago and her mother six months ago. The patient states she took this very well. "I had no regrets. They had a good life, they died close to each other, they couldn't live without each other."

This is an interesting case in that this patient had a complete remission of an illness with only five sessions of psychotherapy, her improvement starting even during the first session. She gave little credit to the interpretations that I had made, other than the one concerning the neighbor's psychosis. Actually, I do not recall ever having made that statement. Catharsis about her father and brothers and possibly some awareness of the similarity of the neighbor to the father would seem to me to be the thing that helped her. It is difficult to evaluate whether her improvement came in any relation to the verbal statements that I made.

C.H. was a twenty-nine-year-old white married female, discussed in the management section. The chief complaint was an obsession that she might kill her six-month-old son. Examination revealed that she was an intelligent, nervous, talkative woman who seemed very concerned about her obsession. Her thought content was permeated with morbid and violent thoughts about which she commented with less concern than her obsession. She was appropriately friendly, cooperative and occasionally smiled. I did not feel she was schizophrenic.

The patient's description of her childhood and parents was as follows: "We were a close family. . . . Mother was perfect and always did things for my sister and me. . . . I was always mean to my Mother. I always felt she would die before I could repay her. . . . Grandmother was like me— a hypochondriac. She died of cancer. . . . Mother told me to watch out for men when I was little. A few men followed me home. . . . I was always afraid someone might stab me. I feared leaving the door open. I always felt guilty for not being a good daughter. . . . Mother was calm but did spank us. Father was sensitive and couldn't take criticism. He would get mad, then brood. He once said he understood why people killed themselves. Years ago he took a gun and was going to kill himself. I bit his hand, grabbed the gun and ran outside with it."

The patient had three years of college and has been writing mystery stories for children since that time. She admitted to sexual activity with her husband and others before marriage. She stated that she has always enjoyed sex and never felt guilty about it. She had one year of psychotherapy after her third year of college for reasons never discussed. She dated her history of nervousness, phobias, obsessions and compulsions to her teen years. Her sister, who is five years younger, has been hospitalized more than once and received electroshock treatment. The exact nature of her illness was not made clear.

The patient's main preoccupation was with violence, sickness and death. At our first meeting she brought up the Texas Tower slaying, the murder of eight nurses in Chicago and the movie "Psycho." Throughout therapy she revealed multiple fears: cancer, permanent nervousness, the birth of an abnormal baby, that her husband would get killed, that her son will get germs from old people or a dirty kitchen floor, that if she went outside a bee might sting her, leading to her falling and hurting her baby, and that she'd be bitten by a deadly spider. Three years ago, after her husband had one episode of impotence when she was trying to get pregnant, a fear was aroused in her that "he may become schizophrenic and kill me."

Some interesting relationships were noted in her thinking:

1. She was bombarded by multiple thoughts on every issue that came to mind. These consisted of the pros and cons of that particular issue.
2. Every time she got a pleasant or optimistic thought, an unpleasant or pessimistic one seemed to get triggered off.
   a. "I can't believe I have a normal baby. I keep thinking something is going to happen to him."
   b. "If people say I'm better, I ask a lot of questions, to show them I'm still bothered."
   c. "If I take my son outside, he'll get sick."
   She said of these phenomena, "I get afraid when I get a happy thought. If I think bad things, it will be a big surprise when something good happens."
3. She tried to plan her present according to how she might feel in the future. "Maybe we should have another baby, so I won't feel so bad in the future if we lose my son." This planning ahead seemed to have a protective function for her.
4. While most of her thoughts involved violence, death or some harm to herself or others, and her obsession involved killing her son, she denied angry feelings or even annoyance toward anyone. Even the thought of asserting herself with people, such as asking a relative to care for a child, made her feel bad or guilty.
5. She thought in extremes. This especially involved the baby: "I'm his mother I *should* love him. No one else *should* have to care for him. I *shouldn't* get thoughts like that about my son or husband."
6. She seemed markedly dependent on her parents. "I'm afraid to be away from my parents. I've never gone away without them. I'm afraid of what would happen if I got sick while away from them."

Treatment, other than the initial advice to the patient and her husband to have the baby taken care of by others, involved reducing the patient's data into terms of the recurring thought processes just described and repeatedly pointing these out to her.

a. "You have an active mind, you get many thoughts, both pro and con, and carefully think into things. This has its benefits because you get many ideas for your books, but it always makes you miserable by putting you in a state of indecisiveness." This remark was made to point out her characteristic type of thinking. Eventually she could be trained to say, "There I go again trying to think of every single possibility." Realizing the latter helps control overthinking.

b. "You seem to be superstitious. Every time you get a pleasant thought or good feeling, you get worried that something bad is bound to happen. To prevent the bad event from happening, you bring up bad thoughts. There is no reason that good things always precede bad ones and there is no reason to expect you can prevent misfortunes from occurring just by thinking they will." Repeatedly pointing out to patients their irrational thinking results in their becoming aware of it. This awareness gives them control over it.

c. "It might be more helpful to think of things in terms of probabilities. The poisonous spider has struck only five people in the State and none were in this geographical area. It would seem that the probabilities or odds of your getting bitten are low." This was an attempt to counteract her tendency to overgeneralize. (If one person is bitten, all will be.)

d. "You seem to have a need for certainty. There is no absolute, right or wrong, good or bad answer as to whether you should have another child or not. In two years when, you say, you might want one, why don't you come in and we'll discuss the pros and cons of your having additional children." The first remarks were to point out and challenge her thinking in extremes. The latter was to stop her from obsessing now on an issue that is two to four years away.

e. "From what you and your husband tell me, your son is quite sensitive and hard to manage. He keeps you so busy you can't do any of the things you enjoy. It would seem to me that most people would feel some annoyance in this situation." This remark was intended to make her realize certain children would annoy most people. When one has this type of child, one should limit his exposure to him.

f. "I get the feeling that you feel very guilty even if you experience a small amount of annoyance." This was said to make her realize annoyance is normal and not something one should feel guilty about.

g. "What relationship does a single episode of impotence have to schizophrenia? Even if your husband were schizophrenic, what percentage of schizophrenics are homicidal?" These two remarks were designed to point out her making predictions without any factual material to back them. The purpose was to get her to challenge some of her automatic predictions.

h. The patient revealed two techniques she tried on herself that she found helpful.

"I just thought of the worst things that could happen, then the less worse and I climbed out of things."

"I thought of an iron man to whom I could direct my hostility since he's invulnerable. I used to imagine my son's head over a toilet, then my husband's. Now I imagine the iron man's."

The patient was seen fourteen times over a six-month period. After the first visit, the couple placed the child with the patient's mother for a two-week period and the patient visited the baby two hours daily. After the two-weeks, the patient kept the baby with her for a few hours each day, gradually increasing the time so that after six months the baby was living at home full-time. After four visits (or one month of therapy), the patient stated she no longer had the obsession to kill the son. By the sixth meeting the patient reported she was sleeping better and enjoying sex more with her husband. She had also resumed her working. Her husband called me and stated she was vastly improved. The patient also planned to make a trip with her husband to a resort four hundred miles away—something she had never done without her parents. "I've been feeling less fearful about going out of town lately." She gave examples of some change in her thinking. She acknowledged the presence of every thought process discussed. A few statements she made are as follows:

"I think you're right when you said I *shouldn't* expect myself to be with my son all the time."
"How can I get out of this reflexive thinking?"
"How can I stop thinking so deeply into everything?"

This woman's presenting symptom was relieved by cognitive therapy. She also felt better in general and returned to old activities and tried out some new ones. She became aware of her thinking processes. Despite her improvement I do not think she was exposed to therapy long enough to get the mastery over her automatic thought processes necessary to avoid residual distortions or to prevent recurrence of some of her previous symptoms. She has not been seen for five months, but I would expect some recurrence to bring her in for future visits. Continued cognitive therapy had been suggested to her but the deterring factors were her realistic financial status and her mother's remark, "Psychiatrists will keep you coming forever. They'll tie you to their apron strings."

N.A. is a twenty-nine-year-old research physicist who presented with a chief complaint of: "I can't work; I can't concentrate." This case is significant from three points of view:

1. The patient is an intelligent, verbal, psychological-minded, young man who would be regarded as the perfect psychoanalytic patient.
2. He has a previous history of having had traditional psychotherapy for a one-year period two years ago while in graduate school. He went twice a week for four months and then, once a week for eight months.

When questioned about the therapy, he stated that he had done most of the talking, and that there was much discussion about his relationship with his father. He was told by the therapist after a year of therapy, "I have been looking for indications that you fear you might surpass your father, but I have been unable to find any." The patient, who had been seen for the same symptoms for which he is now seeing me, said that the therapy gave him moderate tension relief and helped him over some bad times, but "that's all it did for me."

3. After one year with his traditionally oriented therapist, he was sent to a very well-known behavior therapist. He was treated once a week for three months. This treatment was described as follows: "He imposed discipline by regimenting. . . . I guess his method would be good for children. . . . I had to keep a record of the time I got up and note whether I quickly got to work. I then discussed this with the therapist each week. He then told me to go right to work after waking and not to diddle my time away. . . . Also, he told me to do all my serious work in one place, to create a special environment. I was not to read a magazine there."

Neither therapy gave the patient symptom relief. He had hoped that moving to a new environment and being in an academic position would help him, but shortly after starting his research work, the same symptoms began plaguing him.

The patient presented as a thin, neat, intelligent, soft spoken white male with slightly depressed affect. The diagnosis was obsessive-compulsive personality. He was quite spontaneous and needed no prompting to talk. The first notable occurrence in therapy was his preoccupation with his childhood. He discussed in detail the lives of his two older brothers, both of whom had problems similar to his. He seemed to believe that there was one single reason buried in his childhood, perhaps in relation to his father, that was responsible for the patient and his two brothers turning out the same way. My impression was that this preoccupation was due to his long exposure to traditional therapy.

My initial therapeutic goals were to challenge his thinking in extremes, urge him to discuss his present-day attitudes and feelings, and elucidate what his reinforcers were.

His thinking in extremes was demonstrated by such remarks as: "I *ought* to be enjoying my work. . . . To be a good physicist one *must* know everything in his field." I decided to confront him on these in the hope that combatting them successfully would help take some of the pressure off him. (An initial thought on my part relative to this man's extreme attitudes was that his expectations of himself were so high that doing his work only held reward if it were done in great detail involving a marked amount of time. The reward was so far off that it could not act as a motivating factor.) The patient was not receptive to my challenging his "oughts" and "shoulds" and after frequent attempts with this method, over a three-session period (third to sixth session), it was discontinued. At this point, after twenty sessions, the patient only occasionally shows evidence that he is using extremes less. He has only minimally incorporated my challenging remarks into his thinking.

I tried to get him to discuss his present attitudes and feelings. On one occasion, when I was actually feeling exasperated with him, calling his attention to his dwelling in the past led, much to my surprise, to what appeared to be an "insight" response.

Therapist: "You continue to discuss your childhood, and I keep trying to get you back in the present."

Patient: "I always go back to the beginning, even in my work, instead of working at the problem at hand. My brother and I always got stuck on the first paragraph rather than going ahead."

The insight response was noted as a widening of his eyes, a "Say, that's right" appearance on his face and a nodding of his head. After twenty sessions he still goes to the past on occasion, but has increased his discussion of the present markedly. I do not know if "the insight," the "demand characteristics of the situation" or other factors led to this.

I felt it important to learn what was reinforcing to him, what he enjoyed doing. The rationale behind this was that many conscientious people function poorly when denying themselves enjoyment. He listed activities he liked, played down their having any real significance and essentially spoke little on this topic.

My impression after six sessions was that, although the patient was discussing the present more, he was not receptive to the "interruptions" I had made with comments, questions, challenges or any form of "activity." I felt that he had come to talk and that he wanted me to listen. Doing anything but listening at this point, I felt, would lead to his leaving therapy. In essence, this patient "trained me" to use, in part, a psychoanalytic approach—that of being silent. However I did not combine this with the other usual ingredients such as aloofness and distance.

In the ensuing sessions the patient has revealed interesting information that leads one to make numerous conceptualizations of what his attitudes, beliefs and themes might be. Several excerpts from our meetings are as follows:

1. "I have a desire to be a great physicist, not just ordinary, having complete freedom with no one telling me what to do."
2. "Marriage interferes with becoming great."
3. "When I read the biographies of Einstein and Bertrand Russell, I wonder what motivated them to become great."
   "To understand what motivated Franklin at age eighty-four to discover bifocals."
4. "To achieve greatness one has to go deeply into every subject and know it completely before one can develop new ideas in it. However, going into things deeply might turn out to be a waste of time. Even if one went deeply into a subject and knew everything about it, he

might not be able to plan the research and therefore all his time would go to waste . . . therefore, why bother."

5. "Father was not an authoritarian. He didn't tell me to study. However, I do remember him saying, 'Did you do your homework?' That got me mad. I don't feel free to enjoy things. This problem has been in the back of my mind at least ten years. I guess my father taught me this. He said it's a man's duty to work. I was raised strictly, under the protestant ethic."

6. "I'm concerned with my performance rather than the sheer joy of doing it. I would like to do something out of the ordinary, to not conform. In a sense, I would like to conform—to work, publish, get a good job, satisfy my employer and my professor. But if I fall into this trap, then I'm going through the mill like everyone else. I haven't stood out, just in a rut, like the middle class. I want to insist that I run my own life, not let external circumstances run it. The great physicists were not afraid to do something out of the ordinary. I'm restless at night if I have a good workday. I am afraid to be successful. It will mean that I have made my commitment. There will be demands on me, and I won't be able to brood as much. In the past, I worked evenings till 3:00 a.m. I'm afraid that if I get a good idea, I may get anxious for staying successful. I'll end up working every evening. This would make it hard to live with my wife and kids. (Patient is unmarried.) If I work well in the morning, I might formulate a different opinion of what I'll end up as in the future—possibly, being an eight-to-five worker and coming up with good ideas during the day and enjoying my family in the evening."

7. "The image of marriage in America is one of tenderness and care, as if love is at its height when one partner is sick or one partner is not doing well, so the other can comfort him."

8. "If I made a great discovery, it would make me feel uncomfortable. I'd get attention from others, but I couldn't command the subject to explain it to them."

9. "There is a mixed expression of independence on my part, yet a reluctance to jump into it. Is it just not wanting to get dependent?"

10. "I'd like to reach an age, seventy, fifty or even thirty-five, and look back and feel pleased with what I've done."

11. In discussing the only girl he has been seeing for one and one-half years he said: "This is not the type of girl . . . if I was sure of my own life. She has no initiative, not an intellectual, only wants a family, kids and happy married life. Dating her is like reverting to home and childhood. It's a drifting—the easy way out—requires no effort on my part. When I feel good this girl is too slow for me. I'd want to be more active and do things. I'd feel more comfortable with a girl who wants to take the initiative."

12. "If married it would intrude on my rights to introspect and be alone, and the girl would see a part of me she hadn't seen when dating."

13. At about the eighth session, the patient reported a dream—"I was climbing a wall—trying to get to the top. I finally got to the top after a hard climb. When I'm on top of the wall, I see a woman there and feel terrified." He awakened screaming. The meaning of the dream to him was "a woman is a threat to my progress."

14. Some of the remarks the patient made about the author were:
    a. "Coming in here makes me bring out my inadequacies. You have to talk about your failures and that you are being dependent."
    b. "I don't like when you say, 'It's a good session.' Or 'You're doing well. That makes me feel like a little boy.'"
    c. "I felt more equal to you today—not as the patient coming in to show his failure."
    d. "I would like you to say that I'm perceptive and intelligent."
    e. "One of the advantages of coming to you is that you're not much older than I—yourself just out of graduate school, so you may appreciate what I'm feeling."
    f. "I wish you were more experienced—an experienced therapist would have a deeper and quicker understanding of the situation. Your questions are in a faltering tone, as if they are not strongly formulated."
    g. "I feel good after leaving here. I work better for three hours. I always learn something here that sets my mind at ease. This has happened several times. It makes me feel free to do what I want and that what I've been doing is alright."

Some signs of improvement may be noted by reports and attitudes discussed in the past five sessions (fifteenth to twentieth): He has had an increased frequency of good work days and more enjoyable weekend activities. He has sent out sixty-three job applications for next year—an activity which he stated early in therapy he should do, but was unable to. Also he had decided, on his own, to come once weekly rather than twice.

Some of his attitudes which appear changed are:

a. "When reading an article, I'm not as bothered as I used to be that the author is smarter than me."
b. "I was able to read a review on a subject without it bothering me."
c. "I guess no one understands everything. This is the proper attitude."
d. "I've been getting some new research ideas lately."
e. "A year ago I felt that not working *should* bother me. Now I don't feel I *should* be bothered."
f. "I was out with my girlfriend this weekend and wasn't thinking of physics."
g. "Why am I such a perfectionist? Most people don't look for a girl that has the perfect reaction to them."
h. "I think these paradoxes are very real—I can exhibit opposite moods."

The plan of therapy is to allow the patient to do the talking, only interrupting him when he's felt to be "receptive."

Concepts that will be pointed out to him involve:

a. His tendency to think of all the pros and cons of the issues that face him.
b. The presence of any negatives deters him from proceeding with enthusiasm in any area.
c. Positive thoughts tend to trigger negative ones.

For example:

He'd like to read an interesting physics topic but he then thinks—'It might be a waste of time; if I come across something I don't know, I'll feel inadequate; if it's an article written by someone my age, it will make me realize how I've wasted my life; if I get interested in the topic, I will want to read everything in that field, and that might waste time (or I might be bored); reading an interesting article takes me away from work I *should* be doing.'

In relation to girls and marriage some of his thoughts might be: 'I'd like to get married and have a family; if one has a family, one *should* devote evenings and week-ends to being with them; if I were to get involved in a physics problem, I might want to work on it into the night; if I worked on my physics at night or on the weekend, I would not be a *proper* husband or father.'

In both cases the chain of thoughts leads to an imperfect situation. Since he cannot tolerate imperfect situations, he refrains from beginning any potentially rewarding activity.

Therapy must be aimed at familiarizing him with his thoughts and helping him to challenge them. This is the only way I feel he can achieve symptom relief, and function effectively. A more appropriate thought pattern might be:

'I'll read this article since it might be interesting. I won't be wasting time because this could add to my knowledge or, if not, may just be enjoyable. If there is some area I'm not familiar with, I can look it up or try to get as much out of the article as possible without knowing that information. Some men my age have done better than I have, but I don't *have* to be the best. I'm doing a good job and am satisfied with my work.'

CONCLUSION

In this chapter I have tried to describe the thinking that goes into the planning of the therapies I use, the techniques themselves and the results obtained.

I see myself at this time as being between two categories of therapist. On the one hand are those traditionalists with their strong belief in stereotyped "dynamics" and rigid rules of therapy (one to one, noninvolvement of relatives, and the fifty-minute hour). On the other hand are those few extraordinary and talented people who have not only familiarized themselves with multiple techniques from many different schools (cognitive therapy, behavior therapy, rational emotive therapy, implosive therapy, eidetic imagery, psychodrama, morita therapy, etc.), but who realize the importance of techniques designed to *influence* people toward favorable change.

I would like to progress still further from my original traditional background to this latter one. I would also hope that the training programs of future therapists will take this same direction.

Index

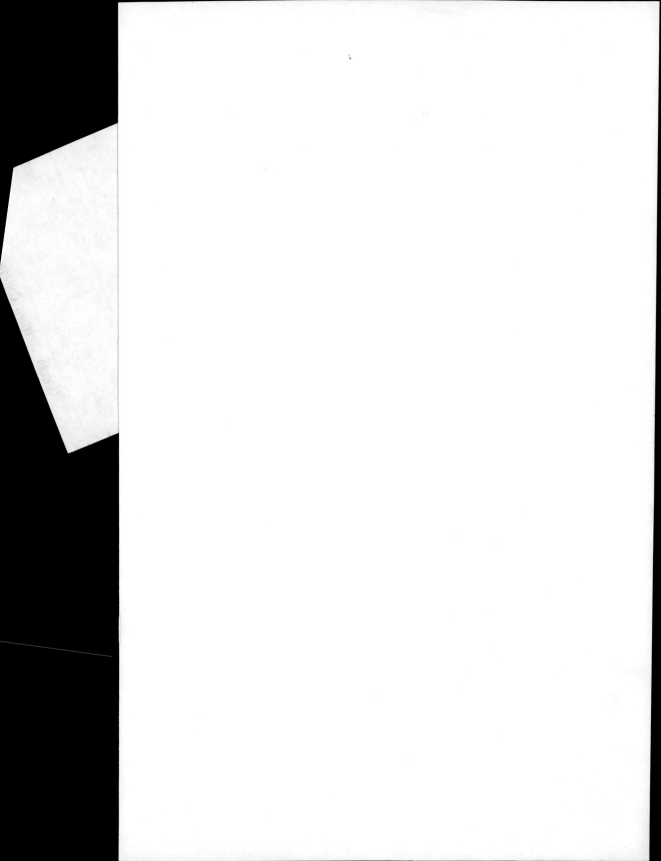

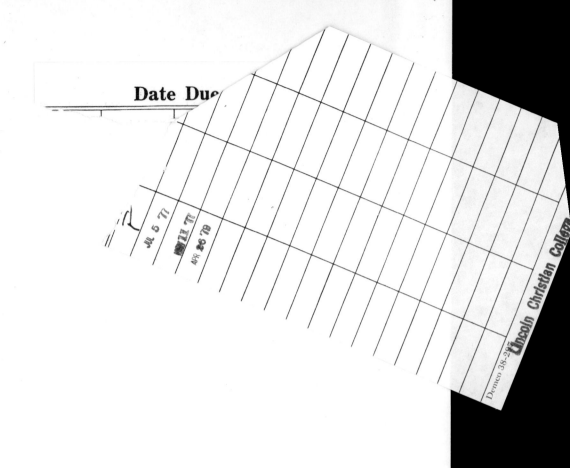

Date Due

JUL 5 77

NOV 14 77

APR 26 '79

Demco 38-297

Lincoln Christian College

Praise for *Mind to Matter*

"If you've been wondering whether your thoughts really do affect your life, this marvelous book will make you a believer. From the level of the atom to the level of our bodies to the level of the galaxies, Dawson Church's painstaking research shows that mind is profoundly creative. Synthesizing hundreds of studies in the fields of biology, physics, and psychology, he shows that moment by moment, the energy fields of our brains are literally creating reality. These insights can have a radical effect on your health and prosperity, and I highly recommend you apply them in your life."

— John Gray, #1 *New York Times* best-selling author of *Men Are from Mars, Women Are from Venus*

"We have entered an era of healing in which the influence of consciousness in health and illness is being validated as never before. For a view of these crucial insights, researcher Dawson Church's Mind to Matter *is invaluable."*

— Larry Dossey, M.D., author of *One Mind: How Our Individual Mind Is Part of a Greater Consciousness and Why It Matters*

"Dawson Church's careful scientific work shows that the Law of Attraction isn't just a metaphysical proposition—it's a scientific reality. Drawing from hundreds of studies, and illustrated with inspiring real-life stories, it demystifies the intricate mechanisms by which thoughts become things. As the boundaries of what you believe is possible for your life are stretched by Dawson's work, they may never snap back to their old shape."

— Marci Shimoff, #1 *New York Times* best-selling author of *Happy for No Reason*

"I love this book. It constantly fascinated me with delicious facts and so many captivating stories. And it is wonderful to see science catching up with what the shamans and sages have always known!"

— Donna Eden, author of *Energy Medicine*

"Once in a long while, a profoundly disruptive vision shatters the scientific paradigm, refocuses the entire way we see the world, and opens up vast new horizons of human potential. For our generation, this book is that vision."

— Raymond Aaron, *New York Times* best-selling author of *Chicken Soup for the Parent's Soul*

"Dawson Church has again proven himself to be one of the great thinkers of our time, demystifying the most complex principles in the universe that influence our lives, with a story-telling ability that makes it all fun and easy to understand. By weaving eye-opening research into engaging, heart-warming stories, an awareness emerges of the power your own mind has to not only direct your life but influence the collective consciousness of the universe itself which binds us together as one."

— Robert Hoss, co-author of *Dreams That Change Our Lives*; Director, DreamScience Foundation

"This groundbreaking book presents the exciting new scientific evidence demonstrating that our thoughts have a direct impact on the world around us, and it shows us how to harness this knowledge for joyful and effective lives."

— David Feinstein, Ph.D., co-author of *Personal Mythology*

"I believe that Mind to Matter *is one of the most important books ever written. Chapter after chapter it shows us how we are masters of our bodies and the world around us. It's filled with mind-blowing research that has completely changed the way I approach my life. The results I'm getting by applying the techniques are astonishing. They can transform your mind and the world of matter around you. I can't recommend this book highly enough."*

— Matt Gallant, author of *Triple Your Productivity*

"Mind to Matter *challenges the core principles of modern medicine and conventional science. Dawson Church makes a compelling case that the mind/body link is more profound than we ever suspected, and that science must expand its paradigm to include forces like consciousness, resonance, and energy. Profusely illustrated, the book includes an impressive compendium of research citations, from classic papers to recent breakthroughs. Many practical examples and exercises provide tools to work on our own personal transformation and, if the book's thesis of interconnection is correct, our social transformation as well. I highly recommend this book."*

— Eric Leskowitz, M.D., Department of Psychiatry,
Harvard Medical School

"Dawson Church has been a pioneer in the field of healing for decades, his research far ahead of its time. His book Mind to Matter *is perfectly timed for an era in which people are opening up to the science and research behind energy techniques. Dawson offers a brilliant and insightful guide to how our thoughts create our reality. Packed with fascinating history from the dawn of evolution to the latest brain research, his work is a blueprint for both experts and non-professionals looking for effective healing strategies. Dawson succinctly shows us not just that these methods work, but the empirical basis for how they work. If you have ever wanted to learn the science of manifestation and how your thoughts affect your material world, this book is a must-read. It will change your thoughts, and applying these principles every day will in turn change your reality. The question is—what will you create after you read it?"*

— Peta Stapleton, Ph.D., School of Psychology,
Bond University, Australia

"Many in our culture are shifting from powerless victims to powerful co-creators. Yet as this evolutionary impulse toward greater power emerges, we are coming face to face with what happens when power is abused. As we face global crises of unpredictable proportions, we need heart-based creators of deep integrity in touch with their power now more than ever. What would be possible in our lives and on our planet if we connected our power with our hearts? What does science have to say about such manifesting power? Mind to Matter explores this edge of how our power to participate in the co-creation of reality functions from the scientific perspective. It also calls us out on how to avoid overstating our human power, as so many 'law of attraction' books mistakenly promise. As our power grows, we are called to acknowledge with humility the paradoxical nature of how powerful we are as creators, yet how uncontrollable the great Mystery really is. May those who read this book step fully into their power, their hearts, and their integrity, and may the world be blessed by how this book affects you."

— Lissa Rankin, M.D., *New York Times* best-selling
author of *Mind Over Medicine*

MIND
TO
MATTER

ALSO BY DAWSON CHURCH

BOOKS

*The Genie in Your Genes: Epigenetic Medicine
and the New Biology of Intention**

*Soul Medicine: Awakening Your Inner Blueprint
for Abundant Health and Energy**

*The EFT (Emotional Freedom Techniques) Manual**

*EFT for Weight Loss**

*EFT for PTSD**

*EFT for Love Relationships**

*EFT for Fibromyalgia and Chronic Fatigue**

*EFT for Back Pain**

EFT for Golf

Psychological Trauma: Healing Its Roots in Body, Brain and Memory

*The Clinical EFT Handbook Volume 1 (co-editor)**

*The Clinical EFT Handbook Volume 2 (co-editor)**

*Communing with the Spirit of Your Unborn Child**

Facing Death, Finding Love

*Available from Hay House
Please visit:

Hay House USA: www.hayhouse.com®
Hay House Australia: www.hayhouse.com.au
Hay House UK: www.hayhouse.co.uk
Hay House India: www.hayhouse.co.in

———

mind
TO
matter

THE ASTONISHING
SCIENCE OF HOW
YOUR BRAIN CREATES
MATERIAL REALITY

DAWSON CHURCH

HAY HOUSE, INC.
Carlsbad, California • New York City
London • Sydney • New Delhi

Copyright © 2018 by Dawson Church

Published in the United States by: Hay House, Inc.: www.hayhouse.com® • *Published in Australia by:* Hay House Australia Pty. Ltd.: www.hayhouse.com.au • *Published in the United Kingdom by:* Hay House UK, Ltd.: www.hayhouse.co.uk • *Published in India by:* Hay House Publishers India: www.hayhouse.co.in

Cover design: Victoria Valentine • *Interior design:* Riann Bender
Indexer: Joan Shapiro

All rights reserved. No part of this book may be reproduced by any mechanical, photographic, or electronic process, or in the form of a phonographic recording; nor may it be stored in a retrieval system, transmitted, or otherwise be copied for public or private use—other than for "fair use" as brief quotations embodied in articles and reviews—without prior written permission of the publisher.

The author of this book does not dispense medical advice or prescribe the use of any technique as a form of treatment for physical, emotional, or medical problems without the advice of a physician, either directly or indirectly. The intent of the author is only to offer information of a general nature to help you in your quest for emotional, physical, and spiritual well-being. In the event you use any of the information in this book for yourself, the author and the publisher assume no responsibility for your actions.

Library of Congress Cataloging-in-Publication Data

Names: Church, Dawson, 1956- author.
Title: Mind to matter : the astonishing science of how your brain creates
   material reality / Dawson Church, Ph.D.
Description: Carlsbad, California : Hay House, [2018] | Includes
   bibliographical references and index.
Identifiers: LCCN 2017060615 | ISBN 9781401955236 (hardcover : alk. paper)
Subjects: LCSH: Neuropsychology. | Brain. | Cognition. | Mind and reality.
Classification: LCC QP360 .C4848 2018 | DDC 612.8--dc23 LC record available at
https://lccn.loc.gov/2017060615

Hardcover ISBN: 978-1-4019-5523-6
10 9 8 7 6 5 4 3 2 1

1st edition, June 2018

Printed in the United States of America

CONTENTS

FOREWORD

Science has become the contemporary language of mysticism. In my experience from teaching audiences around the world, the moment terminology related to religion, ancient traditions, secular cultures, or even new age idealisms is spoken in public, audiences become divided. Yet science unifies—and thus creates community.

Thus, when some of the principles of quantum physics (how mind and matter are related) and electromagnetism are combined with the latest discoveries in neuroscience and neuroendocrinology (the study of how the brain regulates the hormone system of the body), then a little *psychoneuroimmunology (*the study of how the brain, nervous system, and the immune system impact each other—*that's the mind-body connection*) is added and finally the last findings in epigenetics (the study of how the environment affects gene expression) are included in the equation, you can demystify the mystical. In doing so, you will also uncover the mystery of the self and unravel the true nature of reality.

All these new areas of research point the finger toward possibility. They prove we are not hardwired to be a certain way for the rest of our lives, and we are not doomed by our genes—rather, we're marvels of adaptability and change.

Each time you learn something new, unique possibilities you were not previously aware of open up before you, and as a result you are changed. This is called knowledge, and knowledge causes you to no longer see things the way *they* are, but the way *you* are. This is the process of learning, and the more you learn, the more you make new synaptic connections in your brain. And as you'll learn in this wonderful book, recent studies show that just an hour of focused concentration on any one subject doubles the number of connections in your brain related to that subject. The same research tells us that if you don't repeat, review, or think about what you've learned, those circuits prune apart within hours or days. Thus, if learning is making new synaptic connections, remembering is maintaining those connections.

In the research I've conducted with literally thousands and thousands of people all over the world, I now know that once a person understands an idea, a concept, or new information—and they can turn to the person next to them and explain that information—they are firing and wiring certain circuits in their brain. These circuits add new stitches into the three-dimensional tapestry of their brain matter, allowing them to successfully wire the circuits necessary to initiate that new knowledge into a new experience. In other words, once you can remember and discuss the new model of understanding, you are beginning to install the neurological hardware in preparation for an experience.

The more you know what you're doing and why, the easier the *how* gets. That's why this is a time in history when it's not enough to simply *know*—it's a time to *know how*. It makes sense, then, that your next job is to initiate the knowledge by applying, personalizing, or demonstrating what you've philosophically and theoretically learned. This means you're going to have to make new and different choices—and get your body involved. And when you can align your behaviors with your intentions, make your actions equal to your thoughts, or get your mind and body working together, you are going to have a new experience.

So if you are given the proper instructions on what to do, and you follow the directions and perform it properly, you are going to create a new experience. Once you embrace a new experience, the new event will add to (and further enhance) the intellectual circuitry in your brain. This is called experience, and experience enriches the circuitry in the brain. The moment those circuits organize into new networks in the brain, the brain makes a chemical. That chemical is called a feeling or an emotion. That means the instant you feel freedom, abundance, gratitude, wholeness, or joy from that novel event, now you're teaching your body chemically to understand what your mind has intellectually understood.

It's fair to say, then, that knowledge is for the mind and experience is for the body. Now you are beginning to *embody the truth* of that philosophy. In doing so, you're rewriting your biological program and signaling new genes in new ways. That's because new information is coming from the environment. As we know from epigenetics, if the environment signals new genes, and the end product of an experience in the environment is an emotion, you are literally signaling the new genes in new ways. And since all genes make proteins and proteins are responsible for the structure and function of your body (the expression of proteins is the expression of life), you are literally changing your genetic destiny. This suggests that it's quite possible your body can be healed.

If you can create an experience once, you should be able to do it again. If you can reproduce any experience repeatedly, eventually you will neurochemically condition your mind and body to begin to work as one. When you've done something so many times that the body knows how to do it as well as the mind, it becomes automatic, natural, and effortless—in other words, a skill or a habit. Once you've achieved that level, you no longer have to consciously think about doing it. That's when the skill or habit becomes the subconscious state of being. Now it's innate and you're beginning to *master that philosophy.* You have become that knowledge.

This is how common people around the world are beginning to do the uncommon. In doing so they are transitioning from philosopher to initiate to master; from knowledge to experience to wisdom; from mind to body to soul; from thinking to doing to being; and from learning with their head to practicing it by hand and knowing it by heart. The beauty of it is, we all have the biological and neurological machinery to do this.

The side effect of your repeated efforts will not only change who you are, but it should begin to create possibilities in your life that reflect your efforts. Why else would you do it? What do I mean when I say possibilities? I'm talking about healing from diseases or imbalances of the body as well as the mind; creating a better life by consciously directing energy and attention into a new future—the manifestation of new jobs, new relationships, new opportunities, and new adventures—equal to our ability to imagine it; and initiating mystical experiences that literally transcend language.

It makes sense that when the synchronicities, coincidences, and new opportunities appear in your life, you'll pay attention to what you have been doing and it should inspire you to do it again. That's how you go from being the victim in your life to being the creator of your life.

And that's what this powerful book is all about. *Mind to Matter* is your personal guide to prove to yourself how powerful you truly are when you organize your thoughts and feelings into coherent states. It was written for you to not just intellectually understand the content but to consistently use the practices and apply them to your life so that you reap the rewards of your efforts.

It's no short order to create a scientific model of understanding that suggests that our subjective mind (our thoughts) can influence our objective world (our life), never mind write a book about it. Finding the research alone is a task in and of itself. And yet, my dear friend and colleague Dawson Church has taken this task on in this fantastically well-written book.

I'd like to tell you a bit about Dawson Church. I met Dawson at a conference in Philadelphia, Pennsylvania, in 2006. The moment we met, there was an instant connection. I quickly realized when we first were introduced that this was going to be a long and healthy friendship. The energy from the exchange of ideas between us felt like a thunderstorm. And every time we talked about something we both believed to be true, it was like lightning struck. We were both changed from our first interaction. Since then, we have worked together on several different projects. Not only has Dawson published several of his own well-researched studies on energy psychology, but he has been part of my research team that has been busy quantitatively measuring the effects of meditation on the brain and the body. He has impeccably led several of our studies and he has become the voice of reason in our research.

Dawson is one of those people I can e-mail or call and ask, *How long does it take for trauma to consolidate in the brain as a long-term memory?* And he will—without hesitation—tell me the exact time it takes, the best reference, the particular research studies as well as the scientists who conducted those studies. It's as if he were giving me directions to the local supermarket. When I discovered this, that's when I realized I was not working with an average scientist, I was in the presence of a super mind. Dawson is brilliant, charismatic, loving, and full of life. He and I share a passion—to understand and to know more about who we really are and what is possible for human beings, especially during these present times of change.

I loved reading this book because it provided answers to some of my own personal questions about the relationship between mind and the material world as well as the connection between energy and matter. I learned new concepts and it helped me see the world differently. I was changed from my time reading it. It is my hope that not only will it change you and help you to see the world differently, but it will also inspire you to apply the principles so that you embody the truth of what is possible for you in your life. If science is the new language of mysticism, then you are learning from a contemporary mystic—my dear friend Dawson Church. He wants you to become your own mystic too and to prove to yourself that your thoughts matter—they literally become matter.

Dr. Joseph Dispenza
New York Times best-selling author
of *You Are the Placebo: Making Your Mind Matter*

INTRODUCTION

Metaphysics Meets Science

Thoughts become things. This is manifestly true. I am sitting on a chair right now. It began as a thought in someone's mind—every detail of it. The frame, the fabric, the curves, the color.

Thoughts become things. This is manifestly untrue. I will never be a quarterback for the National Football League, no matter how earnestly I think about it. I will never be 16 years old again. I will never pilot the starship *Enterprise.*

Between the ways in which thoughts become things and the ways in which thoughts can never become things there is a wide middle ground.

This book explores that middle ground.

Why? We want to be able to create to the outermost limits of our thought, expanding our lives to the limits of our potential. We want to be as happy, healthy, wealthy, wise, fulfilled, creative, and loved as possible. We also don't want to chase pipe dreams, thoughts that are never going to become things.

When we apply the rigorous standards of science to the inquiry, that middle ground turns out to be enormous. Research shows us that with thought, used deliberately, we can create things beyond the ordinary.

The idea that thoughts are things has become a meme in popular culture. It's held as a firm proposition in metaphysics, and some spiritual teachers ascribe infinite powers to the mind. Yet there are clearly limits to human creative abilities; I cannot manifest an aircraft carrier simply by thinking about one. I cannot become Indonesian, jump over Mount Everest, or turn lead into gold.

New discoveries in epigenetics, neuroscience, electromagnetism, psychology, cymatics, public health, and quantum physics, however, are showing that thoughts can be profoundly creative. The page or device on which you now read these words began as a thought. So did democracy, the bikini, space travel, immunization, money, the four-minute mile, and the assembly line.

THE SCIENTIST VERSUS THE MYSTIC

Science and metaphysics are generally considered to be polar opposites. Science is experimental, practical, rigorous, empirical, materialistic, objective, and intellectual. Metaphysics is spiritual, experiential, abstract, mystical, ephemeral, internal, irreplicable, imprecise, subjective, otherworldly, impractical, and impossible to prove. Science studies the world of matter while metaphysics seeks to transcend it.

I have never perceived science and metaphysics as separate and have delighted in being both a mystic and a scientific researcher. When I bring the rigor of science to the questions of consciousness, each illuminates the other.

This book examines the science behind the creative powers of the mind. It reviews the studies that show, step-by-step, exactly how our minds create material form. As each piece of the puzzle falls into place, the science turns out to be even more astonishing than the metaphysics.

This book is also full of case histories—real, up close, authentic personal accounts of people who had an experience of mind-into-matter. Drawn from the worlds of medicine, psychology, sports, business, and scientific discovery, these stories run the gamut from profound to inspiring to heart-wrenching. They show us that thoughts can become things in ways that stretch the fabric of our space-time reality.

Keys in the Ocean

In 2004, I faced a tight deadline to finish my book *The Genie in Your Genes*. The material, on how our emotions turn genes on and off in our bodies, was fascinating. But finding the time to research and write an emotionally engaging yet scientifically impeccable text—amid the demands of my busy life as a single dad, the owner of two businesses, and a doctoral candidate—was a challenge.

I decided to flee to Hawaii for two weeks for a writing intensive. I booked a room at the Prince Kuhio condo complex, a funky 1950s relic on the beach in Poipu, Kauai. I rented a Jeep Wrangler so I would have a rugged four-wheel-drive vehicle to reach more remote beaches and a place to store my snorkeling gear. That way I could swim each day as well as apply myself to completing the project.

One bright, sunny day, I went for a swim at a gorgeous spot called Lawai Beach. Five hundred feet long, with a turtle colony in a reef 300 feet from shore and a healthy population of tropical fish, it was one of my favorite places. I grabbed my snorkeling gear out of the Jeep, locked up, pocketed the keys, and jumped in the water. An hour later, after swimming all over the bay, wet and happy, I rinsed my goggles and flippers to put them back in the car.

When I reached into my pocket for the keys, it was empty.

Could I have dropped them on the path from the car to the beach? I retraced my steps, looking over every inch of ground. I sifted through the sand between the road and my entry point to the water. Nothing.

The only possible conclusion was that my keys had fallen out of my pocket somewhere in the bay. Not only did the key ring hold the car keys, I'd clipped the apartment keys to it as well. I was now locked out of both the car and the condo.

I decided not to panic. I centered my consciousness in my heart, and I imagined the keys gently drifting back to me. Then I dove into the water and started swimming with a purpose. I was determined to find those keys.

The bay covered about 150 square yards or meters, and the coral on the bottom was 6 to 12 feet down. It twisted into thousands of colorful crannies, and finding something as tiny as a key ring seemed impossible.

I worked my way systematically back and forth across the bay, searching each yard intently. My head told me I was on a fool's errand, but I kept my heart soft and receptive. Each time my thinking brain began to panic, I refocused my consciousness in my heart area. I certainly intended to find the keys, but I didn't let my thoughts take me out of the state of flow.

> I had searched for an hour without success, and it was getting dark. The visibility was dropping as the sun set, and I couldn't see clearly down to the coral anymore. I decided to abandon my quest and swim back to shore.
>
> Though most of the other bathers had left and the day was ending, I saw a father and three sons snorkeling nearby. They were diving to the bottom and coming up in turns.
>
> My intuition gave me a nudge. I swam up to them and asked, "Did you guys find anything on the bottom?" The youngest boy held up my keys.

THE CHAIN OF EVIDENCE
FROM MIND TO MATTER

My skeptic's mind tells me there is a logical explanation for every piece of the key event. I just happened to swim around looking for the keys for the exact length of time it took the boy to find them. I just happened to turn toward the shore at the same moment the family began diving. They just happened to start diving at the spot where my keys had fallen to the bottom. The boy just happened to notice a tiny key ring 12 feet down in an enormous bay after the sky was already dark. It was all a matter of random chance.

But after decades of hundreds of similar experiences, my skeptic's mind has to think again. How can so many highly unlikely things come together at once to produce a desired result?

They led to a quest to determine if there is any scientific link between thoughts and things. As a researcher who has conducted many clinical trials, the editor of a peer-reviewed journal called *Energy Psychology,* and a science blogger for the *Huffington Post,* I read all or part of more than a thousand scientific studies per year. I started to see a pattern. There are multiple links in the chain between thought and thing, and I realized that science could explain many of them. I wondered if anyone had ever connected all the dots to see just how strong the evidence was. Where was the chain strongest, and where were links missing?

If I were to treat the idea of mind creating matter as a scientific rather than a metaphysical hypothesis, would it hold up? I began seeking out research that addressed this question and interviewing some of the brightest minds in the field.

With mounting excitement, I realized that much of the evidence was hiding in plain sight, like pearls scattered in the sand. But no one had strung the facts together in a necklace before. Most of the research is new, and pieces of it are astonishing.

The first pearls I began to pick up from the sand were the easy ones. Research on the human body has been going on since medieval alchemists dissected cadavers. But recently, technology has given scientists unprecedented insight into how our bodies work at the level of cells and molecules.

Nobel Prize–winning physician Eric Kandel showed that when we pass signals through a neural bundle in our brains, that bundle grows rapidly. The number of connections can *double* in *just one hour* of repeated stimulation. Our brains are rewiring themselves along the pathways of our neural activity in real time.

As the thoughts and feelings of our consciousness are carried through our neural network, they trigger the expression of genes. These in turn trigger the synthesis of proteins in our cells. These cellular events produce electrical and magnetic fields that can be measured by sophisticated medical imaging devices such as EEG and MRI.

THE 11-DIMENSIONAL UNIVERSE

The next set of pearls was more challenging. The world of quantum physics is so strange that it confounds our conventional experience of space and time. String theory posits that what we perceive as physical matter is actually composed of strings of energy. What we measure as heavy molecules are fast-moving energy strings, while what we experience as light molecules are energy strings that are vibrating more slowly. The closer science looks at matter, the more it looks like pure energy.

String theory requires a universe with 11 dimensions, not just the 4 required by classical physics. How do our 4-dimensional brains contemplate 11 dimensions? Physicist Niels Bohr said, "If quantum mechanics hasn't profoundly shocked you, you haven't understood it yet."

Then came the pearls that connect consciousness with energy. Energy is entwined with consciousness on both a personal and a cosmic scale. Albert Einstein said: "A human being is a part of the whole, called by us 'Universe,' a part limited in time and space. He experiences

himself, his thoughts and feeling as something separated from the rest—
a kind of optical delusion of his consciousness." When we begin to "free
ourselves from this prison," as Einstein phrased it, then we expand our
consciousness to "embrace all living creatures and the whole of nature."
Our consciousness interacts with the energy of the universe.

CONSCIOUSNESS AND NONLOCAL MIND

Physician Larry Dossey calls this expansive consciousness that
embraces the whole of nature "nonlocal mind." While we live our lives
in our local minds and ordinary reality, we're unconscious participants
in the larger consciousness of nonlocal mind. Moments of synchronicity
like finding my keys remind me of the presence of nonlocal mind. Dossey presents compelling evidence for the existence of nonlocal mind and
inspires us with the potential of living our local lives in synchrony with it.

That's a choice we can make in consciousness. Nobel Prize–winning
physicist Eugene Wigner says that "the very study of the external world
led to the scientific conclusion that the content of the consciousness is
an ultimate reality." Though there are many definitions of consciousness,
the one I prefer is the simplest: simply being aware.

The way we use that consciousness—the way we direct our awareness—produces profound and immediate changes in the atoms and molecules of our bodies. Science also shows us that our consciousness affects
the material reality around us. As our consciousness changes, so changes
the world.

Writing this book, I began to string the pearls together, study by
study. Additional evidence began showing up in my life in the same synchronous manner in which my lost keys had appeared. When I looked
at all the pearls strung together in sequence, I realized that science can
explain every link in the chain from thought to thing.

THE DANCE OF CREATION

I am excited to share each one of these links with you. Through story
and analogy, through experiment and research, through case histories
and anecdotes, we'll trace every part of the process by which your mind
creates the material world around you.

You'll discover that you are a potent creator, and that your thoughts lead to things. You'll learn how to use your mind deliberately, as a creative tool, to think nurturing thoughts. You'll understand how you can nudge material reality effortlessly toward your desires. You'll grasp just how powerful you really are and how capable you are of creating change by simply changing your mind.

You'll also discover how the process works on a grand scale, from the molecule to the cell to the body to the family to the community to the country to the species to the planet to the universe. We'll investigate the dance of creation happening at the scale of nonlocal universal consciousness and how your local mind participates in that dance.

This perspective lifts our awareness from the confines of our ordinary reality into a vast field of potential. As we align our individual local minds with the consciousness of the universal nonlocal mind, the beauty of the material reality we create surpasses anything our limited local minds can even dream of.

PUTTING THESE IDEAS INTO PRACTICE

At the end of each chapter, you'll find a list of practical exercises for implementing the ideas of the chapter in your own life. You'll also find a link to an online Extended Play version of the chapter, with resources to expand your experience. These resources include videos, audios, links, lists, case histories, and previews of ideas explored in following chapters. I encourage you to enrich your transformational journey with the activities in the Extended Play version.

The Extended Play version of this chapter includes:

- Audio interview with Daniel Siegel, M.D., author of *Mind: A Journey to the Heart of Being Human*

- Centering in Your Heart exercise

- Additional case histories and references

To access the Extended Play version, visit: MindToMatter.club/Intro

CHAPTER 1

How Our Brains Shape the World

Mrs. Hughes was short, red-faced, and round. Her hair had a life of its own, throwing off incandescent wisps like solar flares escaping from the grip of the sun's gravity. The bobby pins with which she attempted to confine it were unequal to the task. Her face alternated between pinched disapproval and resigned boredom. As her students suffered through her high school biology classes, she managed to stamp out every trace of curiosity and wonder in us.

I remember looking at line drawings of the human brain in the biology textbooks provided by Mrs. Hughes. The whole structure was fixed and unchanging, just like another organ such as a liver or a heart. In the 1970s, the science Mrs. Hughes taught "knew" that the brain grew until we were roughly 17 years old. After it had filled our skulls, it remained static for a lifetime, faithfully coordinating the many processes of life through its network of neurons.

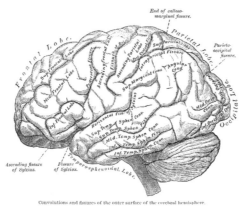

Traditional illustration of the brain.

MIND AS AN EPIPHENOMENON
OF COMPLEX BRAINS

We also had some idea what the mind was. As evolution produced more and more complex brains, going from the simple ganglia of nematode worms to the massive prefrontal cortex that crowns the human head, mind arose. To scientists of Mrs. Hughes's day, *mind* was an "epiphenomenon" of the brain's increasing complexity. Humans could write poetry, record history, make music, and perform calculus because of the power of the mind residing in the brain locked inside the bony circumference of the skull.

As they say in *The Big Short*, "It ain't what you don't know that gets you into trouble. It's what you know for sure that just ain't so." Most of what science knew, as recorded in the biology textbooks of Mrs. Hughes's day, like the static brain, just ain't so.

Our brains are on the boil. Frenetic cellular activity cycles through the brain constantly, creating and destroying molecules and cells, whether we are awake or asleep (Stoll & Müller, 1999).

Even the structure of neurons is constantly changing. Microtubules are the scaffolding that gives cells their rigidity, similar to the way girders shape a building. The microtubules in the brain's nerve cells have a shelf life of just 10 minutes between creation and destruction (Kim & Coulombe, 2010). That's how quickly our brains are changing.

Microtubules are the rigid skeletal structures giving cells their shape.

In this seething mass of activity, selected neural circuits are enhanced. The ones that grow are the ones we use. Pass an information signal repeatedly through a neural bundle and the bundle starts to enlarge. Just as the arms of a bodybuilder get bigger as he practices lifting heavier weights, our neural circuits grow when we exercise them.

THE SPEED OF NEURAL CHANGE

Studies published in the 1990s stunned neuroscientists with findings that even people in their 80s rapidly add capacity to frequently used neural circuits. On November 5, 1998, the headline "news of the week" in the most prestigious research journal, *Science*, read: "New Leads to Brain Neuron Regeneration" (Barinaga, 1998).

The speed of the process caused an earthquake in the world of our scientific knowledge. When the neurons in a neural bundle are stimulated repeatedly, the number of synaptic connections can double in just an hour (Kandel, 1998). If your house acted like your body, it would notice which lights you were turning on, and every hour it would double the amount of electrical conduit going to that light circuit.

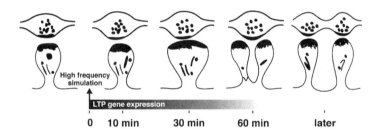

**Within an hour of repeat stimulation,
the number of synaptic connections in a neural pathway doubles.**

To obtain the raw materials to rewire the rooms in which you turned on the lights the most, your smart home would strip wiring from other sources. Our bodies do the same. Within three weeks of inactivity in an existing neural signaling pathway, the body starts to disassemble it in order to reuse those building blocks for active circuits (Kandel, 1998).

INCREASING THE MASS OF
THE BRAIN'S MOST USED REGIONS

This process of neural plasticity is evident when we learn new mechanical or intellectual skills. Take an adult education class in Russian at your community college; by the end of the first hour, you've already learned a few words. By the end of a year of practice, you've built up those neural bundles enough to speak simple Russian sentences without conscious effort.

Or you might decide that chess is a mental challenge that will keep your mind sharp into old age and start playing. At first, you're terrible; you can't remember whether it's the castle or the knight that moves diagonally. But after a few games, you move the pieces around purposefully and even develop plans for long-term strategies.

Youngster engrossed in a chess match.

Maybe you decide you'd like to manage your money better. You take a look at your retirement plan statements and notice that under the tender loving care of your fund manager, they've been growing at 2 percent a year. Someone's getting rich here, but it's certainly not you. You think you might do better on your own, so you take an online course in stock market investing. At first, even the language seems baffling. What's a covered call? How is return on investment (ROI) different from return on equity (ROE)?

Your first few trades might not make money. But after looking at charts and reading investment news for a few months, you gain confidence and discover that you're getting better at the money game.

Whether you're learning a new language, mastering a new hobby, navigating a new relationship, grappling with a new job, or starting a meditation practice, your brain's process of building and unbuilding is at work. You're adding capacity to the neural circuits you're using the most actively, while old ones wither away, a process called pruning.

Eventually, whole regions of the brain that are being actively used start to gain mass. With MRI scans, researchers are able to measure the volume of each part of a living human brain. They find that people who use their memory actively, like London cabbies who navigate a tangle of ancient streets, have a larger volume of tissue in the hippocampus, a part of the brain responsible for memory and learning. Dancers develop more mass in the part of the brain that manages proprioception, the holographic understanding of the body's location in space.

Your mind is constantly making decisions, such as whether to enroll in that Russian class or join the chess club. What the mind does then determines which brain circuits are engaged. The neural pathways in the brain that the mind's choices stimulate are the ones that grow. In this way, the mind literally creates the brain.

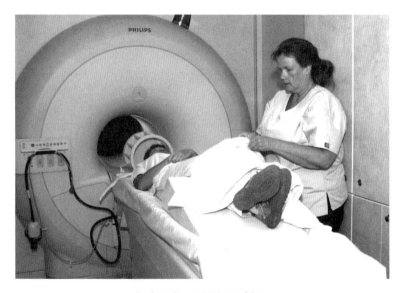

Patient in an MRI machine.

Mindfulness Changes the Brain of a Skeptical TV Journalist

Graham Phillips, Ph.D., is an Australian astrophysicist and TV journalist. Skeptical about feel-good techniques like meditation, he decided to put meditation to the test (Phillips, 2016). In his words, "I'd never really contemplated whether meditation could do anything for me. But the more I hear about the research, the more keen I am to see whether it has any effect. So I'm going to try it myself for two months. . . . For me, to take meditation seriously, I need some hard evidence that it's changing my brain for the better."

Before he began, he was evaluated by a team at Monash University led by biological psychology professor Neil Bailey, Ph.D., and clinical psychologist Richard Chambers, Ph.D. They put him through a battery of tests to evaluate his memory, reaction time, and ability to focus. They also used an MRI to measure the volume of each region of his brain, especially those responsible for memory and learning, motor control, and emotional regulation.

After just two weeks of practicing mindfulness meditation, Phillips felt less stressed and more able to handle the challenges of his job and life. He reported that he "notices stress but doesn't get sucked into it."

Eight weeks later, he returned to Monash for testing. Bailey and Chambers put Phillips through the same battery of tests again. They found that he was better at behavioral tasks, even though he showed diminished brain activity. The researchers noted that his brain had become more energy efficient. It showed an overall decrease in neural activity, doing a better job but exerting less energy. His memory tests also improved.

His reaction time to unexpected events had been cut by almost half a second. Phillips imagined the benefits, such as a quicker reaction time if a pedestrian steps out in front of him when he's driving on a busy street.

One of the brain regions the researchers measured was the hippocampus. They looked especially at the dentate gyrus, the part of the hippocampus responsible for regulating emotion in other parts of the brain. It exerts control over the default mode network, the part of the brain that's active when we aren't engaged in a task. They found that the volume of nerve cells in the dentate gyrus had *increased by 22.8 percent.*

That's an enormous change. Such brain reconfiguration is occasionally seen in young people whose brains are still growing, but it is rarely seen in adults. The change in Phillips's brain indicated a dramatically increased ability to regulate emotions. Psychological tests showed that Phillips's cognitive abilities had increased by several orders of magnitude as well.

There are many studies showing that meditation changes the structure of the brain. A review of the research on mindfulness-style meditation was published in the prestigious journal *Nature Reviews Neuroscience*. It found 21 studies in which participants were placed inside MRI machines to measure the volume of each part of their brain before and after meditation, just like Graham Phillips.

This accumulation of a large body of evidence identified neural growth in "multiple brain regions . . . suggesting that the effects of meditation might involve large-scale brain networks." The review found increases in the volume of "brain regions involved in attention control (the anterior cingulate cortex and the striatum), emotional regulation (multiple prefrontal regions, limbic regions and the striatum) and self-awareness (the insula, medial prefrontal cortex and posterior cingulate cortex and precuneus)" (Tang, Hölzel, & Posner, 2015).

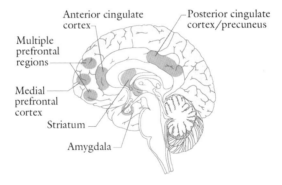

Brain regions in which neural growth occurs as a result of meditation.

WHAT EMOTIONAL REGULATION CAN DO FOR YOU

Like the brain of Graham Phillips, your brain is rewiring itself constantly. The brain adds neural capacity to regions you exercise. Choose a different experience, like meditation, and your brain begins working differently. Change your mind, and information starts to flow along new neural pathways in the brain. The brain's neurons reconfigure themselves accordingly, firing and wiring to fit the new pattern. As the mind directs, the brain responds.

Let's unpack the key elements of Graham's story for a moment. There are five:

- A 22.8 percent increase in the volume of the part of the brain responsible for emotional regulation
- Enhanced brain response time, better memory, increased cognitive powers, improved behavioral abilities
- A more relaxed and energy-efficient brain
- Changes in the brain in just 8 weeks
- No drugs, surgery, supplements, or major life changes—just mindfulness

Imagine having 22.8 percent more nerve cells in your brain to handle the task of emotional regulation. *Emotional regulation* may be jargon from neuroscience, but those two words have a big impact on your daily life. Better emotional regulation means that you're not derailed by common challenges such as:

- Getting triggered by co-workers at your job
- Annoying things your spouse or partner says or does
- Being startled by sudden noises or sights
- The problematic behavior of your children
- What politicians say and do
- Being stuck in traffic
- Stories in the news
- The way your body looks and functions
- Winning or losing at games or conflicts with others
- Religious conflicts or views held by others
- The stock market, your investments, and the economy
- Staying calm when people around you are stressed out
- Being short of time or feeling overwhelmed

- The amount of money you have or expect to have

- The way other people drive their cars

- Your age and how your body is changing

- Crowds, shopping, and close physical proximity to other people

- Other people's opinions that clash with yours

- Your expectations about the way your life ought to be

- The way your parents think and what they say

- Having to wait in line or wait for something you want

- The enviable lifestyles of movie stars and celebrities

- People who make unwanted demands on your time and attention

- The possessions you have or don't have

- Annoying relatives you interact with at family gatherings

- Random mishaps of daily life

- Getting or not getting promotions, rewards, and other things you want

- . . . and anything else that routinely annoys you

Imagine having a brain with vastly increased ability to master those challenges, preventing them from compromising your happiness. Meditation doesn't just change your state—the way you feel at the moment. It changes your traits—the enduring aspects of personality engraved in your brain that govern your outlook on life. Among the positive traits fostered by meditation are greater resilience in the face of adversity, more sympathy for others, and increased compassion for oneself (Goleman & Davidson, 2017). It also leads to a greater degree of self-regulation, making you the master of your emotions rather than a slave to them.

A classic 1972 study called the Stanford marshmallow experiment tested emotional regulation in preschool children. A marshmallow was put in front of them, after which they were left alone in a room. They were promised that they would get a second marshmallow if they could refrain from eating the first one for 15 minutes. Thirty years later, the lives of those who could regulate their emotions were better in many ways. They achieved higher scores on college entry exams. They earned more money and created happier marriages. They had a lower body mass index (BMI) and fewer addictive behaviors (Schlam, Wilson, Shoda, Mischel, & Ayduk, 2013).

The parts of the brain tasked with emotional regulation are also the ones that handle working memory, as revealed by MRI scans (Schweizer, Grahn, Hampshire, Mobbs, & Dalgleish, 2013). Working memory involves awareness, enabling you to remain focused on an activity and to sort relevant from irrelevant information. When your emotions are disturbed, those parts of the brain go offline for use by working memory. You then make poor decisions. When you learn effective emotional regulation, as Graham Phillips did, you are able to control your emotions, freeing up the brain's memory circuits to run your life wisely.

YOUR EVERYDAY SUPERPOWER

This is the everyday superpower that you possess: second by second, you are changing your brain by the way you use your mind. The consciousness of your mind is becoming the cells of the matter of your brain.

We're impressed when we see on-screen superheroes who can change their bodies at will. They may develop mental brilliance, like the hero in the movie and TV series *Limitless,* who takes an experimental drug called NZT that unlocks the full potential of his brain. Or the X-Men, each one of whom has a unique superpower gift.

Yet you, at this very moment, possess the superpower to change your brain. With each thought you think, as you direct your attention, you're signaling your brain to create new neural connections. Use this power deliberately, rather than allowing random thoughts to flow through your mind, and you start to consciously direct the formation of neural tissue. After a few weeks, your brain changes substantially. Keep it up for years, and you can build a brain that's habituated to process the signals of love, peace, and happiness.

This isn't a comic book or sci-fi movie; this is your life! Changing your brain is something you're doing every day. Now it's time to direct the process deliberately in a way that improves your life. Just as you upgrade the operating system of your computer or smartphone, you can upgrade your brain by changing your mind. Mind to matter.

ELECTRICAL CONDUCTORS
GENERATE ENERGY FIELDS

Tiny electrical currents run through the neurons in your brain, just like the electricity that runs through the copper wire in the electrical cords powering your appliances. As a whole, the brain seethes with electrical activity. This produces an energy field around the brain. When you get an MRI or EEG, medical professionals can read the energy field of your brain. It's a magnetic field in the case of an MRI, and it's an electrical field in the case of an EEG. Electricity and magnetism are two sides of the same coin: electromagnetism.

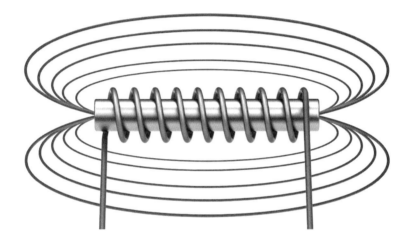

When an electric current is passed through a conductor, it produces a magnetic field. This is true whether the conductor is a power cord or a neuron.

There are many other forms of energy as well, and your brain and mind are constantly interacting with them. One of these is light. All living tissues emit photons, or light particles, and the type and intensity of the photons they emit vary. Even individual cells emit photons. A healthy cell emits a steady stream, while a dying cell sprays out its photons all at once like the burst of radiation from a collapsing supernova.

Light, electricity, and magnetism create the energy fields used in biological signaling. Biologist James Oschman states, "Energy is the currency in which all transactions in nature are conducted" (Oschman, 2015).

THE ANTENNAE IN YOUR CELLS

Imagine two magnets. Sprinkle iron filings around them and you'll see the lines of energy their fields produce. The copper cords powering your appliances and the neurons firing in your brain work the same way. They generate fields.

Now place a bigger magnet nearby. It will exert an influence on the iron filings, and the pattern of the whole energy field will change. Add an even bigger magnet and the field shifts again. Fields within fields produce complex patterns of energy.

The neurons in your brain act like those magnets. They generate fields. Those fields shape the matter around them, just the way the magnets cause the iron filings to form symmetrical patterns.

Bigger fields outside the body, such as the gravitational field of the Earth, act like the bigger magnets. They shift the pattern of your body's fields. They act on your brain and your cells, while your body also exerts a tiny influence on those bigger fields. Our bodies are influencing these big fields while also being influenced by them.

Your body's electromagnetic field extends about five yards or meters from your body. When you're five meters away from another person, your field begins interacting with their field. The two of you might be saying nothing, yet your energy fields are shaping each other in an invisible dance of communication (Frey, 1993).

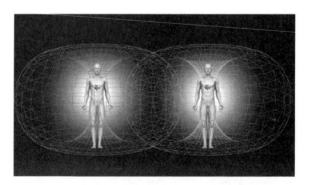

When two people are in close proximity, their fields interact.

For decades, microtubules, with their rigid form, were assumed to be no more than structural elements of the cell. Just as your body has a skeleton that provides a rigid structure to which other structures of the body attach, microtubules are the girders and scaffolding of the cell.

However, like antennae, microtubules are hollow. They are long cylinders. This property allows them to resonate, like a drum. And like antennae, their structure makes them capable of receiving signals from energy fields (Hameroff & Penrose, 1996). Microtubule signaling has been proposed as a method by which the body's complex systems are coordinated among trillions of cells (Oschman, 2015).

The Shaman and the Cardiac Surgeon

The fields of your body can interact with the fields of other people at great distances. A former cardiac patient named Richard Geggie told me this story during my research for a book called *The Heart of Healing* (Smith, 2004):

"In the early 1990s I was in Toronto, Canada. I went to see my doctor because I felt tired and listless. He sent me to have an electrocardiogram. Later that day, when he got the results back, he told me that my heart was at serious risk. He told me to stay calm, not exert myself, keep nitroglycerine pills with me at all times, and to not go outside alone.

"The doctors administered several tests over the course of the following three days, and I failed them all because my arteries were severely clogged. They included an angiogram, another electrocardiogram, and a treadmill stress test. When I started the bicycle test, the clinic staff didn't even let me finish. They stopped me partway. They were afraid I was going to die on the spot, my arteries were so clogged. As a high-risk patient, I was given an immediate appointment for heart bypass surgery.

"The day before the surgery, I woke up feeling much better. I went to the hospital and I was given an angiogram. This involved shooting dye into my arteries through an injection in my thigh. The surgeons wanted to discover the exact location of the blockages prior to the operation. I was prepared for surgery. My chest was shaved, and the doctors were about to mark my skin where they planned to make the incision.

"When the new angiograms came back from the lab, the doctor in charge looked at them. He became very upset. He said he had wasted his time. There were no blockages visible at all. He said he wished his own arteries looked as clear. He could not explain why all the other tests had shown such severe problems.

"I later discovered that my friend Lorin Smith [a Pomo Indian medicine man] in California, upon hearing of my heart trouble, had assembled a group of his students for a healing ceremony the day before the second angiogram. He covered one man with bay leaves and told him that his name was Richard Geggie. For the next hour, Lorin led the group in songs, prayers, and movement. The next day, I was healed."

When I last followed up, 13 years later, Geggie was still in excellent health. The phenomenon of distant healing is well documented, with scores of studies showing its effects (Radin, Schlitz, & Baur, 2015).

DIRECTING THE FLOW OF CONSCIOUSNESS

You can direct your consciousness, the way Lorin Smith did toward Richard Geggie's healing. Consciousness isn't something that simply is; it's something that can be controlled and pointed in a desired direction. When you direct your consciousness, you harness the power of your mind, activate the splendid machinery of your brain, and influence the environment around you (Chiesa, Calati, & Serretti, 2011).

You do that in visibly obvious ways, like deciding to plant a vegetable garden. After your mind makes the decision, you use your consciousness to direct the project. Your brain signals your body to drive your car to the local gardening store, where you buy fertilizer, tools, and seeds. You plant, water, and tend your garden, and a few months later, you have a crop. Your crop began in consciousness and ended in the material reality of a homegrown meal. A thought eventually produced a thing.

Take a look around you right now. The colors in the carpet began as a thought in someone's mind. That person chose the particular shades and textures that wound up in the finished product. Someone else decided the dimensions of your cell phone and laptop computer. Every proportion in your home began as a thought in the consciousness of the builder. We use invisible fields such as cell signals, Bluetooth, and wireless networks every day. A wireless network uses a router to send a signal into the surrounding environment. In the presence of a receiver, such as your smartphone or laptop, information is exchanged. The field of energy created by the router makes communication possible between your laptop and every device accessible to the router.

Though the fields are invisible, they are efficient conductors of information. Even electricity can now be transmitted wirelessly from one device to another.

You also interact with your environment in invisible ways, through the energy fields in which you're immersed. Through your brain, mind, and cells, your consciousness projects signals into the fields around you (Oschman, 2015).

Genius inventor Nikola Tesla is often quoted as saying, "If you wish to find the secrets of the universe, think in terms of energy, frequency, and vibration."

We use invisible energy fields, such as cellular networks, to transmit information every day.

When we originate an idea in consciousness, we send signals into the universal field. Transmission requires hardware, in the form of the brain, as well as software, in the form of the mind. Signals traveling through neural pathways create energy fields, and those fields change depending on the content of consciousness. Healing involves field effects, whether local or distant.

CURING MICE OF CANCER

My friend and colleague Bill Bengston, Ph.D., is a professor of sociology at St. Joseph's College. With various teams of researchers, he has conducted provocative experiments that demonstrate the healing potential of energy fields (Bengston, 2010).

Bill started out as a skeptic. When he finished his degree in sociology in 1971, he had no time for people who claimed paranormal powers. But he was an open-minded skeptic, and when he met healer Bennett Mayrick, he put him to the test. Ben said there was something wrong with Bill's car, and Bill was disappointed. He happened to have had the car inspected the day before, and he knew there was absolutely nothing wrong with it.

Bill's skepticism remained intact for half the drive home—when the car's entire exhaust system crashed to the ground.

Bill got to know Ben well over the next few years and eventually had an opportunity to apply real science to test Ben's skills. Bill had joined the faculty at City University of New York, and one of his fellow faculty members, Dave Krinsley, designed an objective experiment to measure whether human energy could produce healing (Bengston & Krinsley, 2000).

The design was simple. Mice would be injected with mammary cancer, or adenocarcinoma, a procedure that had been used in scores of other studies. In cancer studies, tumors are induced in the mice, after which researchers try various chemicals to see if they will alter the course of the disease. The longest an injected mouse had ever survived was 27 days. After injection, the cancer tumors grow rapidly in the mice, and they die in 14 to 27 days (Lerner & Dzelzkalns, 1966).

The mice in Krinsley's study would be randomized into two groups in order to provide a control. The control mice would be kept in a different building to eliminate the possibility of healing effects due to proximity to the treated mice.

Unfortunately, the shipment of mice did not arrive at the lab on schedule. There were repeated delays, and Ben lost interest in the experiment, as he had other priorities. Dave encouraged Bill to do the healing in Ben's stead.

Eventually, the mice arrived and were injected. Bill began to hold the cage of experimental mice in his hands for an hour each day. His hypothesis was that if healing energy were real, the mice would not develop tumors in the way they normally did.

A week into the treatment, two of the mice developed visible tumors. Bill was bitterly disappointed. When all five developed tumors, Bill asked Dave to put the mice out of their misery, as the experiment had clearly failed.

When Dave arrived, he commented on how healthy Bill's mice appeared to be despite the tumors. They were running around their cages, full of energy, behaving as though they were healthy. The control mice in the other lab, he told Bill, weren't doing well. Two had already died.

He argued, "Perhaps the treatments are slowing down the cancer even if they can't prevent it. There's no record of a single mouse living past day 27. Get one to live 28 days and we'll have a world record. Experiments rarely turn out the way they're supposed to. That's why they're called experiments!"

Around day 17, much to everyone's surprise, the tumors on Bill's mice began to change. They became ulcerated, with scabs replacing the hair on their skin. By day 28, Bill confided to the mice that they were making history. The ulcerations began to disappear and the fur grew back.

Mouse with tumor.

A week later, Bill's mice were examined by a biologist, who relayed the news to Dave: "The mice are cancer-free."

SKEPTICISM IS NO BARRIER TO
BEING A HEALER

The experiment was replicated at different times by different researchers who extended the design in interesting ways. The research teams found that when more mice were treated, the effect was stronger. When the effect was very strong, even mice in the control group in a different building began to improve, and some did not die (Bengston, 2007).

In some studies, Bill trained graduate students to perform the healing. He chose people who, like himself, were skeptics. He eliminated true believers from the pool of healers.

The cages in which the mice were kept were held by Bill or the students.

This made no difference. The mice recovered whether treated by Bill or by skeptical students. Not only did the mice recover, but they also developed immunity to adenocarcinoma. If they were injected later, they no longer developed cancer. Bill also tried treating water that was then given to the mice. This was as effective as using the healing practice on the mice themselves.

Bill required the students to keep notebooks describing their personal experiences. Examination of their notes revealed that at first many of them did not believe they were taking part in an experiment in healing. They thought that they, not the mice, were the subjects being studied. They believed they were unconscious stooges being secretly tested to determine just how gullible they were.

This is called the nocebo effect. It's the opposite of the placebo effect. With placebo, people's belief that they will get better can produce a cure. Patients with nocebo can make themselves sick through their beliefs. People who don't believe in the possibility of healing, like the skeptical grad students, introduce the nocebo effect into their work.

The mice had no opinions, which is what makes animals useful for studies in which researchers wish to eliminate the placebo effect. Bill's skeptical students also didn't believe in healing. So it wasn't belief that was producing the healing.

The most likely explanation for the healing is energy fields. Many of the students, as well as Bill himself, described feeling their hands getting hot as they felt the healing energy begin to flow. They also described a cessation of that feeling when the healing session was complete. They learned to discern exactly what the flow of healing energy through their hands felt like.

Variants of the experiment found that distance was not an obstacle. Whether the mice were in close proximity to or far from the healer did not matter. Energy healing does not appear to be confined by the usual barriers of time and space (Oschman, 2015). Distant intentionality can be as effective as the presence of a healer in the room (Schmidt, Schneider, Utts, & Walach, 2004).

In her book *The Intention Experiment,* medical journalist Lynne McTaggart summarizes six studies using EEG or MRI machines to show that healers are able to affect the brain waves of people at a distance. She concludes that "the receiver's brain reacts as though he or she is seeing the same image at the same time" (McTaggart, 2007).

Bill Bengston also found that he personally was able to change the EEG of a distant human subject. After the experiments with mice, Bill began to offer energy healing to human beings and found that tumors, whether cancerous or benign, often disappeared.

Her Doctor Said: "This Doesn't Make Sense"

Bill Bengston has recorded many case histories from his work with patients with tumors. Here's one in which a patient's doctors were baffled by the changes they saw after energy healing.

"Janis, who was in her 20s, had been diagnosed with ovarian torsion, which means twisted fallopian tubes, along with cysts, causing the ovarian tissue to die. An operation was scheduled, carrying with it the chance that she would become infertile. After I treated her a few times . . . when Janis went for her pre-op exam, her doctor was astonished: 'There are no growths!'

"He referred her to a specialist, who was just as puzzled. He mused aloud while looking at her slides, 'You've got growths in this photo, but they're gone in the next one. You've got twisted tubes in this photo, but now they're gone. This doesn't make sense.' . . . Janis's doctors cancelled her operation" (Bengston, 2010).

CAN HEALING BE LEARNED?

As Bill's skeptical graduate students discovered, healing can be learned. My friends Donna Eden and David Feinstein manage the largest energy medicine program in the world, Eden Energy Medicine. Their program has over 1,000 graduates. Hundreds of stories confirm that energy healing works for humans as well as mice (Eden & Feinstein, 2008).

In the 1980s, I argued that healing was a special ability that only certain gifted individuals possessed. Throughout history, there have been remarkable people who demonstrated verifiable healing powers.

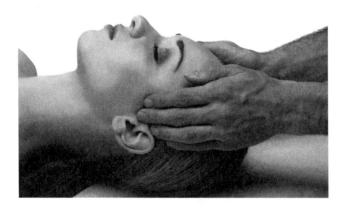

Hands-on healing session.

In *Soul Medicine,* a book I co-authored with Norm Shealy, M.D., founder of the American Holistic Medical Association, we talk about several of these people (Shealy & Church, 2008). Our standard of a verifiable cure was a doctor's diagnosis showing that the patient had a disease, followed by a second diagnosis after healing showing that the patient did not have that disease. Studying these practitioners suggested to me that healing was an unusual gift. Bill, David, Donna, and many others have proved me wrong.

Energy medicine programs such as those offered by Bill and Donna now show that healing is a skill that can be taught. Case studies written by their students include patients who have recovered from serious conditions such as cancer, heart disease, and autoimmune diseases.

I founded a nonprofit called the National Institute for Integrative Healthcare (niih.org). On our website, we maintain a list of studies of energy healing published in peer-reviewed scientific journals. To be included on this list, studies need to meet the following criteria:

- They assess the use of hands-on healing or interventions in the body's energy field.

- They use energetic exercises or techniques to balance the body's energy systems.

- The explanation they use for the effects of treatment is based on changes to the body's energy field.

The list excludes methods such as acupuncture and EFT (emotional freedom techniques) because these have their own online databases. Nonetheless, there are over 600 studies on the list. If you include EFT, acupuncture, and other energy healing methods, there are over 1,000 studies showing that energy healing is effective for a wide range of conditions, including those listed in Table 1.

Alzheimer's	HIV/AIDS
Anxiety	Insomnia
Arthritis	Irritable bowel syndrome
Asthma	Low back pain
Autism	Memory
Burnout	Menstrual distress
Burns	Migraines
Cancer	Mood disorders
Cardiovascular disease	Motion sickness
Carpal tunnel syndrome	Obesity
Children's behavioral issues	Pain
Cognitive impairment	Post-traumatic stress disorder (PTSD)
Cortisol	Prostate cancer
Dementia	Pulmonary disease
Depression	Skin wounds
Diabetes	Smoking
Drug addiction	Stroke
Fibromyalgia	Substance abuse
Headache	Thyroid dysfunction
High blood pressure	

Table 1. Conditions for which energy healing has been shown to be effective.

This compelling body of evidence shows that consciousness—directed by intention, working through energy fields—can produce radical changes in matter. "Skull and skin are not limiting boundaries of energy and information," says UCLA psychiatrist Dan Siegel in his book *Mind* (Siegel, 2017).

Though healing can occur at the level of small animals, such as mice, as well as at the level of larger animals, such as *Homo sapiens*, and can happen at a distance, just how large can the effect get?

The answer is: very large. Whole societies have been changed by a change of mind in a single person. In every age, there are people who have asked "Why?" and "Does it have to be this way?" and "How can we do things differently?" Even when facing a social condition that has been unchanged for centuries, the mind of a single person is sometimes able to change the matter of an entire society.

Mind is able to change matter at the level of the very small—atoms and molecules. Scaling up, it can change matter at the level of cells, organs, and bodies. Getting bigger still, it can change social groups and even whole countries. There are many historical examples of people who've changed first at the level of their own minds and then gone on to have an impact that shapes the world. We'll look at several examples of how individual mind change can scale up to produce enormous social shifts.

HOW A MIND CHANGE ELIMINATED INFECTIOUS DISEASE

Josephine Baker was the first woman to graduate with a doctorate in public health from New York University. In 1908, she was appointed head of the city's new Bureau of Child Hygiene.

She understood the link between poverty and illness and was possessed by a single-minded desire to eliminate human suffering. She introduced many reforms in New York City (Baker, 1925).

Baker instituted a program called the Little Mothers' League to train girls 12 and up in basic infant care. At a time when both parents were usually working outside the home, this improved the health of small children.

Josephine Baker.

Baker standardized the dosage of silver nitrate being placed in the eyes of newborns to prevent syphilis. Before her innovation, there was no standard dose, and some babies were given so much silver nitrate that they went blind.

She established standards for the quality of milk. At that time, the milk fed to most youngsters was watered down and then adulterated with other substances such as flour, starch, or chalk to make it look like the real thing.

Nineteenth-century cartoon depicting the health hazards of tainted milk.

In the middle of World War I, Baker published an editorial in the *New York Times* in which she calculated that the mortality rate of children in New York City was higher than that of soldiers on the Western front. This caused a sensation and highlighted the need for public health reforms (King, 1993).

Baker was determined to control the spread of typhoid fever, one of the major killers of both adults and children. The disease had taken the life of her father, a factor that motivated her choice of career. With a colleague named George Soper, she began to map areas of the city marked by outbreaks of typhoid. At a time when the germ theory of disease was not yet widely accepted, her team identified individuals at the epicenter of each outbreak.

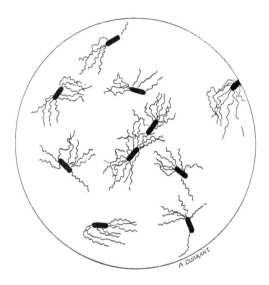

Typhoid bacillus.

TYPHOID MARY

One of these individuals was Mary Mallon, an immigrant from County Tyrone in Ireland. Mary served as a cook to various wealthy families. Josephine Baker and George Soper discovered that wherever Mary worked, outbreaks of typhoid followed shortly thereafter. When she prepared food, she transmitted the typhoid bacillus to those who ate it.

Mary was taken for evaluation and testing, and enormous quantities of the typhoid bacillus were found in her blood. She had no symptoms herself, however, and did not believe she was sick.

Though she was released on a promise to pursue a profession other than cooking, she soon went back to her old ways. Josephine Baker tracked her down again and knocked on the family's front door with a police escort.

Mary ran out the back door and eluded the police. But Josephine, more determined than the boys in blue, tracked her down in a neighbor's potting shed. Mary was huddled in a corner. Josephine sat down on top of Mary and yelled for help until the police arrived. Typhoid Mary was out of circulation for good.

Typhoid Mary.

Josephine Baker's reforms were bitterly contested by the medical establishment. When her campaign against typhoid fever became successful, a group of Brooklyn pediatricians petitioned the mayor to abolish her office. They complained that the supply of sick children to their practices was drying up.

Hearings were held in Congress to stop her. She was mocked as a woman, and critics declared that her efforts would eliminate medicine as a profession for promising young men. Nevertheless, she persisted—and eventually prevailed. By the time she retired, New York had the lowest rate of infant mortality in the United States.

Baker's reforms spread quickly. Her standards were adopted by 35 other states and in 1912 became the basis for the national Children's Bureau. Within a few years, terrifying diseases such as smallpox, typhoid, and cholera were virtually wiped out. That's the power of mind change as it plays out on a large social scale. Anthropologist Margaret Mead is famously supposed to have said, "Never think that a small group of thoughtful, committed citizens cannot change the world. Indeed, it's the only thing that ever has."

AN IDEA WHOSE TIME HAS COME

When you change your mind, sending new signals through the neural pathways of your brain, altering the energy fields all around you, interacting with the fields of others, you have no idea how far the effect might travel.

We see this in great social movements such as the abolition of slavery. In about 50 years, slavery went from an institution that had been with us since the dawn of humankind to being abolished worldwide. Women's suffrage and civil rights followed the same trajectory.

Women's suffrage poster.

Great social movements begin in the consciousness of just a few people. They spread slowly at first, then propagate with accelerating speed. As French novelist Victor Hugo said, "One withstands the invasion of armies; one does not withstand the invasion of ideas" (Hugo, 1877)—or, as it is more popularly paraphrased, "There is nothing more powerful than an idea whose time has come."

An idea that begins in just one mind can take over the world. What are the ideas with which you fill your consciousness every day?

CREATING FROM THE INSIDE OUT

In my first career, in book publishing, I came into contact with many best-selling authors. One day, I asked myself, *What do they have in common?* Reflecting on that question changed the direction of my life.

One of the characteristics common to best-selling authors is a focus on creation. They are much more interested in producing information than consuming it. The flow of words and images tends to be from the inside out, not the outside in. They certainly read and watch videos like the rest of us. But they tend to spend much more time pouring information out of their consciousness than sucking information into their consciousness. Given a choice of reading (inflow) or writing (outflow), they write.

Most people are passive. They take information in. They listen to the radio, watch shows and movies, and read the occasional book. They are consumers of information rather than producers of information. They are constantly influenced by the information they are consuming.

When it comes to best-selling authors, the flow of information tends to run in the opposite direction. They are much more interested in the information they can produce than what they can consume. They are active producers of information rather than passive consumers of information.

DELILAH AND THE INFORMATION FIELD

I remember a picnic with a group of friends a few years back. One member of the group was a woman in her 50s named Delilah who I hadn't seen for a couple of years but with whom I'd previously shared many warm conversations. She had always been pretty, bright, and healthy. Financially secure, she had no need to work, but she enjoyed a moderately successful career as a classical pianist.

We were sitting on the grass in the park on a beautiful spring day after a morning of group free-form dance. As we talked, Delilah shared her distress about what was happening in the world.

There were a lot of problems for her to be distressed about. Wars in several regions. Refugees. Natural disasters. Pollution. The loss of ground water. Mass extinction. Rising sea levels. The poor quality of governance. Deforestation.

News will rarely make you happy.

As we talked, I got a clear picture of the flow of information in Delilah's life. Whenever she was driving, she had her car radio tuned to an all-news station; she read the newspaper daily and watched television news. Note the use of the word *news* three times in that sentence. She was absorbing all this information from the outside world and spent much of her time engaged in the process.

This did not make her happy. I noticed how much Delilah seemed to have aged since our last conversation, and how heavy her energy felt as she described the flood of problems that filled her worried mind. Even though she was healthy, smart, and financially set for life, her mind was consumed by worry. She attuned her consciousness to the bad stuff, like a vacuum cleaner sucking in garbage. Filling her mind with problems led to a mind filled with garbage.

The places to which she turned her attention led to Delilah's immersion in the energy field of bad news. Conditioned by her consciousness, her brain was busy growing the neural circuits of stress. Her mind was guiding her brain to enhance those neural pathways, making them larger and more efficient at carrying their habitual signals. With every increase in capacity, her mind became more attuned to bad news.

Delilah believed that the bad things she heard on the news were happening "out there." She could claim with complete justification that the news items with which she was filling her thoughts were objectively true.

Yet the truth was that she was creating her own stress-filled reality by the direction in which she chose to turn her attention. Focusing on the news sparked the creation of new neurons in those circuits, which created stronger electromagnetic fields, which in turn sensitized her further to similar signals. Her stress had as much to do with her subjective creation of mind as it did with the objective state of the world.

SELF-DIRECTED NEURAL PLASTICITY

That's the risk you take when you're a consumer of information rather than a producer. When the flow of information is from the outside in, you hold your consciousness hostage to the consciousness of the people producing the information. When the container of your mind is being filled with unhappy input, it's hard to maintain a happy state.

When you allow others to fill your consciousness, you are at the mercy of their consciousness.

My wife, Christine, also consumes information constantly. However, she chooses inspirational material. She listens to her favorite transformational speakers during the long drives she takes to work. She reads inspirational books and watches nature shows on television. Her family and friends share inspirational quotes in their e-mail exchanges. She is bathing her mind in information from the outside, and her choice of uplifting material makes her a happy and wise presence.

That's the place from which she then creates. She'll tell you about an exciting new art project she's designed or a powerful new idea she's learned. Those are the things that fill her mind.

The thoughts, beliefs, and ideas that fill your consciousness exert a powerful influence on the world outside your brain. You are constantly creating. You can use that power to create intangibles such as a nurturing emotional environment. You can also use that power to create tangible material conditions. There are many examples of changes that have begun inside the mind of a single person like Josephine Baker and expanded to change the world.

Launching Mind into Space

In the sphere of technology, one person whose personal vision has reshaped entire industries is Elon Musk.

Elon Musk is famous as the founder of several successful businesses, including Tesla and Solar City. He sold his first product at the age of 12. It was a game called Blastar for which he'd written the code.

After applying unsuccessfully for a job at Netscape and dropping out of Stanford University, he founded a company called Zip2, which Compaq later purchased for $307 million. He then cofounded PayPal and cashed out when eBay purchased it.

While Musk's businesses thrived, his personal life hit some rough patches. On a vacation in his native South Africa, he contracted cerebral malaria, which is fatal in about 20 percent of cases. He lost 45 pounds and had a near-death experience. Two years later, his first son died at the age of 10 weeks.

Musk founded his third company, SpaceX, in 2002, with the audacious goal of making commercial spaceflight possible.

The launch of the first SpaceX rocket in 2006 ended in a fireball. Along with the incinerated rocket went the millions of dollars Musk had put into the venture. He was undeterred, however, and afterward wrote: "SpaceX is in this for the long haul and, come hell or high water, we are going to make this work" (Malik, 2006).

The following year, the company launched its second rocket. It failed to reach orbit when the engines shut down prematurely, leaving SpaceX with two strikes against it, and a founder who was desperately short of cash.

In the third launch, in 2008, the two stages of the rocket collided after separating. Its payload—which included Musk's first cargo for NASA, as well as the ashes of Star Trek's James "Scotty" Doohan—wound up in the ocean.

SpaceX launch.

Musk was now completely out of money and on the verge of bankruptcy. He was saved only by an eleventh-hour investment from eccentric billionaire Peter Thiel.

Today, Musk's companies—Tesla, SpaceX, and Solar City—are enormously successful. Yet it took perseverance through setback after setback to get to that point. Musk's mind-set is relentlessly positive, whatever the challenge. His mind has been the source of multiple game-changing material realities.

WHAT WORLD WILL YOU SHAPE WITH YOUR BRAIN?

What's in your mind, and what kind of material world might you create with it?

You have this magnificent brain and mind, capable of creating wealth, happiness, health, and well-being in your own life and the lives of those around you. Your consciousness is powerful—much more powerful than you realize.

Most of us are using just a tiny fraction of our ability, not even realizing that our minds create matter. This book is about harnessing your superpower consciously to make a wonderful life for yourself and those around you. You're already turning thoughts into things. You're doing it every day unconsciously. Now it's time to do it systematically and deliberately.

In the coming pages, you will meet many people like Josephine Baker, Elon Musk, Lorin Smith, and Bill Bengston, who have turned thoughts into things. Information flows out from them into the universal field, and their consciousness conditions the space around them to produce manifestations in material reality.

The concept that mind creates matter is not a metaphysical proposition. It's a biological one. In the chapters ahead, you'll begin to experience for yourself how your brain creates matter in the form of neurons and synapses in response to your consciousness. Consciousness and matter interact with the fields around you, and the result is material reality.

You'll begin to use your consciousness deliberately, building matter through intention flowing from the inside rather than by accident based on what's coming at you from the outside. You'll discover the community of conscious people who are building reality for the highest and best for the whole planet, and discover that you're part of an enormous creative community working for good. Welcome to the future of mind and matter!

PUTTING THESE IDEAS INTO PRACTICE

Activities to practice this week:

- As soon as you wake up in the morning, place your hand over your heart and feel love.

- Buy a journal. Write down a list of your intentions. What are 10 things that would transform your life?

- Breathe and send healing intentions to someone who is sick.

- Make a donation of 10 percent of your next paycheck to a charity dedicated to social change.

The Extended Play version of this chapter includes:

- An audio interview with Bill Bengston, Ph.D.

- Stanford marshmallow experiment video and full story

- A full list of conditions improved by energy therapies

- Women whose inventions changed the world

To access the Extended Play version, visit:
MindToMatter.club/Chapter1

CHAPTER 2

How Energy Builds Matter

"Land ho!" the lookout sang. The day was September 6, 1522, and the port ahead was Sanlúcar de Barrameda, Spain. The ship was the *Victory,* commanded by Captain Juan Sebastián de Elcano.

The *Victory* was the last survivor of five ships commanded by Portuguese mariner Ferdinand Magellan. With a well-equipped fleet, he set out from Spain on September 20, 1519, with the goal of circumnavigating the globe via the Spice Islands.

Magellan first sailed south to Africa. From there, he crossed the Atlantic to Brazil. He followed the Brazilian coast, searching for a strait that would lead to the Pacific Ocean. Traversing the entire length of South America, he spent the winter in the sheltered bay at Puerto San Julián, Argentina, near the southern end of the continent.

On Easter day, his captains mutinied, but Magellan was able to subdue the rebellion. He executed one mutineer and beached one of the others.

On October 21, he finally found the passage he'd been looking for, now called the Strait of Magellan. By that time, one ship had been wrecked and a second one had deserted the convoy.

It took the remaining three ships 38 days to round the treacherous promontory of Tierra del Fuego. When Magellan saw the Pacific at the other end of the strait, he wept for joy. Ninety-nine days later, after sailing across the tranquil ocean, he landed at the island of Guam on March 6, 1521. His men were starving. They had chewed the leather straps of their tunics to stay alive.

The survivors resupplied in the Philippine islands. In two ships, laden with spices, they began the journey home. One ship was lost at sea, and only the *Victory* straggled back to Spain. Only 22 of the original 270 men survived.

FERDINAN MAGELLANVS SVPER ATIS
ANTARCTICI FRETI ANGVSTIIS CLARISS

Ferdinand Magellan.

Magellan was not one of the survivors. He had died en route. On April 27, while fighting as an ally of the chief of the Philippine island of Cebu against a tribe on the neighboring island of Mactan, Magellan was struck by a poisoned arrow. His retreating comrades left him to die.

Magellan's voyage was made possible by a remarkable electromagnetic invention, the compass. Invented in China, the first reference to it appeared in a manuscript written in 1040 (Vardalas, 2013). It describes an "iron fish" that when suspended in water, always pointed south.

A Song dynasty scholar named Shen Kuo wrote another account in 1088. He said that when "magicians rub the point of a needle with lodestone, then it is able to point to the south. . . . It may be made to float on the surface of water, but it is then rather unsteady. . . . It is best to suspend it by a single cocoon fiber of new silk attached to the center of the needle by a piece of wax. Then, hanging in a windless place, it will always point to the south." Indeed, this must have looked like magic in the 11th century, when electromagnetic fields were unknown.

Nineteenth-century Chinese compass.

About 200 years before Magellan's voyage, the first European compass was used in Amalfi, Italy. Mariners of seafaring nations such as England, France, Holland, Spain, and Portugal recognized the importance of this technological marvel and developed and refined the design.

Without the compass, Magellan's remarkable feat of navigation would have been impossible. A thin sliver of magnetized metal suspended in the center, it points to Earth's magnetic north pole regardless of where on the globe it is located. Lines of magnetic force surround Earth's mantle and are detected by the compass's needle.

Earth's magnetic field.

Celestial bodies such as stars and planets have electromagnetic fields. Small objects such as crystals and rocks have them too. So do living beings. You have a field around your body, and it extends about five yards or meters out.

FIELDS ARE BEAUTIFUL—AND EVERYWHERE

Electromagnetic fields are now being measured around increasing numbers of plants and animals. In a study published in the prestigious journal *Science,* a research team investigated the electromagnetic relationship between flowers and the bees that pollinate them.

They found that bees can detect the fields around flowers and use the information to determine which flowers have the most nectar (Clarke, Whitney, Sutton, & Robert, 2013). Study co-author Daniel Robert, a biologist at the University of Bristol, says, "We think bumblebees are using this ability to perceive electrical fields to determine if flowers were recently visited by other bumblebees and are therefore worth visiting."

The electromagnetic properties of the fields around living beings came as a surprise to scientists immersed in matter-bound explanations. Thomas Seeley, a behavioral biologist at Cornell University, commented after reading the study, "We had no idea that this sense even existed."

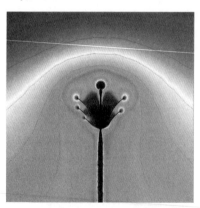

A flower's electromagnetic field.

The ability to perceive electromagnetic fields has now been measured in algae, worms, ants, insects, anteaters, platypuses, and hummingbirds.

Research has recently shown that dolphins are also able to detect electromagnetic fields. The Guiana dolphin is a species that lives close to estuaries in protected waters off the coast of South America. German researchers tested these river dolphins and found that they were sensitive to even very weak electrical currents (Czech-Damal et al., 2011).

The researchers then investigated how the dolphins were able to detect these fields, and they found small hair follicles around the dolphins' mouths. The indentations are surrounded by nerve endings, well supplied with blood vessels, and are filled with gel. Scientists believe these are the sensory organs by means of which the dolphins detect fields.

FIELDS CREATE THE SHAPES OF MOLECULES

I vividly remember my first experience with electromagnetism. In my first-grade science class, we sprinkled iron filings onto a piece of paper. As we moved magnets around under the paper, they rearranged the iron filings. Without touching, even at a distance, fields were able to rearrange matter. Because this simple experiment is repeated millions of times each year around the world, it's easy to forget how amazing it is. We take it for granted that fields exist and are able to shape matter, yet we somehow forget to apply this concept when we're struggling with the challenges of everyday material life. Whether we scale up large—to the size of a planet or a galaxy—or scale down small—to the size of a single atom—we find fields. Each cell of your body has its own unique electromagnetic field. The molecules of which your cells are built also have fields. Electromagnetism is central to the processes of biology.

Aside from water, most of the molecules in our bodies are proteins. Our bodies manufacture more than 100,000 different types of proteins. They're large and complicated molecules, with strings of atoms folded around each other to make intricate designs. When a cell is synthesizing a protein, it creates these folds the same way my first-grade science class moved iron filings.

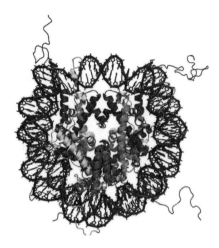

Protein molecules are intricately folded.

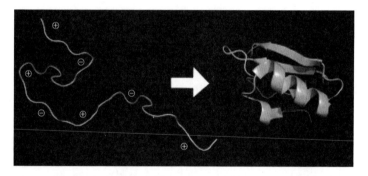

Protein before and after folding. Electrical charges at different points on the molecule determine how it shapes itself.

Each part of the string of molecules making up a protein has its own positive or negative charge. If two parts of the string are both negatively charged, they repel each other. The same is true of positively charged parts. On the other hand, negatives and positives are attracted to each other. These forces of attraction and repulsion mold the big and complicated protein string into its designated shape.

STALKING THE WILD FIELD

Willem Einthoven was an eccentric Dutch physician born in 1860. In the late 1890s, he set out to measure the electromagnetic field of the human heart. He began building a device called a galvanometer. Einthoven faced a great deal of skepticism and opposition, and to many of his medical colleagues, who were used to looking only at matter, the notion of invisible energy fields seemed suspect.

His first attempts were unpromising. His machine weighed 600 pounds (270 kg) and needed five people to operate it. A water-filled radiator system was required to cool the powerful electromagnets on which it relied.

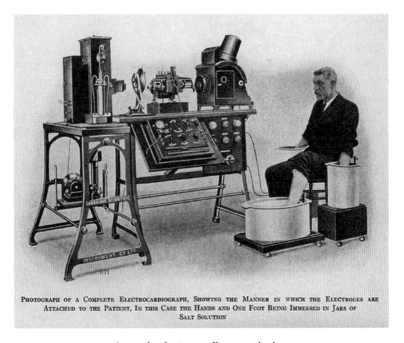

PHOTOGRAPH OF A COMPLETE ELECTROCARDIOGRAPH, SHOWING THE MANNER IN WHICH THE ELECTRODES ARE ATTACHED TO THE PATIENT, IN THIS CASE THE HANDS AND ONE FOOT BEING IMMERSED IN JARS OF SALT SOLUTION

An early electrocardiogram device.

After years of painstaking work, Einthoven developed a galvanometer much more sensitive than any available at the time. He was able to hook up subjects and measure their heart rates. He eventually built up a substantial theory of how the heart functioned and what the readings of electrocardiograms (EKGs) meant for diagnosis and treatment.

As for his critics? Einthoven had the last laugh, winning the Nobel Prize for medicine in 1924. He inspired the search for the field of the brain, which was discovered in 1926. Later researchers were able to map the field of even a single cell.

An early EEG recording, showing the electromagnetic activity of the brain.

WHAT ARE FIELDS DOING?

Harold Saxton Burr was a visionary researcher who became a professor at Yale School of Medicine in 1929. He began to study the energy fields around animals and plants, measuring ways in which matter (atoms, molecules, and cells) is organized by those fields as organisms develop and grow. In a key paper in 1949, he mapped the electromagnetic field around a single nerve. His careful measurements showed a field much like the iron filings around the magnet in my first-grade science class. The field was strongest closest to the nerve and became weaker moving outward from the nerve (Burr & Mauro, 1949).

Burr's huge insight was that fields weren't just *produced by* living organisms, but that fields *created* matter, providing lines of force around which matter could arrange itself into atoms, molecules, and cells.

Harold Saxton Burr.

In his book *The Fields of Life* (1973), Burr used the analogy of the iron filings with which I played as a child. If you shake the iron filings off the paper and add new ones, they arrange themselves into the same patterns as the discarded ones. It is the field that is organizing the filings; the field is not being produced by the filings.

Burr wrote: "Something like this . . . happens in the human body. Its molecules and cells are constantly being torn apart and rebuilt with fresh material from the food we eat. But, thanks to the controlling [life]-field, the new molecules and cells are rebuilt as before and arrange themselves in the same pattern as the old ones" (Burr, 1973, pp. 12–13).

For instance, when you cut your finger and your skin regrows, the field provides the blueprint around which the new cells organize themselves. Energy is not an epiphenomenon of matter; energy is *organizing* matter.

For many of his experiments, Burr used salamanders. He measured the voltages on the outer membranes of salamander eggs, and found that one spot had maximum voltage, while a spot 180 degrees opposite had minimal voltage. He marked both spots.

When the salamanders grew to maturity, he found that what had been the point with the strongest field in the egg had become the head. The point with lowest electrical activity was always the tail. The field appeared to be organizing the matter of the egg during gestation and development.

Burr used mice to determine if the energy field played a role in cancer. He measured their fields and noted which mice later developed cancer. After taking more than 10,000 measurements, he found that the electromagnetic signature of cancer appeared in the mouse's energy field before any detectable cellular malignancy was evident.

Thermography scan of a couple doing yoga.

ENERGY CREATES MATTER

In a landmark study published in 1947, Burr turned his attention to human disease to determine if his observations might have therapeutic value. He and his colleagues examined women with uterine cancer. They found that these women's uteruses had an electromagnetic charge that was different from the charge of healthy uteruses (Langman & Burr, 1947).

Burr then looked at a group of healthy women who did not have a diagnosis of uterine cancer. Those women who had the electromagnetic signature of uterine cancer—even though they were apparently healthy—were the ones who went on to develop cancer later. Cancer was showing up *in the field of energy* before it showed up *in the cells of matter.* Burr's work demonstrated that it is not the case that material organs and organisms like hearts and uteruses and salamanders and mice create energy fields. Energy fields form the templates around which matter condenses. Change the field and you change matter.

Though this understanding may be relatively recent in modern science, it is actually not an entirely new concept. An ancient saying in traditional Chinese medicine is "The mind controls the qi, and the blood follows the qi." By *qi* (also spelled *chi*) the ancient sages were referring to life energy, and by *blood* they meant the matter of the body. Energy directs matter.

WHAT IS H_2O?

Water is so familiar to us that many of us take it for granted. It makes up 70 percent of the volume of our bodies and comprises a similar percentage of the surface of the planet. We drink it and bathe in it every day without giving it a second thought. While people other than chemists can't recite the formula for any other molecule, everyone knows that the formula for water is H_2O. Yet it turns out that this most common of substances holds profound lessons about the relationship of energy to matter.

If I ask you, "What is H_2O?" you're likely to answer, "Water, of course." Certainly, if I hand you a glass of H_2O at room temperature, it's water. But if I add energy to the water by placing it on the stove, it becomes steam. It's still H_2O, but the increase in energy has completely changed the material form it takes.

If I take the same H_2O and place it in the freezer, subtracting energy, the matter changes form again. It becomes ice. The decrease in energy has again completely altered the form of the matter. This is one analogy that my colleague Eric Leskowitz, M.D., of Harvard Medical School, an expert on energy in acupuncture, uses to explain the effect of energy on matter. In similar ways, energy underlies the form matter takes in a huge number of ways that we don't usually notice.

H_2O can exist in several different states yet still be water.

WATER AND HEALING

In a remarkable series of experiments at McGill University, pioneering researcher Bernard Grad examined the effect of healing energy on animals and plants.

The healing was provided by a former Hungarian cavalry officer named Oskar Estebany, who could heal people by projecting energy from his hands. He was not trained in any way, and he had discovered his gift by accident when massaging horses. He believed that this energy was electromagnetic in nature and that it was a natural human ability. Grad first tested Estebany's abilities on mice. Four rows of small puncture wounds were made on their backs, and Estebany was instructed to "heal" only the two center rows. Sure enough, these rows healed faster than the outer rows. Estebany's mice also healed significantly faster than those held by students.

Grad then tested the effect of treated water on the growth rate of barley seeds. When provided with water held by Estebany for 30 minutes, more of the seeds germinated and the resulting plants grew taller. Their chlorophyll content increased, and the quality of leaf growth was significantly enhanced (Grad, 1963). Other researchers also found highly significant improvements in plant growth or seed germination after healers treated the plants (Scofield & Hodges, 1991; Kronn, 2006).

One rigorous study examined water treated by therapeutic touch practitioners (Schwartz, De Mattei, Brame, & Spottiswoode, 2015). The molecule H_2O has two hydrogen atoms bonded to a single oxygen atom. The angle of the bond between them can be measured, just as you can open a hinge partially and measure the angle it forms. The angle of the molecular bond of normal water is 104.5 degrees.

After 45-minute therapeutic touch sessions, the water showed highly statistically significant changes in its absorption of infrared light, which demonstrated that the bonding angle between the oxygen and two hydrogen atoms was altered by contact with the healing field. This particular experiment was very carefully blinded and controlled. Other researchers have also found alterations in the molecular structure of water after contact with a healer (Lu, 1997; Kronn, 2006).

Penn State University materials science professor Rustum Roy conducted many studies of the structure of water. He found that water molecules have a variety of potential configurations in which they can bond together. These can be altered by passing specific frequencies through the water. Water resonates with these frequencies, and the resulting water can have healing properties (Rao, Sedlmayr, Roy, & Kanzius, 2010).

Chinese qigong master Xin Yan has demonstrated the ability to alter the molecular structure of water dramatically, even at a distance. Researchers from the Chinese Academy of Sciences conducted 10 experiments with Dr. Yan. In the first, he stood near the water. In the other nine, he was at a distance of between 7 km and 1,900 km. In all cases, he was able to affect the water while allowing a control sample to remain unchanged.

When performing studies showing that energy healing cured cancer in mice, Bill Bengston noted similar changes in the infrared properties of water held by the healer (Bengston, 2010). He also reviewed research showing that the energy fields of a healer's hands can change how fast cellular enzymes catalyze and, in red blood corpuscles, increase the content of hemoglobin, the compound that carries oxygen to our cells.

H_2O is an oxygen atom bonded to two hydrogen atoms at an angle of 104.5 degrees.

ADELINE AND THE HEALING STARS

In the early 1980s, I interviewed a cancer survivor named Adeline. I was working on a project recording spontaneous remissions. Among the many stories I heard, hers stands out to me.

By the time Adeline was diagnosed with uterine cancer in her early 30s, it had spread throughout her body. Adeline's doctors recommended surgery followed by chemotherapy and radiation. Her chances of survival were small.

Unwilling to surrender her body to the ravages of treatment, she decided that instead, she would make her last months as serene as possible.

Adeline began to take long walks in the redwoods of Northern California where she lived. She also took long baths each day, letting water out as it cooled and topping the bath off with hot water. As she lay in the tub and walked through the forest, she imagined tiny glittering healing stars raining from heaven. They passed through her body, and whenever the point of a star touched a cancer cell, she imagined the cancer cell popping like a burst balloon.

Adeline ate the healthiest diet possible, meditated every day, read inspirational books, and terminated her relationships with people whose company was upsetting to her. Aside from a couple of close friends, most of her time was spent in solitude.

Her walks became longer, and she found herself feeling better physically than she'd felt her entire life.

When she went back to the hospital for a checkup nine months later, Adeline's doctors could find no trace of cancer in her body.

Adeline changed her energy in every possible way. She changed the energy of her physical environment by immersing herself in nature. She filled her mind with positive and specific images like the healing stars and with the uplifting energy of inspirational books. She ate food with an elevated energetic signature. She eliminated the negative energy of unhappy friends. She bathed daily, a practice that fills the body with electrons, countering the free radicals that are a major source of oxidative stress and cell degeneration.

In this pervasive environment of positive healing energy, directed by consciousness, the matter of Adeline's body began to change. Her cells responded, and her body began to eliminate the malfunctioning cancerous tissue. She used energy to heal her material body, and she never went back to her old habits.

Adeline became so accustomed to feeling good that it became her new normal. When I interviewed her seven years later, she was still meditating, eating clean, and living a low-stress lifestyle—and she was still cancer-free.

Adeline's story shows that it's not just gifted healers like Oskar Estebany who heal with energy. We can heal ourselves as well when we adjust our consciousness to the frequency of healing. The matter of our cells responds to the energy of our consciousness.

We're all familiar with the parlor trick of an opera singer breaking a wine glass. When the frequency of the singer's voice raises the energy of the molecules in the glass to the critical limit, they shatter. This is a well-known illustration of a little-known field of study called cymatics, the science of how sound affects matter. Dive deeper into cymatics, and we find that sound is as full of astonishing properties as water.

The resonant frequency of sound vibration can shatter a wine glass.

CYMATICS: HOW FREQUENCY
CHANGES MATTER

Ernst Chladni was a 19th-century German physicist and musician. He is called the father of acoustics for his pioneering experiments with sound. His father was a strict disciplinarian who did not allow young Ernst outside to play each day until he had finished his rigorous studies.

Chladni had an extremely sensitive musical ear, able to discern very small differences between frequencies. After obtaining two degrees, one in law and one in philosophy, Chladni became interested in the study of sound. Inspired by other scientists who had made energy fields visible, he developed a new device.

Fine sand was placed on top of a thin metal plate and a violin bow was drawn along the side of the plate. This caused the plate to vibrate. Different vibrational frequencies produced different patterns in the sand.

Chladni plate.

Chladni became famous for his public demonstrations, and he traveled throughout Europe year after year. This brought him into contact with many other scientists, and he progressively developed his ideas. He published his seminal work, *Acoustics,* in 1802, founding a new scientific field.

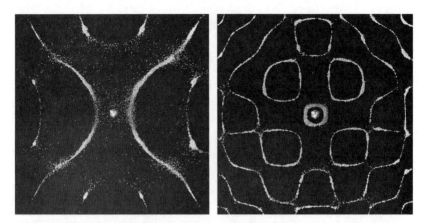

The frequency of sound passed through a Chladni plate produces different patterns. Above, 1305 Hz and 5065 Hz. Below, 2076 Hz and 2277 Hz.

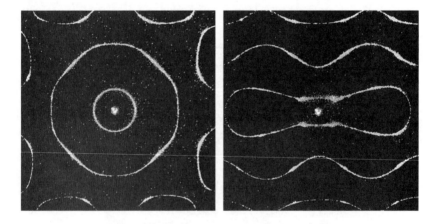

The study of how sound affects matter is called cymatics. Following Chladni's pioneering work, scientists have been examining the effects of vibrational tones on various substances. Vibrations can change the configuration of material objects dramatically and immediately.

A modern Chladni plate is attached to a scientific instrument called a vibration generator. When the frequency is adjusted, the metal vibrates at different rates. When a substance with a contrasting color, such as white sand, is sprinkled on the plate, patterns are visible. That's because when certain frequencies are passed through molecules, they produce distinct shapes. Generally, the higher the frequency, the more complex the pattern it produces in matter.

Various types of matter can be used to illustrate the effect of energy passing through Chladni plates. Salt and sand are popular media. Living organisms such as seeds also respond.

A large Chladni plate at the Harvard University natural sciences laboratory.

Chladni plates and vibration generators are popular items in high-school science classes. They can be purchased online or easily made at home using simple materials. Yet as a demonstration of how energy organizes matter, they are a powerful reminder that every frequency that passes through our bodies and minds is organizing the molecules of our bodies.

SOUND VIBRATIONS
CREATE SQUARE WATER

Water can also be made to change shape in response to vibration. When water comes out of a tube, the shape of the stream is round. If certain frequencies are played nearby, however, it changes its regular form into a series of right angles or a spiral.

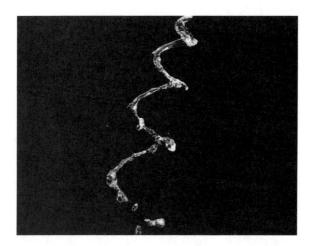

A stream of water changes shape in response
to sound vibration from a speaker.

Another way to visualize the impact of energy frequencies on matter is to pass sound waves through a dish of water. As the frequency is changed, the patterns in the water change too. Certain types of classical music produce complex and beautiful patterns in the water, while other frequencies, such as those found in harsh music, produce chaotic and disorganized wave forms.

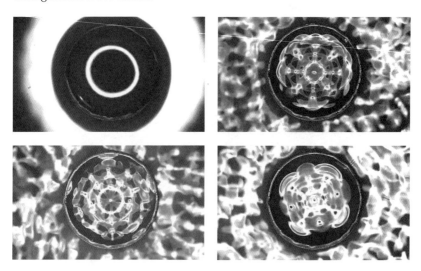

Water in a backlit glass dish changing shape as various
energy frequencies are passed through it.

YOUR PERSONALITY IN A DROP OF WATER

A fascinating series of experiments at the Aerospace Institute (officially, the Institute for Static and Dynamics for Aerospace Constructions) in Stuttgart, Germany, used water as a medium. The studies, performed by Professor Dr. Bernd Helmut Kröplin, measured the effect of different people on water.

A large group of students participated in one experiment. Each one filled a hypodermic syringe with water and squeezed a series of droplets onto a microscope slide. Kröplin's team then took photographs of the droplets.

They found that each person's group of droplets looked quite different from the droplets produced by the others. The droplets produced by the same person, however, were virtually the same. Even if the person squeezed out 20 droplets, a similar pattern was discernable in all 20. But that group of droplets looked different from the droplets produced by the next person, and the next. It seemed that passage through the energy field of a person produced an indelible and consistent impact on the matter, in the form of water, that they handled.

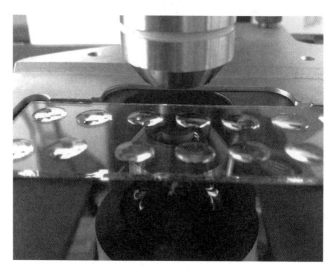

A subject produces a series of droplets on a microscope slide.

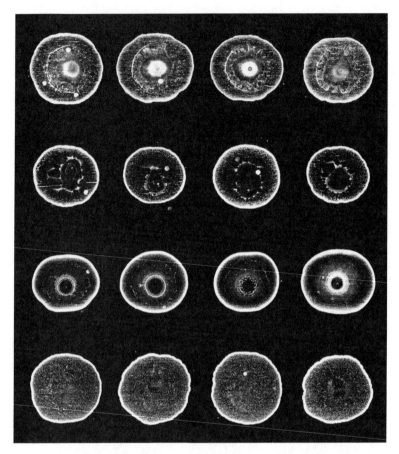

However many droplets are produced by a person, they all look similar. Yet they are completely different from a series of droplets produced by another person.

Just as the fingerprints of every one of the eight billion people on the planet are unique, the energy field of each person is unique. When water passes through a person's energy field, the shapes it assumes are always the same, while different from the shapes produced by any other person. Kröplin and his associate Regine Henschel describe their latest research in their book *Water and Its Memory*, saying, "To our surprise, we could demonstrate that the drop image is changed in the vicinity of the experimenter by the individual energy field around him or her. Each experimenter creates an individual, reproducible set of drop images without any special mind or thought activity" (Kröplin & Henschel, 2017).

Another study, this time on the effects of distant intention on water, was performed by a research group at the Institute of Noetic Sciences (IONS) in Petaluma, California.

A group of 2,000 people in Tokyo focused positive intentions on water samples inside an electromagnetically shielded room in Petaluma. Such rooms, also known as Faraday cages, are lead-lined chambers designed to screen out all known forms of radiation. Fiber-optic cables connect the instrumentation inside the room to the lab outside, so that even conventional electromagnetic fields are screened out.

Unknown to the group of earnest intenders in Tokyo, however, similar water samples were being held in a different location as controls.

Photographs of ice crystals formed from both sets of water were then viewed by 100 independent judges. They found the shapes in the treated water more beautiful than those in the untreated water (Radin, Hayssen, Emoto, & Kizu, 2006).

  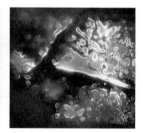

| **Water exposed to the music of Mozart.** | **Water exposed to the music of Vivaldi.** | **Water exposed to heavy metal music.** |

Your body is 70 percent water. That water is responding to the vibrations around it as certainly as the particles on the Chladni plates or the droplets on Dr. Kröplin's microscope slides. When you are flooding the water molecules of your body with the vibrations of healing energy, you are entraining them in sympathy with wellness, while discordant vibrations have the opposite effect. Immerse your mind in positive energy and at least 70 percent of the matter in your body comes into sync with that elevated state.

How Sound Cured Jim's Alcoholism and Cardiac Disease

By Frances Dachelet, R.N., licensed acupuncturist, acutonics practitioner

Jim, a 40-year-old married man, sought treatment for intermittent heart palpitations that had been active over the previous month. He reported that when his heart started to race, he felt anxiety, shortness of breath, and chest pain.

He was admitted to the hospital the first time it happened and had a complete heart workup that was negative for myocardial infarction or any specific heart problem. Jim had been married for one year and was the father of a six-month-old baby boy. He worked full-time as a physician's assistant in an emergency care setting and found his work busy and rewarding.

Jim had a long family history of alcoholism. His father had been physically abusive to him, his siblings, and his mother. Jim had received some therapy in the past to deal with particular childhood problems.

Jim admitted that he hides and covers many of his feelings with humor and sarcasm. He worries about being a good enough father, husband, and physician's assistant. When he doubts himself, he uses alcohol to calm his worries. He admitted to having a problem with drinking, although he had reduced the number of times he drank to excess.

Jim eats a vegetarian diet and has hot meals with his family that his wife prepares. He reported consuming too much dairy and cheese and had gained weight since getting married. He acknowledged the need to drink more water, that he will go for long periods of time not drinking liquids at all during a day, then having a beer or cocktails at night.

He was assessed energetically with:

- Shen disturbance (agitation of the spirit)
- Imbalances of the liver, spleen, and kidney meridian energies
- Intergenerational alcoholism
- Heart chakra issues
- Fear

At the first treatment, Jim came in with heart palpitations and was visibly uncomfortable and frightened. Treatment strategies for this visit were to calm the spirit, slow the heart rate and breathing, and strengthen the kidney energy to anchor the energy of the heart and lung acupuncture meridians.

The treatment was started with tuning forks for grounding, centering, and stabilizing kidney meridian energy. Tuning fork intervals were applied to points for calming the spirit and nourishing and balancing the heart energy.

Grounding on kidney points was repeated, and Jim reported feeling calm and a sensation he described as his heart slowing down. He was less anxious and visibly relaxed on the treatment table.

Extraordinary vessels were used to address the intergenerational issues, drawing on their primordial connection to Source to open to those deep-seated childhood issues. Tuning fork combinations were used to break through the familial issues.

The session ended with additional grounding, using kidney points located on the feet. Jim reported feeling calm and rested.

Dietary, hydration, and exercise recommendations were made to Jim. He reported no palpitations or panic symptoms following his first treatment.

Subsequent treatments focused on nourishing kidney energy and balancing the nervous system while continuing to address familial patterns and to provide nurturance.

High-octave tuning forks were added and sounded above the body to clear and heal the body's subtle energy field.

The treatment series ended by grounding the energy shifts, using kidney points on the feet.

Jim reported that after his first treatment, the palpitations did not return. Though he still experienced occasional stress and anxiety, he felt much better. He continued to work on his diet and stopped drinking alcohol. He was investigating an outpatient rehabilitation program and considering treatment.

ENERGY FLOWS ALONG
ACUPUNCTURE MERIDIANS

Acupuncture meridians such as the kidney, liver, and spleen merid-ians used in Jim's treatment sequence have been used for healing for thousands of years. The meridians and the acupoints along them were identified in a Chinese book called *The Yellow Emperor's Classic of Internal Medicine* that is more than 2,000 years old.

Meridians were also known in Europe. A mummified body found in the Alps in 1991 exhibits 61 tattoos. Some are shaped like crosses or targets. Scientists have studied the mummy, called Otzi, extensively and can identify the diseases from which he suffered. Some of the tattoos are directly on the acupoints for those particular conditions. Otzi's corpse is some 5,400 years old, making it apparent that human beings have known for millennia about the link between these points and healing.

Some of the tattoos on Otzi's body are on acupoints.

FINDING ACUPOINTS ON YOUR BODY

Nowadays it is easy to find acupoints on a body using a handheld skin galvanometer. Acupoints are excellent conductors of electricity, since they have only 1/2000th of the resistance of the surrounding skin. Low resistance equals high conductance, as with wires that run through a power cord. When these low-resistance points are stimulated, energy flows through them easily.

When I teach live workshops, I often use a galvanometer to find acupoints on a volunteer's body. This makes it apparent to participants that acupoints aren't just some ancient Chinese fiction. They're real and they're measurable, and when energy therapies use them for healing effect, the flow of energy in the body is altered.

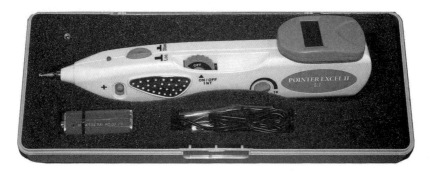

Acupoints can easily be identified using a handheld galvanometer.

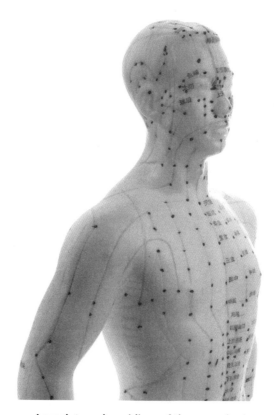

Acupoints and meridians of the upper body.

An energy psychology method that uses acupoints is called Emotional Freedom Techniques (EFT). This is the most popular of the more than 30 different energy psychology methods that exist today. EFT is used by over 20 million people worldwide. It stimulates acupoints on the body's meridians by tapping on them with the fingertips. For this reason, EFT is often simply called tapping. Its popularity has grown rapidly over the last two decades because it's easily learned, quickly applied, and effective. I wrote the most recent edition of the handbook describing the method, *The EFT Manual,* to make the version of EFT used in studies more widely available (Church, 2013).

That evidence-based form is called clinical EFT, and there are now over 100 clinical trials published in peer-reviewed psychology and medical journals attesting to its efficacy. Meta-analyses of EFT for depression, anxiety, and PTSD show that its treatment effects are much greater than those of drugs or talk therapy.

EFT uses some simple elements drawn from talk therapy but adds the ingredient of tapping on acupoints. It takes less than a minute to tap through them all, and psychological distress usually diminishes immediately.

I've presented EFT workshops at many medical and psychology conferences and noticed that doctors usually take readily to EFT. They are very aware of the contribution that stress makes to physical disease. I've had several doctors tell me that after tapping, patient issues resolved without further need for conventional allopathic treatment. As Chuck Gebhardt, M.D., observed in the following account after seeing swelling subside immediately after acupoint tapping, "Nothing in my traditional medical training in anatomy, physiology, or pathology even hinted at what I am now witnessing."

ᴀ Fʟᴜ Sʜᴏᴛ Gone Wʀᴏɴɢ

By Chuck Gebhardt, M.D.

I am a traditionally trained American physician who has been using a somewhat modified version of EFT for about six months. As readers would expect, I have been seeing great success and tremendous value to my patients. I specialize in internal medicine and I am one of six physicians in a private practice in southwest Georgia.

I typically treat my patients as I always have, but if they are experiencing acute discomfort during our visit, I will try to treat the discomfort with tapping or pressure on acupoints (if circumstances allow). Before I introduce this technique, though, I examine, diagnose, and treat all important problems as I usually do, including their acute problems that I am about to target with a new and unusual intervention after the traditional work is done. Now for the story.

Bill received a flu shot from my very able assistant with no initial problem. He is a 60-year-old gentleman whom I treat for hypertension and hypercholesterolemia. He is otherwise completely healthy, well balanced, and down to earth, with no psychological problems of any kind.

Early the next morning, he called and reported that within hours of the shot his left arm began to throb with pain and swell. . . . In my office, the area of swelling was the size of about a half of a hardboiled egg (very dramatic indeed). It throbbed and hurt him so much, he couldn't stand for his shirt sleeve to touch it. It was intensely red and very warm to touch. His temperature was 100.5°F, and he had beads of cold sweat on his forehead (called diaphoresis).

I prescribed an antihistamine, pain medicine, and a steroid dose pack to be started immediately and instructed him to call us right away if he had any trouble breathing or felt like he might pass out.

As he was about to leave with his prescriptions in hand, I decided to tap on some of the meridians on his head, left shoulder, and left arm to see if I could relieve his discomfort somewhat until the medications would take effect.

Tapping on several spots seemed to help a little, but when I tapped on the inside of his left elbow at a spot that acupuncturists call L5, he said: "Wow! That is helping a lot." Over the next 30 seconds, while I continuously tapped on L5, the inflamed, swollen lump shrunk to about one-tenth its initial size, the redness faded, and it stopped hurting.

His low-grade temperature and diaphoresis resolved, and his feeling of malaise was also gone. This response was jaw-dropping amazing for both me and him. He even pounded on the previously exquisitely tender spot with his fist to show how well it now felt. His grin was ear to ear. When I saw him again about a month later, he said the pain and swelling never came back, so he didn't see any need to fill the prescriptions I had written for him.

> This was one of the most dramatic responses to acupoint stimulation I have witnessed, but it is only one of many I see on a daily basis in my practice.
>
> Nothing in my traditional medical training in anatomy, physiology, or pathology even hinted at what I am now witnessing. As you know, anyone who watches these dramatic improvements knows immediately that our previous understanding of how our bodies and our minds work is in need of important revisions and redirected research. This is very exciting.

Dr. Gebhardt is one of many physicians using EFT for physical ailments. At one conference, a doctor came up to me, grasped my hands, and expressed his gratitude for the training in EFT I had given at that same conference two years earlier. He told me that at his clinic they now use EFT with every new patient during the intake process. This typically clears the emotional aspects of the presenting problem, and after that the doctors can address what's left—the parts of the problem that are truly medical.

Energy Healing for Champion Swimmer Tim Garton after Stage 2 Non-Hodgkin's Lymphoma

Tim Garton, a world-champion swimmer, was diagnosed in 1989 with stage 2 non-Hodgkin's lymphoma. He was 49 years old and had a tumor the size of a football in his abdomen. It was treated with surgery followed by four chemotherapy treatments over 12 weeks, with subsequent abdominal radiation for 8 weeks. Despite initial concern that the cancer appeared to be terminal, the treatment was successful, and by 1990 Tim was told that he was in remission. He was also told that he would never again compete at a national or international level. In 1992, however, Tim Garton returned to competitive swimming and won the 100-meter freestyle world championship.

In early July of 1999, he was diagnosed with prostate cancer. A prostatectomy in late July revealed that the cancer had expanded beyond the borders of his prostate and could not all be surgically removed.

Once again, he received weekly radiation treatment in the area of his abdomen. After eight weeks of treatment, the cancer had cleared.

In 2001, the lymphoma returned, this time in his neck. It was removed surgically. Tim again received radiation, which left severe burns on his neck. The following year, a growth on the other side of his neck, moving over his trachea, was diagnosed as a fast-growing lymphoma that required emergency surgery.

He was told that the lymphoma was widespread. An autologous bone marrow and stem cell transplant was done at this time, but it was not successful. There was concern that the tumors would metastasize to his stomach. His doctors determined at this point that they could do nothing more for him. He was told that highly experimental medical treatments, for which there was little optimism, were the only alternative. He was given an injection of monoclonal antibodies (Rituxan), which had been minimally approved for recurrent low-grade lymphoma. Rituxan is designed to flag the cancer sites and potentially help stimulate the immune system to know where to focus.

At this point, Tim enlisted the services of Kim Wedman, an energy medicine practitioner trained by Donna Eden. Tim and his wife went to the Bahamas for three weeks and took Kim with them for the first week. Kim provided daily sessions lasting an hour and a half. These sessions included a basic energy balancing routine, meridian tracing, a chakra clearing, and work with the electrical, neurolymphatic, and neurovascular points.

Kim also taught Tim and his wife a 20-minute twice-daily energy medicine protocol, which they followed diligently, both during the week Kim was there and for the subsequent two weeks. The protocol included a basic energy balancing routine and specific interventions for the energy pathways that govern the immune system and that feed energy to the stomach, kidneys, and bladder.

Upon returning to his home in Denver, in order to determine how quickly the cancers might be spreading, Tim scheduled a follow-up assessment with the oncologist who had told him, "There is nothing more that we can do for you." To everyone's thrill and surprise, Tim was cancer-free. He has remained so during the four years between that assessment and the time of this writing. He has been checked with a PET scan each year, with no cancer detected.

CREATING MATTER FROM INFINITE MIND

The big picture in all this research is that energy builds matter. We know that we are immersed in energy fields, from Earth's magnetic field to the fields produced by the hearts of the people closest to us. We know that our organs have fields and our cells have fields. These fields change in response to intention and the activity of a healer—and that healer can be us.

We know that disease shows up in a person's energy field before it becomes evident at the level of matter and that the water that makes up our bodies is sensitive to the energy fields around it. We know that sound frequencies change matter and that even the act of observing subatomic particles can change their behavior.

Finally, we see that when energy is applied with the intention of healing, matter often follows. Ancient healing systems such as acupuncture, as well as modern variants such as EFT, all show the effect of energy on our cells. Over a thousand studies of energy healing show that it is effective for both psychological conditions (e.g., anxiety and depression) and physical symptoms, including pain and autoimmune diseases.

Although science used to regard energy fields as epiphenomena of matter, the evidence now suggests that matter is an epiphenomenon of energy. The implication for healing is that when we change our energy fields, the cells of our material bodies respond.

Albert Einstein understood the relationship of energy to matter. His famous equation is $E = mc^2$. The E stands for "energy" and the m stands for "matter." They are in balance on opposite sides of the equation. He wrote, "What we have called *matter* is *energy,* whose vibration has been so lowered as to be perceptible to the senses. There is no matter."

We can choose to remain materialists. Faced with imbalances in our lives, disturbances in our emotions, and diseases in our bodies, we can look for material solutions like pills or surgery or recreational drugs to make us feel better.

We can also choose the path of energy. When people change energetically, matter follows right along. Faced with the inevitable challenges of being human, we can take Einstein's advice and shift the E side of the equation. Simple, broadly effective, and elegant, working at the level of energy frees us from the tyranny of matter. We address our problems at the level of cause rather than effect.

As we free our attention from fascination with matter, we perceive the intelligence innate in energy. Shifting to the level of detached consciousness opens us to the infinite possibilities contained in the nonlocal field of infinite intelligence.

When we create in alignment with this universal nonlocal field, we are in touch with the field of infinite possibilities. We are no longer bound by the limited subset of possibilities offered by matter. This interaction patterns the cells of our bodies, from water molecules to neurons, and aligns our material form with the endless possibilities in the field of infinite intelligence. Habituating ourselves to living there, we create entirely different lives than are possible when we remain bound by the limitations of material thinking.

PUTTING THESE IDEAS INTO PRACTICE

Activities to practice this week:

- Sing for at least a few minutes each day when you're alone.

- Experience water deeply. Take a walk by a body of water, enjoy a bath, splash in a fountain. Notice the ripples and reflections.

- Before you drink a glass of water, hold it to your heart and radiate blessing toward it.

- Use sound consciously. For the entire week, fast from all music other than meditation music channels.

- Write your observations of your experiences of sound and water in your journal.

The Extended Play version of this chapter includes:

- Studies of life-forms able to detect electromagnetic fields

- Best cymatics videos

- The sound patterns of Ernst Chladni

- Sound healing case histories

- Dawson's galvanometer video

- Water memory videos

- Professor Rustum Roy's presentation on the changes in the properties of water

To access the Extended Play version, visit: MindToMatter.club/Chapter2

CHAPTER 3

How Our Emotions Organize Our Environment

On a bright spring morning in 1892, a young German soldier named Hans Berger was riding high. He was taking part in military exercises in the town of Würzburg, and his unit was pulling artillery pieces into position with their horses.

Suddenly, Berger's horse reared up on its hind legs, throwing him to the ground right in front of one of the wagon wheels. At the last second, Berger's desperate companions halted the momentum of the gun just before it crushed him. Berger escaped death with nothing more than a dirty uniform.

That evening, he received a telegram from his father in Coburg, asking about his well-being. His father had never sent him a telegram before. That morning, Berger's older sister had been "overwhelmed by an ominous feeling . . . convinced that something terrible had happened to him" and urged her father to send the telegram.

Berger struggled to understand how his feelings of terror might have been communicated to his sister over 100 kilometers away. He had been planning to become an astronomer but now changed his mind, and after his discharge from the army, he became a psychiatrist instead, studying the workings of the brain (Millett, 2001).

In June of 1924, he had the opportunity to study the brain of a 17-year-old boy who had a gap in his skull as a result of an earlier surgery to remove a brain tumor. He wanted to see if he could measure brain activity. After weeks of modifications to his equipment in the wake of unsuccessful readings, to Berger's excitement, he finally observed "continuous oscillations of the galvanometer."

He wrote in his journal: "Is it possible that I might fulfill the plan I have cherished for over 20 years and even still, to create a kind of brain mirror: the electroencephalogram!" (Millett, 2001).

Hans Berger.

In 1929, after refining his equipment and skills, Berger described the first two brain waves ever discovered: alpha and beta. Unfortunately, Berger's work ran counter to the brain theories then prevalent in contemporary medicine, and his work was rejected by most of his colleagues. British and American scientists believed that what he was measuring was the result of an electrical artifact, and one wrote that he was "highly skeptical of the possibility of recording anything of significance from the surface of the brain."

Berger was forced into retirement from his university professorship and his health worsened. He sank into depression and took his own life in 1941. It was not until consciousness researchers began to investigate the link between mind and brain in the 1960s that EEGs came into widespread use. They're now used to map states of consciousness as well as brain function, and new waves such as gamma continue to be discovered (Hughes, 1964).

THE COMMUNICATING BRAIN: CLAPPING "THE WAVE"

I travel to New York often, and I love going to see Broadway musicals. When *The Book of Mormon* opened, I was one of the first to buy tickets.

Members of the audience were laughing all the way through. At the end, the cast got a standing ovation.

Suddenly, the applause changed. Rather than a thousand people clapping separately, everyone began to clap in rhythm. *Clap, clap, clap, clap.* The rhythmic clapping become so insistent that the actors came back onstage for an encore. The clapping communicated approval to the actors, and they responded with another song.

The neurons in your brain do something similar. They fire together in rhythmic patterns, communicating with each other across the brain. These patterns are measured in cycles per second, or Hertz (Hz). Imagine an audience clapping together slowly. That's a slow brain wave, with millions of neurons firing together slowly. Imagine an audience clapping quickly. That's a fast brain wave, with millions of neurons firing together quickly.

Today's EEGs calculate wave patterns from each of the brain's many different parts. They typically use 19 electrodes attached to the surface of the scalp.

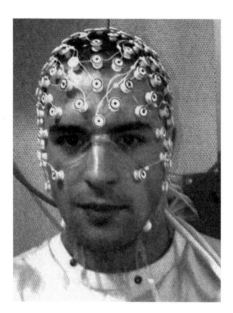

A typical 19-electrode array.

One research team observed, "Scientists are now so accustomed to these EEG correlations with brain state that they may forget just how remarkable they are. . . . A single electrode provides estimates of synaptic action averaged over tissue masses containing between roughly 100 million and 1 billion neurons" (Nunez & Srinivasan, 2006). When we see brain wave changes on an EEG, it indicates that the firing patterns of billions of neurons in our brains are also changing.

WHAT BRAIN WAVES ARE AND WHAT THEY DO

There are five basic brain waves that are picked up by a modern EEG. Gamma is the highest brain wave frequency (40 to 100 Hz). It's most prevalent at times when the brain is learning, making associations between phenomena and integrating information from many different parts of the brain.

A brain producing lots of gamma waves reflects complex neural organization and heightened awareness. When monks were asked to meditate on compassion, large flares of gamma were found in their brains (Davidson & Lutz, 2008).

They were compared to novice meditators who had meditated for an hour a day the week before. The novices had brain activity similar to that of the monks. But when the monks were instructed to evoke a feeling of compassion, their brains began to fire in rhythmic coherence, like the audience clapping at *The Book of Mormon* musical.

The flares of gamma waves measured in the brains of the monks were the largest ever recorded. The monks reported entering a state of bliss. Gamma is associated with very high levels of intellectual function, creativity, integration, peak states, and of feeling "in the zone." Gamma waves flow from the front to the back of the brain about 40 times per second (Llinás, 2014). Researchers look to this oscillating wave as a neural correlate of consciousness (NCC), a state linking the brain's activity with the subjective experience of consciousness (Tononi & Koch, 2015).

Brain researchers talk about the amplitude of a brain wave and that simply means how big it is. A high amplitude of gamma means a big gamma wave, while a low amplitude means a small one. Measurements of brain waves show peaks and valleys. The distance from the peak to the trough is the amplitude. Amplitude is measured in microvolts, and brain waves typically measure between 10 and 100 microvolts, with the faster waves like gamma having the lowest amplitude.

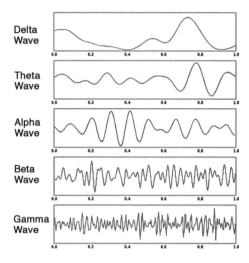

EEG brain waves from slowest to fastest.

The next fastest wave is beta (12 to 40 Hz). Beta is typically divided into two parts: high beta and low beta. High beta is your monkey mind. High beta (15 to 40 Hz) is the signature brain wave of people with anxiety, people experiencing frustration, and people under stress.

The more stressed people become, the higher the amplitude of the beta their brains produce. Negative emotions such as anger, fear, blame, guilt, and shame produce large flares of beta in the EEG readout.

This shuts down the brain regions that handle rational thinking, decision making, memory, and objective evaluation (LeDoux, 2002). Blood flow to the prefrontal cortex, the "thinking brain," is reduced by up to 80 percent. Starved of oxygen and nutrients, our brains' ability to think clearly plummets.

Low beta is the band that synchronizes our bodies' automatic functions, so it's also called the sensorimotor rhythm frequency, or SMR (12 to 15 Hz).

Beta is required for processing information and for linear thinking, so normal levels of beta are fine. When you focus on solving a problem, composing a poem, calculating the best route to your destination, or balancing your checkbook, beta is your friend. SMR represents a calm, focused mental state. It's stress that produces high beta, especially above 25 Hz.

Alpha (8 to 12 Hz) is an optimal state of relaxed alertness. Alpha connects the higher frequencies—the thinking mind of beta and the associative mind of gamma—with the two lowest frequency brain waves, which are theta (4 to 8 Hz) and delta (0 to 4 Hz).

Theta is characteristic of light sleep. When we dream vividly, our eyes move rapidly and our brains are primarily in theta. Theta is the frequency of rapid eye movement (REM) sleep. Theta is also the dominant frequency of people under hypnosis, healers, people in trances, and people in highly creative states (Kershaw & Wade, 2012). The recollection of emotional experiences, both good and bad, can trigger theta.

The slowest frequency is delta. Delta is characteristic of deep sleep. Very high amplitudes of delta are also found in people who are in touch with nonlocal mind, even when they're wide awake. The brains of meditators, intuitives, and healers have much more delta than normal.

The eyes of people who are in deep dreamless sleep don't move. Delta waves also predominate in such non–rapid eye movement (NREM) sleep.

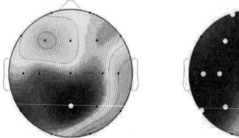

On this type of chart (a "z-score" chart), the middle shade indicates normal activity, and the two lighter shades progressively reduced activity. The two darker shades indicate increased activity. The brain on the left shows a variety of activity. The brain on the right is highly active at the middle frequencies of theta, a common pattern in experienced healers.

AWAKENING FROM EVERYDAY REALITY

EEG pioneer Maxwell Cade noticed that alpha, in the middle of the range of frequencies, forms a bridge between the two high frequencies of beta and gamma and the two low frequencies of theta and delta (Cade & Coxhead, 1979). Biofeedback and neurofeedback skills focus on teaching people how to get into an alpha state. The ideal state is enough alpha to link all of the other brain rhythms together. High beta is minimized, so that there is very little monkey mind and anxiety. There is a balanced amount of gamma and theta, and a wide base of delta.

Maxwell Cade.

A biophysicist, Cade had worked on radar for the British government before turning his attention to measuring states of consciousness. He developed his own machine, the "mind mirror," in 1976. It is unique among EEG devices in that it provides a clear visual snapshot of brain waves.

His student Anna Wise described the machine as follows: "What sets the Mind Mirror apart from other forms of electroencephalography was the interest, on the part of its developer, not in pathological states (as in the case of medical devices), but in an optimum state called the Awakened Mind. Instead of measuring subjects with problems, the inventor of the Mind Mirror sought the most highly developed and spiritually conscious people he could find. In the flicker of their brainwaves, he and his colleagues found a common pattern, whether the subject was a yogi, a Zen master or a healer."

THE AWAKENED MIND

Using the mind mirror, over 20 years, Cade recorded the brain wave patterns of more than four thousand people with strong spiritual practices. He found the Awakened Mind state was common in this group. Cade also noticed another similarity: they all had high amounts of alpha.

As noted, alpha waves are right in the middle of the spectrum, with beta and gamma above, and theta and delta below. When someone in the Awakened Mind state has lots of alpha, it creates a link between the high frequencies above and the low frequencies below. Cade called this the alpha bridge, because it bridges the conscious mind frequencies of beta with the subconscious and unconscious mind frequencies of theta and delta. This allows a flow of consciousness, integrating all the levels of mind.

Cade wrote: "The awakening of awareness is like gradually awakening from sleep and becoming more and more vividly aware of everyday reality—only it's everyday reality from which we are awakening!" (Cade & Coxhead, 1979).

Max Cade with first 1970s version of the mind mirror.

I developed a meditation method called EcoMeditation that's very simple, yet it's consistently and automatically able to bring people into the Awakened Mind EEG pattern. EcoMeditation uses EFT tapping to clear obstacles to relaxation. It then takes you through a series of simple physical relaxation exercises that send signals of safety to the brain and body. It does not rely on belief or philosophy; instead, it's based on sending the body physiological cues that produce a deeply relaxed state automatically. The instructions are free at EcoMeditation.com.

During EcoMeditation, we see lots of delta brain waves as well. Delta is where we connect with many resources above and beyond the local self. As noted, people in trance states, as well as healers, artists, musicians, and intuitives, tend to have plenty of delta.

Those in a creative trance, such as a composer making music or a child at play, usually have lots of delta. They lose all awareness of the outer world as they become absorbed in their creativity. They're mostly in delta, with some theta and alpha, and just enough beta to function (Gruzelier, 2009).

It's been fascinating to me to speak to people whose brains show a high amplitude of delta during meditation. They report transcendent experiences. They describe feeling one with the universe, an exquisite sense of harmony and well-being (Johnson, 2011). Albert Einstein referred to this as an expansive state of consciousness in which we "embrace all living creatures and the whole of nature." Scientists can be mystics too!

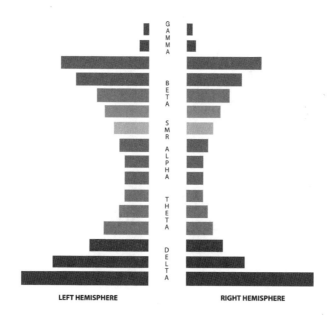

LEFT HEMISPHERE   RIGHT HEMISPHERE

Display from the mind mirror. Normal brain function: note that all six frequencies are present, with balance between left and right hemispheres.

Anxiety: A person with anxiety has a lot of high
beta and little alpha, theta, or delta.

Increase in alpha activity: A subject breaking through to integration
has flares of alpha, even though they still have a pronounced anxiety,
which shows up as beta. They're also amplifying theta, though the waves
are not balanced equally between left and right hemispheres.

G A M M A

B E T A

S M R

A L P H A

T H E T A

D E L T A

LEFT HEMISPHERE   RIGHT HEMISPHERE

Balance between brain activities: The "Awakened Mind" pattern, with large amounts of delta and theta, and lowered beta. Plentiful alpha provides an "alpha bridge" between conscious mind (beta) and unconscious and subconscious levels (theta and delta).

The Musician Trapped inside the Programmer

At a live workshop, I taught EcoMeditation to Prem, a 42-year-old man with moderate anxiety. He was a computer programmer who wanted to bring more creativity into his life. Prem played the guitar but rarely made time for it, even though it was his favorite hobby. "I just don't have time for myself," he said. One of his core beliefs was "Life is tough. You have to apply yourself. There's no time for play."

When we began the session, Prem's EEG showed a high degree of beta waves in both the left and the right hemispheres of his brain. Beta is the wave typical of stress. His alpha waves were minimal.

Alpha is the ideal wave, one of relaxed alertness, linking the high and low frequencies.

Prem's EEG readout showed plenty of theta and delta, but his minimal alpha amplitude was like a bottleneck; he didn't have access to his creative side. His high amplitude of beta is also characteristic of people with chronic anxiety, stress, and burnout (Fehmi & Robbins, 2007).

Once Prem settled into the EcoMeditation routine, he had big flares of alpha in both the right and the left hemispheres of his brain, though larger on the right. His anxious, stressed-out beta waves disappeared. His brain began to produce gamma waves, which it had not been doing before.

Prem was not a meditator and said that he had taken meditation classes but never succeeded in establishing a routine meditation practice. However, EcoMeditation quickly settled him into a deep state. His brain waves stabilized in the Awakened Mind pattern.

In the absence of stress, the blood rushed back into his prefrontal cortex, and his thinking became clear as he gained access to the biological and intellectual assets in the executive centers of his brain.

At that workshop, we tested the biological responses of participants as well as their psychological states before and after the workshop. Prem's set point for cortisol, the primary stress hormone, dropped significantly. When our stress levels drop, biological resources are freed up for cell repair, immunity, and other beneficial functions.

This was evident in Prem's levels of salivary immunoglobulin A (SIgA), a key immune marker. They rose significantly between the beginning and the end of the workshop. His resting heart rate dropped from 79 to 64 beats per minute (bpm), while his blood pressure dropped from 118/80 to 108/70. All these indicators reflected the newly balanced function of his brain.

Similar positive effects were noted for other workshop participants. For the whole group, average cortisol levels declined and SIgA levels rose. Resting heart rate dropped from 70 to 66 (Groesbeck et al., 2016).

Once we reversed the stress response with EcoMeditation, Prem began to see the light side of life. The blood began to flow back into his forebrain and his whole hard drive came back online. He felt empowered. He knew he had resources. He knew he had the capacity for play. He regained a sense of control in his life. He had a sense of agency, of self-efficacy, and his whole story changed.

When I tested Prem afterward by having him repeat his opening statement that "Life is tough . . . there's no time for play," he burst into laughter. "That sounds like my dad speaking," he observed, and he scowled and wagged his finger as he mimicked a stern father rebuking his playful child.

Prem practiced EcoMeditation throughout the workshop and, by the end, could quickly induce that relaxed state. He began planning time to play guitar and honor his creative side.

Session at a workshop with a participant hooked up to an EEG.

WHEN CONSCIOUSNESS CHANGES, BRAIN WAVES CHANGE

The energy fields of brain waves and the matter of neural pathways are in a constantly evolving dance. When consciousness changes, brain waves change and different neural pathways are engaged.

The extremes are love and fear. When we're in a state of fear, our alpha bridge disappears. We may still have theta and delta, but we're cut off from the resources of our subconscious mind and its connection with the universal whole.

Beta waves flood the fearful brain. It's in survival mode.

When we're in a state of bliss, our brains show the Awakened Mind pattern. A step beyond, they can also move to a symmetrical pattern Cade called the Evolved Mind. As our consciousness is filled with love, our brains function very differently, with large amounts of theta and delta, plus an alpha bridge to connect our conscious with our subconscious mind.

Emotions create brain states. Brain waves measure the fields generated by consciousness. Passing signals through the neural bundles engaged by love, joy, and harmony creates a characteristic energy field (Wright, 2017). When monitoring the brains of people doing EcoMeditation, EEG expert Judith Pennington observed that "theta and delta progressed their patterns from the Awakened Mind to the Evolved Mind state."

Emotions also create neurotransmitters. Among these are serotonin, dopamine, endorphins, oxytocin, and anandamide (Kotler & Wheal, 2017). Serotonin is associated with satisfaction, and dopamine with a sensation of reward. Endorphins block pain and increase pleasure. Oxytocin is the "bonding hormone," and it stimulates feelings of closeness and intimacy with others. Anandamide is called the "bliss molecule," and it's named after the Sanskrit word for happiness. It binds to the same receptors in the brain as THC, the primary psychoactive molecule in marijuana. When mind changes, it creates molecular facts in the form of these neurotransmitters. As they flood our brains, we feel satisfied, secure, bonded, blissful, and serene. When our minds enter elevated emotional states, we're literally getting high—on drugs produced by our bodies.

BRAIN WAVES EXPRESS THE FIELDS GENERATED BY EMOTION

An influential study examined the brain wave patterns of meditators from five different contemplative traditions ranging from qigong to Zen (Lehmann et al., 2012). It compared their brain function in a normal state of consciousness and in meditation.

One of the challenges of such research is that a single hour of EEG recordings of a single subject yields millions of pieces of data. It tells you the predominant frequencies of each part of the brain millisecond by millisecond, and these frequencies are changing constantly. Interpreting this huge mass of data requires experience and a model to describe what you're looking for.

After building a complete picture of how the entire brain functions, the investigators in this study concluded that the most informative model was to compare beta with delta. They measured the ratio of beta to delta before meditation, during meditation, and after meditation. While the meditation traditions offered very different teachings, from chanting to movement to sitting still, what they all had in common was a reduction in beta and an increase in delta.

The researchers identified "globally reduced functional interdependence between brain regions," a change in brain function suggesting a dissolution of the sense of an isolated local self. This brain pattern of low beta and high delta typified what they termed "the subjective experience of non-involvement, detachment and letting go, as well as of all-oneness and dissolution of ego borders" as the consciousness of meditators shifted into oneness with the nonlocal universal field.

That is the same brain wave pattern I've seen in the EEG readouts of hundreds of meditators who are describing states of flow, altered consciousness, and connection with the universal nonlocal field in which the borders of the local self dissolve.

THE EXPERIENCE OF THE MYSTICS

At one workshop, we videotaped statements from people whose brains showed enormous amounts of delta. We asked them what they had experienced during the meditations. One woman named "Julie," who suffered from depression, described it like this:

"At first, having my eyes closed was annoying. I could feel every little scratchy itchy feeling in my skin. My throat tickled, and I wanted to cough. I could hear the guy next to me breathing, and that was annoying too. But then I began to forget about all that stuff, and a feeling of peace came over me.

"I could feel the breath going inside my body. And going out again. It felt like a river flowing. I started to float, like I was a helium balloon or something.

"I seemed to go to another place, and it was beautiful. I could feel the rocks and trees and ocean, and I seemed to be part of it all, like I was absorbed into this perfection of everything there is in the cosmos.

"These four huge blue beings drifted near me, and I felt incredible love and connection flowing out of them. They were like outlines of people but transparent and about 15 feet high. Made out of a beautiful royal blue mist.

"I've been so worried about all the stuff going on in my life lately, but one of the beings drifted close to me and I felt reassured. Like she was telling me everything is going to be okay. My heart filled up with love, and I realized that love is everything.

"She gave me a shiny diamond crystal to remind me that she's always there for me. I put it in my heart. It melted all the miserable, depressed pain that's been living there for too long, and the pain became drops of water that fell into the ground.

"When you told us to come back into the room, I felt like I was a million miles away. I brought that feeling of peace back into my body. It was hard to come back, and I realize part of me is there all the time."

COMMONALITIES IN MYSTICAL EXPERIENCE

What Julie described is a typical mystical experience. Human beings have been having transcendent experiences since the dawn of consciousness, and hers had characteristics similar to many others:

- A pervasive feeling of peace
- The falling away of worry and doubt
- A felt sense of detachment from local self and the limitations of the body
- An experience of oneness with nonlocal mind, including nature, the universe, and all of life
- A meeting with a symbolic guide
- Receiving a symbolic gift that carries healing power
- The integration of the gift with her body and her local self
- A sense of being changed by the experience

The neuroscientists I've worked with have instructed experienced meditators to provide prearranged signals during meditation, such as tapping their forefinger three times when they feel the experience of oneness. We can time-stamp this spot on the EEG readout. This has allowed us to correlate their internal experience with brain states.

When their local self abandons its preoccupation with the body to merge with nonlocal mind, we see large flares of delta. The high-amplitude delta wave becomes stable when the meditators integrate the two states, such as when Julie communed with the blue being who gave her the gift (Pennington, 2017).

Once people start to make meditation part of their daily lives, they develop higher amplitudes of alpha, theta, and delta than they had before.

Mystical experiences throughout history show similarities. Tukaram, an Indian saint of the 17th century, wrote the following poem, "When I Lose Myself in Thee" (Hoyland, 1932):

> When thus I lose myself in Thee, my God,
> Then do I see, and know,
> That all Thy universe reveals Thy beauty,
> All living beings, and all lifeless things,
> Exist through thee.
>
> This whole vast world is but the form
> In which Thou showest us Thyself,
> Is but the voice,
> In which Thyself Thou speakest unto us.
>
> What need of words?
> Come, Master, come,
> And fill me wholly with Thyself.

In Tukaram's poem, we can see characteristics similar to Julie's experience. He loses his sense of local self, disappearing into nonlocal consciousness. He has an experience of oneness with the universe. He feels the universe communicating with him, a state of unity in which no words are necessary.

Though there were no EEGs around in the 17th century to map the brain waves of mystics such as Tukaram, we can infer the types of neural signaling occurring in their brains by examining similar experiences in people like Julie.

**Indian saint Ramakrishna often spontaneously
entered states of mystical experience.**

Indian saint Ramakrishna (1836–1886) would go into states of bliss
that lasted for hours at a time. His body became stiff, and he became so
absorbed in his transcendent experience that he was unaware of his surroundings. When he emerged from meditation, he was often unable to
speak for a while. Once, after regaining the power of speech, he described
seeing a light like a million suns. A luminous form emerged from the
light, took human shape, then reintegrated with the light.

Theologian Huston Smith is the author of the textbook *The World's
Religions* and an expert on mystical experience. He states that experiences
of oneness are common to mystics throughout history. The experience
is not dependent on time or culture. Mystics aren't talking secondhand
about oneness; they're talking firsthand about experiences of oneness
(Smith, 2009).

When they descend from the mountaintop, they share their experience with those around them. Inspired, their listeners often venerate
them and may even build religions around them. What all the mystics
are pointing to, however, is the direct experience of oneness. This is an
order removed from the secondhand experience mediated by intercessors
such as priests and religious rites.

Mystics don't disagree with one another or believe their own path is superior to another, because they've all had the same experience. Only second-tier religious authorities come into conflict. While religions are different, the mystical experience is one. Smith holds that the mystical experience is the pinnacle of human consciousness (Smith, 2009).

The breakthrough of modern science is that we can now chart the information flow in the brains of mystics, just as the ancient mariners charted the unknown seas. Science is now showing us objectively what mystics like Smith have known subjectively, that mystical experience produces common and predictable patterns in the brain.

The brain's right parietal lobe is responsible for positioning the body in relationship to its surroundings and distinguishing the boundary between self and other. Neuroimaging studies show that in ecstatic states, this region goes offline (Kotler & Wheal, 2017). When Ramakrishna and other mystics describe their sense of local self fading into a merger with a universal nonlocal mind, the experience is echoed in the objective function of their brains. As their oxytocin spikes, they bond with the universe, and as their brains flood with anandamide, they enter bliss.

DELTA WAVES AND CONNECTION WITH NONLOCAL CONSCIOUSNESS

My friend and colleague Dr. Joe Dispenza has been collecting brain scans at meditation workshops for many years and now has a compendium of over 10,000 scans. Studying the patterns that are common to this group of mind maps gives us fascinating insights into the experience of workshop participants.

What we see in Joe's collection is people with much more theta and delta than usual. The baseline amount of delta in the brains of meditators is much greater than those in "normal" brains (Thatcher, 1998). Meditators have practiced releasing their attachment to local mind and immersing themselves in experiences of oneness with nonlocal mind.

Repeated meditation moves the brain into a new zone of functioning that includes much more delta than the old normal. When Joe tested first hundreds and then thousands of such brains, what he noticed was that they were processing information in a way that was very different from the average brain (Dispenza, 2017).

Activity in many of these people is in the red zone, which means that the amount of delta is two deviations from the mean greater than that found in a database of normalized mind maps (Thatcher, 1998). The practical meaning of this statistic is that only 2.5 percent of the general population has the delta function we're seeing in experienced meditators. Neuroscientists measuring the changes in brain waves during Joe's advanced workshops found that over the four days of a workshop, the brain's baseline delta activity increases by an average of 149 percent (Dispenza, 2017).

Delta brain waves range in amplitude from 100 to 200 microvolts from peak to trough (ADInstruments, 2010). When testing people in Eco-Meditation workshops, we often see amplitudes of over 1,000 microvolts. Sometimes we see surges of over a million microvolts. Most EEG equipment is not even able to measure so much delta.

This correlates with powerful spiritual experiences such as the ones reported by today's Julie and yesterday's Tukaram. They have been reported by mystics from all traditions for thousands of years. We can't objectively measure an experience like the sense of local self and local mind dissolving into nonlocal self and universal mind. We can, however, measure how the brain having such an experience processes information. The common denominator is enormous amplitudes of delta waves. This energy is matched by molecules like serotonin and dopamine, as well as the ecstasy neurotransmitter anandamide and the bonding hormone oxytocin. These types of experience are not isolated exceptions. Research shows that 40 percent of Americans and 37 percent of Britons have had at least one transcendent experience that took them beyond local mind. Often they describe it as the most important experience of their lives, shaping everything that came later (Greeley, 1975; Castro, Burrows, & Wooffitt, 2014).

Few talked about their experiences with others, however. Children didn't tell parents. Patients didn't tell doctors. Wives didn't tell husbands. Because this type of conversation is outside our normal social conventions, we don't have the language or context to conduct it.

That doesn't mean these experiences aren't happening. When we start to look for them, encounters with nonlocal mind are all around us.

THETA WAVES AND HEALING

Sometimes such altered brain states are accompanied by rapid healing. In a meditation workshop taught by Joe Dispenza, a Mexican man we'll call "José" described similar mystical experiences (Dispenza, 2017).

José had come to the workshop shortly after being diagnosed with a cancerous brain tumor. He was due for a life-threatening operation soon. During one of the meditations, José—like Julie—saw otherworldly beings. One of them reached his hand into José's skull and rooted around inside for a while. José felt vivid physical sensations as though his scalp were being cut open and his brain tissue rearranged.

The day after the workshop, José rearranged his schedule so that he could get a new X-ray. He flew to Houston to consult with doctors at MD Anderson, a famous cancer clinic, before returning home. The new scan, taken just a day after the workshop, showed that all traces of the tumor had disappeared.

During intense healing experiences, we often see high amplitudes of theta waves on the EEG. Theta has been mapped as the signature brain wave during energy healing sessions (Benor, 2004). If one person is offering healing to another, we see big theta waves in first the healer, then the healee. The switch often happens at the moment the healer feels his or her hands becoming warm—the subjective experience of energy flow (Bengston, 2010).

In one study, a healer and client were both hooked up to EEGs. The healer's EEG readout showed 14 periods of sustained theta at the frequency of exactly 7.81 Hz. The client's EEG shifted to the same frequency, demonstrating entrainment between healer and healee (Hendricks, Bengston, & Gunkelman, 2010).

THE DOCTOR WHO COULDN'T HEAL

In one of my trainings, "Anise," a brilliant doctor, volunteered to work on her issues in front of the whole group while hooked up to an EEG monitor. Anise had earned not only an M.D. but also a doctorate in pharmacology. In addition, she was certified in healing touch and several other modalities.

Anise had been diagnosed with fibromyalgia 13 years earlier. The symptoms, such as joint pain, fatigue, and "brain fog," were sometimes severe, other times less so. She had eventually become so debilitated, however, that she was no longer able to work.

On the day of the training, her pain level was 7 out of 10, and her brain fog was so extreme that she was barely able to comprehend the lectures. She walked with difficulty and needed to prop herself up with three pillows in order to feel comfortable enough to function.

Anise had a high degree of frustration and anger at herself because her husband, "Dal," who was also attending the workshop, now had the whole financial burden of providing for the family, including their two teenage daughters. Another source of anger was the experience that "despite all my training, I can't heal myself."

Although we sometimes see "one-minute wonders" during workshops, this was not the case for Anise. Hers was a long and complicated session. She had difficulty creating a vision for her future because she could not imagine herself getting better.

Gestalt therapist Byron Katie has clients ask themselves provocative questions that challenge their assumptions about self and the world. One of these questions is "Who would I be without this story?" Another way of asking it is "What contribution is this disability making to my life?"

I asked this of Anise. The question triggered a memory of a time when she was eight years old and being emotionally abused by a family member. She got sick, and her illness became her shield. When Anise was bedridden, she could retreat into her bedroom and didn't have to deal with her tormentor.

Once we identified the core issue that sickness might be a solution masquerading as a problem, we used energy psychology techniques to release all her anger at her childhood persecutor, who was still very much present in her life.

Her pain went down to a 1 out of 10, and she began to smile and then laugh at the predicament she'd created for herself. "My nemesis has never become successful," she realized, and she felt empowered in that relationship for the first time in her adult life.

She began to talk about the possibilities for her future. She'd been offered a great job in Brazil but hadn't considered it because she didn't think she could function physically without the resources she enjoyed in the United States. Now that possibility opened up for her. "How about it?" she asked her husband. "I would love to," Dal responded, his eyes shining.

At the end of our session, Anise stood up and walked around the room. As her pain subsided completely, she swung her arms and legs freely, with a full range of motion. She left the workshop that day to have dinner with Dal and discuss their positive future. Not only had her consciousness shifted, but her body had been freed up dramatically as well.

CONSCIOUSNESS SHIFTS THE WAY THE BRAIN PROCESSES INFORMATION

During sessions with clients hooked up to an EEG, what we typically see at the start of a session is a lot of high beta, indicating worry and stress. There's little alpha, gamma, or theta. The absence of alpha means clients are unable to bridge their conscious minds (beta) and their creativity, intuition, and connection to the universal field (theta and delta).

As clients experience flashes of insight, we see large flares of alpha in both the left and the right hemispheres of the brain. During Anise's aha moment of realizing that her tormentor had never become anything like as successful as she was, her alpha flared out so wide that it exceeded the measuring capability of our device.

By the end of the session, we saw the typical Awakened Mind pattern in Anise's brain. She had a small amount of high beta, indicating that her critical thinking capacities were online. But she had more SMR (low beta), showing that she was in touch with her body. She had large amounts of theta and an even greater amplitude of delta, showing a connection with her creativity, intuition, and the universal information field. Her gamma had increased, demonstrating a greater ability to make connections between disparate parts of the brain and process information in an integrated way.

While her psychological breakthroughs were profound, her physiological functioning as diagrammed on her EEG readouts showed real-time brain changes. She wasn't simply experiencing a psychological change; the way her brain organized information was shifting too.

This is more than simply a change in the mind. This is a change in the brain itself, as new neural bundles wire themselves together. New neural bundles are constantly being formed and old ones pruned throughout our lives (Restak, 2001).

When we meditate, tap, use another form of energy psychology, or otherwise shift our consciousness, the brain changes quickly. The brain can be intentionally changed by the mind, especially by what is known as attention training (Schwartz & Begley, 2002). True transformation repatterns neural pathways. Eventually, the entire state of the brain shifts and establishes a new and healthy level of homeostasis.

One research team notes that "an accelerating number of studies in the neuroimaging literature significantly support the thesis that . . . with appropriate training and effort, people can systematically alter neural circuitry associated with a variety of mental and physical states that are frankly pathological" (Schwartz, Stapp, & Beauregard, 2005). We can take our dysfunctional brain networks and alter them with our minds.

It's not just mystics and healers who produce large alpha bridges and theta flares when they're in ecstatic states. Groups for whom high performance is critical are finding that tuning the brain in this way produces big leaps in achievement. U.S. Navy SEALs need to operate effectively in rapidly changing combat conditions. Using millions of dollars of advanced EEG equipment in a "Mind Gym" specially constructed in Norfolk, Virginia, they learn to enter a state they call ecstasis (Cohen, 2017). Once they "flip the switch" into ecstasis, their brains are in a state of flow, an altered reality in which super-performance becomes possible. Other peak performers, such as elite courtroom lawyers, Olympic athletes, and Google executives, also train themselves to enter ecstasis.

The characteristics of these flow states are described in the book *Stealing Fire* (Kotler & Wheal, 2017). Among them are selflessness and timelessness. People in ecstasis transcend the boundaries of local mind. EEG readings show that the prefrontal cortex of their brains, the seat of a sense of self, shuts down. Beta-wave mental chatter ceases. They gain distance from the anxious obsessions of local mind. Their internal chemistry changes as "feel-good" neurotransmitters like serotonin, dopamine, anandamide, and oxytocin flood their brains.

In this state they gain a nonlocal perspective. They are open to an infinite range of possible options and outcomes. The self, rather than being trapped in a limited fixed local reality, is able to try on different possibilities. This "knocks out filters we normally apply to incoming information," leading to associative leaps that facilitate problem solving and super-creativity. Kotler and Wheal (2017) review the research on the performance gains produced by these brain wave states. These include a 490 percent improvement in mental focus, a doubling of creativity, and a 500 percent increase in productivity.

During ecstasis, whether found in the ancient accounts of Tukaram or the modern experiences of Julie and the Navy SEALs, people have common experiences. These are linked to neurotransmitters: entering a state of bliss (anandamide), a sense of detachment from the body that encapsulates the local self (endorphins), local self bonding with the nonlocal universe (oxytocin), serenity (serotonin), and the reward of being changed by the experience (dopamine).

These are the characteristics of upgraded minds, and we now have EEGs and neurotransmitter assays to measure the changes they produce in matter. In the past, ecstatic states were attainable only by mystics, and it took decades of study, rigorous practice, ascetic discipline, and spiritual initiation. Today, "we now know the precise adjustments to body and brain that let us recreate them for ourselves" at will; technology is providing us with "a Cliff Notes version of . . . how to encounter the divine" (Kotler & Wheal, 2017). Today, the highest-performing humans in the fields of sports, business, combat, science, meditation, and art are inducing them routinely. Tomorrow, as we map the physiology of these states and turn ecstasis into a learnable skill, they will be available to everyone.

My Brief Career as an Artist, or Dodging the Bullets of Belief

My career as an artist began at age five and started off badly.

My family had just transplanted themselves to America, and I found myself involuntarily incarcerated in Howard Elementary School in Colorado Springs, Colorado. My British accent attracted unfavorable attention from the teachers. To fix the problem, they consigned me to remedial speech classes, where I developed a stutter and a speech impediment.

One day, I brought an art project home to show my parents. Along with all the other kindergartners, I'd been instructed to draw a cowboy. I did my best, and my teacher noticed how good the drawing looked. Flushed with this rare show of approval, I took my drawing home and showed my mother.

She burst out laughing and ridiculed the drawing. She danced around the dining room, shrieking and pantomiming the anatomically inaccurate angles of the cowboy's arms and legs. Crushed, I retreated to the bunk bed on the enclosed porch that I shared with my sister. I never drew another human form again, confining my doodles to ships and aircraft.

Until I turned 45 years old.

I began to meditate daily as well as tap regularly. I examined my core beliefs. One of these was *I'm no good at art*.

Is that really true? I asked myself. Along with a woman I was close to at the time, who happened to own an art gallery, I signed up for a one-day watercolor class at the local college.

The moment I picked up the brush, it felt alive in my hand. I entered an effortless state of flow. I felt as though I'd been painting for a century. I was a sponge for knowledge, learning every technique the teacher knew in just that one day. My artsy girlfriend couldn't believe I was a novice and suspected I'd obtained a clandestine degree in art somewhere along the line.

Next, I took a two-day class in painting the human face in watercolor. I again sucked the teacher dry, insisting on knowing her advanced techniques before the end of the first day.

I then began to paint regularly. Being a methodical sort, I numbered each painting in the order I completed it—1, 2, 3, and so on—instead of giving them names. They were mostly faces. I painted my love. I painted my confusion. I painted my pain.

Watercolor #13: Angel of destiny.

Once I had eight paintings, I took the best four to a local coffee-shop-cum-art-gallery. The owner was impressed and booked me for a one-man show. The opening was in six weeks. "Come the day before and hang 36 pieces," he said.

I tried to look nonchalant as I walked out the door, but inside I was quaking. Thirty-six pieces! He didn't know I'd only done eight in my whole life, if you exclude the cowboy. Now I had to come up with around 30 more in six weeks, on top of my 60-hour workweek and being a single dad to my two young children!

During breaks at work, I began to paint methodically. I realized I could meet the deadline, but only if I took a cue from Henry Ford and set up my paintings on a production line. Very un-artsy, but necessary.

I arranged three easels side by side in a row. Each watercolor wash takes about 10 minutes to dry before you can apply the next one. So I would apply a layer to one easel and then work on the following one. Then on to the third. By the time I circled back to the first painting, the wash had dried, and I could repeat the process.

Watercolor is a demanding medium. The paint is transparent, so you can't cover up a mistake the way you can using opaque media like oil or acrylic. If you mess up a wash or allow a drop of the wrong color to fall on the paper, the painting is ruined. The pressure was on to finish and frame those 30 paintings. As I entered the flow state, I found that I could hold the plan of each of the three paintings in my mind while simultaneously applying the paint effortlessly.

I met the deadline and opened my first art show. People loved the images, and I sold several pieces. Emboldened, I approached the most prestigious local venue, City Hall. They rotated local artists every few weeks. Again, the manager immediately booked me for a one-man show. Again, I painted and enjoyed the process of exhibiting.

Then the opportunity arose to co-author a book, called *Soul Medicine*, with my mentor, Dr. Norm Shealy. I decided to switch my energies and very limited free time into writing instead of painting. Halfway through the largest and most ambitious piece I'd ever painted, I laid down my brushes forever and began to write instead.

Art show invitation.

The experience was full of lessons for me. One is that our heads are full of beliefs that aren't true—in my case, things like the core belief *I'm no good at art*. Another lesson is that these core beliefs arise from early childhood experiences. They shape our entire lives, and unless we challenge them, we can spend our lives demonstrating the lies we were told as children. Most of my subsequent career has been spent helping other people identify and challenge their limiting core beliefs.

One of the friends who came to the grand opening of my City Hall exhibit was a woman named Alice. She was a fused-glass artist who had been struggling to make a living at her craft for years. Alice said to me, "I'm awed. One-person shows are impossible to get. I've never been able to land one." I didn't reply to Alice. Inside my head, I wiped my metaphorical brow and thought, *Whew, I'm glad I didn't know that. I've only had two shows. I had no idea they were hard to land.*

Another watercolor artist at the reception painted landscapes. She exclaimed, "But you paint portraits. Faces are the most difficult thing to paint in watercolor!" My mental self-talk was: *Who knew? Not me . . . Dodged another belief bullet.*

Once I disintegrated one belief, I began to disintegrate others. I began to question all the beliefs that had kept me small and limited. I began to reclaim parts of myself that I'd disowned because of the disapproval of parents, teachers, partners, and friends. I began to find out who I was and become that person, instead of confining myself to the limitations set up by the people around me.

That's what the human potential movement is all about. We have vast abilities, powers, and insights within. They may be constrained by the blindness of the people around us, but they're still there. We're much bigger than we've believed. Once we begin to take off the blinders and step into our full magnificence, we become shapers of the world around us rather than reflections of the limitations of the past.

Watercolor #21: Heart's Too Big.

Every moment is the moment you decide: Will I be that magnificence, or will I continue to pretend I'm less than what I know I am?

Imagine if I had played it safe and stuck with my trusty tried-and-true core belief I'm no good at art. Imagine if I'd consulted my experienced friends in advance and discovered that one-man shows are impossible to obtain and that faces are the most difficult thing to paint. The result would have been no art classes, no one-man shows, no explosion of creativity, perhaps no book and no life-changing career in writing and research. That's the consequence of living in the box of your old beliefs: no new mind, no new matter—instead of living in an open world of new mind, new matter.

As a thought experiment, imagine that you continue, for the rest of your life, to hold the beliefs about yourself that you hold today. That's one option at the fork in the road ahead. If you take the other direction at the fork, you challenge every limiting belief in your head and reach out far ahead for your potential. You succeed sometimes, you fail at other times, but either way you grow. You start to discover the boundaries of who you really are instead of the boundaries your teachers and parents held about you. Your new mind becomes your new matter.

You truly are at the crossroads at this very minute. Which direction will you choose? My mission in this book is to encourage you to say, "I know I have greatness in me, and I'm determined to express it fully!"

Social scientists used to believe that our personality is formed very early in life and does not change much over time. A 1989 headline in the *New York Times* proclaimed "Personality: Major Traits Found Stable through Life" (Goleman, 1987). It reported on a study showing that our core traits, such as anxiety, friendliness, and appetite for new experiences, are fixed.

The longest personality study ever conducted, however, shows that our personalities can change beyond recognition over the course of our lives (Harris, Brett, Johnson, & Deary, 2016). It began with data from a 1950 survey of 1,208 14-year-olds. Six questionnaires were used by their teachers to evaluate six personality traits.

Sixty years later, researchers tracked down the original respondents, now aged on average 77. They found that there was little overlap with their teenage selves. Where they expected to find a good deal of stability of personality traits, they were surprised to find little, with one exclaiming that "there is hardly any relationship at all" (Goldhill, 2017).

Our childhood beliefs and traits don't have to dog us through life. As we take responsibility for change and practice desirable habits of mind consistently, we can shift dramatically. The changes might not show up in a week or a month, but consistent practice over time can turn you into a completely different person.

EMOTIONS SHAPE THE WORLD AROUND US

We think of ourselves as autonomous individuals, making our own decisions and leading our own lives. In reality, we are part of a matrix of connection. We are connected to each other through our neural networks and by means of invisible energy fields.

Our thoughts and emotions are not contained within our minds and bodies. They affect people around us, often without their knowledge. Their thoughts and emotions are affecting us too—at the subconscious and unconscious levels.

Prior research has shown that brains synchronize when sharing information. When one person speaks while another listens, the brain regions active in the speaker light up in the listener too.

Biomedical engineers at Drexel University, in collaboration with psychologists at Princeton, developed a wearable brain-imaging headband to measure this phenomenon (Liu et al., 2017). It builds on work using functional magnetic resonance imaging (fMRI) to examine the activity of the language areas of the brain. Especially when the speaker is describing a vivid and emotional experience, the listener's brain activity mirrors that of the speaker.

The researchers recorded one English-speaking subject and two Turkish-speaking subjects telling a real-life story. Their brains were scanned while they were speaking. The recording was then played back to 15 English-only speakers while the investigators measured activity in the parietal and prefrontal areas of the listeners' brains. These regions are involved in our ability to discern the goals, desires, and beliefs of other people. Those areas lit up when the listeners heard the English story but not the Turkish ones. The researchers also found that the greater the degree of "coupling" between brain areas in listener and speaker, the better the degree of comprehension. This shows that the better our brains are at mirroring the experience of others, the more we understand them.

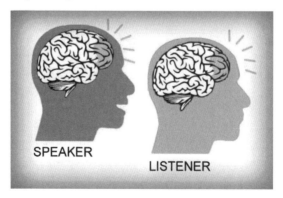

Brain coupling during communication.

ENERGY FIELDS AT A DISTANCE

Energy fields can affect others at a distance as well. Eric Leskowitz, M.D., a psychiatrist from Harvard Medical School's Spaulding Rehabilitation Hospital, visited the Institute of HeartMath in Boulder Creek, California, in 2007. While blindfolded and meditating, his heart rate and heart coherence were continuously monitored by the lab technicians.

Heart coherence is associated with increased alpha brain wave activity. It is a state in which the interval between heartbeats is regular and constant. It's produced by positive emotions such as love and compassion. Negative emotions disrupt heart coherence.

At random intervals unknown to Leskowitz, expert meditators standing behind him were given a signal to enter heart coherence themselves. As they did so, Leskowitz's heart coherence also increased (Leskowitz, 2007). Without touching him, they were able to shift his heart-brain function.

A follow-up study measured the same effect in 25 volunteers in a series of 148 ten-minute trials, and it found the same phenomenon of heart entrainment at a distance (Morris, 2010). The author stated that "a coherent energy field can be generated and/or enhanced by the intentions of small groups of participants. . . . The evidence of heart rhythm synchronization across participants supports the possibility of heart-to-heart bio-communications."

Our bodies and brains are synchronizing with people around us all the time. When we observe others being touched, our brains light up in the same way as if we were being touched (Schaefer, Heinze, & Rotte, 2012). That's because our brains contain mirror neurons that echo the sensations we're observing. These mirror neurons even fire in sympathy with facial expressions and tones of voice, indicating that we are very sensitive to both verbal and nonverbal emotional cues provided by those around us.

It is not only positive emotions that can be transmitted from person to person. Our brains are also attuned to the pain of another. Researchers in Birmingham, England, showed college students images of people suffering from localized sports injuries or from receiving injections. Almost a third of the students felt pain at the same site portrayed in the photographs they were looking at.

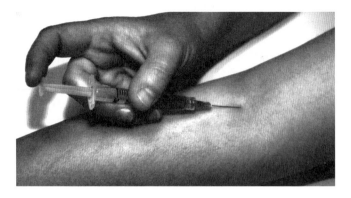

Receiving an injection.

The researchers then used an fMRI machine to compare the brains of 10 students who had felt only an emotional reaction to the images against another 10 students who had actually felt physical pain. All 20 students showed increased activity in the areas of the brain that process emotions. But only those who had actually felt the pain physically had activity in the brain regions that process pain (Osborn & Derbyshire, 2010).

As another example, babies cry not just when family members are in distress, but even when strangers are upset (Zahn-Waxler, Radke-Yarrow, Wagner, & Chapman, 1992). Their nervous systems have a high degree of entrainment with those around them, and the structures in the emotion-processing parts of their brains light up in response to the emotions of others.

EMOTIONAL CONTAGION

Emotions are contagious (Hatfield, Cacioppo, & Rapson, 1994). When your best friend laughs, you're likely to laugh along with her. When she's depressed, you're equally likely to feel blue too. Just as you can get the flu by walking into a classroom full of sick second-graders, you can pick up emotions from the people around you—for instance, walking into that classroom and feeling happy when you hear all the second-graders laughing at a joke. Emotions are contagious in the same way infectious diseases are contagious. This isn't only true of negative emotions such as fear, stress, and sadness. It is also the case for joy and contentment (Chapman & Sisodia, 2015).

Framingham is a charming New England town in Massachusetts, 19 miles from Boston. Now home to 17,000 families, it was first settled in the mid-1600s. Late in that century, Framingham received an influx of families from nearby Salem, people who were seeking to escape the infamous Salem witch trials. That part of town is still called Salem's End.

In medical literature, the town is famous for the Framingham Heart Study. In 1948, a farsighted group of researchers from the National Heart Institute set up an ambitious research project to find the cause of heart disease and stroke, both of which had been rising steadily in the first half of the century.

Framingham Common.

They recruited 5,209 Framingham residents between the ages of 30 and 62 and performed a comprehensive battery of psychological and physical tests. Subjects returned every two years for follow-up. In 1971, the study enrolled a second generation, consisting of 5,124 of the original participants' children and the children's spouses, and today many of the grandchildren and great-grandchildren of the original participants still participate.

The gold mine of data obtained by the study has enabled researchers to look at much more than heart disease. A sub-study of 4,739 people over 20 years looked at their happiness levels and how these levels affected those around them (Fowler & Christakis, 2008).

This study found that one person's happiness can boost that of another for time periods as long as a year. When a person in the Framingham social network became happy, the chances that a neighbor, spouse, sibling, or friend would become happy increased up to 34 percent. Living within a mile of a friend who became happy increased a participant's chance of happiness by 25 percent.

"You would think that your emotional state would depend on your own choices and actions and experience," observed study co-author Nicholas Christakis, a medical sociologist at Harvard University. "But it also depends on the choices and actions and experiences of other people, including people to whom you are not directly connected. Happiness is contagious." Barbara Fredrickson, the author of *Love 2.0,* calls this positivity resonance (Fredrickson, 2013). When the frequency of our consciousness is love, we naturally connect with others who resonate with that shared energy field.

THE RIPPLE EFFECT OF HAPPINESS

Not only did happy people affect those around them, but happiness also showed a ripple effect. Three degrees of separation out, people became happier. Having a friend know someone who was happy increased the chances of happiness by as much as 15 percent, and even in the next layer out, the likelihood was still 6 percent.

Negative emotions were also contagious, but not as much. Having an unhappy connection increased the chances of unhappiness by an average of 7 percent, as opposed to 9 percent for happiness.

Emotional contagion is present in groups too (Barsade, 2002). It can influence group dynamics and can lead to improved cooperation, enhanced task performance, and decreased conflict. "Emotional contagion, through its direct influence on employees' and work teams' emotions, judgments, and behaviors, can lead to subtle but important ripple effects in groups and organizations," says Sigal Barsade, author of several influential studies of emotional contagion. Positive emotion and mood in a team member, especially the leader, enhances the performance of the whole team. But stressed leaders will degrade the performance of everyone around them.

an Organizational Culture Corroded by emotional Contagion

By Stacene Courvallis

Our company manufactures specialized construction equipment, and is admired by others in our industry as an example of tightly-focused growth.

As the recent construction boom expanded, so did we. We hired a lot of new people quickly, and one of those was Wilma, a senior executive who reported to me. Her resume looked perfect, and she'd passed the interviewing process with flying colors.

Three months into her job, her performance was good, but Wilma had begun sharing concerns with me about various projects and people. A couple of other executives who usually left work early. A budget overrun in another department. An engineer with sensitive proprietary information who was friends with a peer at a competing company.

She framed her observations in terms of concern for the health of our organization, and I was grateful to her for pointing them out.

Emotional energy, whether positive or negative, spreads throughout a team.

Soon Wilma's gripe sessions became a regular part of my workload, and she continued to discover problems. She felt that the corporate culture was too lax and that the other executives didn't give me enough respect. She believed we needed to sharpen our mission statement and our goals. She believed we could downsize our workforce and increase our profit margins.

I started to wonder if there was much more wrong with the company than I had perceived, and I became suspicious of other members of the executive team. The exuberant, fun tone of our office began to erode, despite our accelerating financial success.

Then our CFO, Jason, asked for a confidential meeting with me. He told me that Wilma had been talking to him about the failings of others in the office, and Jason did not believe her concerns were warranted. As I dug deeper, I discovered a pattern. She took other executives into her confidence, smearing all the managers except the person she was talking to.

I also realized that the real problem was me. I had been sucked into Wilma's stories, and lost my own sense of trust in our people, and security in the company's direction. I had been unconsciously transmitting this to the rest of the team, leading to the loss of our emotionally uplifting organizational culture.

Some quick web searches soon revealed that this malaise had a name: emotional contagion. Unhealthy emotions can spread among people in close proximity just the way diseases spread. Our whole company had become infected.

Once I identified emotional contagion, I could see it in every organization I encountered. I went into a courtroom and felt the thick fog of discontent and unhappiness that filled the building. I went into the local music store and noticed that the smiles of employees seemed genuine, and they were truly having fun as they interacted together.

I let Wilma go late on a Friday afternoon. On Monday morning, the mood in the entire office had changed. People were relaxed once again. Our company felt like a fun and creative place to work once more. The flow of conversation was no longer guarded. Trust had returned. With the carrier of the bad feelings removed, the previous positive emotional tone quickly reasserted itself. Best of all, I felt good about myself and the company again.

EMOTIONAL CONTAGION SHAPES THE WORLD

Emotions aren't contagious just at the level of a team, family, or community. They're contagious on the much larger scale of social networks.

A massive experiment with 689,003 Facebook users found that emotional contagion doesn't even require contact between people (Kramer, Guillory, & Hancock, 2014). Entire groups of people can come into emotional coherence, and their brain waves change, potentially generating a huge combined field.

The study used an automated system to change the amount of emotional content in the news feeds of Facebook users. When user timelines were manipulated to reduce positive emotions, according to the study authors, "People produced fewer positive posts and more negative posts; when negative expressions were reduced, the opposite pattern occurred."

This demonstrates that "Emotions expressed by others on Facebook influence our own emotions, constituting experimental evidence for massive-scale contagion via social networks." It showed that nonverbal cues and personal interaction weren't necessary for emotional contagion to occur.

Though it's happening below the level of our conscious awareness, we're sharing our emotions with others all the time, including through online social networks. A study conducted by the University of Vermont found that photographs posted on Instagram reflect the mood of the person posting them. The researchers compared photos posted by depressed people with those posted by people who were not depressed. They compared 43,950 photos posted by 166 individuals. Half of these had been diagnosed with clinical depression during the previous three years (Reece & Danforth, 2017).

The investigators discovered that depressed people manipulated their photos to have darker tones. Their most popular choice of filter was one called Inkwell, which removes color and makes photos black and white. Happy people were more likely to use a filter called Valencia, which gives photos a warmer and brighter tone. Depressed people literally drained the color out of what they shared with others.

Using these color choices as a tool for diagnosing depression was successful 70 percent of the time. That's substantially higher than the 42 percent success rate of general practice doctors.

THE NUREMBERG RALLIES

The unconscious spread of negative emotions has been directing human societies for millennia, long before social media came along. It's nothing new. Examples of mass hysteria can be found throughout the pages of history. In the 1930s, Adolf Hitler staged huge rallies in Nuremberg, Germany, to whip up enthusiasm and showcase the power of Germany and the National Socialist Party to the nation and the world.

Huge banners, goose-stepping marchers, martial songs, torchlit processions, fireworks, and bonfires enthralled the hundreds of thousands of spectators. Long speeches by Adolf Hitler and other Nazi Party luminaries laid out party ideology. The emotional contagion of the spectacular events helped unite the country behind Hitler's vision.

The 1934 rally drew over a million people. The American journalist William Shirer had recently arrived to cover Germany for the Hearst newspaper group and decided to attend. In his diary, he records his impressions of his first evening in the grand medieval city. He found himself carried along in a wave of humanity. In front of the hotel where Hitler was staying, 10,000 people chanted, "We want our Führer!"

Adolf Hitler addressing the 1934 Nuremberg rally.

Shirer wrote, "I was a little shocked at the faces, especially those of the women, when Hitler finally appeared on the balcony for a moment. They reminded me of the crazed expressions I once saw in the back country of Louisiana on the faces of some Holy Rollers. . . . They looked up at him as if he were a Messiah, their faces transformed into something positively inhuman."

The following morning, Shirer attended the opening ceremony of the rally. He wrote, "I'm beginning to comprehend, I think, some of the reasons for Hitler's astounding success. . . . This morning's opening meeting . . . was more than a gorgeous show; it also had something of the mysticism and religious fervor of an Easter or Christmas Mass in a great Gothic cathedral. The hall was a sea of brightly colored flags. Even Hitler's arrival was made dramatic. The band stopped playing. There was a hush over the thirty thousand people packed in the hall. Then the band struck up the *Badenweiler March*. . . . Hitler appeared in the back of the auditorium and followed by his aides, Göring, Goebbels, Hess, Himmler, and the others, he strode slowly down the long centre aisle while thirty thousand hands were raised in salute."

To those attending, the event was intoxicating. Shirer records that "Every word dropped by Hitler seemed like an inspired Word from on high. Man's—or at least the German's—critical faculty is swept away at such moments, and every lie pronounced is accepted as high truth itself" (Shirer, 1941).

That's the power of emotional contagion. Like the reign of Hitler, the Salem witch trials, the Red Scare of the 1960s, the 1994 Rwandan genocide, the 2003 Iraq war, the Great Recession of 2007, and the North Korean nuclear standoff, such times of mass hysteria usually end badly for all concerned.

MARKET AND COMMODITY BUBBLES

Stock market bubbles are another example of emotional contagion. Investors forget the ups and downs of the business cycle in a wave of speculative buying. In 1996, Federal Reserve Board chairman Alan Greenspan called it "irrational exuberance." In his book *The Ascent of Money*, historian Niall Ferguson states, "Booms and busts are products, at root, of our emotional volatility" (Ferguson, 2008).

Ratios of the stock prices of companies relative to their income as of February 20, 2018 (Shiller, 2017). The historic median is 16, meaning that company stocks are typically valued at 16 times their historic earnings. Ratios above 16 indicate a bubble. In early 2018, the ratio stood at 33.

On October 16, 1929, Irving Fisher, an economics professor at Yale University, announced that American stock prices had "reached what looks like a permanently high plateau."

He was very wrong. The market slipped a few days later, then crashed and crashed again. Over the next three years, the market declined by 89 percent. It did not regain its 1929 level until 1954.

In seeking to explain the crash, legendary economist John Maynard Keynes was well aware of the emotional contagion that had gripped the national psyche, calling it a "failure of the immaterial devices of the mind" (Ferguson, 2008).

Bubbles have been seen throughout history. In 1634, the prices of Dutch tulip bulbs began to rise, and speculators entered the market. The Dutch tulip mania began. Some bulbs changed hands 10 times a day, at ever higher prices. By January 1637, rare tulip bulbs sold for more than the price of a house. On February 5, the bubble abruptly collapsed.

Wagon of Fools **by Hendrik Gerritsz Pot.**

The emotional contagion of tulip mania was captured in a 1637 painting by Hendrik Gerritsz Pot called *Wagon of Fools*. It depicts a group of Dutch weavers who have dropped their looms to follow a wagon topped by Flora, goddess of flowers. She carries bouquets of tulips in her arms and is accompanied by alcoholics, moneylenders, and the double-faced goddess Fortuna. The assembly is being led to their deaths in the sea.

The feelings we feel when our brain wave patterns are hijacked by emotional contagion are real. We have a spike in stress-related beta waves and a drop in alpha. It takes a strong mind to remain unaffected by the mass hysteria around us. We can't easily discern an emotion being given to us secondhand from one arising within our own neural network.

MAPPING THE ENLIGHTENED BRAIN

Historical observers have been able to describe the extremes of consciousness. The continuum ranges from the emotional contagion that drives whole civilizations to war to the enlightened states of the mystics.

Modern neuroscience, however, gives us the ability to map the neural signaling involved in consciousness and describe the signaling pathways active in the emotional brain.

When we record the brain waves of people having mystical experiences, we translate subjective states of consciousness into objective pictures of brain function. As consciousness shifts away from fear, distress, and the worries of the local mind, brain waves change. This indicates that different neural pathways are being engaged, which in turn alters the brain's electromagnetic field. Subjective feelings of inner peace can now be mapped objectively using EEGs to provide an objective picture of information flow in the brain.

During mystical experiences, mind leaves matter. Consciousness ceases to identify exclusively with the local self, and EEG readings show large flares of alpha waves as the alpha bridge is created between conscious and unconscious reality.

Consciousness then transcends attachment to the local self to merge with nonlocal mind. The EEG shows first flares and then large, steady amplitudes of delta waves, the signature wave of nonlocal mind and connection with the universal field.

When altered states are experienced, the EEG records large amplitudes of alpha, theta, and delta simultaneously. When physical healing takes place, such as the dissolution of José's tumor, flares of theta are usually evident.

In this union of local brain and nonlocal mind, a transformation occurs. Symbols such as the beings Julie saw and the crystal she received become emblems of a new personal reality that integrates local and nonlocal mind. At the conclusion of the mystical experience, the person returns to local reality. However, they are changed. They may have brought back a gift representing emotional or physical healing, such as the crystal Julie placed in her heart. The process produces a release of old stuck energy—in Julie's case, the depression that melted like raindrops and fell to the ground. They may experience physical healing, such as the disappearance of José's brain tumor.

Matter is changed by mind. Many studies show that meditators have higher volumes of brain tissue, better sleep, fewer diseases, increased immunity, enhanced emotional health, reduced inflammation, slower aging, increased intercellular communication, balanced neurotransmitters, greater longevity, and less stress.

Our transformed mental, emotional, and physical states then radiate around us. As we become happier, we affect the people we associate with. They in turn affect people around them, and the effects of mind change ripple through the community. Positive emotional contagion occurs.

Jesuit philosopher Pierre Teilhard de Chardin coined the term *noosphere*, sometimes translated as *orb of awareness*, to describe the field of consciousness produced by humankind. Include all the rest of life on Earth and you have the *psychosphere*, or orb of consciousness of everything in the field. I also use the term *emosphere* to describe the collective emotional tone of the planet.

We are part of the field of healing in the psychosphere of humankind. Our energy is out of phase with the negative emotions infecting society; we don't participate in those fields. Our change of mind has produced a new material reality, one that supports our health and spiritual transformation.

PUTTING THESE IDEAS INTO PRACTICE

Activities to practice this week:

- Practice EcoMeditation for at least 10 minutes each morning and evening.
- Foster positive emotional contagion by deliberately connecting with other people.
- Spend at least 10 minutes with your spouse at the beginning and end of each work day.
- Talk about the things your spouse wants to discuss and practice summarizing what they tell you.
- When you're in a store, look the people helping you in the eye.
- Practice smiling at other people to foster positive emotional connections.
- In your journal, note any petty annoyances that trigger you.

The Extended Play version of this chapter includes:

- Audio interview with psychiatrist Eric Leskowitz, M.D.
- The seven steps of EcoMeditation
- Emotional contagion videos
- Additional case histories and references

To access the Extended Play version, visit: MindToMatter.club/Chapter3

CHAPTER 4

How Energy Regulates DNA and the Cells of Our Bodies

You are not the same person you were a second ago, let alone yesterday. Your body is replacing cells and rejuvenating its systems at a frantic pace.

Your body contains some 37 trillion cells (Bianconi et al., 2013). That's a much bigger number than the count of galaxies in the known universe. Old cells are dying and new ones replacing them all the time. Each second, over 810,000 cells are being replaced.

Your body produces one trillion new red blood cells per day (Wahlestedt et al., 2017). That's a big number; with all its zeros it can be expressed as 1,000,000,000,000.

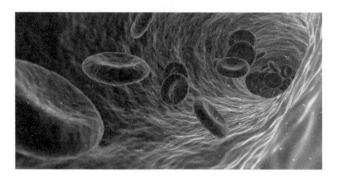

Red blood cells circulating.

As they circulate through your veins and arteries, red blood cells carry oxygen and nutrients to every other cell in your body. Each blood cell has a lifetime of about four months, after which the liver extracts its vital ingredients and sends the rest to the spleen for recycling. You don't have a single red blood cell in your body that you had six months ago. Every one has been replaced.

YOUR BODY IS CONSTANTLY REGENERATING ITSELF

The lining of your digestive tract also undergoes rapid turnover. It's replaced every four days. Your lung tissue? Every eight days. Even the densest of tissues, your bones, are constantly regenerating, with 10 percent of your skeleton being replaced each year.

There are about 84 billion neurons in the brain, along with a similar number of non-neural cells (Azevedo et al., 2009). Our brains are growing new neural cells continuously, and each cell can connect with thousands of others, weaving an interconnected web of an estimated 150 trillion synapses (Sukel, 2011). Our brains are replacing at least one neuron per second (Walløe, Pakkenberg, & Fabricius, 2014).

The hippocampus is the part of the brain responsible for memory and learning. It's constantly adding new neurons and synapses while pruning others. Some neural pathways are shrinking, and the volume of those parts of the hippocampus diminishes. Other neural pathways are growing, with their volume expanding.

When a patient has a liver transplant, half the liver of the donor is typically removed and transplanted into the body of the new host. Yet so fast do liver cells regenerate that within eight weeks the donor's liver has grown back to its original size (Nadalin et al., 2004). The oldest cell now in your liver is about five months old

Cell Type	Turnover Time	BNID
blood neutrophils	1-5 days	101940
bone osteoblasts	3 months	109907
bone osteoclasts	2 weeks	109906
cardiomytes	0.5-10% per year	107076, 107077, 107078
cervix	6 days	11032
colon lining cells	3-4 days	107812
fat cells	8 years	103455
Intestine Paneth cells	20 days	107812
lens cells	lifetime	109840
liver hepatocyte cells	0.5-1 year	109233
lungs alveoli	8 days	101940
oocytes (female gametes)	lifetime	111451
pancreas beta cells (rat)	20-50 days	109228
platelets	10 days	111407, 111408
red blood cells	4 months	101706, 107875
skeleton	10% per year	107076, 107077, 107078
skin epidermis cells	10-30 days	109214, 109215
small intestine epithelium	2-4 days	107812, 109231
sperm (male gametes)	2 months	110319, 110320
stem cells	2 months	109232
stomach	2-9 days	101940
tongue taste buds (rat)	10 days	111427
trachea	1-2 months	101940
white blood cells Eosinophils	2-5 days	109901, 109902

The regeneration of cells occurs at different rates in different tissues. This table shows the renewal rates of some of these. The acronym BNID refers to the Harvard University Database of Useful Biological Numbers.

Even the heart regenerates. Until very recently, scientists believed that the heart does not regenerate and that once heart cells have died, they are not replaced. But recent research shows that heart tissue contains regions of stem cells that are available to replace damaged or dead cells and that the entire heart regenerates at least three times in the course of a person's life (Laflamme & Murry, 2011).

The corneal cells on the surface of your eye can regenerate within 24 hours. Your skin is being entirely replaced every month. The lining of your stomach is renewing itself every week and your colon even faster. The self you were yesterday is not the self you are today.

Cell division.

Welcome to the new you!

This continual turnover of the fundamental building blocks of our bodies has profound implications for how quickly and completely we can heal.

Our bodies are programmed to heal. Healing is not something we get from a prescription, a doctor, an herb, or an alternative therapist. Healing is what our bodies do naturally and normally every second of every day. The deeper our understanding of the healing process, the better equipped we are to turn mind to matter.

YOUR BODY USES THE MATERIAL YOU MAKE AVAILABLE TO IT

When you look in the mirror each morning, you might believe you're seeing yesterday's face staring back at you. But during the previous day, your body replaced some 60 billion cells. You're a different physical being than you were the day before.

This extensive daily remodeling of the body isn't happening in a vacuum. You are shaping the quality of cells your body produces with material inputs such as the food you eat and the water you drink. When you eat high-quality food, your body has the raw materials with which to create high-quality proteins, the molecular building blocks of cells.

When you eat low-quality food, the body only has substandard materials out of which to fashion new proteins. When your food lacks vital nutrients, your body is forced to make compromises, and those trade-offs can eventually damage your health.

Most of us know to choose healthy food and not eat junk, yet we're often much less discriminating about the energy we absorb.

Think of your body as a factory and the cells it produces as cars. If the finest steel is being delivered to its loading docks by freight companies, and it has excellent glass, flexible rubber, and advanced composites at its disposal, the factory can build high-quality cars.

But if the rubber is brittle or the glass opaque or the steel weak, the final product is compromised. The factory can't build excellent cars out of shoddy ingredients. If the matter going in is inadequate, the matter emerging from your body's manufacturing cycle will be of poor quality. Garbage in, garbage out.

That's the matter end of the equation. What about energy?

CELLS REGENERATE IN A FIELD

Cells also replicate in an energy environment. Just as poor-quality matter is going to produce poor-quality cells, inferior energy is going to result in inferior molecules. Energy fields bathe our bodies, and the type of energy in which cell regeneration takes place determines the biological outcome.

Right now, I'm enjoying a delicious cup of Earl Grey tea. I went to the kitchen, popped a tea bag into a cup, filled the cup with the tangy water from my well, and put the cup inside the microwave. I set the timer for two minutes, sufficient to bring the water to a boil.

Though they're invisible, the waves inside the microwave oven caused the water in my teacup to change state. In two minutes, the water went from a room temperature of 70°F to boiling, 212°F. Matter was changed by energy.

In the same way, our cells are bathed in the surrounding energy fields. These fields change the matter of our cells, even though they're invisible. Strong radiation, such as that released in nuclear reactor disasters, can cause cells to mutate.

What happens when your cells are bathed in the energy of love, appreciation, and kindness created by a vibrant and coherent brain? Just the opposite. They're nurtured in the radiant fields of positive emotion.

Here is one of my favorite healing stories. Glenda Payne faced a truly desperate situation as her body began to degenerate. How she used her mind to save herself has inspired thousands of people.

From Terminal Muscular Degeneration to Dancing around the Room

By Glenda Payne

I had a job I loved. I was the wholesale program manager for a greenhouse manufacturing company. I was just expanding our market into France when I began to notice strange symptoms. Climbing the stairs was becoming more and more of a struggle. I would feel as though I had just run a mile up a steep hill. My thigh muscles would hardly lift my legs. By the time I reached the top stair, I would be gasping for breath.

Despite taking time off to rest, I found that the muscle pain and weakness escalated, with a frightening new symptom: terrible shortness of breath leading to blackouts. Simple activities such as hand-washing dishes, standing in line at a public counter, or pushing a grocery cart would leave me in an embarrassed heap on the floor, desperately gasping for breath and fighting blackout. One afternoon, I was standing in the office talking with a co-worker and

I helplessly slid to the floor, lost in a black tunnel. After that, I could no longer drive. I never went back to work again.

My doctors could find no explanation. After five years of expensive tests, going to specialist after specialist, I finally got a diagnosis: a rare condition called mitochondrial inclusion body myositis. I was told there was nothing they could do for me.

My life spiraled down into one of hopeless despair. I was ready to give up. My world was reduced to my living room couch or my bed.

One spring, my sister shared a five-minute video demonstration of EFT tapping. We became hooked on tapping. That summer, we heard Dawson Church interview Dr. Joe Dispenza in a webinar.

In the interview, Dr. Dispenza related his own medical miracle story. He had been a professional bicycle racer. During an event, he was directly hit by a large truck as he was navigating a turn. His injuries were serious, with little hope that he would recover enough to walk again. He shared how he used his mind to communicate to the nerves and cells of his body while he was strapped to a bed, utterly motionless. He projected an image of his healthy body into what he called the unified field of consciousness. It worked.

As I lay there in my constant state of painful, exhausted fatigue, I latched onto the hope that if he could find full recovery, I could too!

Dawson worked with me on a live call during that same webinar. Hearing Dr. Dispenza's story and tapping with Dawson for a few minutes on that call changed my life. My sister and I both knew that tapping was helping us clear major issues we'd been plagued with our whole lives. We chose to pursue certification.

In October, we enrolled in our first certification class with Dawson. He worked with me again in a demonstration. At the end of the four-day workshop, I approached Dawson with the words, "Notice what's missing?" I dropped my cane and proceeded to dance in front of the whole room. I had arrived at the hotel for that workshop in a wheelchair. I left dancing. I haven't used my scooter since that day.

In the three years since I first listened to that interview with Joe and Dawson, I've completed my EFT practitioner certification program, simultaneously completed energy psychology certification, written and published a book, and completed an initiation as a shaman. I'm currently working on material for a second book and a blog.

I still have good days and bad days. I still need lots of rest. My cane is still my companion on most outings, though I find I am using it less and less. I am able to go on hikes again, though they are brief, of short distance, and must be on level ground. Inclines can still do me in. And I have to plan at least one full day of rest after. I've learned to listen to my body.

Glenda four years later.

The happier I get using all of the tools now available to me, the happier my body is too, and the more activity I can handle. I have turned what was once a hopeless existence full of lonely despair into a life of joyful inspiration. I enjoy whatever life chooses to offer me in each moment.

I have a limited, part-time practice, but the people I work with provide the impetus to continue being kind to my body. A well-rested me can be more available to my clients and my readers. *I love this work!* I hope that one day my story will prove to be as life-changing and inspirational to them as hearing Dr. Joe's story was to me.

WHEN SERIOUS DISEASES SIMPLY DISAPPEAR

I believe that many cases of remission from serious diseases are influenced by mental fields. The bodies of these people are being bathed in positivity while the cells are replicating and growing. When every one of those 810,000 new cells that your body creates each second is born in an energetic environment of kindness and love, it shapes their development.

When we create mental, emotional, and spiritual fields of love and kindness, we provide a healthy energetic ecosystem in which our bodies regenerate.

The spontaneous remission of cancer without treatment has historically been viewed by the medical profession as a rare phenomenon. One of the first authors to make an estimate stated that it probably happened in 1 out of every 80,000 cases (Boyd, 1966). A contemporary estimate was 1 in 100,000 cases (Boyers, 1953).

Modern studies, however, are discovering that remission is common. One found that about a fifth of breast cancers are healed by mind and body without the need for medical intervention (Zahl, Mæhlen, & Welch, 2008). Others report a similar percentage of patients healing spontaneously from a type of cancer that affects white blood cells (Krikorian, Portlock, Cooney, & Rosenberg, 1980). A bibliography of medical reports of spontaneous remission found over 3,000 cases reported in the medical literature (O'Regan & Hirshberg, 1993).

The spread of cancer requires signaling and cooperation between groups of cancer cells. This signaling is triggered by stress (Wu, Pastor-Pareja, & Xu, 2010). Adrenaline, also called epinephrine, is one of our two main stress hormones, the other being cortisol. High levels of adrenaline trigger the spread of ovarian cancer cells far away from the primary tumor. They also activate an enzyme called FAK that inhibits the destruction of cancer cells and hastens death (Sood et al., 2010). A different enzyme, one that destroys prostate and breast cancer cells, is immobilized by adrenaline (Sastry et al., 2007).

When we lower our stress levels, we reverse these effects, sometimes quickly. Researchers report tumors shrinking to less than half their original size within a few hours of an emotional healing session (Ventegodt, Morad, Hyam, & Merrick, 2004). Among those who experience spontaneous remission or survive much longer than usual after a diagnosis, a change in worldview is common. They become more altruistic in their relationships with others and actively involve themselves in their treatment (Frenkel et al., 2011). Anandamide, the "bliss molecule" generated by meditation, also inhibits the formation of cancer cells. As mind changes, so does matter.

Altruism and connection with others are hallmarks of those who heal.

The Shrinking Tumors

Energy healing researcher Bill Bengston, whom you read about in a previous chapter, was the subject of several randomized controlled trials in which he and his graduate students were consistently able to heal cancerous tumors in mice. He then began to apply his method to people. The following story is an example of the healing that can occur when cells are bathed in positive energy fields (Bengston, 2010).

One of Bill's students, Laurie, was diagnosed with terminal breast cancer. It had spread first to her lymph nodes and then metastasized throughout her body. She was given four months to live. Bill recounts:

> "Against all advice, she opted to be treated by me. . . . For two months I treated Laurie six days a week, sometimes many hours a day. So intense was the process that I developed alarming lumps in my own armpits and groin, which disappeared when I physically disconnected from her.
>
> "The usual medical tests administered by her doctors, including X-rays, blood work, and CAT scans, showed her tumors to be shrinking. Eventually, they disappeared. . . . Laurie and I celebrated the fifth and tenth anniversary of her remaining cancer-free."

The invisible microwaves of kindness might be bathing the regenerating cells of the bodies of people like Laurie to produce healing. When those 810,000 cells that are being created by our bodies every second are marinating in the energy of positive emotion, they're being shaped by the field.

When our consciousness shifts, and we begin to make deliberate changes, as Glenda and Laurie did, we change the character of the energy in which our new cells are being formed. Maintain those positive mental states for a few weeks and trillions of new cells have now been shaped by them.

Let's now look at the direct evidence for the influence of human-generated energy on cell formation.

ENERGY GUIDES CELL FORMATION

As researchers have exposed cell cultures to ranges of frequencies, they have shown that some are particularly beneficial to the growth of certain types of cells. Some of the frequencies that stimulate the growth of healthy cells are the very frequencies generated by our brains. The electromagnetic fields of our brains, generated by our consciousness, may produce direct effects on cellular regeneration.

Most of the signals to which our cells are most sensitive are at the very lower end of the frequency spectrum. These microcurrents aren't involved in carrying energy. Instead, they carry information (Foletti, Ledda, D'Emilia, Grimaldi, & Lisi, 2011).

Cells are typically sensitive to very narrow frequency bands. These are called frequency windows because cells will respond to frequencies in these narrow ranges but not to those above or below that range.

Frequency windows are the narrow bands of energy to which particular cells respond.

A review of 175 papers published in the scientific literature from 1950 to 2015 found that certain frequencies triggered cell regeneration and repair. In the words of the authors, "Waves affect cells . . . only at specific frequencies, being separated by wide ranges of non-effective frequencies" (Geesink & Meijer, 2016, p. 110). These frequencies are similar to a musical scale, with harmonic resonance between frequencies on the scale, just as there are in a pleasing chord played on the piano. The authors listed the physical effects that various frequencies exert:

- Stimulate the formation of nerve cells and synapses
- Repair spinal cord tissue
- Reduce the symptoms of Parkinson's disease
- Inhibit the growth of cancer cells
- Improve memory
- Synchronize the firing of neurons in different parts of the brain
- Increase attention

- Speed wound healing
- Decrease the activity of inflammatory cells
- Increase bone regeneration
- Reduce the degeneration of nerves in diabetics
- Trigger the expression of beneficial genes
- Promote the growth of connective tissue like ligaments and tendons
- Increase the amount of stem cells circulating in the body
- Stimulate stem cells to differentiate into muscle, bone, and skin
- Enhance the activity of white blood cells in the immune system
- Catalyze the synthesis of growth hormone
- Regulate free radicals (oxygen atoms regarded as the primary cause of aging)
- Repair heart muscle by inducing cells to assemble and graft onto damaged tissue

BIOMARKERS AS INDICATORS OF HEALTH

As we look at the fascinating research showing the effect of energy fields on cells, you'll be captivated by the healing potential of this work. You'll see the possibility of radically improving your health and that of the people around you.

You'll also notice that there are several common biological markers that scientists examine. These include gene expression, growth hormone (GH) levels, aging markers called telomeres, and numbers of circulating stem cells. The reason researchers use these biomarkers is that they correlate with the activation of our immune and inflammation systems.

Healthy activities reduce inflammation and boost immunity. The goal for health is to have a highly functional immune system and as little systemic inflammation in the body as possible.

Stem cells are "blank" cells that can turn into any other type of cell. They circulate through the body, and when we need to repair skin cells from a cut on our finger or lung tissue damaged by smoke, stem cells turn themselves into whatever specific type of cell is required. They can change into bone cells, muscle cells, lung cells, or skin cells, depending on the body's needs. Their versatility makes stem cells extremely important to healing, and researchers use a count of their numbers as a proxy for how effectively an immune system is functioning.

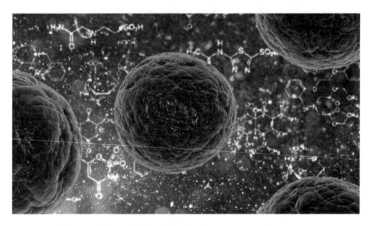

**Stem cells are "blank" cells that can turn into any
other type of cell as required by the body.**

Another common substance of interest is growth hormone, or GH. Though the word *growth* is in its name, that doesn't mean it makes us grow larger. GH repairs and regenerates our cells. When we sleep, we typically produce more GH as our bodies repair the tissues damaged by the day's activities. To keep our bodies young, healthy, and strong, we need high levels of GH. Patients whose vitality is depleted often have low levels of GH. So if a treatment produces a higher concentration of GH, it's beneficial to our system.

Oxidative stress is another common focus of research. Though the type of oxygen we breathe in the air is stable, that's because it is composed of two oxygen atoms bonded together (O_2). However, single oxygen atoms, unpaired with a second atom, damage our cells. They're called free radicals. Oxidative stress, the product of free radicals, is regarded as the most universal cause of aging.

Another much-studied molecule is telomerase. Telomeres are the endcaps of the chromosomes in our cells, and they shorten slightly every time a cell divides. Telomerase is an enzyme that adds DNA molecules to the ends of telomeres. As we grow older, the chains of DNA in the telomeres on the ends of our chromosomes decline at a rate of about one percent a year. This makes telomere length an extremely stable marker of biological aging.

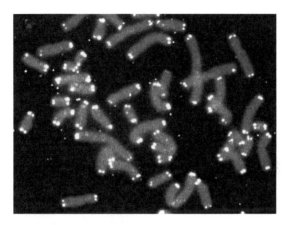

The bright spots at the ends of the chromosomes are telomeres.

When people are stressed, their cells die more quickly because of the wear and tear on their molecules. To replace the cells killed by stress, the body's cells have to divide more often to make replacements. As cells divide more frequently, their telomeres shorten more quickly. Stressed people lose telomere length fast, while healthy people have long telomeres. This is one reason why stressed people die at younger ages than those who know how to relax. Scientists can tell our biological age from the length of our telomeres, making this a popular genetic test.

BRAIN WAVES AS WINDOWS TO THE MIND

There are thousands of studies showing the energy field frequency windows that affect cells and molecules. What I'm particularly interested in is the frequencies generated by our own brain waves, especially delta, theta, alpha, and gamma. That's because these are naturally occurring frequencies in our bodies. As our brain frequencies change, they affect our cells. I'm fascinated by how we can change our cellular environment using our own naturally generated brain waves.

When in my trainings I teach people to meditate and tap, their levels of these four brain waves increase. They are frequencies you can induce yourself—no medications, herbs, beliefs, or mind-altering substances required!

A century of study has demonstrated that our brains produce the energy fields we measure as brain waves. It's also shown that mental states such as the ones we generate during meditation and tapping produce unique energy fields. Very slow waves like delta, theta, and alpha, as well as very fast waves like gamma, change dramatically when we induce these states of mind. As we examine the research associated with each of the five brain wave frequencies, from slowest to fastest, you'll notice an exciting range of healing events associated with each.

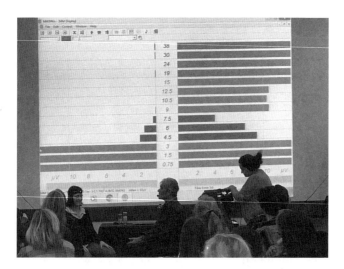

A conference participant hooked up to an EEG during a live therapy session. The entire audience can see her brain waves.

Delta

The slowest brain wave, delta, from 0 to 4 Hz, is associated with many beneficial changes in living tissues. Key studies of normal brains have pointed to some of the links between healing and frequencies in the 0–4 Hz range.

A group of sleep investigators hooked men up to EEG monitors before they went to bed in order to study sleep patterns (Gronfier et al., 1996). In addition to the EEG readings, growth hormone levels were measured every 10 minutes. The researchers found that when delta waves were at their peak in the brain, the secretion levels of GH were highest.

In a different group of men of a wide range of ages, from teenagers to octogenarians, an association was found between delta and GH production (Van Cauter, Leproult, & Plat, 2000). Production of both of these declined progressively, the older the men were. GH is synthesized during periods of delta wave sleep.

Ahmed and Wieraszko (2008) took slices of live tissue from the hippocampus, the part of the brain that governs memory and learning. They found that a very low frequency in the delta band, 0.16 Hz, increases activity in the synaptic connections between neurons in the hippocampus. This suggests that memory and learning may be enhanced by delta activity.

Researchers from Washington University School of Medicine in St. Louis, Missouri, looked at beta-amyloids, sticky plaques between neurons in the brain characteristic of Alzheimer's disease (Kang et al., 2009). They found that during sleep, when brains are primarily in theta and delta brain wave states, beta-amyloid production in the brain ceases, and toxic material is cleared away. The effect was greater in deep sleep, the phase of sleep in which our brains are in delta.

When analyzing RNA and five proteins that are involved in the production of telomerase, a group of researchers found peak resonance in these molecules in the frequency bands of 0.19 and 0.37 Hz (Cosic, Cosic, & Lazar, 2015). What is striking about this study is that other frequencies did not affect telomerase. The molecule was exquisitely sensitive to just a tiny frequency window within delta.

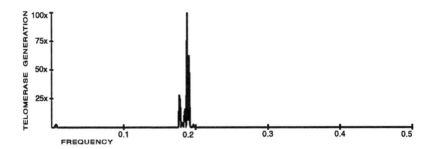

**The resonant peaks for 10 telomere sequences clustered
around a frequency window of 0.19 Hz.**

A research team inspired by the work of Marko Markoff, who has published more than 100 scientific reports on biological electromagnetism, found that delta frequencies between 0.5 Hz and 3 Hz stimulate the regeneration of nerve cells (Sisken, Midkiff, Tweheus, & Markov, 2007).

Delta is the wave that we see in EEG readouts when people are having a sense of connection with the infinite. They typically report mystical experiences in which the local self merges with the nonlocal self. Meditators with large amplitudes of delta feel connected to all of nature, to other human beings, and to the infinite. They lose the sense of being an isolated individual, or what Albert Einstein called the delusion of separateness. Instead, they experience oneness with all that is.

When our brains are producing delta, we are bathing our cells in a frequency that has the potential to produce a whole gamut of beneficial physiological changes at the level of our cells, from growing our telomeres and boosting our GH levels to regenerating our neurons and sweeping our brains clear of beta-amyloid plaques. We are not just having a nice subjective experience; in the delta state, we are creating an objective energy environment in which our bodies thrive.

People who are in transcendent states, experiencing oneness with nonlocal mind, show large amplitudes of delta brain waves.

Theta

Theta is the second slowest brain wave, with oscillations ranging from 4 to 8 Hz. It's the frequency most commonly observed in healers. Becker (1990) found that when healers were in the midst of an energy healing session, theta was the most common wave in their brains. Before starting the healing session, they might have had high beta or delta or other brain wave patterns indicative of ordinary consciousness, but once they placed their hands on or near a sick person and began the healing encounter, they reverted to theta.

This was true regardless of which healing school they belonged to or what set of beliefs they held. Some were qigong masters. Others were Native American shamans. Some were kabbalistic practitioners. Still others were Christian faith healers. Regardless of affiliation, their brains went into theta when they immersed themselves in the healing state (Kelly, 2011).

Healing session.

Theta is associated with many beneficial changes in the body. A group of researchers studied the effect of various frequencies on DNA repair. They found that electromagnetic fields between 7.5 Hz and 30 Hz were able to enhance molecular bonding (Tekutskaya, Barishev, & Ilchenko, 2015). Within that range, 9 Hz proved most effective.

There are many studies of human and animal cartilage cells, because repair of these cells is essential to wellness, as anyone who has had a sprained ankle or a pulled ligament can attest. A research group using pulsing electromagnets found that human cartilage cells are regenerated by the frequency of 6.4 Hz, right in the middle of the theta band (Sakai, Suzuki, Nakamura, Norimura, & Tsuchiya, 1991). This frequency also increases the activity of antioxidants, the molecules that neutralize the free radicals regarded as the most common cause of aging.

A research group at the Toho University School of Medicine in Japan looked at the EEG signatures of subjects practicing deep abdominal breathing. They found that their levels of the "feel-good" neurotransmitter serotonin rose, and theta as well as alpha and delta waves increased (Fumoto, Sato-Suzuki, Seki, Mohri, & Arita, 2004). Another study found that frequencies alternating between 5 Hz and 10 Hz produced a large reduction in lower back pain in 17 patients (Lee et al., 2006).

A pair of Russian scientists examined the effect of frequencies between 5.5 Hz and 16.5 Hz on DNA in a water solution. They found that the molecules were most highly stimulated at 9 Hz and that the effect was more than twice as great as it was on the untreated control molecules (Tekutskaya & Barishev, 2013).

Alpha

If you've undergone neurofeedback or biofeedback training, you've heard a lot about alpha. These trainings are designed to educate you to induce an alpha brain wave state at will. Alpha oscillates at 8 to 13 Hz.

Alpha is right in the middle of the frequency bands, between beta and gamma above and theta and delta below. Legendary brain pioneer Maxwell Cade believed that alpha serves as a bridge between the upper and lower frequencies. Beta reflects the activity of the conscious mind, while theta and delta represent the subconscious and unconscious minds. Cade believed that the alpha bridge connects the conscious mind with both the intuitive wisdom of the unconscious and the nonlocal resource of the universal field. A truly integrated person is able to generate large amplitudes of alpha.

It turns out that alpha also does good things for our bodies. It improves our levels of mood-enhancing neurotransmitters such as serotonin. When the alpha brain wave level increased in a group of exercisers, they gained a boost in serotonin, and their emotional state was elevated (Fumoto et al., 2010). In another study, Zen meditators received the same benefits from cultivating an alpha state (Yu et al., 2011).

Meditation produces beneficial changes in brain waves. The "alpha bridge" is the key to connecting our conscious minds with our unconscious resources.

A pioneering study exposed DNA to various frequencies. It found that the alpha frequency of 10 Hz resulted in significantly increased synthesis of the DNA molecule (Takahashi, Kaneko, Date, & Fukada, 1986).

Neurons in the brain's hippocampus also fire in this range (4–12 Hz), and at 10 Hz and higher frequencies, the synapses in the learning and memory circuits of the brain are enhanced (Tang et al., 1999). Other regions of the brain also use the 8–10 Hz band to communicate, with their neurons oscillating at those frequencies (Destexhe, McCormick, & Sejnowski, 1993).

Alpha, therefore, tunes the brain to peak performance, as well as facilitating gene expression and improving mood. The expansive emotional feelings reported by meditators after their regular sessions aren't simply subjective self-assessments. They are objective biological facts that can be measured in DNA, neurotransmitters, and brain waves.

Beta

Beta waves range from 13 to 25 Hz. There are two types of beta, and many modern researchers split beta into two different types of wave. Low beta, from 13 to 15 Hz, is also called SMR, which is short for sensorimotor rhythm. It's associated with the body's housekeeping functions.

High beta ranges from 15 to 25 Hz. It's always present in the thinking brain but increases when we focus on a task. Look up the route to a destination on your smartphone, write a blog post, take a language class, or cook with a complicated recipe, and your brain's amplitude of high beta increases.

Stress results in abnormally large amplitudes of high beta. When you're arguing with a friend, under an impossible deadline at work, hearing scary sounds in a dark house at night, remembering a childhood trauma, or thinking negative thoughts, your brain kicks into high beta. It's the signature brain wave of stress. It's associated with a rise in cortisol and adrenaline and a large number of adverse reactions in your body. Fear and anxiety produce high beta, and it inhibits many beneficial cellular functions. Your body ages much faster when your brain is bathed in high beta waves.

Gamma

Gamma is the most recently discovered brain wave. It is associated with the integration of information from all of the brain's regions, as well as with coherence as they all synchronize (Gray, 1997). Imagine having a flash of insight about a problem that has been bothering you for weeks. Imagine the satisfaction of doing a difficult task perfectly. Think about the synchronized brain function of a child at play, an artist painting, or a composer writing a masterpiece. That's gamma. It starts where beta leaves off, at 25 Hz, and goes up to 100 Hz and above.

Researchers build an extremely low-frequency electromagnetic field generating system using a transformer, multimeter, solenoids coils, teslameter, and probe (Razavi, Salimi, Shahbazi-Gahrouei, Karbasi, & Kermani, 2014).

A team led by Li-Huei Tsai of MIT tested the effect of gamma waves on Alzheimer's disease. They had mice run a maze while they recorded the brain waves in the hippocampus, which is responsible for navigation and memory. When a mouse hit a dead end, its brain would display a sharp burst of gamma. The brains of mice genetically engineered to be prone to Alzheimer's didn't react the same way. They produced less gamma, with poor synchronization between groups of neurons.

The researchers then flashed light into the brains of the mice at a gamma frequency of 40 Hz. In just an hour, the levels of beta-amyloid decreased by half. "We were very, very surprised," says Tsai (Iaccarino et al., 2016).

Looking for a mechanism, she found that gamma had mobilized a class of brain cells called microglia. These are the scavengers of the brain, gobbling up malformed proteins and dead cells. After exposure to gamma, the size and number of the microglia doubled as they began to scoop up the beta-amyloid plaques.

Vikaas Sohal of the University of California says, "If gamma oscillations are part of the software of the brain, this study suggests that running the software can alter the hardware" (Yong, 2016).

A pilot study that used light to stimulate the hippocampi of five patients with the cognitive decline characteristic of Alzheimer's found that their symptoms improved (Saltmarche, Naeser, Ho, Hamblin, & Lim, 2017). Newer versions of this technology combine both 10 Hz (alpha) and 40 Hz (gamma) stimulation (Lim, 2014, 2017).

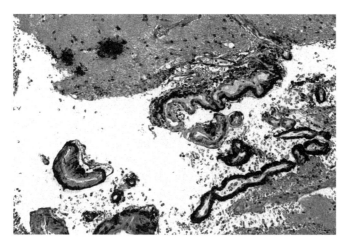

Alzheimer's disease produces plaques in the
brain that impede neural signaling.

Gamma is associated with many other beneficial changes in our bodies. A frequency of 75 Hz is epigenetic, triggering the genes that produce anti-inflammatory proteins in the body (De Girolamo et al., 2013). On the lower end of the gamma spectrum, a frequency of 50 Hz results in the body increasing its production of stem cells, the "blank" cells that differentiate into muscle, bone, skin, or whatever other specialized cells are required (Ardeshirylajimi & Soleimani, 2015). The frequency of 60 Hz regulates the expression of stress genes, those that code for stress hormones like cortisol. The same frequency also activates a key gene called Myc that in turn regulates around 15 percent of all the other genes in the body (Lin, Goodman, & Shirley-Henderson, 1994).

High beta, the signature brain wave of a stressed-out consciousness, actually suppresses DNA synthesis. When bone cells were exposed to a beta frequency of 25 Hz, it inhibited their growth. Gamma frequencies of 75 Hz or more, however, increased their growth. A peak was reached at 125 Hz, with that frequency producing three times the growth rate of the beta frequency (Ying, Hong, Zhicheng, Xiauwei, & Guoping, 2000).

The previous studies are suggestive rather than definitive, because in many of them, the frequencies were produced by external devices such as pulsed electromagnetic field (PEMF) machines. Others, such as those linking brain waves to cell changes, demonstrate association between the two phenomena rather than causation.

The big picture, however, is that our bodies are sensitive to the frequencies generated by our brains, from the slowest waves of delta to the fastest waves of gamma, and that by understanding these links, we can use our brain waves to heal our cells.

MIND CHANGE = FIELD CHANGE = CELL CHANGE

The sheer number and variety of cell changes associated with brain waves is remarkable. Armed with the knowledge that the brain waves we generate are producing massive shifts in our body moment by moment, how can we nudge the process in the direction of optimal health?

Studies show that many spiritual practices change brain waves. Mindfulness produces a host of beneficial changes in brain waves. A meta-analysis including 56 papers and a total of 1,715 subjects found increased alpha and theta waves (Lomas, Ivtzan, & Fu, 2015). Other research shows that heart coherence produces alpha and gamma even while it calms the anxiety bands of beta (Kim, Rhee, & Kang, 2013). When you practice mindfulness meditation for just three months, you start to grow your telomeres (Jacobs et al., 2011).

Research I've done at Joe Dispenza's advanced workshops shows that thousands of people are routinely able to increase their levels of delta and gamma (Church, Yang, Fannin, & Blickheuser, 2016). I've hooked up meditators to EEG monitors at my EcoMeditation workshops and observed increases in gamma, alpha, theta, and delta brain waves while the monkey mind characteristics of beta disappear.

EEG expert Laura Eichman talked about what she observed in one participant at a workshop: "The changes I saw in Stephanie's brain waves were typical of everyone we measured. Ten minutes into the EcoMeditation exercise, people tune in to their heart energy and send it out to connect with someone else. I saw a huge increase in Stephanie's delta amplitude, and shortly after that, her gamma. Her higher gamma frequency bands were riding on her low delta.

"I had the screen readout on a standard 10-millivolt setting, which is fine to measure the usual brain activity. But Stephanie's brain was producing so much delta that I had to adjust the window all the way out to 20 millivolts. That still wasn't enough, I had to go out progressively further, to 30 and then to 40 millivolts to capture her brain activity.

"This link between the high and low frequency bands—delta and gamma—is one we've seen a few times in healers and psychics. Afterward, I asked Stephanie about her experience. It matched her brain map. She reported an 'inner knowing' that she was filled with light."

EcoMeditation combines tapping, mindfulness, heart coherence, and neurofeedback in a simple yet elegant package that integrates the benefits of all those methods. All of these are ways we can shift the energy fields in which our cells are reproducing.

The magic pill to increase well-being and happiness.

If I offered you a pill that could increase your levels of circulating stem cells, lengthen your telomeres, dissipate beta-amyloid plaques in your brain, improve your memory and attention levels, boost your serotonin, repair your DNA, regulate inflammation, boost your immune system, repair your skin, bone, cartilage, and muscle cells, power up your GH levels for cell repair, and enhance the neural connections in your brain, how much would you pay for it?

Though it's priceless, it's all free. EcoMeditation has been free on the Internet for over a decade. I've taught it to thousands of people all over the world. It's ironic that what might be the biggest medical breakthrough of our generation is freely available to everyone, from the poorest to the richest.

All of the beneficial brain wave states are available to us by simply touching our screens and following simple instructions. As we make this choice, our fields change, and the 810,000 cells that our bodies are creating each second are bathed in the health-promoting waves coming from our very own brains.

YOUR IDEAL BRAIN WAVE RECIPE

There are an infinite number of possible brain wave states. There is a brain wave state that you are accustomed to being in every day. It is the one your regular mental function produces. That's the way your very own personal brain processes information. It feels familiar to you, because you have a set range for the amplitude of each wave in which your brain normally functions. You are accustomed to a certain amplitude of beta relative to theta, alpha, and delta.

Your personal brain wave ratio is like a recipe. Your habitual mix is like the food you eat most frequently. You are familiar with the smell, taste, and texture of the dish, and you hardly notice you are eating it.

A peak state is different. It's like a gourmet meal with exquisite brain waves as the ingredients. Add more delta, and you feel one with the universe. Add more theta, and you experience a wave of healing. Increase the amplitude of alpha, and your conscious and subconscious minds start communicating with one another.

Perhaps your personal everyday recipe (expressed in μV, or microvolts) is this:

- Beta: 20
- Alpha: 25
- Theta: 30
- Delta: 100

That's a fairly normal set of numbers. There's nothing wrong with it, and most people's brains are somewhere in that range every day.

When you have a peak experience, the numbers change. The recipe your brain experiences when you enter an elevated state is different. Alpha swells from your usual 25 to 60 μV. Worry-driven beta shrinks from 20 μVto 5. Theta and delta balloon to 50 μV and 200 μV respectively. You have a profound inner experience of connection with the infinite field and feel one with all beings. This might be triggered by an experience such as:

- The first day of spring
- An inspirational movie
- Your favorite song
- A baby grasping your finger
- A foot massage
- A tender moment with a friend
- An inspirational talk
- Running a mile
- Receiving applause after a speech
- The perfect cup of coffee
- A new book from your favorite author
- Completing a long-overdue task
- Contemplating open space after throwing out clutter
- A smile from a stranger
- Dunking a basketball in the hoop
- Witnessing the birth of a puppy
- A perfect sunset
- Falling in love
- A walk on the beach

By accident, triggered by an external stimulus, you've experienced a new brain wave recipe, and it feels great. If at that moment of peak experience, I had you hooked up to an EEG, your brain wave recipe might look like this:

- Beta: 5
- Alpha: 60
- Theta: 50
- Delta: 200

Look at how different those numbers are from your everyday recipe. All that high-stress beta has disappeared. Your alpha has flared way up, as have theta and delta. You have a completely different ratio of waves as your brain processes information in a new way.

When we take a bite of a gourmet recipe, our palate is startled by how delicious the food is. We savor each mouthful. The recipe is unfamiliar and exotic. In the same way, the ratio of brain waves we experience during a peak state is one that is not familiar to us. It's special.

We might call it being in the zone or a transcendent state, or on a high or in an altered state, or channeling a discarnate being, or falling in love, or having a visitation by an angel, or feeling euphoric, or touching heaven, or living a magic moment, or having a peak experience, or seeing a spirit guide. Whatever label we give it, we recognize this novel experience as being special. We're sampling a recipe that is much more delicious than our normal fare. It doesn't feel like us, which is why we might think it's a divine visitation or a personality separate from our own.

Yet it's your brain that has created this recipe, even if only for a moment. The brain that creates that particular ratio of brain wave ingredients is able to create it again. It can be trained to do so at will.

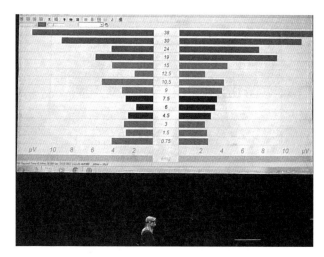

The habitual brain wave recipe of this workshop participant had lots of fear-induced beta, little theta and delta, and only a small alpha bridge.

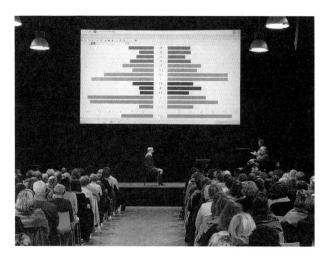

After treatment, we see large flares forming an alpha bridge, expanded theta and delta, and a disappearance of high amplitudes of beta.

When we first hook people up to EEGs during our workshops, we see the combinations of brain waves that represent their personal recipes. Often they are stressed and anxious, with a lot of high-frequency beta waves. They have little alpha, theta, or delta. To them, this state of being cut off from their unconscious and the universe, without an alpha bridge, is normal.

After treatment, the entire way their brains process information changes. They've sampled a new recipe and they like it. They have a big alpha bridge connecting their conscious and subconscious minds. They're in touch with the healing frequency of theta and the transcendent frequency of delta.

If we can persuade them to make this a consistent practice, with their brains enjoying the delicious new brain wave recipe every day, they become habituated to feeling good. It becomes the new normal. In time, their set point changes, and the gourmet recipe becomes their staple. Their bodies are bathed in the fields of healing every day.

Here is one example of a workshop participant who experienced a breakthrough when his brain flipped into this elevated state.

Hearing the Waves Breaking on the Distant Shore

Harold was in the middle of a profound crisis. A top official at the United Nations, he'd blacked out and fallen to the ground in the middle of a hostage negotiation three months before. His doctors told him he was stressed, and while they could find nothing wrong with his 52-year-old body, they advised him to relax and learn meditation. He'd made a complete recovery except for his hearing, which he had lost when he blacked out. Tests showed that he'd lost 80 percent of the hearing in his left ear.

He decided to enroll in a weeklong training I was offering at Esalen Institute in Big Sur, California. He had been visiting Esalen for various classes for 15 years, and the combination of massage, hot tubs, homegrown food, and oceanside views usually rejuvenated him.

When I met him, I was awed by his intelligence, humor, and expansive worldview. He had a satisfying long-term marriage, a successful son, a best-selling book, professional kudos, and every material benefit. Yet he was haunted by a gnawing sense that he'd made a wrong turn somewhere in his life. He wanted coaching to help him decide whether to take early retirement from his stressful job and to develop a robust health plan.

To help create the changes he envisioned, Harold volunteered to be my subject for a coaching demonstration in front of the whole group.

Before the training began, we used a panel of tests to assess the well-being of the people in the group. These tests included psychological evaluations of depression, anxiety, pain, happiness, and post-traumatic stress disorder (PTSD). We also measured Harold's physiological profile. The panel of tests included cortisol (the main stress hormone), salivary immunoglobulin A (SIgA, a primary marker of immune function), and resting heart rate. We hooked Harold up to an EEG during his session so we could monitor his brain waves.

Working with me in front of the whole group, Harold described his fears of growing older, of getting sicker, of becoming irrelevant. He recounted how shocked he felt when he abruptly lost consciousness during the hostage negotiation: "Suddenly, I hit the floor." While he was reconciled to the loss of hearing he'd suffered, he worried that it was the start of a progressive physical decline.

As I worked with him, Harold began to relax and tune in to his emotions. His breathing slowed and his muscles relaxed. His EEG readings showed flares of theta and delta waves, expanded alpha frequencies, and a reduction in beta. These were all indications that he was getting out of his anxious "monkey mind" and back in tune with his intuition and his bodily sensations. As his mind changed, his brain functions shifted.

We worked through a succession of his fears and disappointments and identified goals that he might achieve if he combined relaxation with creativity. Energy psychology helped him resolve all the jagged emotions left over from his health crisis, while coaching psychology clarified the opportunities before him and the fresh goals he could set for himself.

Eventually, I asked him, "How is that 80 percent hearing loss in your left ear?" He looked surprised, and said, "It's almost gone . . . maybe 15 percent loss now."

"How do you know it's an 80 percent hearing loss?" I wondered.

"The doctor told me," he affirmed. "It's a medical diagnosis."

"Let's work on that belief," I suggested.

We then focused on beliefs like *It's a medical diagnosis* and *The doctor said it, so it must be true.*

After coaching him through a process that questioned those beliefs, I asked him again about his left ear. He closed his eyes, focused intently on his hearing. Suddenly, his eyes popped wide open. Almost shouting, he exclaimed, "I can hear the waves breaking on the shore! I've been coming to Esalen for 15 years, and I've never been able to hear the ocean. Now I can!"

PRACTICE HABITUATES THE BRAIN TO BALANCE

During my EcoMeditation retreats, on the first morning, we teach people to attain these peak states. It isn't hard if you have the right combination of signals to the body. At first, it takes about four minutes to drop into the recipe. By the afternoon session, participants can do it in 90 seconds.

They feel wonderful and think they've arrived in heaven every time they close their eyes and start meditating. Yet that brain wave state is just the beginning. We then train them to evoke the magic recipe with their eyes open, at first in the meditation room. Once they become stable in the EcoMeditation state in that safe location, we start sending them into the environment outside.

They walk along the footpaths or through the gardens, learning to maintain that state. They come back into the meditation room and close their eyes again, increasing their amplitude of alpha. We then have them go outside again. We alternate inside and outside, eyes open and eyes closed, over and over again.

After the third day, they are usually able to maintain their new state with eyes open outside the room. At that stage, we've begun to change their set point and install a new normal. A doctor named Susan Albers describes it this way: "The morning following the class was the first time I had ever successfully meditated—in my entire life. All 52 years of it. I'm not someone who's calm, ever. And I was. What a revelation!"

Another participant, Maaike Linnenkamp, said: "EcoMeditation makes me calmer, more relaxed, and gives me a clearer mind. It was powerful for me to break the old thinking process and let go of the unpleasant memories that I usually dwell on. For the first time in my life, when I remembered bad events, I didn't become anxious. I just could not believe it when I talked to a friend about it later and still felt no anxiety. I feel very grateful and I will apply this technique on a regular basis."

Participants at an EcoMeditation workshop at Esalen Institute in California.

Susan, Maaike, and their friends have learned to take that gourmet brain wave recipe and turn it into their everyday brain food. They've trained their brains to be able to cook that delicious meal consistently. Just as it is hard to go back to bad wine once you've experienced fine wine, or start wearing harsh fabrics after you've enjoyed soft microfibers, or revert to your ancient cell phone after you've become used to the features of the latest model, it is hard to go back to the old normal recipe. Your previous brain state is the one that now feels foreign. You've upgraded your brain.

COHERENT BRAIN STATES TRIGGER GENE EXPRESSION

I have served as the chief investigator in many studies showing the effects of emotional healing on both physical and psychological symptoms. My latest work examines the epigenetic effects of stress reduction. The number and importance of the genes affected is astonishing.

After the first groups of U.S. veterans began returning from Iraq and Afghanistan, therapists told me they were encountering many clients with PTSD. Linda Geronilla, Ph.D., a clinical psychologist at Marshall University's medical school, shared with me that in just a few sessions of

EFT tapping with veterans, PTSD symptoms such as nightmares, flashbacks, and hypervigilance were gone.

Linda and I designed a study to determine if EFT was effective in treating PTSD. Our pilot study involved just seven veterans, but it was so successful that we were able to achieve statistical significance (Church, Geronilla, & Dinter, 2009). When you get statistical significance (which means that there is just one possibility in 20 that the results are due to chance) in a very small sample, it means you have a very effective treatment.

With a group of colleagues, I then launched a full-scale nationwide randomized controlled trial. We compared veterans getting standard care for PTSD, usually at a VA hospital, with a second group getting standard care plus EFT.

The study took several years to complete, but the results were the same. PTSD symptoms dropped by over 60 percent (Church et al., 2013). Once the study was published, Linda conducted a replication study, with almost identical results (Geronilla, Minewiser, Mollon, McWilliams, & Clond, 2016).

I wondered what was happening inside the bodies of these veterans, especially at the level of the genome. In 2009, I initiated a study of gene expression in veterans receiving 10 sessions of EFT. It took six years to complete, but eventually it showed that six stress genes were being regulated. Inflammation was being dialed down even while immunity was being dialed up (Church, Yount, Rachlin, Fox, & Nelms, 2016).

EFT PRODUCES DRAMATIC GENE SHIFTS

Beth Maharaj, an imaginative psychotherapist friend, designed a groundbreaking study for her doctoral dissertation. She had discovered a new type of gene test. While the earlier clinical trials required veterans to provide blood samples at a lab, the new test was saliva based. Participants had only to spit in a cup, and we could measure expression in hundreds or even thousands of genes.

Beth gave four subjects an hour-long placebo session, followed a week later by an hour-long EFT therapy session, and compared saliva samples before and after each session. She found that EFT produced regulation of an astonishing 72 genes (Maharaj, 2016). The functions of those genes proved to be fascinating. Among them were:

- The suppression of cancer tumors
- Protection against the sun's ultraviolet radiation
- Type 2 diabetes insulin resistance
- Immunity from opportunistic infections
- Antiviral activity
- Synaptic connectivity between neurons
- Creation of both red and white blood cells
- Enhancement of male fertility
- Building white matter in the brain
- Regulating metabolism
- Increasing neural plasticity
- Strengthening cell membranes
- Reducing oxidative stress

These shifts in gene expression were substantial, and when Beth retested participants a day later, about half of the effects persisted. That's a big payoff for just one hour of therapy.

MEDITATION REGULATES CANCER GENES

Inspired by Beth's example, my friend Joe Dispenza decided to test participants at one of his advanced workshops. I obtained saliva samples from 30 people, and when the results came back from the lab, we found that eight genes were significantly upregulated during the four days of meditation.

With a research team, I examined the data from over 100 EEG scans from another of Joe's workshops. We found that after practicing for four days, people entered a meditative state 18 percent faster and the ratio of anxiety-producing beta to integrative delta had improved by 62 percent (Church, Yang, et al., 2016).

As people's brains were being regulated by Joe's powerful meditation practices, their genes were also shifting. The functions of the eight genes we found changed tell a powerful story of physiological shift. They are involved in neurogenesis, the growth of new neurons in response to novel experiences and learning. They are also implicated in protecting our body against the influences that age our cells.

Several of these genes regulate cell repair, including the ability to move stem cells to the sites in the body where they can repair damaged or aging tissue. These genes are also involved in the building of cellular structures, especially the cytoskeleton, the framework of rigid molecules that gives our cells shape and form.

Three of these eight genes help our bodies identify and eliminate cancerous cells, suppressing the growth of cancer tumors. Their names and functions are as follows:

CHAC1 regulates the oxidative balance in cells. The hormone glutathione is key to reducing free radicals, and CHAC1 helps control the levels of glutathione in cells (Park, Grabińska, Guan, & Sessa, 2016). CHAC1 has several other functions. It also helps neural cells form and grow optimally (Cantagrel et al., 2010). It is believed to assist with the proper formation of the protein molecules that regulate oxidation and neuron formation.

CTGF (connective tissue growth factor) plays an important role in many biological processes (Hall-Glenn & Lyons, 2011). These range from the healing of wounds to the development of bones to the regeneration of cartilage and other connective tissue. CTGF helps new replacement cells migrate to the sites of wounding and damage in the body. It regulates the growth of new cells and the binding of cells to each other during the healing process. Decreased expression of this gene is linked to cancer and to autoimmune diseases such as fibromyalgia.

TUFT1 has a variety of functions in cell repair and healing (Deutsch et al., 2002). It helps regulate the functioning of a class of stem cells. During a child's development of teeth, TUFT1 acts to start the mineralization process of enamel. It is also thought to be involved in regulating oxygen levels in cells and in the differentiation of neurons.

DIO2 is important to the function of many types of brain and endocrine tissue (Salvatore, Tu, Harney, & Larsen, 1996). As well as being prevalent in thyroid tissue, it is highly expressed in other tissues, synchronizing local cells with thyroid gland function. It helps regulate metabolism by reducing insulin resistance, which in turn reduces the risk of metabolic disease (Akarsu et al., 2016), while also playing a role in craving and addiction. It helps regulate mood, especially depression.

C5orf66-AS1 is a gene associated with the suppression of tumors (Wei et al., 2015). It codes for a type of RNA that acts to identify and eliminate cancerous cells from the body.

KRT24 codes for the synthesis of a protein molecule that gives cells their structure. It also helps these molecules organize themselves in regular arrays (Omary, Ku, Strnad, & Hanada, 2009) and suppresses certain types of cancer cells such as those involved in colorectal cancer (Hong, Ho, Eu, & Cheah, 2007).

ALS2CL is one of a class of genes that suppress tumors, especially those contributing to a type of cancer called squamous cell carcinoma that affects the head and neck (Lee et al., 2010).

RND1 helps cells in the growth phase organize the molecules that give them their rigid structure. RND1 also catalyzes the growth of the parts of neural cells that reach out to connect with other neurons. It suppresses certain types of cancer cells such as those found in throat cancer and breast cancer (Xiang, Yi, Weiwei, & Weiming, 2016).

New technologies are allowing us to peer into the nuclei of our cells and the information flow in our brains and find out what happens during EFT, meditation, and other stress-reduction practices. What we are discovering is that the changes these techniques produce in the body are far from trivial. The picture emerging is that changes of mind produce profound changes in the matter of which our bodies are formed.

Bryce Rogow is a former Marine medic who served in four combat deployments in Iraq. He was there during some of the most bitter fighting and witnessed carnage and horror. After being discharged with PTSD, he set out on a quest for self-healing. Here's his story.

From a Combat Zone to Inner Peace

By Bryce Rogow

A lot of my friends say I'm a walking contradiction: on one hand a spiritual seeker; I've studied meditation at a Zen monastery in Japan, am a yoga teacher, and I've been learning mind-body medicine from some of the top healers around the world.

On the other hand, I'm a veteran of four combat deployments to Iraq as a corpsman, or medic, with the U.S. Marines. After getting out of the military, I was diagnosed with PTSD, and after some time of feeling lost and hopeless, I embarked on a journey of self-discovery and healing, intent on learning the most effective techniques for cooling the fires of mental and physical distress.

My first deployment with a U.S. Marine recon battalion (the Marines' version of Special Forces) led me to the second battle of Fallujah in November 2004, a massive assault on a city that has been described as the most intense urban combat U.S. forces have seen since Hue City in Vietnam.

All of us who deployed carry with us images that stay with us for the rest of our lives, images we have to learn how to live with.

For me, the first image of that kind came after my first buddy in my unit was killed while digging up an IED (improvised explosive device)—one of the homemade bombs insurgents would bury in fields and roadsides.

My method for preserving my own mental function, in addition to becoming addicted to the painkillers we medics had available, was to accept the fact that I was already dead, and so I would constantly remind myself that nothing that happened to me would matter, because I was already dead.

When I received my honorable discharge from the U.S. military in 2008, I was surprised to have survived the war. I expected a huge flood of relief when I was released from any possibility of future deployments, but that relief never came. I walked and drove around U.S. cities with the same tense fear I'd experienced in Iraq.

I spent a good deal of time heavily dependent on alcohol and drugs, including drugs such as clonazepam prescribed by well-meaning psychiatrists at the VA, drugs that were extremely addictive and led to a lot of risky behavior.

After getting out and realizing I needed to start helping myself, I decided that I wanted to learn meditation from an authentic Asian master, so I went to Japan to train at a traditional Zen monastery, called Sogenji, in the city of Okayama, Japan. Spending hours in the half-lotus position reminded me of the "stress positions" we used during enhanced interrogations after waterboarding became forbidden.

I am profoundly grateful to Shodo Harada-Roshi, a true modern Zen master, for facilitating that experience. However, after leaving the monastery, I realized that I would not be able to maintain that level of meditation on my own, that I would need faster and easier ways, and a better understanding of mind and body, to make meditative practices a useful part of my life.

I was really amazed, then, to come across, one day while researching on the Internet, a man, Dawson Church, who had already put together such a program, a "meditation of meditations" he calls EcoMeditation.

When I first came across his EcoMeditation, I simply read from the web page and followed the steps, and within two minutes found myself activating all these healing resources and entering a state of profound relaxation and well-being that I'd previously achieved only after hours, if not days and weeks, of meditation.

Bryce has become a passionate advocate for the use of EcoMeditation in the Department of Veterans Affairs. He believes that simple, low-cost self-help methods should be available to all veterans.

Thousands of people have now followed the seven simple steps at EcoMeditation.com and had the same profound and immediate experience of peace that Bryce had. As we investigate their physical changes, we find that their cortisol drops, along with their heart rate (Groesbeck et al., 2016). Their levels of immune hormones rise, as does their happiness. Depression, anxiety, and pain drop significantly. Inner peace reduces stress and produces beneficial changes in the body down to the level of gene expression.

YOUR INNER STATE IS YOUR GENETIC REALITY

Personal genetic testing is now widespread. Many people know what genes they have and understand their susceptibility for specific diseases based on their genetic profile. At workshops, I often get the question, "I have the XYZ gene. Doesn't that mean I'm destined to get XYZ disease?"

People get so worried about the results of gene tests. Yet as you see from the previous lists of genes, many are dramatically shifted by tapping and meditation.

It's not the genes you have that determine your destiny as much as what you do with them. Subject your body to high levels of stress over long periods of time and you upregulate the expression of cancer genes.

But make the opposite choice, and tap and meditate daily, and you reduce your stress. Along with it, your gene expression shifts. When those

810,000 cells that are being formed every second are birthed in an energy field of love and kindness, their gene expression is regulated by that field.

Mind to matter is not an abstract metaphysical proposition. It is a physical fact, as material as the bodies we live in. Thought by thought, moment by moment, our minds are creating the energy fields in which our cells reproduce. Positive thoughts provide our cells with an energy culture in which they thrive. Thoughts that nurture our cells as they regenerate become thriving molecular matter. Energy is epigenetic, regulating the processes of life and healing. When we elevate our consciousness to the infinite, generating the energy recipe of incandescence in our brains, our cells take form within the inspired energetic template we provide.

PUTTING THESE IDEAS INTO PRACTICE

Activities to practice this week:

- Practice altruism:

  Smile at strangers today.
  Thank people who help you in stores.
  Do an unexpectedly nice thing for someone
  close to you.

- Write a brief letter or e-mail to someone you love and send it to them.

- Listen to EcoMeditation on your mobile device as you walk, run, or exercise.

The Extended Play version of this chapter includes:

- Brain scan videos
- The database of energy healing research
- Audio interviews with EEG neurofeedback experts
- Additional case histories and references

To access the Extended Play version, visit:
MindToMatter.club/Chapter4

CHAPTER 5

The Power of
Coherent Mind

I'm lying on the beach in Hawaii. It's a beautiful day, with a cloudless sky and a light breeze ruffling the ocean. Children are playing around me, and happy vacationers are splashing in the water. Snorkelers are ogling the turtle colony on the reef offshore, while kayakers and paddle-boarders ply the bay.

I'd flown to Hawaii to finish my book. The publisher's deadline was perilously close and I hadn't been making much progress at home, torn between the demands of single-parenting two young children and running a demanding business. Escaping to Hawaii seemed like a good way to give myself a window to complete the manuscript.

After working all morning, I decided to give myself a break. As I had pounded away on my laptop earlier, I could see the happy scene and the beach. My mind said, *You're in Hawaii! Why are you sitting here cooped up in this dark condo instead of playing on the beach?*

After those thoughts had driven me crazy for a few hours, I succumbed to their logic and headed for the beach.

Now, lying on the warm sand, my mind starts chattering again. *What are you doing here on the beach?* it demands. *The whole purpose of getting away to Hawaii was to write the book. You aren't writing a thing. You're just lying around doing nothing.*

How true, I reflect. I give a sigh, roll up my blanket, and head for the condo.

That's the double bind in which we live. Our inner critics give us hell regardless of which choice we make. When I was writing inside the condo, my inner critic savaged me for not enjoying the beach. As soon as I went outside, it began lambasting me for not writing. Damned if I do, damned if I don't. Nothing I could do could please my inner critic. Many of us are trapped on a similar hamster wheel of endlessly repetitive negative thoughts.

NEGATIVE THOUGHTS BESIEGE THE MIND

A study of psychologically normal people found that they had about 4,000 distinct thoughts each day. Of those, between 22 percent and 31 percent were unwanted and uncontrollable intrusive thoughts, while 96 percent of them were repetitive thoughts about daily activities (Klinger, 1996). The Cleveland Clinic's Wellness Program says that 95 percent of our thoughts are repetitive and 80 percent of them are negative.

Two thousand years ago, the Buddha identified the mind as the source of our suffering. In the Bhagavad Gita, Arjuna laments, "The mind is very fickle indeed O Krishna, turbulent, strong and obstinate." Most of us are trapped in the cycle of negative thinking, with no idea how to escape. But why did our huge and complex brains evolve to work that way?

THE EVOLUTIONARY VALUE OF NEGATIVE THINKING

Both repetitive thinking and negative thinking make sense from the perspective of evolutionary biology. For our distant ancestors, repetitive thinking handled routine life tasks in the background, while hypervigilant negative thinking gave them a survival advantage by keeping them attuned to possible threats from the environment.

The brain is designed to default to beta brain waves under survival conditions. Beta is the signature brain wave of fear. Fear was what kept our ancestors alive. Their degree of paranoid hypervigilant alertness was in direct proportion to their degree of survival. Miss the tiger in the grass, even for a second, and you got eaten.

Consider the tale of two teenage sisters 100,000 years ago. We'll call one Hug and the other Gug.

Hug is the happiest of people. As she carries water from the stream to the village each day, she sings for joy. She stops to smell the fragrant yellow roses. She pauses to listen to the sound of children laughing. She's filled with wonder as she gazes on the orange and grey hues cast by the rising sun. She notices the good in all the other people in the village.

Her sister, Gug, is the opposite. Suspicious and paranoid, Gug is always looking for what's wrong. Show her a silver cloud, and she'll point out the dark lining. She sees problems at every turn. She notices every imperfection in her fellow villagers. When she carries water from the stream to the village, others avoid her. Except for Hug, who searches for the good in everyone and tolerates Gug's company.

One day, they're ambushed by a hungry tiger hiding in the grass. Gug, always on the lookout for threats, spots the tiger a split second before Hug. She screams and starts running just a nanosecond before Hug sees the tiger and runs too.

Hug gets eaten by the tiger. She never makes it to puberty. But Gug reproduces, passing her threat-detection genes on to the next generation.

Multiply this by 1,000 generations, with each one getting a little bit better at finding the bad stuff. The ability to notice what's wrong in the environment has now been honed by natural selection to a fine art. That brings us to today, and to you and me. Even when absolutely nothing is wrong, the caveman brains we've inherited from Gug are diligently scanning the horizon for threats.

Our distant ancestors could make two kinds of mistakes. One was thinking that there was no tiger hiding in the grass when there was, and the other was thinking that there was a tiger in the grass when there wasn't (Hanson, 2013).

**Our brains evolved to be exquisitely sensitive
to environmental cues that signal danger.**

The second kind of mistake carries no immediate evolutionary penalty. Being attuned to threats, looking for the bad stuff, just makes you a miserable curmudgeon like Gug. It also guarantees your survival.

The first kind of mistake carried the death penalty. Miss the tiger in the grass just one time and you get eaten. People like Hug who lacked the ability to focus relentlessly on threats got weeded from the gene pool.

If she'd been watching me on the beach in Hawaii, Mother Nature would have given me gold stars for having such a well-developed ability to find the bad stuff everywhere I went. Unfortunately, caveman brain cares nothing for my happiness. Whatever my choice, my inner critic chews me to shreds.

THE ORANGE APRON THAT COULD NOT CUT KEYS

The Home Depot chain is famous for the orange aprons worn by staff. I walked into my local Home Depot one day to get a key cut. It was for my old RV, a 1983 Ford Econoline. The man who ran the key-cutting machine was at his station and I showed him the key.

He took it like it was an infected kidney and shook his head, saying, "I don't think we carry that style of key."

I pointed out that the Ford Motor Company had manufactured about three million of these vehicles, so they weren't exactly rare. He said, doubtfully, "It's a double-sided key," as though that represented an insurmountable difficulty.

"You cut the same key for me last week," I offered, helpfully.

He inserted the key into the laser reader, and after a scan, a red light flashed.

"No," he said mournfully, "we don't carry that one."

"Could you try it again?" I pleaded.

He punched the ON switch again, the laser scanned the key, and this time a green light appeared.

"We're really low on blanks," he said next, shaking his head.

"Can you just look?" I asked, politely.

He perused his stock, found the blank, and cut the key. All with the air of a man who has been let down by the world. His superpower could even make the laser malfunction.

The impatient part of me wanted to grab him by the shoulders and cheer him up. Buy him a copy of *The Power of Positive Thinking*. Give him a free pass to one of my workshops. Deliver one of my rousing keynote speeches.

The compassionate part of me extended itself into his consciousness. What might it be like to live in a mind that sees difficulties where there are none? Where your thinking defeats the simplest of enterprises before you even begin? What is it like to inhabit a mind predisposed to failure?

CAVEMAN BRAIN

Even though our ancestors left the savanna thousands of years ago, most of us still look much harder for what's wrong around us than for what's right.

When we wake up in the morning, our brains have been in theta and delta sleep states. We emerge into alpha, and it feels like we're in suspended animation as our brains gradually wake up to the day. Then beta kicks in and we start thinking. And worrying. The evolutionary mechanism that identified the tiger springs into action. A parade of paper tigers flows through our minds. We start thinking thoughts like this:

Is this the day that report is due on my boss's desk? Or is it next week?

What will I have for breakfast? Will it make me fat?

Did I hear my husband snoring last night?

What kind of mood are my kids in today? Will they make my life miserable?

I don't think the shoes I was planning to wear today are right for my outfit.

Did we run out of coffee?

I need to catch up on that disaster I watched on the news last night.

What's the weather like?

If Jane didn't leave a comment on my Facebook post, I'm going to be mad.

How much red is there in the commuter lane on Google Maps?

Once you wake up, your brain starts to drive you crazy with worry. Yet this is exactly what our brains evolved to do. When Gug woke up, she needed to be alert to a hostile environment from the second she opened her eyes. Might a tiger have crept up to the cave while she was sleeping? The Neanderthal who woke up grumpy, suspicious, and paranoid lived. Her sister who woke up happy, content, and peaceful missed those tiny survival cues that made the difference between life and death.

Today, without predators, we still wake up and immediately start to worry. Thoughts flood into our minds. The floodgates open and our minds churn in a torrent of anxiety. Before we've even walked out the front door to start our day, we've been consumed by anxious thoughts.

There are two basic survival questions: Can I eat it? Will it eat me?

Caveman brain takes a toll on our bodies. In an eight-year study of 68,222 adults published in the *British Medical Journal*, researchers found that even mild anxiety produces a 20 percent greater risk of death (Russ et al., 2012). The very skill that kept our ancestors alive—looking for the bad stuff and ignoring the good stuff—is killing us today. Our minds have become a major threat to our survival. Caveman brain is a fatal condition.

CARRYING THE Woman FOR a Day

There's a charming Zen story about two celibate monks who were on a long journey. One morning they came to a stream that was swollen with floodwater. On the bank was a young woman who couldn't get across. The older of the two monks hoisted her onto his broad shoulders, and both monks walked into the water and crossed safely to the other side. After thanking the old monk, the woman went on her way.

The two monks walked in silence till dusk, but there was tension in the air. The dam of emotional intensity in the younger monk eventually burst. "The rules of our religion forbid us to touch women," he said. "How could you have done that?"

"My son," said the older monk, "I picked her up and set her down this morning. You have been carrying her all day."

The angry inner ruminations of the younger monk had been raising his stress level long after the event was over. That's what we do when we obsess about the past or fear for the future. Using the system designed by Mother Nature to be engaged only when we are in true danger, we send stressful messages to our bodies with our thoughts, compromising our ability to regenerate and heal.

With Audrey Brooks, Ph.D., a research psychologist at the University of Arizona, I did a study of health-care workers. Professionally, they worked as chiropractors, nurses, psychotherapists, doctors, or alternative practitioners. We measured their levels of psychological distress before and after a one-day EFT tapping workshop. We assessed participants at five workshops, and the final study included 216 participants (Church & Brooks, 2010).

The health-care workers tapped together in groups.

We found that symptoms of anxiety, depression, and other mental health issues dropped an average of 45 percent in the course of the day. When we followed up six months later, those who had kept tapping had the lowest stress levels.

But one of our striking findings was just how stressed health-care workers are. On the scale we used for the study, a score of 60 represents such severe anxiety and depression that you need treatment. Their average starting score was 59. That's just one point less than the diagnostic threshold of 60. And that's the average; many individuals were more stressed than their patients. Being a health-care professional doesn't mean you can escape caveman brain.

The Whirlpool of Depression

By Naomi Janzen, EFT Universe trainer

I went through an 18-month period of depression after the end of a terrible relationship. I tried everything to shake it, but I could not. I felt trapped in an endless loop of anger and grief. I was being dragged around and around by this whirlpool of negative thoughts and feelings.

It used to exasperate me when I would read helpful pamphlets on depression that would say, basically, "Snap out of it."

I had a lot of tools. If anyone was capable of snapping out of it, it was me. But I'd wake up every morning at 3:11 A.M., when my defenses were down. I couldn't stop thinking about the man who had hurt me. The loop kept going. I was obsessed with justice I knew I would never get. The whirlpool dragged me around in a circle of repetitive thoughts.

If you have a friend who, maybe 20 years after a breakup, keeps talking about it, with nothing new to say, have compassion on them. They're in the whirlpool of looping anger and grief.

EFT rescued me from the endless loop, the whirlpool, and got me to dry land. Now my job is to help other people escape from their whirlpools!

The whirlpool that Naomi Janzen describes, in which the mind loops endlessly through a list of negative thoughts, is what kept her ancestors alive, but it's worse than useless today. These patterns rob us of peace of mind, drive our cortisol through the roof, and deprive our bodies of the resources they need to regenerate and heal. Even very smart people like Naomi often find, to their frustration, that they can't talk themselves out of the whirlpool. It takes a powerful psychospiritual tool like EFT to break the looping mental patterns of caveman brain.

SLOW-BURNING AND FAST-BURNING STRESS HORMONES

After completing the health-care workers study, I was intrigued by how quickly people could shed stress with EFT. I looked for a way of measuring changes in the body, and I found it in cortisol.

Cortisol is one of our two primary stress hormones, the other being adrenaline (also called epinephrine). You can think of adrenaline as our short-acting fight-or-flight hormone. When we're stressed, it kicks in immediately. In under three seconds, it speeds up our heart rate, contracts our blood vessels, and dilates our lungs. That gives our caveman the physical boost required to escape from danger.

Cortisol is our long-acting stress hormone. It rises and falls on a regular, slow curve throughout the day. It rises sharply in the morning, perking us up and getting us ready for an active day. It's at its lowest level around 4 A.M., when we're in deep sleep. It peaks at 8 A.M. When it starts declining, between 8 P.M. and 10 P.M., we become drowsy.

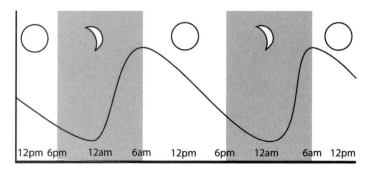

The cortisol cycle.

Like adrenaline, however, cortisol rises in just a few seconds when we're stressed. Stress disrupts the slow, even, daily cortisol rhythm. When you're running from a tiger, cortisol rises along with adrenaline. When you're worried, cortisol also rises.

Our bodies are designed to flourish with normal levels of cortisol synthesized along the smooth curve of the cortisol cycle. They are not designed to handle high levels of cortisol continuously. Chronic high cortisol leads to widespread body damage, including:

- High blood pressure
- Death of neurons in the brain's memory centers
- High blood sugar
- Heart disease
- Diminished cell repair
- Accelerated aging
- Alzheimer's disease
- Fatigue
- Obesity
- Diabetes

- Slow wound healing

- Reduced bone repair

- Fewer stem cells

- Reduced muscle mass

- Increased skin wrinkling

- Fat around the waist and hips

- Osteoporosis

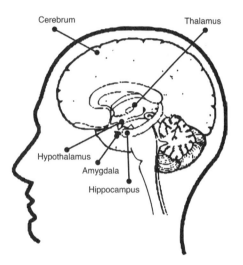

**Cortisol kills neurons in the hippocampus, one
of the structures of the emotional midbrain.**

Over time, high cortisol disrupts cell metabolism so that excessive
calcium enters brain cells and produces free radicals, the most harmful
molecules in the body. Free radicals trigger a range of degenerative illnesses and rapid aging (McMillan et al., 2004). High cortisol also leads
to dysfunction in our mitochondria, the "energy factories" of cells (Joergensen et al., 2011). We then feel tired and our energy levels crash. Cortisol kills neurons in the brain's hippocampus, which governs emotional
regulation, memory, and learning (Sapolsky, Uno, Rebert, & Finch, 1990).
Cortisol is accompanied by high beta brain waves, the signature waves of
stress and anxiety.

CHRONIC HIGH CORTISOL

So when we get stressed for a few minutes, are we wrecking our bodies?

The answer is no. Bodies are designed to handle quick spikes of stress and then return rapidly to their normal baseline. Just two minutes after a stressful event, our body has already disassembled the fast-acting adrenaline molecules it built in response to danger (Ward et al., 1983). Slow-burning cortisol takes about 20 minutes to dissipate (Nesse et al., 1985). Your body is designed to generate cortisol quickly in response to an objective threat and dissipate it quickly when the threat is gone.

So if cortisol and adrenaline molecules dissipate rapidly, how can our levels stay high over time?

By *thought*—especially thought that triggers strong emotion. This sends signals through the neural pathways of negativity in our brains.

We cause chronic cortisol production by turning our attention to those factors in the environment that stress us out. Negative thinking drives high cortisol even when there is no tiger in the grass. Our brilliant brains are able to ruminate about the bad thing that happened in the past or the bad thing that might happen in the future. Even if it never happened and will never happen, we can nonetheless focus on it, picture it, contemplate it, imagine it, talk about it, and catastrophize about it.

The body cannot distinguish between an actual threat and a perceived threat. It has no way of knowing that the imaginary threat we are conjuring up in our minds using negative thinking is not an actual threat to our survival. Purely by thought alone, we can drive cortisol up and produce corrosive effects on our cells.

RESETTING STRESS HORMONE LEVELS

As I watched clients sigh and relax after EFT tapping sessions, I wondered what might be happening invisibly, inside their bodies, to their stress hormones. To answer this research question, I designed a study to examine their cortisol levels. With colleagues from the California Pacific Medical Center and the University of Arizona, I conducted the first study that examined psychological conditions such as anxiety and depression as well as cortisol levels before and after EFT (Church, Yount, & Brooks, 2012).

The study was ambitious and took several years to complete. It was conducted at five integrative medical clinics in California and included 83 subjects. It was a triple-blind randomized controlled trial, the gold standard of scientific proof. The results were provocative, and the study was published in a prestigious journal, the oldest peer-reviewed psychiatry journal in North America.

We assessed subjects' mental health, and also measured their cortisol, before and after a single therapy session. One group received EFT, a second group talk therapy, and a third group simply rested.

The results were striking. Psychological symptoms such as anxiety and depression declined in the talk therapy and rest groups, but they dropped more than twice as much in the EFT group. Cortisol dropped by 24 percent, showing that EFT was having an effect inside the body.

Devastated by the Loss of the Love of His Life

Dean, one of the participants in the cortisol study, was a 58-year-old male psychiatric nurse who had been randomized to the talk therapy group. Dean's scores on psychological distress were as high after the therapy session as before, and I was concerned about his well-being.

In the second treatment session, instead of talk therapy, we used EFT. We worked on a memory around which he had a high emotional charge: breaking up with his girlfriend. He told me that he thinks about the breakup every day.

He said that on the last day, he drove his girlfriend to the airport and put her on an airplane. He teared up as he remembered, "with stunned regret," the image of her walking down the jetway.

The adult event reminded him of a childhood incident. When he was five years old, he saw a television advertisement in which Gina Lollobrigida was touted as "the most beautiful woman in the world."

After watching the advertisement, little Dean went to the bathroom, climbed up onto a stool, and looked at himself in the mirror. He concluded that he was not good-looking and realized he never would be. When he described the memory, he experienced a sharp pain in his solar plexus, but after tapping, he felt much better at the end of the session.

When Dean's cortisol results arrived back from the lab (SabreLabs.com) a few days later, they showed that his cortisol levels had dropped from 4.61 ng/ml to 2.42 ng/ml, or 48 percent, after the tapping session. But after his earlier talk therapy session, Dean's cortisol had risen from 2.16 ng/ml to 3.02 ng/ml, an increase of 40 percent (Church, 2013). This echoes other research showing that therapies that engage the body are usually more effective than those that engage the mind alone.

Later, I had the opportunity to find out just what was happening inside the bodies of people taking a five-day residential EFT workshop. This particular workshop was held at California's Esalen Institute, the place where Gestalt therapy, Rolfing, humanistic psychology, and many other groundbreaking approaches were first developed.

Esalen Institute front gate.

The research team measured a comprehensive panel of physiological markers as well as psychological conditions such as anxiety, depression, and PTSD (Bach et al., 2016). As anticipated, large improvements in mental health occurred during the week.

However, the changes in physiological markers of health were extraordinary. Cortisol dropped by 37 percent. Salivary immunoglobulin A, an immune marker, rose by 113 percent. Resting heart rate dropped by 8 percent, and blood pressure was reduced by 6 percent. The blood pressure, cortisol, and heart rate figures showed that participants were much less stressed at the end of the week than at the beginning.

While an hour of EFT had reduced cortisol by 24 percent in the previous study, five days of tapping was associated with an even bigger stress-reduction effect. Participant pain dropped by 57 percent, while happiness increased by 31 percent. When we reassessed psychological symptoms six months later, most of the improvements had held. This close association between physical health and mental health is a pervasive finding in research in meditation, EFT, and other stress-reduction techniques.

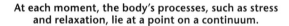

At each moment, the body's processes, such as stress
and relaxation, lie at a point on a continuum.

Tapping and meditation dial down stress. Stress isn't like a light switch, either on or off. It's like a dimmer switch, getting brighter or darker. When we relax, this nudges our cortisol levels and beta brain waves lower. When we get stressed, we move the needle in the opposite direction. Gene expression, hormones, brain states, and stress all operate on this type of continuum. Each strong emotion we have, positive or negative, moves the needle in one direction or the other.

COHERENT MIND = COHERENT MATTER

The caveman brain is not efficient. Addled by beta waves and intoxicated with cortisol, it's chaos. Imaging studies show that the four lobes of the brain fall out of synchrony and that groups of neurons fire chaotically rather than in harmony. In the scientific literature, the word for efficiency is *coherence*. When the brain is functioning at peak efficiency, an EEG scan shows coherence between brain regions and neural groups.

When our consciousness is disrupted by stress, our brains are not coherent. In this state, the creations of our minds are not coherent either.

But when we drop our stress, train our unruly minds to remain calm, and release negative thinking from our consciousness, our brains become coherent. In highly coherent states, our minds are able to create effects in the physical world that are astonishing.

THE POWER OF COHERENT LIGHT

Lasers use coherent light, while non-laser light sources such as LEDs or incandescent bulbs use incoherent light. Put another way, a laser is set up so that all the light rays are parallel to each other rather than going off in random directions. This characteristic of coherence makes lasers extraordinarily powerful. Light from a 60-watt incandescent light bulb can faintly illuminate objects two to four yards or meters away. It converts only about 10 percent of its energy into light, and that light is not coherent.

Organize that same 60 watts of light into a coherent laser, however, and it can cut through steel.

Coherent Laser Light

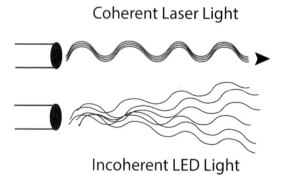

Incoherent LED Light

Coherent versus noncoherent light.

An ordinary handheld laser pointer of the kind used in lectures, with a tiny power source of just 5 thousandths of a watt, can illuminate a point 12 miles or 20 kilometers away (Nakamura, 2013). Using a trillion times more power (1 billion watts), scientific lasers can even bounce off the moon and reflect back to earth (Shelus et al., 1994).

Mental coherence is similar. When our brain waves are coherent, the quality of thought they produce is focused and efficient. We can turn our attention to problems, focus on them, and solve them.

BRAIN FOG

When our brains are not coherent, we aren't able to think clearly. We're afflicted by "brain fog," and our wooly brains can't think clearly. When we're upset, problems seem opaque, we're easily confused, and our cognitive abilities plummet. Brain researcher Joseph LeDoux calls this "the hostile takeover of consciousness by emotion" (LeDoux, 2003).

Laser used for astronomical observations at the Goddard Space Flight Center.

Brain studies have found that it takes less than a second for a statement or even a single word to trigger an emotional reaction (Davidson, 2003). By the time we recognize that we're under stress, our brains have already been triggered. We can be overwhelmed by emotional reactions in just a fraction of a second, producing brain fog and the inability to think clearly.

When that happens, our access to remembered skills and rational thinking is greatly impaired. We are unable to be objective and consider a problem realistically. Stress can result in a drain of more than 70 percent of the blood from the frontal lobes, the cognitive centers of the brain. As blood carries oxygen, this means that the brain is not getting its normal supply of oxygen either. We can't think straight when the blood and oxygen flow to our brains is reduced as a result of being stressed. The caveman doesn't have to be able to do long division in his head; he just needs to be able to escape from the tiger.

When that primitive survival response is triggered by thought and emotion, the result is a huge reallocation of biological resources. Blood flows out of the prefrontal cortex into the muscles. Suddenly, all those wise skills you have in your prefrontal cortex, your thinking brain, are no longer available to you. It's like a computer, which has masses of data stored on its hard drive. If you unplug the computer, all the stored information is still there, but you can no longer access it; there is no power to make it useable.

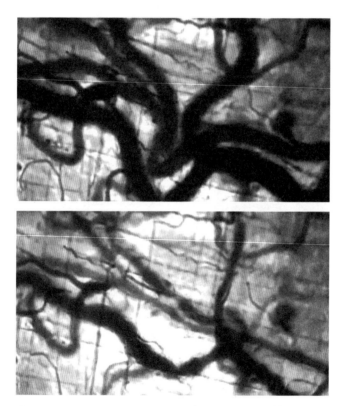

**Capillaries before (above) and 14 seconds after (below) a stress signal.
They can contract by over 70 percent.**

When you lose the blood supply to your prefrontal cortex, it's like a computer that's unplugged. All the resources that are stored in that part of your brain—the skills learned in therapy, the brilliant solutions you've read in books, the methods you've practiced in classes, the strategies you've learned from experts—all these are unavailable to caveman brain.

Come into coherence, however, and your resources come online. Like the laser pointing at the moon, you're able to perform inspired long-range planning. You think clearly about problems, you focus on your goals, your imagination is unlocked, and your creativity soars. That's the power of a coherent mind.

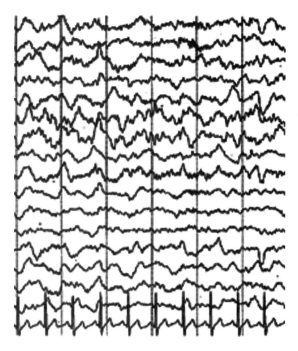

Incoherent brain waves.

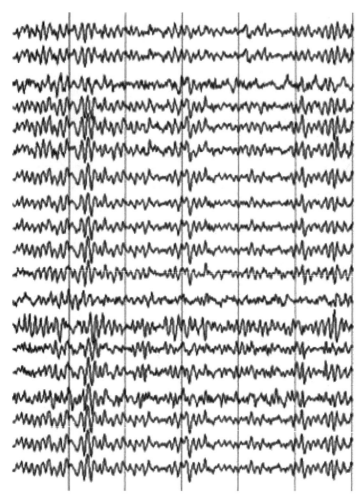

Coherent brain waves. In coherence, all the parts of the brain
are working together.

COHERENT MIND AND THE FOUR
FORCES OF PHYSICS

A coherent mind focuses the power of attention the way a laser
focuses the power of light. People who achieve high levels of coherence
are able to do extraordinary things. Remarkable research now shows that
a coherent mind can literally bend the forces of the material universe.

There are four fundamental forces in physics: gravity, electromagnetism, the strong nuclear force, and the weak nuclear force.

The strong force is what holds atoms together. The protons and neutrons in the nucleus of an atom contain huge amounts of energy, and the force required to hold them together is enormous, which is why it's called the strong force. It operates at very short distances between components of an atom.

The weak nuclear force is the one that gives rise to radioactive decay. In this process, the nuclei of atoms break down because they do not have enough energy to hold together. Energy and matter are released from these unstable nuclei over a period of time until they form a different, stable element that is not radioactive.

Different radioactive substances have different rates of decay. Some are very long while others are very short. The half-life of uranium-238 is very long, about 3.5 billion years. The half-life of another element, francium-233, is just 22 minutes.

These half-lives are so consistent that you can set your watch by them. Scientists who need precise measures of time use an atomic clock and reference their experiments by International Atomic Time, a scale that uses the combined output of 400 highly precise atomic clocks in various parts of the world. One second is defined as the period it takes for one cesium-133 atom to oscillate 9,192,631,770 times.

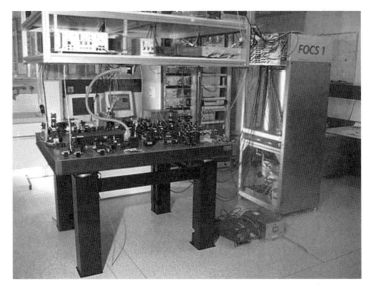

A cesium atomic clock constructed in 2004 for a lab in Switzerland that operates with an uncertainty period of 1 second every 30 million years.

A radioactive element often used in studies is americium-241. Discovered in 1944, it has a half-life of 432 years, emits what are known as alpha particles, and is stable at room temperature. It's also ubiquitous in our homes, where it powers most smoke detectors. It's safe, since its alpha radiation travels only 3 cm (under 1.5 inches) and is stopped by almost any solid object. If smoke particles enter the detector, they're hit by the alpha particles, triggering a drop in electrical current, which sets off the alarm.

The weak nuclear force is not affected by electromagnetism or gravity. In fact, it is 10 trillion trillion times stronger than gravity.

Given the stability of atomic radiation, so consistent that it powers atomic clocks, you might imagine that it would be very hard to change. Yet that is exactly what a number of researchers have tried to accomplish using the human energy field as the agent of change.

QI = MC2

A qigong master named Dr. Yan Xin projects qi, or life energy, to his patients. Scientists at the Institute of High Energy Physics, part of the Chinese Academy of Sciences, decided to put Dr. Yan's powers to a rigorous objective test.

They asked him to alter the rate of decay of a tiny 2-mm americium-241 disk inside a plexiglass container. One of the four fundamental forces of physics, the decay rate of radioactive substances is immune to high temperatures, strong acids, massive electromagnetic fields, or extreme pressures.

For the first eight sessions, Dr. Yan projected qi energy to the americium for 20 minutes while standing nearby. A second americium disk was used as a control. He was able to change the decay rate of radioactive alpha particles in the target disk while leaving the control disk unchanged. He could either slow down or speed up the decay rate, whichever was requested of him (Yan et al., 2002).

For the next three sessions, the researchers decided to study whether the effect diminished with distance. They placed Dr. Yan 100 to 200 meters away from the americium source. This made no difference in the results.

They then tested whether being in a distant city would weaken the effect. Over the next five years, they had him project qi into the target disk from progressively greater distances, starting 1,500 km away and eventually moving as far as 2,200 km away. A series of 39 additional trials showed that he was able to produce the same effect from a distance as he could standing in the same room.

These 50 separate experiments showed that Dr. Yan could lower the radioactive decay rate by 11.3 percent and raise it by up to 9.5 percent in the 20-minute course of the experiments. It normally takes 432 years for americium to decay, a rate of only 0.0006 percent per day, so the passage of time could not explain the results.

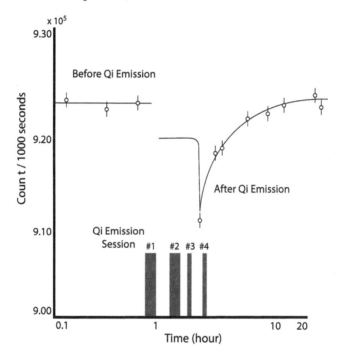

**Readings from the spectrometer with Dr. Yan Xin
in the same location as the americium source.**

Nuclear physicist Feng Lu, one of the researchers, observed that "Dr. Yan's research transformed the accepted view of the nature of the world. The results of his research have demonstrated that the human potential is far greater . . . than that which has been previously thought."

In his book *The Energy Cure,* Dr. Bill Bengston describes his empirical tests of the healer Bennett Mayrick (Bengston, 2010). On one occasion, Bennett was hooked up to a device that measures the rate of radioactive decay. The technician instructed him to concentrate on making the

radioactive material decay more rapidly. Bengston observed, "The technician gave a yelp. 'Something's wrong. This thing says the decay is occurring faster than I believe can be possible.'

"Ben playfully replied, 'Then I'll slow it down.'

"Soon the technician was mumbling something about the decay
slowing to almost one-half its normal rate."

When Bengston asked Ben how he did this, Ben said that to speed up
the decay, he imagined a cloud, which he then dissolved with his mind.
To slow it down, he imagined a frozen rock.

My Eureka Moment

On June 26, 2017, I nervously unpacked my very own Geiger
counter. For the past few months, I'd e-mailed colleagues—with far
more experience than I—copies of the Bengston and Yan experiments and urged them to conduct replications. No one seemed
interested.

The equipment required was simple and inexpensive, just a Geiger counter and a smoke detector containing an americium-241 disk.

The methodology was elementary. Either a healer could slow
down the rate of radioactive decay or he could not. A Geiger counter
can measure radiation as either microsieverts, a standard scientific
unit, or counts per minute (CPM). CPM is a count of how many
electrons are being released by the radioactive source.

I set up the equipment on my dining room table and figured out
how to get a basic radiation reading. I discovered that the baseline
in my house fluctuated between 12 and 22 CPM, with an average
of 18 CPM.

I then placed the Geiger counter over the radiation source, a
simple household smoke detector. The radiation readings rose to an
average of 60 CPM. Just a couple of inches away, the readings were
normal; a Geiger counter has to be very close to a smoke detector to
measure any radiation since the devices are designed to be safe for
household installation.

I performed the seven steps of EcoMeditation and then filled my
mind with the same image that Ben Mayrick had used, a frozen rock.
The Geiger counter didn't register any change.

Well, that's it, I thought. *It didn't work. That ability may be something only a few people, like Ben or Dr. Yan, possess.*

But I decided to continue meditating, my hands on either side of the smoke detector. I sent energy through my hands, just as I would with a client to whom I was offering healing.

The numbers began to rise. First to the high 60s and then into the 70s. By the time I'd meditated for a while, it rose to over 80 CPM. I ran the test for 10 minutes, and it averaged 80 CPM.

I then stopped meditating, and the numbers dropped back to 60 CPM. After another 10 minutes, I moved the Geiger counter two feet away from the smoke detector, and the background readings averaged the same 18 CPM as when I began.

The first experiment on June 26, 2017.

I paced around the house with questions exploding in my brain.

- Could I get the same result a second time?

- Why was I not able to lower the count, only raise it?

- Could other people do this? Is the effect more pronounced with gifted healers than it is with ordinary people?

- Can anyone be trained to do this? Is it a skill that can be taught? Does this ability improve with practice?

- Was my belief in energy healing enhancing the results?

- Would skepticism be a barrier to replicating them?

- What force could be producing the change in the radiation levels? How can I test this in a way that is methodologically impeccable?

- Did it happen because of my magic T-shirt? (just kidding)

I had so much energy that I couldn't go back to my office to do routine work. I jumped into my venerable relic of a car, a bright red 1974 Jensen Healey, and drove to the gym to exercise, screaming and shouting and punching the air around me. When life hands us such moments, it's worth celebrating!

I now knew that people other than Yan Xin and Ben Mayrick could produce the effect. The club of radioactivity changers had just expanded from two to three!

When my wife, Christine, came back from work that afternoon, I sat her down at the dining room table to see if we could boost the number of club members from three to four.

Ten minutes of measuring background radiation gave us an average of 17 CPM. When I put the Geiger counter on top of the smoke detector, a 10-minute test gave an average CPM of 60. When Christine placed her hands around the source and meditated for 10 minutes, the CPM dropped to 57, and when I asked her to visualize her youngest grandchild's face, it dropped to 52.

Christine was able to maintain 52 CPM for 10 minutes. When I asked her to raise the CPM by using Ben Mayrick's imagery, the dial didn't move upward for more than a few seconds before dropping again. She tried other imagery, but still was not able to raise it. This was interesting: I could raise it but not lower it, while Christine could lower it but not raise it.

After she stopped, I tested the unattended Geiger counter for 10 minutes and it averaged 61 CPM. Another 10-minute test, away from the smoke detector, gave us a background radiation count of 18 CPM. There were officially now four members of the club . . . and maybe millions more!

THE FIFTH FORCE

The ability to alter the rate of radioactive decay, one of the four fundamental forces of physics, raises several questions: If one force can be altered by a force that is not one of the other three, can any of those other three be altered? Can gravity or electromagnetism, forces far weaker than the two nuclear forces, be changed?

Joie Jones, Ph.D., late professor of radiological sciences at the University of California–Irvine, teamed up with Russian physicist Yuri Kronn to devise an ingenious experiment to determine if electromagnetism is susceptible to change. They pointed out that a "fifth force" is required to do this, and they called it "subtle energy" (Kronn & Jones, 2011).

They measured the electrical conductivity of various substances that were deliberately infused with subtle energy. They found that compared to baseline controls, electromagnetism was decreased by 25 percent.

An experiment with healing intention measured the magnetic fields around the targets of healing (Moga & Bengston, 2010). These were mice who had been injected with a substance that caused cancer. The healer sent intentional healing energy to them locally (with the healer present in the room) for 30 minutes on the first day of the study, and then nonlocally (with the healer in a distant location) for 12 weeks. Measuring devices in the mice's cages found an increase in the magnetic field to 20–30 Hz, followed by a decrease to 8–9 Hz, then a further drop to below 1 Hz. The effect then reversed.

Local healing and nonlocal healing produced the same effects. The researchers subsequently tested various healing modalities and found similar changes in the magnetic field during tai chi and healing touch sessions as well. They also reviewed five other studies that measured similar phenomena (Moga & Bengston, 2010).

This research suggests that at least two of the four fundamental laws of physics—electromagnetism and the weak nuclear force—can be altered by a coherent mind holding healing intentions.

Kronn and Jones found that their experiments could be done successfully in certain labs but not in others. They were puzzled as to why, and it took them some time to figure out the difference. It turned out that the labs where replications were unsuccessful were those in which experiments on dead animals were performed. Kronn developed an energy protocol, called "clean sweep," for those labs, after which they could successfully host replications (Kamp, 2016).

Kronn has found that scientists affect what they're studying. He says that "Your own energy will distort the energy pattern you are recording. Similarly, if you repeat an experiment and you don't want it to work, then it won't. Or, when one of my collaborators has a 'bad—out-of-tune—day,' we can't accurately test energy patterns" (Kamp, 2016).

When Christine and I were near the Geiger counter in ordinary consciousness, nothing much happened. But when we meditated, the readout changed. Similarly, Ben Mayrick used vivid mental imagery, while Dr. Yan projected qi energy into the americium sample, with the intention of either speeding up or slowing down its radioactive decay.

Changing matter in this way requires a coherent state of mind. When brain waves are incoherent, with anxiety-laden beta waves predominating and stress hormones such as cortisol and adrenaline infusing our cells, we're out of the state of flow. Our intentions lack clarity or power.

But when we slow ourselves down into a meditative state, with a broad alpha bridge connecting our conscious minds to high-amplitude theta and delta waves, we access the power of coherent mind. In this state, our intentions affect matter.

COHERENT MIND AND ACTIVE INTENTION

Led by Rollin McCraty, Ph.D., the Institute of HeartMath in Boulder Creek, California, has been studying the effects of coherent heartbeats for more than two decades.

Heart rate variability (HRV) readouts for anger (above) and appreciation (below) (McCraty, Atkinson, & Tomasino, 2003).

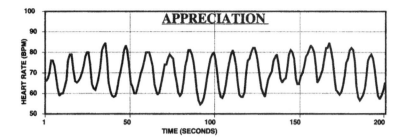

Heart coherence is a reliable marker of overall physical health, associated with pervasive effects throughout the body. It reduces cortisol secretion and expands the amplitude of alpha waves in the brain. It brings not only the brain but other organ systems such as circulation and digestion into coherence too, while also boosting the immune system (McCraty, Atkinson, & Tomasino, 2003).

McCraty writes: "The current scientific conception is that all biological communication occurs at a chemical/molecular level through the action of neurochemicals fitting into specialized receptor sites, much like keys open certain locks. However, in the final analysis, the message is actually transmitted to the interior of the cell by a weak electrical signal.

"From these and related findings, a new paradigm of energetic communication occurring within the body at the atomic and quantum levels has emerged—one which is compatible with numerous observed phenomena that could not be adequately explained within the framework of the older chemical/molecular model. 'Fight or flight' reactions to life-threatening situations . . . are too immediate and manifold to be consistent with the key-lock model of communication. However, they are comprehensible within the framework of quantum physics and an internal and external electromagnetic or energetic signaling system, which may also explain . . . the energetic communication links between cells, people, and the environment.

"Several of the brain's electrical rhythms, such as the alpha and beta rhythm, are naturally synchronized to the rhythm of the heart and this heart-brain synchronization significantly increases when an individual is in a physiologically coherent mode. This synchronization is likely to be mediated at least in part by electromagnetic field interactions. This is important as synchronization between the heart and brain is likely involved in the processes that give rise to intuition, creativity, and optimal performance" (McCraty, Atkinson, & Tomasino, 2003).

DNA CHANGE IN A COHERENT STATE

An ingenious HeartMath experiment used human placental DNA to test the effect of human intention in a coherent state. The degree of molecular twist in a sample of DNA can be measured by the molecule's absorption of ultraviolet light. This test can determine whether the molecule's double helix coils are more tightly or less tightly wound.

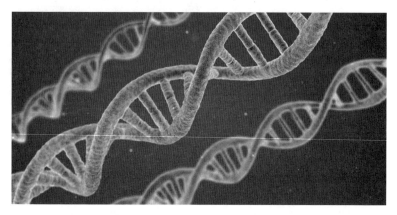

The DNA molecule has a double helix structure, and the degree of its twist can be measured by its absorption of ultraviolet light.

In the study, individuals trained in HeartMath techniques generated feelings of love and appreciation while holding a specific intention to either wind or unwind the DNA in an experimental sample.

The results were profound. In some cases, there was a change of 25 percent in the conformation of the DNA. Similar effects occurred whether participants were given the instruction to wind the helixes tighter or to unwind them.

When these participants entered that state of coherence but had no intention of changing the DNA, it changed no more than it did with a control group, which was composed of untrained local residents and students. When trained participants held the intention of changing the DNA but did not move into a coherent state, the DNA likewise remained unchanged.

In order to determine just how specific and local the effect might be, in one experiment with a highly trained volunteer, three separate vials of DNA were prepared. The volunteer was asked to wind the DNA spirals tighter in two of the samples but not in the third. Those were exactly the results measured under later UV analysis in the laboratory; changes showed up only in the two samples to which the volunteer had directed his intention.

This suggests that the effects are not simply the result of an amorphous energy field, but are highly correlated with the intender's intentions.

The researchers speculated that the effects might be due to the proximity of the samples to the participants' hearts, since the heart generates a strong electromagnetic field. They therefore performed similar experiments at a distance of half a mile from the DNA samples. The effects were the same. Five nonlocal trials showed the same effect, all to statistically significant levels.

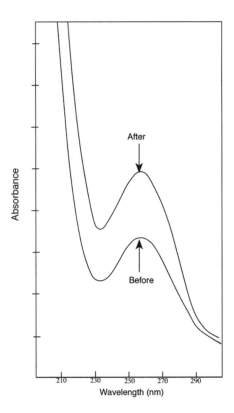

Ultraviolet absorption in DNA before and after being exposed to human intention (McCraty, Atkinson, & Tomasino, 2003).

These studies demonstrate that the DNA molecule can be altered through intentionality. The better participants were at generating a state of heart coherence, the better they were at affecting DNA with their intentions. Control group participants who were untrained and unskilled at heart coherence were unable to produce an effect despite the strength of their intentions. Both intention and coherence were required in order to alter the DNA molecules.

The researchers suggested that "an energetic connection exists between structures in the quantum vacuum and corresponding structures on the physical plane," and that "this connection can be influenced by human intentionality."

McCraty and his colleagues also speculated that the positive emotions affecting DNA might play a role in phenomena such as spontaneous remissions, the health and longevity rewards of faith, and the positive effects of prayer.

Legend holds that the Chinese medicine modalities of herbs and acupuncture are a secondary form of healing. Near the start of the 2,000-year-old book *The Yellow Emperor's Classic of Internal Medicine,* the basic text of acupuncture, the Yellow Emperor says, "I have heard that in early ancient times, there were the Enlightened People who could . . . breathe in the essence of qi, meditate, and their spirit and body would become whole."

In the distant past, the original acupuncturists believed, healing occurred by means of coherent intention and energy alone. This was a belief in the West as well. Romantic poet William Blake asked the question: "Does a firm persuasion that a thing is so make it so?" and replied to himself, "In ages of imagination this firm persuasion removed mountains" (Blake, 1968, p. 256).

The qi energy of traditional Chinese medicine has also been focused by Dr. Yan on living cells, not just on americium-241. When he applied five minutes of coherent mind to cancer cells and healthy cells, the DNA in the cancer cells disintegrated while the healthy cells were not harmed (Yan et al., 2006). In other studies, similar effects were noted in colorectal, prostate, and breast cancer cells.

The effect of human-generated healing energy has been measured in a large number of studies. A systematic review of 90 randomized controlled trials of healing methods—mainly qigong, healing touch, and Reiki—found that two-thirds of the higher-quality trials showed that the techniques were effective (Hammerschlag, Marx, & Aickin, 2014).

OKAY, IT HAPPENS. BUT HOW?

In science, *that* something is happening is usually observed before we understand *how* something is happening. EFT tapping studies showed *that* anxiety, depression, and phobias could be healed a decade before they showed *how* these conditions were being healed (cortisol reduction, brain coherence, gene expression). Medicine knew *that* aspirin cured pain a century before it understood *how*. *That* penicillin killed bacteria was discovered more than 30 years before science understood *how* it worked.

How are the intentions of a coherent mind able to affect matter?

We think of material realities as facts, but in the quantum world, all possibilities exist simultaneously and then condense into probabilities. Theoretically, any of the swarm of infinite possibilities present in the possibility wave can become reality. But only one possibility does. The swarm is then said to have "collapsed" into a particular reality.

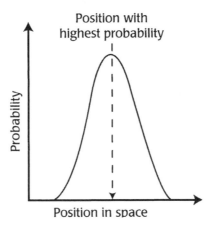

Distribution of quantum probability.

One of the factors that determine the direction in which the swarm of possibilities collapses is the act of observation. In a quantum universe, phenomena and space and time are affected by the observer. All possibilities exist in the quantum field; the act of observation collapses them into probability.

This is called the observer effect. When subatomic particles are observed, they collapse from an infinite number of possibilities to a single probability. Without the observer, they remain in a state of indeterminate possibility. Only when observed do they become a single defined probability. The scientific discovery that it requires observation to create material fact has profound implications for our understanding of the material world and the role of consciousness in creating it.

THE OBSERVER EFFECT

The observer effect is measured in a classic physics demonstration called the double-slit experiment. It has been repeated hundreds of times in the past century. It shows how the presence of an observer changes the outcome of what is observed.

While subatomic particles like electrons are supposed to behave according to the fixed laws of physics, they don't always cooperate. The double-slit experiment demonstrates that the act of observing a particle affects its behavior.

Electrons are fired at a barrier with two slits in it, and where they end up is recorded. If they behaved as particles, you'd expect to see two vertical areas of impact on the other side. It would be as if you'd thrown paint-covered tennis balls at the slits and they'd produced two vertical paint splashes on the wall.

But the electrons don't behave like tennis balls. Instead, they interact with each other to produce a wave. This also happens with photons of light, with water, and with sound.

What happens when you shoot a single photon through the double slits? It still forms an interference pattern, just as if it were traveling through both slits simultaneously.

However, if you place a detector near the slits and observe the process, the electrons behave like tennis balls. The wave interaction pattern disappears.

If you pass larger particles through the slits, they also behave like tennis balls. But on the level of the subatomic, electrons and photons behave like waves unless they are observed, in which case they show up as predictable tennis-ball particles. The act of observation completely changes the outcome of the experiment, collapsing waves into particles, energy into matter.

Setup of the double-slit experiment.

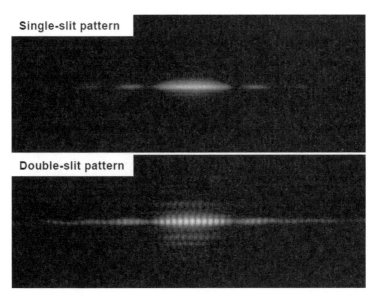

Interference patterns. *Top:* a single slit produces the expected line.
The double slit produces a wave pattern as observed electrons interact.

The double-slit experiment shows that subatomic particles can combine the characteristics of a particle and a wave and that the act of observation changes their behavior. Nobel prize–winning physicist Richard Feynman called it "a phenomenon which is impossible . . . to explain in any classical way, and which has in it the heart of quantum mechanics. In reality, it contains the only mystery [of quantum mechanics]" (Feynman, Leighton, & Sands, 1965).

Electrons and photons exist in waves of possibility. The act of observation triggers the collapse of the wave into a probability. Being measured by a machine produces the observer effect, and so does measurement by a human observer.

ENTANGLEMENT BETWEEN DISTANT PARTICLES

A second important principle from quantum physics is the phenomenon of entanglement. Physicists can produce entanglement by firing a laser through a crystal. Both photons of light and electrons of matter can be entangled. If two electrons become entangled, one will spin clockwise and the other counterclockwise. The act of measuring the spin determines the direction of rotation.

Once a pair of electrons has become entangled, they remain so regardless of distance. If a physicist in Paris measures one spinning clockwise, a colleague in San Francisco might observe its entangled partner spinning counterclockwise. No matter how great the degree of separation, the effect persists.

In a key experiment, researchers at the Delft University of Technology began with two unentangled electrons. Each electron was entangled with a photon, after which both photons were taken to a third location where they were entangled with each other. This caused both of their partner electrons to become entangled as well (Hensen et al., 2015).

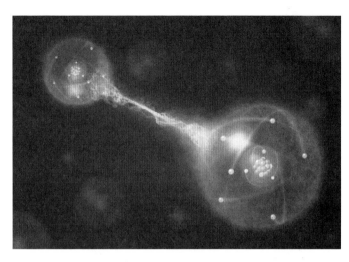

Entanglement between distant atomic particles.

An ingenious study performed by Dean Radin and Arnaud Delorme of the Institute of Noetic Sciences tested the effect of observation by human minds compared to robot observation. They had a double-slit experiment "observed" either by a robot or by human observers. The human observers participated online in a total of 5,738 sessions over two years. The results of the experiment showed that human observation—real live minds—produces a greater observer effect than machine observation (Radin, Michel, & Delorme, 2016).

THE OBSERVER EFFECT AND ENTANGLED PARTICLES

The observer effect also shows up in entangled particles. In a study using two entangled photons, each had a possible position of being either horizontal or vertical. Left to their own devices in their own little universe, the two photons remain in an indeterminate state. But when an observer intrudes on this closed system by observing one photon, the possibility wave collapses into a probability and the photon becomes either horizontal or vertical. Its entangled partner then responds by taking up the opposite position (Moreva et al., 2014).

Physicist Werner Heisenberg said, "What we observe is not nature in itself, but nature exposed to our method of questioning" (1962).

Not until they are observed do entangled photons take up opposite polarities (Fickler, Krenn, Lapkiewicz, Ramelow, & Zeilinger, 2013).

"In the realm of possibility," says quantum physicist Amit Goswami, Ph.D., "the electron is not separate from us, from consciousness. It is a possibility of consciousness itself, a material possibility. When consciousness collapses the possibility wave by choosing one of the electron's possible facets, that facet becomes actuality" (Goswami, 2004).

So the scientific mind, rather than impartially witnessing objective phenomena, is itself influencing which of the infinite sea of potentials winks into existence as a phenomenon. Goswami continues, "The agency that transforms possibility into actuality is consciousness. It is a fact that whenever we observe an object, we see a unique actuality, not the entire spectrum of possibilities. Thus, conscious observation is sufficient condition for the collapse of the possibility wave."

IS SCIENCE THE OBJECTIVE MEASUREMENT OF MATERIAL PHENOMENA?

Science is usually thought of as the objective measurement of material phenomena. When a scientist reports that she has found a molecule that kills cancer cells and the results are published in a reputable journal, we believe that they are true. When a team investigates a social phenomenon such as emotional contagion and provides a statistical analysis demonstrating the effect, we confidently assume that it exists.

But what if all of science is swayed by the observer effect? What if scientists are finding things they expect to find, not just at the level of electrons and photons but stars and galaxies as well? What if the minds of scientists are shaping the matter they observe? What if the strength of their belief is producing all or part of the effects they're observing? What if the degree of belief scientists possess determines the outcome of their experiments?

Belief permeates and shapes the entire field of science. Scientists set out to measure something because they believe there is something to be measured. If they don't believe something is there, they don't look for it, so they have no way of finding it.

An example of this comes from the research into the spiritual states of AIDS patients. Early AIDS research focused on the disease as a biological phenomenon to be targeted at the level of matter. Only after hundreds of studies had been performed with that mind-set did a research team include a questionnaire that assessed the spiritual states of patients.

To their astonishment, they found that the beliefs patients held about God and the universe affected the progression of the disease. The quantity of AIDS virus in the bloodstreams of those who believed in a punishing God increased three times faster than those who believed in a benevolent God. Beliefs predicted whether patients would live or die more strongly than factors such as depression, risky behavior, and coping skills (Ironson et al., 2011).

Before that landmark study, the importance of spiritual belief was unknown. Not because it didn't exist, but because no one had thought to look for it.

The beliefs held in the minds of scientists shape the material reality they discover at every turn.

THE EXPECTANCY EFFECT

In an influential 1963 animal trial at Harvard University, researchers tested what is known as the expectancy effect. If you expect something to happen, you're more likely to perceive it happening. Professor Robert Rosenthal gave students two groups of lab rats. He told them that one group had been specially bred to be good at running mazes, or "maze bright." The others had been bred to be "maze dull." In reality, the rats had been randomly allocated between the two groups. The students conducted their tests and duly found the "maze bright" rats to outperform the others (Rosenthal & Fode, 1963).

Rosenthal then performed a similar experiment with teachers. He told them that tests showed that certain of their students were entering a year of academic flourishing. In reality, these students had also been selected at random. At the end of the year, the IQ scores of the designated students were higher than the control group (Rosenthal & Jacobson, 1963). Mind had produced matter, with belief making significant changes in performance in the material world.

The Freshman Whose Ignorance Could Precipitate Crystals

A grad student who supervised a chemistry lab at MIT described to me one of the procedures she and her fellow students were required to learn as part of the curriculum. They had to precipitate sodium acetate crystals out of a supersaturated solution. It was tricky to accomplish and required focused attention from the budding chemists. Most had to make many attempts and even then were not always successful. They knew that the procedure was difficult, and successful precipitation was akin to a rite of passage in the lab.

That semester, a first-year student joined the lab as an assistant. The first time he attempted the experiment, he was able to precipitate the sodium crystals immediately. The supervisor was very surprised. When the student tried it again, the result was the same. The freshman was able to precipitate the crystals effortlessly every time he tried. "He just has a knack for it," the supervisor exclaimed, with puzzlement tinged with envy. The student was so green that he hadn't yet received the memo that the procedure was fraught with difficulty.

Variability in the results obtained among individual scientists isn't supposed to happen in empirical sciences such as physics and chemistry. Molecules and atoms are supposed to behave the same way under the same conditions at all times. There is no room in the standard scientific paradigm for scientists' intentions, beliefs, or energy fields to be influencing the results.

Yet reports reveal that certain chemists are better than others at making elements behave and can use their intention to "will" them to conform (Sheldrake, 2012). Physicist Fred Alan Wolf speculates that "the laws of the universe may simply be the laws of our own collective minds" (Wolf, 2001). Neuroscience expert Robert Hoss says, "Solid matter is just an illusion. At our most fundamental level we may look something like this—an organized soup of subatomic particles popping in and out of existence within the infinite energy field of the universe" (Hoss, 2016).

THE MIND OF SCIENCE

The sciences can be classified by the scale and type of their subjects. First comes physics, which studies the most fundamental levels of matter such as atoms and subatomic particles. Then comes chemistry, which looks at how those particles assemble themselves into molecules and interact with each other. These sciences are called the physical sciences—or "pure" sciences or "hard" sciences—because they measure the cold, hard objective fact of physical matter. They're based on mathematics rather than the squishy unpredictability of living things.

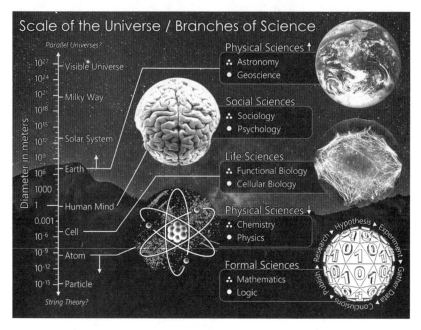

The scale of the universe mapped to the branches of science, with physical sciences as the foundation.

Biology and the other life sciences build on physics and chemistry to study living cells, tissues, and organisms. These interact in complex systems that are often unstable and evolving in unpredictable directions. Geology and astronomy also study solid physical matter. Geology examines the composition of the planet. Astronomy scales up by a large order of magnitude to look at the material structure and motion of stars, galaxies, and the universe.

Then come the "soft" sciences of the mind. Psychology examines individual behavior, while sociology studies the interactions of groups. Those in the hard sciences often feel superior to those in the soft sciences because they deal with the level of matter rather than that of mind. Physicist Ernest Rutherford, who in 1907 discovered that the atom was mostly empty space and that subatomic particles are bound together by electromagnetic fields, had a low opinion of the other sciences, sniffing contemptuously, "In science there is only physics. All the rest is stamp collecting."

THE REPLICATION CRISIS

When they publish their papers, scientists are required to provide a "methods" section. This outlines how the experiment was set up and does this so clearly that other scientists can run the same experiment in an attempt to replicate the previous study's findings.

A discovery published in a single paper may represent an actual effect. But when an independent research team comes up with the same result, it's likely that the effect found in the first study is real. For this reason, replication studies are important in science.

So much so that before it approves a new drug, the U.S. Food and Drug Administration (FDA) requires two studies demonstrating the drug's efficacy. When formulating standards for "empirically validated therapies," the American Psychological Association borrowed the same standard, requiring a replication of a study before declaring the therapy evidence based (Chambless & Hollon, 1998).

In the early 2000s, a giant biotech company, Amgen, set out to replicate some important studies. The company was pouring millions of dollars into research on cancer biology based on earlier research. If the effects found in the original studies were robust, then the next stage of development of cancer drugs would be built on solid ground. They asked their scientists which previous studies were most important to their work and came up with 53 "landmark" studies.

In 10 years of work, Amgen was able to replicate only 6 of the 53 studies. The researchers called this "a shocking result" (Begley & Ellis, 2012).

A few months earlier, another giant pharma company, Bayer, had published a similar analysis. This led to a sustained effort to determine how many key studies were replicable. An attempt to replicate five cancer biology trials was successful for only two (eLife, 2017). Epidemiologist John Ioannidis of Stanford University summarized the findings by saying, "The composite picture is, there is a reproducibility problem" (Kaiser, 2017).

What about the soft sciences? An international group of 270 researchers set out to replicate 100 studies published in 2008 in three top psychology journals. They found that they were able to replicate fewer than half of them (Open Science Collaboration, 2015).

The journal *Nature* conducted a survey of 1,576 researchers to identify their experiences with replication. It found that over 70 percent of them had failed when attempting to reproduce another scientist's research findings. Over half could not even replicate their own research (Baker, 2016).

There are many roots to the "reproducibility crisis" in science. A variety of factors stand in the way of successful replications. Among them are haphazard laboratory management, sample sizes too small to provide a high degree of statistical power, and the use of specialized techniques that are uniquely hard to repeat.

Selective reporting plays a big role, too, as positive results are usually reported while negative ones are swept under the rug. These are called file drawer studies because, metaphorically, they are thrown into the bottom drawer of a filing cabinet, never to see the light of day. An analysis of psychology studies estimates that 50 percent are never published (Cooper, DeNeve, & Charlton, 1997).

Another factor making studies hard to replicate is that beliefs can influence the results. Scientists have beliefs. They're human. They are not godlike intellects immune from glory seeking, egotism, jealousy, and territorialism. They have whims, preferences, and needs. They need successful research to obtain grants, jobs, and tenure. They fall in love with their work, the "Pygmalion effect" immortalized in the musical *My Fair Lady*. Scientists approach their work with as many presuppositions as any other demographic group has.

Scientists believe in what they're doing and look for effects they expect to find. The strength of their beliefs may skew their results, a phenomenon called the expectancy effect. To control for this, most medical research is carried out blind. The statisticians analyzing two groups of data don't know which sample is from the experimental and which from the control group.

Experiments in the physical sciences, such as chemistry and physics, are assumed to be independent of the observer effect, so they are blinded in fewer than one percent of cases.

The same is not true in the hard sciences, such as physics and chemistry. Surveys show that under one percent of studies in these fields are performed blind (Sheldrake, 1999; Watt & Nagtegaal, 2004). The researchers carrying them out know which of the samples is the experimental one, and the beliefs and expectations in their minds may well be producing the effects they observe in matter. The observer effect has been measured at the level of atoms and molecules in the physical sciences as well as on the scale of people and societies in the soft sciences.

MEASURING THE STRENGTH OF SCIENTISTS' BELIEF SYSTEMS

How strong are the beliefs of scientists? An interesting test comes from the work of Daryl Bem, a social psychologist at Cornell University, who performed experiments on precognition. In a series of nine experiments with over 1,000 participants, he found a statistically significant link supporting foreknowledge of future events (Bem, 2011).

Bem's critics so strongly believed that precognition was not true that they applied a radically more stringent approach. First, they analyzed each of the nine experiments separately, instead of combining the results to provide the largest possible pool of data (Radin, 2011). It's always more difficult to find an effect in a smaller data pool. They then used a statistical test very different from those normally used in psychology studies (Wagenmakers, Wetzels, Borsboom, & Van Der Maas, 2011).

The technique they used requires the formulation of two prior beliefs about the phenomenon. The first is the belief that it is true, the other that it is false. They set their level of belief that precognition cannot exist at 100,000 trillion to 1 (Radin, 2011). Unsurprisingly, this made the effect go away.

Bem's research team used this same method to re-analyze their own data. They found that even if you had a tiny belief that precognition might be true, the collective result of their nine experiments showed that it exists. How tiny? You needed only a prior belief there was 1 chance in 100 million that premonition might occur (Bem, Utts, & Johnson, 2011).

You didn't need to be a true believer in precognition to identify the effect. Even if you were a firm skeptic whose mind allowed just a sliver of belief—1 possibility in 100 million—the study validated precognition: "If one begins with the possibility that retrocausal effects might be real, even when that possibility is extremely small, then the strength of the existing evidence will substantially shift one's belief towards [precognition]" (Radin, 2011).

UNWAVERING FAITH

An independent team failed to replicate Bem's study (Ritchie, Wiseman, & French, 2012). This led to a large-scale research effort, involving 90 experiments in 33 different labs in 14 countries. This time, Bem used both the unconventional statistical methods of his critics as well the standard tests of probability and found that both supported the existence of premonition (Bem, Tressoldi, Rabeyron, & Duggan, 2015).

Most skeptics don't believe in premonition.

Bem's first experiment and the re-analysis of his data by his critics provides a fascinating but unintentional statistical comparison of just how strong beliefs among scientists can become. Bem's detractors could not tolerate a belief of just 1 possibility in 100 million that premonition might exist and set the threshold of their faith at an astonishing 100,000 trillion to 1 (Radin, 2011). That's the kind of unwavering certainty that the most hardened fundamentalist would be proud of.

The survey in *Nature* showing that 70 percent of scientists fail at replication didn't make much of a dent in their confidence in science. Their belief remained strong. Most still trust published papers. They're much more optimistic than they might be expected to be, based on the data: "Seventy-three percent said that they think that at least half of the papers in their field can be trusted, with physicists and chemists generally showing the most confidence" (Baker, 2016).

What we find when we examine the way science is conducted is that for better or for worse, it is heavily influenced by belief. The ideal of the scientist as an objective assessor of facts is at odds with reality. Scientists are believers, especially in their own work. They cannot separate mind from matter.

Science is not, in fact, the objective measurement of matter. It's a dance between the inner consciousness, or mind, of the scientist and the material world of matter. Change mind, and matter changes right along with it.

AT WHAT SCALE DO ENTANGLEMENT AND THE OBSERVER EFFECT OPERATE?

The consensus in physics up through the early 21st century was that entanglement and the observer effect occurred only on a micro scale. They were peculiar properties of the subatomic world, but for structures larger than an atom, good old-fashioned common-sense cause-and-effect Newtonian physics applied. Because entanglement requires communication between particles faster than the speed of light, Einstein detested it and called it "spooky action at a distance" (Born, 1971).

So for a century, physicists confined spooky action to the realm of the tiny. It could not possibly be operating at the large scales of things like cells and organisms. In 2011, however, researchers were able to entangle millions of atoms together at one time (Lee et al., 2011). In 2007, quantum effects were discovered in the way light is used by bacteria for photosynthesis. In 2010, this phenomenon was measured at room temperature, and in 2014, researchers discovered that this quantum coherence in living organisms is organized by fields (Romero et al., 2014).

On the human level, research has shown that our sense of smell is able to detect molecules based on their quantum energetic signature rather than just their shape (Gane et al., 2013). In the human brain, groups of neurons seem to have their own version of quantum entanglement. Widely spaced neural regions are able to fire in coherence, at the same time, in a process called phase locking, possibly synchronized by quantum communication (Thiagarajan et al., 2010).

Another important experiment seeking quantum effects in human brains examined seven pairs of subjects hooked up to EEGs. They enclosed one person from each pair in a soundproof room shielded from all known forms of electromagnetic radiation. At random intervals, 100 times during the course of the experiment, the brain of the member of the pair outside the room was stimulated briefly. When the two groups of brain wave samples were compared, they showed that the brains of those inside the shielded room responded to the stimulation of the partner outside (Grinberg-Zylberbaum, Delaflor, Attie, & Goswami, 1994).

In an experiment on a planetary scale, the Chinese government in 2016 launched the Quantum Experiments at Space Scale (QUESS) mission. Its goal is to use quantum coherence at distances of thousands of miles to provide ultra-secure data transmission.

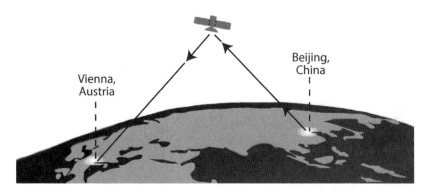

**The QUESS teleportation system uses photon
entanglement to transmit data securely.**

When data are transmitted through fiber-optic cables, the data get scattered or absorbed. Preserving the quantum state of photons over large distances is not possible using this technology. The goal of the Chinese project is to teleport quantum states using entangled pairs of photons.

Data are encrypted by polarizing a string of photons, which are then transmitted through space by bouncing the data off a satellite to a distant location on the planet. This eliminates the scattering that occurs when data are transmitted using fiber-optic cables and results in secure transmission.

GLOBAL CYCLES

The serious study of the effects of the fields of the earth, sun, and planets on human beings is a recent and exciting new branch of science. The interactions between these global fields and life-forms, and the effects that living beings are having on the planet's field, are just starting to be mapped.

The largest-scale project to gather data on these interactions is called the Global Coherence Initiative (GCI). It uses large, recently developed magnetometers to measure changes in the Earth's magnetic field. They are located all over the world. They measure "biologically relevant information that connects all living systems" (McCraty & Deyhle, 2016).

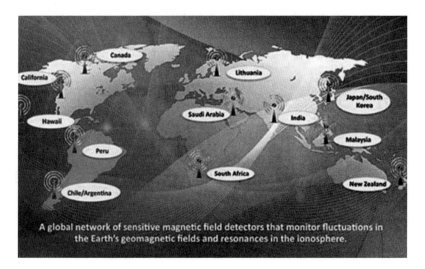

A global network of sensitive magnetic field detectors that monitor fluctuations in the Earth's geomagnetic fields and resonances in the ionosphere.

The six operating and six proposed Global Coherence Initiative (GCI) monitoring sites.

The GCI sensors monitor changes triggered by shifts in the Earth's magnetic field, by solar storms, and by changes in the speed of the solar wind. They also test the hypothesis that collective human consciousness affects this information field, and they seek to determine whether "large numbers of people creating heart-centered states of care, love and compassion will generate a more coherent field environment that can benefit others and help offset the current planetary discord and incoherence."

Russian scientist Alexander Tchijevsky noticed a striking fact when looking at sunspot flares that occurred early in the 20th century. They coincided with the most violent battles of World War I (Tchijevsky, 1971). This led him to analyze earlier periods dating from 1749 to 1926. He looked at major historical events in the histories of 72 countries such as the onset of social revolutions and wars and found the same relationship going back centuries. He identified an 80 percent correlation between social upheaval and sunspot activity.

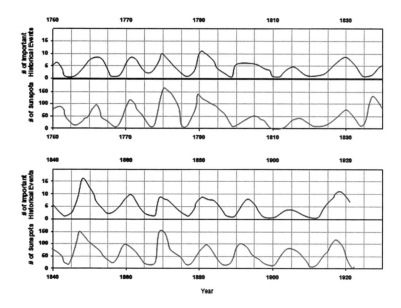

The upper line represents historical events and the lower line represents the number of sunspots during the same period.

This effect works in the opposite direction too. Solar activity has been related to periods of cultural flourishing and positive social evolution with leaps in the arts, science, architecture, and social justice (McCraty & Deyhle, 2016).

When a person is in a heart coherent state, they also radiate a coherent signal all around their body. When such a person comes together with others, that produces a group field effect (McCraty & Childre, 2010). This brings people nearby into coherence too. The goal of GCI is both to measure and to influence these interactions. Large numbers of people in coherence may be able to nudge the whole psychosphere of the planet toward positive evolutionary shifts.

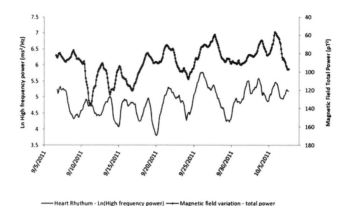

One participant's heart rate variability (HRV) and the magnetic field at the California GCI site over a 30-day period.

This process is expected to "greatly accelerate cooperation, collaboration, innovative problem-solving and intuitive discernment for addressing society's significant social, environmental and economic problems. This will become increasingly apparent as countries adopt a more coherent and inclusive planetary view. This planetary view will be critical for meaningfully and successfully addressing social and economic oppression, wars, cultural intolerance, crime and disregard for the environment" (McCraty & Deyhle, 2016).

Shifts in human consciousness can also be measured using random number generators (RNGs). These are computers that simply generate a continuous stream of zeros and ones at random. Because they're designed to produce random output, they should not, in principle, do anything else. At moments of peak collective experience, however, the streams of digits that they are constantly generating do indeed change. They deviate from randomness, sometimes so far that the results are statistically significant, meaning that there's only 1 possibility in 20 that the results are due to chance. At large sporting events, when the crowd is going wild, RNGs have been found to deviate significantly from baseline (Leskowitz, 2014).

MEASURING SHIFTS IN COLLECTIVE GLOBAL CONSCIOUSNESS

The Global Consciousness Project (GCP) is an international collective of scientists and engineers. It collects data from 70 host sites around the world and transmits the data to a central repository at Princeton University (Nelson, 2015).

When dramatic events engage large numbers of people around the globe and global consciousness becomes coherent, the behavior of the RNGs changes. It deviates from randomness. For around two decades, the GCP has been tracking these changes. It finds these correlate with significant global events that involve the awareness of large groups of people. Examples of these events include:

- 1998: The bombings of the U.S. embassies in Kenya and Tanzania

- 1999: The aerial bombardment of Yugoslavia by NATO in an effort to stop the massacre of Serbs

- 2000: The first visit by the pope to Israel

- 2000: The explosion on board the Russian submarine *Kursk*

- 2003: A global candlelight vigil for peace organized by Desmond Tutu and various organizations

- 2004: The Democratic Party convention

- 2004: The Beslan massacre in which 150 hostages died in Russia

- 2005: The Iraqi elections

- 2005: The earthquake in Kashmir, Pakistan

- 2006: The magnitude 6.2 earthquake in Indonesia in which over 3,000 people died

- 2008: The nomination of Barack Obama as president

- 2010: The passage of the Obamacare reform act

- 2010: The Israeli attack on a flotilla of pro-Palestinian activists that killed nine civilians

- 2010: The rescue of 33 Chilean miners after 18 days underground

- 2011: A global meditation called by New Reality Group, a group of "physicists and mathematicians that believe our very own consciousness defines our reality"

- 2013: A global meditation organized by the Peace Portal Activations group

- 2013: The death of Nelson Mandela

- 2015: International Peace Day

The GCP calculates the statistical probability of these changes occurring. It also tracks the cumulative possibility that these correlations are happening purely by chance. Those odds are one in a trillion (Nelson, 2015).

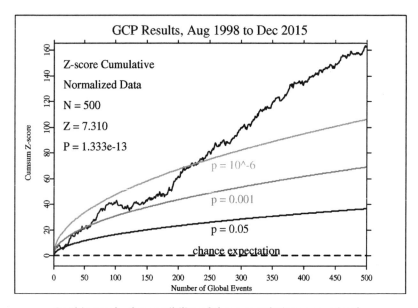

On this graph, the possibility of these correlations occurring by chance is indicated by the bottom dashed line. The three smooth curves represent increasing levels of statistical significance. The final result is the jagged top line (Nelson, 2015).

These large-scale measurements show that collective human consciousness interacts with the material world. Carl Jung believed that some elements of personal experience spring from a much larger consciousness shared by all humankind, which he termed the collective unconscious. He believed that "The collective unconscious contains the whole spiritual heritage of mankind's evolution, born anew in the brain structure of every individual" (1952).

Large-scale scientific projects such as the GCP and the GCI are now allowing us to measure the effects of shared experience. We are finding that what we experience collectively is having an effect on the material world. Group mind is affecting the matter of the entire psychosphere in which we live.

PERSONAL COHERENCE INFLUENCES GLOBAL COHERENCE

When we come into personal coherence, we feel much better emotionally, spiritually, and physically. Our cortisol levels go down, while the neurotransmitters serotonin and dopamine balance in our brains. We have high levels of all the brain waves that promote healing and low levels of anxiety-linked high beta. We feel good subjectively, and this translates into objective changes in the biology of our cells. Mind becomes matter as our brains are flooded with pleasure-inducing endorphins, intimacy-producing oxytocin, and the bliss molecule anandamide.

We're also then resonant with the corresponding global frequencies. We aren't living our lives as isolated human beings but as resonant nodes that are part of a great universal whole. As we increase our personal coherence, we add our measure to the sum of coherence being generated by everyone else on the planet resonating in synchrony with those energies.

In this way, we play a small but significant part in nudging the whole planet into flourishing. The following story by Joe Marana is an example of the synchronicities that sometimes tie geological and personal events together.

My Sister's Love FROM BEYOND THE Grave

By Joe Marana

I had lent a cassette set of Wayne Dyer's audio program *Real Magic* to a friend.

It contains six cassettes. When they were returned to me, they were all rewound except for one cassette. I was a little bit annoyed and thought, *Why didn't he rewind this one?*

Then I thought, *Maybe there's a message here for me.* So I went over to my elaborate stereo system with its fancy cassette player, dropped the tape in, and hit the play button.

I heard Wayne Dyer's voice saying, "What if you hadn't heard from your sister in three years and you're thinking about how nice it would be to talk to her?"

I was stunned. It was the three-year anniversary of my sister's death, and I had been missing her terribly.

When the mail arrived that day, it included a letter from a lady from Paraguay named Juanita Lopez. She has multiple sclerosis, and a few times each year I send her money. Each time, Juanita would write back and give me a detailed list of what she'd spent the money on. Shoes for her niece. New thatch on her roof. A water purifier.

I opened the letter. At the very top, in block capitals, in handwriting completely different from Juanita's, it said, "I am your everlasting sister and I remember you every day and send you love."

I fell to the ground, and I couldn't stop sobbing for a long time.

I fired off an airmail letter to Juanita asking, "Why did you say that?"

The next day, there was an earthquake in Paraguay. It killed four people, and one of them was Juanita Lopez. So I never got a reply.

I shared this story with a scientist from the Institute of Noetic Sciences, and he said that the most likely explanation is entanglement. The letter had been mailed before I heard the message from Wayne Dyer. Yet somehow they were all connected.

To add to the synchronicities, I heard Joe's story on a radio show while I was parked outside a hotel in my car, waiting for my wife, Christine, to check us out. I had just finished keynoting the annual conference of . . . (you guessed it) . . . the Institute of Noetic Sciences.

ENTANGLED LIVES

Entanglement might be at work in distant healing and nonlocal communication. People who are emotionally close are also neurologically close, no matter the distance. Research teams at Bastyr University in Seattle and the University of Washington examined the EEG signatures of people with close emotional bonds. They found that when a partner was shown an image, the other partner, even though distant, immediately developed the same pattern of EEG brain function (Standish, Kozak, Johnson, & Richards, 2004).

A gifted faith healer might be considered, in quantum terms, to be an observer who routinely collapses space-time possibilities into the probability of healing. A prayer is an intention that might also collapse the swarm of possibilities present in the possibility wave in the direction of a certain probability.

In *The Intention Experiment,* her book about large international experiments that gauge the effect of human intention on physical matter, Lynne McTaggart states that the observer effect implies that "living consciousness is somehow central to this process of transforming the unconstructed quantum world into something resembling everyday reality," and that "reality is not fixed, but fluid, and hence possibly open to influence" (McTaggart, 2007). According to Bill Bengston, "This suggests that human consciousness, individually and collectively, produces what we call 'reality'" (Bengston, 2010).

Robert Hoss, an expert on the neuroscience of extrasensory phenomena such as near-death experiences and precognitive dreams, asks a provocative question: If it is only the act of observation that is collapsing the waves of energy into the particles of matter that make up the world around us, *who or what is doing the observing?* Who is the grand observer catalyzing the creation of all the matter in the physical world? Hoss believes it is consciousness: the great nonlocal consciousness of the universe itself. That is, the universe itself is consciousness, continually creating matter out of mind (Hoss, 2016).

This view has increasing support from mainstream scientists. Gregory Matloff is a veteran physicist at the New York City College of Technology. He argues that our individual local minds may be linked to the nonlocal mind of the cosmos through a "proto-consciousness field" that extends through all of space. In this model, the minds of stars might be controlling their orbital journeys through matter. The entire universe may be self-aware. His views are shared by many others (Powell, 2017).

When we as human beings release the fixation our local minds have on local reality and instead align our local consciousness with the nonlocal consciousness of the universe, we bring local mind into coherence with nonlocal mind. In this coherent state, what we create with local mind is a reflection of nonlocal mind. We're no longer limited by our old, conditioned thinking, so we no longer create the same present-day reality out of the stale experiences of our past.

Instead, we think outside the box. We see possibilities we were blind to when trapped in local mind. We explore the potential of our lives found in the expansive awareness of nonlocal mind. We perceive ways in which the world can change that we simply don't see when stuck in a noncoherent personal reality field. The observer effect demonstrates that reality is plastic. Bringing the power of coherent mind to our experience, our perception creates events that are extraordinary.

In my own life, I find it easy to get sucked into the conventional view that "facts are facts" and that the outside world just is the way it is. To correct this tendency, I practice framing my experiences, good or bad, in ways that support my goals. When I'm acting with awareness, I use my mind to create and maintain a "reality field" that is congruent with what I want.

Maintaining the Reality Field

I had a career change at the age of 45. I'd left the book publishing world a few years earlier and purchased a small hotel. While I raised my two children, I lived a semiretired life.

I was also bored to tears, feeling cut off from the world of healing and ideas I'd participated in as a publisher.

To get back in the game, I decided to publish an anthology called *The Heart of Healing,* a reprise of a successful anthology I'd published in the 1980s.

I sent letters of invitation to 30 of the best-known names in healing, people like Larry Dossey, Deepak Chopra, Donna Eden, Bernie Siegel, and Christiane Northrup.

Inside each letter was a stamped blue postcard. I asked each person to check a box saying yes or no and write a line explaining why they were responding that way.

For the following month, I ran out to my mailbox eagerly each day, awaiting the return of blue postcards. The first one came from Bernie Siegel with a yes! I went back to my office and told my assistant how relieved I felt that at least one person, Bernie, hadn't forgotten me after 15 years!

Then came one from Larry Dossey with a no.

I ran back into my office. I waved the postcard above my head excitedly. After seeing the no, my assistant looked at me with a puzzled frown.

"I've opened a dialogue with Larry Dossey!" I exclaimed.

That's how I framed every no. That blue postcard didn't represent a closed door, it was the start of a dialogue. I maintained my reality field of a successful anthology even when faced with evidence to the contrary.

Eventually, almost all the no's did appear in the anthology, which went on to win an award for best health book of the year. As for Larry, he has become a friend and sent me one of the very first endorsements for *Mind to Matter*.

CULTIVATING COHERENT MIND

We can retrain our scattered and chaotic minds to function coherently. EEG scans show that this produces flares of gamma waves, signaling increased creativity as well as orchestration of all the regions of the brain. Add to that synchronization entrainment with the nonlocal mind of the universe and our intentions have the focused power of a laser.

As Christine and I discovered with the Geiger counter, the ability to use intention to affect molecular matter isn't a superhuman anomaly. It's something a trained and coherent mind can easily accomplish. Entanglement and the double-slit experiments demonstrate that consciousness is influencing the material world around us every day.

Stanford University professor William Tiller reminds us of the difference between incoherent light in an incandescent bulb and the power of organized light in the form of a laser. He says: "Just like the light bulb example, vast unutilized potential exists within us, the basic ingredients are already there but they are relatively incoherent with respect to each other. Our task is to transform the largely incoherent ingredients into a completely coherent system" (Tiller, 1997).

Think deliberately. Use this remarkable gift of consciousness to direct your thoughts rather than being pushed around by reality. Even adverse circumstances can propel us to greatness if we've mastered our minds, deliberately filling them with love and purpose rather than doubt and fear.

A coherent mind has the power of a laser, able to cut through steel. Consciousness, holding an elevated reality, organizes our neural pathways. It brings our brain waves into coherence, along with our hearts and every other system in our bodies. It rewires our neural networks. In this state, we're able to operate at levels that transcend the known laws of physics.

We then join naturally together with other people, aligning with the large social energy fields of positive resonance. Synchronicities become the norm rather than the exception. As philosopher C. S. Lewis exclaimed, "Miracles are a retelling in small letters of the very same story which is written across the whole world in letters too large for some of us to see" (Lewis, 1970).

Cultivating coherent local mind starts with aligning our consciousness with the fields of love and creativity found in nonlocal mind. That's why meditating first thing in the morning, while your brain is in an alpha state, before beta kicks in, is so effective. Trying to quiet the mind after the floodgates of thought have already opened is hard. Extending the alpha state you've been in when your eyes were closed during sleep is much easier.

When I wake up in the morning, I want to stretch out that alpha connection as long as possible, so I meditate immediately. I then start my day with coherent mind rather than caveman brain. These positive mental states have profound effects on health and longevity. Optimists have half the mortality rate of pessimists, and lowering your stress can add 10 years to your life span (Giltay, Geleijnse, Zitman, Hoekstra, & Schouten, 2004; Diener & Chan, 2011).

A mind attuned to the infinite is a wonderful place to live. It nudges the matter of our bodies toward health and well-being. It unlocks our creativity. It shifts our family and community relationships to a state of love, compassion, and pleasure. It nurtures the natural world and influences the psychosphere of the entire planet. Our minds, organized into coherence, can illuminate the realm of miracles.

PUTTING THESE IDEAS INTO PRACTICE

Activities to practice this week:

- Continue to practice EcoMeditation for at least 10 minutes each morning and evening.

- Touch the people in your household every day deliberately. This can be:

  > An encouraging squeeze on the shoulder
  > A pat on the back
  > A longer hug than usual

- In your journal, take a look at the entries for the past few weeks. Do you notice any synchronicities? Mark them with an *S*.

The Extended Play version of this chapter includes:

- Audio interview with Bob Hoss

- Statistics on the causes, symptoms, and impact of stress

- The Global Consciousness Project (GCP)

- The Global Coherence Initiative (GCI)

To access the Extended Play version, visit:
MindToMatter.club/Chapter5

CHAPTER 6

Entraining Self with Synchronicity

Molokai is often called the most Hawaiian island. Though 260 miles square, it boasts not a single traffic light. There are two gas stations serving the 7,000 inhabitants, along with one modest grocery store. Visitors stay at an establishment called the Hotel Molokai—"the" hotel because that's the one and only hotel on the island. Visitors can buy postcards entitled "Molokai Nightlife." They're solid black.

My wife, Christine, and I visited Molokai for the first time a few years back. We had 10 days to relax there, and we had a strong intention of connecting with some of the local residents and events. Synchronistically, the day before we flew from Maui to Molokai, we met a musician and shaman from Molokai named Eddie Tanaka. He offered to show us around when he got back to the island a few days after we were due to land there.

On our first day, after driving the oceanfront road for a few miles, we decided to take a walk and try to find a trailhead. We got ready to leave our condo, then got distracted and pottered aimlessly around the living room instead. About 45 minutes later, we finally wandered downstairs to start our planned walk.

My eye was caught by a bumper sticker on a car in the parking lot. It said: "Don't change Molokai. Let Molokai change you." I took a photo with my phone to share on the Love Bathing Facebook page where Christine and I record our travels.

The owner of the car walked by and noticed me photographing her car, and we fell into conversation. She was a retired accountant named Joy, and she turned out to be a fountain of information. She told us where the nearest trails were and about the community sing-alongs where people connect. She shared the locations of heiaus, Hawaiian sacred sites that we love to visit, soaking in the energy fields of these ancient places of worship.

A restored Hawaiian heiau, or ancient temple.

It turned out that Joy and her husband lived in the condo below ours. She knew Eddie and often played ukulele with him. She told us about his distinctive house, with a front wall topped with hundreds of glass bottles. We'd driven past it that morning.

Joy invited us to a community sing-along at the Hotel Molokai the following day, where we met her friends. People welcomed us warmly. At the end of the performance, everyone held hands in a big circle and sang "Hawaii Aloha" together. My heart was so touched that I cried all the way through the beautiful song. We enjoyed 10 days in which we "talked story" with Joy, Eddie, and our other new friends.

But the synchronicities had begun long before that. The year before, the 20-something daughter of a friend of ours took a whole year off work to explore the Caribbean, "looking for the perfect island." I envied her and imagined taking a year off to do that myself. Because of my speaking engagements and my life mission of training people in advanced healing methods, it was impossible.

Then one morning after meditation, I realized, *You don't have to move your body all over the place in a search for the perfect island. The universe already knows! Just ask your inner guidance.* I asked the question, and a still small voice said, *Check out Molokai.* I'd been visiting the Hawaiian Islands for 20 years and it had never occurred to me to visit Molokai before that morning meditation. That nudge led to booking the 10-day vacation.

Christine and I had a wonderful time. Molokai has miles of sandy beaches, and they are usually deserted. Often ours were the only footprints in the sand. On our hikes, we discovered remote *heiaus* so overgrown with vegetation that they were invisible till we stumbled upon them. Magic was in the air every day.

Miles of sandy beaches on Molokai, with a rainbow
thrown in for good measure.

Since I was a toddler, I've been fascinated by rainbows. On a number of occasions, I've driven my car for miles, whimsically trying to locate the base of a particularly vivid rainbow. But I've never found a rainbow's end.

One afternoon, as Christine and I drove around a bend on the rugged west side of Molokai just after a rainstorm, there it was. The rainbow ended on the road just in front of the car. Or rather, one of the rainbows—there were two others ending in the steaming foliage on either side of the road. I'd been granted more than I'd wished for.

We left Molokai feeling loved, rested, and renewed. The morning before our flight left, we went to our last sing-along, at an old coffee plantation, where a sizable percentage of the island's population had turned out to enjoy the homemade entertainment. I left with tears in my eyes, feeling as though I'd found a second home.

None of the connections we made on that first day on the island would likely have happened unless . . .

- We decided to go on a walk our first morning.

- We got distracted and left 45 minutes later than planned.

- I stopped to look at a bumper sticker and stayed long enough to take a photo.

- Joy walked by at that exact moment.

We would never even have been on Molokai if I had not tuned in to my intuition.

Sure, all of this could have happened quite by chance. Yet synchronicities like this happen to Christine and me all the time. Since we met, we've kept a relationship journal in which we record events and epiphanies in our lives.

A few years back, we were struck by just how many unlikely synchronicities happen to us and how things we think about seem to manifest as if by magic. We began writing a big *S* in our journal to identify those entries and to remind ourselves to be grateful for a happy and harmonious life. Journal entries from our time in Molokai contain *S* after *S* after *S*.

GOD'S WAY OF REMAINING ANONYMOUS

Ours is not the first generation to notice synchronicity. It's fascinated human beings for millennia. Two thousand years ago, the father of modern medicine, Hippocrates, observed, "There is one common flow, one common breathing, all things are in sympathy. The whole organism and each one of its parts are working in conjunction for the same purpose. . . . The great principle extends to the extremist part, and from the extremist part it returns to the great principle, to the one nature, being and not-being" (Jung, 1952). Roman emperor and philosopher Marcus Aurelius believed, "Everything is connected and the web is holy."

In the early 20th century, the great Swiss psychiatrist Carl Jung became intrigued by the phenomenon of synchronicity. He defined it as "a meaningful coincidence of two or more events, where something other than the probability of chance is involved" (Jung, 1952, p. 79).

One of his most quoted examples of synchronicity occurred during a therapy session. A young woman who was a patient of Jung's but who was not making progress in her therapy recounted a dream. In it she saw a piece of jewelry shaped like a golden scarab beetle. In ancient Egyptian cosmology, scarabs are the symbol of rebirth.

While they were discussing the dream, Jung heard a rapping at the window. Opening it to investigate, he found a beetle of the scarab family. He gave it to the woman, a symbol of her potential to move past her obstacles and renew her life. Jung wrote, "Synchronicity reveals the meaningful connections between the subjective and objective world."

Albert Einstein was a frequent guest at Jung's house during the time he was developing his theory of relativity. Their conversations about the relativity of time and space played a role in the development of Jung's concepts of synchronicity. Einstein quipped, "Synchronicity is God's way of remaining anonymous."

SYNCHRONICITY AND DREAMS

Dreams are often harbingers of synchronicity. Jung analyzed his patients' dreams, paying particular attention to the symbols they contained. He looked for connections between dream images and waking life, like the scarab beetle. These turn up with surprising frequency.

Dreams can change the course of our lives. They're often filled with symbols and events that contain synchronous links to the real-life challenges we face. They give meaning to our experience and can provide information far beyond the abilities of the waking mind.

One category of synchronous dreams are those that carry information about our health. In dreams, people often gain knowledge about their bodies that transcends the scope of ordinary consciousness.

Radiologist Larry Burk, M.D., has been collecting and studying breast cancer dreams for years. Analyzing stories from women around the world, he finds that many of these dreams are life-changing experiences (Burk, 2015). They also share common characteristics. Among these are that the dreamer senses that the dream is important (94 percent of cases). In 83 percent of cases, the dream is more intense and vivid than other dreams. Most dreamers experience a feeling of dread, and in 44 percent of cases, the words *cancer* or *tumor* appear.

In over half the cases Dr. Burk has collected, the dream resulted in the woman seeking medical consultation. Dreams led directly to diagnosis and frequently highlighted the precise location of the tumors.

The Debris Hidden under the Ledge

One of the participants in Dr. Burk's study is named Wanda Burch. She had a series of dreams about a tumor and followed up by getting a physical exam and mammogram. Neither definitively showed the existence of a tumor. Her physician, Dr. Barlyn, was an open-minded clinician and willing to consider her story. As she tells it:

"Dr. Barlyn listened to my dream and handed me a felt-tip marker. 'Draw the location on your breast.' I drew a dot far underneath the right side of the left breast and told him that another dream had shown me a ledge, with the 'dream debris'—or tumor—hidden underneath the ledge. Dr. Barlyn inserted the biopsy needle in the area I designated and felt resistance, an indication of a problem. The surgical biopsy gave Dr. Barlyn the details of a fast-moving, extremely aggressive breast cancer whose cells were not massing in a fashion that allowed them to be seen on a mammogram."

This led Wanda to successful treatment and to sharing her story with other women in the form of a book called *She Who Dreams* (Burch, 2003).

A friend of Dr. Burk's was not as fortunate in her interaction with her doctor. Sonia Lee-Shield had a warning dream and described her symptoms during a consultation:

"I had a dream that I had cancer. I went to the G.P. complaining of a lump and spasm-like feelings on my sternum. The G.P. concluded it was normal breast tissue, and the feeling in my sternum was dismissed, a devastating mistake. A year later, a different doctor diagnosed stage 3 breast cancer."

At that late stage, treatment was unsuccessful, and Sonia did not survive. Her tragedy gave Dr. Burk the impetus he needed to publicize the importance of synchronous warning dreams. He has found cases in which the diagnosis of many other types of cancer was preceded by dreams. These include skin, lung, brain, prostate, and colon cancers (Burk, 2015).

Dreams are filled with symbolism uniquely meaningful to the dreamer.

The dreams of cancer patients like Wanda and Sonia demonstrate the intricate dance of mind and matter. Consciousness, speaking to the mind in dreams, highlights problems in the body. It not only shows that a problem exists, but it can also pinpoint exactly where the problem is. Consciousness is able to present refined levels of information beyond the most sophisticated scans and instruments available to modern medicine.

Dreams don't just warn us of malfunctions in our bodies and our lives. They can also play a role in healing. There are many accounts of people who've had dreams in which they healed their bodies or facilitated healing for others. The dream messages were corroborated by subsequent medical diagnoses. The following case history describes a dream a therapist had about her client. It comes from a provocative collection of stories called *Dreams That Change Our Lives* (Hoss & Gongloff, 2017).

MOTHER MARY AND THE ORBS

By Carol Warner

I was seeing a client and her daughter, whom I will call Jennifer. Jennifer had been brutally beaten and sexually abused by a male relative who had been living with them. She had not disclosed this early on because he had repeatedly threatened to kill her mother and her. When, after many years, she did disclose, the man was arrested but then acquitted. Inexplicably, the judge blamed the mother.

Jennifer entered into a downward spiral. She ended up in a relationship that replicated her years of beatings; she got into drugs, ran away, worked at a strip club, and was raped again. Jennifer was emotionally unreachable, and her mom's grief was enormous.

After some time, her mom moved to another city to start a business, so we no longer met for sessions, but one day she called and said Jennifer had asked to return home. She said she was ready to start her life over and "face her past." Mother wisely insisted on therapy as a condition of Jennifer's return home. Jennifer said she only trusted me—and I lived three hours away!

Since Jennifer had lost her driver's license, her mother, in an extraordinary offer, agreed to take one day off her job weekly to drive Jennifer the six-hour round trip to my office to see me. In our first meeting, I asked Jennifer if she had received a gynecological exam. She had never had one. I strongly encouraged Jennifer to see a gynecologist for a thorough exam.

In our next meeting, Jennifer and her mom came together to my office, long-faced, with very sad news. A biopsy revealed several large spots of ovarian cancer, a cancer with a very poor prognosis.

Shocked, Jennifer went for a second opinion. This gynecologist said she could easily see three large spots of cancer on Jennifer's ovaries. The second biopsy also revealed cancer. The prognosis was terminal. Jennifer's estimated life span was now only six months. Mother and daughter were devastated.

Jennifer commented how "my life has been shit" and how ironic it was that now that she was making a fresh start, she would likely die. Her mother was heartbroken, and felt hopeless and helpless. I, too, was stunned and extremely saddened. I had a heartfelt connection with them.

That night I included Jennifer and her mom in my prayers. I asked God to help them. During the middle of the night, I had the following dream:

Mary, mother of Jesus, is descending from the sky. She is luminous, glowing, surrounded by the most beautiful ethereal blue light imaginable. As she floats down toward me, I see that she is dressed in a beautiful blue gown, perhaps with gold specks in it. She emanates an incredible aura of peace and love. As I watch Mary, her arms are outstretched, and three glowing globes of golden-white light issue forth from her hands. Somehow, I have the knowledge that each of the globes of light goes to one of the three cancerous spots on Jennifer's ovaries. I watch as each globe surrounds a spot completely and envelops it. As I watch this amazing sight, I awaken with absolute certainty that Jennifer is now totally healed of her cancer.

I experienced this absolute certainty both in the dream and upon wakening. As the day went on, I thought often about the dream. In my day consciousness, I was having doubts. I wondered whether to tell Jennifer the dream. I did not wish to give her false hope. I decided to tell her, while cautioning that I did not know what the dream meant. It seemed to me I had no right to keep this dream from Jennifer, since it was about a visitation from Mary to Jennifer.

When I spoke next with Jennifer, her eyes grew wide as I told her the dream. Despite my cautions, she said she knew it was true, that Mary healed her.

Jennifer went back to the same doctor who had told her the spots were visible. The doctor expressed disbelief that just one week later, there was now absolutely no trace of cancer. Two repeat biopsies verified that the cancer was gone. We were all thrilled and awed at what had happened. Fifteen years later, she is cancer-free.

It is not surprising that dreams can play a role in healing. The most vivid dreams occur in REM (rapid eye movement) sleep. In this state, our eyes are moving around rapidly, just as they might do while we're looking at things when we're awake.

The dominant brain wave frequency in the REM dreaming state is theta. Theta is also observed in the brains of healers at the height of the healing experience (Oschman, 2015). The EEG frequency window of healing corresponds with that of dreaming. In both dreams and healing, the brain is in a theta state. Brain and consciousness are sharing an experience, one measured in matter, the other in mind.

PRECOGNITION AND THE ARROW OF TIME

Another anomalous experience that has been extensively studied is precognition, the ability to sense events before they occur. While there are over 100 studies of precognition, a series of decisive experiments was carried out by Daryl Bem.

Bem used standard psychological tests, such as giving students a long list of words and asking them to remember as many as possible. Later, words were randomly selected from the list and given to the students to type out. Their recollection of the typed words was compared to their recall of those they weren't asked to type. They had significantly better recollection of words they were later asked to type.

Another experiment showed two curtains on a computer screen. In a series of 36 trials, students were told that an erotic image was behind one of the curtains and asked to guess which one it was. Chance would have dictated a 50 percent probability of success, but they scored 53.1 percent, significantly above chance.

Bem's meticulously designed and conducted studies took 10 years to complete and involved a large sample of over 1,000 participants. His results were echoed by an analysis of 101 studies of precognition spanning 75 years performed by Dean Radin of the Institute of Noetic Sciences (Radin, 2011). They were performed in 25 different laboratories located in various countries, including the United States, Italy, Spain, Holland, Austria, Sweden, England, Scotland, Iran, Japan, and Australia. The analysis showed that 84 percent of them reported statistically significant results.

Bem later replicated his initial work on an even larger scale (Bem, Tressoldi, Rabeyron, & Duggan, 2015). His studies produced a storm of criticism among skeptics and those who simply couldn't believe that precognition might exist. Human beings tend to stick firmly to their worldviews regardless of the findings of science.

Yet quantum physics does not require the arrow of time to move only in a forward direction. Many equations work both forward and backward. Einstein said, "The distinction between past, present, and future is only a stubbornly persistent illusion" (as cited in Calaprice, 2011).

ATHEISTS AREN'T EXEMPT

What we have come to call anomalous experiences, such as precognition and out-of-body states, are far from uncommon. In a poll of students at American, Chinese, and Japanese universities, many report anomalous experiences, while over 30 percent report having them frequently (McClenon, 1993). At least 59 percent had experienced déjà vu, and many described out-of-body experiences.

Being religious or believing in the supernatural was not a requirement for such experiences: atheists and agnostics had them too. The researchers analyzed whether believers were more prone to anomalous experiences and found that they were not. Even famed skeptic and editor of the *Skeptic* magazine, Michael Shermer, described an event that shook his belief system "to the core" (Shermer, 2014).

THE BROKEN RADIO THAT PLAYED LOVE MUSIC

June 25, 2014, was the wedding day of Michael Shermer and Jennifer Graf. She was from Cologne, Germany, and had been raised by her mother and grandfather Walter.

Three months before the wedding, Graf shipped her possessions to Shermer's home in California. Many of the boxes were damaged and several heirlooms lost. One that arrived intact was Walter's 1978 Philips radio, and when it was unpacked, Shermer inserted batteries and set out to "bring it back to life after decades of muteness."

His attentions were in vain. He even opened it up to see if there were any loose wires inside that he could solder, but the radio refused to emit even static.

On her wedding day, Graf was feeling lonely. Her beloved grandfather was not there to give her away. She and Shermer walked to the back of the house, where music was playing in the bedroom.

They looked at their computers and phones to locate the source of the music. They even opened the back door to see if was coming from a neighbor's house.

Then Graf opened the drawer of Shermer's desk to reveal her grandfather's radio. It was playing a love song. The couple sat in stunned silence, broken only by Graf's sobbing. Shermer's daughter also heard the music.

The following day, the radio fell silent, and has never worked since.

In the survey of anomalous experiences, even students in the hard sciences were disposed to them. Ethnic background didn't make a big difference; anomalous experiences were common in both white and black American students. As Jung observed, "Synchronicity is an ever-present reality for those who have eyes to see."

Jung witnessed a snake swallowing a fish on the shore of the lake at Bollingen and afterward had the image carved into a rock in his garden.

Jung continues to tickle us with synchronicity from beyond the grave. One of the most comprehensive texts on the subject is *Synchronicity: Nature and Psyche in an Interconnected Universe* by prominent Jung scholar Joseph Cambray (2009). David Rosen, editor of Cambray's book, shares a striking synchronicity related to working on the text:

"In my backyard there is a Japanese garden with a pond containing numerous koi. Shortly before Joseph Cambray arrived [to deliver the lectures that became the synchronicity book], a snake caught and swallowed a koi. When I saw figure 1 of 'Jung's carving of a snake swallowing a fish,' I wondered if this was an example of synchronicity. . . . I had not observed such an event before or after this occurrence (Cambray, 2009)."

WHAT CAN EXPLAIN SYNCHRONICITY?

That synchronicity happens is well established. *How* it happens is another question. What could possibly be coordinating processes in so many different dimensions of reality? How can a biological phenomenon such as the proliferation of cancer cells be linked to a state of consciousness such as a dream or premonition?

Cancer cells are matter. They are physical units inside living bodies. They grow and divide at a rapid pace, exempt from the signals that cause normal cells to self-destruct when they are old or damaged. Cancer cells lose the molecular bonds on their membranes that keep them in place, allowing them to detach from the surrounding tissue. They then migrate to distant parts of the body. In stage 3 and 4 cancers, rogue cells metastasize throughout the body. They are matter gone wild, molecular clusters on a path of self-destruction.

Dreams are pure mind. They are completely subjective, with a meaning unique to the dreamer. They are filled with images that engage our emotions and senses. They engage the full spectrum of our consciousness whenever we sleep. How can a subjective experience such as dreaming connect with an objective reality such as cell proliferation?

Synchronicity ties the subjective and objective together. It connects the immaterial world of mind and energy with the material world of matter and form. The worlds of mind and matter resonate together in the course of synchronous events.

RESONANCE IN SMALL AND LARGE SYSTEMS

There are many videos online showing pendulums coming into resonant coherence. There is a link at the end of this chapter for a video showing 64 metronomes being activated one after the other. At first, they all swing independently and randomly.

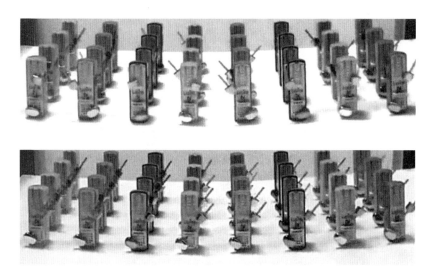

In the first image, 32 metronomes begin ticking independently. Within three minutes, resonance produces coherence and all the metronomes tick together.

Then, slowly but surely, a remarkable change occurs. Two of the pendulums begin to swing in synchrony. A short while later, a third one joins them. The fourth one comes into coherence quicker than the third. Within three minutes, the entire collection is swinging away together, precisely in sync.

This type of resonance was described in 1665 by Dutch physicist Christiaan Huygens. Eight years earlier, he had patented the pendulum clock. While recovering from an illness during which he had plenty of time to observe his surroundings, including the two pendulum clocks in his room, he noticed an odd phenomenon: regardless of the position in which the pendulums began, they would slowly entrain to swinging in unison.

Resonance is a property of all systems, from the very small to the infinitely large. At the atomic level, we find molecules with similar properties resonating together (Ho, 2008). At the cellular level, cells use resonance to communicate, propagate, and heal (Oschman, 2015).

Ascending the scale, we find resonance operating in organisms, from tiny ones such as viruses to large ones such as human beings. Scaling up even bigger, resonance is found at the level of the entire planet.

Getting still larger, we find resonance in "the music of the spheres," at the level of solar systems, galaxies, and the universe. From the infinitesimally small to the unimaginably large, resonance is the song sung by matter.

Not only do similar systems resonate together, they resonate with other systems as well. The very large can resonate with the very small. Our human bodies can be entrained by the resonance of Earth, picked up by the brain's pineal gland, 30 percent of whose molecules are metallic and hence magnetically sensitive (Oschman, 1997).

FIELD LINE RESONANCES

Our planet has an electromagnetic field of its own, just like a big magnet. It has a north and a south pole, and the lines of force generated by this enormous magnet radiate out hundreds of thousands of miles into space.

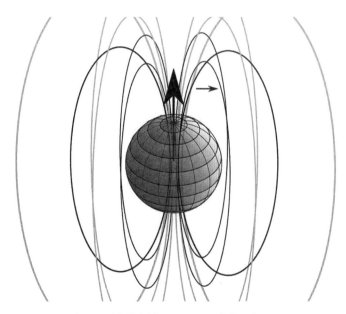

The Earth's field lines surround the planet.

Imagine these lines as strings on an instrument such as a violin. When you pluck a string, it resonates. In a similar way, the field lines of Earth resonate when they are plucked. As the solar wind sweeps by the planet at a speed of two million miles an hour (3 million km/h), it is constantly plucking those strings.

Several common "notes" are played on Earth's geomagnetic strings. Some of these notes play all the time, like a continuous chord, while others sound intermittently, like a string that is plucked occasionally. For this reason, field line resonances are divided into continuous and irregular pulsations (Jacobs, Kato, Matsushita, & Troitskaya, 1964; Anderson, Engebretson, Rounds, Zanetti, & Potemra, 1990).

One of the most important continuous geomagnetic pulsations that scientists measure is in the frequency window of 0.1 to 0.2 Hz. Another is in the range of 0.2 to 5 Hz. Irregular pulsations in the lowest frequency range are from 0.025 to 1 Hz.

The lowest of Earth's continuous geomagnetic frequencies, 0.1 Hz, is exactly the same frequency as the rhythm of the human heart when in coherence. If we practice a relaxation method like the Quick Coherence Technique developed by the HeartMath Institute, our heart begins to beat in coherence. In that state, our individual human heart is sounding the same note as the slowest of the frequencies of Earth's magnetic field (McCraty, 2017).

The 0.1 Hz frequency also happens to be the frequency of human cardiovascular systems. The same frequency is used by a variety of animals and even individual cells to communicate and entrain the systems that surround them, just like metronomes in synchronous alignment.

If you've ever held a guitar or violin on your lap while someone else was playing an instrument in the same room, you'll have felt the vibration that the music sets up. The strings and sound box of your instrument vibrate in harmony with the instrument being played nearby, even though no one is plucking the strings of the instrument you hold.

That's resonance. Resonance entrains objects tuned to similar frequencies even at a distance.

Certain of Earth's field line frequencies resonate with exactly the same frequencies that occur in the human brain and heart. As the planet plays its chords, our brains and bodies are humming along and possibly even using that constant music to regulate biological processes.

SCHUMANN RESONANCES

Have you ever blown air out of your mouth across the opening of a bottle? It makes a low-frequency whistling sound. Sound waves bounce back and forth between the sides of the bottle, traveling through the air inside. The pitch produced depends on the volume of the bottle.

A German physicist named Winfried Schumann used mathematics to postulate that a similar effect occurs on a global scale. In this case, the volume determining frequency is not that of a bottle but of the space between the surface of the planet and the edge of the ionosphere.

The ionosphere is a bubble of plasma that encircles Earth. One of the properties of plasma is that low-frequency magnetic waves bounce off it. Like a mirror, the inside of the plasma bubble reflects waves.

That is how radio works. A signal is sent up, it bounces off the ionosphere's mirror, and it is then captured at a distant location by a person with a receiver tuned to that frequency. When magnetic pulses are introduced into the cavity between the planet's surface and the top of the plasma bubble, some are dissipated while others aren't. Only resonant waves propagate consistently, like the whistle you hear when you blow across a bottle. These are the Schumann resonances.

Schumann resonances bounce off the plasma bubble surrounding the planet.

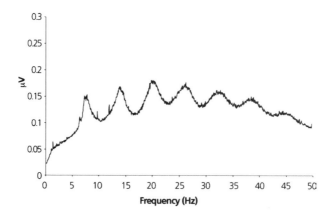

Schumann resonance data recorded from sensor
site in Boulder Creek, California. Note that the
frequencies correspond to those of human brain waves.

In 1960, long after Schumann predicted mathematically that such
waves must exist, they were measured experimentally. The primary
Schumann resonance is 7.83 Hz. Harmonics are resonant multiples of the
original frequency, and Schumann's wave produces harmonics at 14.3,
20.8, 27.3, and 33.8 Hz.

These frequencies are also found in the waves originating in our
brains as they process information: 7.83 Hz is in the theta band, in the
exact same frequency window measured in brain waves during peak
healing moments (Oschman, 2015; Bengston, 2010).

The next harmonic of the Schumann resonance, 14.3 Hz, is in the
frequency range of low beta brain waves, typical of the housekeeping
functions of the body. The third harmonic of the basic Schumann resonance, 27.3 Hz, is in the same frequency range our brains use when
we're focused on a task and thinking hard. The harmonic of 33.8 Hz falls
within the frequency range of gamma, the waves produced by our brains
at moments of integration and insight.

It's striking that the primary resonance of Earth's plasma sheath as
well as its harmonics fall into the same frequency windows as the primary human brain waves. Our mental states, generated by the fields our
brains produce as they process information, resonate with the frequencies of the planet on which we live. When we increase a particular wave,
such as the surge of theta that accompanies energy healing treatments,
we increase our resonance with that planetary information signal. Planet
and healer are entrained in an intense energetic union.

BODIES AND BRAINS ENTRAINED
BY EARTH'S FREQUENCIES

Dr. Franz Halberg of the University of Minnesota Medical School coined the term *circadian rhythms* to describe the body's daily cycles (Halberg, Tong, & Johnson, 1967). Until his death in his late 90s, he conducted research in his lab seven days a week. In 2017, research on the genetics of the body clock won the Nobel Prize in medicine.

Halberg believed that the reason that the delta through gamma frequencies are pervasive in our brains and our bodies is that we evolved on planet Earth, entrained in its frequencies. Studies conducted by his Halberg Chronobiology Center and by other researchers have demonstrated links between Earth's field lines and Schumann resonances and markers of human health (Selmaoui & Touitou, 2003; Brown & Czeisler, 1992).

Human emotions, behavior, health, and cognitive function are all affected by solar and geomagnetic fields (Halberg, Cornélissen, McCraty, Czaplicki, & Al-Abdulgader, 2011). Earth's field is hypothesized to be a "carrier of biologically relevant information that connects all living systems" (McCraty, 2015).

Rollin McCraty, director of research at HeartMath, says, "We're all like little cells in the bigger Earth brain—sharing information at a subtle, unseen level that exists between all living systems, not just humans, but animals, trees, and so on" (McCraty, 2015). Information is flowing throughout this living matrix of the "Earth brain," synchronizing the activity of all life-forms, down to the level of cells and molecules.

The human brain is attuned to electromagnetic fields.

The human brain, an electromagnetic organ pulsing with neural connections and impulses, is exquisitely sensitive to electromagnetic fields: "Changes in the Earth's magnetic field have been shown to affect human heart rhythms and have been associated with the following: changes in brain and nervous-system activity; athletic performance, memory and other tasks; synthesis of nutrients in plants and algae; the number of reported traffic violations and accidents; mortality from heart attacks and strokes; and incidence of depression and suicide" (HeartMath Institute, n.d.).

Given the pervasiveness of these frequencies on a planetary scale and the fact that we evolved in them over the course of hundreds of millions of years, it's hardly surprising that our bodies, minds, hearts, and cells are entrained to them.

HOW ANOMALOUS EVENTS ASSEMBLE INTO SYNCHRONICITIES

A team of Dutch researchers performed a systematic review of 175 studies of biological fields. They suggest that coherent quantum frequencies regulate the processes of living organisms. They found that electromagnetic fields influence neural systems and consciousness and may represent "a universal electromagnetic principle, that underlies the observed life-sustaining effects and also may have been instrumental in the creation of biological order in first life and quantum consciousness" (Geesink & Meijer, 2016).

Parallels between quantum mechanics, biological systems, and consciousness were drawn by many of the movement's founders, including Albert Einstein, Erwin Schrödinger, Werner Heisenberg, Wolfgang Pauli, Niels Bohr, and Eugene Wigner. These pioneers perceived energy, space, time, consciousness, and matter not as separate entities but instead as interacting in a vast synchronistic dance.

Geesink and Meijer found that the human electromagnetic (EM) field "communicates bi-directionally with a global EM field, via wave resonance [and] comprises a universal consciousness, that experiences the sensations, perceptions, thoughts and emotions of every conscious being in the universe" (2016, p. 106). Connect the dots between all the scientific findings and synchronicity suddenly doesn't seem mysterious at all.

Frequencies may function as the resonators that entrain micro and macro events in synchronicity. Though we can't see these frequencies, they permeate both mind and matter. We swim in them as a fish swims in water, unaware of the existence of the fundamental fields that shape consciousness and everything in the material world.

I believe that the intercommunication between these levels of reality provides a plausible scientific explanation for synchronicity. Multidirectional intercommunication throughout the emosphere, psychosphere, and magnetosphere allows information to pass rapidly throughout all levels of reality, those of both mind and matter. Fields link us continuously, even if we are unaware of their existence. That linking is how all the unlikely components of anomalous events are able to assemble into synchronicities.

The Boy Who Flew for Peace

The 1980s were a time of huge international tension. The United States and the Soviet Union glared at each other across a vast arsenal of nuclear weapons. If either fired first, the result would be mutually assured destruction, which bears the appropriate acronym of MAD.

The two empires fought proxy wars in Asia and Africa. Their European allies (NATO for the United States and the Warsaw Pact for the USSR) lived tensely together. Some states were split in two, such as East and West Germany. If the Cold War turned hot, they would be the front lines.

Any incident had the potential to set off the powder keg, and the leaders of the two countries maintained a hotline from one capital to the other to head off disaster.

In 1983, a South Korean airliner, flight KAL 007, was shot down by a Soviet MiG fighter. All 269 passengers on board were killed.

Ronald Reagan was the U.S. president at the time. The Soviet Union was in flux as two hardline presidents, Yuri Andropov and Konstantin Chernenko, died in office. The youngest man to hold the job, Mikhail Gorbachev, was installed in 1985.

In Reykjavik, Iceland, in 1986, Regan and Gorbachev met in a summit. Their goal was to reduce the number of nuclear warheads each possessed. At the last minute, the talks collapsed.

A teenager in West Germany named Matthias Rust was following the negotiations closely "because if there was a conflict, we all knew we would be the first to be hit" (Dowling, 2017). Just 18 years old, Rust had been taking flying lessons, learning to fly the venerable Cessna 172. The aircraft had been designed in the early 1950s, using pre–World War II technology such as an air-cooled engine and wings above the fuselage.

Deeply affected by the failure of the peace talks, Rust hatched a plan to build a metaphorical "bridge of peace" between East and West. He booked his Cessna for three weeks, not telling anyone what he planned to do. He took off from Uetersen Airfield, near Hamburg, on May 13, 1989.

He flew to Iceland, where he prepared for the next leg of his journey. He visited Hofdi House, where the failed talks between Gorbachev and Reagan had taken place, and later reported, "It gave me motivation to continue."

He then flew to Norway and on to Finland, the country closest to the Soviet Union, and the one with the most porous border.

Before he took off again, on May 28, he filed a flight plan with the authorities, telling them he was bound for Stockholm, Sweden. But after leaving the air traffic control zone, he turned off the plane's transponder, the device that allows any plane to be tracked, and headed for the Soviet border.

Soon he was spotted by Soviet radar in Latvia. As he approached the border, he entered the air above the most sophisticated air defense system in the world. Missiles and fighter planes stood ready to repel attackers 24/7. The fleet included extraordinary craft such as the MiG-25, which can fly nearly three times the speed of sound, and the largest fighter plane ever constructed, the Tu-128, which fires missiles 17 feet (5m) in length and is the size of a World War II bomber.

The day of Rust's flight happened to be Border Guards Day, a national holiday on which most of the men guarding the border were off on vacation.

Nonetheless, radar detected Rust's plane and directed MiG fighters in close to identify it visually, since its transponder was not responding. They reported that it was a Yak-12, a Soviet training plane that looked similar to the Cessna 172. Clouds then concealed Rust's whereabouts, but the next wave of MiGs spotted him again. One pilot flew in close, then reported to headquarters that the aircraft was actually a West German intruder.

Upstream in the command chain, that pilot's superiors were convinced that the pilot was mistaken: how could a West German plane have made it all the way across the border?

Because of the negative publicity from the attack on KAL 007, Soviet commanders were cautious. They wanted the order to shoot Rust down to come from the highest level, in this case Defense Minister Sergei Sokolov.

Other ground commanders still believed that Rust's plane was a Yak-12, and near Moscow he entered an air control zone in which Yak-12 pilots were training in their aircraft.

To navigate, Rust had only simple maps he'd purchased off the shelf in West Germany. Late in the day, he identified Moscow. After seeing the onion domes of Saint Basil's Cathedral, he scouted for a safe place to land.

He found a clear runway on the eight-lane Bolshoy Moskvoretsky Bridge, connecting Red Square with the districts to the south of the city. Normally, the bridge was a tramway route, but that morning one section of cables had been removed for maintenance. There was just enough room for him to land.

After Rust touched down, Muscovites surrounded the plane. Everyone was friendly. A British doctor, Robin Stott, had just decided to get some fresh air and walked out of his hotel for an evening stroll, taking his video camera with him. Hearing the noise of the plane's engine, he pointed his lens at the sky in time to video the landing and its aftermath. KGB agents arrived but stood around talking to each other, unsure of what to do next.

They eventually detained Rust and took his Cessna to a nearby airport for examination; no one could believe that a teenager had just penetrated the air defense system of the mighty Soviet Union. After nearly a year in jail, Rust was returned to West Germany.

The military confusion that facilitated Rust's flight gave Soviet leader Mikhail Gorbachev an excuse to get rid of hardliners who opposed his reforms, including Sokolov. Gorbachev's reforms, such as the economic revolution called perestroika and the opening of society called glasnost, gained momentum. The Soviet Union collapsed three years later.

Rust's Cessna is now on display in a German museum.

Matthias Rust could never have known what the full effects of his action on the consciousness of other people would be. He just followed his vision and made a personal statement so dramatic that the world took notice. He never flew a plane again.

Rust's story is an example of how the personal and the global come together. Global stories are often dramatized by personal stories. Like the man standing in front of the tank during the Tiananmen Square protests in China the same year as Rust's flight, one individual's actions often highlight momentous events. Huge information fields involving millions of people can come into focus through the lens of a single person.

Notice how many synchronicities had to be in place for Rust's trip:

- Most of the men normally guarding the Soviet border were off duty, celebrating Border Guards Day.

- The first Soviet fighters to spot Rust's plane took it for a Soviet training plane.

- Low clouds obscured most of Rust's journey.

- The Soviet pilot who correctly identified his plane as a West German aircraft was not believed by his superiors.

- The Soviet authorities were cautious because of the huge negative publicity recently generated by shooting down a South Korean civilian airliner.

- The defense minister, Sergei Sokolov, was unavailable because he was attending a high-level meeting.

- Ground controllers assumed Rust's was a Soviet training plane whose transponder had malfunctioned.

- Rust accidentally flew over a training range where similar aircraft were practicing.

- The tram cables spanning the bridge on which Rust landed had been removed that morning for maintenance.

- Peace activist Dr. Robin Stott had decided to walk outside to get some fresh air just before Rust landed.

- Stott happened to take his video camera with him.

- Stott heard the sound of the plane's engine and was able to train his camera in the right direction just before it landed.

At pivotal moments in history, synchronicities can abound. Many highly unlikely events stack up, one on top of the other, which nudge the future in a certain direction. As we read the accounts of great social, political, or military changes, they're often laced with huge numbers of improbable synchronous events.

Though we perceive the world as stable, it is actually changing rapidly. Of those companies that were in the Fortune 500 list of the world's largest companies in 1950, only 10 percent appear there today. Even the best-organized and most information-rich organizations in the world aren't usually able to maintain their positions as the cosmos swirls and changes around them.

SPONTANEOUS SYNCHRONIZED ORDER IN NATURE

Cornell University mathematician Steven Strogatz says that a tendency toward spontaneous synchronized order is a primary characteristic of nature, from the subatomic scale to the most distant reaches of the universe (Strogatz, 2012). From inanimate molecules to complex living systems, spontaneously arising order may be a fundamental tendency in all of nature.

Strogatz points to examples such as the synchronization of schools of fish, flocks of birds, and the internal clocks of the human body. He even shows how waves of movement propagate through flocks of birds and schools of fish. There's no leader, master plan, or supercomputer coordinating these millions of intricate movements. Organization arises spontaneously from within the flock, herd, or cell, synchronized by nature.

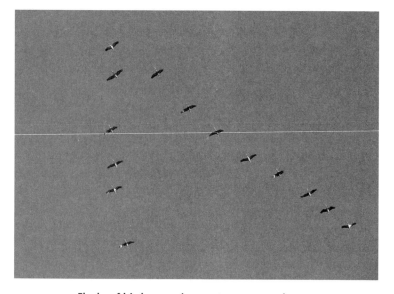

Flocks of birds move in spontaneous synchrony.

Strogatz notes that spontaneous order arises at every level of the universe, from the smallest to the largest. It extends from superconductivity in elements to the nuclei of individual cells, to the flashing tails of fireflies, to the tissue that signals our hearts to pump, to traffic patterns, and to the farthest edges of the cosmos. The clock genes in the human body entrain with the diurnal cycle of the planet and even with the bodies of other human beings nearby.

Spontaneously arising order is also evident in the functioning of our cells. Each cell undergoes some 100,000 metabolic processes per second. Groups of millions of cells, sometimes in distant regions of the body, coordinate their activities. They use fields to do this.

Fields are a far more efficient method of coordination than chemical or mechanical signaling. If you are walking up to your locked car and want to unlock the door, you can insert the key in the lock and turn it. That's the mechanical approach to getting the job done. But it's much faster to press the button on your remote and use the field approach instead.

Our bodies communicate through fields in a similar way.

Strogatz uses many examples of resonance drawn from human behavior, including fads, mobs, and stock trading. One of his examples is the unexpected saga of London's Millennium Bridge.

The Millennium Bridge

The Millennium Bridge over the Thames River was intended to be a marvel. Opened on June 10, 2000, it was the first crossing to be constructed over the venerable river in a century.

The bridge's designers extolled it as "a pure expression of engineering structure," comparing its sleek lines to a blade of light. Engineers called it "an absolute statement of our capabilities at the beginning of the 21st century." At the opening ceremony, thousands of enthusiastic spectators swarmed all over the bridge.

Then something unexpected happened. The bridge began to sway slightly from side to side.

The wobble became more pronounced. Pedestrians didn't know what to do. They began to walk with wide strides to counteract the bridge's motion. Like entrained pendulums, they stepped to the left and then to the right.

The wobble increased, and the people scrambled off the bridge as soon as they could. It was closed immediately.

Why did the bridge fail, after the brightest design and engineering minds in the world had done their utmost to make it perfect?

When they first felt the first tiny sway, the pedestrians on the bridge adjusted their behavior to compensate. This unintentionally brought them into resonance. They began to walk together, exacerbating the movement of the bridge.

In an example of what scientists call emergent systems, there was no plan or leader guiding the Millennium Bridge wobble. It took place as an emergent response to resonance.

The bridge's problems were soon solved by installing dampers to cushion the bridge's movement, and the bridge reopened. But the event remains an example of how resonance can trigger unexpected consequences in complex systems.

The Millennium Bridge.

JUNG, EMERGENT PROPERTIES, AND SELF-ORGANIZATION

One of the first scientists to study self-organizing systems was Nobel laureate Ilya Prigogine. He explored ways in which order can emerge out of apparent chaos. His work contributed to the establishment of the Santa Fe Institute, which studies complexity and chaos theory.

One branch of the Santa Fe Institute's work examines systems that have self-organizing features, also known as emergent properties. They are termed *emergent* because they don't originate within the systems themselves but are stimulated by forces in the external environment. In the book *Emergence: The Connected Lives of Ants, Brains, Cities, and Software,* researcher Stephen Johnson writes, "In these systems, agents residing on one scale start producing behavior that lies one scale above them. . . . The movement from low-level rules to higher-level sophistication is what we call emergence" (Johnson, 2002, p. 18).

There are five characteristics of emergent structures (Corning, 2002). They are:

- Radical novelty: they spontaneously develop new features.
- Coherence: they maintain themselves over a period of time.
- Higher holistic order: they exhibit the property of wholeness.
- Dynamic process: they evolve.
- Apparent: they can be perceived.

One example of emergence is the evolution of distinct neighborhoods in large cities. Like-minded people get together and organize the businesses, social clubs, schools, and religious institutions most relevant to them. The process is organic and bottom-up, resisting the top-down control systems of zoning laws and planning commissions.

These types of "emergent intelligence" organize without consciousness and in response to changing stimuli. Assimilating and responding to information, emergent systems adapt and self-organize into new patterns. Physicist Doyne Farmer said: "It's not magic, but it feels like magic" (Corning, 2002).

A Nova Science television program on emergence uses the example of an ant colony: "Ants are not mental giants, and they can't see the big picture. Yet out of their simple behaviors—follow the strongest pheromone trail, say, or save the queen at all costs when under attack—arises a classic example of emergence: the ant colony. The colony exhibits an extraordinary ability to explore and exploit its surroundings. It is aware of and reacts to food sources, floods, enemies, and other phenomena, over a substantial piece of ground. Each ant dies after days or months, but the colony survives for years, becoming more stable and organized over time" (Nova, 2007).

Ants provide an example of emergent behavior.

Jung's concept of synchronicity represents an application of the idea of self-organizing systems to psychology. Synchronicity incorporates emergent properties of personal experience, brain, fields, and environment (Hogenson, 2004). Jungian researcher Joseph Cambray says that "Emergent phenomena, especially in the human realm, can appear to ordinary, individual consciousness as meaningful, if inexplicable, coincidences. . . . Synchronicities can be explored as a form of emergence of the Self and have a central role in individuation or psychological maturation" (Cambray, 2002).

Members of the Santa Fe Institute argue that self-organizing systems may be as important in evolution as natural selection: "Life and its evolution have always depended on the mutual embrace of spontaneous order and [natural] selection's crafting of that order" (Kaufman, 1993).

In 1959, Jung wrote a letter to his friend Erich Neumann, observing, "In this chaos of chance, synchronistic phenomena were probably at work, operating both with and against the known laws of nature to produce, in archetypal moments, syntheses which appear to us miraculous. . . . This presupposes not only an all-pervading, latent meaning which can be recognized by consciousness, but during that preconscious time, a psychological process with which a physical event meaningfully coincides" (Jung, 1975).

Cambray concludes that "Meaningful coincidences are psychological analogues that spur the evolution of both the personal and the collective psyche, organizing images and experiences into previously unimagined forms" (Cambray, 2009).

Synchronicities are part of how we grow and evolve as people, as societies, and as a species.

September 11 Synchronicities

Like most people, I remember where I was on September 11, 2001. I was living in a cottage in Guerneville, California, with my two young children. My ex-wife, knowing I don't watch TV, phoned and told me to turn it on. Horrified, I watched as the second jet crashed into the towers and they collapsed. Along with millions of others, I felt as though the world as we knew it had come crashing down too.

Estimates of those killed in the towers exceeded 6,000. That number was arrived at by reporters who calculated how many people would normally be working in the two towers at 8:46 A.M., when the first jet hit. The official estimate from the New York Police Department almost two weeks later, after the dust had settled, was 6,659 dead.

However, as the months went by and the story kept unfolding, the numbers kept dropping. The final death toll was 2,753. That's less than half the initial estimate. What explains such a huge disparity between the numbers?

Part of the answer is that the evacuation efforts were largely successful. Most of those who worked below the impact points managed to escape. Yet there were many more who were supposed to be at their desks above the impact points that morning but were not. Where were they?

According to a careful analysis of this question by *USA Today*, "Many companies did head counts after the attack. . . . Counts from more than 50 floors indicate the buildings were barely half full" (Cauchon, 2001). Where were the missing people?

There are many reasons why people weren't in the World Trade Center that morning. When talking to survivors, some describe having been warned by intuition, dreams, or precognition. Others experienced unexpected delays due to crowded trains or family problems.

Rebeka Javanshir-Wong is one of our energy psychology practitioners. Her husband is one of those who was absent when the planes hit. Here's how she tells the story:

"My husband, who worked at Tower 2, also had an out-of-routine day when he went to work later than usual and was on his way to the office when the planes crashed.

"His company had invited two of their young employees from Malaysia to come for training. They had arrived the night before, and since it was their first time in the U.S., my husband, along with other colleagues, had taken them out to dinner and helped them settle in an apartment the company had rented for them near the Twin Towers. Knowing that these two had big jet lag, they all decided to start work a little later the next morning and give them time to rest."

The delay saved all their lives.

Celebrities often make their schedules public, so their comings and goings are easy to track. There are many stories of well-known people who weren't at the World Trade Center that morning as scheduled. Among them are these:

- Sarah Ferguson, Duchess of York, was scheduled to be on the 101st floor for a charity event. She ran late and was still doing an interview in the NBC television studio at 8:46 A.M. when the first plane hit.

- With a group of friends, actor Mark Wahlberg was due to fly on American Airlines flight 11. They changed their plans and, at the last minute, chartered their own plane.

- Actor and producer Seth McFarlane was also booked on American Airlines flight 11. His travel agent gave him the wrong takeoff time and he arrived at the gate after it had closed.

- Actress Julie Stoffer had a fight with her boyfriend and missed the same plane.

- Michael Lomonaco, head chef of the restaurant at the top of the towers, Windows on the World, was heading up to his office half an hour before the first plane hit. He had a noon appointment to have his glasses fixed at the optometry store in the lobby, and he decided to go back down again to see if they could fit him in early. The half-hour delay saved his life.

- The developer who held the lease on the World Trade Center, Larry Silverstein, had a dermatology appointment that morning. He had decided to skip the appointment and go to work, but his wife persuaded him to visit the doctor instead.

- Olympic swimmer Ian Thorpe was out for a jog that he planned to end at the observation deck on the World Trade Center. He realized he'd forgotten his camera and returned to his hotel room. When he turned on his TV, he saw the north tower on fire.

- Corporate director Jim Pierce was due to attend a meeting on the 105th floor of the south tower. But by the evening before, the organizers realized that there were too many people in the group to fit in the meeting room, so they switched the venue to the Millennium Hotel across the street. Pierce later learned that 11 of the 12 people who'd been in the original conference room died in the tragedy.

- Lara Lundstrom was rollerblading down a street in lower Manhattan when she realized that the driver of a silver Mercedes SUV stopped at a light was actress Gwyneth Paltrow. Lara stopped to talk for a few minutes. This resulted in her missing her train to the south tower and her absence in her office on the 77th floor.

Sometimes small synchronicities—the forgotten camera, jet lag, the chance meeting with an actress, the eyeglasses repair—have a disproportionate effect on our lives. Big events like 9/11 seem to spawn many synchronicities—or perhaps we just notice them when they're dramatized by a global event.

SYNCHRONICITY IS SCIENCE

Synchronicity, which seems to be so mysterious when we first encounter it, turns out to have solid scientific explanations behind it. Spontaneous order arises in living systems, from the atom to the galaxy.

Our brains are attuned to the same frequencies as the planet on which we live. In altered states of consciousness such as dreams, trance, meditation, hypnosis, and epiphany, we enjoy access to a nonlocal information field that extends far beyond our local senses.

Fields permeate the cosmos, including our planet and our bodies. When resonance is established between macro and micro, such as between a Schumann and brain wave frequency, the macro and the micro can fire in coherence. Bodies entrain to fields, and two-way intercommunication occurs between them. Information flows between all levels of reality, including both mind and matter, permeating the emosphere, psychosphere, and magnetosphere. That's how all the seemingly mysterious parts of synchronous events are able to come together.

The psychosphere.

The great scientists of the early quantum age in the first part of the 20th century were aware of the great fields in which our local human minds operate. Einstein said: "Everyone who is seriously involved in the pursuit of science becomes convinced that some spirit is manifest in the laws of the universe, one that is vastly superior to that of man" (as cited in Calaprice, 2002).

Max Planck, a founding father of quantum physics, said: "All matter originates and exists only by virtue of a force which brings the particles of an atom to vibration and holds this most minute solar system of the atom together. . . . We must assume behind this force the existence of a conscious and intelligent Mind. This Mind is the matrix of all matter" (as translated in Braden, 2008). The deeper scientists delve into the workings of matter, from subatomic particles to the enormous scale of galaxies, the more they notice the synchronous coordination present in the whole.

BRAIN AS TRANSDUCER OF UNIVERSAL FIELD

The view of skeptics and materialists is that the mind is *in* the brain: "Mind is what brain does." Mind is believed to be an epiphenomenon of brain, a consequence of brain. As brains evolved, becoming larger and more complex, goes this theory, they gave rise to mind. When enough neurons fire together, they produce this artifact called consciousness. Sir Francis Crick, the co-discoverer of the double helix structure of DNA, summed up this proposition with the words: "A person's mental activities are entirely due to the behavior of nerve cells, glial cells, and the atoms, ions, and molecules that make up and influence them" (Crick & Clark, 1994).

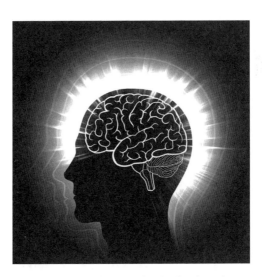

The theory that the complex brain gives rise to
consciousness is unsupported by science.

There is no proof supporting the theory that consciousness lives inside the brain. A review by the Cambridge Center for Behavioral Studies notes, "Brain-centered theories of consciousness seem to face insuperable difficulties" (Tonneau, 2004). Despite the lack of evidence at present, however, materialist skeptics assure us that science will eventually fill in the gaps.

Nobel Prize–winning neurophysiologist Sir John Eccles called this "promissory materialism." He regarded it as "a superstition without a rational foundation . . . a religious belief held by dogmatic materialists . . . who confuse their religion with their science. It has all the features of a messianic prophecy" (as cited in Dossey, 2009).

There is, on the other hand, plenty of evidence that consciousness exists outside the brain. The mind does not behave as though it is confined to the brain, and there are many experiences of nonlocal consciousness that cannot be explained by a local mind trapped inside the confines of the human skull.

CONSCIOUSNESS BEYOND THE BORDERS OF THE SENSES

In altered states, our consciousness is able to go far beyond the borders of our senses and obtain information that comes from far beyond our local minds. In the past few decades, dozens of scientific papers studying altered states such as near-death experiences (NDEs) and out-of-body experiences (OBEs) have been published (Facco & Agrillo, 2012). While people who are medically dead can experience NDEs, in 37 percent of NDE cases, the person was not close to death (Clark, 2012).

These experiences have some characteristics in common. People having OBEs and NDEs report a sense of having actually left their physical body. They have full use of their senses, which are often greatly enhanced. They have freedom of movement and a sense of well-being. They can see things that would normally not be visible to them, such as objects on top of cabinets in the operating room or on the rooftops of nearby buildings, or family members not present in the room. They may know the thoughts of those present in the room with them or report precise details of conversations that occurred when they were under general anesthesia.

Having an out-of-body or near-death experience changes people.

Once people come back from an OBE or NDE, they are changed. They are not afraid of death, and they believe in a loving and compassionate universe. They have a sense of certainty about what they perceived.

Dr. Mario Beauregard, author of *Brain Wars,* believes that the function of the brain is to act as a filter. The consciousness of each person exists in this all-knowing state of infinite perception, which is characteristic of OBEs and NDEs. That infinite mind is then filtered by the brain into a manageable experience in order to exist in a physical body (Beauregard, 2012).

Dr. Kenneth Ring and Sharon Cooper performed a study examining the NDEs of people who have been blind from birth (Ring & Cooper, 2008). The results offer particularly compelling evidence of the existence of consciousness beyond the body, because these people have never been able to see. Unlike sighted people having NDEs who are describing objects and people they have witnessed before, blind people have no such frame of reference.

The Blind Woman Who Saw

During their NDEs, blind people have been able to describe details of objects they have never seen. One such experiencer was a 45-year-old woman named Vicki Umipeg, whose optic nerve had been destroyed at birth by an overdose of oxygen. She reported, "I don't see anything, not even in my dreams, not even black."

After a car accident, she was taken to the emergency room. She found her awareness floating above her body: "I found myself in the hospital looking down at what was happening, frightened since I had never 'seen' before." Vicki was disoriented and had difficulty recognizing that the body she was staring down at was hers: "I knew that it was mine because I wasn't in mine."

Vicki was later able to describe the doctor and nurse who were working on her unconscious body, as well as their words: "They kept saying, 'We can't bring her back.' I felt very detached from my body and couldn't understand why they were upset. I went up through the ceiling hearing beautiful sounds of wind chimes. Where I was I could see trees, birds, and people but all made of light. I was overwhelmed because I couldn't imagine what light was like. It was like a place where all knowledge was. I was then sent back and into my body in excruciating pain."

Vicki was also able to describe details of objects she had never been able to see, such as the patterns on her rings: "I think I was wearing the plain gold band on my right ring finger and my father's wedding ring next to it. But my wedding ring I definitely saw. . . . That was the one I noticed the most because it's most unusual. It has orange blossoms on the corners of it." Vicki later said that this experience was "the only time I could ever relate to seeing and to what light was, because I experienced it."

Thirteen hundred years ago, the Tibetan Book of the Dead described states of nonlocal consciousness. In a place suspended between life and death called the bardo state, the bardo body is able to perceive the world without the mediation of the senses. It can move through solid objects and travel to any place in the cosmos instantly, just like the consciousness described by people having OBEs and NDEs.

Indian Vedic philosophy holds that the great nonlocal universal consciousness is reflected in each of us. The analogy is that of buckets of water in which the sun is reflected. Though there are many different buckets, it is the same sun reflecting in all of them.

Shamans were believed to move between the local and nonlocal world.

Only in recent times has the belief arisen that nonlocal consciousness is "paranormal" or "psychic" and that study of these phenomena is off-limits to conventional science. For most of the thousands of years of human history, the holy person or shaman was a special member of the tribe. Such people were believed to "travel between the worlds" of local awareness and nonlocal mind, bringing back wisdom and healing from realms beyond those of ordinary consciousness (Eliade, 1964).

Shamans were able to commune with animals and beings outside of local awareness and were often gifted with dreams and visions that conveyed meaning from the nonlocal universe. Only recently have altered states such as those experienced in dreams, mystical ecstasy, oneness with nature, NDEs, and OBEs come to be regarded as anything other than a normal part of human experience.

NDEs and OBEs can be transformative. John is a gay African American man with an advanced degree, but after being diagnosed with AIDS, he hit rock bottom. Then, while participating in a study of AIDS patients, he found himself transcending preoccupation with his own suffering and helping a drunk white man who was in distress. Right afterward, he had an OBE. Here's how he describes the experience (Church, 2013).

No One Has a Monopoly on God

"I felt like I was floating over my body, and I'll never forget this, as I was floating over my body, I looked down, it was like this shriveled-up prune, nothing but a prune, like an old dried skin. And my soul, my spirit was over my body. Everything was so separated. I was just feeling like I was in different dimensions, I felt it in my body like a gush of wind blows. I remember saying to God, 'God! I can't die now, because I haven't fulfilled my purpose,' and, just as I said that, the spirit and the body became one, it all collided, and I could feel this gush of wind and I was a whole person again.

"That was really a groundbreaking experience. Before becoming HIV-positive, my faith was so fear based. I always wanted to feel I belonged somewhere, that I fit in, or that I was loved. What helped me to overcome the fear of God and the fear of change was that I realized that no one had a monopoly on God. I was able to begin to replace a lot of destructive behavior with a sort of spiritual desire. I think also what changed [was] my desire to get close to God, to love myself, and to really embrace unconditional love."

The study of AIDS patients found that those who believed in a loving God or benevolent universe had much better health outcomes than those who believed in a punishing one (Ironson et al., 2011). It also found that a diagnosis was often followed by a crisis leading to a spiritual breakthrough.

IS THE MIND IN THE BRAIN?

The mind is not in the brain any more than the picture on your computer is inside the screen.

When you turn on your TV and watch *Comedy Central*, the show is not inside your screen. There is certainly a close correlation between your device and the show. If your screen has a crack in it, it won't display the show properly. That doesn't mean that the existence of *Comedy Central* is dependent on your screen. The show has an existence independent of your screen and its degree of functionality.

Many experts looking at the research on brain and mind have suggested that the brain functions in a similar way (Kelly, 2011; Dossey, 2013). It is a transducer of mind in the same way that your screen is a transducer of the signal that carries the show. Mind and consciousness are independent of the screen.

Research shows that consciousness is not located in the brain. Dr. Bruce Greyson, who performed a study of NDEs in a cardiac care unit, concludes, "No one physiological or psychological model by itself explains all the common features of NDE. A clear sensorium and complex perceptual processes during a period of apparent clinical death challenge the concept that consciousness is localized exclusively in the brain" (Greyson, 2003). Your consciousness extends far beyond your local self, and your brain is akin to the receiver that translates it into your everyday experience.

In ordinary waking states, consciousness is firmly anchored to local reality. When you're driving to work or watching your child's baseball game or walking your dog or filling out your tax returns, your mind is focused on local reality. What you perceive as "you" is driving the car, looking at the traffic, and noticing the surrounding vehicles. Nonlocal fields are still there, but your mind isn't tuned in to them.

In anomalous states, we're no longer bound by local reality.

During times of anomalous states, such as dreaming, trance, meditation, mystical ecstasy, or hypnosis, our consciousness is no longer tethered to local reality. We lose identification with our bodies and our local sense of self. Like souls in the bardo state, we can move instantly to distant parts of the universe, unconfined by the constraints of local reality.

Some anomalous states are unremarkable regular experiences, like our nightly dreams. Others are transcendent experiences, like the oneness with nature we might experience during a mindful moment deep in the woods or splashing our toes in the ocean. At such times, our sense of a local self falls away and we feel one with all that is. In a mystical state, the boundaries of local self dissolve, and we become one with the universe.

THE BRAIN AS BRIDGE BETWEEN LOCAL AND NONLOCAL REALITY

The brain is also capable of bridging local and nonlocal reality. As well as providing the biological anchor through which we participate in nonlocal mind, it is constantly processing information from our surroundings.

This information flow is a two-way street. If we're lost in a daydream, our consciousness far away from our body, and a car backfires outside our window, our attention is shocked immediately back into the present. If we're in the middle of a dream at night, traveling far beyond the limits of waking awareness, and we smell smoke, our brain alerts us to danger and brings us back to earth in a hurry.

Our brain takes the information from the outside world and conveys it to our mind.

The ability of the brain to engage with and interpret the outside world is key to our functioning as human beings. But if we devote all our attention to the outside world and the local thoughts that cycle through our brains, we can miss out on the ecstatic states available to us when we are connected to nonlocal mind. A human experience that is focused only on local awareness and phenomena is an impoverished one, partaking in only a tiny sliver of the consciousness available to it.

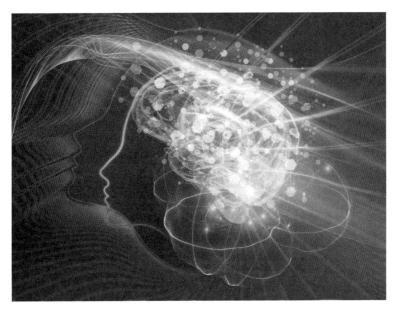

The brain bridges local and nonlocal reality.

Recent research has shown that large-scale fields exist around the planet and that they both entrain human consciousness and are affected by it (McCraty & Deyle, 2016). The human brain is a plausible biological mediator between these large-scale nonlocal fields and individual human awareness, the bridge between the local and the universal.

CHOOSING THE SIGNAL TO WHICH WE ATTUNE

We can choose the frequency to which we attune our minds. Like a streaming music service with millions of choices of stations, there are millions of competing nonlocal signals to choose from all the time.

Some of these signals are permutations of fear, while others are permutations of love. We can choose to attune the transceiver of our local mind with any one of the infinite varieties available.

We can choose magical experiences, orienting our awareness to them consciously. Rather than an occasional random fluke, they then become our default setting. We can decide to meditate when we wake up each morning, not leaving it up to chance whether or not we feel in tune with the cosmos that day. When we're stressed, we can tap, restoring equilibrium to our troubled emotions and maintaining our ability to connect with a larger perspective.

We can decide to go to our favorite spot in nature or listen to a piece of music that lifts us into a state of ecstasy. We can change the broadcast channel, turning off the news and tuning to the words and energy of an inspirational teacher instead. We can make a conscious decision to lift our attention from ordinary local reality to the sublime nonlocal signal of the universal mind.

By choosing these practices, we use our minds deliberately in order to induce transcendent states. Such states become not an inadvertent happy accident, but a lifestyle upgrade that we have deliberately installed.

THE BILL ON THE BEACH

In my dream, I am giving a speech. The auditorium is dark, but in the blackness and via live streaming, millions of people are listening intently. I'm using a PowerPoint presentation.

The next-to-last slide is one of a gateway. It has a big wooden post on either side. In the middle hangs a yellow sign with crenellation on top. It says, "The Happy Universe."

I tell the audience that every one of them deserves to live there. There's nothing stopping them. Well, almost nothing. I flip to my last slide.

It's a ticket that says, "Admit one."

I tell them that they have to pay for this ticket. The price of admission is their suffering. They can't get in if they hang on to even one atom of it. They have to give up absolutely every shred of suffering to purchase the ticket. Do that, and you're in.

The ticket only admits one person. You can't take your loved ones in there with you. They have to make the choice to buy a ticket themselves. Each person has to give up his or her suffering to get in, and you can't let go of it for someone else.

That's the end of the dream. I awake with the images embossed on my mind.

That was the dream I had the day I finished this book. Every part of the writing process was laced with synchronicities.

The previous New Year's Eve, my primary prayer for the year was that I be able to enter a deep meditative state quickly. Usually, it took me a while to shed all the mental chatter, and I wanted to be able to dive right in without spending so much time quieting my mind.

In a few weeks, this began to happen. I could invoke alignment quickly.

Two months later, taking a break from a conference at which I was speaking, I took a walk on the beach in San Diego. I was becoming obsessed with the idea of writing a book about the scientific evidence linking mind and matter. But I already had another book project half finished, too much other work, and no publisher. There were far more reasons not to proceed with the project than to go ahead.

It was a chilly winter's day, so my wife, Christine, had decided to stay in the car. I paced for a mile, wrestling with the book idea. I dodged children, dogs, and kites, all of which were out in force despite the cold weather. I could find no clarity, and I asked the universe for a clear sign.

I didn't receive any great epiphany, so I turned to walk back to the car. My eye caught something at the tide line. It was a $10 bill. There was no one around who it might belong to, and I picked it up.

The bill on the beach.

I got back in the car and showed it to Christine. Like any other bill, it said, "In God We Trust."

That seemed like an appropriate though unexceptional message. But why a $10 bill, rather than $1, $5, or $20?

Then the association hit me. In all my work, I use a rating scale from 0 to 10. If you believe something strongly, your belief is a 10 out of 10. The symbolism seemed to indicate that I could trust the universe to proceed with this project and it would be a 10 out of 10 grand slam.

A week later, the outline had written itself. Two weeks after that, I had a talk with Reid Tracy, the president of Hay House, who loved the idea. He preferred the title *Mind to Matter* to my alternative title *Thoughts to Things*, so the first option became the book title while *Thoughts to Things* became the title of my accompanying online course.

I wrote up a detailed proposal, and the day I mailed it in, a message arrived in my e-mail inbox from Mike Dooley, another Hay House author who sends daily messages to his subscribers. The subject line was "Thoughts become things and dreams come true." Another synchronicity.

I carved out several three-to-four-day blocks of time to write. Those days, I found myself wide awake at 4 A.M. I would spend an hour in meditation, getting my mind perfectly aligned, after which I would read and write obsessively for about 15 hours.

My friend David Feinstein gave me valuable feedback after I'd written the first three chapters. One morning after meditation, I had a strong urge to thank him. I decided to phone him later that morning. I hardly ever use my phone because I prefer e-mail, and I know he travels most of the year and rarely turns on his phone. So I knew I'd get his voicemail and be able to leave a warm message of appreciation.

I was surprised when, instead, David answered the phone. He told me he'd just returned the day before from a trip and turned on his cell phone a few minutes before I called. When the call came through, the phone displayed no caller ID, and he doesn't usually answer such calls. But he received an intuitive nudge to do so. Yet another synchronicity.

When I was writing this chapter on planetary-scale effects, I was struggling to understand the Schumann resonances. That month, I had also inadvertently double-booked myself to speak at two confer-ences the same weekend. One was in the Caribbean and the other at the opposite side of the continent in California. I had to split my time by speaking at one on Saturday, then flying back to California early Sunday morning to speak at the other.

Sunday afternoon, I was on a science panel at the second con-ference. Sitting next to me was HeartMath research director Rollin McCraty. He had just published a major paper on . . . you guessed it. Besides Schumann resonances, he also told me about field line resonances, which I had never even heard of before. They became a major part of the chapter. Synchronicities abounding!

Christine and I visited our friends Bob and Lynne Hoss in Arizona on the way to another conference. Bob is an expert on the neurosci-ence of dreaming. He had recently keynoted a conference and pre-pared a presentation on Carl Jung, the collective unconscious, and the double-slit experiments. His PowerPoint filled in crucial gaps in my knowledge. Synchronicity again!

On the same day, Jack Canfield, John Gray, and Rick Leskowitz all e-mailed me to say they'd endorse the book.

The June 12, 1982, peace rally.

When the publisher gave me the official publication date, June 12, a shiver ran up my spine. That date is highly significant for me. On June 12, 1982, I was in Central Park, New York, joining hundreds

260 MIND TO MATTER

of thousands of people protesting against the nuclear standoff between the U.S. and the USSR. After the rally, Secretary of State George Schultz went on television to say that the rally would make absolutely no difference in U.S. policy.

A few months later, U.S. president Ronald Reagan made an astonishing U-turn. The most hawkish of presidents amazed the world by proposing the START (Strategic Arms Reduction Treaty) nuclear reduction talks. Every year, on the anniversary of June 12, I remember the day when, in a powerful collective act of group mind, we decided not to blow up the planet and ourselves along with it.

Finally, on the very last day I had available to complete the manuscript of this book, I visited a neighborhood grocery store for breakfast. Near the checkout stand, my eye was caught by the latest special from *Time* magazine, entitled "The Science of Emotions." I opened it to a random page, and saw the headline of an article on how synchronicity can be predictable and not simply a matter of chance. That piece led me to the last four studies I needed to complete the synchronicity chapter.

Each day, I begin with attunement. I know that if I begin resonating with the fields of fear and lack that are present in the psychosphere, they will absorb my attention. Instead, I deliberately align my mind with the highest possibilities for me and for the planet.

We can choose to attune to the fields of love, peace, and joy. Like selecting the stations on a radio dial, we can allow the instrument of our brain and body to play the melodies of beauty and wonder that resonate through the planetary field. When we align ourselves with these fields, they resonate through our worlds, connecting us synchronistically with the highest possibilities in our destiny.

ATTENTION BUILDS BRAINS

Research into the brains of people in elevated spiritual states tells us that they are processing information very differently from the way they function in ordinary consciousness. The ratio of delta, beta, alpha, theta, and gamma waves changes drastically as the brain functions in an entirely different way. When these patterns of neural firing are changed on a regular basis, they quickly begin to build new synaptic connections. The volume of the various parts of our brain begins to change as the matter of brain tissue reconfigures itself to match the mind of deliberate creation.

The brain then becomes more skilled at transducing these signals. With more neural connections to carry the information flow, the brain is better at picking signals up from the universal field. It's more attuned to signaling from the field, with a higher degree of the neural circuits that facilitate synchrony.

A study performed by researchers at the University of Zurich compared people who were making a choice about how generous to be. A sum of money was promised to 50 participants at the start of the experiment. Half committed to spending the money on themselves alone, and the other half committed to spending it on someone else. Both groups were then asked to make a series of decisions indicative of generous behavior.

The investigators used MRIs to measure brain activity during and after the decision-making process. They found that participants who behaved the most generously had the biggest changes in brain regions associated with happiness. The researchers were surprised that the mere intent to spend money on someone else, before the generous act occurred, was sufficient to trigger changes in neural patterns (Park et al., 2017).

**Of the choices available to us each moment,
where will we direct our awareness?**

Every moment, we're faced with choices about where to direct our consciousness. Will we focus on the agonizing suffering with which the media tries to trap our awareness? Or will we orient our attention to the eternal now? Will we get sucked into the petty dramas of the human condition or align our thoughts with the wisdom of universal mind? With each choice we make, we shape our brain. Choose consistently for months and years, and you literally create a brain in synchrony with nonlocal mind.

Sir John Eccles, who earned a Nobel Prize for his work on the brain's neural synapses, says that "We have to recognize that we are spiritual beings with souls existing in a spiritual world as well as material beings with bodies and brains existing in a material world" (Popper & Eccles, 2012). When we live as though we are spiritual beings with material bodies and orient our consciousness in that way each day, the matter we create with our minds is very different.

ENTRAINING SELF WITH SYNCHRONICITY

Does synchronicity just happen, or can we encourage it? Is it a phenomenon that appears randomly by chance or can we step into a reality in which synchronicity is common?

Rather than being just an occasional accident, synchronicity, I've found, is a state that can be cultivated. We can deliberately entrain our local minds to the nonlocal consciousness of the universe in which the spontaneous coordination of nature is ever present. With practice, living synchronously and in harmony with the unfolding patterns of the universe becomes our minds' default setting.

Since I've started writing those big S's into my journal whenever synchronicities happen, they seem to be happening more often. Because I'm observing them, I'm attuned to them. As we do when practicing any new skill, I'm building the neural pathways that carry that type of information. I'm using the observer effect consciously, collapsing the possibility wave into the probabilities that I desire.

That doesn't mean that I can magically create anything I want like a magician pulling a rabbit out of a hat. It's a process of nudging reality consistently rather than manifesting something out of nothing immediately. It's *using* the principles of nature rather than defying them.

For instance, I've wanted to learn some French to use during my frequent trips to that country. Collapsing the possibility wave doesn't mean that I can instantly speak French. I still need to buy the online course, practice my pronunciation, and learn the vocabulary.

Ordinary things then happen that support my intent. A friend mentions a book that's available. It contains stickers with French words that you place on those items in your house. Seeing the objects and French words together every day builds your vocabulary quickly.

French language stickies adorn common objects in my house.

Next, I start to notice correspondences between Spanish words I already know and French words I don't know. I meet a Frenchman at a farmer's market and exchange a few words of French. Another friend tells me you can turn on French subtitles when you watch movies or watch them dubbed in French with English subtitles. My wife and I occasionally have dinner with our tablets next to us, with a translation window open, and practice having a simple French conversation. And on and on. Once I decide to learn French, the whole universe appears to conspire to support my goal.

THOUGHT BY THOUGHT AND NEURON BY NEURON

You cultivate synchronicity with consistently held thought. Perhaps you're making supper, and you discover that you're missing white pepper, which is essential to the recipe. The nearest convenience store is two miles away. You get in your car, leave your driveway, make the turns required, park, go in the store, and find the aisle in which white pepper is kept. You don't just go from standing in your kitchen, needing white pepper, to standing in the spice aisle. There are many steps along the way. That's the way consistently held thoughts produce things.

Researchers at New York University found that romance-minded students who believed they would get a date were significantly more likely to do so. Golfers who were told that they were playing with a lucky ball scored better during putting practice. In games of chance, optimists win more prizes than pessimists. People who see a silver lining around dark clouds, using their minds to positively reframe negative events, deactivate the amygdala, the midbrain structure that processes fear. According to psychologist Richard Wiseman, these people "expect the best outcomes, and these expectations become self-fulfilling prophecies" (Rockwood, 2017). Best-selling author Tim Ferriss says, "The most fulfilled and effective people I know—world-famous creatives, billionaires, thought leaders, and more—look at their life's journey as perhaps 25 percent *finding* themselves and 75 percent *creating* themselves" (Ferriss, 2017).

Over the course of 15 years, a team led by Dr. Robert Gramling of the University of Rochester surveyed 2,816 adults between the ages of 35 and 75. His study was aimed at identifying those at risk for heart disease. The results showed that beliefs made a huge difference in their health.

Those who believed they were at low risk of heart disease had only a third the incidence of strokes and heart attacks. The effect held even after controlling for variables such as cholesterol level, smoking, high blood pressure, family history, and other risk factors (Gramling et al., 2008). The belief in—and fear of—heart problems was associated with contracting cardiovascular disease.

That's the way mind becomes matter. Thought by thought, we're engaging neural pathways. When you have a belief about your heart, and you practice that belief in your mind year after year, you're building new neurons, neuron by neuron. It's not that you have a single negative thought about heart disease and drop dead instantly. It's not that you have a single positive thought and find yourself healed forever—just the way you don't desire white pepper and find yourself instantly in the grocery store. There are steps in between, as beliefs are rehearsed and thoughts become things and neurons shape biology. Hold a thought consistently, and you create the biological and environmental conditions that draw that thing to you.

THOUGHT FIELDS AND THE COLLECTIVE UNCONSCIOUS

In my live workshops, I've noticed that generally people seem to be effortless masters of one aspect of life. We work with five life areas:

- Work (including career and retirement)
- Love (including all close relationships)
- Money
- Health (including weight, diet, and exercise)
- Spirituality

Typically, people have no problem at all with at least one of these areas. Some, for instance, are career masters, enjoying fast-track success from their teenage years. Others effortlessly maintain a deep and abiding spiritual practice, woven into the fabric of their lives. Some, like my wife, automatically create great marriages and wonderful relationships with family and children.

One of my friends, Phil Town, is a money master. He's one of the most successful hedge fund managers in the business. He's written two best-selling books on taking charge of your own money. Money is his medium, and he talks, thinks, and acts effortlessly in this sphere of influence.

Another of my friends, Andrew Vidich, is a spiritual master. He has meditated every day of his life since his teen years. He spends over an hour in meditation every morning, and kindness and joy sparkle out of his eyes and his being. He is in the energy field of spirituality, and people feel transformed in his presence without a word being spoken. When you read his books, *Light upon Light* and *Love Is a Secret,* you share the energy field he inhabits, and you feel uplifted.

While we may be effortless masters of one of the five life areas, we may struggle with another. A friend of mine who started a hugely successful personal growth company in the late 1980s became a multimillionaire in his 20s. He's healthy and has enjoyed all the trappings of success. Yet after two glasses of wine at a mastermind group meeting, he confided in me how desperately unhappy he was in his love life. "I just got divorced from my third wife," he said disconsolately. "I had to sell my executive jet to get the money to pay her off. I understand why she divorced me . . . I'm a jerk, and I've screwed up every relationship in my life." Being a master in one life area is no guarantee of success in another.

One of the pioneers in the use of acupressure for healing was a clinical psychologist named Roger Callahan. He developed a method called thought field therapy. The term *thought field* is striking. Callahan believed that we have habitual patterns of consciousness, which he called thought fields. When we participate in a thought field, we inhabit the energy of that field, and we perceive the material world through the lens of that field.

Thought fields can also be large scale, akin to Jung's collective unconscious. Jung believed that most of our behavior is driven by the unconscious. The part of the mind we're aware of is like the tip of an iceberg protruding from the top of the sea. We think that's all there is. In reality, our behavior is being shaped by the collective thought fields below the surface, even though we're not conscious of them.

The collective unconscious is like an iceberg. We're only aware
of the tip, our conscious thought processes above the surface.
Below is the collective unconscious, driving behavior.

Types of energy in the collective unconscious can form thought fields. These can be simple and innocuous, like the thought field associated with the hobby of quilting. I once attended a workshop at a big conference center that was hosting several other groups. One of these was a quilting convention.

I didn't know a thing about quilts when I walked in the door. So I sat at a table with the quilters for some of the meals. Sucked into their thought field, resonating with their enthusiasm, quilting seemed like the most fascinating activity in the world.

Those who have mastery in one of the five life areas inhabit that particular thought field. Get two investors together and they begin sharing their investing insights as they resonate together. Put two meditators together and they reinforce the thought field of meditation as they interact.

Other thought fields are not so benevolent. Spend time with drug addicts or alcoholics and you can sense the thought fields holding their habits in place. People with similar patterns resonate together. That's why it is impossible for addicts to get and stay clean if they keep the company of other addicts. They are used to resonating with that thought field, and it sucks them in when they are close.

When you are in a fearful state of mind, fear breeds fear. The thought field of fear seeks out external stimuli to be afraid of. The fearful mind precipitates fearful probabilities out of the infinite potentials in the possibility wave. You might believe that the problems are "out there" in your environment, caused by other people, corporations, the government, or random events. In reality, you are inhabiting a thought field that shapes the material space around you. Mind can produce matter in negative as well as positive ways. In the Bible, the ancient philosopher Job laments: "What I feared has come upon me."

EMBODYING THE FIELDS OF MASTERY

When you're in a meditation workshop with Andrew Vidich, meditation seems easy. In his thought field, sharing in his unwavering attunement with the field of spiritual experience, similar frequencies are activated in you. Those frequencies resonate with similar frequencies in Andrew's local field and, through him, the same frequencies in the nonlocal field. While connected in powerful resonance patterns with the field produced by meditation, you participate in that energy.

I've had a similar experience in money workshops with Phil Town. While you're in the field of money expertise Phil generates, his explanations seem clear and simple. You have breakthroughs in your understanding of stocks and financial reports as you align your consciousness with Phil's field. In a room with 200 people all entrained to the same money frequency, you condition your mind and brain in resonance.

It's easy to meditate when resonating with the local field of a meditation group.

After you leave the meditation workshop or money seminar, the concepts soon become fuzzy. You start to forget what you learned and the state you attained, unless you practice. When you rehearse attunement with that thought field by reading books, watching videos, and learning more, you maintain your resonance with the field. Soon you've built the neural pathways and brain states that are characteristic of that thought field. You've moved from touching the field to embodying the field. You're on your way to mastery.

When we use our minds in this way, we condition matter. When we make a conscious choice to attain mastery in a field, we activate resonance with all the components of that field. Some may be local to us right where we are. Others may be nonlocal, distant in time or space.

Our intent, filling our consciousness, opens the doors to synchronicity. Opportunities and connections appear seemingly out of the blue. Yet they are generated by our participation in that particular thought field.

As an author and trainer, I'm fortunate to spend personal time with many transformational leaders. Individually, they generate inspiring energy fields. When they're together, the effect is enhanced. Being with them conditions my thinking and my energy as we come into resonance. Surrounding yourself with uplifting people is one of the best things you can do for both mental and physical health.

The following story, told by one of those leaders, is a remarkable story of manifestation. Who hasn't dreamed of manifesting a million dollars? This type of aspiration might seem beyond the pale of possibility. Yet as the German philosopher Goethe exclaimed (1887):

> What you can do, or dream you can, begin it,
> Boldness has genius, power, and magic in it.

Manifesting a Million Dollars

By Raymond Aaron

I lead transformational retreats, and in one exercise at the start of each event, we ask people to define what they'd most like to manifest during the course of the workshop.

As we went around the group, people chose the usual goals, like sleeping through the night, a revelation about which career path to choose, or having no conflicts with their spouse during the event.

But one man said he wanted a million dollars. He had started a company with a new technology to harvest stem cells, at the leading edge of health research. His goal was to have the financial freedom to pursue his dreams.

I didn't comment out loud, but I thought, *Wow, that's a huge goal.*

When the turn came for the next participant, he decided to copy the man who'd just spoken. He said he wanted a million dollars too!

I groaned inside. Two men who both want a million dollars to manifest during the retreat! It seemed impossible.

Three days later, the two men were bursting with excitement, and shared their news with the group. The second man's father was an investment banker. He'd told his father about the stem cell company, set up a meeting with the first man, and his father had become incredibly excited by the potential of the startup company. He'd told the first man that he'd be able to raise $100 million for him. Not $1 million, $100 million!

"And I get a one percent finder's fee!" said the second man. "That's a million dollars!"

ATTUNING YOUR MIND TO THE HIGHEST POSSIBLE STATE

Synchronicity is much more than meets the eye. It seems like a series of events that mysteriously line up to produce a significant result.

In reality, synchronicity represents the coordination of all life, from the most distant nonlocal reaches of space to the most intimate local environment of our thoughts. All are synchronized by resonant fields, and as we make choices with our minds, we set up resonance patterns that extend to infinity.

Our thoughts are profoundly creative. Once we realize this, we direct our thoughts consciously. We do what it takes to attune the functioning of our minds with the most elevated possibilities. We use our creative power deliberately. Goethe said, "We all have certain electric and magnetic powers within us and ourselves exercise an attractive and repelling force" (as cited in Jung, 1952). Understanding the creative power of our thoughts empowers us to use them wisely and deliberately, attuning to the thought fields of love, kindness, and creativity.

When I wake up in the morning, my first priority is attunement. My mind is swirling and my attention scattered, often focusing on the problems and negative aspects of the day ahead. Fragments of bad dreams and disturbing images I've seen on TV pop in and out at random.

If I were to start my day that way, I would bring that swirling, negative, scattered thought field to my material reality. I would condition my material world with the energy of that dysfunctional field.

So the first thing I do is attune my thoughts to the highest possible state. I tap away my worry and stress, and sit calmly in meditation. I know what my body feels like when I'm in that state of attunement to the infinite, with my brain producing high amplitudes of alpha, theta, and delta waves, and get in touch with that frequency. Once I'm attuned, I bask in that state for a long time. My thoughts escape from the swirl of confusion in which I woke up.

I feel happiness and optimism surging up within me like the exuberance of spring. I celebrate that wonderful feeling and tap again to anchor it in mind and body. If there's a patch of grass nearby, I walk outside, stand barefoot in the dew, and ground myself in Earth's frequencies. I might listen to an inspirational audio to give my thoughts direction. If I'm home, I look at my vision board and affirm my goals. I write in my journal, recording positive intentions for the life journey ahead. I fill my mind with gratitude for the blessings of my life. I savor the anticipation of the synchronicities that will appear to delight me in the hours ahead.

Then, centered and inspired, I walk into my day.

Making attunement the first priority each day conditions your local field.

Do this for just one month, every day, and your life will start to change. Use your mind deliberately, and matter will change. You will call synchronicity to you. Whether your challenges are with money, health, love, work, or spirituality, you'll find that you quickly move to a new level of mastery when you begin using your mind for conscious creation. Attune to those energy fields, and matter follows right along. Synchronicities line up all around you, and you live a life attuned to the music of the spheres.

Sometimes, right in the middle of an ordinary day, the beauty of life hits me like a cloudburst. I stop in my tracks, overwhelmed, tearful, too stunned to be able to take it all in. I stop what I'm doing and allow the feeling to expand. I open my heart big enough to stretch around the full extent of my blessings.

I relish those moments, savoring them as I expand my sense of self to accommodate the full measure of life's beauty and perfection. A life lived in conscious synchrony with the universe is a life well lived.

PUTTING THESE IDEAS INTO PRACTICE

Activities to practice this week:

- As you practice EcoMeditation morning and evening, hold the intention that you align your life with synchronicity.

- Notice emergence when it appears in your personal world. You might observe this in:

    Colonies of insects
    Flocks of birds
    Schools of fish
    The flow of traffic in cities

- In your journal, write down three or more big synchronous events that have happened in your life.

- Also in your journal, make a brief note of any experiences of emergence you've witnessed in the past few days.

The Extended Play version of this chapter includes:

- Video and full report of Mathias Rust's flight

- How emergence permeates our daily life

- Metronome entrainment videos

- "Hawaii Aloha" sung by IZ, on YouTube

- The extraordinary healing story of concentration camp survivor Jack Schwarz

- Ten famous people who eluded death on 9/11

To access the Extended Play version, visit:
MindToMatter.club/Chapter6

CHAPTER 7

THINKING FROM
BEYOND LOCAL MIND

Muir Woods National Monument is one of the loveliest places in California. It is named after conservationist John Muir. When he was 11 years old, his family emigrated from Scotland to the United States. He became an avid outdoorsman, with a wanderlust that took him all over the continent. Just before his 30th birthday, he walked from Indianapolis to the Gulf of Mexico, a distance of a thousand miles.

Muir eventually settled in California, writing an influential series of articles called Studies in the Sierra. He published 10 books expounding his philosophy of naturalism. His 1901 book *Our National Parks* brought him to the attention of president Theodore Roosevelt, who made a trip to Yosemite Valley to visit Muir in 1903. Muir's life became a tribute to connection with nature.

The forest in the park itself is primeval. Coast redwoods are the tallest living beings on the planet, reaching heights of over 100 yards or meters. The oldest trees alive were saplings when Jesus walked the earth 2,000 years ago, while some alive today were 1,000 years old when Columbus sailed the Atlantic. Fossilized examples show that the species has been around for over 200 million years.

The giant redwoods carry a powerful presence.

The land on which Muir Woods is located was purchased in 1905 by conservationists William and Elizabeth Kent. Believing the place was sacred, they wanted to protect the giant redwoods from loggers. The Kents were forced to take out a bank loan to acquire the property. Elizabeth was nervous about their financial exposure, but William responded, "If we lost all the money we have and saved these trees, it would be worthwhile, wouldn't it?" In 1908, President Theodore Roosevelt proclaimed the land the Muir Woods National Monument.

In the historic spring following World War II, delegates from all the primary nations of the world met in San Francisco to draft the charter of the United Nations. Just before he was due to open the conference, President Franklin D. Roosevelt died. On May 19, 1945, to honor him, the delegates held a ceremony in Muir Woods' Cathedral Grove. Today, around a million people a year visit Muir Woods to gape in wonder at trees that have been around longer than recorded human history.

WHEN THE UNIVERSE SIGNALS A U-TURN

One afternoon on the way to visit a friend, Christine and I drove past Muir Woods—accidentally. We'd missed a turn at an intersection a mile away.

It was the Memorial Day holiday weekend, the official start of summer in the United States. There were thousands of people at the park. Traffic was backed up before and after the entrance. All the parking lots were full to overflowing, and visitors were parked along the side of the road more than a mile away. Pedestrians were walking along both sides of the narrow road in a steady stream of coming and going.

We talked about how much we would like to visit Muir Woods but that we'd wait for a time when it wasn't so crowded.

We enjoyed our evening with our friends and decided to spend the night in their spare room. We left the following morning, heading for home. Suddenly, Christine exclaimed, "We're so close to Muir Woods, why don't we go there now?" We made a quick U-turn and drove back to the park.

It was 7:45 A.M., and the parking lot was almost empty. We walked down the path toward Cathedral Grove, the heart of the forest. We drank in the beauty of the trees, the air, and the sounds of birds, squirrels, and the stream. Christine said, "Let's treat this as a walking meditation." We walked in silence.

We walked for more than a mile, all around the most popular loop in Cathedral Grove. It took an hour. Frequently, we stopped in awe to gaze up at the grandeur of the trees.

The redwood trunks draw the eye upward.

We didn't see a single person anywhere along the way. On the return journey, we headed for the park entrance, our souls deeply nourished, feeling profoundly connected with nature, one with the great universal field.

When we got back to our starting point in the parking lot, the morning's visitors were streaming into the park. Four tour buses had arrived, disgorging hundreds of people. The crush of humanity at the entrance was so thick that we had to elbow our way out.

Yet we'd been able to enjoy the forest, all to ourselves, basking in the sacred space of nature, between the two invasions. Just following our bliss, with no fixed plan, going with the flow, we had our wish to enjoy Muir Woods without the crowds—on the most crowded weekend of the year.

BEING IN THE FLOW OF NONLOCAL MIND

Alignment with the universal flow unlocks alignment with all the synchrony, grace, beauty, and wisdom of the universe. As you, an individual human being, a local mind, move into alignment with the great nonlocal mind—the mind behind all mind, the mind that gives rise to all consciousness—as you merge and become one with that mind, your mind, your individual local mind, is no longer functioning as an isolated, separate, lonely fragment, cut off from the whole by the illusion of separateness.

Instead, the flow of nonlocal mind is now in you, and you are in the flow. You are now no longer local consciousness. You are now universal consciousness. You have stepped from the position of that which is acted on to the perspective of that which acts.

Horizons of creativity open up to you. Vistas of possibility flood your awareness. You know yourself to be one with universal wisdom, with universal power, with universal intelligence, with universal love. From that place in consciousness, you live a life of wisdom, intelligence, and love. You no longer ask for love, need love, or crave love, because you are love. You no longer pray for wisdom, because you are wisdom. You no longer seek inner peace, because your very nature is peace. Standing in that place, you have access to all the wisdom, peace, and love in the universe.

This is the transcendent state that has been experienced and described by mystics throughout the ages. It is the state of flow that elite athletes experience at times of peak performance. It is the state into which artists enter when they create their most inspired work. It is the state children naturally inhabit when they lose themselves in play.

It is the state we're meant to live our lives in all the time. It's been perceived as a special, occasional exception to the grind of daily life. Yet it's actually meant to be the way we start and end each day. Each day is meant to flow in an unfolding of synchronous possibilities.

When I meet people in my workshops and they tell the stories of their lives, I'm moved by their suffering. Yet I'm also struck by the way this suffering accumulates as they move through life. They weren't born suffering. As toddlers, they knew how to laugh, love, and play. They then have negative experiences and gradually move from the spontaneously joyful childhood state to the worried, diminished, stressed adult state.

PUTTING FLOW INTO PRACTICE

How can we reverse the process? That may be the most important question of our lives. We can learn to be proactive, doing those things in consciousness and in practice that bring us back into synchrony with the universe. We can learn to release our suffering and learn to play again.

We can rehearse the states of consciousness that we knew as children and turn our adult lives into a joyful playground of possibility.

The way to put this into practice is simple.

When you wake up every morning, simply align your consciousness with the highest possible frequency of which you are capable. Sit quietly, read the words that inspire you the most, and enter a contemplative state. Before you begin your day, before you begin to think or create, align yourself. Align yourself to the highest possible vibrational frequency that you know. Align yourself with the most elevated energy field of which you are conscious.

The first conscious act of the day is to align with the nonlocal universal field.

Use this gift called consciousness to constantly align yourself to that highest possible energy field at the start of every day. As you do this, you will feel a shift in your body. You will feel a physical sense of shifting to a new plane, of moving into an altered state.

The physical sensation of being aligned with the universal field, one with nonlocal mind, is quite different from the physical experience generated by the illusion of being a separate local mind cut off from the love, the wisdom, the brilliance, the elevated perspective of the great nonlocal intelligence.

Then, in this space you create for yourself every morning, at one with the universe, the thoughts you think will be different. The actions you take will be different. The aspirations you have will be completely different. The expectations you hold will change. The assumptions you make will be nothing like the assumptions made in a state of isolated local mind. The worldview from which you see life and creation will be expansive. The possibility fields you perceive will be infinite. Your very sense of self, who you are as a human being, will shift completely.

LIVING IN ATTUNEMENT WITH THE UNIVERSAL FIELD

A *you* living in attunement with the universal field has an entirely different sense of self than a *you* living as a self isolated in local mind. Perceiving yourself as one with this synchronized universe, you move into your day with a sense of equanimity, power, peace, joy, love, and exuberance. You align with creative genius, and you shape the world outside of yourself based on a sense of high vision drawn from the reality field of that universal mind.

Suddenly, you are no longer an isolated individual bumping into this or that problem or challenge. Instead, you are part of an orchestra of synchronized movement. One with the universe, you are one with everyone else who is one with the universe. One with the universe, you are one with every force and phenomenon in nature that is also one with the universe. One with the universe, you dance to the tune of the natural harmonics of creation.

**When we're in resonance with the universal field, we're in
synchrony with everyone else who is resonating with the field.**

THE RESONANT SYMPHONY OF ALL MIND

When you align with the universe, your individual mind is automatically synchronized with every other mind that is also synchronized
with the universe, and the only minds with whom you are out of tune are
those who are themselves out of tune with the universe.

You love them, you bless them, and by your attunement, you invite
them to attunement as well. You cannot help those you love by moving
out of attunement and into the place of non-attunement in which they
live. You can only help them by being vibrantly attuned to universal self.
You are then a beacon of invitation, welcoming them to the possibility of
joining you in the dance of attunement.

If they do join you, they are naturally and effortlessly attuned with
you, and if they choose otherwise, you bless them on their path. You
need not persuade them or induce them. They will join the dance whenever they are ready. Let them go; you will find that there are thousands

of people, millions of people, billions of people, ready to dance with you in attunement with life.

This is the universe's wish for you: That you find and remain in this attunement. That you start your day calibrating yourself to the universal field. That you start each day by dropping the illusion that you are a struggling local entity and by accepting the reality that you are one with all that is. That is what the universe most wants for you.

RELINQUISHING THE ILLUSION OF LOCALITY

The universe knows that once you let go of the illusion that you are an isolated, local entity and embrace the reality that you are one with universal mind, suddenly you are part of the flow. Synchronously, you dance with every being who is part of the universal dance. Your life flows easily and organically. All of the friction, all of the static that you experience at the level of local mind falls away. Your life is easy, happy, and naturally creative. You feel one with this universal reality of oneness. The kind of life you create for yourself from that perspective is radically different from the life you create from the perspective of an isolated local self.

We move through our lives in conscious alignment with the universal field.

Making this choice day after day, this choice to align every morning, sends your life off on a completely new trajectory, one rich in possibilities. One suffused with joy. One bursting with vitality and enthusiasm.

You are at a crossroads in this moment. A choice point. The point at which you either embrace the reality of yourself as one with a benevolent universe or continue in the illusion that you are not. You face this choice this moment. You face this choice every moment.

THE MOST IMPORTANT CHOICE
YOU'LL EVER MAKE

This is the most important choice you will make in your entire life: aligned or not aligned. And as you make that choice now, as you align in the next moment, and the next and the next, and the next day, the next week, the next month, as you make that choice an infinite number of times, it becomes not a choice but a fact. It becomes not a decision but a way of life. As it becomes a way of life, as it becomes the default setting for your consciousness, you begin to build the neural wiring that anchors it in matter. The matter of your body becomes the vehicle not for your local mind but for nonlocal mind.

Nonlocal mind, driving the neural circuits of your brain and body, creates a new brain and body. It builds cells. Regenerates DNA. Creates a field of connection. Generates coherence in your thoughts, words, and deeds. Opens possibilities in your sphere of influence. Co-creates with you at the level of your material reality.

The material reality you create when one with the universal mind is completely different from the material reality you create when cut off from universal mind. You think these thoughts in alignment with universal mind and they become things in alignment with universal mind. The matter of your body is shifted and changed. The matter of your material reality is shifted and changed. And after moment after moment after moment of alignment, you live in an entirely different material reality from the one you would have created had you remained locked in the prison of local mind and local self.

What will we create together in this unified field? Let's find out!

PUTTING THESE IDEAS INTO PRACTICE

Activities to practice this week:

- Take a walk in nature and practice walking slowly. Feel each footfall.

- Walk or stand barefoot on sand or wet grass for a few minutes each day.

- During your EcoMeditation practice morning and evening, consciously tune your local self to nonlocal mind.

- One day, after meditating, in your journal, draw an illustration of your local self and nonlocal reality. You don't have to be a great artist—just a simple line drawing is fine.

- Ask nonlocal mind, *What is your highest vision for me?* and write whatever pops into your head down in your journal.

The Extended Play version of this chapter includes:

- Video of fields of the human heart

- Instruction for how to ground and center yourself in Earth's fields

- Researcher Stephan Schwartz on anomalous experiences and quantum consciousness

To access the Extended Play version, visit: MindToMatter.club/Chapter7

AFTERWORD

Where Mind Takes Us Next

I'm privileged to live among awesome creators. You and I are creating the world around us by our thoughts in this very moment. And in every moment.

We are members of a community of artists, painting our world into existence moment by moment. The visions we see in our mind's eye translate themselves, thought by thought, into the concrete reality of material form all around us. As we choose our thoughts, we are in fact choosing our material reality, whether we are consciously aware of it or not.

What sort of world will we create in the coming moments, days, months, years, and decades?

I'm convinced it will be a world of peace, of compassion, of beauty, of opportunity, of wisdom. In the past centuries, we've practiced creating survival, fear, anger, war, resentment, competition, shame, guilt, rivalry, and other forms of strife. As a species, we've had thousands of generations to experience the material circumstances that result from that type of thinking.

We have seen the suffering it produces. Now, I believe, we are ready for a new experience. We are ready to paint a new world. As we realize our ability to choose that world, we begin to select thoughts, feelings, experiences, and beliefs that facilitate its creation.

When we first make the discovery that we create with our minds, we produce our first small deliberate creations. Like a baby taking its first steps, we're tentative and uncertain.

But if you've ever watched a child learn to walk, you know that this hesitancy quickly gives way to exuberant confidence. Now free to explore the world, the child strides about enthusiastically. She goes places she has never been able to go before. Her circle of influence expands ever wider, as she ventures farther and farther from her point of origin. She quickly adjusts her mind to the new reality and assumes a degree of mobility and freedom she never knew before she took the first step.

That's us today. As a species, we have just begun to scratch the surface of our power. We have no idea yet what we are capable of. We've hardly taken even our very first step. We are only just beginning to realize what we might accomplish.

While the future is unknown, shrouded in mystery, we can look back and see clearly what has happened in the past. We see the two world wars of the 20th century, and the even bloodier conflicts of the 19th century and earlier times. We see the ignorance, poverty, starvation, injustice, and cruelty in which our species has been bred for millennia. While a millennium of progress in science and philosophy has given us the first glimmers of enlightenment, human existence has been driven by the stark requirements of survival for most of our history.

As a species, we've been there, done that, and bought the T-shirt. Now it's time for more. When we didn't know that our thoughts created our reality, we assumed that all the suffering in which we lived was a fixed and objective reality.

Now we know better. We have begun to understand the immense potential of our minds to create reality. We understand the leverage we possess over both the microscopic and the macroscopic levels of form. On the microscopic scale, we understand that our thoughts are shaping the anatomy and physiology of our cells at every moment, calling molecules into and out of existence, like a medieval alchemist's fantasy.

On the macroscopic level, our thoughts combine with those of the rest of our species to create the broad sweep of history. The history we create once we understand our power is very different from the history we created when we labored blindly under the illusion that reality was composed of random events that simply happened to us.

As conscious creators, we choose differently. When our survival needs push us to think angry and bitter thoughts, born out of the illusion of scarcity and competition, we choose not to think them. Not thinking them, we join with the millions of other people making similar choices. We find ourselves drawn into the reality fields of that new community. Multiplying the resonance of those shared fields, we shift the direction of society.

When you choose not to think that negative thought, and you replace it with a positive one instead, you aren't just shifting your own reality. You're shifting reality for the whole human species. You're adding to the sum of kindness and compassion in the world. You're reinforcing that new reality field. You're one of millions of people adding their positive energy to the new reality. You're helping transform it into an irresistible force that turns the tide of history.

While the forces of misery—people driven by survival and ignorant of the fact that they were creating the same dark world that they feared—may have been running the show for millennia, today is different. We understand our power. We make different choices. We use our power to shape first our own personal reality and then, collectively, the reality of the planet.

Having experimented with fearful thinking and its consequences, I believe that we have now embarked on a new experiment. Like that toddler taking her first steps, we are shining light into the darkness of our old conditioned thinking. That first beam of light, like that first step, gleams hesitantly. Yet the light feels good. The molecules we create in our bodies when we lighten our thinking feel good. The circumstances we create in the world around us when we enlighten our minds are infinitely more enjoyable. In a positive feedback loop, this reinforces our desire for more of the same.

Growing increasingly confident in our newfound power to create a positive world, we begin to think boldly. We imagine what a world without war, hunger, or poverty might look like. That subjective immaterial vision is the embryo of objective material reality.

This is the work we now do together. Joining with the millions of other people all over the world who have made the commitment to a positive future for themselves and humankind, we produce an irresistible field of love. The field of love we create opposes no one. We don't judge, condemn, or complain. We simply love.

As the field of love grows stronger, it bathes everything within its circumference. Out of this shared reality field of love, a new material reality is born. The material reality reflects the energy of the vibrational reality. In the new material reality, people act instinctively with kindness and compassion. Respect and altruism are the new normal in human relationships.

From the moment they are conceived, the children of the future grow up with these assumptions. Bathed in love from conception onward, children experience nothing else. They become vibrant creators, with their play, social interactions, and life expectations saturated with the certainty of love. Growing up in a world of love, they create love in their careers and families. The world changes to reflect their expectations.

I have no idea what our children, or our children's children, might create. I am certain that the types of creations produced by human beings saturated with love will be the products of happiness. I believe that their fresh creations will take science, technology, education, art, music, philosophy, religion, architecture, the environment, civilization, and society to places far beyond what our generation can conceive of.

That's the world I plan to live in for the rest of my life. That's the world I choose to create with my personal thoughts from the moment I open my eyes at the start of each new day. That's the world I invite you to join me in creating with your personal thoughts moment by moment. There is no better place to live.

Thank you for partnering with me in this journey of exploration. We have seen how the proposition that mind creates matter is not mere metaphysical speculation, but scientific fact. We have discovered that our minds create reality and become aware of the potential each of us has to create a benevolent reality using the astonishing power of thought. As we play together from this point on, I look forward to co-creating this delicious world of love and joy with you.

REFERENCES

CHAPTER 1

Baker, S. J. (1925). *Child hygiene.* New York: Harper.

Barinaga, M. (1998). New leads to brain neuron regeneration. *Science, 282*(5391), 1018–1019. doi:10.1126/science.282.5391.1018b.

Bengston, W. F. (2007). A method used to train skeptical volunteers to heal in an experimental setting. *The Journal of Alternative and Complementary Medicine, 13*(3), 329–332.

Bengston, W. F. (2010). *The energy cure: Unraveling the mystery of hands-on healing.* Boulder, CO: Sounds True.

Bengston, W. F., & Krinsley, D. (2000). The effect of the "laying on of hands" on transplanted breast cancer in mice. *Journal of Scientific Exploration, 14*(3), 353–364.

Chiesa, A., Calati, R., & Serretti, A. (2011). Does mindfulness training improve cognitive abilities? A systematic review of neuropsychological findings. *Clinical Psychology Review, 31*(3), 449–464.

Church, D. (Ed.). (2004). *The heart of healing.* Santa Rosa, CA: Elite Books.

Eden, D., & Feinstein, D. (2008). *Energy medicine: Balancing your body's energies for optimal health, joy, and vitality.* New York: Penguin.

Frey, A. H. (1993). Electromagnetic field interactions with biological systems. *FASEB Journal, 7*(2), 272–281.

Goleman, D., & Davidson, R. J. (2017). *Altered traits: Science reveals how meditation changes your mind, brain, and body.* New York: Penguin.

Hameroff, S., & Penrose, R. (1996). Orchestrated reduction of quantum coherence in brain microtubules: A model for consciousness. *Mathematics and Computers in Simulation, 40*(3–4), 453–480.

Hugo, V. (1877). *The history of a crime.* (T. H. Joyce & A. Locker, Trans.). New York: A. I. Burt.

Kandel, E. R. (1998). A new intellectual framework for psychiatry. *American Journal of Psychiatry, 155*(4), 457–469.

Kim, S., & Coulombe, P. A. (2010). Emerging role for the cytoskeleton as an organizer and regulator of translation. *Nature Reviews Molecular Cell Biology, 11*(1), 75–81.

King, C. R. (1993). *Children's health in America: A history.* New York: Bantam.

Lerner, L. J., Bianchi, A., & Dzelzkalns, M. (1966). Effect of hydroxyurea on growth of a transplantable mouse mammary adenocarcinoma. *Cancer Research, 26*(11), 2297–2300.

Malik, T. (2006, March 26). Fuel leak and fire led to falcon 1 rocket failure, SpaceX says. *Space.com.* Retrieved from www.space.com/2200-fuel-leak-fire-led-falcon -1-rocket-failure-spacex.html.

McTaggart, L. (2007). *The intention experiment: Using your thoughts to change your life and the world.* New York: Free Press.

Oschman, J. L. (2015). *Energy medicine: The scientific basis.* London: Elsevier Health Sciences.

Phillips, G. (2016). Meditation. *Catalyst.* Retrieved May 16, 2017, from www.abc .net.au/catalyst/stories/4477405.htm.

Radin, D., Schlitz, M., & Baur, C. (2015). Distant healing intention therapies: An overview of the scientific evidence. *Global Advances in Health and Medicine* 4(Suppl.):67–71. doi:10.7453/ gahmj.2015.012.suppl. Retrieved from http://deanradin.com/evidence/RadinDistantHealing2015.pdf.

Schlam, T. R., Wilson, N. L., Shoda, Y., Mischel, W., & Ayduk, O. (2013). Preschoolers' delay of gratification predicts their body mass 30 years later. *The Journal of Pediatrics, 162*(1), 90–93.

Schmidt, S., Schneider, R., Utts, J., & Walach, H. (2004). Distant intentionality and the feeling of being stared at: Two meta-analyses. *British Journal of Psychology, 95*(2), 235–247.

Schweizer, S., Grahn, J., Hampshire, A., Mobbs, D., & Dalgleish, T. (2013). Training the emotional brain: Improving affective control through emotional working memory training. *Journal of Neuroscience, 33*(12), 5301–5311.

Shealy, N., & Church, D. (2008). *Soul medicine: Awakening your inner blueprint for abundant health and energy.* Santa Rosa, CA: Energy Psychology Press.

Siegel, D. (2017). *Mind: A journey into the heart of being human.* New York: Norton.

Smith, L. (2004). Journey of a Pomo Indian medicine man. In D. Church (Ed.), *The heart of healing* (pp. 31–41). Santa Rosa, CA: Elite Books.

Stoll, G., & Müller, H. W. (1999). Nerve injury, axonal degeneration and neural regeneration: Basic insights. *Brain Pathology, 9*(2), 313–325.

Tang, Y. Y., Hölzel, B. K., & Posner, M. I. (2015). The neuroscience of mindfulness meditation. *Nature Reviews Neuroscience, 16*(4), 213–225.

CHAPTER 2

Bengston, W. (2010). *The energy cure: Unraveling the mystery of hands-on healing.* Boulder, CO: Sounds True.

Burr, H. S. (1973). *The fields of life: Our links with the universe.* New York: Ballantine.

Burr, H. S., & Mauro, A. (1949). Electrostatic fields of the sciatic nerve in the frog. *Yale Journal of Biology and Medicine, 21*(6), 455.

Church, D. (2013). *The EFT manual* (3rd ed.). Santa Rosa, CA: Energy Psychology Press.

Clarke, D., Whitney, H., Sutton, G., & Robert, D. (2013). Detection and learning of floral electric fields by bumblebees. *Science, 340*(6128), 66–69.

Czech-Damal, N. U., Liebschner, A., Miersch, L., Klauer, G., Hanke, F. D., Marshall, C., Dehnhardt, G., & Hanke, W. (2017). Electroreception in the Guiana dolphin (*sotalia guianensis*). *Proceedings of the Royal Society, Biological Sciences, 279*(1729), 663–668. doi:10.1098/rspb.2011.1127.

Grad, B. (1963). A telekinetic effect on plant growth. *International Journal of Parapsychology, 5*(2), 117–133.

Grad, B. (1967). The "laying on of hands": Implications for psychotherapy, gentling, and the placebo effect. *Journal of the American Society for Psychical Research, 61*(4), 286–305.

Kaplan, M. (2013, February 21). Bumblebees sense electric fields in flowers. *Nature News Online.* Retrieved from www.nature.com/news/bumblebees-sense-electric-fields-in-flowers-1.12480.

Kronn, Y. (2006, April 6). *Subtle energy and well-being.* Presentation at California State University, Chico, CA.

Kröplin, B., & Henschel, R. C. (2017). *Water and its memory: New astonishing results in water research.* Germany: GutesBuch Verlag.

Langman, L., & Burr, H. S. (1947). Electrometric studies in women with malignancy of cervix uteri. *Obstetrical and Gynecological Survey, 2*(5), 714.

Lu, Z. (1997). Laser raman observations on tap water, saline, glucose, and medemycine solutions under the influence of external qi. In L. Hui & D. Ming (Eds.), *Scientific qigong exploration* (pp. 325–337). Malvern, PA: Amber Leaf Press.

Radin, D., Hayssen, G., Emoto, M., & Kizu, T. (2006). Double-blind test of the effects of distant intention on water crystal formation. *Explore: The Journal of Science and Healing, 2*(5), 408–411.

Rao, M. L., Sedlmayr, S. R., Roy, R., & Kanzius, J. (2010). Polarized microwave and RF radiation effects on the structure and stability of liquid water. *Current Science, 98*(11), 1500–1504.

Schwartz, S. A., De Mattei, R. J., Brame, E. G., & Spottiswoode, S. J. P. (2015). Infrared spectra alteration in water proximate to the palms of therapeutic practitioners. *Explore: The Journal of Science and Healing, 11*(2), 143–155.

Scofield, A. M., & Hodges, R. D. (1991). Demonstration of a healing effect in the laboratory using a simple plant model. *Journal of the Society for Psychical Research, 57*(822), 321–343.

Vardalas, J. (2013, November 8). A history of the magnetic compass. Retrieved from http://theinstitute.ieee.org/tech-history/technology-history/a-history-of-the-magnetic-compass.

Wheatstone, C. (1833). On the figures obtained by strewing sand on vibrating surfaces, commonly called acoustic figures. *Philosophical Transactions of the Royal Society of London 123*, 593–633. Retrieved from http://archive.org/stream/philtrans07365800/07365800#page/n17/mode/2up.

Yan, X., Lu, F., Jiang, H., Wu, X., Cao, W., Xia, Z., . . . Zhu, R. (2002). Certain physical manifestation and effects of external qi of Yan Xin life science technology. *Journal of Scientific Exploration, 16*(3), 381–411.

CHAPTER 3

ADInstruments. (2010). *Electroencephalography.* Retrieved May 21, 2017, from web.as.uky.edu/Biology/_./Electroencephalography%20Student%20Protocol.doc

Barsade, S. G. (2002). The ripple effect: Emotional contagion and its influence on group behavior. *Administrative Science Quarterly, 47*(4), 644–675.

Bengston, W. (2010). *The energy cure: Unraveling the mystery of hands-on healing.* Boulder, CO: Sounds True.

Benor, D. J. (2004). *Consciousness, bioenergy, and healing: Self-healing and energy medicine for the 21st century* (Vol. 2). Bellmar, NJ: Wholistic Healing Publications.

Cade, M., & Coxhead, N. (1979). *The awakened mind: Biofeedback and the development of higher states of awareness.* New York: Dell.

Castro, M., Burrows, R., & Wooffitt, R. (2014). The paranormal is (still) normal: The sociological implications of a survey of paranormal experiences in Great Britain. *Sociological Research Online, 19*(3), 16.

Chapman, R., & Sisodia, R. (2015). *Everybody matters: The extraordinary power of caring for your people like family.* New York: Penguin.

Cohen, S. (2017). Science can help you reach enlightenment—but will it mess with your head? *New York Post,* February 26, 2017, retrieved at https://nypost.com/2017/02/26/science-can-help-you-reach-instant-enlightenment-but-will-it-mess-with-your-head/.

Davidson, R. J., & Lutz, A. (2008). Buddha's brain: Neuroplasticity and meditation. *IEEE Signal Processing Magazine, 25*(1), 176.

Dispenza, J. (2017). *Becoming supernatural.* Carlsbad, CA: Hay House.

Fehmi, L. G., & Robbins, J. (2007). *The open-focus brain: Harnessing the power of attention to heal mind and body.* Boston: Trumpeter Books.

Ferguson, N. (2008). *The ascent of money: A financial history of the world.* New York: Penguin.

Fowler, J. H., & Christakis, N. A. (2008). Dynamic spread of happiness in a large social network: Longitudinal analysis over 20 years in the Framingham Heart Study. *British Medical Journal, 337,* a2338.

Fredrickson, B. (2013). *Love 2.0: Finding happiness and health in moments of connection.* New York: Plume.

Goldhill, O. (2017, February 19). You're a completely different person at 14 and 77, the longest-running personality study ever has found. *Quartz Media.* Retrieved from https://qz.com/914002/youre-a-completely-different-person-at-14-and-77-the-longest-running-personality-study-ever-has-found.

Goleman, D. (1987, June 9). Personality: Major traits found stable through life. *New York Times.* Retrieved from www.nytimes.com/1987/06/09/science/personality-major-traits-found-stable-through-life.html.

Greeley, A. M. (1975). *The sociology of the paranormal: A reconnaissance.* Beverly Hills, CA: Sage Publications.

Groesbeck, G., Bach, D., Stapleton, P., Banton, S., Blickheuser, K., & Church, D. (2016, October 12). *The interrelated physiological and psychological effects of EcoMeditation: A pilot study.* Presented at Omega Institute for Holistic Studies, Rhinebeck, NY.

Gruzelier, J. (2009). A theory of alpha/theta neurofeedback, creative performance enhancement, long distance functional connectivity and psychological integration. *Cognitive Processing, 10*(Suppl. 1), S101–109.

Harris, M. A., Brett, C. E., Johnson, W., & Deary, I. J. (2016). Personality stability from age 14 to age 77 years. *Psychology and Aging, 31*(8), 862.

Hatfield, E., Cacioppo, J. T., & Rapson, R. L. (1994). *Emotional contagion.* New York: Cambridge University Press.

Hendricks, L., Bengston, W. F., & Gunkelman, J. (2010). The healing connection: EEG harmonics, entrainment, and Schumann's Resonances. *Journal of Scientific Exploration, 24*(4), 655.

Hoyland, J. S. (1932). *An Indian peasant mystic: Translations from Tukaram.* London: Allenson.

Hughes, J. R. (1964). Responses from the visual cortex of unanesthetized monkeys. In C. C. Pfeiffer & J. R. Smythies (Eds.), *International review of neurobiology 7* (pp. 99–153). New York: Academic Press.

Kotler, S., & Wheal, J. (2017). *Stealing fire: How silicon valley, the navy SEALs, and maverick scientists are revolutionizing the way we live and work.* New York: HarperCollins.

Johnson, M. L. (2011). Relationship of alpha-theta amplitude crossover during neurofeedback to emergence of spontaneous imagery and biographical memory. Doctoral dissertation, University of North Texas. Retrieved from http://citeseerx.ist.psu.edu/viewdoc/download?doi=10.1.1.842.2019&rep=rep1&type=pdf.

Kershaw, C. J., & Wade, J. W. (2012). *Brain change therapy: Clinical interventions for self-transformation.* New York: W. W. Norton.

Kramer, A. D., Guillory, J. E., & Hancock, J. T. (2014). Experimental evidence of massive-scale emotional contagion through social networks. *Proceedings of the National Academy of Sciences, 111*(24), 8788–8790.

LeDoux, J. (2002). *Synaptic self: How our brains become who we are.* New York: Penguin.

Lehmann, D., Faber, P. L., Tei, S., Pascual-Marqui, R. D., Milz, P., & Kochi, K. (2012). Reduced functional connectivity between cortical sources in five meditation traditions detected with lagged coherence using EEG tomography. *Neuroimage, 60*(2), 1574–1586.

Leskowitz, E. (2007). The influence of group heart rhythm on target subject physiology: Case report of a laboratory demonstration, and suggestions for further research. *Subtle Energies and Energy Medicine Journal, 18*(3), 1–12.

Liu, Y., Piazza, E. A., Simony, E., Shewokis, P. A., Onaral, B., Hasson, U., & Ayaz, H. (2017). Measuring speaker-listener neural coupling with functional near infrared spectroscopy. *Scientific Reports, 7,* 43293.

Llinás, R. R. (2014). Intrinsic electrical properties of mammalian neurons and CNS function: A historical perspective. *Frontiers in Cellular Neuroscience, 8,* 320.

Millett, D. (2001). Hans Berger: From psychic energy to the EEG. *Perspectives in Biology and Medicine, 44*(4), 522–542.

Morris, S. M. (2010). Achieving collective coherence: Group effects on heart rate variability coherence and heart rhythm synchronization. *Alternative Therapies in Health and Medicine, 16*(4), 62–72.

Nunez, P. L., & Srinivasan, R. (2006). *Electric fields of the brain: The neurophysics of EEG.* New York: Oxford University Press.

Osborn, J., & Derbyshire, S. W. (2010). Pain sensation evoked by observing injury in others. *Pain, 148*(2), 268–274.

Pennington, J. (in press). The brainwaves of creativity, insight and healing: How to transform your mind and life. *Energy Psychology: Theory, Research, and Treatment.*

Reece, A. G., & Danforth, C. M. (2017). Instagram photos reveal predictive markers of depression. *EPJ Data Science, 6*(1), 15.

Restak, R. M. (2001). *The secret life of the brain.* New York: Joseph Henry Press.

Schaefer, M., Heinze, H. J., & Rotte, M. (2012). Embodied empathy for tactile events: Interindividual differences and vicarious somatosensory responses during touch observation. *Neuroimage, 60*(2), 952–957.

Shiller, R. J. (2015). *Irrational exuberance* (3rd ed.). Princeton, NJ: Princeton University Press.

Shirer, W. (1941). *Berlin diary: The journal of a foreign correspondent, 1934–1941.* New York: Alfred A. Knopf.

Schwartz, J. M., & Begley, S. (2009). *The mind and the brain.* New York: Springer Science & Business Media.

Schwartz, J. M., Stapp, H. P., & Beauregard, M. (2005). Quantum physics in neuroscience and psychology: A neurophysical model of mind-brain interaction. *Philosophical Transactions of the Royal Society of London B: Biological Sciences, 360*(1458), 1309–1327.

Smith, H. (2009). *The world's religions* (50th anniv. ed.). San Francisco: HarperOne.

Thatcher, R. W. (1998). EEG normative databases and EEG biofeedback. *Journal of Neurotherapy, 2*(4), 8–39.

Tononi, G., & Koch, C. (2015). Consciousness: Here, there and everywhere? *Philosophical Transactions of the Royal Society of London B: Biological Sciences, 370*(1668), 20140167, 1–17.

Wright, R. (2017). *Why Buddhism is true: The science and philosophy of meditation and enlightenment.* New York: Simon and Schuster.

Zahn-Waxler, C., Radke-Yarrow, M., Wagner, E., & Chapman, M. (1992). Development of concern for others. *Developmental Psychology, 28*(1), 126.

CHAPTER 4

Ahmed, Z., & Wieraszko, A. (2008). The mechanism of magnetic field-induced increase of excitability in hippocampal neurons. *Brain Research, 1221,* 30–40.

Akarsu, E., Korkmaz, H., Balci, S. O., Borazan, E., Korkmaz, S., & Tarakcioglu, M. (2016). Subcutaneous adipose tissue type II deiodinase gene expression reduced in obese individuals with metabolic syndrome. *Experimental and Clinical Endocrinology and Diabetes, 124*(1), 11–15.

Ardeshirylajimi, A., & Soleimani, M. (2015). Enhanced growth and osteogenic differentiation of induced pluripotent stem cells by extremely low-frequency electromagnetic field. *Cellular and Molecular Biology, 61*(1), 36–41.

Azevedo, F. A., Carvalho, L. R., Grinberg, L. T., Farfel, J. M., Ferretti, R. E., Leite, R. E., . . . Herculano-Houzel, S. (2009). Equal numbers of neuronal and nonneuronal cells make the human brain an isometrically scaled-up primate brain. *Journal of Comparative Neurology, 513*(5), 532–541.

Becker, R. O. (1990). The machine brain and properties of the mind. *Subtle Energies and Energy Medicine Journal Archives, 1*(2).

Bengston, W. (2010). *The energy cure: Unraveling the mystery of hands-on healing.* Boulder, CO: Sounds True.

Bianconi, E., Piovesan, A., Facchin, F., Beraudi, A., Casadei, R., Frabetti, F., . . . Perez-Amodio, S. (2013). An estimation of the number of cells in the human body. *Annals of Human Biology, 40*(6), 463–471.

Boyd, W. (1966). *Spontaneous regression of cancer.* Springfield, Il: Thomas.

Boyers, L. M. (1953). Letter to the editor. *JAMA, 152,* 986–988.

Cantagrel, V., Lefeber, D. J., Ng, B. G., Guan, Z., Silhavy, J. L., Bielas, S. L., . . . De Brouwer, A. P. (2010). SRD5A3 is required for the conversion of polyprenol to dolichol, essential for N-linked protein glycosylation. *Cell, 142*(2), 203.

Church, D., Geronilla, L., & Dinter, I. (2009). Psychological symptom change in veterans after six sessions of Emotional Freedom Techniques (EFT): An observational study. *International Journal of Healing and Caring, 9*(1), 1–14.

Church, D., Hawk, C., Brooks, A., Toukolehto, O., Wren, M., Dinter, I., & Stein, P. (2013). Psychological trauma symptom improvement in veterans using Emotional Freedom Techniques: A randomized controlled trial. *Journal of Nervous and Mental Disease, 201*(2), 153–160. doi:10.1097/NMD.0b013e31827f6351.

Church, D., Yang, A., Fannin, J., & Blickheuser, K. (2016, October 14). *The biological dimensions of transcendent states: A randomized controlled trial.* Presented at Omega Institute for Holistic Studies, Rhinebeck, New York. Submitted for publication.

Church, D., Yount, G., Rachlin, K., Fox, L., & Nelms, J. (2016). Epigenetic effects of PTSD remediation in veterans using clinical Emotional Freedom Techniques: A randomized controlled pilot study. *American Journal of Health Promotion*, 1–11. doi:10.1177/0890117116661154.

Cosic, I., Cosic, D., & Lazar, K. (2015). Is it possible to predict electromagnetic resonances in proteins, DNA and RNA? *EPJ Nonlinear Biomedical Physics, 3*(1), 5.

De Girolamo, L., Stanco, D., Galliera, E., Viganò, M., Colombini, A., Setti, S., . . . Sansone, V. (2013). Low frequency pulsed electromagnetic field affects proliferation, tissue-specific gene expression, and cytokines release of human tendon cells. *Cell Biochemistry and Biophysics, 66*(3), 697.

Destexhe, A., McCormick, D. A., & Sejnowski, T. J. (1993). A model for 8–10 Hz spindling in interconnected thalamic relay and reticularis neurons. *Biophysical Journal, 65*(6), 2473–2477.

Deutsch, D., Leiser, Y., Shay, B., Fermon, E., Taylor, A., Rosenfeld, E., . . . Mao, Z. (2002). The human tuftelin gene and the expression of tuftelin in mineralizing and nonmineralizing tissues. *Connective Tissue Research, 43*(2–3), 425–434.

Foletti, A., Ledda, M., D'Emilia, E., Grimaldi, S., & Lisi, A. (2011). Differentiation of human LAN-5 neuroblastoma cells induced by extremely low frequency electronically transmitted retinoic acid. *Journal of Alternative and Complementary Medicine, 17*(8), 701–704. doi:10.1089/acm.2010.0439.

Frenkel, M., Ari, S. L., Engebretson, J., Peterson, N., Maimon, Y., Cohen, L., & Kacen, L. (2011). Activism among exceptional patients with cancer. *Supportive Care in Cancer, 19*(8), 1125–1132.

Fumoto, M., Sato-Suzuki, I., Seki, Y., Mohri, Y., & Arita, H. (2004). Appearance of high-frequency alpha band with disappearance of low-frequency alpha band in EEG is produced during voluntary abdominal breathing in an eyes-closed condition. *Neuroscience Research, 50*(3), 307–317.

Fumoto, M., Oshima, T., Kamiya, K., Kikuchi, H., Seki, Y., Nakatani, Y., . . . Arita, H. (2010). Ventral prefrontal cortex and serotonergic system activation during pedaling exercise induces negative mood improvement and increased alpha band in EEG. *Behavioural Brain Research, 213*(1), 1–9.

Geesink, H. J., & Meijer, D. K. (2016). Quantum wave information of life revealed: An algorithm for electromagnetic frequencies that create stability of biological order, with implications for brain function and consciousness. *NeuroQuantology, 14*(1).

Geronilla, L., Minewiser, L., Mollon, P., McWilliams, M., & Clond, M. (2016). EFT (Emotional Freedom Techniques) remediates PTSD and psychological symptoms in veterans: A randomized controlled replication trial. *Energy Psychology: Theory, Research, and Treatment, 8*(2), 29–41. doi:10.9769/EPJ.2016.8.2.LG.

Gray, C. M. (1997). Synchronous oscillations in neuronal systems: Mechanisms and functions. *Pattern Formation in the Physical and Biological Sciences, 5,* 93.

Groesbeck, G., Bach, D., Stapleton, P., Banton, S., Blickheuser, K., & Church, D. (2016, October 15). *The interrelated physiological and psychological effects of EcoMeditation: A pilot study.* Presented at Omega Institute for Holistic Studies, Rhinebeck, New York.

Gronfier, C., Luthringer, R., Follenius, M., Schaltenbrand, N., Macher, J. P., Muzet, A., & Brandenberger, G. (1996). A quantitative evaluation of the relationships between growth hormone secretion and delta wave electroencephalographic activity during normal sleep and after enrichment in delta waves. *Sleep, 19*(10), 817–824.

Hall-Glenn, F., & Lyons, K. M. (2011). Roles for CCN2 in normal physiological processes. *Cellular and Molecular Life Sciences, 68*(19), 3209–3217.

Hong, Y., Ho, K. S., Eu, K. W., & Cheah, P. Y. (2007). A susceptibility gene set for early onset colorectal cancer that integrates diverse signaling pathways: Implication for tumorigenesis. *Clinical Cancer Research, 13*(4), 1107–1114.

Iaccarino, H. F., Singer, A. C., Martorell, A. J., Rudenko, A., Gao, F., Gillingham, T. Z., . . . Adaikkan, C. (2016). Gamma frequency entrainment attenuates amyloid load and modifies microglia. *Nature, 540*(7632), 230–235.

Jacobs, T. L., Epel, E. S., Lin, J., Blackburn, E. H., Wolkowitz, O. M., Bridwell, D. A., . . . King, B. G. (2011). Intensive meditation training, immune cell telomerase activity, and psychological mediators. *Psychoneuroendocrinology, 36*(5), 664–681.

Kang, J. E., Lim, M. M., Bateman, R. J., Lee, J. J., Smyth, L. P., Cirrito, J. R., . . . Holtzman, D. M. (2009). Amyloid-β dynamics are regulated by orexin and the sleep-wake cycle. *Science, 326*(5955), 1005–1007.

Kelly, R. (2011). *The human hologram: Living your life in harmony with the unified field.* Santa Rosa, CA: Elite Books.

Kim, D. K., Rhee, J. H., & Kang, S. W. (2013). Reorganization of the brain and heart rhythm during autogenic meditation. *Frontiers in Integrative Neuroscience, 7,* 109. doi:10.3389/fnint.2013.00109.

Krikorian, J. G., Portlock, C. S., Cooney, D. P., & Rosenberg, S. A. (1980). Spontaneous regression of non-Hodgkin's lymphoma: A report of nine cases. *Cancer, 46*(9), 2093–2099.

Laflamme, M. A., & Murry, C. E. (2011). Heart regeneration. *Nature, 473*(7347), 326–335.

Lee, P. B., Kim, Y. C., Lim, Y. J., Lee, C. J., Choi, S. S., Park, S. H., . . . Lee, S. C. (2006). Efficacy of pulsed electromagnetic therapy for chronic lower back pain: A randomized, double-blind, placebo-controlled study. *Journal of International Medical Research, 34*(2), 160–167.

Lee, D. J., Schönleben, F., Banuchi, V. E., Qiu, W., Close, L. G., Assaad, A. M., & Su, G. H. (2010). Multiple tumor-suppressor genes on chromosome 3p contribute to head and neck squamous cell carcinoma tumorigenesis. *Cancer Biology and Therapy, 10*(7), 689–693.

Lim, L. (2014, July 21). The potential of treating Alzheimer's disease with intranasal light therapy. *Mediclights Research.* Retrieved from www.mediclights.com/the-potential-of-treating-alzheimers-disease-with-intranasal-light-therapy.

Lim, L. (2017). *Inventor's notes for Vielight "Neuro Alpha" and "Neuro Gamma."* Retrieved September 4, 2017, from http://vielight.com/wp-content/uploads/2017/02/Vielight-Inventors-Notes-for-Neuro-Alpha-and-Neuro-Gamma.pdf.

Lin, H., Goodman, R., & Shirley-Henderson, A. (1994). Specific region of the c-myc promoter is responsive to electric and magnetic fields. *Journal of Cellular Biochemistry, 54*(3), 281–288.

Lomas, T., Ivtzan, I., & Fu, C. H. (2015). A systematic review of the neurophysiology of mindfulness on EEG oscillations. *Neuroscience and Biobehavioral Reviews, 57,* 401–410. doi:10.1016/j.neubiorev.2015.09.018.

Maharaj, M. E. (2016). Differential gene expression after Emotional Freedom Techniques (EFT) treatment: A novel pilot protocol for salivary mRNA assessment. *Energy Psychology: Theory, Research, and Treatment, 8*(1), 17–32. doi:10.9769/EPJ.2016.8.1.MM.

Nadalin, S., Testa, G., Malagó, M., Beste, M., Frilling, A., Schroeder, T., . . . Broelsch, C. E. (2004). Volumetric and functional recovery of the liver after right hepatectomy for living donation. *Liver Transplantation, 10*(8), 1024–1029.

Omary, M. B., Ku, N. O., Strnad, P., & Hanada, S. (2009). Toward unraveling the complexity of simple epithelial keratins in human disease. *Journal of Clinical Investigation, 119*(7), 1794–1805. doi:10.1172/JCI37762.

O'Regan, B., & Hirshberg, C. (1993). *Spontaneous remission: An annotated bibliography.* Novato, CA: Institute of Noetic Sciences.

Park, E. J., Grabińska, K. A., Guan, Z., & Sessa, W. C. (2016). NgBR is essential for endothelial cell glycosylation and vascular development. *EMBO Reports, 17*(2), 167–177.

Razavi, S., Salimi, M., Shahbazi-Gahrouei, D., Karbasi, S., & Kermani, S. (2014). Extremely low-frequency electromagnetic field influences the survival and proliferation effect of human adipose derived stem cells. *Advanced Biomedical Research, 3,* 25–30.

Sakai, A., Suzuki, K., Nakamura, T., Norimura, T., & Tsuchiya, T. (1991). Effects of pulsing electromagnetic fields on cultured cartilage cells. *International Orthopaedics, 15*(4), 341–346.

Saltmarche, A. E., Naeser, M. A., Ho, K. F., Hamblin, M. R., & Lim, L. (2017). Significant improvement in cognition in mild to moderately severe dementia cases treated with transcranial plus intranasal photobiomodulation: Case series report. *Photomedicine and Laser Surgery, 35*(8): 432–441.

Salvatore, D., Tu, H., Harney, J. W., & Larsen, P. R. (1996). Type 2 iodothyronine deiodinase is highly expressed in human thyroid. *Journal of Clinical Investigation, 98*(4), 962.

Sastry, K. S., Karpova, Y., Prokopovich, S., Smith, A. J., Essau, B., Gersappe, A., . . . Penn, R. B. (2007). Epinephrine protects cancer cells from apoptosis via activation of cAMP-dependent protein kinase and BAD phosphorylation. *Journal of Biological Chemistry, 282*(19), 14094–14100.

Sisken, B. F., Midkiff, P., Tweheus, A., & Markov, M. (2007). Influence of static magnetic fields on nerve regeneration in vitro. *Environmentalist, 27*(4), 477–481.

Sood, A. K., Armaiz-Pena, G. N., Halder, J., Nick, A. M., Stone, R. L., Hu, W., . . . Han, L. Y. (2010). Adrenergic modulation of focal adhesion kinase protects human ovarian cancer cells from anoikis. *Journal of Clinical Investigation, 120*(5), 1515.

Sukel, K. (2011, March 15). The synapse—a primer. *Dana Foundation*. Retrieved from www.dana.org/News/Details.aspx?id=43512.

Takahashi, K., Kaneko, I., Date, M., & Fukada, E. (1986). Effect of pulsing electromagnetic fields on DNA synthesis in mammalian cells in culture. *Experientia, 42*(2), 185–186.

Tang, Y. P., Shimizu, E., Dube, G. R., Rampon, C., Kerchner, G. A., Zhuo, M., . . . Tsien, J. Z. (1999). Genetic enhancement of learning and memory in mice. *Nature, 401*(6748), 63–69.

Tekutskaya, E. E., & Barishev, M. G. (2013). Studying of influence of the low-frequency electromagnetic field on DNA molecules in water solutions. *Odessa Astronomical Publications, 26*(2), 303–304.

Tekutskaya, E. E., Barishev, M. G., & Ilchenko, G. P. (2015). The effect of a low-frequency electromagnetic field on DNA molecules in aqueous solutions. *Biophysics, 60*(6), 913.

Van Cauter, E., Leproult, R., & Plat, L. (2000). Age-related changes in slow wave sleep and REM sleep and relationship with growth hormone and cortisol levels in healthy men. *JAMA, 284*(7), 861–868.

Ventegodt, S., Morad, M., Hyam, E., & Merrick, J. (2004). Clinical holistic medicine: Induction of spontaneous remission of cancer by recovery of the human character and the purpose of life (the life mission). *Scientific World Journal, 4,* 362–377.

Wahlestedt, M., Erlandsson, E., Kristiansen, T., Lu, R., Brakebusch, C., Weissman, I. L., . . . Bryder, D. (2017). Clonal reversal of ageing-associated stem cell lineage bias via a pluripotent intermediate. *Nature Communications, 8,* 14533.

Walløe, S., Pakkenberg, B., & Fabricius, K. (2014). Stereological estimation of total cell numbers in the human cerebral and cerebellar cortex. *Frontiers in Human Neuroscience, 8.*

Wei, G., Luo, H., Sun, Y., Li, J., Tian, L., Liu, W., . . . Chen, R. (2015). Transcriptome profiling of esophageal squamous cell carcinoma reveals a long noncoding RNA acting as a tumor suppressor. *Oncotarget, 6*(19), 17065–17080.

Wu, M., Pastor-Pareja, J. C., & Xu, T. (2010). Interaction between RasV12 and scribbled clones induces tumour growth and invasion. *Nature, 463*(7280), 545–548.

Xiang, G., Yi, Y., Weiwei, H., & Weiming, W. (2016). RND1 is up-regulated in esophageal squamous cell carcinoma and promotes the growth and migration of cancer cells. *Tumor Biology, 37*(1), 773.

Ying, L., Hong, L., Zhicheng, G., Xiauwei, H. & Guoping, C. (2000). Effects of pulsed electric fields on DNA synthesis in an osteoblast-like cell line (UMR-106). *Tsinghua Science and Technology, 5*(4), 439–442.

Yong, E. (2016, Dec 7). Beating Alzheimer's with brain waves. *Atlantic.* Retrieved from www.theatlantic.com/science/archive/2016/12/beating-alzheimers-with -brain-waves/509846.

Yu, X., Fumoto, M., Nakatani, Y., Sekiyama, T., Kikuchi, H., Seki, Y., . . . Arita, H. (2011). Activation of the anterior prefrontal cortex and serotonergic system is associated with improvements in mood and EEG changes induced by Zen meditation practice in novices. *International Journal of Psychophysiology, 80*(2), 103–111.

Zahl, P. H., Mæhlen, J., & Welch, H. G. (2008). The natural history of invasive breast cancers detected by screening mammography. *Archives of Internal Medicine, 168*(21), 2311–2316.

CHAPTER 5

Bach, D., Groesbeck, G., Stapleton, P., Banton, S., Blickheuser, K., & Church, D. (2016, October 15). *Clinical EFT (Emotional Freedom Techniques) improves multiple physiological markers of health.* Presented at Omega Institute for Holistic Studies, Rhinebeck, New York.

Baker, M. (2016). 1,500 scientists lift the lid on reproducibility. *Nature, 533*(7604), 452–454.

Begley, C. G., & Ellis, L. M. (2012). Drug development: Raise standards for preclinical cancer research. *Nature, 483*(7391), 531–533.

Bem, D. J. (2011). Feeling the future: Experimental evidence for anomalous retroactive influences on cognition and affect. *Journal of Personality and Social Psychology, 100*(3), 407.

Bem, D., Tressoldi, P., Rabeyron, T., & Duggan, M. (2015). Feeling the future: A meta-analysis of 90 experiments on the anomalous anticipation of random future events. *F1000Research, 4,* 1188.

Bem, D. J., Utts, J., & Johnson, W. O. (2011). Must psychologists change the way they analyze their data? *Journal of Personality and Social Psychology, 101*(4), 716–719.

Bengston, W. (2010). *The energy cure: Unraveling the mystery of hands-on healing.* Boulder, CO: Sounds True.

Blake, W. (1968). *The portable Blake.* New York: Viking.

Born, M., (Ed.). (1971). *The Born–Einstein letters: Correspondence between Albert Einstein and Max and Hedwig Born from 1916–1955* (I. Born, Trans.). New York: Macmillan.

Chambless, D., & Hollon, S. D. (1998). Defining empirically supported therapies. *Journal of Consulting and Clinical Psychology, 66,* 7–18.

Church, D. (2013). Clinical EFT (Emotional Freedom Techniques) as single session therapy: Cases, research, indications, and cautions. In M. Hoyt & M. Talmon (Eds.), *Capture the moment: Single session therapy and walk-in service.* Bethel, CT: Crown House.

Church, D., & Brooks, A. J. (2010). The effect of a brief EFT (Emotional Freedom Techniques) self-intervention on anxiety, depression, pain and cravings in health-care workers. *Integrative Medicine: A Clinician's Journal, 9*(5), 40–44.

Church, D., Yount, G., & Brooks, A. J. (2012). The effect of Emotional Freedom Techniques on stress biochemistry: A randomized controlled trial. *Journal of Nervous and Mental Disease, 200*(10), 891–896. doi:10.1097/NMD.0b013e31826b9fc1.

Cooper, H., DeNeve, K., & Charlton, K. (1997). Finding the missing science: The fate of studies submitted for review by a human subjects committee. *Psychological Methods, 2*(4), 447.

Davidson, R. J. (2003). Affective neuroscience and psychophysiology: Toward a synthesis. *Psychophysiology, 40*(5), 655–665.

Diener, E., & Chan, M. Y. (2011). Happy people live longer: Subjective well-being contributes to health and longevity. *Applied Psychology: Health and Well-Being, 3*(1), 1–43.

eLife. (2017). Reproducibility in cancer biology: The challenges of replication. *eLife, 6,* e23693. doi: 10.7554/eLife.23693.

Feynman, R. P., Leighton, R. B., & Sands, M. (1965). The Feynman lectures on physics (Vol. 1). *American Journal of Physics, 33*(9), 750–752.

Fickler, R., Krenn, M., Lapkiewicz, R., Ramelow, S., & Zeilinger, A. (2013). Real-time imaging of quantum entanglement. *Nature–Scientific Reports,* 3, 2914.

Gane, S., Georganakis, D., Maniati, K., Vamvakias, M., Ragoussis, N., Skoulakis, E. M., & Turin, L. (2013). Molecular vibration-sensing component in human olfaction. *PLoS one, 8*(1), e55780.

Giltay, E. J., Geleijnse, J. M., Zitman, F. G., Hoekstra, T., & Schouten, E. G. (2004). Dispositional optimism and all-cause and cardiovascular mortality in a prospective cohort of elderly Dutch men and women. *Archives of General Psychiatry, 61*(11), 1126–1135.

Goswami, A. (2004). *Quantum doctor: A physicist's guide to health and healing.* Hampton Roads, VA: Hampton Roads Publishing.

Grinberg-Zylberbaum, J., Delaflor, M., Attie, L., & Goswami, A. (1994). The Einstein-Podolsky-Rosen paradox in the brain: The transferred potential. *Physics Essays, 7,* 422.

Hammerschlag, R., Marx, B. L., & Aickin, M. (2014). Nontouch biofield therapy: A systematic review of human randomized controlled trials reporting use of only nonphysical contact treatment. *The Journal of Alternative and Complementary Medicine, 20*(12), 881–892.

Hanson, R. (2013). *Hardwiring happiness: The practical science of reshaping your brain—and your life.* New York: Random House.

Heisenberg, W. (1962). *Physics and philosophy: the revolution in modern science.* New York: Harper & Row.

Hensen, B., Bernien, H., Dréau, A. E., Reiserer, A., Kalb, N., Blok, M. S., . . . Amaya, W. (2015). Loophole-free Bell inequality violation using electron spins separated by 1.3 kilometres. *Nature, 526*(7575), 682–686.

Hoss, R. (2016, June 12). *Consciousness after the body dies.* Presentation at the International Association for the Study of Dreams, Kerkrade, Netherlands.

Ironson, G., Stuetzle, R., Ironson, D., Balbin, E., Kremer, H., George, A., . . . Fletcher, M. A. (2011). View of God as benevolent and forgiving or punishing and judgmental predicts HIV disease progression. *Journal of Behavioral Medicine, 34*(6), 414–425.

Joergensen, A., Broedbaek, K., Weimann, A., Semba, R. D., Ferrucci, L., Joergensen, M. B., & Poulsen, H. E. (2011). Association between urinary excretion of cortisol and markers of oxidatively damaged DNA and RNA in humans. *PLoS ONE, 6*(6), e20795. doi:10.1371/journal.pone.0020795

Jung, C. G. (1952). The structure of the psyche. In *Collected works, vol. 8: The structure and dynamics of the psyche.* London: Routledge & Kegan Paul.

Kaiser, J. (2017, January 18). Rigorous replication effort succeeds for just two of five cancer papers. *Science.* Retrieved from www.sciencemag.org/news/2017/01/rigorous-replication-effort-succeeds-just-two-five-cancer-papers.

Kamp, J. (2016). It is so not simple: Russian physicist Yury Kronn and the subtle energy that fills 96 percent of our existence but cannot be seen or measured. *Optimist,* Spring, 40–47.

Klinger, E. (1996). The contents of thoughts: Interference as the downside of adaptive normal mechanisms in thought flow. In I. G. Sarason, G. R. Pierce, & B. R. Sarason (Eds.), *Cognitive interference: Theories, methods, and findings* (pp. 3–23). Hillsdale, NJ: Lawrence Erlbaum.

Kronn, Y., & Jones, J. (2011). Experiments on the effects of subtle energy on the electro-magnetic field: Is subtle energy the 5th force of the universe? *Energy Tools International.* Retrieved July 5, 2017, from www.saveyourbrain.net/pdf/testreport .pdf.

LeDoux, J. (2003). The emotional brain, fear, and the amygdala. *Cellular and Molecular Neurobiology, 23*(4), 727–738.

Lee, K. C., Sprague, M. R., Sussman, B. J., Nunn, J., Langford, N. K., Jin, X. M., . . . Jaksch, D. (2011). Entangling macroscopic diamonds at room temperature. *Science, 334*(6060), 1253–1256.

Leskowitz, R. (2014). The 2013 World Series: A Trojan horse for consciousness studies. *Explore: The Journal of Science and Healing, 10*(2), 125–127.

Lewis, C. S. (1970). *God in the dock: Essays on theology and ethics.* London: Eerdmans.

McCraty, R., Atkinson, M., & Tomasino, D. (2003). *Modulation of DNA conformation by heart-focused intention.* Boulder Creek, CA: HeartMath Research Center, Institute of HeartMath, Publication No. 03-008.

McCraty R. & Childre, D. (2010). Coherence: Bridging personal, social, and global health. *Alternative Therapies in Health and Medicine, 16*(4), 10.

McCraty, R., & Deyhle, A. (2016). *The science of interconnectivity.* Boulder Creek, CA: HeartMath Institute.

McMillan, P. J., Wilkinson, C. W., Greenup, L., Raskind, M. A., Peskind, E. R., & Leverenz, J. B. (2004). Chronic cortisol exposure promotes the development of a GABAergic phenotype in the primate hippocampus. *Journal of Neurochemistry, 91*(4), 843–851.

McTaggart, L. (2007). *The intention experiment: Using your thoughts to change your life and the world.* New York: Free Press.

Moga, M. M., & Bengston, W. F. (2010). Anomalous magnetic field activity during a bioenergy healing experiment. *Journal of Scientific Exploration, 24*(3), 397–410.

Moreva, E., Brida, G., Gramegna, M., Giovannetti, V., Maccone, L., & Genovese, M. (2014). Time from quantum entanglement: An experimental illustration. *Physical Review A, 89*(5), 052122–052128.

Nakamura, T. (2013, November 14). One man's quest to prove how far laser pointers reach. Retrieved from http://kotaku.com/one-mans-quest-to-prove-how -far-laser-pointers-reach-1464275649.

Nelson, R. (2015). Meaningful correlations in random data. *The Global Consciousness Project.* Retrieved August 20, 2017, from http://noosphere.princeton.edu/ results.html#alldata.

Nesse, R. M., Curtis, G. C., Thyer, B. A., McCann, D. S., Huber-Smith, M. J., & Knopf, R. F. (1985). Endocrine and cardiovascular responses during phobic anxiety. *Psychosomatic Medicine, 47*(4), 320–332.

Open Science Collaboration. (2015). Estimating the reproducibility of psychological science. *Science, 349*(6251), aac4716.

Powell, C. S. (2017, June 16). Is the universe conscious? Some of the world's most renowned scientists are questioning whether the cosmos has an inner life similar to our own. National Broadcasting Company (NBC). Retrieved from www.nbcnews.com/mach/science/universe-conscious-ncna772956.

Radin, D. I. (2011). Predicting the unpredictable: 75 years of experimental evidence. *AIP Conference Proceedings, 1408*(1), 204–217.

Radin, D., Michel, L., & Delorme, A. (2016). Psychophysical modulation of fringe visibility in a distant double-slit optical system. *Physics Essays, 29*(1), 14–22.

Ritchie, S. J., Wiseman, R., & French, C. C. (2012). Failing the future: Three unsuccessful attempts to replicate Bem's 'Retroactive Facilitation of Recall' Effect. *PLoS ONE, 7*(3), e33423.

Romero, E., Augulis, R., Novoderezhkin, V. I., Ferretti, M., Thieme, J., Zigmantas, D., & Van Grondelle, R. (2014). Quantum coherence in photosynthesis for efficient solar-energy conversion. *Nature Physics, 10*(9), 676–682.

Rosenthal, R., & Fode, K. (1963). The effect of experimenter bias on performance of the albino rat. *Behavioral Science, 8,* 183–189.

Rosenthal, R., &. Jacobson, L. (1963). Teachers' expectancies: Determinants of pupils' IQ gains. *Psychological Reports, 19,* 115–118.

Russ, T. C., Stamatakis, E., Hamer, M., Starr, J. M., Kivimäki, M., & Batty, G. D. (2012). Association between psychological distress and mortality: Individual participant pooled analysis of 10 prospective cohort studies. *British Medical Journal, 345,* e4933.

Sapolsky, R. M., Uno, H., Rebert, C. S., & Finch, C. E. (1990). Hippocampal damage associated with prolonged glucocorticoid exposure in primates. *Journal of Neuroscience, 10*(9), 2897–2902.

Sheldrake, R. (1999). How widely is blind assessment used in scientific research? *Alternative Therapies in Health and Medicine, 5*(3), 88.

Sheldrake, R. (2012). *Science set free: 10 paths to new discovery.* New York: Deepak Chopra Books.

Shelus, P. J., Veillet, C., Whipple, A. L., Wiant, J. R., Williams, J. G., & Yoder, C. F. (1994). Lunar laser ranging: A continuing legacy of the Apollo program. *Science, 265,* 482.

Standish, L. J., Kozak, L., Johnson, L. C., & Richards, T. (2004). Electroencephalographic evidence of correlated event-related signals between the brains of spatially and sensory isolated human subjects. *Journal of Alternative and Complementary Medicine, 10*(2), 307–314.

Tchijevsky, A. L. (1971). Physical factors of the historical process. *Cycles, 22,* 11–27.

Thiagarajan, T. C., Lebedev, M. A., Nicolelis, M. A., & Plenz, D. (2010). Coherence potentials: Loss-less, all-or-none network events in the cortex. *PLoS Biology, 8*(1), e1000278.

Tiller, W. A. (1997). *Science and human transformation: Subtle energies, intentionality and consciousness.* Walnut Creek, CA: Pavior Publishing.

Wagenmakers, E. J., Wetzels, R., Borsboom, D., & Van Der Maas, H. L. (2011). Why psychologists must change the way they analyze their data: The case of psi: Comment on Bem (2011). *Journal of Personality and Social Psychology, 100*(3), 426–432.

Ward, M. M., Mefford, I. N., Parker, S. D., Chesney, M. A., Taylor, B. C., Keegan, D. L., & Barchas, J. D. (1983). Epinephrine and norepinephrine responses in continuously collected human plasma to a series of stressors. *Psychosomatic Medicine, 45*(6), 471–486.

Watt, C., & Nagtegaal, M. (2004). Reporting of blind methods: An interdisciplinary survey. *Journal of the Society for Psychical Research, 68,* 105–116.

Wolf, F. A. (2001). *Mind into matter: A new alchemy of science and spirit.* Newburyport, MA: Red Wheel/Weiser.

Yan, X., Lu, F., Jiang, H., Wu, X., Cao, W., Xia, Z., . . . Zhu, R. (2002). Certain physical manifestation and effects of external qi of Yan Xin life science technology. *Journal of Scientific Exploration, 16*(3), 381–411.

Yan, X., Shen, H., Jiang, H., Zhang, C., Hu, D., Wang, J., & Wu, X. (2006). External Qi of Yan Xin Qigong differentially regulates the Akt and extracellular signal-regulated kinase pathways and is cytotoxic to cancer cells but not to normal cells. *International Journal of Biochemistry and Cell Biology, 38*(12), 2102–2113.

CHAPTER 6

Anderson, B. J., Engebretson, M. J., Rounds, S. P., Zanetti, L. J., & Potemra, T. A. (1990). A statistical study of Pc 3–5 pulsations observed by the AMPTE/CCE Magnetic Fields Experiment. *Journal of Geophysical Research: Space Physics, 95*(A7), 10495–10523.

Beauregard, M. (2012). *Brain wars: The scientific battle over the existence of the mind and the proof that will change the way we live our lives.* San Francisco: HarperOne.

Bem, D. J. (2011). Feeling the future: Experimental evidence for anomalous retroactive influences on cognition and affect. *Journal of Personality and Social Psychology, 100*(3), 407.

Bem, D., Tressoldi, P., Rabeyron, T., & Duggan, M. (2015). Feeling the future: A meta-analysis of 90 experiments on the anomalous anticipation of random future events. *F1000Research, 4,* 1188.

Bengston, W. (2010). *The energy cure: Unraveling the mystery of hands-on healing.* Boulder, CO: Sounds True.

Braden, G. (2008). *The spontaneous healing of belief: Shattering the paradigm of false limits.* Carlsbad, CA: Hay House.

Brown, E. N., & Czeisler, C. A. (1992). The statistical analysis of circadian phase and amplitude in constant-routine core-temperature data. *Journal of Biological Rhythms, 7*(3), 177–202.

Burch, W. (2003). *She who dreams: A journey into healing through dreamwork.* San Rafael, CA: New World Library.

Burk, L. (2015, October 13). Dreams that warn of breast cancer. *Huffington Post blog.* Retrieved from www.huffingtonpost.com/larry-burk-md/dreams-that-warn-of-breas_b_8167758.html.

Calaprice, A. (Ed.). (2002*). Dear Professor Einstein: Albert Einstein's letters to and from children.* Amherst, NY: Prometheus.

Calaprice, A. (Ed.). (2011). *The ultimate quotable Einstein.* Princeton, NJ: Princeton University Press.

Cambray, J. (2002). Synchronicity and emergence. *American Imago, 59*(4), 409–434.

Cambray, J. (2009). *Synchronicity: Nature and psyche in an interconnected universe* (Vol. 15). College Station: Texas A&M University Press.

Cauchon, D. (2001, December 20). For many on Sept. 11, survival was no accident. *USA Today.* Retrieved from http://usatoday30.usatoday.com/news/sept11/2001/12/19/usatcov-wtcsurvival.htm.

Church, D. (2013). *The genie in your genes: Epigenetic medicine and the new biology of intention.* Santa Rosa, CA: Energy Psychology Press.

Clark, N. (2012). *Divine moments.* Fairfield, IA: First World Publishing.

Corning, P. A. (2002). The re-emergence of "emergence": A venerable concept in search of a theory. *Complexity, 7*(6), 18–30. doi:10.1002/cplx.10043.

Crick, F., & Clark, J. (1994). The astonishing hypothesis. *Journal of Consciousness Studies, 1*(1), 10–16.

Dossey, L. (2009). *The science of premonitions: How knowing the future can help us avoid danger, maximize opportunities, and create a better life.* New York: Plume.

Dossey, L. (2013). *One mind: How our individual mind is part of a greater consciousness and why it matters.* Carlsbad, CA: Hay House.

Dowling, S. (2017, May 26). The audacious pilot who landed in Red Square. *BBC Future.* Retrieved from www.bbc.com/future/story/20170526-the-audacious-pilot-who-landed-in-red-square.

Eliade, M. (1964). *Shamanism: Archaic techniques of ecstasy.* London: Routledge & Kegan Paul.

Facco, E., & Agrillo, C. (2012). Near-death experiences between science and prejudice. *Frontiers in Human Neuroscience, 6,* 209.

Ferriss, T. (2017). *Tribe of mentors: Short life advice from the best in the world.* New York: Houghton Mifflin Harcourt.

Geesink, H. J., & Meijer, D. K. (2016). Quantum wave information of life revealed: An algorithm for electromagnetic frequencies that create stability of biological order, with implications for brain function and consciousness. *NeuroQuantology, 14*(1).

Goethe, J. W. (1887). *The first part of Goethe's Faust* (J. Anster, Trans.). London: George Routledge & Sons.

Gramling, R., Klein, W., Roberts, M., Waring, M. E., Gramling, D., & Eaton, C. B. (2008). Self-rated cardiovascular risk and 15-year cardiovascular mortality. *Annals of Family Medicine, 6*(4), 302–306.

Greyson, B. (2003). Incidence and correlates of near-death experiences in a cardiac care unit. *General Hospital Psychiatry, 25*(4), 269–276.

Halberg, F., Cornélissen, G., McCraty, R., Czaplicki, J., & Al-Abdulgader, A. A. (2011). Time structures (chronomes) of the blood circulation, populations' health, human affairs and space weather. *World Heart Journal, 3*(1), 73.

Halberg, F., Tong, Y. L., & Johnson, E. A. (1967). Circadian system phase—an aspect of temporal morphology; procedures and illustrative examples. In H. von Mayersbach (Ed.), *The cellular aspects of biorhythms* (pp. 20–48). New York: Springer-Verlag.

HeartMath Institute. (n.d.). Global coherence research: The science of interconnectivity. Retrieved August 6, 2017, from www.heartmath.org/research/global -coherence.

Ho, M. W. (2008). *The rainbow and the worm: The physics of organisms.* London: World Scientific.

Hogenson, G. B. (2004). Archetypes: Emergence and the psyche's deep structure. In J. Cambray & L. Carter (Eds.), *Analytical psychology: Contemporary perspectives in Jungian analysis.* London: Routledge.

Hoss, R. J., & Gongloff, R. P. (2017). *Dreams that change our lives.* Asheville, NC: Chiron.

Ironson, G., Stuetzle, R., Ironson, D., Balbin, E., Kremer, H., George, A., . . . Fletcher, M. A. (2011). View of God as benevolent and forgiving or punishing and judgmental predicts HIV disease progression. *Journal of Behavioral Medicine, 34*(6), 414–425.

Jacobs, J. A., Kato, Y., Matsushita, S., & Troitskaya, V. A. (1964). Classification of geomagnetic micropulsations. *Journal of Geophysical Research, 69*(1), 180–181.

Johnson, S. (2002). *Emergence: The connected lives of ants, brains, cities, and software.* New York: Simon & Schuster.

Jung, C. G. (1952). Synchronicity: An acausal connecting principle. In *Collected works, vol. 8: The structure and dynamics of the psyche*. London: Routledge & Kegan Paul.

Jung, C. G. (1975). *Letters, vol. 2: 1951–1961*. G. Adler & A. Jaffé (Eds.). Princeton, NJ: Princeton University Press.

Kaufman, S. A. (1993). *The origins of order: Self-organization and selection in evolution*. Oxford: Oxford University Press.

Kelly, R. (2011). *The human hologram: Living your life in harmony with the unified field*. Santa Rosa, CA: Elite Books.

McClenon, J. (1993). Surveys of anomalous experience in Chinese, Japanese, and American samples. *Sociology of Religion, 54*(3), 295–302.

McCraty, R. (2015). Could the energy of our hearts change the world? *GOOP*. Retrieved from http://goop.com/could-the-energy-of-our-hearts-change-the-world.

McCraty, R. & Deyle, (2016). *The science of interconnectivity*. Boulder Creek, CA: HeartMath Institute.

Nova. (2007, July 10). Emergence. *NOVA*. Retrieved from www.pbs.org/wgbh/nova/nature/emergence.html.

Oschman, J. L. (1997). What is healing energy? Part 3: Silent pulses. *Journal of Bodywork and Movement Therapies, 1*(3), 179–189.

Oschman, J. L. (2015). *Energy medicine: The scientific basis*. London: Elsevier Health Sciences.

Park, S. Q., Kahnt, T., Dogan, A., Strang, S., Fehr, E., & Tobler, P. N. (2017). A neural link between generosity and happiness. *Nature Communications, 8*.

Popper, K. R., & Eccles, J. C. (2012). *The self and its brain*. New York: Springer Science & Business Media.

Ring, K., & Cooper, S. (2008). *Mindsight: Near-death and out-of-body experiences in the blind* (2nd ed.). iUniverse.

Radin, D. I. (2011). Predicting the unpredictable: 75 years of experimental evidence. In *AIP Conference Proceedings 1408*(1), 204–217.

Rockwood, K. (2017). *Think positive, get lucky*. In Gibbs, N. (Ed.), *The science of emotions* (pp. 62–65). New York: Time.

Selmaoui, B., & Touitou, Y. (2003). Reproducibility of the circadian rhythms of serum cortisol and melatonin in healthy subjects: A study of three different 24-h cycles over six weeks. *Life Sciences, 73*(26), 3339–3349.

Shermer, M. (2014, October 1). Anomalous events that can shake one's skepticism to the core. *Scientific American*. Retrieved from www.scientificamerican.com/article/anomalous-events-that-can-shake-one-s-skepticism-to-the-core.

Strogatz, S. H. (2012). *Sync: How order emerges from chaos in the universe, nature, and daily life*. London: Hachette.

Tonneau, F. (2004). Consciousness outside the head. *Behavior and Philosophy, 32*(1), 97–123.

INDEX

ACKNOWLEDGMENTS

It takes a village to create a book of this magnitude, and I am deeply grateful to all the people who have played a part in making it possible.

Sir Isaac Newton said that we stand on the shoulders of giants. No scientist creates alone. We build on the discoveries of others. I am so grateful to the hundreds of visionary researchers whose work is cited in these pages, and upon whose foundations I have built. Wherever I looked for evidence, I usually found it, and the breadth of mind and imagination I discovered in the work of my colleagues often humbled and astounded me.

Everyone in the healing field, especially me, owes a debt of gratitude to clinical psychologist David Feinstein. His intellectual rigor, brilliant academic writing skills, and ethical awareness have shaped the work of an entire generation of energy healing professionals. He provided detailed feedback on the first few chapters and helped shape this book.

Many other professionals read sections dealing with their areas of expertise and corrected errors and misunderstandings. EEG expert Gary Groesbeck gave me detailed feedback on the brain wave chapters, while his colleague Judith Pennington provided clear explanations of the Awakened Mind and Evolved Mind patterns. Psychiatrist Ron Ruden alerted me to the importance of delta brain waves and the many ways we can increase them.

Rollin McCraty of the Institute of HeartMath gave me clear and explicit explanations of Schumann resonances and field line resonances, as well as conducting primary research on the topic. Dean Radin of the Institute for Noetic Sciences helped me understand the statistical basis of the research on premonition and maintains the most current website listing scientific publications of extraordinary human experiences. His remarkable experiments have provided a sound scientific basis for this work.

My close friend Bob Hoss is a brilliant polymath whose mind knows no boundaries. He's an expert on the neuroscience of dreaming and how the brain uses symbolism to solve problems. He provided the pillars for the passages on Carl Jung, the collective unconscious, the emotional brain, and quantum phenomena.

I'm grateful to Lissa Rankin for fascinating conversations that led to clearer insights into how mind becomes matter. Also to Bill Bengston for his provocative work on using energy to heal cancer and for helping me understand both the animal and human dimensions of this research.

I'm grateful to all the institutes and conferences that sponsor my live workshops, like Esalen, Kripalu, Omega, and the New York Open Center. At these modern gathering places of mind and spirit, I meet a variety of fascinating teachers whose insights enrich my understanding.

I'm privileged to interact with many other like-minded people who are members of the Transformational Leadership Council. Thank you, Jack Canfield, for founding and fostering this remarkable group of visionaries. Many of those who endorsed this book are fellow members.

I'm also grateful to the skeptics. There are many professional naysayers who claim that humans are beings of matter rather than energy. Their attacks on the field of energy healing, especially in the entries in Wikipedia that they control, and their denial of the science described in this book serve a useful purpose. Many of these experiments have been designed to rebut their arguments. The relentless barrage of skeptical criticism is indirectly responsible for the thousands of studies of energy healing published in peer-reviewed journals.

I'm especially grateful to my friend and Hay House president Reid Tracy. This book was born in a conversation with him, and he suggested the title. His entire team at Hay House, including publisher Patty Gift, editor Anne Barthel, and marketing director Richelle Fredson, has been a joy to work with, on both a personal and a professional level.

I've had an amazing professional relationship with my friend and editor Stephanie Marohn for over a decade, and I'm so thankful for her keen eye and warm encouragement. Karin Kinsey's expert eye is responsible for the illustrations and typesetting, and she's given me enthusiastic support all along. I'm also grateful for the inspired editorial guidance of Hay House editor Anne Barthel and the eagle eye of copyeditor Rachel Shields.

I cannot even begin to express how much the genius of Heather Montgomery, General Manager of my organization Energy Psychology Group, makes in my life. Heather manages a complex organization with wisdom and humor. Her hand-picked team, including Seth Buffum, Marion Allen, Kendra Heath, Jackie Viramontez, and Mack Diesel, maintain high professional standards and make work fun even under pressure. There are many more laughs in the office than tears!

I'm also grateful for the board members and volunteers of the National Institute for Integrative Healthcare, the nonprofit I founded. We've now conducted or helped catalyze over 100 scientific studies and treated more than 20,000 veterans with PTSD. Giving back is a cornerstone of my life and I'm inspired by the hundreds of NIIH volunteers who do the same.

Many of my fellow transformational entrepreneurs supported the launch of this book, and I'm grateful to Nick Ortner, Mastin Kipp, Lissa Rankin, Joe Dispenza, Natalie Ledwell, Joe Mercola, Dave Asprey, and many others who shared it with their communities.

During the wildfire that consumed my home and office in October 2017, a committed group of people came together to help us recover. I traveled for most of the month while my wife, Christine, navigated our family's next steps at home. Her daughters, Julia and Jessie, as well as my children, Rexana and Lionel, together with Julia's husband, Tyler, formed an impromptu committee to take care of hundreds of details, from finding us emergency shelter to making lists of destroyed items. This huge disruption could have derailed the book, but thanks to their efforts it did not.

I'm blessed with a large extended family. Tens of thousands of people visit my EFT Universe website each month, and thousands train with us every year. The depth of emotional intimacy and heart sharing we experience both in person and in our social networking sites makes it impossible to ever feel alone. We know we're part of a huge global movement.

My wife, Christine, makes magic with her beautiful energy. Just being near her feels like being enfolded in a warm, soft blanket of love. She provides me with an energy environment that is filled with goodwill and happiness. It was Christine who encouraged me to work with Reid Tracy and Hay House and who every day creates the beautiful home environment and energy ecology in which this book was written.

ABOUT THE AUTHOR

Dawson Church is an award-winning author whose best-selling book *The Genie in Your Genes* (www.YourGeniusGene.com) has been hailed by reviewers as a breakthrough in our understanding of the link between emotions and genetics. He founded the National Institute for Integrative Healthcare (www.NIIH.org) to study and implement promising evidence-based psychological and medical techniques. In his undergraduate and graduate work at Baylor University, he became the first student to successfully graduate from the academically rigorous University Scholars program in 1979. He earned a doctorate at Holos University under the mentorship of neurosurgeon Norman Shealy, M.D., Ph.D., founder of the American Holistic Medical Association. After an early career in book publishing as editor and then president of Aslan Publishing (www.aslanpublishing.com), Church went on to receive a postgraduate Ph.D. in Natural Medicine as well as clinical certification in Energy Psychology (CEHP certification# 2016). Church's groundbreaking research has been published in prestigious scientific journals. He is the editor of *Energy Psychology: Theory, Research & Treatment,* a peer-reviewed professional journal (www.EnergyPsychologyJournal.org), and a blogger for the Huffington Post. He shares how to apply the breakthroughs of energy psychology to health and athletic performance through EFT Universe (www.EFTUniverse.com). EFT Universe was the first organization to have its courses accredited for CME (continuing medical education) for all of the major professions, including doctors (AMA), psychologists (APA), and nurses (ANCC). He has trained thousands of practitioners in energy psychology techniques and offers the premier certification program in the field (EnergyPsychologyCertification.com).

IMAGE CREDITS

CHAPTER 1

Page 4. Shoobydooby/CC-by-2.0

Page 5. Mountain Home Air Force Base

Page 11. Michael Beer / Dreamstime.com

Page 12. Courtesy of HeartMath® Institute

Page 25. Wellcome Images/CC-by-4.0, images@wellcome.ac.uk

Page 27. Library of Congress Prints and Photographs Division Washington, D.C; LC-DIG-ppmsca-12512/Benjamin M. Dale, 1951

CHAPTER 2

Page 37. top. Rama// Cc-by-sa-2.0-fr

Page 40. Richard Wheeler/CC-By-SA-3.0

Page 43. Thermal Vision Research / Wellcome Images / CC by 4.0, images@wellcome.ac.uk

Page 48. Steven Duong / Flickr /

Page 53 & 54. Courtesy of Prof. Dr. Bernd Helmut Kröplin, www.worldinadrop.com

Page 55. © Office Masaru Emoto, LLC.

Page 58. South Tyrol Museum of Archaeology

Page 49. bottom. iStock.com/olyniteowl

CHAPTER 3

Page 69. Douglas Myers/CC-By-SA-3.0

Page 105. Bundesarchiv, Bild 102-04062A/CC-By-SA-3.0

CHAPTER 4

Page 125. US Department of Energy Human Genome Program

Page 133. © 2011 Michael Bonert / /CC SA 3.0 U

CHAPTER 5

Page 167. © NASA

Page 178 & 179. Courtesy of HeartMath® Institute

Page 185. Jordgette / CC BY-SA 3.0

Page 187. Mark Garlick/Science Photo Library / Alamy Stock Photo

Page 188. McMillan / Nature / Fickler et al., 2013 / CC 3.0 U

Page 192. Eric Fisk / CC-By-SA- 3.0 U

CHAPTER 6

Page 224. Naturefriends/CC-By-SA-4.0

Page 229. © NASA

Page 231. iStock.com/Agsandrew

Page 236. RonnyNB / CC-By-SA-3.0 U

Page 246. iStock.com/MariaArefyeva

Page 255. iStock.com/Agsandrew

Page 247. iStock.com/ValeryBrozhinsky

Page 259. Getty Images

Page 266. iStock.com/Niyazz

Hay House Titles of Related Interest

YOU CAN HEAL YOUR LIFE, the movie, starring Louise Hay & Friends
(available as a 1-DVD program, an expanded 2-DVD set,
and an online streaming video)
Learn more at www.hayhouse.com/louise-movie

THE SHIFT, the movie, starring Dr. Wayne W. Dyer
(available as a 1-DVD program, an expanded 2-DVD set,
and an online streaming video)
Learn more at www.hayhouse.com/the-shift-movie

———

*BECOMING SUPERNATURAL: How Common People
Are Doing the Uncommon,* by Dr. Joe Dispenza

*THE BIOLOGY OF BELIEF 10th ANNIVERSARY EDITION:
Unleashing the Power of Consciousness, Matter & Miracles,*
by Bruce Lipton, Ph.D.

*MIND OVER MEDICINE: Scientific Proof That
You Can Heal Yourself,* by Lissa Rankin, M.D.

*RESILIENCE FROM THE HEART: The Power to Thrive
in Life's Extremes,* by Gregg Braden

All of the above are available at your local bookstore,
or may be ordered by contacting Hay House (see next page).

We hope you enjoyed this Hay House book. If you'd like to receive our online catalog featuring additional information on Hay House books and products, or if you'd like to find out more about the Hay Foundation, please contact:

Hay House, Inc., P.O. Box 5100, Carlsbad, CA 92018-5100
(760) 431-7695 or (800) 654-5126
(760) 431-6948 (fax) or (800) 650-5115 (fax)
www.hayhouse.com® • www.hayfoundation.org

———

Published in Australia by:
Hay House Australia Pty. Ltd., 18/36 Ralph St., Alexandria NSW 2015
Phone: 612-9669-4299 • *Fax:* 612-9669-4144 • www.hayhouse.com.au

Published in the United Kingdom by:
Hay House UK, Ltd., Astley House, 33 Notting Hill Gate, London W11 3JQ
Phone: 44-20-3675-2450 • *Fax:* 44-20-3675-2451 • www.hayhouse.co.uk

Published in India by: Hay House Publishers India,
Muskaan Complex, Plot No. 3, B-2, Vasant Kunj, New Delhi 110 070
Phone: 91-11-4176-1620 • *Fax:* 91-11-4176-1630 • www.hayhouse.co.in

———

<u>Access New Knowledge.</u>
<u>Anytime. Anywhere.</u>

Learn and evolve at your own pace
with the world's leading experts.

www.hayhouseU.com

Free e-newsletters
from Hay House, the Ultimate
Resource for Inspiration

Be the first to know about Hay House's free downloads, special offers, giveaways, contests, and more!

 Get exclusive excerpts from our latest releases and videos from *Hay House Present Moments*.

 Our *Digital Products Newsletter* is the perfect way to stay up-to-date on our latest discounted eBooks, featured mobile apps, and Live Online and On Demand events.

 Learn with real benefits! *HayHouseU.com* is your source for the most innovative online courses from the world's leading personal growth experts. Be the first to know about new online courses and to receive exclusive discounts.

 Enjoy uplifting personal stories, how-to articles, and healing advice, along with videos and empowering quotes, within *Heal Your Life*.

 Have an inspirational story to tell and a passion for writing? Sharpen your writing skills with insider tips from *Your Writing Life*.

Sign Up Now!

Get inspired, educate yourself, get a complimentary gift, and share the wisdom!

Visit www.hayhouse.com/newsletters to sign up today!

Tune In to
Hay House Radio—
Radio for Your Soul

HAY HOUSE RADIO offers inspirational and personalized advice from our best-selling authors, including Anthony William, Dr. Christiane Northrup, Doreen Virtue, James Van Praagh, and many more!

Enjoy **FREE** access to life-changing audio 24/7 on HayHouseRadio.com, and with the Hay House Radio mobile app.

Listen anytime to the Hay House Radio archives of over 13,000 episodes (and more added daily!) with a Hay House Radio All Access Pass.

Learn more at www.HayHouseRadio.com

Hay House Podcasts
Bring Fresh, Free Inspiration Each Week!

Hay House proudly offers a selection of life-changing audio content via our most popular podcasts!

Hay House Meditations Podcast

Features your favorite Hay House authors guiding you through meditations designed to help you relax and rejuvenate. Take their words into your soul and cruise through the week!

Dr. Wayne W. Dyer Podcast

Discover the timeless wisdom of Dr. Wayne W. Dyer, world-renowned spiritual teacher and affectionately known as "the father of motivation." Each week brings some of the best selections from the 10-year span of Dr. Dyer's talk show on HayHouseRadio.com.

Hay House World Summit Podcast

Over 1 million people from 217 countries and territories participate in the massive online event known as the Hay House World Summit. This podcast offers weekly mini-lessons from World Summits past as a taste of what you can hear during the annual event, which occurs each May.

Hay House Radio Podcast

Listen to some of the best moments from HayHouseRadio.com, featuring expert authors such as Dr. Christiane Northrup, Anthony William, Caroline Myss, James Van Praagh, and Doreen Virtue discussing topics such as health, self-healing, motivation, spirituality, positive psychology, and personal development.

Hay House Live Podcast

Enjoy a selection of insightful and inspiring lectures from Hay House Live, an exciting event series that features Hay House authors and leading experts in the fields of alternative health, nutrition, intuitive medicine, success, and more! Feel the electricity of our authors engaging with a live audience, and get motivated to live your best life possible!

Find Hay House podcasts on iTunes, or visit
www.HayHouse.com/podcasts for more info.